THE DEAD SEA SCROLLS AFTER FIFTY YEARS

VOLUME I

THE DEAD SEA SCROLLS AFTER FIFTY YEARS

A Comprehensive Assessment

EDITED BY

PETER W. FLINT
AND
JAMES C. VANDERKAM

With the Assistance of Andrea E. Alvarez

VOLUME ONE

WIPF & STOCK · Eugene, Oregon

Wipf and Stock Publishers
199 W 8th Ave, Suite 3
Eugene, OR 97401

The Dead Sea Scrolls After Fifty Years, Volume 1
A Comprehensive Assessment
By Flint, Peter and Vanderkam, James C.
Copyright©1998 Koninklijke Brill N. V.
ISBN 13: 978-1-5326-8068-7
Publication date 1/30/2019
Previously published by Brill, 1998

CONTENTS
Volume One

Contents v
Preface vii
Terms, Sigla and Abbreviations ix
List of Contributors xv
Introduction to Volume One xvii
List of Plates xxi

PART ONE
REVIEW OF SCHOLARSHIP

ADAM S. VAN DER WOUDE
Fifty years of Qumran Research 1

PART TWO
QUMRAN ARCHAEOLOGY

JODI MAGNESS
Qumran Archaeology: Past Perspectives and Future Prospects 47

PART THREE
QUMRAN TEXTS

EUGENE ULRICH
The Dead Sea Scrolls and the Biblical Text 79

LEONARD J. GREENSPOON
The Dead Sea Scrolls and the Greek Bible 101

MOSHE J. BERNSTEIN
Pentateuchal Interpretation at Qumran 128

HANNAH K. HARRINGTON
Biblical Law at Qumran 160

SARIANNA METSO
Constitutional Rules at Qumran 186

JOHN I. KAMPEN
The Diverse Aspects of Wisdom in the Qumran Texts 211

ESTHER G. CHAZON
Hymns and Prayers in the Dead Sea Scrolls 244

GEORGE J. BROOKE
Parabiblical Prophetic Narratives 271

AL WOLTERS
The Copper Scroll 302

PART FOUR
TECHNICAL STUDIES

MARTIN G. ABEGG, JR.
The Hebrew of the Dead Sea Scrolls 325

EDWARD M. COOK
The Aramaic of the Dead Sea Scrolls 359

FRANK MOORE CROSS
Palaeography and the Dead Sea Scrolls 379

EMANUEL TOV
Scribal Practices Reflected in the Texts from the Judaean Desert 403

GREG DOUDNA
Dating the Scrolls on the Basis of Radiocarbon Analysis 430

GREGORY BEARMAN, STEPHEN J. PFANN, AND SHEILA I. SPIRO
Imaging the Scrolls: Photographic and Direct Digital Acquisition .. 472

DONALD W. PARRY, DAVID V. ARNOLD, DAVID G. LONG,
SCOTT R. WOODWARD
New Technological Advances: DNA, Databases, Imaging Radar 496

ANNETTE STEUDEL
Assembling and Reconstructing Manuscripts 516

ESTHER BOYD-ALKALAY AND ELENA LIBMAN
Preserving the Dead Sea Scrolls and Qumran Artefacts 535

PREFACE

This is the first volume of *The Dead Sea Scrolls After Fifty Years: A Comprehensive Assessment*, to be followed by a second later in 1998. Since the goals of this two-part collection and details of the individual essays are provided in the Introduction, the main function of the Preface is to comment briefly on style and to thank several people who have contributed to the success of the project.

With respect to language, the editors decided not to adopt a single style for the two volumes that comprise *The Dead Sea Scrolls After Fifty Years*. Some of the essays are thus in British English and others in U.S. English.

Thanks are extended to three groups of people. First, to the contributors for meeting various deadlines and striving to make their material both comprehensive and accessible to the non-specialist. Second, to two individuals whose research and assistance have proved indispensable to the present volume: Taylor Kim and Andrea E. Alvarez, both of Trinity Western University. In particular, Ms. Alvarez has been closely involved with all aspects of the project from the start. Finally, we extend thanks to the team at E. J. Brill NV, including Production Editors Wouter Kool, Mattie Kuiper and Pim Rietbroek. Above all, we recognize Senior Religion Editor Hans van der Meij, who conceived and proposed these volumes to mark the fiftieth anniversary following the discovery of the first Dead Sea Scrolls. In view of this distinguished publisher's extensive involvement with Scrolls research (notably via the series "Studies on the Texts of the Desert of Judah"), it seems most fitting that this volume and its companion appear under the Brill imprint.

Peter W. Flint 31 March, 1998
Langley, British Columbia

James C. VanderKam
Notre Dame, Indiana

TERMS, SIGLA AND ABBREVIATIONS

See *Biblia Hebraica Stuttgartensia*; *Septuaginta. Psalmi cum Odis* (ed. A. Rahlfs); the DJD series; and the Indices in Volume Two of this Fiftieth Anniversary collection. For journals and other secondary sources, cf. "Instructions for Contributors" in the *Catholic Biblical Quarterly* 55 (1993) 888-97 and the *Membership Directory and Handbook* of the Society of Biblical Literature (1994) 223-40. For Qumran sigla, see J. A. Fitzmyer, *The Dead Sea Scrolls: Major Publications and Tools for Study* (rev. ed.; SBLRBS 20; Atlanta: Scholars Press, 1990) 1-8.

TERMS AND SIGLA

→	A passage is continuous with the one before it (e.g. Ps 38→71).
(?)	Some doubt exists as to the identification of a verse or reading.
X	Denotes a verse/section that is absent from MT (e.g. Ps 118:1, 15, 16, 8, 9, X, 29), or an uncertain cave (e.g. XḤev/Se4)
[ ]	The bracketed portions are not extant, but were originally written.
[ ]	Space between fragments or where the leather surface is missing.
\	Division between lines in a manuscript.
//	Two or more parallel texts (e.g. Ps 18//2 Sam 22)
○	Ink traces of an unidentified letter remain.
+	Word(s) or a verse have been added.
>	Word(s) or a verse have been omitted.
*	What the scribe originally wrote (e.g. 4QPse^*)
—	Denotes Heb. pagination (e.g. "11QPsa^a המגילה," 123*–128*)
corr	The corrected form (e.g. 4QPse^{corr})
1°, 2°	The first, second occurrence of a form
2:4–5	The second extant column of the manuscript, lines 4–5
frg. 10 ii 4–5	Fragment 10, column 2, lines 4–5
א א א	A certain letter, a probable letter, a possible letter, respectively
Ant.	Josephus, *Antiquities*
bis	Two times
BP	"Before Present" (the number of radiocarbon years before 1950)
BYU	Brigham Young University
c.	*cum*, with
CALIB	The University of Washington's Quaternary Isotope Laboratory Radiocarbon Calibration Program
col(s).	Column(s)
corr.	*correctus, -a, um*, the corrected reading
DNA	Deoxyribonucleic Acid
aDNA	Ancient DNA

TERMS, SIGLA AND ABBREVIATIONS

mtDNA	Mitochondrial DNA
e, ex	Out of, from
ed(s).	Edition, editor(s), or edited
eras.	*erasum*, erased
FARMS	Foundation for Ancient Research and Mormon Studies
fin.	*finis,* end (e.g. $144:13^{fin}$)
frg(s).	Fragment(s)
𝔊 or LXX	The Old Greek (as in the Göttingen editions)
𝔊*	The (reconstructed) original reading of the Old Greek
GHz	Gigahertz
hab	*habet, habent,* it has, they have
HUBP	Hebrew University Bible Project
IAA	Israel Antiquities Authority (photograph accession numbers)
init.	*initium,* beginning
JPL	Jet Propulsion Laboratory
La	The Vetus Latina or Old Latin translation of the LXX
LXX	The Septuagint
𝔐 or MT	The Masoretic Text
𝔐^{ed}	An edition of the Masoretic Text (usually *BHS*)
𝔐^L or B^{19A}	Codex Leningradensis
𝔐$^{ms(s)}$	Masoretic manuscript(s)
𝔐^q	*qere* for the Masoretic Text
m.	Mishnah (as in *m.Yadayim*)
MS(S)	Individual manuscript(s)
Mus. Inv.	Museum Inventory Number (e.g. in the Rockefeller Museum)
n.	*nota,* note
n.p.	No publisher (cited)
n.s.	New series
NASA	National Aeronautics and Space Administration
OG	The Old Greek (original Septuagint)
ORTH.?	A form that may be only an orthographic variant
p.	Pesher (e.g. 4QpPs^a)
PAM	Palestine Archaeological Museum (photograph accession numbers)
PCR	Polymerase Chain Reaction
pr.	*praemitte, -mittit, -mittunt,* place before, it places before, they place before; or *praemittendum,* to be placed before
Ra	Rahlfs' edition of the Septuagint
recte	Correctly
recto	The front, inscribed side of a MS: the hair side of a leather scroll, or the side of a papyrus having horizontal ridges
rel.	*reliqui, -ae, -a,* the remaining MSS
repr.	Reprint(ed)

TERMS, SIGLA AND ABBREVIATIONS

rev.	Revised
SAR	Synthetic Aperture Radar
tris	Three times
v(v)	Verse(s)
vacat	Indicates that the leather or papyrus was intentionally left blank
VAR.?	A form that may be a variant
verso	The reverse side of a manuscript: the flesh side of a leather scroll, or the side of a papyrus having vertical ridges
vid.	*ut videtur, -entur*, as it seems, as they seem from the available evidence
Vorlage	Hebrew text used by the translator of the Greek or other Version
y. ʿErubin	The Palestinian Talmud, Tractate *ʿErubin*.
y. Šabbat	The Palestinian Talmud, Tractate *Šabbat*.
YSAR	Brigham Young University SAR

JOURNALS, BOOKS AND SERIES

AASOR	Annual of the American Schools of Oriental Research
ABD	D. N. Freedman (ed.), *The Anchor Bible Dictionary* (6 vols., New York: Doubleday, 1992)
AbrN	*Abr-Nahrain*
AGJU	Arbeiten zur Geschichte des antiken Judentums und des Urchristentums
AnBib	Analecta biblica
ANTJ	Arbeiten zum Neuen Testament und Judentum
ANYAS	Annals of the New York Academy of Sciences
ANZSTR	Australian and New Zealand Studies in Theology and Religion
ASOR	American Schools of Oriental Research
ATTM	K. Beyer, *Die aramäischen Texte vom Toten Meer* (Göttingen: Vandenhoeck & Ruprecht, 1984)
ATTME	K. Beyer, *ATTM Ergänzungsband* (1994)
BA	*Biblical Archaeologist*
BAR	*Biblical Archaeologist Reader*
BARev	*Biblical Archaeology Review*
BASOR	*Bulletin of the American Schools of Oriental Research*
BASORSup	*Bulletin of the American Schools of Oriental Research, Supplements*
BBB	Bonner biblische Beiträge
BBR	*Bulletin for Biblical Research*
BETL	Bibliotheca ephemeridum theologicarum lovaniensium
BHK	*Biblia Hebraica*
BHS	*Biblia Hebraica Stuttgartensia*
Bib	*Biblica*
BibOr	Biblica et orientalia

BIOSCS	*Bulletin of the International Organization for Septuagint and Cognate Studies*
BIS	Biblical Interpretation Series
BJRL	*Bulletin of the John Rylands University Library of Manchester*
BJS	Brown Judaic Studies
BTB	*Biblical Theology Bulletin*
BZAW	Beihefte zur ZAW
Cahiers RB	Cahiers de la *Revue Biblique*
CATSS	Computer Assisted Tools for Septuagint Studies
CBQ	*Catholic Biblical Quarterly*
CBQMS	Catholic Biblical Quarterly Monograph Series
CCJC	Cambridge Commentaries on Writings of the Jewish and Christian World 200 BC to AD 200
CJA	Christianity and Judaism in Antiquity
ConB	Coniectanea biblica
ConBNT	Coniectanea biblica, New Testament
ConBOT	Coniectanea biblica, Old Testament
CRAIBL	*Comptes rendus de l'Académie des inscriptions et belles-lettres*
CRINT	Compendia rerum iudaicarum ad novum testamentum
CTSRR	College Theology Society Resources in Religion
DBSup	*Dictionnaire de la Bible, Supplément*
DJD	Discoveries in the Judaean Desert
DJDJ	Discoveries in the Judaean Desert of Jordan
DSD	*Dead Sea Discoveries*
EI	*Eretz Israel*
ETL	*Ephemerides theologicae lovanienses*
FB	Forschung zur Bibel
GKC	Gesenius' Hebrew Grammar (ed. E. Kautzsch, tr. A. E. Cowley)
HBC	*Harper's Bible Commentary*
HBD	*Harper's Bible Dictionary*
HS	*Hebrew Studies*
HSM	Harvard Semitic Monographs
HSS	Harvard Semitic Studies
HTIBS	Historic Texts and Interpreters in Biblical Scholarship
HTR	*Harvard Theological Review*
HTS	Harvard Theological Studies
HUCA	*Hebrew Union College Annual*
HUCM	Hebrew Union College Monographs
IBR	Institute for Biblical Research
IDBSup	G. A. Buttrick (ed.), *Interpreter's Dictionary of the Bible, Supplement*
IEJ	*Israel Exploration Journal*

INJ	*Israel Numismatics Journal*
JAOS	*Journal of the American Oriental Society*
JBL	*Journal of Biblical Literature*
JBS	Jerusalem Biblical Studies
JDS	Judean Desert Studies
JEA	*Journal of Egyptian Archaeology*
JFA	*Journal of Field Archaeology*
JJS	*Journal of Jewish Studies*
JNES	*Journal of Near Eastern Studies*
JNSL	*Journal of Northwest Semitic Languages*
JNSLSup	*Journal of Northwest Semitic Languages*, Supplement Series
JQR	*Jewish Quarterly Review*
JQRMS	Jewish Quarterly Review Monograph Series
JRA	*Journal of Roman Archaeology*
JSJ	*Journal for the Study of Judaism in the Persian, Hellenistic and Roman Period*
JSJSup	*Journal for the Study of Judaism in the Persian, Hellenistic and Roman Period*, Supplement Series
JSNT	*Journal for the Study of the New Testament*
JSNTSup	*Journal for the Study of the New Testament*, Supplement Series
JSOT	*Journal for the Study of the Old Testament*
JSOTSup	*Journal for the Study of the Old Testament*, Supplement Series
JSP	*Journal for the Study of the Pseudepigrapha*
JSPSup	*Journal for the Study of the Pseudepigrapha*, Supplement Series
JSS	*Journal of Semitic Studies*
JTS	*Journal of Theological Studies*
LA	*Liber Annuus*
LCL	Loeb Classical Library
McCQ	*McCormick Quarterly*
MSU	Mitteilungen des Septuaginta-Unternehmens
NJBC	R. E. Brown et al (eds.), *The New Jerome Biblical Commentary*
NovT	*Novum Testamentum*
NovTSup	*Novum Testamentum*, Supplements
NTOA	*Novum Testamentum et Orbis Antiquus*
NTOAArch	*Novum Testamentum et Orbis Antiquus.* Series Archaeologica
NTS	*New Testament Studies*
OBO	Orbis biblicus et orientalis
OTE	*Old Testament Essays*
OTS	*Oudtestamentische Studiën*
PAAJR	*Proceedings of the American Academy of Jewish Research*
PEQ	*Palestine Exploration Quarterly*
PLO	Porta Linguarum Orientalium

PMPCAC	Publicaciones del Monte de Piedad y Caja de Ahorros de Córdoba
RB	*Revue biblique*
REJ	*Revue des études juives*
RevQ	*Revue de Qumran*
RHPR	*Revue d'histoire et de philosophie religieuses*
SAOC	Studies in Ancient Oriental Civilization
SBLDS	Society of Biblical Literature Dissertation Series
SBLMasS	Society of Biblical Literature Masoretic Studies
SBLMS	Society of Biblical Literature Monograph Series
SBLRBS	Society of Biblical Literature Resources for Biblical Study
SBLSBS	Society of Biblical Literature Sources for Biblical Study
SBLSCS	Society of Biblical Literature Septuagint and Cognate Studies
SBLSP	Society of Biblical Literature Seminar Papers
SBLSS	Society of Biblical Literature Semeia Studies
SBLSym	Society of Biblical Literature Symposium Series
SBLTT	Society of Biblical Literature Texts and Translations
SBT	Studies in Biblical Theology
SCS	Septuagint and Cognate Studies
SDSSRL	Studies in the Dead Sea Scrolls and Related Literature
SEÅ	*Svensk exegetisk årsbok*
Sem	*Semitica*
SIJD	Schriften des Institutum Judaicum Delitzschianum
SJLA	Studies in Judaism in Late Antiquity
SNTS	Society for New Testament Studies
SNTSMS	Society for New Testament Studies Monograph Series
SPB	Studia postbiblica
SQA	T. Muraoka (ed.), *Studies in Qumran Aramaic* (Abr-Nahrain Supplement 3; Louvain: Peeters, 1992)
SSN	Studia semitica neerlandica
STDJ	Studies on the Texts of the Desert of Judah
SUNT	Studien zur Umwelt des neuen Testaments
SVTP	Studia in veteris testamenti pseudepigrapha
TA	*Theologische Arbeiten*
ThR	*Theologische Rundschau*
TZ	*Theologische Zeitschrift*
TLZ	*Theologische Literaturzeitung*
UTB	Uni-Taschenbücher
VT	*Vetus Testamentum*
VTSup	*Vetus Testamentum*, Supplements
ZAH	*Zeitschrift für Althebraistik*
ZAW	*Zeitschrift für die alttestamentliche Wissenschaft*
ZTK	*Zeitschrift für Theologie und Kirche*

LIST OF CONTRIBUTORS

Martin G. Abegg, Jr.
Director, Dead Sea Scrolls Institute and Associate Professor of Religious Studies
Trinity Western University, British Columbia

David V. Arnold
Assistant Professor of Electrical and Computer Engineering
Brigham Young University, Provo, Utah

Gregory Bearman
Ancient Near Eastern Image, Pasadena, California

Esther Boyd-Alkalay
Conservator, Israel Antiquities Authority, Rockefeller Museum, Jerusalem

Moshe J. Bernstein
Associate Professor of Bible, Yeshiva University, New York

George J. Brooke
Professor of Biblical Studies, University of Manchester

Esther G. Chazon
Lecturer and Associate Director of the Orion Center, Institute of Jewish Studies
Hebrew University of Jerusalem

Edward M. Cook
Cincinnati, Ohio

Frank Moore Cross
Hancock Professor of Hebrew and Other Oriental Languages, Emeritus
Harvard University

Greg L. Doudna
Dead Sea Scrolls Initiative, University of Copenhagen

Peter W. Flint (Editor)
Director, Dead Sea Scrolls Institute and Associate Professor of Religious Studies
Trinity Western University, British Columbia

Leonard J. Greenspoon
Philip M. and Ethel Klutznick Chair in Jewish Civilization
Creighton University, Omaha, Nebraska

Hannah K. Harrington
Associate Professor of Old Testament, Patten College, Oakland, California

LIST OF CONTRIBUTORS

John I. Kampen
Vice President and Dean of Academic Affairs and Professor of Religion
Bluffton College, Bluffton, Ohio

Elena Libman
Conservator, Israel Antiquities Authority, Rockefeller Museum, Jerusalem

David G. Long
Associate Professor of Electrical and Computer Engineering
Brigham Young University, Provo, Utah

Jodi Magness
Associate Professor of Classical and Near Eastern Archaeology
Tufts University, Medford, Massachussetts

Sarianna Metso
Finnish Academy Researcher, University of Helsinki, Finland

Donald W. Parry
Assistant Professor of Hebrew Language and Literature
Brigham Young University, Provo, Utah

Stephen J. Pfann
Director, Center for the Study of Early Christianity, Jerusalem

Sheila I. Spiro
Ancient Near Eastern Image, Pasadena, CA and
Ancient Biblical Manuscript Centre, Claremont, California

Annette Steudel
Researcher and Lecturer in Second Temple Judaism and New Testament
University of Göttingen

Emanuel Tov
J. L. Magnes Professor of Bible, Hebrew University of Jerusalem

Eugene Ulrich
Professor of Hebrew Scriptures, University of Notre Dame

James C. VanderKam (Editor)
Professor of Hebrew Scriptures, University of Notre Dame

Scott R. Woodward
Professor of Microbiology, Brigham Young University, Provo, Utah

Adam S. van der Woude
Emeritus Professor of Old Testament and Early Judaism
Qumran Instituut of the Theological Faculty, Rijksuniversiteit, Groningen

Al Wolters
Professor of Biblical Studies, Redeemer College, Ancaster, Ontario

INTRODUCTION TO VOLUME ONE

A fiftieth anniversary is a fitting time for reflection and planning. The first of the Dead Sea Scrolls were recovered from a cave in 1947, and those scrolls and subsequent discoveries have occasioned the birth and flourishing of an entirely new area of research. By now the bibliography on the Qumran finds has become staggering, far more than any one scholar is likely to read through, much less control, in a lifetime. There have been two major phases of Qumran study, the first coming in the decade and a-half after the first texts became available for study, and the second continuing and thriving at present. The latest surge in Qumran studies was caused by the controversial process of opening the scrolls to more general scholarly access in the early 1990's. Not only can the expert now view the originals in the museums but photographs of all the texts are also widely available, and most of the texts have been published, either preliminarily or officially and definitively. With all this newly-available evidence, it is not surprising that editions are appearing rapidly and publications on the scrolls have increased geometrically in the last decade.

The E. J. Brill Publishing Company NV, and Senior Religion Editor Hans van der Meij in particular, recognized that the jubilee of the first discoveries was an appropriate time for assessing where we now stand and looking to the future in scrolls scholarship. The result is *The Dead Sea Scrolls After Fifty Years*, in two volumes. From the outset the editors decided that it would be most helpful to those working in the field and to others in related disciplines if the essays that were commissioned focused especially on those aspects of Qumran research where there was something new to say, although the two volumes together offer a comprehensive assessment. The editors also determined that a wide range of opinion would be solicited and that experts at various stages in their careers would be invited to contribute.

The first two essays in this volume cover broad subjects and thus stand by themselves. A. S. van der Woude, himself a participant in scrolls research for decades, kindly took on the daunting task of surveying the vast field over its first 50 years. J. Magness, a more recent entrant into the field, has contributed a survey of the all-important archaeological data from Khirbet Qumran and offers her own proposal for phases of occupation at the site. The two larger sections that complete the first volume each comprise nine essays and are entitled "Qumran Texts" and "Technical Studies." In the former, a first part devoted to the so-called "biblical" texts includes E. Ulrich's assessment of the situation and the significance of the evidence for the Hebrew Bible, while L. Greenspoon deals with the contributions that the Qumran finds have made to study of the Septuagint and its history. The remaining essays in this section focus on types of texts and, in some cases, especially interesting and important individual compositions. M. Bernstein concentrates on the Qumran texts that offer interpretations of legal passages in the Pentateuch. The many Qumran rules are the subject of two essays: H. Harrington deals with those that may be termed "legal" (e.g. MMT), while S. Metso centers her attention on those texts that set forth rules for the life and beliefs of communities. One of the newest fields in Qumran research is the wisdom texts that are only now being published; an analysis of these and of their significance is presented by J. Kampen. The many hymns and prayers found in the caves are studied and classified by E. Chazon, while G. Brooke surveys the recently available narrative texts about prophets such as Jeremiah, Ezekiel and Daniel. The Copper Scroll has been a controversial work for many years; the final essay in this section offers a special study by A. Wolters, one of the foremost experts on this enigmatic document.

The last decade of Qumran study has been marked by the application of several kinds of sophisticated scientific techniques to the manuscript fragments and other artefacts. The final nine essays in Volume One provide full coverage of these exciting developments. M. Abegg has written a study of the linguistic traits of Qumran Hebrew, and E. Cook has provided a comparable analysis for Qumran Aramaic. The field of Semitic palaeography which has played so large a role in dating the scrolls and scroll fragments continues to be enriched by new textual finds, and F. M. Cross, who has written the most influential study of the evidence, provides an overview and update on the scribal hands evident in the Qumran texts. E. Tov, the Editor-in-Chief of the "Discoveries in the Judaean Desert" series, has contributed an essay surveying the data relevant for determining whether there was a special Qumran scribal school. G. Doudna provides an in-depth analysis of carbon-14 and Accelerator Mass Spectrometry dating techniques and the results they have yielded for the scrolls and fragments that have been tested. S. Pfann has written a history of photographing the Dead Sea Scrolls, while G. Bearman and S. Spiro, in the second part of the same article, take us through the amazing world of modern digital imaging which has produced improved photographs of the texts. D. Parry, S. Woodward, and other experts from FARMS furnish descriptions of the CD-Rom of the scrolls produced there, DNA analysis of the skins on which many of the texts were written, and the sonor techniques used in searching for hidden underground cavities. The process of reconstructing scrolls when only parts remain and placing fragments within them is described by A. Steudel, while conservators E. Boyd-Alkalay and E. Libman of the Israel Antiquities Authority report preserving the scrolls and other finds.

The first volume of *The Dead Sea Scrolls After Fifty Years* will be followed soon by a second which will contain essays on specific topics in the Qumran texts as well as the contributions and relations of the scrolls to Early Judaism and Early Christianity. A number of appendices and indices, including a list of all the Qumran texts and a register of all the passages represented on the biblical scrolls, will support the two volumes and provide for easier access to their rich contents.

The Editors

LIST OF PLATES
(See end of Book)

PLATE 1
Khirbet Qumran: Plan of Site in Periods Ib and II

PLATE 2
Khirbet Qumran: Plan of the Iron Age Settlement

PLATE 3
Khirbet Qumran: Plan of Period Ia

PLATE 4
Khirbet Qumran: Plan of Period Ib

PLATE 5
Khirbet Qumran: Plan of Period II

PLATE 6
Khirbet Qumran: The Pool in L48-49, split by the earthquake

PLATE 7
Khirbet Qumran: Pottery in the Pantry (L89)

PLATE 8
Fragment from 4QSam[a] (1 Samuel 14:47-49) at 200%

PLATE 9
Early Aramaic and Proto-Jewish Scripts

PLATE 10
The Evolution of the Formal Hand in the Hasmonaean and Herodian Periods

PLATE 11
Early Semicursive Scripts

LIST OF PLATES

PLATE 12
Semicursive Scripts from Qumran

PLATE 13
Herodian and Post-Herodian Cursive Scripts

PLATE 14
An Old Hebrew Script and a Palaeo-Hebrew Script from Qumran

PLATE 15
Four SAR Images of Sites in Israel

FIFTY YEARS OF QUMRAN RESEARCH

ADAM S. VAN DER WOUDE

1. INTRODUCTORY COMMENTS

After fifty years of research on the Dead Sea Scrolls even a specialist can hardly take a comprehensive view of all the contributions that have been devoted to the Qumran findings. It is, of course, also not possible for one person to deal adequately with all their aspects and ramifications—the variety and richness of the subjects evoked by the discovery of the documents are no less than overwhelming. This is not only exemplified by the wide range of contributions to the present volumes on the Dead Sea Scrolls after fifty years, but also by the more than 10,000 that have been itemized in the bibliographies of Ch. Burchard, W. S. LaSor, B. Jongeling, and F. García Martínez and D. W. Parry.[1] We feel, therefore, quite justified to offer this treatment in broad outline and even to impose other restraints on our presentation. We have chosen here to concentrate mainly upon the newest developments and not to deal with the history of the discoveries (which has often been told), nor with the constitution of the first editorial committee and the process of editing the texts (which has been criticised by a number of scholars).[2] We wish to present a critical treatment of important and

---

[1] Ch. Burchard, *Bibliographie zu den Handschriften vom Toten Meer* (BZAW 76; Berlin: Töpelmann, 1957); idem, *Bibliographie zu den Handschriften vom Toten Meer II* (BZAW 89; Berlin: Töpelmann, 1965); W. S. LaSor, *Bibliography of the Dead Sea Scrolls 1948-1957* (Pasadena, CA: Fuller Theological Seminary, 1958); B. Jongeling, *A Classified Bibliography of the Finds in the Desert of Judah 1955-1969* (STDJ 7; Leiden: Brill, 1971); F. García Martínez and D. W. Parry, *A Bibliography of the Finds in the Desert of Judah 1970-95* (STDJ 19; Leiden: Brill, 1996). See also C. Koester, "A Qumran Bibliography: 1974-1984," *BTB* 15 (1985), 110-20; J. A. Fitzmyer, *The Dead Sea Scrolls: Major Publications and Tools for Study* (2nd ed., SBLRBS 20; Atlanta: Scholars Press, 1990).

[2] For example, see Z. J. Kapera, "The Unfortunate Story of Qumran Cave Four," in idem (ed.), *Qumran Cave IV and MMT. Special Report* (Kraków: Enigma Press, 1991) 5-53.

currently-debated questions that pertain to the provenance of the scrolls and their contents, as well as the origins, history and character of the Qumran community, its beliefs and practices, and the significance of these ancient documents for the study of the Old Testament, early Judaism and the New Testament.

> Apart from introductory monographs on the Dead Sea Scrolls,[3] earlier overviews and critical evaluations of investigations into the findings were offered by Hans Bardtke in *ThR* 29 (1963) 261-92; 33 (1968) 97-117, 185-236; 35 (1970) 196-230; 37 (1972) 97-120, 193-219; 38 (1973-1974) 257-91; 39 (1974) 189-221; 40 (1975) 210-26; and 41 (1976) 97-140; E. M. Laperrousaz et al., "Qumrân et les découvertes au désert de Juda," in *Supplément au Dictionnaire de la Bible* 51 (Paris: Letouzey et Ané, 1978) cols. 737-1014; D. Dimant, "Qumran Sectarian Literature," in M. E. Stone (ed.), *Jewish Writings of the Second Temple Period* (CRINT 2.2; Assen: Van Gorcum; Philadelphia: Fortress, 1984) 483-550; J. Murphy-O'Connor, "The Judean Desert," in R. A. Kraft and G. W. E. Nickelsburg (eds.), *Early Judaism and Its Modern Interpreters* (Philadelphia: Fortress; Atlanta: Scholars Press, 1986) 119-56; G. Vermes, "Biblical Studies and the Dead Sea Scrolls 1947-1987: Retrospects and Prospects," *JSOT* 39 (1987) 113-28; idem, *The Dead Sea Scrolls Forty Years On* (Oxford: Postgraduate Hebrew Centre, 1987); G. Vermes, F. Millar and M. Goodman, "The Writings of the Qumran Community," in Emil Schürer, *The History of the Jewish People in the Age of Jesus Christ (175 B.C.–A.D. 135)*, revised by G. Vermes et al. (3 vols., Edinburgh: Clark, 1986) 3.1.380-469; F. García Martínez, "Estudios Qumránicos 1975-1985: Panorama crítico I–VI," *Estudios Bíblicos* 45 (1987) 125-205, 361-402; 46 (1988) 325-74, 527-48; 47 (1989) 93-118, 225-66; A. S. van der Woude in *Theologische Rundschau* 54 (1989), 221-61; 55 (1990), 274-307; 57 (1992), 1-57, 225-53.

2. THE PROVENANCE OF THE SCROLLS

That the manuscripts recovered from the caves of Qumran are remnants of the library of the religious community which flourished

---

[3] The most recent introductions include: F. M. Cross, *The Ancient Library of Qumran* (3rd ed., The Biblical Seminar 30; Sheffield: Sheffield Academic Press, 1995); G. Vermes, *The Dead Sea Scrolls. Qumran in Perspective* (rev. ed., London: SCM, 1994); H. Stegemann, *Die Essener, Qumran, Johannes der Täufer und Jesus* (Freiburg: Herder, 1993. English translation: *The Library of Qumran. On the Essenes, Qumran, John the Baptist, and Jesus* [Grand Rapids: Eerdmans, 1998]); J. C. VanderKam, *The Dead Sea Scrolls Today* (Grand Rapids: Eerdmans; London: SPCK, 1994); L. H. Schiffman, *Reclaiming the Dead Sea Scrolls* (Jerusalem and Philadelphia: The Jewish Publication Society, 1994).

from the second part of the 2nd century BCE until 68 CE near the northwestern shore of the Dead Sea, has been the opinion of the majority of scholars since the very dawn of Qumran research. Doubts about dating these documents to the time around the beginning of the common era were expressed by some scholars during the earlier years following their discovery,[4] but these were undermined by the results of palaeographical research[5] which have more recently been confirmed by carbon-14 tests.[6]

Evidently not all the manuscripts that were found in the caves were composed by members of the community of Qumran. Not only the manuscripts of the Hebrew Bible (which make up about a fourth part of the scrolls), but many other writings were written prior to the establishing of the community—although we cannot in every case be sure of their origin. In similar vein, the long editorial history of various works also points to the composition of their earliest levels before the Qumranites settled in the Judean Desert. Yet in spite of their huge quantity, these texts—whether written outside Qumran or within its community, and with their different characters and provenances—are surprisingly homogeneous with respect to their contents. They form a unity which is best described as a *religious library* belonging to, and reflecting upon, the theological and halakhic interests of a particular "sectarian" community. Even the astronomical and calendrical texts are closely related to works dealing with the festive calendar and the priestly courses.

We may conclude that these manuscripts derive from one and the same library for at least three reasons: (a) The collections housed in the caves (with the exception of Cave 7) present the same pattern of biblical, apocryphal and sectarian works; (b) Exemplars of the same apocryphal and sectarian compositions were stored in different caves; (c) Some of the manuscripts that have been found in different

---

[4] Note J. Murphy-O'Connor's overview, "The Judean Desert," in Kraft and Nickelsburg (eds.), *Early Judaism and Its Modern Interpreters*, 119-56, esp. 121ff.

[5] Cf. F. M. Cross, "The Development of the Jewish Script," in G. Ernest Wright (ed.), *The Bible and the Ancient Near East: Essays in Honor of William Foxwell Albright* (Garden City, NY: Doubleday, 1961) 133-202.

[6] G. Bonani et al., "Radiocarbon Dating of the Dead Sea Scrolls," ʿAtiqot 20 (1991) 27-32; G. Bonani et al., "Radiocarbon Dating of Fourteen Dead Sea Scrolls," *Radiocarbon* 34 (1992) 843-49; A. J. T. Jull, D. J. Donahue, M. Broshi and E. Tov. "Radiocarbon Dating of Scrolls and Linen Fragments from the Judean Desert," *Radiocarbon* 37 (1995) 11-19.

caves were copied by the same scribe. It also seems clear that the library belonged to the community of Qumran; this is both suggested by the physical proximity between the caves and the buildings of Qumran, and corroborated by the identity of the pottery found in the caves and in the buildings.

We also know that the Qumran community was a sectarian group because of: the theological outlook of its own compositions (which in many respects differs from the religious ideas of the mainstream of early Judaism); its different calendar and halakhah; its highly-structured organization; and its members' conviction that they were the true Israel and the repository of the authentic traditions of the religious body from which they had seceded (G. Vermes). Although several nonbiblical works found in the caves were written prior to the settlement of the community in the desert of Judah, these writings were apparently regarded by the members as compatible with their own ideology and halakhah, since they attested to the apocalyptic and Essene traditions which eventually gave rise to the world-view and halakhah of the Qumranites.[7]

In contrast to these considerations, K. Rengstorf already in 1960 suggested that the Qumran scrolls should be viewed as part of the Temple library of Jerusalem, which was moved to the desert in the first years of the first Jewish revolt against the Romans.[8] In similar vein, N. Golb has recently denied that any type of relationship existed between the scrolls and the Qumran community.[9] In his opinion, the manuscripts found in the caves come from different libraries in Jerusalem, and represent the literature of early Judaism as a whole. Golb's thesis is based on the assumption that Qumran was a fortress which could not have been the residence of a group like the Essenes, nor the location of an important library. Furthermore, in his view the absence of documentary records (letters, deeds, contracts, etc.) in the caves, the small number of sectarian texts, and

---

[7] Cf. F. García Martínez and A. S. van der Woude, "A 'Groningen' Hypothesis of Qumran Origins and Early History," *RevQ* 14 (1990), 521-41, esp. 521ff.

[8] K.-H. Rengstorf, *Hirbet Qumran und die Bibliothek vom Toten Meer* (Stuttgart: Kohlhammer, 1960).

[9] N. Golb, "The Dead Sea Scrolls: A New Perspective," *American Scholar* 58 (1989), 177-207; idem, "Who Hid the Dead Sea Scrolls?," *BA* 48 (1985) 68-82; idem, *Who Wrote the Dead Sea Scrolls? The Search for the Secret of Qumran* (New York: Scribner, 1995).

their contradictory outlooks and points would exclude a sectarian library. He also stresses that the copy of the Songs of the Sabbath Sacrifice found at Masada shows this work was not unique to Qumran, and that Pliny in his *Natural History* was not describing the site of Qumran and its inhabitants. Golb further regards it as inconceivable that all the literature of early Judaism would have disappeared except for that from a small fringe group.

Golb's objections against the scrolls belonging to the library of the Qumran community are unconvincing, to say the least. Although Qumran was an Israelite stronghold in the 8th century BCE and became a military outpost of the Roman army after 68 CE, in view of its workshops, meeting places, common rooms and the big cemetery with more than a thousand tombs it must have been a community centre in the last centuries before the beginning of the common era.[10] The alleged absence of documentary texts in the Qumran caves (in contrast to the finds at Murabbaʿât) turns out to be an incorrect assumption in view of a number of documents that were found relating to business dealings (cf. 4Q342–358).

Golb also seems to underestimate the quantity of clearly sectarian texts, plays down the fact that they cover all aspects of the religious thought and life of a sectarian community, and cannot explain why other groups' distinctive views are shown in a negative light throughout the scrolls if the library really represented a cross-section of Jewish literature at the time. He fails to see that even the Damascus Document (CD) and the Manual of Discipline (1QS)—which respectively legislate for the "camps community" and the Qumran community—are related to one another at the basic level of doctrine, aims and principles. Of course, we cannot trace exactly how the copy of the Songs of the Sabbath Sacrifice reached Masada, but it is quite feasible that a member of the Qumran community brought it to the fortress after the destruction of the Qumran settlement by the Romans. The fact that Pliny's description of the Essenes is not without its difficulties by no means warrants that he had a site other than Qumran in mind.[11] Finally, Golb's thesis that it is inconceivable for all the literature of early Judaism to have disappeared and only the literature of a small fringe group to have been preserved, is really irrelevant to the attribution of the Dead Sea

---

[10] García Martínez and van der Woude, "A 'Groningen' Hypothesis," 521-41.

[11] VanderKam, *Dead Sea Scrolls Today*, 71ff., 95ff.

Scrolls to the Qumran community. To sum up, then, the thesis that the scrolls represent all the literature of the Judaism of the time cannot ultimately be substantiated.

One more consideration which points to the sectarian character of the Qumran library may be added. After the members of the community founded by the Teacher of Righteousness moved to the desert of Judah in about 125 BCE, they do not seem to have included in their library one single book which was later composed outside Qumran. It can be shown that all the apocryphal and pseudepigraphical writings that were discovered in the caves originated before the end of the 2nd century BCE. This is remarkable because (with a few exceptions) all pre-Maccabean Jewish literature that is known to us has been preserved among the Dead Sea Scrolls: not only apocalyptic writings, but also portions of other compositions (the Letter of Jeremiah, Ecclesiasticus, Tobit and Jubilees). This seems to confirm that the members of the Qumran community considered themselves as the true heirs of early Jewish religious traditions, but formed from the end of the 2nd century BCE onwards a "sect" that did not allow the intrusion of religious texts and halakhic ideas that were cherished in other circles.

3. THE CONTENTS OF, AND RESEARCH ON, THE SCROLLS

The few documentary texts that were found among the Dead Sea Scrolls do not disprove that the Qumran library is essentially a collection of religious literature. Apart from the remnants of biblical scrolls and apocryphal compositions, the library of Qumran contains: (a) sectarian works which represent the thought and halakhah of the community in its most developed form; (b) works of the formative period which attest to visions and persuasions as yet not clearly differentiated from the Essenism which was their ultimate source; (c) works which reflect Essene thought and accord with the classical information about Essenism; and (d) works belonging to the apocalyptic tradition which gave rise to Essenism. A number of these writings reveal a composite character and reflect ideological developments that pertain both to the formative period and to later times.

A conspicious feature of Qumran research in its initial phase was that the major scrolls were usually studied as homogeneous literary units. Only the last decades have seen a thorough analysis of the literary layers of such important documents as the Rule of the Community (1QS), the War Scroll (1QM) and the Temple Scroll

(11QT). The recently realized access to all the materials from Cave 4 has shown beyond doubt that the major Qumran scrolls have undergone a number of redactional processes.

3.1 1QIsa^a and 1QIsa^b

Of the two Isaiah manuscripts among the scrolls of Cave 1, 1QIsa^a (sometimes abbreviated 1QIs^a) in particular has led to a number of investigations with divergent results. J. Siegel[12] pointed to the close relationship between 1QIsa^a and the Severus scroll, a Hebrew Pentateuch which—according to a statement in the Midrash Bereshit Rabbah of R. Moshe HaDarshan—was brought in 70 CE to the "synagogue of Severus" in Rome. A list of variant readings in the Severus scroll has been preserved in the Midrash, in the Farḥi-Bible of 1382, and in a Paris manuscript. Although Siegel may well have shown that many of these variant readings and a number of orthographic peculiarities go back to the time when the Qumran documents were written, his conclusion that the Severus scroll and 1QIsa^a belong to the category of *Vulgärtexte* which were later withdrawn from circulation (because of their variants and different orthography), must be doubted. In a similar vein, E. Kutscher[13] considered 1QIsa^a as a popular text-type that was primarily used for personal study and eventually replaced by the standard text. A. van der Kooij[14], however, has criticized an exclusive reliance on linguistic criteria for explaining the variant readings and has drawn attention to interpretative variants in 1QIsa^a. He concludes that the writer of this document was not only a copyist, but in the first place a scribe who actualized the prophetic message according to the same exegetical methods which guided the authors of the "Biblical Commentaries" of Qumran. Van der Kooij identifies the writer of 1QIsa^a with the Teacher of Righteousness himself. J. Hoegenhaven[15]

---

[12] J. P. Siegel, *The Severus Scroll and 1QIs^a* (SBLMasS 2; Missoula, MT: Scholars Press, 1975).

[13] E. Y. Kutscher, *The Language and Linguistic Background of the Isaiah Scroll (1QIs^a)* (STDJ 6; Leiden: Brill, 1974). Cf. also E. Qimron, *The Language and-Linguistic Background of the Isaiah Scroll (1QIs^a). Indices and Corrections* (STDJ 6A; Leiden: Brill, 1979).

[14] A. van der Kooij, *Die alten Textzeugen des Jesajabuches. Ein Beitrag zur Textgeschichte des Alten Testaments* (OBO 35; Freiburg [Schweiz]: Universitätsverlag; Göttingen: Vandenhoeck & Ruprecht, 1981).

maintained that 1QIsa^a and the Masoretic text of the book of Isaiah had different backgrounds, although both stem from a common text-family. In his view, therefore, one should not contend that the writer of the scroll deliberatedly changed his *Vorlage* in order to conform with a certain interpretative point of view, or deny that 1QIsa^a represents a certain textual tradition, as van der Kooij does.

3.2 *The Rule of the Community (1QS)*

The content of the *Rule*—whose oldest copy (4QS^a) derives from the end of the 2nd century BCE—was regarded in the first years of Qumran research as an arbitrarily reassembled collection of distinct sources broken up in fragments,[16] yet also as a literary unity.[17] Apart from a vague reference to multiple sources, P. Wernberg-Møller[18] did not pay attention to the literary genesis of 1QS in his introduction to and translation of the document. But A. Leaney[19] attempted to define and date the various sources involved, regarding 8:1-9:26 as the oldest element, written before the advent of the Teacher of Righteousness (to whom he attributed 10:1–11:11). Analyses of various portions of 1QS by other scholars have confirmed its composite character, but the first attempt to construct a general theory explaining the composition of the document was made by J. Murphy-O'Connor in 1969.[20] In his essay, which became fundamental to further research, Murphy-O'Connor propounded a four-stage evolution of 1QS:

Stage 1: The Manifesto (8:1-16; 9:3-10:8), in which the Teacher of Righteousness proposed to move to the wilderness.

---

[15] J. Hoegenhaven, "The First Isaiah Scroll from Qumran (1QIs^a) and the Massoretic Text. Some Reflections with Special Regard to Isaiah 1-12," *JSOT* 28 (1984) 17-35.

[16] H. E. del Medico, *L'énigme des manuscrits de la Mer Morte* (Paris: Plon, 1957) 160.

[17] P. Guilbert, "Le plan de la 'Règle de la Communauté'," *RevQ* 1 (1958-1959) 323-44.

[18] P. Wernberg-Møller, *The Manual of Discipline* (STDJ 1; Leiden; Brill, 1957).

[19] A. R. C. Leaney, *The Rule of Qumran and Its Meaning. Introduction, Translation and Commentary* (New Testament Library; London: SCM; Philadelphia: Westminster, 1966).

[20] J. Murphy-O'Connor, "La génèse littéraire de la Règle de la Communauté," *RB* 76 (1969) 528-49.

Stage 2: A penal code for a small community (8:16–9:2) was added.
Stage 3: The community redefined itself (5:1-13) and enacted more elaborate legislation (5:15–7:25).
Stage 4: Columns 1-4 and the hymn of 10:9–11:22 were added.

In a thorough study of the composition of 1QS J. Pouilly[21] found the analysis of Murphy-O'Connor to be substantially correct, but assigned 8:10b-12a to stage two (rather than stage one), and 5:13b–6:8a to stage four. While Murphy-O'Connor accepted Pouilly's conclusions, P. Mantovani[22] refused to make a distinction between stages 1 and 2. According to her, the initial clauses of columns 1:1ff., 5:1ff. and 8:1ff. point to three redactionally-combined blocs of tradition. Moreover, D. Dimant[23] rejected altogether the idea of textual stages reflecting different life-situations in the Qumran community.

A renewed analysis of the textual development of 1QS with due regard to the ten copies of the work from Cave 4[24] has recently been undertaken by S. Metso.[25] The Finnish scholar concludes that no standard edition of the work ever existed, and that the sections included in the Community Rule varied to some extent. She proposes that 4QS^d and 4QS^e seem not to have contained 1QS 1–4 at all, and the final hymn is lacking in 4QS^e—in which, however, the calendrical text Otot was directly attached to the regulations of 9:12-26a. 4QS^b is the only manuscript which can be stated with certainty to have included all the same sections of the Rule as does 1QS; yet its text was much shorter than that of 1QS. In comparison to the latter,

---

[21] J. Pouilly, *La Règle de la Communauté de Qumrân. Son évolution littéraire* (Cahiers de la RB 17; Gabalda: Paris, 1976).

[22] P. A. Mantovani, "La stratificazione letteraria della Regola della Communità: a proposito di uno studio recente," *Henoch* 5 (1983) 69-91.

[23] "Qumran Sectarian Literature," in M. E. Stone (ed.), *Jewish Writings of the Second Temple Period* (CRINT 2.2; Assen: Van Gorcum; Philadelphia: Fortress, 1984) 483-550, esp. 501-2.

[24] A transcription and annotated translation of the fragments appears in the new edition of the Community Rule by J. H. Charlesworth and E. Qimron in Charlesworth et al. (eds.), *The Dead Sea Scrolls. Hebrew, Aramaic, and Greek Texts with English Translations*, Vol. 1. *Rule of the Community and Related Documents* (Tübingen: Mohr-Siebeck; Louisville: Westminster John Knox, 1994) 53-103.

[25] S. Metso, *The Textual Development of the Qumran Community Rule* (STDJ 21; Leiden: Brill, 1997).

4QS^{b,d} lack both the additions which strenghtened the self-understanding of the community and the biblical quotations that were intended to provide a Scriptural legitimation for regulations already prevailing in the community. While the text of Otot (a list of the weekly service of the priestly families in the Temple) was included in 4QS^e, it soon lost its relevance for a community that had rejected the Temple as defiled and was replaced by the final psalm in 4QS^{b,d}. Metso identifies four stages of redaction, which are represented in turn by 4QS^e; 4QS^{b,d}; 1QS; and the corrections and additions of the second scribe in columns 7-8 of 1QS.

3.3 The Rule of the Congregation (1QSa) and the Blessings (1QSb)

Only a few studies have been devoted to these two works. A major contribution to the explanation of 1QSa was published by L. Schiffman in 1989.[26]

3.4 The War Scroll (1QM)

This text has often been commented upon ever since E. L. Sukenik published its contents in 1954.[27] A. Dupont-Sommer[28] considered cols. 15–19 to be a supplementary rule added to the corpus of columns 2–14 with col. 1 as an introduction to the whole, but J. Carmignac[29] and B. Jongeling[30] advocated the literary unity of 1QM. Y. Yadin[31], whose commentary is particularly useful because of his analysis of military tactics and armament, was not specific on this particular point. However, J. P. M. van der Ploeg[32] showed already in 1959 that the document is a composite work, by discerning a primitive document containing cols. 1:10–12:15-19 (and possibly 13–

---

[26] L. H. Schiffman, *The Eschatological Community of the Dead Sea Scrolls. A Study of the Rule of the Congregation* (SBLMS 38; Atlanta: Scholars Press, 1989).

[27] E. L. Sukenik, אוצר המגילות הגנוזות (Jerusalem; Bialik Foundation and the Hebrew University, 1954); English translation by N. Avigad and Y. Yadin (eds.), *The Dead Sea Scrolls of the Hebrew University* (Jerusalem: Magnes Press, 1955).

[28] A. Dupont-Sommer, *Les écrits esséniens découverts près de la Mer Morte* (Paris: Payot, 1959).

[29] J. Carmignac, *La Règle de la Guerre* (Paris: Letouzey et Ané, 1958).

[30] B. Jongeling, *Le rouleau de la guerre des manuscrits de Qumrân* (Assen: Van Gorcum, 1962).

[31] Y. Yadin, *The Scroll of the War of the Sons of Light against the Sons of Darkness* (Oxford: Oxford University Press, 1962).

[32] Van der Ploeg, *Le rouleau de la guerre* (STDJ 2; Leiden: Brill, 1959).

14), which were expanded by the addition of cols. 2–9. The main contribution to the literary analysis of 1QM was presented by P. Davies in his revised dissertation in 1977.[33] According to Davies, columns 2–9 are a literary compilation of sources dealing with the war between the tribes of Israel and the nations, mainly reaching back to Maccabean times, and edited in the Hasmonean period. This section, he adds, should not be termed a typical Qumranic writing because dualistic viewpoints are lacking, the perspective is pan-Israelite, and (with the exception of the solar calendar) distinct sectarian ideas do not occur. In cols. 15–19 the final war between the sons of light and the sons of darkness is described with explicit ethical and dualistic features. This section is the end-product of a long development from a original Maccabean war-rule that is represented by 14:2-12, and underwent its final redaction in the second half of the 1st century BCE. For Davies, cols. 10–12 form a collection of hymns and prayers, many of which reflect a Maccabean setting. Cols. 13 and 14, however, once circulated separately. Col. 1 is a redactional introduction to 1QM as a whole, because it presents a summary of the final war as described in cols. 2–9 and 15–19, and stems from the first half of the 1st century CE.

Although Davies could have taken the preliminary remarks of M. Baillet[34] on the fragments of 1QM and related documents from Cave 4 more seriously, his work was unduly criticized by J. Carmignac[35] because of the latter's distaste for literary criticism. Davies' study, of course, must be supplemented and corrected in view of the new texts from Cave 4 and on the basis of subsequent criticism. Referring to the dualism between light and darkness, J. Collins[36] has asserted that

---

[33] P. R. Davies, *1QM, the War Scroll from Qumran: Its Structure and History* (BibOr 32; Rome: Biblical Institute Press, 1977).

[34] Cf. M. Baillet, "Les manuscrits de la Règle de la Guerre de la grotte 4 de Qumrân," *RB* 79 (1972) 217-26. The texts were subsequently published by Baillet in *Qumrân Grotte 4.III (4Q482-4Q520)* (DJD 7; Oxford: Clarendon Press, 1982). See now J. H. Charlesworth et al. (eds.), *The Dead Sea Scrolls. Hebrew, Aramaic, and Greek Texts with English Translations*, Vol. 2. *Damascus Document, War Scroll, and Related Documents* (Tübingen: Mohr-Siebeck; Louisville: Westminster John Knox, 1995) 80-203.

[35] Cf. his review in *RevQ* 9 (1978) 599-603.

[36] J. J. Collins, "The Mythology of Holy War in Daniel and the Qumran War Scroll: A Point of Transition in Jewish Apocalyptic," *VT* 25 (1975) 596-612; idem, "Dualism and Eschatology in 1QM. A Reply to P. R. Davies," *VT* 29 (1979) 212-

columns 15–19 are the core of 1QM, while P. Skehan[37] has correctly pointed out that the palaeography of 1QM excludes the very late date of the final redaction as postulated by Davies.

Davies did not investigate the question of the literary genre of 1QM, a void that has been filled by J. Duhaime.[38] In contrast to H. Michaud who regarded the document as an apocalypse, and Carmignac who viewed it as a liturgy for the holy war, Duhaime confirmed Yadin's thesis that the War Scroll is an authentic military textbook. Its unrealistic character should be explained by assuming that the author antithetically made use of this genre in order to show how the prescriptions of the Law could be observed during the final war. Quite another view was put forward by M. Krieg,[39] according to whom 1QM 15–19 is a cultic drama of a relatively late date and influenced by the mystery cults. In Krieg's opinion, col. 1 of 1QM stems from pre-Qumranic Hellenistic times and cols. 2–14 from the Qumran community itself. It is no surprise that these idiosyncratic views were not positively received.

3.5 The Hymns (Hodayot)

The Hodayot scroll from Cave 1 (1QH) has suffered a good deal of physical damage. After E. Sukenik[40] reconstructed 18 columns but could not locate the 66 fragments of the document, J. Carmignac[41] proposed a different order for the columns. Some years later, É. Puech[42] succeeded in reconstructing the original order of 24 columns

---

16. See also P. R. Davies, "Dualism and Eschatology in the Qumran War Scroll," *VT* 28 (1978) 28-36; idem, "Dualism and Eschatology in 1QM. A Rejoinder," *VT* 30 (1980) 93-97.

[37] Cf. Skehan's review of Davies' book in *CBQ* 40 (1978), 602-03.

[38] J. Duhaime, "The War Scroll from Qumran and the Greco-Roman Tactical Treatises," in F. García Martínez and É. Puech (eds.), *Etudes Qumrâniennes. Mémorial Jean Carmignac* (Paris: Gabalda, 1988) 133-51.

[39] M. Krieg, "Moʿēd Nāqām: Ein Kultdrama aus Qumran. Beobachtungen an der Kriegsrolle," *TZ* 41 (1985) 3-30.

[40] E. L. Sukenik, אוצר המגילות הגנוזות.

[41] J. Carmignac and P. Guilbert, *Les textes de Qumrân traduits et annotés* (Paris; Laetouzey et Ané, 1961) 129.

[42] É. Puech, "Quelques aspects de la restauration du Rouleau des Hymnes (1QH)," *JJS* 39 (1988) 38-55. See also idem, "Un hymne essénien en partie retrouvé et les Béatitudes. 1QH V 12–VI 18 (= col. XIII–XIV 7) et 4QBéat.," in García Martínez and Puech (eds.), *Mémorial Jean Carmignac*, 59-88; idem,

together with the location of the fragments. This reconstruction is remarkably consistent with an earlier analysis by H. Stegemann proposed in his unpublished Heidelberg dissertation.[43] The thesis of the homogeneity of 1QH that was advocated by Sukenik and A. Dupont-Sommer[44] (who considered the Teacher of Righteousness as the author of the collection), was disputed by S. Holm-Nielsen[45] and G. Morawe.[46] Working independently, these two scholars categorized cols. 2:3–7:25 and 8:4–9:36 as individual thanksgiving psalms, and the remaining compositions as hymns. Despite resorting to different arguments, G. Jeremias,[47] J. Becker[48] and H.-W. Kuhn[49] attributed the vast majority of the psalms in 2:1–8:40 to the Teacher of Righteousness.

In 1981 B. Kittel[50] conceded that the Teacher may have written some of the poems, but remarks that the "I" of the hymns "could be embraced by the whole community as their experience, too"—a statement which contradicts G. Jeremias' earlier observation[51] that no prayer could repeat what the Teacher of Righteousness in his poems claimed as his particular and own experience. For the same

---

"Restauration d'un texte hymnique à partir des trois manuscrits fragmentaires: 1QH^a xv 37–xvi 4 (vii 34–viii 3), 1Q35 (H^b) 1,9-14, 4Q428 (H^b) 7," *RevQ* 16 (1995) 543-58.

[43] H. Stegemann, "Rekonstruktion der Hodajot" (diss., Heidelberg: Heidelberg University, 1963).

[44] A. Dupont-Sommer, *Aperçus préliminaires sur les manuscrits de la Mer Morte* (Paris: Maisonneuve, 1950), esp. 86.

[45] S. Holm-Nielsen, *Hodayot: Psalms from Qumran* (Aarhus: Universitetsforlaget, 1960) 312-23.

[46] G. Morawe, *Aufbau und Abgrenzung der Loblieder von Qumran* (TA 16; Berlin: Evangelische Verlagsanstalt, 1961) 107.

[47] G. Jeremias, *Der Lehrer der Gerechtigkeit* (SUNT 2; Göttingen: Vandenhoeck & Ruprecht, 1963).

[48] J. Becker, *Das Heil Gottes: Heils- und Sündenbegriffe in den Qumrantexten und im Neuen Testament* (SUNT 3; Göttingen: Vandenhoeck & Ruprecht, 1963).

[49] H.-W. Kuhn, *Enderwartung und gegenwärtiges Heil: Untersuchungen zu den Gemeindeliedern von Qumran* (SUNT 4; Göttingen: Vandenhoeck & Ruprecht, 1966).

[50] B. P. Kittel, *The Hymns of Qumran. Translation and Commentary* (SBLDS 50; Chico, CA: Scholars Press, 1981).

[51] G. Jeremias, *Der Lehrer der Gerechtigkeit* (Göttingen: Vandenhoeck & Ruprecht, 1963) 168-267.

reason Holm-Nielsen's, Kittel's and Kuhn's assumption that 1QH had a cultic *Sitz im Leben* in the liturgy of the Qumran community is to be doubted. A didactic use of the poems by its members is just as feasible, although admittedly uncertain. While the artistic quality of the hymns has often been characterized as a poor imitation of canonical poetry and as a biblical mosaic, Kittel attributed this evaluation to an inadequate understanding of the poetic forms used at Qumran and modern distaste for apocalyptic imagery. She tried to counter this disqualification by illuminating then-current literary techniques and the stylistic features of the poetry by which attention is drawn to linguistic and formal dependence on the canonical psalms on the one hand, and to the author's distinct personal contribution on the other.

3.6 The Genesis Apocryphon (1QapGen)

The Genesis Apocryphon from Cave 1, which was composed in Aramaic, has been judiciously commented upon by J. Fitzmyer.[52] The severely damaged scroll, probably written in the 1st century BCE, has been described as an early form of midrash but is (with Fitzmyer and C. Evans)[53] better defined as an exemplar of the "rewritten Bible." In its extant portions, the document draws on embellishments of the birth and life of Noah and Abraham and glosses over the moral weaknesses of the patriarchs. More recently, J. Greenfield and E. Qimron[54] have succeeded in reconstructing the major part of col. 12, which deals with Noah and his vineyard.

3.7 The Habakkuk Commentary (1QpHab)

The Habakkuk Commentary from Cave 1 is an example of the genre of the *pesharim*, i.e. Bible commentaries which interpret the prophetic message as a prediction referring to the history of the Qumran community and the final age. M. Horgan[55] dealt with the available documents of this genre and rightly observed that not all of

---

[52] J. A. Fitzmyer, *The Genesis Apocryphon of Qumran Cave 1. A Commentary* (BibOr 18A; Rome: Pontifical Biblical Institute, 1966 [2nd ed., 1971]).

[53] C. A. Evans, "The Genesis Apocryphon and the Rewritten Bible," in García Martínez and Puech (eds.), *Mémorial Jean Carmignac*, 153-65.

[54] J. C. Greenfield and E. Qimron, "The Genesis Apocryphon Col. XII," in T. Muraoka (ed.), *Studies in Qumran Aramaic* (Leuven: Peeters, 1994) 70-77.

[55] M. P. Horgan, *Pesharim. Qumran Interpretation of Biblical Books* (CBQMS 8; Washington, DC: Catholic Biblical Association, 1979).

them are autographa. However, the problems which the *pesharim* present appear to be insufficiently solved in her work.

Notwithstanding the use of the term *midrash* in 4QFlorilegium 1, line 14, I. Rabinowitz[56] maintained that a pesher cannot be regarded as a type of midrash, whether in method or in form, comparable to those that are known in Rabbinic literature. While admitting that the Habakkuk commentary provides revelatory interpretation, L. H. Silberman[57] found instead a strong structural and methodological relationship between the Qumran pesharim and the rabbinical *petira*. F. García Martínez[58] protested this view by asserting that, although the hermeneutical rules of the pesher-method are no different from those of the Rabbinic midrashim, the Qumranic type of interpretation rests on a revelation given to the Teacher of Righteousness. In order to articulate the relationship between the pesharim and the Rabbinic midrashim, and the differences between them, E. Slomovic[59] and W. Brownlee[60] spoke of a "midrash pesher." According to the latter scholar, who as a rule translated the term *pesher* by "prophetic meaning," the Targums may well have been models for the organization of the pesharim. In his opinion, the Teacher of Righteousness may have used the pesher as his method of instruction. Although the pesharim were committed to writing several decades after his death, many of their interpretative features go back to the Teacher and (as in the case of Daniel) to divine revelation that was accorded to him.

D. Dimant[61] views the relationship of the historical eschatological exegesis of the pesharim to the community of Qumran, rather than their interpretative features, as decisive for the definition of their literary genre. Yet she also states that the pesharim can only be

---

[56] I. Rabinowitz, "Pesher/Pittarôn. Its Biblical Meaning and its Significance in the Qumran Literature," *RevQ* 8 (1972-1976) 219-32.

[57] L. H. Silberman, "Unriddling the Riddle. A Study in the Structure and Language of the Habakkuk Pesher 1QpHab," *RevQ* 3 (1961-1962) 323-64.

[58] F. García Martínez, "El pesher: interpretacíon profética de la Escritura," *Salmanticensis* 26 (1979) 125-39.

[59] E. Slomovic, "Towards an Understanding of the Exegesis of the Dead Sea Scrolls," *RevQ* 7 (1969-1971) 3-15.

[60] W. H. Brownlee, *The Midrash Pesher of Habakkuk* (Missoula, MT; Scholars Press, 1979).

[61] D. Dimant, "Qumran Sectarian Literature," 503ff.

understood with the aid of a divinely inspired interpretation, i.e. by the Teacher of Righteousness. G. Brooke,[62] however, seems to have doubts about a *Sonderoffenbarung*:

> Inspiration, if any, does not lie in the result of the exegesis as such, in its contents, but rather in the ability of any member of the community and especially the Teacher of Righteousness to interpret scripture through the correct application of exegetical techniques. If the techniques had not been used, then there would have been no objective means whereby the Qumran audience could have judged the validity or otherwise of the 'inspired interpretation.'[63]

In his book on the literary genre of the Habakkuk Commentary,[64] H. Feltes pointed out that 1QpHab 7:4ff. (where it is said that God disclosed all the mysteries of his servants, the prophets, to the Teacher of Righteousness) does not refer to exegetical mysteries but to the eschatological decisions of God. Therefore, he added, this passage should not be adduced as evidence of biblical exposition by divine revelation. This seems to be a correct observation: the pesharim of Qumran as such are not inspired writings, although they take the view revealed to the Teacher of Righteousness that the prophetic message predicted the history of the community and the final age.

K. Elliger's commentary on 1QpHab[65] (1953) was an admirable interpretation in the early years of Qumran research, and was followed twenty-five years later (1979) by W. Brownlee's exposition which summarized his lengthy occupation with the scroll.[66] Brownlee's exegesis, however, was mainly concerned with linguistic questions and proposals for filling out the lacunae of the available text, paying scant attention to the identification of the persons and events that are referred to in the document. In connection with the "Groningen hypothesis," we will shortly deal with the latter questions.

---

[62] G. J. Brooke, *Exegesis at Qumran. 4QFlorilegium in its Jewish Context* (JSOTSup 29; Sheffield: JSOT Press, 1985).

[63] Brooke, *Exegesis at Qumran*, 43-44.

[64] H. Feltes, *Die Gattung des Habakukkommentars von Qumran (1QpHab). Eine Studie zum frühen jüdischen Midrasch* (FB 58; Würzburg: Echter Verlag, 1986).

[65] K. Elliger, *Studien zum Habakuk-Kommentar vom Toten Meer* (Tübingen: Mohr-Siebeck, 1953).

[66] Brownlee, *Midrash Pesher*.

3.8 The Damascus Document (CD)

After the discovery in 1896 of medieval manuscripts of the Damascus Document (CD) in the Ezra synagogue of Old Cairo, and their edition by Solomon Schechter in 1910 (re-edited in 1970 with a prolegomenon by J. Fitzmyer),[67] it came as somewhat of a surprise that copies of the same work appeared in Caves 4, 5 and 6 at Qumran. Because the oldest manuscript (from Cave 4) stems from the first half of the 1st century BCE, this work must have been composed not much later than 100 BCE. Their presence there confirms the early intuition of Israel Levi[68] that the work was of Sadducean (Essene?) origin and has led to the conclusion that the medieval manuscripts have only partially preserved the original text. The original sequence of its component parts is as follows:[69]

(a) Introduction (lacking in CD, but partially preserved in 4QD^a and 4QD^b)
(b) CD cols. 1–8, 19–20
(c) Ordinances (preserved in different manuscripts from Cave 4)
(d) CD cols. 15–16, 9–14
(e) Other ordinances (found in 4QD^b)
(e) A codex of atonement (preserved in 4QD$^{b, d, e}$)
(f) A ritual pertaining to the excommunication of members and the conclusion of the work (found in 4QD^b and 4QD^e).

The complete Damascus Document work falls into two parts: the Admonition and the Laws. The structure of the former is complex and has led to a number of literary analyses. Three sources were

---

[67] S. Schechter, *Documents of Jewish Sectaries* (Prolegomenon by J. A. Fitzmyer; New York: Ktav, 1970). A new edition is to be found in M. Broshi (ed.), *The Damascus Document Reconsidered* (Jerusalem: Israel Exploration Society–Shrine of the Book–Israel Museum, 1992), in which partial account is taken of the fragments from Caves 4-6 and which contains a full bibliography for the years 1970-1989 compiled by F. García Martínez (supplementing the bibliography provided by J. A. Fitzmyer in *The Dead Sea Scrolls: Major Publications and Tools for Study*, 25-34). A transcription and annotated translation of CD and the fragments from Caves 4-6 is published in Charlesworth et al. (eds.), *Dead Sea Scrolls* (Vol. 2), 4-79. The critical edition was recently published: J. M. Baumgarten at al. (eds.), *Qumran Cave 4.XIII: The Damascus Document (4Q266-273)* (DJD 18; Oxford: Clarendon Press, 1996).

[68] I. Levi, "Un écrit sadducéen antérieur à la destruction du Temple," *REJ* 63 (1912) 1-19.

[69] This was already observed by J. T. Milik, *Ten Years of Discovery in the Wilderness of Judaea* (London: SCM Press, 1959) 58-60.

identified by A.-M. Denis[70] (1:12–4:6; 4:6–6:11; 7:4–8:21 = 19-20), which in his opinion successively reflect the developing self-understanding of the Qumran community. In a series of articles,[71] J. Murphy-O'Connor distinguished four documents which had existed independently prior to the settlement of some Essenes at Qumran: a Missionary Document (2:14–6:1) dating to the time of the Maccabees; a Memorandum (6:2–8:3) from a later period; the Critique of the Princes of Judah (8:3-18) from the time of Jonathan; and the Appeal to Fidelity (19:33–20:1b, 8b-13, 17b-34) from the period after the death of the Teacher of Righteousness. P. Davies[72] concurred with Murphy-O'Connor's hypothesis that the Admonition contains pre-Qumranic material, but in his opinion the original work comprised 1:1–7:9 and 20:27-34; for him not only the "Missionary Document," but the Admonition as a whole, should be characterized as catechetical rather than apologetic. In Davies' view the warnings of 7:10–8:19 supplemented the original work in a second redaction. A third redaction added 19:33–20:26 to the whole and reworked the former editions, *inter alia* by transposing 1:1–2:1 into a *Heilsgeschichte* of the community of Qumran.

But D. Dimant[73] rejected the theses of Murphy-O'Connor and Davies as speculative and advocated instead the literary unity of CD, including the Laws. Although J. Boyce[74] supposed a gradual growth of the Damascus Document, he arrived[75] at conclusions that clearly differ from Davies' analysis. In Boyce's opinion, CD and 1QS are contemporaneous, with the former document intended for the

---

[70] A.-M. Denis, *Les thèmes de connaissance dans le Document de Damas* (Louvain: Publications universitaires, 1967).

[71] J. Murphy-O'Connor, "An Essene Missionary Document? CD II,14–VI,1," *RB* 77 (1970) 201-29; idem, "A Literary Analysis of Damascus Document VI,2–VIII, 3," *RB* 78 (1971) 210-32; idem, "The Original Text of CD 7:9–8:2 = 19:5-14," *HTR* 64 (1971) 379-86; idem, "The Critique of the Princes of Judah (CD VIII, 3-19)," *RB* 79 (1972) 200-16; idem, "A Literary Analysis of Damascus Document XIX,33–XX,34," *RB* 79 (1972) 544-64.

[72] P. R. Davies, *The Damascus Covenant. An Interpretation of the "Damascus Document"* (JSOTSup 25; Sheffield: JSOT Press, 1982).

[73] D. Dimant, "The Damascus Document," in M. E. Stone (ed.), *Jewish Writings from the Second Temple Period*, 490-97.

[74] J. M. Boyce, "The Poetry of the Damascus Document and Its Bearing on the Qumran Sect," *RevQ* 14 (1989) 615-28.

[75] Because of his distinction between poetic and midrashic passages.

Essenes outside Qumran, and the latter for the Qumran community itself. While this view is attractive and has also been adopted by other authors, it hardly explains the fact that the Teacher of Righteousness (who founded the Qumran community) figures in the text of CD. Moreover, the precise identification of the "land of Damascus," where the "converts of Israel" who left Judah found refuge, remains a serious problem which until now has not been satisfactorily resolved.[76] Meanwhile, the assertion of C. Rabin and H. Stegemann[77] that the Admonition once formed a separate writing which was independent from and without relationship to the Laws, seems to be contradicted by the fragments of CD that were found in Cave 4. A series of useful studies on the laws of CD and the Cave 4 fragments of the work has been presented by J. Baumgarten.[78]

3.9 The Temple Scroll (11QT^a)

This, the longest manuscript discovered in the Qumran caves, was copied in Herodian times and published in 1977 by Y. Yadin in modern Hebrew (three volumes and a supplement).[79] This was

---

[76] On this problem see, for example, P. R. Davies, "The Birthplace of the Essenes: Where is 'Damascus'?" *RevQ* 14 (1990) 503-19.

[77] C. Rabin, *The Zadokite Documents* (Oxford: Clarendon Press, 1958) x; H. Stegemann, "Das Gesetzeskorpus der 'Damaskusschrift' (CD IX–XVI)," *RevQ* 14 (1989-90) 409-34.

[78] J. M. Baumgarten, "4Q Zadokite Fragments on Skin Disease," *JJS* 41 (1990) 153-65; idem, "The Laws of the Damascus Document in Current Research," in Broshi (ed.), *Damascus Document Reconsidered*, 51-62; idem, "The Disqualification of Priests in 4Q Fragments of the Damascus Document. A Specimen of the Recovery of pre-Rabbinic Halakha," in J. Trebolle Barrera and L. Vegas Montaner (eds.), *Proceedings of the International Congress on the Dead Sea Scrolls—Madrid, 18-21 March 1991* (2 vols., STDJ 11; Leiden: Brill; Madrid: Universidad Complutense, 1992) 2.503-15.

[79] Y. Yadin, מגילת המקדש (Jerusalem: The Israel Exlporation Society–Institute of Archaeology of the Hebrew University of Jerusalem–Shrine of the Book, 1977; English translation: *The Temple Scroll* [Jerusalem: Israel Exploration Society, 1983]). A popular introduction to the Temple Scroll was published by Yadin in his *The Temple Scroll: The Hidden Law of the Dead Sea Sect* (New York: Random House, 1985). Cf. also J. Maier, *Die Tempelrolle vom Toten Meer übersetzt und erläutert* (Munich: Reinhardt, 1978; English translation: *The Temple Scroll. An Introduction, Translation, and Commentary* [Sheffield: JSOT Press, 1985]). As to the measurements of the Temple courts, Maier advocates a "maximal solution" over against Yadin's "minimal solution."

followed in 1983 by an English edition which is basically identical with the Hebrew one, apart from a discussion of textual corrections proposed by other scholars, and a short treatment of the literature on the scroll since 1977. A new critical edition based upon all previous studies, all available photographs and the original scroll itself—together with a full listing of all possible alternative readings—was produced by E. Qimron in 1996 and includes a classified bibliography by F. García Martínez.[80] Yadin was able to make use of fragments of another copy of the work (11QT[b]), which was also found in Cave 11 and copied in Herodian times, and had been allotted for publication in 1961 by the Jordanian authorities to the Royal Dutch Academy of Sciences and Arts.

In a lecture delivered by J. van der Ploeg on these fragments at the Leuven Qumran congress of 1976,[81] Yadin is reported to have been ignorant of the agreement and to have claimed that Father R. de Vaux had given him permission to include the new material in his edition of the Temple Scroll. F. García Martínez[82] re-edited these fragments with joins which were unknown to Yadin, and the present writer showed that the Israeli scholar had overlooked a fragment belonging to the second manuscript of the work.[83] While Yadin thought that 4Q364-365,[84] which date to Hasmonaean times, were also parts of the Temple Scroll, they seem to belong instead to a Paraphrase of the Pentateuch.[85]

The Temple Scroll deals with instructions pertaining to the erection and the furnishings of the Temple in the holy city, its courts and festival calendar, as well as purity laws and prescriptions mainly

---

[80] E. Qimron, *The Temple Scroll. A Critical Edition with Extensive Reconstructions*, with a Bibliography by F. García Martínez (Beer-Sheva: Ben-Gurion University of the Negev ; Jerusalem: Israel Exploration Society, 1996).

[81] J. P. M. van der Ploeg, "Un halakha inédite de Qumrân," in M. Delcor (ed.), *Qumrân: Sa piété, sa théologie et son milieu* (BETL 46; Paris and Gembloux: Duculot, 1978) 107-13.

[82] F. García Martínez, "11QTemple[b]: A Preliminary Publication," in Trebolle Barrera and Vegas Montaner (eds.), *The Madrid Qumran Congress*, 2.363-91.

[83] A. S. van der Woude, "Ein bisher unveröffentlichtes Fragment der Tempelrolle," *RevQ* 13 (1988) 89-92.

[84] 4Q364-365 were published by E. Tov and S. White in H. Attridge et al. (eds.), *Qumran Cave 4.VIII: Parabiblical Texts, Part I* (DJD 13; Oxford: Clarendon Press, 1994).

[85] Which, however, may have been one of its sources.

based on Deuteronomy 12-26. It has been the focus of a plethora of comments—especially concerning its character, provenance and composition. According to Yadin, the scroll is a real Torah that contains divine revelation for the whole of Israel, and constitutes the fundamental law of the Essene movement. Its author based himself on biblical traditions, which he either reproduced or modified, and then harmonized and joined, adding passages of his own in the process. Yadin thus regarded him as an editor rather than an author. B. Z. Wacholder,[86] however, tried to show that the Temple Scroll was the work of a real author, whom he identified with the Teacher of Righteousness (the Zadok of CD 5:5!). This author's intention was to replace the old Mosaic Law by a new and superior Torah, which he composed about 200 BCE. Wacholder's idiosyncratic identifications of figures that are mentioned in CD and 1QpHab—and the fact that he totally ignores the complicated redactional history of 1QS—are only two reasons why his study did not produce a serious alternative to the views of Yadin.

Yadin claimed that 11QT is of Qumranic origin,[87] on the basis of parallels with CD, 1QM and the Nahum Commentary from Cave 4 (4QpNah) and on the grounds that a solar calendar of 364 days is presupposed; however, this view has been vigorously challenged by B. Levine,[88] L. Schiffman,[89] H. Stegemann[90] and others. While Stegemann's dating of the composition of 11QT in the 5th or 4th century BCE does not seem to be convincing, Levine's and García Martínez's[91] thesis that it slightly antedates the settlement of the

---

[86] B. Z. Wacholder, *The Dawn of Qumran. The Sectarian Torah and the Teacher of Righteousness* (HUCM 8; Cincinnati, OH: Hebrew Union College, 1983).

[87] Y. Yadin, "Is the Temple Scroll a Sectarian Document?," in G. M. Tucker and D. A. Knight (eds.), *Humanizing America's Iconic Book: Society of Biblical Literature Centennial Addresses 1980* (Chico, CA: Scholars Press, 1982) 153-69.

[88] B. A. Levine, "The Temple Scroll: Aspects of Its Historical Provenance and Literary Character," *BASOR* 232 (1978) 5-23.

[89] L. A. Schiffman, "The Temple Scroll in Literary and Philological Perspective," in W. S. Green (ed.), *Approaches to Ancient Judaism II* (BJS 11; Chico, CA: Scholars Press, 1980) 143-58.

[90] H. Stegemann, "The Origins of the Temple Scroll," in J. A. Emerton (ed.), *Congress Volume Jerusalem 1986* (VTSup 40; Leiden: Brill, 1988) 235-56.

[91] F. García Martínez, "Essénisme qumrânien: Origines, caractéristiques, héritage," in B. Chiesa (ed.), *Correnti culturali e movimenti religiosi del giudaismo*

Qumran community in the desert carries conviction. This proposal explains both the affinities of the Temple Scroll with certain sectarian writings and the dissimilarities between its contents and distinct compositions of the community. These differences include the following: the interests found in 11QT differ from those expressed in typical Qumran documents; the way in which Holy Scripture is interpreted seems to be at variance with the Qumran commentaries; the halakhah in the document shows evidence of alterations; the covenant festival mentioned in 1QS is not alluded to in 11QT; and attitudes towards the Temple and its authorities differ in the Temple Scroll and in the writings authored by members of the Qumran community.

M. Wilson and L. Wills[92] have convincingly shown that the Temple Scroll is a composite work. A major contribution to the study of 11QT^a has been published by M. Wise,[93] in which two decades of research are critically summarized and an elaborate compositional analysis of the document is provided. Wise distinguishes between: (a) a "Deuteronomy Source" (cols. 51–56; 60–66), which was taken over by the author of 11QT without notable modifications; (b) a "Temple Source" (roughly cols. 3–13; 30–47); (c) a "Midrash to Deuteronomy Source" (cols. 57:1–59:21; 60:2-11; 64:6b-13a), which according to Wise[94] cannot be used as a means to date the Temple Scroll; and (d) a "Festival Calendar Source" (cols. 13:8–29:2). He assumes that the redactor inserted into these sources many different laws that derive from the community described in CD, from which the redactor himself must have originated. In Wise's opinion, the redactor—who intended his work as a law for the eschaton—was the Teacher of Righteousness, who composed the final redaction about 150 BCE.

(Atti del V Congresso internazionale dell' AISG; Associazione italiana per lo studio del giudaismo. Testi i studi 5; Roma: Carucci, 1987) 37-57.

[92] A. M. Wilson and L. Willis, "Literary Sources in the Temple Scroll," *HTR* 75 (1982) 275-88.

[93] M. O. Wise, *A Critical Study of the Temple Scroll from Cave 11* (SAOC 49; Chicago: The Oriental Institute of the University of Chicago, 1990). See also F. García Martínez, "Sources et rédaction du Rouleau du Temple," *Henoch* 13 (1991) 219-32 and his review in *JSJ* 22 (1991) 155-61.

[94] Consequently, Wise criticizes the standpoint of M. Hengel, J. H. Charlesworth and D. Mendel, in "The Polemical Character of 'On Kingship' in the Temple Scroll. An Attempt at Dating 11QTemple," *JJS* 37 (1986) 28-38.

3.10 Miqṣat Maʿaśe Ha-Torah (4QMMT)

One of the most intriguing and controversial documents from Cave 4 is מקצת מעשי התורה ("Some of the Works of the Torah"), also known as the *Halakhic Letter* (4Q394-399).[95] This work most likely contained an opening formula,[96] a calendar,[97] a list of halakhot in which the senders differed from their opponents,[98] and an epilogue outlining the reasons for their withdrawal from the rest of the people and offering a surprisingly friendly appeal to the leader of the addressees to return to the right way. While the six fragmentary copies of 4QMMT date from the second half of the 1st century BCE to the first half of the 1st century CE, the work seems to have been composed in the second half of the 2nd century BCE. It is written in a type of Hebrew that seems to be intermediate between biblical and Mishnaic Hebrew, probably the colloquial language of the time.

In a preliminary publication, E. Qimron and J. Strugnell[99] thought that MMT was a letter from a leader of the Qumran sect (possibly the Teacher of Righteousness) to the leader of its opponents (possibly Jonathan or Simon). In their final edition, however, they have somewhat changed their views by suggesting that the document may be a treatise dealing with some points of the Sadducean halakhah, or a codex treating controversies which had forced the "Zadokite" Essenes to dissociate themselves from another group (later known as the Pharisees). There is a conspicuous similarity between the legal views found in 4QMMT and the positions which Rabbinical literature attributes to the Sadducees (cf. *m. Yadayim* 4:6-7). This fact has led L. Schiffman[100] to propose that the Qumranites were pious Sadducees, although he admits that they are not to be identified with

---

[95] E. Qimron and J. Strugnell, *Qumran Cave 4.V: Miqṣat Maʿaśe ha-Torah* (DJD 10; Oxford: Clarendon Press, 1994).

[96] Now entirely lost.

[97] Only partly preserved in 4Q394.

[98] Most of these are partially or completely preserved.

[99] E. Qimron and J. Strugnell, "An Unpublished Halakhic Letter from Qumran," in *Biblical Archaeology Today: Proceedings of the International Congress on Biblical Archaeology, Jerusalem, April 1984* (Jerusalem: Israel Exploration Society–Israel Academy of Sciences and Humanities–ASOR, 1985) 400-07.

[100] L. H. Schiffman, "The New Halakhic Letter (4QMMT) and the Origins of the Dead Sea Sect," *BA* 53 (1990) 64-73; idem, "Origins and Early History of the Qumran Sect," *BA* 58 (1995) 37-48.

the Hellenized Sadducees that are described by Josephus and mentioned in the New Testament. Aside from the fact that it is not surprising for some of the legal views held by the conservative Qumranites (who called themselves "sons of Zadok") to coincide with those of the Sadducees, Schiffman's use of the term "Sadducee" is too ambiguous to allow the identification which he suggests. Moreover, Josephus' description of the differences between the Sadducees, Pharisees and Essenes, as well as the anti-Saducean doctrines found in the Qumran writings, render it improbable that the Qumran community arose from Saducean origins. Meanwhile, the twin problem of just who the senders of 4QMMT were, and who their addressees were, remains a moot question. It seems safe to presume that the latter were the Jerusalem clergy and their leader. Identifying the sender of the document as the Teacher of Righteousness cannot be excluded; however, this has not been substantiated so far. In any case, "scholarship is just beginning to scratch the surface of this fragmentary document" (M. Bernstein).[101]

3.11 1 Enoch

The publication by J. T. Milik[102] of Aramaic fragments from eleven manuscripts of 1 Enoch that were found in 1952 in Cave 4 has more or less revolutionized research into this pseudepigraphon. Four of these represent the Astronomical Book of 1 Enoch (chapters 72–82); the rest contain portions of the other Enochic booklets, with the exception of the Similitudes (chapters 37–71).

According to Milik, the *Astronomical Book* is the oldest Enochic writing known to us. 4QEnastr^a (late 3rd or early 2nd century BCE) and 4QEnastr^b (beginning of the 1st century CE) contain parts of a lengthy, summarized "calendar"[103] which synchronises the phases of the moon with the course of the sun during a solar year of 364 days, and describes the course of the celestial bodies from one gate of heaven to the next. The rest of 4QEnastr^b and 4QEnastr^c (mid-1st century BCE) offer a text that only approximately corresponds with parts of the Ethiopic version of chapters 76–79 and 82. 4QEnastr^d

---

[101] Cf. the studies collected in J. Kampen and M. J. Bernstein (eds.), *Reading 4QMMT. New Perspectives on Qumran Law and History* (SBLSS 2; Atlanta: Scholars Press, 1996) 50.

[102] J. T. Milik, *The Books of Enoch. Aramaic Fragments of Qumran Cave 4* (Oxford; Clarendon Press, 1976).

[103] In the Ethiopic version, this calendar is found in 73:1–74:9.

(second half of the 1st century BCE) completes, by its description of the winter, the picture of spring and summer that abruptly ends in the Ethiopic text. The rest of this document deals with the courses of the stars and with the firmament.

Whether this is the original conclusion of the Astronomical Book (thus Milik) or has to be placed before chap. 79 (thus J. VanderKam)[104] is difficult to decide. O. Neugebauer[105] dealt in great detail with the Astronomical Book, whose Ethiopic version in his opinion is extremely composite. In his commentary, M. Black[106] essentially accepted Neugebauer's ideas, denying the existence of a separate Astronomical Book in Aramaic. VanderKam, on the other hand, advocated the literary unity of chapters 72-78; 82:9-20, 79; and 82:1-8. F. García Martínez[107] rejected Black's thesis completely, on the grounds that Eupolemus and Jub. 4:17 presuppose an Astronomical Enochic writing. Just why the Astronomical Book bases itself on an early stage of Babylonian astronomy is so far unexplained; as pointed out by J. Greenfield and M. Stone,[108] there are no compelling reasons for dating its origin earlier than the 3rd century BCE. What it does show, however, is that a 364-day solar calendar was being used in that century, although it is unclear whether this calendar was sectarian (R. Beckwith)[109] or not (VanderKam).[110]

The Aramaic fragments of the *Book of the Watchers* (1 Enoch 1-36) evidence in principle the same textual tradition as the Greek and

---

[104] J. C. VanderKam, *Enoch and the Growth of an Apocalyptic Tradition* (CBQMS 16; Washington, DC: The Catholic Biblical Association of America, 1984).

[105] O. Neugebauer, *The "Astronomical" Chapters of the Ethiopic Book of Enoch (72-82)* (Copenhagen: Kongelige Danske Videnskabernes Selskab, 1981).

[106] M. Black, with J. C. VanderKam, *The Book of Enoch or 1 Enoch. A New English Edition with Commentary and Textual Notes* (SVTP 7; Leiden: Brill, 1985).

[107] F. García Martínez, "Estudios Qumránicos 1975-1985: Panorama crítico I," *Estudios Bíblicos* 45 (1987) 125-205.

[108] J. C. Greenfield and M. E. Stone, "The Books of Enoch and the Traditions of Enoch," *Numen* 26 (1979) 89-103.

[109] R. T. Beckwith, "The Earliest Enoch Literature and its Calendar. Marks of their Origin, Date and Motivation," *RevQ* 10 (1979-1981) 365-403.

[110] J. C. VanderKam, "Some Major Issues in the Contemporary Study of I Enoch," *Maarav* 3 (1982) 85-97.

Ethiopic versions, and have made it possible to solve a number of long-debated questions. On the basis of 4QEn^a (early 2nd century BCE) and 4QEn^b (mid-2nd century BCE), chapters 1–5 now seem to be an introduction to the Book of Watchers[111] and were apparently already part of this work in the 2nd century BCE. The thesis that the Book of Watchers as we have it dates to the 3rd century BCE is now widely accepted, but Milik's contention that chapters 6–19 form a literary unity has been sharply criticized by C. Newsom,[112] Collins,[113] Black and García Martínez on the following grounds: chapters 12–16 must be clearly distinguished from 17–19 and 6–11; and the latter contain at least two different traditions (the cycles of Shemichaza and Asael). We may conclude that early Jewish writers knew already in the 3rd century BCE the myth of the fallen angels,[114] that the throne vision of Enoch suggests early roots of the much later Merkabah mysticism, and that Jewish apocalypticism originated much earlier than the final redaction of Daniel.

To demonstrate that the *Book of Dream Visions* (chapters 83–90) once circulated separately is not possible on the basis of 4QEn^c (end 1st century BCE), 4QEn^d (same period) and 4QEn^e (first half of the 1st century BCE); however, its contents and Jub. 4:19 suggest that this was indeed the case during the mid-2nd century BCE. Because the "big horn" (90:9) symbolizes Judas Maccabaeus (not John Hyrcanus I) and the latter's death is not yet presupposed, the Book of the Dream Visions must have been composed before 161 BCE. This is corroborated by 4QEn^f (150-125 BCE), which contains a small fragment of 1 Enoch 86:1-3.

The *Letter of Enoch* (chapters 91–108) is fragmentarily represented by 4QEn^g (mid-1st century BCE), which confirms the generally-accepted original sequence in the Apocalypse of the Ten Weeks (93:3-10; 91:11-17), and by 4QEn^c. Although the Letter may have once circulated separately (in view of its relatively archaic orthography [Milik]), it had doubtlessly been incorporated in the

---

[111] But not to 1 Enoch as a whole.

[112] C. A. Newsom, "The Development of 1 Enoch 6-19: Cosmology and Judgement," *CBQ* 42 (1980) 310-29.

[113] J. J. Collins, "The Apocalyptic Technique: Setting and Function in the Book of Watchers," *CBQ* 44 (1982) 91-111.

[114] Which is possibly told in the Book of Noah; cf. F. García Martínez, *Qumran and Apocalyptic* (STDJ 9; Leiden: Brill, 1992) 29-30.

Enochic corpus by the 1st century BCE, as is shown by 4QEn^c which also includes parts of the Book of Watchers and of the Dream Visions. 1 Enoch 105 appears not to be a *Fremdkörper* in the Letter; however, a few Aramaic remnants in 4QEn^c reveal that the original text deviated from the Ethiopic version, a fact which may confirm a Christian redaction of its contents. Whether chapters 106–107 reflect passages from the Book of Noah (thus Milik), or are to be viewed as an inclusio with 91:1-10 (thus VanderKam),[115] is a moot question; however, the two blank lines between chapters 105 and 106–107 in 4QEn^c may indicate that the latter are an addition to the Letter of Enoch.

It was Milik who discovered in the fragments of 4QEn^c (and some others from Caves 1, 2 and 6) remnants of the Book of Giants which was later included in Mani's canon, because he found in these pieces the gnostic theme of the struggle between light and darkness. García Martínez[116] has tried to reconstruct the original sequence of the contents of this work; however, K. Beyer[117] believes it to have originated from the 3rd century BCE and has proposed a different arrangement.

Milik's edition of the Aramaic Enoch fragments has often elicited sharp criticism because of his lengthy supplements to the existing portions of text, his often hypothetical transcriptions, his dating of the Book of Similitudes to about 270 CE, and his thesis that Gen. 6:1-4 depends on a "Book of the Visions of Enoch." Despite these well-founded strictures, Milik's publication is one of the major achievements in the field of Qumran studies. The same can be said of M. Knibb's edition of the Ethiopic text, with its introduction and annotated translation, in which he takes full account of the Aramaic fragments.[118]

Unfortunately, lack of space prevents us from reporting on and evaluating the scholarly discussion of other Qumran texts, many of wich are most interesting.

---

[115] *Growth of an Apocalyptic Tradition*, 174-75.

[116] *Qumran and Apocalyptic*, 110ff.

[117] K. Beyer, *Die aramäischen Texte vom Toten Meer* (Göttingen: Vandenhoeck & Ruprecht, 1984) 260ff.

[118] M. A. Knibb, *The Ethiopic Book of Enoch. A New Edition in the Light of the Aramaic Dead Sea Fragments* (Oxford: Clarendon Press, 1978).

4. ORIGINS, HISTORY AND CHARACTER OF THE QUMRAN COMMUNITY

On the basis of the striking similarities between the descriptions of the Essenes in the writings of Philo of Alexandria and Flavius Josephus, and several indications in the Dead Sea Scrolls,[119] the identification of the Qumran community with the Essenes has dominated the field from the very beginning of Qumran research. This thesis, which was already put forward by E. Sukenik in 1948, has been elaborated by A. Dupont-Sommer,[120] G. Vermes[121] and J. T. Milik,[122] and confirmed by many others. The existing contradictions between the reports of Philo and Josephus and the data offered by the scrolls have usually been played down on the assumption that Philo and Josephus were insufficiently informed, and with the assertion that we have to reckon with historical developments. T. Beall[123] pointed to six "apparent discrepancies" between Josephus' description of the Essenes and the contents of the scrolls which might challenge the identification of the Qumran community with the Essenes. But neither he nor J. VanderKam[124] considers these as serious enough grounds for denying this identification. P. Callaway,[125] however, opines that we should not treat lightly the differences between the classical sources and the Qumran writings, and that we should differentiate the Qumran community (although it was probably of Essene origin) from the Essenes as described by Philo and Josephus.

The Qumran community did not produce any historical works, not even ones pertaining to its own history. Therefore, we can only try to reconstruct indirectly its origins and history on the basis of archaeological data and a number of literary sources (especially the Qumran Bible commentaries whose authors interpreted the prophetic message as a prediction of their own community and the final age).

---

[119] Especially those provided by the Rule of the Community (1QS).

[120] A. Dupont-Sommer, *Les écrits esséniens*.

[121] G. Vermes, "The Essenes and History," *JJS* 32 (1981) 18-31.

[122] J. T. Milik, *Ten Years of Discovery*.

[123] T. S. Beall, *Josephus' Description of the Essenes Illustrated by the Dead Sea Scrolls* (SNTSMS 58; Cambridge: Cambridge University Press, 1988).

[124] J. C. VanderKam, *Dead Sea Scrolls Today*, 87ff.

[125] P. R. Callaway, *The History of the Qumran Community. An Investigation* (JSPSup 3; Sheffield: JSOT Press, 1988) 63-87.

Most notably, the Habakkuk commentary from Cave 1 (1QpHab), the Nahum commentary from Cave 4 (4QpNah or 4Q169), the first Psalms commentary from Cave 4 (4QpPs^a or 4Q171) and the Damascus Document (CD) contain data which in principle can be used in an attempt to unriddle the history of the Qumran community. P. Davies' scepticism as to the value of the pesharim as a possible source of information for the group's history ("we have no warrant to plunder them for historical data"), seems far too negative.[126] Unfortunately, however, the allusions to historical events found in the said scrolls are often obscure because use is generally made of nicknames (e.g. the Wicked Priest, the Liar, the Teacher of Righteousness, the House of Peleg), which were without doubt clear to the members of the sect but pose questions to modern interpreters. Consequently, it does not come as a surprise that scholars have not presented a uniform picture of the sect's origins and history.

As pointed out by F. García Martínez,[127] the reconstruction of the latter must comply with sound methodological procedures. First of all, the delimitations dictated by palaeographical and archaeological research must be constantly kept in mind. Since archaeological data show that phase 1a of the buildings of Qumran hardly preceded the reign of John Hyrcanus I, it is improbable that the Qumran community settled in the Qumran area before ca. 125 BCE. This seems to imply that the Teacher of Righteousness appeared on the stage of history during the second half of the 2nd century BCE, not—as has occasionally been suggested—in the first half of the century. Palaeographical considerations lead us to conclude that the Rule of the Community (1QS) was written between 100 and 75 BCE, the Habakkuk Commentary (1QpHab) and the Nahum Commentary (4QpNah) between 40 and 20 BCE, the first Psalms Commentary from Cave 4 (4QpPs^a) between 30 and 20 CE, and the oldest manuscript of the Damascus Document (4QD^a) in the first decades of the 1st century BCE. This means that the Teacher of Righteousness— who is mentioned in three of the documents (1QpHab, 4QpNah, CD) and whose death is presupposed in CD 19:35-36—must have lived at least before 80 BCE. Assuming that the oldest manuscript of the

---

[126] P. R. Davies, *Behind the Essenes: History and Ideology in the Dead Sea Scrolls* (Atlanta: Scholars Press, 1987) 27.

[127] F. García Martínez, "Qumran Origins and Early History: A Groningen Hypothesis," *Folia Orientalia* 25 (1988) 113-36.

Damascus Document we possess is not an autograph, this date must be moved backwards by a number of decades. These facts militate against B. Thiering's identification of the Teacher of Righteousness with John the Baptist and the Wicked Priest with Jesus of Nazareth,[128] let alone R. Eisenman's identification of the Teacher with James the Just, the brother of Jesus.[129]

Second, we must allow a certain period for the evolution of the ideology that eventually led to the establishment of the Qumran community. It is therefore improbable that the moment at which the members of the community settled in the Qumran region coincided with the time when the Teacher of Righteousness made his first appearance, as has been suggested by J. Murphy-O'Connor.[130]

The oldest, yet most widely-accepted, theory on the origins of the Essene movement traces its beginnings to the "synagogue of the Hasideans" (2 Macc 2:42; 7:13; 2 Macc 14:6) at the time of the Maccabean revolt. Ever since his 1953 publication,[131] G. Vermes has defended this thesis repeatedly,[132] interpreting the "age of wrath" (CD 1:5) as the Hellenistic crisis and the "root of planting" (CD 1:7) as the Hasidean movement. However, this explanation—although adhered to by a wide range of scholars—is beset with a number of difficulties. It has been pointed out that we know very little about the Hasideans, and that no necessary connection between them and the Essenes can be shown.[133] García Martínez remarks that neither Philo nor Josephus mentions Qumran, and that according to these authors Essenes taught in the Jerusalem Temple, were in the service of Herod the Great, and (even during the first Jewish revolt) carried on the government of provinces. Such facts seem hardly compatible with the secluded society that the Qumran community apparently was.

---

[128] See, for example, her *Redating the Teacher of Righteousness* (ANZSTR 1; Sydney: Theological Explorations, 1979).

[129] R. Eisenman, *Maccabees, Zadokites, Christians and Qumran. A New Hypothesis of Qumran Origins* (SPB 34; Leiden: Brill, 1983); idem, *James the Just in the Habakkuk Pesher* (SPB 35; Leiden: Brill, 1986); idem, *Jesus the Brother of James. The Key to Unlocking the Secret of Early Christianity and the Dead Sea Scrolls* (New York: Viking, 1995).

[130] "The Essenes and Their History," *RB* 81 (1974) 215-44.

[131] *Les Manuscrits du désert de Juda* (Paris: Desclée, 1953).

[132] For example, in "The Essenes and History," 18-31.

[133] J. Kampen, *The Hasideans and the Origin of Pharisaism* (SBLSCS 24; Atlanta: Scholars Press, 1988) 158.

With recourse to a detailed exegesis of the Damascus Document Murphy-O'Connor[134] has suggested that the origin of the Essene movement must be sought in the Babylonian diaspora. In his view, a group of conservative Jews came around 165 BCE from Mesopotamia to Jerusalem where they condemned the leading authorities and invited outsiders to join them. Around 152 the Teacher of Righteousness—who was high priest in Jerusalem during the so-called intersacerdotium,[135] but was then driven from office when Jonathan took power in 152 BCE—would have sided with these Jews, and after a conflict with the "Liar" urged them to withdraw with him into the desert. This thesis, which is particularly based on the halakhic rules of CD 9–16 (that seem to presuppose a pagan environment), has been accepted by a number of scholars. It is true that the Damascus Document relates the pre-history of the Essene movement to the Babylonian exile, but it is not entirely clear how this relation is to be interpreted. CD is certainly written from a Palestinian perspective. According to L. Schiffman,[136] the halakhic rules of 9–16 do not necessarily point to Babylonia since they are broadly identical with traditional halakhah. Moreover, the allusion to the Book of Jubilees in these laws (CD 16:3-4) does not favour a Babylonian origin. M. Knibb[137] has suggested that CD refers to a theological schema to be found in contemporary Jewish literature (e.g. 1 En 93:1-10 and 91:11-17, the Enochic Ten Weeks Apocalypse). According to this, the exilic situation will last until the final age in which God will bring about a new beginning for the elect; the Essene movement marks the end of the exilic situation and the re-establishment of the covenant. The objection of Murphy-O'Connor[138] and Davies[139] that CD 1:5-6—which stipulates that God caused a root of planting to grow from Israel and Aaron 390 years after giving them into the hand of Nebuchadnezzar—is a later addition, gives the impression of a *petitio principii*. It is significant that CD never

---

[134] Murphy-O'Connor, "The Essenes and their History," 215-44; idem, "The Damascus Document Revisted," *RB* 92 (1985) 223-46.

[135] According to Murphy-O'Connor.

[136] L. H. Schiffman, "Legislation Concerning Relations with Non-Jews in the Zadokite Fragments and Tannaitic Literature," *RevQ* 11 (1982-1984) 379-89.

[137] M. A. Knibb, "Exile in the Damascus Document," *JSOT* 25 (1983) 99-117.

[138] Murphy-O'Connor, "Damascus Document Revisted," 227f.

[139] P. R. Davies, *The Damascus Covenant*, 61ff., 67.

mentions the *return* of an exilic group to Palestine; the term שבי ישראל does not mean "the returnees of Israel" (as initially thought by Murphy-O'Connor) or "the exiled of Israel" (Davies) but rather "the converts of Israel" (as later admitted by Murphy-O'Connor).

García Martínez[140] finds the origins of the Essene movement in apocalyptic circles of the 3rd and 2nd centuries BCE, making a clear distinction between the Essenes of the classical sources and those of the Qumran community. He points out that according to Josephus (*Antiquities* 18 §11) the three "philosophies" of the Jews (i.e. the Essenes, Sadducees, and Pharisees) were inherited by the Jews "from the most ancient times," that Pliny the Elder assumes an existence of the Essenes *per saeculorum milia* (*Naturalis Historia* 5.73), and that Philo even traces their origins to the Mosaic age (cf. Eusebius, *Praeparatio Evangelica* 8 §6f.). According to García Martínez, a Palestinian-apocalyptic origin of the Essenes is evidenced by the many manuscripts of 1 Enoch that were found at Qumran, and the ideological and halakhic similarities between ideas in the Dead Sea Scrolls and those found in pre-Maccabean literature.[141] He cites as telling examples of the close relationship of the Essene movement and the Qumran community with apocalypticism the "eschatologizing of the prophets" (which continues the apocalyptic transformation of the exegesis of prophetic literature), the recourse to secret writings and heavenly tablets, the conviction of being in community with the angelic world, and the apocalyptic conception of the heavenly temple which would replace the present polluted sanctuary.

R. Beckwith[142] and D. Dimant[143] have also pleaded for a Palestinian-apocalyptic origin of Essenism in the 3rd century BCE,

---

[140] F. García Martínez, "Orígenes apocalipticos del movimiento esenio y origenes de la secta qumránica," *Communio* 18 (1985) 353-68; idem, "Orígenes del movimiento esenio y orígenes qumránicos. Pistas para una solución," in V. Collado Bertomeu and V. Vilar-Hueso (eds.), *Simposio bíblico español (Córdoba 1985)* (Valencia-Córdoba: PMPCAC, 1987) 527-56; idem, "Essénisme qumranien: Origines, charastéristiques, héritage," in B. Chiesa (ed.), *Correnti culturali e movimenti religiosi del giudaismo* (Rome: Carucci, 1987) 37-57; idem, "Qumran Origins and Early History," 113-36.

[141] Notably the Astronomical Book, the Book of the Watchers and the Dream Visions of 1 Enoch, and Jubilees.

[142] R. T. Beckwith, "The Pre-History and Relationships of the Pharisees, Sadducees and Essenes: A Tentative Reconstruction," *RevQ* 11 (1982-1984) 3-46.

[143] D. Dimant, "Qumran Sectarian Literature," 542-47.

while G. Nickelsburg finds in the presence of Enochic material at Qumran strong evidence for the hypothesis that the Enochic writings stem from circles that were in some significant sense ancestral to the Qumran community. He underlines that "the common sectarian experience of association with the angels and the presence of angelic liturgies presume a democratizing of apocalyptic language to explain one's eschatological existence in the community."[144] Nevertheless, formal apocalypses of genuine Qumran origin cannot be identified with certainty among the Dead Sea Scrolls, or are at best extremely rare. For example, the Book of Giants was apparently written outside of Qumran, the New Jerusalem texts were composed by circles from which the Qumran community sprang, and the origin of the Songs of the Sabbath Sacrifice[145] is disputed (although their Qumranic provenance is probable). This does not mean that the Qumran community cannot be described as an "apocalyptic movement"; even if its members did not compose apocalyptic works, their world-view was certainly apocalyptic.[146]

This brings us to the question of the origin and history of the Qumran community. According to Vermes,[147] the Teacher of Righteousness, a Zadokite priest, appeared on the stage of history twenty years after the Hasidean movement had established itself. A conflict with Jonathan, who took over the office of high priest, caused him and his followers to retreat to the Judaean Desert. H. Stegemann[148] elaborated on the thesis of Vermes and revised it in certain respects. In his view, after Menelaus had taken over the high priesthood and Onias III was murdered, the pious (who held to the ancestral laws) lost all confidence in the high priesthood and decided to leave the land of Judah, and then founded the "New Covenant" in the "land of Damascus." According to Stegemann, the Teacher of Righteousness was high priest in Jerusalem during the intersacer-

---

[144] G. W. E. Nickelsburg, "1 Enoch and Qumran Origins. The State of the Question and Some Prospects for Answers," in K. H. Richards (ed.), SBLSP 9 (Atlanta: Scholars Press, 1986) 341-60.

[145] Formally, the Songs do not qualify as an apocalypse.

[146] See the recent publication of J. J. Collins, *Apocalypticism in the Dead Sea Scrolls* (London and New York: Routledge, 1997).

[147] G. Vermes, "The Essenes and History," 18-31.

[148] H. Stegemann, *Die Entstehung der Qumrangemeinde* (Bonn: Rheinische Friedrich-Wilhelms-Universität, 1971).

dotium (159-52 BCE). He was, however, ousted from office by Jonathan and fled to a camp of the members of the New Covenant. At a certain point he visited a camp whose members were not willing to boycott the Temple cult of Jerusalem, and came in conflict with the "Liar" who refused to accept his claims. This event led to the final rupture between the Essenes and the Pharisees. In his recent publications Stegemann has essentially repeated these views.[149]

F. M. Cross[150] also described the Teacher of Righteousness as a Zadokite who sympathized with the Hasideans, but dated his appearance somewhat later to the last days of Jonathan or even to the first regnal years of Simon. J. Charlesworth,[151] who identified the community of Qumran with the Essenes of the classical sources, has posited a priestly conflict concerning the high priesthood which led to a rift between the Teacher of Righteousness and the "Wicked Priest"[152] and their respective followers. Eventually, a rupture took place within the community of the Teacher of Righteousness between those who remained faithful to him and those who followed the "Liar." Like many others, D. Dimant[153] has identified the "Wicked Priest" with the high priest Jonathan, and the members of the Qumran community with the Essenes; but she doubts whether the Teacher of Righteousness and his followers were Zadokites who opposed the Hasmonean priesthood, since the theme of Zadokite descent is totally absent in the scrolls. P. Davies[154] makes essentially the same point and suggests that we are better advised to speak of the non-Zadokite nature of the community of Qumran. H. Burgmann has devoted much energy to the reconstruction of the history of the Qumran community; however, his idiosyncratic ideas published in German have largely been ignored.[155]

---

[149] Note Stegemann's *Die Essener*, 194ff.

[150] F. M. Cross, "The Dead Sea Scrolls and the People Who Wrote Them," *BAR* 3/1 (1977) 23-32, 51.

[151] J. H. Charlesworth, "The Origin and the Subsequent History of the Authors of the Dead Sea Scrolls. Four Transitional Phases Among the Qumran Essenes," *RevQ* 10 (1979-1981) 213-33.

[152] I.e. the Jerusalem high priest.

[153] D. Dimant, "Qumran Sectarian Literature," 542ff.

[154] P. R. Davies, *Behind the Essenes*, 51-72.

[155] Cf. Burgmann's monographs *Vorgeschichte und Frühgeschichte der essenischen Gemeinden von Qumran und Damaskus* (ANTJ 7; Frankfurt: Lang,

P. Callaway[156] has carefully, although not exhaustively, summarized the results of the investigations into the Qumran community's earliest history. His own conclusions, however, seem to be somewhat minimalistic and open to objection. The gist of his analysis is that the Damascus Document mentions the Teacher of Righteousness, the Liar, and the apostates who "looked after easy interpretations," as figures of the early second century BCE, concerning whose relationships and controversies nothing concrete is said. According to Callaway, the Wicked Priest of 1QpHab and 4QpPs[a] was a high priest in the second century BCE, but was not necessarily a Zadokite.

A more positive reconstruction of the earliest history of the Qumranites is offered by the proponents of the "Groningen hypothesis." This schema combines García Martínez's view of the apocalyptic origins of the Essene movement and the conviction that the Qumran community is an Essene splinter-group, with the present author's contention that the designation "Wicked Priest" of 1QpHab refers to various Hasmonean high priests from Judas Maccabaeus to Alexander Jannaeus.[157] This calling into question the current identification of the Wicked Priest with a single high priest (e.g. Jonathan) is reinforced by Davies' suggestion[158] that this figure is possibly the amalgam of several, T. Lim's concession that he cannot be identified with one person,[159] and I. Tantlevsky's recent study[160] distinguishing between two Wicked Priests (Jonathan and Alexander Jannaeus).

A monograph on the history of the ideas of the Essene movement which ultimately gave birth to the splinter group of Qumran, and their relationship with the rest of early Judaism, is a important desideratum. Although such a work would be difficult to write in view of the limited data at our disposal, the task is not an impossible one.

1987); and *Die essenischen Gemeinden von Qumran und Damaskus in der Zeit der Hasmonäer und Herodier (130 ante–68 post)* (ANTJ 8; Frankfurt: Lang, 1988). For a summary of Burgmann's ideas, see A. S. van der Woude, "Fünfzehn Jahre Qumranforschung (1974-1988) IV," *ThR* 57 (1992) 244-47.

[156] P. R. Callaway, *History of the Qumran Community*.

[157] García Martínez and van der Woude, "A 'Groningen' Hypothesis," 521-41.

[158] *Behind the Essenes*, 28.

[159] T. H. Lim, "The Wicked Priests of the Groningen Hypothesis," *JBL* 112 (1993) 415-25.

[160] I. R. Tantlevsky, *The Two Wicked Priests in the Qumran Commentary of Habakkuk* (Kraków-St.Petersburg: Enigma Press, 1995).

5. THE QUMRAN COMMUNITY'S BELIEFS AND PRACTICES

The Qumran community seems to have understood itself as the "true Israel" and the covenant people who remained faithful to the ancestral laws, God's elect of the last days. Stegemann's contention that its members expected a "Wende zum Besseren," by longing for the time when God would exterminate the Hasmoneans and once again a Zadokite priest would officiate as high priest,[161] seems to underestimate the apocalyptic world view of the Qumranites.

Without further evidence, we should not automatically identify the beliefs and the halakhah of the Qumran community with those of the Essene movement from which it sprang, but must take into consideration the various layers and stages of development in the sectarian literature. Reflecting the lack of thorough literary-critical analysis of the documents in the first decades of Qumran research, many authors tended in those years to look upon the corpus of texts as reflecting a homogeneous system of thought; even later on, some scholars have unfortunately advocated this approach.

5.1 The Origin of Evil and the Duality of Human Existence

As to the theme of the origin of evil (cf. P. Sacchi[162] and J. J. Collins),[163] we find remarkably little appeal in the Scrolls to the Enochic tradition of the fall of the angels, which draws upon Genesis 6 and other sources. While it is alluded at in CD 2:15-16, there the fall of the Watchers is not causative, but instead paradigmatic for human sinfulness. In the Damascus Document, the source of evil conduct lies rather in the inclination of the human heart, as was already taught by Ben Sira. The Sapiential Work A (1Q26; 4Q415-418,423, cf. Harrington[164] and Lange)[165] draws on Genesis 1-3 and

---

[161] H. Stegemann, "Die Bedeutung der Qumranfunde für die Erforschung der Apokalyptik," in D. Hellholm (ed.), *Apocalypticism in the Mediterranean World and the Near East* (Tübingen: Mohr-Siebeck, 1983) 495-530.

[162] P. Sacchi, "Riflessioni sull'essenza dell'apocalittica: Peccato d'origine e libertà dell'uomo," *Henoch* 5 (1983) 31-61; idem, "Die Macht der Sünde in der Apokalyptik," *Jahrbuch für Biblische Theologie* 9 (1994) 111-24.

[163] J. J. Collins, "The Origin of Evil in Apocalyptic Literature and the Dead Sea Scrolls," in J. A. Emerton (ed.), *Congress Volume, Paris 1992* (VTSup 61; Leiden: Brill, 1995) 25-38; idem, *Apocalypticism in the Dead Sea Scrolls*, 30-51.

[164] D. J. Harrington, *Wisdom Texts from Qumran* (London: Routledge, 1996).

[165] A. Lange, *Weisheit und Prädestination* (STDJ 18; Leiden: Brill, 1995), esp. 45-92.

speaks of two types of humanity: a spiritual people in the likeness of the holy ones and men of a "spirit of flesh."

This duality of human existence is formulated differently in the Instruction on the Two Spirits (1QS 3:13–4:26), a discourse on creation and human nature,[166] which is indebted to both sapiential and apocalyptic traditions. It displays a dualism that is simultaneously psychological, moral and cosmic (cf. Collins). There it is said that God appointed for man two spirits, and that unlawful deeds are caused by the dominion of the Angel of Darkness. While it is not altogether clear when and where the Sapiential Work and the Instruction originated, the latter work appears to represent the current view of the Qumranites. Since at least one copy (4QS^d) of the Community Rule apparently did not contain the first four columns of 1QS, thus indicating that these were added to the work at a later redactional stage, it seems reasonable to view the Instruction on the Two Spirits as a Qumranic composition, especially since the preceding description of the covenant renewal festival (1:1-3:12) also presupposes a dualistic world-view.

5.2 Predestination and Election

Other major themes in the belief-system of the community are predestination and election. Not only man's life, but also human history, is predetermined; in accordance with the periodization of history found in Daniel 9 and a number of other apocalyptic writings. this forms a sequence of fixed periods preordained by God before creation. Although man's personal fate is dependent upon God's election, human obedience to the Law of Moses is prerequisite for salvation (P. Garnet).[167] In practice, this means that only those who have joined the community of the Qumran covenanters are the elect for eternal life: *extra ecclesiam nulla salus!* Such a doctrine somewhat undermines D. Dimant's dictum: "The freedom given to man is not to choose where to go but to discover where he is" (i.e. by the mystery of knowledge imparted to him).[168]

---

[166] See esp. H. Stegemann, "Zu Textbestand und Grundgedanken von 1QS III,13–IV,26," *RevQ* 13 (1988) 95-131; and Lange, *Weisheit und Prädestination*, 121-70.

[167] P. Garnet, *Salvation and Atonement in the Qumran Scrolls* (Tübingen: Mohr/Siebeck, 1977).

[168] D. Dimant, "Qumran Sectarian Literature" 538.

5.3 Eschatology, Messianism, and Resurrection[169]

It cannot be doubted that the members of the Qumran community believed themselves to be living in the final age. This conviction is already expressed in 4QMMT, while CD 20:14-15 predicts the destruction of "all men of war" forty years after the death of the Teacher of Righteousness. They expected the eschatological prophet and the messiahs of Aaron and Israel (1QS 9:11). But since the present author wrote his dissertation on the messianic conceptions of the community of Qumran,[170] new texts have made it increasingly difficult to synthesize the messianic ideas into one coherent system. García Martínez[171] has identified the figure called "Son of God" and "Son of the Most High" in the "Son of God" text (4Q246, 1st century BCE) with a heavenly messiah; Collins,[172] while speaking in terms of the messianic king, admits that his divine origin is emphasized. But in the wake of others, Stegemann views the figure negatively and identifies him with Antiochus IV Epiphanes who in his arrogance wanted to be called Son of God and Son of the Most High.[173] But the affinities of the text with Daniel 7 and Ezra 13 (cf. also Luke 1:32) strongly suggest a positive figure (with Collins), and seem to indicate that at least in some Jewish circles of the first century BCE the Davidic messiah was related to the Son of Man described in Daniel 7.

The scrolls which derive from the Qumran community contain no unambigious references to a belief in bodily resurrection.[174] Instead, the focus is on sharing the angelic life in the community and thereby transcending death and continuing that life in heaven (Collins).[175]

5.4 Halakhah at Qumran

The most conspicuous and influential contributions to the study of Qumran halakhah have been published by J. Baumgarten and L.

---

[169] For a recent volume with several contributions on these themes, see C. A. Evans and P. W. Flint (eds.), *Eschatology, Messianism, and the Dead Sea Scrolls* (SDSSRL 1; Grand Rapids: Eerdmans, 1997).

[170] A. S. van der Woude, *Die messianischen Vorstellungen der Gemeinde von Qumran* (SSN 3; Assen: Van Gorcum, 1957).

[171] F. García Martínez, "Messianische Erwartungen in den Qumranschriften," *Jahrbuch für Biblische Theologie* 8 (1993) 171-208, esp. 188ff.

[172] *Apocalypticism in the Dead Sea Scrolls*, 82.

[173] *Die Essener*, 341.

[174] However, resurrection may be referred to in 4Q521.

[175] *Apocalypticism in the Dead Sea Scrolls*, 123.

Schiffman.[176] According to the latter, the sectarian rules are the outcome of an inner development of sectarian life. Even the organizational rules and especially the penal code and the rules of entry and expulsion were intended to fulfill ideals that are inherent in the Bible. But M. Weinfeld[177] maintains that the organizational rules of the community simply reflect the way guilds and religious associations of the Hellenistic period used to structure their regulations of order. In his view, *contra* Schiffman, they have nothing to do with inspired biblical exegesis.

5.5 Other Doctrines

Unfortunately, for lack of space several other aspects of the community's beliefs and practices will have to be passed over in this essay. For instance, considerable attention has been paid to Qumran liturgical life and the concomitant religious poetry by J. Maier,[178] M. Weinfeld[179] and B. Nitzan.[180] Several other themes and doctrines are presented in Part Five of this Fiftieth Anniversary collection.[181]

6. THE SCROLLS AND THE CANON AND TEXT OF THE OLD TESTAMENT

6.1 The Scrolls and the Canon

Although the vast majority are preserved in a fragmentary state, the more than 200 biblical scrolls from Qumran[182] throw new light

---

[176] See Baumgarten's *Studies in Qumran Law* (SJLA 24; Leiden: Brill, 1977); and L. H. Schiffman, *The Halakhah at Qumran* (SJLA 16; Leiden: Brill, 1975); idem, *Sectarian Laws and the Dead Sea Scrolls: Courts, Testimony and the Penal Code* (BJS 33; Chico, CA: Scholars Press, 1982).

[177] M. Weinfeld, *The Organizational Pattern and the Penal Code of the Qumran Sect* (NTOA 2; Fribourg [Schweiz]: Editions Universitaires; Göttingen: Vandenhoeck & Ruprecht, 1986).

[178] J. Maier, "Zu Kult und Liturgie der Qumrangemeinde," *RevQ* 14 (1989) 543-86.

[179] M. Weinfeld, "Prayer and Liturgical Practice in the Qumran Sect," in D. Dimant and U. Rappaport (eds.), *The Dead Sea Scrolls: Forty Years of Research* (STDJ 10; Leiden: Brill, 1992) 241-58.

[180] B. Nitzan, *Qumran Prayer and Religious Poetry* (STDJ 12; Leiden: Brill, 1994).

[181] See the second volume.

[182] On the total, E. Ulrich (Chief Editor of the Cave 4 Biblical Scrolls) suggests a number of "just on 200," while J. VanderKam (*The Dead Sea Scrolls Today* [Grand Rapids: Eerdmans; London: SPCK, 1994] 30–31) estimates the number at 202 biblical scrolls at Qumran, with 19 more from other sites in the Judaean desert.

on the textual transmission of the Old Testament and its canonical history. In addition, these new manuscripts have raised many questions which are difficult to answer. All of the books found in the Hebrew Bible are represented among the Dead Sea Scrolls, with the exception of Nehemiah and Esther. The absence of Nehemiah is merely a coincidence, since Ezra-Nehemiah form one book in the Hebrew Bible, and one manuscript of Ezra (4Q117) was found in Cave 4. Esther, however, did not belong to the sacred writings at Qumran—in contrast to some other books now known as "Apocrypha" (Ecclesiasticus, Tobit, the Letter of Jeremiah) or "Pseudepigrapha" (1 Enoch, Jubilees, Testament of Levi, etc.). Thus at the beginning of the Common Era we cannot speak of a "canon" in the sense of a well-defined number of holy writings—at least not for Judaism as a whole.

6.2 Textual Types or Families?

E. Tov[183] has drawn a distinction between the biblical manuscripts that were brought to Qumran from outside and those that were copied in accordance with the rules of the Qumran scribal school in the community. With the exception of the proto-Samaritan manuscripts, the former show both orthographically and materially a conservative tradition, whereas the latter are marked by specific orthographic-linguistic features, the rendition of the divine name in ancient Hebrew script, and (especially) by a free approach to the biblical text. More challenging is Tov's thesis that we should abandon the traditional classification of the biblical manuscripts into textual types and recensions but instead should speak simply of "texts." His grounds for this view is that the Qumran scrolls (with the exception of the proto-Samaritan tradition) lack typological features; for example, a manuscript such as 11QpaleoLev is incompatible with the traditional threefold scheme of proto-masoretic, proto-Septuagint and proto-Samaritan textual types.

On the other hand, Tov is careful not to run to extremes, since a major part of the texts can clearly be specified as proto-masoretic. He also concedes that 4QJer^b apparently represents the *Vorlage* of the Septuagint version of Jeremiah. Although the "local texts" thesis

---

[183] E. Tov, "Hebrew Biblical Manuscripts from the Judaean Desert: Their Contribution to Textual Criticism," *JJS* 39 (1988) 5-37.

that was proposed by Frank Moore Cross[184] is rejected by S. Talmon[185] in view of the plurality of textual types discovered in the library of Qumran,[186] the latter nevertheless finds a limited number of text-families as a result of historical vicissitudes and their acceptance by sociologically-integrated circles. Talmon's thesis, however, can hardly be reconciled with the plurality of text-types that appear at Qumran because from a sociological point of view its community constitutes a striking example of one tightly-knit group.

6.3 Standardization and Uniformity of the Hebrew Text

Surprisingly, neither Masada nor the caves of Wadi Murabbaʿât provide evidence for a pluriform textual tradition as may be seen at Qumran. This raises the question of how and why this uniform textual tradition was reached—a problem that has been answered in various ways. Since a standardization of the text at the so-called synod of Javneh is not supported by Rabbinic sources and is highly doubtful for a number of reasons, M. Greenberg[187] attributed this standardization to scribes living within reach of the Temple at Jerusalem. In his view, from the middle of the 2nd century BCE onwards these scribes made a critical selection among manuscripts and textual variants, and in doing so excluded the proto-Samaritan Pentateuch and the Hebrew *Vorlage* of the Septuagint. But B.

---

[184] F. M. Cross, "The History of the Biblical text in the Light of the Discoveries in the Judaean Desert," in F. M. Cross and S. Talmon (eds.), *Qumran and the History of the Biblical Text* (Cambridge, MA: Harvard University Press, 1975) 177-95.

[185] S. Talmon, "The Old Testament Text," in P. R. Ackroyd and C. F. Evans (eds.), *The Cambridge History of the Bible I* (Cambridge: Cambridge University Press, 1970) 159-99.

[186] For two recent articles on textual pluriformity among the biblical scrolls, see E. Ulrich, "The Bible in the Making: The Scriptures at Qumran," in E. Ulrich and J. VanderKam (eds.), *The Community of the Renewed Covenant: The Notre Dame Symposium on the Dead Sea Scrolls* (CJA 10; Notre Dame, USA: University of Notre Dame Press, 1994) 77-93; and idem, "Multiple Literary Editions: Reflections toward a Theory of the History of the Biblical Text," in D. Parry and S. Ricks (eds.), *Current Research and Technological Developments on the Dead Sea Scrolls. Conference on the Texts from the Judean Desert, Jerusalem, 30 April 1995* (STDJ 20; Leiden: Brill) 78-105 + pls. I-II.

[187] M. Greenberg, "The Stabilization of the Text of the Hebrew Bible Reviewed in the Light of the Biblical Materials from the Judaean Desert," *JAOS* 76 (1956) 157-67.

Albrektson[188] opposed this theory by claiming that the standard Hebrew text was not achieved by deliberate text-critical work. In his opinion, the textual tradition current among the Pharisees gained dominance, and after 70 CE gradually supplanted other textual witnesses in Rabbinic Judaism. Although Albrektson does not stress this point, his thesis implies that the (proto-Masoretic) textual tradition that was supported by the Pharisees must have existed well before 70 CE.

The Greek manuscript of the Twelve Prophets[189] from Naḥal Ḥever (latter half of the 1st century BCE) has a text which is apparently a revision of the Septuagint tradition on the basis of a Hebrew text showing marked similarities with the proto-Masoretic tradition. There are thus indications that the process of adapting the Greek tradition to the proto-Masoretic text had already started in the 2nd century BCE.[190] Such attempts not only presuppose text-critical work among early scribes, but also the existence of a guiding Hebrew prototype and increasing uniformity towards the proto-Masoretic tradition well before 70 CE.

Instead of assuming a gradual development from pluriformity to uniformity in the textual tradition of the Old Testament, as has been postulated by Albrektson, E. Ulrich[191] and others, we should consider another possibility: that a far-reaching uniformity of textual tradition existed in the religious circles around the Temple of Jerusalem well before 70 CE *alongside* a pluriform tradition elsewhere in Palestine, with both traditions being exemplified by the Qumran biblical texts.[192] This explains in simple fashion why the textual tradition supported by the Pharisees, who survived the

---

[188] B. Albrektson, "Reflections on the Emergence of a Standard Text of the Hebrew Bible," in J. A. Emerton (ed.), *Congress Volume Göttingen 1977* (VTSup 29; Leiden: Brill, 1978) 49-65.

[189] D. Barthélemy, *Les devanciers d'Aquila. Première publication intégrale du texte des fragments du Dodécaprophéon* (SVT 10; Leiden: Brill, 1963); E. Tov with R. A. Kraft, *The Greek Minor Prophets Scroll from Naḥal Ḥever (8ḤevXIIgr): The Seiyâl Collection I* (DJD 8; Oxford: Clarendon Press, 1990).

[190] S. P. Brock, "The Phenomenon of the Septuagint," *OTS* 17 (1972) 11-36.

[191] Ulrich, "The Bible in the Making," 77-93, esp. 92-93.

[192] A. S. van der Woude, "Pluriformity and Uniformity. Reflections on the Transmission of the Text of the Old Testament," in J. N. Bremmer and F. García Martínez (eds.), *Sacred History and Sacred Texts in Early Judaism* (Kampen: Kok Pharos, 1992) 151-69.

destruction of Jerusalem and its Temple, could almost abruptly gain the field after 70 CE. The Pharisaic conviction that the Holy Spirit had withdrawn from Israel since the days of Haggai, Zechariah and Malachi excluded appeal to any later divine inspiration, thereby entailing a shift from authority outside Scripture to Scripture alone. This development gradually led to the canonization of Holy (Hebrew) Scripture as God's literally inspired word, and did not admit of various diverging textual recensions. But the situation at Qumran was different; since the community knew its own divinely-inspired authorities, pre-eminently the Teacher of Righteousness, the need to replace textual pluriformity by uniformity was not urgent.

6.4 Availability of All the Biblical Scrolls

Since 1992, many of the biblical scrolls from Cave 4 have been published in the DJD series.[193] The remaining manuscripts from Caves 4 and 11,[194] as well as those from Naḥal Ḥever and Wadi Sdeir,[195] are scheduled to appear by the end of 1998. Besides making this material available to scholars, this development facilitates what was hitherto most difficult: comprehensive analyses of individual biblical books in the light of all the Judaean evidence. Unlike most of the non-biblical ones, several biblical books appear in large numbers of manuscripts (e.g. 39 for Psalms, 29 for Deuteronomy, 21 for Isaiah, and 17 for Exodus).[196] In such cases, it is necessary for scholars to have access to all the relevant scrolls, which is now at last possible. One of the first studies that takes into consideration all the manuscripts of a biblical book (in this case, 36 scrolls from Qumran

---

[193] See P. W. Skehan, E. Ulrich and J. E. Sanderson, *Qumrân Cave 4.IV: Palaeo-Hebrew and Greek Biblical Manuscripts* (DJD 9; Oxford: Clarendon Press, 1992); E. Ulrich and F. M. Cross, *Qumran Cave 4.VII: Genesis to Numbers* (DJD 12; Oxford: Clarendon Press, 1994); E. Ulrich and F. M. Cross (eds.), *Qumran Cave 4.IX: Deuteronomy, Joshua, Judges, Kings* (DJD 14; Oxford: Clarendon Press, 1995); E. Ulrich et al. (eds.) *Qumran Cave 4.X: The Prophets* (DJD 15; Oxford: Clarendon Press, 1997).

[194] E. Ulrich et al. (eds.), *Qumran Cave 4.XI: Psalms to Chronicles* (DJD 16; Oxford: Clarendon Press [forthcoming]); F. García Martinez, E. Tigchelaar and A. S. van der Woude, *Qumran Cave 11.II: 11Q2-18, 11Q20-30* (DJD 23; Oxford: Clarendon Press [forthcoming]).

[195] P. Alexander et al. (eds.), *Qumran Cave 4.XXVI: Miscellaneous Texts from Qumran and Other Sites* (DJD 36: Oxford: Clarendon Press [forthcoming]).

[196] J. C. VanderKam, *Dead Sea Scrolls Today*, 30.

and 3 from elsewhere) is that of P. Flint on the Book of Psalms.[197] Similar investigations of other major biblical books[198] can be expected to appear in the next few years.

7. THE SCROLLS, EARLY JUDAISM, AND THE NEW TESTAMENT

The Dead Sea Scrolls have taught us once again that early Judaism was considerably more variegated than has often been thought by Jewish and Christian scholars. G. Vermes[199] has provided a study on the impact of Qumran on Jewish studies in the first 25 years of research, while H. Stegemann has dealt with the same theme in a more recent publication.[200]

Although the New Testament shows many terminological and ideological affinities with early Judaism, its spiritual climate is remarkably different from that of Qumran. O. Betz,[201] J. Cook,[202] J. Fitzmyer,[203] and C. Evans[204] have provided useful overviews of Qumran studies pertaining to the New Testament. The standard work, edited by K. Stendahl, appeared in 1957, but has recently been revised with a new and enlightening introduction.[205] In addition,

---

[197] P. W. Flint, *The Dead Sea Psalms Scrolls and The Book of Psalms* (STDJ 17; Leiden: Brill, 1997).

[198] "Major" in this sense denotes books that are attested by large numbers of scrolls from the Judaean Desert.

[199] G. Vermes, "The Impact of the Dead Sea Scrolls on Jewish Studies During the Last Twenty-Five Years," *JJS* 26 (1975) 1-14.

[200] H. Stegemann, "Qumran und das Judentum zur Zeit Jesu," *Theologie und Glaube* 84 (1994) 175-94.

[201] O. Betz, "Qumran and the New Testament. Forty Years of Research," in Z.J. Kapera (ed.), *Mogilany 1989: Papers on the Dead Sea Scrolls Offered in Memory of Jean Carmignac. Part I* (Kraków: Enigma Press, 1993) 79-100.

[202] J. Cook, "The Dead Sea Scrolls and the New Testament," *OTE* 6 (1993) 233-47.

[203] J. A. Fitzmyer, "The Dead Sea Scrolls and the New Testament After Thirty Years," *Theology Digest* 29 (1981) 351-67; idem, "The Qumran Scrolls and the New Testament after Forty Years," *RevQ* 13 (1988) 609-20.

[204] C. A. Evans, "Jesus and the Messianic Texts from Qumran: A Preliminary Assessment of the Recently Published Materials," in idem, *Jesus and His Contemporaries: Comparative Studies* (AGJU 25; Leiden: Brill, 1995) 83-154.

[205] K. Stendahl (ed.), *The Scrolls and the New Testament* (New York: Harper, 1957). Rev. ed., with a new introduction by James Charlesworth (New York: Crossroad, 1992).

Fitzmyer has collected a number of his essays bearing on the New Testament and its Semitic background.[206] Instructive are as well the studies on John and Jesus in relation to the Dead Sea Scrolls, edited by J. Charlesworth,[207] and H. Lichtenberger's article on John the Baptist and the texts of Qumran.[208]

---

[206] J. A. Fitzmyer, *A Wandering Aramean: Collected Aramaic Essays* (SBLMS 25; Missoula, MT: Scholars Press, 1979), recently reprinted as Part 2 of idem, *The Semitic Background of the New Testament* (BRS; Grand Rapids: Eerdmans; Livonia, MI: Dove, 1997).

[207] J. H. Charlesworth (ed.), *John and Qumran* (London: Chapman, 1972); idem (ed.), *John and the Dead Sea Scrolls* (New York: Crossroad, 1990); idem (ed.), *Jesus and the Dead Sea Scrolls* (New York: Doubleday, 1992).

[208] H. Lichtenberger, "Johannes der Täufer und die Texte von Qumran," in Kapera (ed.), *Mogilany 1989: Papers on the Dead Sea Scrolls*, 139-52.

QUMRAN ARCHAEOLOGY: PAST PERSPECTIVES AND FUTURE PROSPECTS*

JODI MAGNESS

The discovery of the Dead Sea Scrolls in caves adjacent to Khirbet Qumran (whose ancient name is unknown), prompted archaeologists to carry out excavations at the site in 1951 and 1953-56. The first season was jointly directed by G. Lankester Harding on behalf of the Department of Antiquities of Jordan and Roland de Vaux of the École Biblique et Archéologique Française de Jerusalem. The later seasons were carried out under the direction of de Vaux, who also conducted excavations at the nearby site of Ein Feshkha in 1958. Although de Vaux published a number of preliminary reports and a synthetic overview of the archaeology of Qumran, he never produced a final excavation report before his death in 1971. The finds from the caves were published together with the scroll material in the *Discoveries in the Judaean Desert* series. In 1994, the first volume of the final reports on de Vaux's excavations at Qumran and Ein Feshkha was published by Jean-Baptiste Humbert and Alain Chambon. Most of it is a photo album accompanied by de Vaux's field notes. Four projected future volumes will be devoted to the pottery, stone, glass, metal, bone, and other objects, the coins, and the archaeology (stratigraphy, chronology, architecture).[1]

---

* I would like to thank the British Academy for its generous permission to reproduce the illustrations that appear in this article. The plans of Khirbet Qumran were originally published by Oxford University Press for the British Academy, and were drawn up by Fr. H.-M. Coüasnon.

[1] For the publication of de Vaux's excavations at Qumran, Ein Feshkha, and the ceramic material from the caves, see the following works by him: "Fouilles au Khirbet Qumrân, Rapport préliminaire," *RB* 60 (1953) 83-106; "Fouilles au Khirbet Qumrân, Rapport préliminaire sur la deuxième campagne," *RB* 61 (1954) 206-36; "La poterie," in D. Barthelemy and J. T. Milik, *Qumran Cave 1* (DJD 1; Oxford: Clarendon Press, 1955) 8-13; "Fouilles de Khirbet Qumrân, Rapport préliminaire sur les 3e, 4e, et 5e campagnes," *RB* 63 (1956) 533-77; "Fouilles de Feshkha," *RB* 66 (1959) 225-55; "Archéologie," in M. Baillet, J. T. Milik and R. de Vaux, *Les "Petites Grottes" de Qumran* (DJD 3; Oxford: Clarendon Press, 1962)

1. DE VAUX'S CHRONOLOGY

De Vaux divided the sectarian settlement at Qumran into three phases, which he termed "Period Ia," "Period Ib," and "Period II." A late Iron Age settlement preceded these periods, and they were followed by a brief phase of Roman occupation referred to by de Vaux as Period III. The "periods" were defined on the basis of stratigraphic and architectural evidence. In approximate terms, de Vaux dated Period Ia to the third quarter of the second century BCE, Period Ib from the last quarter of the second century BCE to 31 BCE, and Period II from 4-1 BCE to 68 CE. The following is a brief description of the remains from each of these phases.[2]

Iron Age (see Plate 2)[3]

The site of Qumran was first inhabited during the late Iron Age (eighth to seventh centuries BCE). De Vaux found that the foundations of some of the walls, which lay at a lower level than the others, were embedded in a layer of ash containing numerous sherds of late Iron Age date. Other finds from this phase included a jar handle stamped with the paleo-Hebrew inscription *lamelekh* ("to the king"). De Vaux reconstructed the Iron Age settlement as consisting of a rectangular building with a row of rooms along the eastern side of an open couryard. An enclosure attached to the west side of the building contained a large round cistern (L110), which was fed by surface runoff. He noted the similarity of this building to Israelite strongholds in the Buqeia and Negev, and dated its destruction to the time of the fall of the Kingdom of Judah.

Period Ia (see Plate 3)

The site of Qumran had been abandoned for several hundred years when it was resettled by a new population, which de Vaux identified as sectarian. According to de Vaux, the initial phase of this settlement was modest and short-lived. Parts of the ruined Iron Age building were rebuilt and reoccupied. The round Iron Age cistern

---

3-36; *Archaeology and the Dead Sea Scrolls* (London: Oxford University Press, 1973); and "Le matériel archéologique. La poterie," in R. de Vaux and J. T. Milik, *Qumrân Grotte 4.2* (DJD 6; Oxford: Clarendon Press, 1977) 15-20. See also J.-B. Humbert and A. Chambon, *Fouilles de Khirbet Qumrân et de Aïn Feshkha I* (Göttingen: Vandenhoeck and Ruprecht, 1994).

[2] For the material presented in this section consult the references in note 1.

[3] The Plates appear together at the end of the volume.

was also cleared, a new channel was built to supply it, and two new rectangular cisterns (L117-118) were dug nearby. De Vaux attributed two side-by-side potters' kilns in the southeast corner of the building to this phase. They were covered by the steps leading down to a cistern (L66) constructed during the next period of occupation.

De Vaux had difficulty ascertaining the date of Period Ia because no coins were found, and the few scraps of pottery recovered are identical with those of the next phase, Period Ib. Since the Period Ia remains were scanty, and he dated the beginning of Period Ib to the time of John Hyrcanus (135-104 BCE) or Alexander Jannaeus (103-76 BCE), de Vaux assigned Period Ia to the third quarter of the second century BCE.

Period Ib (see Plates 1 and 4)

According to de Vaux, the sectarian settlement at Qumran acquired its definitive form when it suddenly expanded greatly in size during the reign of John Hyrcanus or Alexander Jannaeus. The main entrance to the settlement was at the foot of a square, two-storey high tower in the center of the northern side (L9-11). The core of the settlement was the reconstructed Iron Age building, consisting of rooms (some of which were two storeys high) grouped around a central courtyard. A large room identified by de Vaux as a dining room and assembly hall (L77), and an adjacent pantry (L86, L89) were erected at this time to the south of the original core. Another group of rooms was added to the western area around the old round cistern, which was still in use. The water system was greatly expanded by the construction of new pools and cisterns, some of which were apparently used as ritual baths (miqva'ot). These were now fed by an aqueduct that brought flash flood waters from nearby Wadi Qumran. This settlement is characterized by the apparent absence of private dwellings; instead, many of the rooms appear to have been used as workshops (including a potters' workshop in L64 and L84, on the eastern side of the site), or for communal purposes (such as the dining room/assembly hall in L77). Exactly where the community lived is disputed; some of the second storey rooms may have been used as dwellings, but many of the inhabitants apparently occupied huts or tents around the site.[4] The presence of certain

---

[4] See J. Patrich, "Khirbet Qumran in Light of New Archaeological Explorations in the Qumran Caves," in M. O. Wise, N. Golb, J. J. Collins, and D. G. Pardee

domestic pottery types, such as cooking pots and oil lamps, suggests that some of the caves in the area were also inhabited. In the open spaces between and around the buildings, sheep, goat, and cow bones were found carefully deposited under potsherds or inside pots. De Vaux interpreted these as the remnants of ritual meals. Others have suggested that they represent sacrifices, though there are no identifiable remains of an altar at Qumran, nor do the Dead Sea Scrolls refer to the offering of animal sacrifices outside the Jerusalem Temple by members of the sect.[5]

According to de Vaux, the end of Period Ib was marked by an earthquake and a fire. The evidence for earthquake destruction, which was found throughout the settlement, is perhaps clearest in the case of one of the cisterns (L49), whose steps and floor were split and whose eastern half had dropped (see Plate 6).[6] The testimony of Flavius Josephus (*Jewish War* 1 §370-380; *Antiquities* 15 §121-147) enabled de Vaux to pinpoint the date of this earthquake to 31 BCE; in addition to this damage there was evidence for a fire in the settlement. De Vaux concluded that the earthquake and fire were simultaneous, because it was the simplest solution, but readily admitted that there was no evidence to confirm this. De Vaux used the numismatic evidence to support his interpretation: all ten identifiable coins of Herod the Great found at Qumran came from mixed levels, where they were associated with later coins. He noted that the Herodian coins were not dated, and cited a then recent study assigning such coins to the period after 30 BCE. Yaakov Meshorer has since suggested that Herod's undated bronze coins were minted after 37 BCE.[7]

Period II (see Plates 1 and 5)

According to de Vaux, the buildings damaged by the fire and/or the earthquake were not repaired immediately. Because the water

---

(eds.), *Methods of Investigation of the Dead Sea Scrolls and the Khirbet Qumran Site, Present Realities and Future Prospects* (ANYAS 722; New York: New York Academy of Sciences, 1994) 73-95; M. Broshi, "The Archaeology of Qumran," in D. Dimant and U. Rappaport (eds.), *The Dead Sea Scrolls, Forty Years of Research* (STDJ 10; Leiden: Brill, 1992) 103-15, esp. 105.

[5] See de Vaux, *Archaeology and the Dead Sea Scrolls* 13-16; J.-B. Humbert, "L'espace sacré à Qumrân," *RB* 101-2 (1994) 161-214.

[6] The Plates appear together at the end of the volume.

[7] For references see J. Magness, "The Chronology of the Settlement at Qumran in the Herodian Period," *DSD* 2 (1995) 58-65.

system ceased to be maintained, the site was flooded and silt accumulated up to a depth of 75 cm. The sediment overlay the layer of ash from the fire, indicating that the period of abandonment was subsequent to the fire (and that the two were presumably related). Following this period of abandonment, the site was cleared and reoccupied by the same community that had left it, as indicated by the fact that the general plan remained the same and many of the buildings seem to have been used for the same purposes as before. Most of the rooms were cleared out, with some debris dumped over the slopes of a ravine to the north of the site. Some of the damaged structures were strengthened, while others were left filled with collapse and abandoned. The tower, for example, was strengthened by the addition of a sloping stone glacis on its exterior, but the store of over one thousand dishes in the pantry (L86, L89), which had fallen and broken in the earthquake, was left lying on the floor of the room and buried. The cistern whose steps had been split by the earthquake (L49) went out of use (see Plates 6 and 7).

De Vaux again relied on the numismatic evidence to date the beginning of Period II. Since only ten identifiable coins of Herod the Great were found, all from mixed contexts, he assigned them to Period II. These coins could, he reasoned, have continued in circulation after Herod's death. De Vaux therefore dated the beginning of Period II to the time of Herod's successor, Herod Archelaus. He based this on several considerations. First, sixteen coins of Archelaus were recovered, after which point the numismatic sequence of Period II continues without interruption to the First Revolt. Second, one of Archelaus' coins was found in a deposit that had been cleared out of one of the buildings. The fact that the other coins in this deposit all dated to Period Ib, and did not include any coins of Herod the Great, suggested that the reoccupation of the site was undertaken during Archelaus' reign. Finally, there is the evidence provided by a hoard of 561 silver coins from L120, which were preserved in three pots. Most of these are Tyrian tetradrachmas from the period after 126 BCE, with the most recent coin in the hoard dating to 9/8 BCE (and several earlier pieces countermarked in the same year). As de Vaux noted, this evidence provides a *terminus post quem* of 9/8 BCE for the burial of the hoard. On the basis of Seyrig's observation that there is a relative lacuna in the issues of Tyrian tetradrachmas from 9/8 BCE until 1 BCE/1 CE (a lacuna which has since been filled), de Vaux dated the beginning of Period II to some time between 4 and 1 BCE—that is, to early in the reign of Herod Archelaus. Thus, the presence of coins of Herod Archelaus provided de Vaux with a *terminus post quem* of 4 BCE, while the absence of Tyrian tetradrachmas of post-1 BCE date in the hoard suggested a *terminus ante quem* for the beginning of Period II.

Aside from the strengthening or abandonment of the structures mentioned above, de Vaux noted that some minor modifications and changes were made to the rooms and the water system when the site was reoccupied in Period II. However, the potters' workshop continued in use (L64, L84), as did the custom of depositing animal bones under potsherds outside the buildings. One of the more controversial installations from this phase of occupation comes from a large room in the central part of the settlement (L30). The collapsed debris from the second storey level yielded the remains of low, plastered mud-brick benches and tables, a platform with two cup-shaped cavities, and two inkwells. De Vaux's interpretation of this room as a scriptorium (writing room) has been challenged because there is no evidence that scribes at this time wrote while seated on a bench at a table. However, the alternative proposal that it was a triclinium (dining room) is even less satisfactory, as the benches are too narrow for reclining.[8]

A cemetery containing about 1,100 tombs is located at a distance of fifty meters to the east of the site. The tombs, which are arranged in neat rows along the top of the plateau, are marked by heaps of stones on the surface. All but one are oriented from north to south. Other tombs located at the edges of the cemetery or on the low hills to the east do not have the same regular alignment and orientation. The bodies were placed in a kind of loculus or niche at the bottom of a rectangular cavity dug into the marl of the plateau. Of the twenty-six tombs excavated by de Vaux, those in the main part all contained adult male burials, while those at the edges included some women and children.[9]

---

[8] See de Vaux, *Archaeology and the Dead Sea Scrolls* 29-33; R. Donceel and P. Donceel-Voûte, "The Archaeology of Khirbet Qumran," in Wise et al. (eds.), *Methods of Investigation*, 1-38, esp. 27-31; R. Reich, "A Note on the Function of Room 30 ("the Scriptorium") at Khirbet Qumran," *JJS* 46 (1995) 157-60.

[9] For the cemetery at Qumran see de Vaux, *Archaeology and the Dead Sea Scrolls* 45-50; Humbert and Chambon, *Fouilles* 346-52; S. H. Steckoll, "Preliminary Excavation Report in the Qumran Cemetery," *RevQ* 23 (1968) 323-36; R.

The Period II settlement suffered a violent destruction by fire which de Vaux attributed to the Roman army at the time of the First Jewish Revolt. He used the numismatic evidence and Josephus' testimony to pinpoint the date to 68 CE. This destruction brought the sectarian settlement at Qumran to an end.

Period III

Following the destruction in 68 CE, the site seems to have been occupied for no more than five years by a small garrison of Roman soldiers who cleared out the debris in parts of the settlement. There is also some evidence for activity or small-scale occupation of the site at the time of the Bar Kokhba Revolt (132-135 CE).

2. QUMRAN: SECTARIAN SETTLEMENT, VILLA, FORTRESS OR ENTREPOT?

De Vaux's interpretation of the site of Qumran as a sectarian settlement inhabited by the same community that deposited the scrolls in the nearby caves has recently been challenged by a number of scholars. Among these are Robert Donceel and Pauline Donceel-Voûte, and J.-B. Humbert, who have suggested that the site functioned as a "villa rustica" during all or part of its main phase of existence, Norman Golb, who believes it was a fortress, and Alan Crown and Lena Cansdale, who have interpreted it as a commercial entrepot.[10] I do not believe that the archaeological evidence supports

---

Hachlili, "Burial Practices at Qumran," *RevQ* 62 (1993) 247-64; Z.J. Kapera, "Some Remarks on the Qumran Cemetery," in Wise et al. (eds.), *Methods of Investigation*, 97-113. For similar cemeteries elsewhere see P. Bar-Adon, "Another Settlement of the Judean Desert Sect at ʿEn el-Ghuweir on the Shores of the Dead Sea," *BASOR* 227 (1977) 1-25; H. Eshel and Z. Greenhut, "Ḥiam el-Sagha, A Cemetery of the Qumran Type, Judean Desert," *RB* 100-2 (1993) 252-59.

[10] See Donceel and Donceel-Voûte, "The Archaeology of Khirbet Qumran," 1-38; P. Donceel-Voûte, "Les ruines de Qumran réinterprétées," *Archeologia* 298 (1994) 24-35; Humbert, "L'espace sacré à Qumrân"; N. Golb, "Khirbet Qumran and the Manuscript Finds of the Judaean Wilderness," in *Methods of Investigation*, 51-72; idem, *Who Wrote the Dead Sea Scrolls?* (New York: Simon and Schuster, 1995) 3-41; A. Crown and L. Cansdale, "Qumran—Was It an Essene Settlement?" *BAR* 20 (1994) 24-36, 73-78. For another interpretation of the settlement see E. Cook, "What was Qumran? A Ritual Purification Center," *BAR* 22/6 (1996) 39, 48-51, 73-75. For my published responses to the villa interpretation, with relevant bibliographical references, see J. Magness, "A Villa at Khirbet Qumran?" *RevQ* 63

any of these alternative interpretations. For example, the presence of the tower and the evidence for a violent destruction by fire at the end of Period II (including the discovery of a few iron arrowheads) cited by Golb do not prove that the site was a fortress. They only indicate that the inhabitants were concerned with protecting the site, and that it was destroyed by a hostile human force, apparently the Romans.

The "villa theory," which was first advanced by Donceel and Donceel-Voûte on the basis of the richness and variety of the finds from the site, has attracted the most attention. However, comparisons between contemporary Judaean and Idumaean villas and the settlement at Qumran are inconsistent with this interpretation. These comparisons include layout and design, architectural style and technique, interior decoration, and ceramic material. The contemporary Judaean and Idumaean palaces and villas that can be compared to Qumran are: (1) the royal Hasmonean and Herodian palaces at Masada, Herodion, and Herodian Jericho (Tulul Abu el-ʿAlayiq; (2) the private, upper-class urban Jewish mansions of the Herodian period in Jerusalem's Jewish Quarter; (3) "Hilkiah's Palace," a private, rural villa of the Herodian period in Idumaea.

All of these palaces and villas share certain features that are not found at Qumran. For example, the Hasmonean palaces uncovered by Ehud Netzer at Jericho typically have a central courtyard surrounded by rooms. A hall with two columns *in antis*, which probably functioned as a triclinium or reception hall, opened on to the southern side of the courtyard. Other features of the Hasmonean palaces at Jericho include swimming pools, gardens, an elaborate water-supply system, bath-houses, and miqvaʾot. The typical features of the plans of Herodian palaces include a main wing with a triclinium, a peristyle courtyard, a bath-house (usually with a Roman-style hypocaust system), and dwelling rooms. The triclinium was a large hall with three rows of columns around the inside and a wide entrance open to the landscape or an inner courtyard. The peristyle courtyard had rows of columns around the sides and a garden in the center. The extended palace complex included entertainment facilities such as large pools for swimming and boating, elaborate gardens, and water channels and installations.

(1994) 397-419; J. Magness, "What was Qumran? Not a Country Villa," *BAR* 22/6 (1996) 38-47, 72-73.

The Herodian mansions in the Jewish Quarter of Jerusalem provide the best comparanda for private, upper-class dwellings, though they are urban, not rural in character, while the villa ("Hilkiah's Palace") at Khirbet el-Muraq is a close analogue, as a private, rural villa in Idumaea. Features common to these sites and Qumran include the presence of numerous miqva'ot at Qumran and in the mansions in the Jewish Quarter, while Qumran and Hilkiah's Palace were both protected by large square towers and had elongated halls identified as dining rooms. However, the settlement at Qumran has none of the characteristics of layout and design found in the Hasmonean and Herodian palaces: the hall with two columns *in antis*, the colonnaded triclinium, the peristyle courtyard with garden, the bath-houses, and the large swimming pools and landscaped gardens. Qumran does have courtyards, without peristyles, around which rooms were grouped. There was a second storey of rooms in at least part of the settlement.[11] Unlike Qumran, Hilkiah's Palace has a bath-house heated by a hypocaust system, and the central courtyard has a peristyle. Though there are elaborate water systems at all of these sites, Qumran differs in having no clearly identifiable bath-houses or built-up bathtubs; only cisterns and pools, some of which were apparently used as miqva'ot.[12] It is also distinguished by the presence of workshops located throughout the settlement, and by the large adjacent cemetery.

However, the most compelling argument against the identification of Qumran as a villa lies in the almost complete absence of interior decoration–such as frescoes, stucco, and mosaic floors–all of which are found at the other sites. Of course, the settlement at Qumran shares some features of plan and decoration with contemporary palaces and villas in Judaea and Idumaea, since the inhabitants expressed themselves in the architectural vocabulary of their environment. However, these shared features, such as the extensive water-system, the central courtyards, and the large dining room are

---

[11] Thirteen columnar elements (drums and bases) that were apparently found in secondary use in Period III contexts indicate that the central courtyard at Qumran may have had a full or partial peristyle in Periods Ib or II. See J. Magness, review of J.-B. Humbert and A. Chambon, *Fouilles de Khirbet Qumrân et de Aïn Feshkha I* (Göttingen: Vandenhoeck and Ruprecht, 1994), *DSD* 3 (1996) 342-45.

[12] For the miqva'ot at Qumran see B. G. Wood, "To Dip or Sprinkle? The Qumran Cisterns in Perspective," *BASOR* 256 (1984) 45-60; R. Reich, "The Great Miqveh Debate," *BAR* 19/2 (1993) 52-53.

too utilitarian to support the identification of Qumran as a villa. On the contrary, it is the differences between Qumran and contemporary palatial and villa sites which are significant.

The character of the ceramic assemblage from Qumran, which contrasts sharply with those from contemporary Judaean sites, also argues against its identification as a villa.[13] The repertoire of types represented at Qumran is limited, repetitive, and plain. The absence or rarity of both imported and local fine ware types (such as imported amphoras and eastern terra sigillata) from the Qumran corpus is suggestive of a deliberate and selective policy of isolation on the part of the inhabitants.[14] For example, imported amphoras, which contained fine wine, fish-sauce *(garum)*, and other products from around the Mediterranean have been found in Herod's palaces at Masada, Jericho, and Herodion, and at the site of Qasr el-Yehud (Khirbet Mazin) near Qumran. The amphoras often bear stamps on the handles or inscriptions on the body certifying the identification and source of their contents. Imported amphoras have even been found in the Jewish Quarter, prompting Avigad's explanation that, "there have always been more and less observant Jews."[15] Some of the "less observant" Jews of Jerusalem's Jewish Quarter apparently consumed the non-kosher contents of the amphoras.

This is not the case at Qumran, where no imported amphoras are published from the excavations. Instead, the inhabitants of Qumran

---

[13] See J. Magness, "The Community at Qumran in Light of Its Pottery," in Wise, Golb, Collins and Pardee (eds.), *Methods of Investigation*, 39-50.

[14] Though the manufacture of Eastern Sigillata A began ca. 140-130 BCE, it is rare at sites in Judea before the reign of Herod the Great. See A. M. Berlin, "Between Large Forces: Palestine in the Hellenistic Period," *BA* 60 (1997) 2-51, esp. 25; R. Bar-Nathan, *The Pottery of Jericho in the Hasmonean Period and the Time of Herod, and the Problem of the Transition from Hasmonean Pottery Types to Pottery Types of the Time of Herod* (unpublished Ph.D. diss., Jerusalem: The Hebrew University, Institute of Archaeology, late 1980's [Hebrew]) 209, 222-23. Thus, while the rarity or absence of imports and fine wares at Qumran is unusual for a Judaean site of the late first century BCE and first century CE, this does not hold true for the pre-31 BCE settlement.

[15] N. Avigad, *Discovering Jerusalem* (Nashville: Thomas Nelson, 1983) 77-79, 87-88. For imported amphoras containing the residue of fish sauce, see H. Cotton, O. Lernau, and Y. Goren, "Fish sauces from Herodian Masada," *JRA* 9 (1996) 223-38. For other references see Magness, "Community at Qumran in Light of Its Pottery," 39-50.

apparently preferred to manufacture and use their own ceramic products, many of which are morphologically similar to types found elsewhere in Judaea, but without decoration. They also produced some ceramic types which are characteristic of or unique to Qumran, such as the "scroll jars," and a peculiar type of oil lamp of Hellenistic inspiration, both of which are discussed below. I believe that most of the pottery found in the excavations at Qumran was produced in the workshops discovered at the site, though this needs to be verified by analysis of the clays. The presence of the same ceramic types (including those unique to Qumran) in the caves and the settlement establishes an important archaeological link, which advocates of the villa theory and other alternative interpretations have attempted to deny. Some scholars have objected to the identification of Qumran as a sectarian settlement because scrolls were found only in the caves, not in the excavations at the site. Not only is this is a dangerous argument from silence, it ignores the fact that any scroll material originally present at the site would likely have been burned in the fires that destroyed it in ca. 9/8 BCE (see below) and in 68 CE.

3. THE THIRTY-YEAR GAP BETWEEN PERIODS IB AND II[16]

Most scholars have accepted de Vaux's conclusions regarding the chronology of the settlement at Qumran, though many have grappled with the problems raised by this thirty-year gap in occupation. For example, it does not make sense that an earthquake would have caused the inhabitants to abandon the site for thirty years. One might expect political turmoil or unstable social conditions to cause such an abandonment, but not an earthquake. Also, how is it that after such a long time, the site was reoccupied by the same population? Where did the community go for thirty years? Because of these problems, some scholars have suggested that the earthquake and fire were not simultaneous. They have proposed that the settlement was burned during the turbulent period of the Parthian invasion and the reign of Mattathias Antigonus (40-37 BCE) and then abandoned. The site would have been ruined and empty when the earthquake struck in 31 BCE. De Vaux argued convincingly against this interpretation, which again fails to account for the whereabouts of the community during such a long gap in occupation.

---

[16] For this section, see Magness, "Chronology of the Settlement at Qumran," 58-65.

I believe that a reconsideration of the archaeological evidence, especially the coins, provides a solution to these problems. As noted above, only ten identifiable coins of Herod the Great were found at Qumran, all undated bronze issues from mixed levels. De Vaux associated these with the Period II settlement, claiming that they remained in circulation after Herod's death. However, there are other coins dating to Herod's reign from Qumran. These are among the silver coins found in the hoard, most of which are Tyrian tetradrachmas dating from 126 BCE to 9/8 BCE. More important, however, is the context of this hoard, which was described by de Vaux as follows: "These three pots [containing the coins] were buried beneath the level of Period II and above that of Period Ib."[17] De Vaux associated the burial of the hoard with the reoccupation of the site at the beginning of Period II. However, the context makes it clear that the hoard could equally be associated with the end of Period Ib, and common sense suggests that this is the case. Hoards are usually buried in times of trouble, and often remain buried because the owner[s] failed to return and retrieve the valuables. It is reasonable to assume that the hoard at Qumran was buried because of some impending danger, and that it remained buried because the site was subsequently abandoned for some time. For whatever reason, the hoard was never retrieved even after the site was reoccupied.

The assignment of this hoard to the end of Period Ib suggests a different chronological sequence for the settlement at Qumran. The site was not abandoned after the earthquake of 31 BCE. The inhabitants immediately repaired and/or strengthened many of the damaged buildings, but did not bother to clear those which were beyond repair. The settlement of Period Ib then continued without apparent interruption until 9/8 BCE or some time thereafter. It is the coin hoard which provides a *terminus post quem* for the abandonment of the site. The fact that this hoard was buried, combined with the presence of a layer of ash, suggests that the fire which destroyed the settlement should be attributed to human agents rather than to natural causes. In other words, in 9/8 BCE or some time thereafter, Qumran seems to have suffered a deliberate, violent destruction. Such a destruction better accounts for the abandonment of the site by the inhabitants. However, it was not the prolonged

---

[17] De Vaux, *Archaeology and the Dead Sea Scrolls*, 34; Humbert and Chambon, *Fouilles*, 329-30.

abandonment postulated by de Vaux. Instead, the site was abandoned in 9/8 BCE or some time thereafter, and reoccupied early in the reign of Herod Archelaus (that is, in 4 BCE or shortly thereafter). On the basis of the presently available evidence, it is impossible to narrow this range any further. The fact that the water system fell into disrepair and silt covered the site indicates that the abandonment lasted for at least one winter season. Since it is impossible to pinpoint the date, the causes leading to the destruction of the site must remain unknown, though it is tempting to associate them with the revolts and turmoil which erupted in Judaea upon the death of Herod the Great.

4. THE POTTERY OF PERIODS IB AND II

My revised sequence for Qumran means that de Vaux's Period Ib includes both pre-31 and post-31 BCE remains. It is possible to distinguish between late Hellenistic ceramic types and types dating to the reign of Herod the Great by isolating those which come from loci abandoned after the earthquake of 31 BCE, and those from loci covered by the ash of the fire of ca. 9/8 BCE. In fact, Qumran provides a unique opportunity to establish a ceramic typology for the reign of Herod the Great.[18]

The only ceramic material published from Qumran is illustrated in de Vaux's preliminary reports, while additional information can be gleaned from his recently published field notes. Though no pottery is illustrated in the latter source, the vessels recovered are listed in the locus descriptions. Their numbers can be correlated with those illustrated in the preliminary reports. Because only a small amount of pottery is published from loci which show clear evidence of destruction by earthquake or by the fire of ca. 9/8 BCE, it is difficult to pinpoint differences between the late Hellenistic and Herodian ceramic types at Qumran. There seems to be a tendency for the walls of the deep cups or beakers with flaring rims to become thicker during the course of the Herodian period. The bases of the cups and bowls also seem to change from ring to disc in form, though this is by no means universal.[19] The peculiar oil lamps of Hellenistic

---

[18] For references for this section see J. Magness, "The Chronology of Qumran, Ein Feshkha, and Ein el-Ghuweir,"*The Qumran Chronicle* 8 (1997) 7-21; idem, "Community at Qumran in Light of Its Pottery," 39-50.

[19] These changes are best seen by comparing the assemblages from L89 (pre-31 BCE), L130-135 (ca. 9/8 BCE), and L114 (probably late 1st century BCE – early 1st

inspiration are apparently represented at Qumran only in contexts dating to the reign of Herod the Great.[20] Jericho and Masada are the only sites aside from the caves and settlement at Qumran where these lamps have been found. At Jericho, they also occur in contexts dating to the time of Herod. The absence of wheelmade, knife-pared ("Herodian") lamps in any of the Period Ib contexts lends support to a growing body of evidence that this type appeared either late in the reign of Herod the Great or after his death.

Another ceramic type not attested from any of the Period Ib contexts at Qumran is the "scroll jars," which were described by de Vaux as "cylindrical jars." All of the published examples come from Period II contexts. Those published in the preliminary reports seem to represent all the examples of this type found at Qumran, since no other "cylindrical jars" are listed in the locus descriptions in Humbert and Chambon. The scroll jars thus seem to belong mainly, if not exclusively to the first century CE, though according to de Vaux they were discovered in Period Ib and II contexts. In addition, Bar-Nathan states that scroll jars are first attested at Jericho in contexts dating to the reign of Herod the Great.[21] Only the final publication of the pottery will make it possible to determine whether scroll jars first appeared at Qumran during the reign of Herod the Great (that is, in post-31 BCE Period Ib contexts), or after his death (in Period II).

One of the problems in discussing the distribution of scroll jars is defining exactly what is meant by the term. Bar-Nathan uses it broadly, to include a variety of jars with wide mouth. According to this definition, scroll jars are found at Qumran, Masada, Herodian Jericho, and Quailba. However, Bar-Nathan also notes that by far the largest variety of scroll jars is represented in the caves and settlement at Qumran. At Qumran, they are more common in the

---

century CE); cf. de Vaux ("Fouilles de Khirbet Qumrân," *RB* 63 [1956] figs. 1-4), who also noted these tendencies (*Archaeology and the Dead Sea Scrolls*, 18).

[20] For a discussion of these lamps see Magness, "Community at Qumran in Light of Its Pottery," 41, 46. The only locus from which lamps of this type are published is 130 (other examples, described by de Vaux as "Hellenistic lamps" but not published, were found in L40 ["lower level"], L44, and L74). There are no examples recorded from earthquake destruction levels, or from Period II contexts. The other published lamps of this type all come from the caves around Qumran.

[21] For references see Magness, "Chronology of Qumran, Ein Feshkha, and Ein el-Ghuweir," nn.40-41.

caves than in the settlement. Even at Herodian Jericho, which seems to have the second largest representation of this type, the selection is mostly limited to a large variant with bag-shaped body. I believe that the pattern of distribution and the morphology of the "classic" scroll jars (Bar-Nathan's Type 2B), which are characterized by a long, cylindrical body, indicate that they were designed to hold scrolls. However, the much larger or smaller variants with bag-shaped or oval bodies published from Qumran and Herodian Jericho were probably put to other uses. Bar-Nathan notes that at Jericho most of the scroll jars, which are the large variant with bag-shaped body, were found in the Herodian industrial area. On the basis of the presently available evidence it is impossible to determine whether the "classic" scroll jars were developed as a variant of a local jar with wide mouth, or visa versa.

The parallels between the ceramic corpus from Herodian Jericho and that from Qumran, which include the scroll jars and the peculiar oil lamps of Hellenistic inspiration, are striking. Bar-Nathan is certainly correct in attributing this phenomenon to regional distribution patterns. Could these parallels also reflect the presence of the same community? Does the presence of scroll jars in Zealot contexts at Masada (mentioned by Bar-Nathan) support Yigael Yadin's suggestion that members of the Qumran community joined the rebels there after Qumran had fallen to the Romans?

5. THE CHRONOLOGY OF EIN FESHKHA[22]

At Ein Feshkha, de Vaux excavated a complex that is at least partly contemporary with the sectarian settlement at Qumran. Though no scroll jars seem to be attested from Ein Feshkha, the rest of the ceramic corpus is similar to that from Qumran. The nucleus of the settlement is a rectangular building consisting of rooms surrounding a central courtyard. The main phase of occupation distinguished by de Vaux is contemporary with Period II at Qumran. Most of the pottery recovered in the excavations belongs to this phase, and the dating is supported by the numismatic evidence. As at Qumran, Period II at Ein Feshkha ended with a destruction by fire. De Vaux also found traces of an earlier phase of occupation, which he called

---

[22] For references for this section see de Vaux, "Fouilles de Feshkha," and other relevant bibliography in Magness, "Chronology of Qumran, Ein Feshkha, and Ein el-Ghuweir."

Period I. The architectural evidence for this phase is scanty, consisting mostly of an earlier level in L6 (the northwest corner of the courtyard), and in L21 and 22 (the long room on the north side of the courtyard). Most of the pottery associated with Period I is fragmentary, and much of it comes from piles of rubbish which were cleared out of the building and discarded outside the north wall when the site was reoccupied at the beginning of Period II. Though he equated it with Period Ib at Qumran, de Vaux noted that there is no evidence that Period I at Ein Feshkha ended with a violent destruction, either by earthquake or fire. Yet the fact that the building was cleared out suggests that it too was abandoned for some time.

The repertoire of ceramic types published from Period I contexts at Ein Feshkha is very limited. What is important, however, is that none of the types has to antedate the Herodian period. The cups, bowls, and beakers appear to have the slightly thicker walls characteristic of the Herodian and post-Herodian period at Qumran. Other types, such as the storage jars with outward folded rim and the piriform unguentarium, should certainly be dated no earlier than the time of Herod the Great. The numismatic evidence supports this revised chronology. Among the coins from Period I are four of Alexander Jannaeus, one of Mattathias Antigonus, and one of Herod the Great, dating to the third year of his reign. As both Avigad and Ariel have noted, since the coins of Alexander Jannaeus are known to have remained in circulation even under Herod, they are not necessarily an indicator of a Hasmonean phase of occupation.[23] Instead, it is the latest pottery and coins which provide the date for the associated building or level. Thus, Period I at Ein Feshkha should be assigned to the Herodian period.

De Vaux was puzzled by the fact that there is no evidence for the earthquake of 31 BCE at Ein Feshkha, which is just 3 km south of Qumran. He attributed this to a different geological formation at Ein Feshkha. However, the ceramic evidence indicates that Period I at Ein Feshkha dates to the Herodian period. I believe that this settlement was first established after the earthquake of 31 BCE, which would account for the absence of evidence for earthquake destruction at the site. Because of the limited nature of the ceramic repertoire, it

---

[23] Avigad, *Discovering Jerusalem*, 85; D. T. Ariel, "A Survey of Coin Finds in Jerusalem (Until the End of Byzantine Period)," *LA* 32 (1982) 273-326, esp. 285-87.

is difficult to determine whether the end of Period I at Ein Feshkha is contemporary with the end of Herodian Period Ib at Qumran, that is, ca. 9/8 BCE or some time thereafter. At any rate, the ceramic evidence does not contradict the possibility that Ein Feshkha was abandoned (but not destroyed) at the same time as Qumran.

6. THE CHRONOLOGY OF EIN EL-GHUWEIR[24]

About fifteen kilometers to the south of Qumran, Pesach Bar-Adon excavated a settlement by the springs at Ein el-Ghuweir. There he uncovered the remains of a long building consisting of a large hall with a kitchen and two rooms to the east. Bar-Adon distinguished two layers of burnt material in the hall and kitchen, which indicated that the complex had been destroyed twice by fire. Regarding the chronology of the settlement, Bar-Adon concluded as follows:

> The coins were identified as belonging to the time of Herod, Archelaus, and Agrippa I, i.e. from the period between 37 BCE and 44 CE. According to these limits, the settlement did not exist for long. In contrast to this, the pottery finds considerably extend the period during which the settlement existed. In accordance with the material discussed above, the types of pottery found both in the large structure at ʿEn el-Ghuweir and in the cemetery are similar to those found in Qumran Ib. Thus, they date from Qumran's most flourishing period—from the days of Alexander Yannai until the beginning of the reign of Herod. The pottery types are also similar to those from Qumran II, the period ending with the Great Revolt and the destruction of the settlement in 68 CE. It is therefore possible that the two layers of burned material at ʿEn el-Ghuweir parallel the double destruction of Qumran and ʿEn Feshkha.[25]

Bar-Adon's chronology is not supported by the ceramic evidence, for clearly pre-Herodian types appear to be absent from the corpus at Ein el-Ghuweir. This parallels the complete absence of pre-Herodian coins from the site. Some of the ceramic types, such as the asymmetrical flasks, have a range throughout the first century BCE and first century CE. However, most of the published types from Ein el-Ghuweir, such as the storage jars with outward folded rim, the piriform unguentaria, the carinated cooking pots, and the wheelmade, hand-pared ("Herodian") oil lamps, do not antedate the

---

[24] For references for this section see Bar-Adon, "Another Settlement of the Judean Desert Sect," and other relevant bibliography in Magness, "Chronology of Qumran, Ein Feshkha, and Ein el-Ghuweir."

[25] Bar-Adon, "Another Settlement of the Judean Desert Sect," 18.

Herodian period. Thus, the numismatic and ceramic evidence indicates that the settlement at Ein el-Ghuweir was established no earlier than the reign of Herod the Great. On the basis of the published evidence, it is impossible to determine when the fire that destroyed the earlier phase of the settlement occurred, and whether it is contemporary with the destruction at Qumran in ca. 9/8 BCE.

7. PERIOD IA AT QUMRAN

Some scholars have suggested that during Period Ia, Qumran was a non-sectarian settlement, and that it was occupied by sectarians only in the later phases. According to J.-B. Humbert, for example, during Period Ia Qumran functioned as a non-sectarian agricultural settlement. He also believes that Period Ia continued until the site was destroyed in 57 BCE (by Gabinius), or in 31 BCE (during Herod's establishment of control over Jericho and the Dead Sea region).[26] Could Qumran originally have been an agricultural settlement or fortress that was later occupied by sectarians?

I do not believe that the archaeological evidence supports such an interpretation. In fact, I do not believe that de Vaux's Period Ia exists at all! As mentioned above, de Vaux found no coins associated with Period Ia, and only a few potsherds that are indistinguishable from those of Period Ib. In this context it should be noted that virtually all of the pottery published (and perhaps saved?) by de Vaux from the excavations at Qumran consists of whole (intact or restored) vessels, as opposed to sherds. Almost all of these whole vessels come from the three destruction levels of 31 BCE, 9/8 BCE, and 68 CE, when they were smashed and left lying on the floors and were buried in the collapse. Thus, this ceramic material dates to the end of each of these occupational phases. Because of this, it is impossible to determine precisely when Period Ia began. However, none of the pottery that de Vaux published from Qumran has to antedate the first century CE. This suggests that most of the architectural remains he attributed to Period Ia probably belong to the Period Ib pre-31 BCE phase, while his Period Ib includes both pre-31 and post-31 BCE remains. One exception to this are the two potters' kilns beneath L66, which must date to the late Iron Age, since they were covered by a cistern destroyed in the earthquake of

---

[26] See Humbert, "L'espace sacré à Qumrân," 161-214.

31 BCE.[27] Only the final publication of all of the material from Qumran, including the pottery, coins and stratigraphy, will make it possible to reconstruct these phases accurately.

Thus, I do not believe that de Vaux's Period Ia existed, or that the sectarian settlement at Qumran was established before the first century BCE. De Vaux dated the beginning of his Period Ib no later than the reign of Alexander Jannaeus because he found 143 coins of that king. However, these only provide a *terminus post quem* for the beginning of his Period Ib, and, as we have seen, the coins of Alexander Jannaeus are known to have remained in circulation down to the time of Herod the Great. This means that the settlement at Qumran was apparently established much later than de Vaux thought, probably some time in the first half of the first century BCE.[28] However, the presence of miqva'ot, the pantry containing over one thousand dishes, and the possible evidence for the custom of depositing animal bones outside the buildings in pre-31 BCE contexts[29] indicate that the settlement was sectarian from the beginning of its establishment.

8. A TOILET AT QUMRAN?

One installation described in de Vaux's field notes is located in L51, a large room to the north of the pool in L48-49, on the eastern side of the site.[30] A terracotta pipe set into a conical, mud-lined pit that was filled with thin layers of coarse, dirty earth was embedded in the floor of this room. Though soil samples are not available for analysis, other evidence suggests that his identification is correct.

---

[27] Circular kilns with a central pillar are attested in Palestine at least from the Bronze Age on, though a "tongued" type was apparently more common in the Iron Age; see G. Delcroix and J.-L. Huot, "Les fours dits 'de potier' dans l'Orient ancien," *Syria* 49 (1972) 35-75, esp. fig. 7:E.2 (a)-(b).

[28] Other scholars have also proposed that Period Ia did not begin before the first century BCE; see for example E.-M. Laperrousaz, "Does the Temple Scroll Date from the First or Second Century BCE?" in G. J. Brooke (ed.), *Temple Scroll Studies* (Sheffield: Sheffield Academic Press, 1989) 91-97, esp. 96.

[29] L132 might provide published evidence for these deposits in Period Ib contexts prior to 31 BCE. There a group of pottery with bones was found lying on virgin soil (see Humbert and Chambon, *Fouilles*, 335). Due to the lack of published section drawings, however, it is impossible to determine whether this deposit lay beneath the plastered basin in this locus, which apparently dates to the time of Herod the Great.

[30] Cf. Humbert and Chambon, *Fouilles*, 309; photographs 148-51.

Perhaps the best-known examples of ancient toilets are Roman luxury latrines, which were often part of a public bath house. They were equipped with wooden or stone seats pierced with holes which lined three sides of the room. The seats were mounted above a constantly running stream of waste water from the bath house, which carried off the sewage. A small gutter on the floor in front of the seats carried water for washing the hands and cleaned the spillage.[31] Since these latrines relied on a constant supply of fresh water brought by aqueduct, they are rarely found outside Roman civic bath houses or other public establishments. Moreover, since Roman luxury latrines first appeared in the second century CE, they postdate the site of Qumran and the Dead Sea Scrolls.[32]

Sanitary arrangements varied greatly in the ancient Mediterranean world, even during the time of the Roman Empire. Since many private dwellings in Roman cities lacked any toilet facilities, residents either had to use a "chamber pot" (such as a broken amphora), or simply went outdoors. When toilet installations are found in Roman houses, they usually consist of a seat built over a cesspit for the waste. When the cesspit was full, a local manure merchant would be called to carry it away for resale as fertilizer. Sometimes the cesspit was dug in the backyard, and connected to the toilet by a terracotta pipe drain. The waste was then "flushed" through the pipe by a bucket of water. However, because of the gentle gradient and the absence of any anti-odor U-bend trap, this arrangement did not represent much of an improvement.[33]

---

[31] A. T. Hodge, *Roman Aqueducts and Water Supply* (London: Duckworth, 1992) 270-71; also see R. Neudecker, *Die Pracht der Latrine, Zum Wandel öffentlicher Bedürfnisanstalten in der kaiserzeitlichen Stadt* (Munich: Friedrich Pfeil, 1994). Luxury latrines of this type have been found at a number of sites in Israel; for a Roman-Byzantine period example at Caesarea see F. L. Horton, Jr., "A Sixth-Century Bath in Caesarea's Suburbs and the Transformation of Bathing Culture in Late Antiquity," in A. Raban and K. G. Holum (eds.), *Caesarea Maritima, A Retrospective after Two Millennia* (Leiden: Brill) 183; and for an early Islamic example near Jericho see R. W. Hamilton, "Mafjar, Khirbet el-," in E. Stern (ed.), *The New Encyclopedia of Archaeological Excavations in the Holy Land* (New York: Simon and Schuster, 1993) 923.

[32] See Neudecker, *Die Pracht der Latrine*, 39.

[33] Hodge, *Roman Aqueducts*, 336-37; A. Scobie, "Slums, Sanitation, and Mortality in the Roman World," *Klio* 68 (1986) 409-17.

Toilets of Late Bronze and Iron Age date have been identified at several sites in Egypt and Palestine. Two stone toilet seats dating from the seventh to sixth centuries BCE were discovered in the excavations in the City of David in Jerusalem. Both were made of large, square blocks of limestone pierced with a hole in the center of the concave top. One of the seats was found in a small cubicle at the back of the House of Ahiel, still sitting in its original position over a cesspit. Similar stone toilet seats, sometimes set over cesspits, have been found elsewhere in Jerusalem, at Buseirah and Tell es-Saidiyeh in Jordan, and in Egypt.[34]

The installation described by de Vaux in L51 at Qumran thus appears to represent the cesspit of a toilet. Perhaps the pipe set into it was intended to carry waste "flushed" down by pouring in water. Since no seat was found over the pipe and cesspit, it may have been made of wood. However, I believe that a pierced stone block from locus 44, which is adjacent to and east of L51, may represent a toilet seat. This object, which is not illustrated, was tentatively identified by de Vaux as part of a conduit or chimney flue.[35]

The published top plans seem to indicate that the toilet in L51 went out of use after the earthquake of 31 BCE, together with the pool in adjacent L48-49.[36] Thus, this toilet belongs to the pre-31 BCE phase of Period Ib. Albert Baumgarten has recently argued that the sanitation arrangements described in the Temple Scroll (11QT) and by Josephus differ so fundamentally that they could not reflect the practices of the same sect. He concluded that the Temple Scroll is not an Essene document, or, at least, that the group living according to its rules is not to be equated with the Essenes described by Josephus.[37]

How do the sanitary arrangements in these ancient sources compare? In the scrolls, latrines are referred to by the Hebrew term "the hand" or "the place for a hand."[38] The relevant passage from the Temple Scroll (Col. 46:13-16) says:

---

[34] See J. Cahill, K. Reinhard, D. Tarler and P. Warnock, "Scientists Examine Remains of Ancient Bathroom," *BAR* 17/3 (1991) 64-69.

[35] Humbert and Chambon, *Fouilles*, 307.

[36] Humbert and Chambon, *Fouilles*, 72-73.

[37] A. I. Baumgarten, "The Temple Scroll, Toilet Practices, and the Essenes," *Jewish History* 10 (1996) 9-20. I am grateful to Lawrence H. Schiffman for sending me a copy of this article.

[38] Y. Yadin, *The Temple Scroll* (New York: Random House, 1985) 178.

> And you shall make them a place for a hand outside the city, to which they shall go out, to the north-west of the city—roofed houses with pits within them, into which the excrement will descend, so that it will not be visible at any distance from the city, three thousand cubits.[39]

Yadin noted that the prohibition and much of the phraseology of this passage are based on the text of Deut 23:9-14. The War Scroll (1QM) mandates the placement of latrines at a distance of 2000 cubits from the camps, which is 1000 cubits less than the distance from the city prescribed by the Temple Scroll:

> There shall be a space between all their camps and the place of the hand about two thousand cubits, and no unseemly evil thing shall be seen in the vicinity of their encampment.[40]

Josephus describes the sanitation practices of the Essenes as follows:

> (On the Sabbath) they do not even go to stool. On other days they dig a trench a foot deep with a mattock–such is the nature of the hatchet which they present to neophytes–and wrapping their mantle about them, that they may not offend the rays of the deity, sit above it. They then replace the excavated soil in the trench. For this purpose they select the more retired spots. And though this discharge of the excrements is a natural function, they make it a rule to wash themselves after it, as if defiled.[41]

As Baumgarten noted, though all these sources describe a practice secluded from the public eye, they differ in the way this was achieved. Whereas the Temple Scroll and War Scroll describe permanent, roofed facilities, Josephus's Essenes dug a new hole in the ground in an open, remote spot each time they had to relieve themselves.[42] However, I disagree with Baumgarten's conclusion that this reflects the practices of two different groups or sects, since it assumes that our sources provide complete accounts. Instead, it appears that only those practices which deviated from the norm are described by Josephus and mandated by the Temple Scroll and War Scroll. Furthermore, Baumgarten's chronological argument is flawed. He suggests that the Temple Scroll could not represent an earlier stage of the sect than Josephus's Essenes because this would reverse the development of ancient latrines, which were usually a later phenomenon associated with the rise in economic standards.[43]

---

[39] Yadin, *Temple Scroll*, 178.
[40] Yadin, *Temple Scroll*, 178.
[41] *JewishWar* 2 §147-49.
[42] Baumgarten, "The Temple Scroll," 13.
[43] Baumgartem, "The Temple Scroll," 14.

However, as we have seen, private toilets (consisting of a cesspit covered with a seat) are attested in Egypt and Palestine already in the Late Bronze Age and Iron Age.

The textual evidence combined with the presence of the toilet at Qumran indicates that the sectarians attended to their bodily functions in various ways. When they did not have access to built latrines in permanent settlements, they relieved themselves in the manner described by Josephus. The location of the toilet in L51 on the eastern edge of the settlement suggests that the regulations prescribed for the holy camps in the War Scroll and the holy city of Jerusalem in the Temple Scroll did not apply to the settlement at Qumran. These sources seem to single out specific instances where a special sanitation practice is employed or mandated. Josephus was struck by the fact that the Essenes secluded themselves when defecating outdoors–in contrast to the usual contemporary practice of openly relieving oneself.[44]

The Temple Scroll describes the type of latrine found at Qumran and undoubtedly in other permanent settlements, but it and the War Scroll add a distance regulation because of the state of purity required in the ideal holy city or during a holy war. Similarly, Yadin noted that the distances for latrines mandated by the Temple Scroll and War Scroll would have placed them beyond the Sabbath limits.[45] This accords with Josephus' statement that the Essenes did not defecate on the Sabbath. If this regulation was observed at Qumran, the inhabitants may have refrained from using the toilet in L51 on the Sabbath. As Baumgarten and others have noted, the sect differed from contemporary Jews and non-Jews in regarding defecation as a polluting activity.[46] It is this difference which led to the practice described by Josephus and the regulations prescribed by the Temple Scroll and War Scroll. Similarly, the Sabbath prohibition is mentioned in all three sources because it differed from normative contemporary practice.

It is interesting to note that de Vaux's description of the toilet in L51 corresponds with the physical description of the latrines in the Temple Scroll as "roofed houses with pits within them, into which

---

[44] See Hodge, *Roman Aqueducts*, 37; Scobie, "Slums," 417.
[45] Yadin, *Temple Scroll*, 179.
[46] Baumgarten, "The Temple Scroll," 11-12.

the excrement will descend."⁴⁷ According to de Vaux's notes, the remains of collapsed burnt reeds and marly earth indicate that L51 was roofed. The fact that the only doorway in L51 opened on to the pool in L48-49 recalls Josephus's description of the Essene custom of washing themselves as if defiled after attending to their bodily functions. This is another instance where Josephus singled out a practice that differed from contemporary norms. Similarly, he was struck by the fact that new initiates into the sect were presented with a hatchet for digging a hole in the ground each time they defecated. De Vaux tentatively suggested that an iron tool found in the excavations in Cave 11 may represent this kind of hatchet.⁴⁸

Thus, I believe that the sectarians attended to their bodily needs in various ways, using whatever facilities were available. Our sources describe or mandate only distinctive sanitation practices, which stem from the unique sectarian belief that defecation is a polluting activity. Because of this, the sectarians washed themselves after defecating, refrained from defecating altogether on the Sabbath, chose isolated spots when relieving themselves in the open, and required the placement of latrines at a certain distance from their ideal holy city of Jerusalem and the camps of a holy war. It is not clear whether another toilet was constructed elsewhere in the settlement at Qumran to replace the one in L51, which was apparently destroyed in the earthquake of 31 BCE.

9. THE HOARD OF TYRIAN TETRADRACHMAS AND THE TEMPLE TAX

As noted above, in L120 de Vaux discovered a hoard of 561 silver coins deposited in three pots, which contained 223, 185, and 153 pieces, respectively. The hoard consisted almost exclusively of Tyrian tetradrachmas.⁴⁹ Here I would like to consider the nature of this hoard. According to the excavation inventory register, a total of 1231 coins and coin fragments was recovered at Qumran, including the coins in the hoard.⁵⁰ However, the only silver coins listed in de Vaux's field notes from contexts outside the hoard are: one Tyrian tetradrachma of Antiochus VII from locus 7; a didrachma of Antiochus VII Euergetes from locus 9; a Roman imperial coin of

---

⁴⁷ Yadin, *Temple Scroll*, 178.
⁴⁸ De Vaux, "Une hachette Essenienne?," *VT* 9 (1956) 399-407.
⁴⁹ See de Vaux, *Archaeology and the Dead Sea Scrolls*, 34-35.
⁵⁰ Donceel and Donceel-Voûte, "The Archaeology of Khirbet Qumran," 3.

Vespasian from locus 35; one autonomous Tyrian tetradrachma from locus 45; an illegible coin from locus 52; two didrachmas, of Demeterius II and Antiochus VII respectively, from locus 77; and one sigla of Antiochus Euergetes of Tyre from Trench A. Thus, virtually all of the Tyrian tetradrachmas at Qumran appear to have been deliberately collected together. The fact that some, if not all of the scattered examples could come from post-Period Ib contexts suggests the possibility that all of the Tyrian tetradrachmas from Period Ib were gathered in this hoard. Though some scholars have noted that such coins were used for the annual half-shekel tax paid by Jews to the Temple during the Second Temple period, no one has considered the presence of this hoard at Qumran in relation to the beliefs and practices of the sect.

Two scrolls from Cave 4 at Qumran deal with the matter of the Temple tax: 4Q159 and 4Q513, which have been described as a treatise expounding several biblical texts, or collections of assorted halakhot. They are legislative in nature, based on or dealing with biblical laws drawn almost exclusively from the Pentateuch. Because this legislative material was intended for practical observance by the author's audience, these texts are categorized as "Ordinances."[51]

The development of the annual half-shekel tax to the Temple has been traced by J. Liver. The original obligation to give a half shekel as an offering to the Lord appears in Exod 30:11-16 in relation to the taking of the census. This offering, which was binding on all those who were numbered, represented a once in a lifetime payment. Eventually this one-time offering became linked with the annual third of a shekel payment instituted in the time of Nehemiah for the maintenance of the Temple. Since the sources relating to the period prior to Roman rule in Judaea do not mention the annual half-shekel offering, it does not appear to have become an obligatory payment until the end of the Hasmonean period or later. Liver concluded that the regulation making the half-shekel an annual offering was introduced only after the Pharisees gained ascendancy over their opponents, the Sadducees and Boethusians.[52]

---

[51] See L. H. Schiffman, "Ordinances and Rules," in J. H. Charlesworth (ed.), *The Dead Sea Scrolls. Hebrew, Aramaic, and Greek Texts with English Translations*. Vol. 1, *Rule of the Community and Related Documents* (Tübingen: Mohr-Siebeck; Louisville: John Knox, 1994) 145-75; and J. Liver, "The Half-Shekel Offering in Biblical and Post-Biblical Literature," *HTR* 56 (1963) 173-98.

[52] Liver, "The Half-Shekel Offering."

In 4Q159, the Pentateuchal regulation of the half-shekel is understood as referring to an offering made only once in a lifetime by those included in the census. Lawrence H. Schiffman has noted that the absence of the notion of a one-time payment in 4Q513 suggests that these are different recensions of the same text.[53] According to Liver, the sect must have objected to the half-shekel sanctuary offering because it was instituted as an annual obligation for all Israel only after they had segregated themselves from the Jerusalem Temple and the rest of Israel, and because it was a halakhah that had originated outside the sect.[54] As other scholars have previously noted, opposition to the establishment of an annual Temple tax may have existed in other Jewish circles, as expressed for example in Matt 17:24-27, where Jesus rebukes Peter for indicating to the tax collectors of Capernaum that his master paid the annual tribute.[55]

Liver also discussed the correlation between 4Q159 and 4Q513 on the one hand, and sectarian regulations concerning censuses in general. According to the Manual of Discipline, the sect had an annual census that included the registration of its members. The Damascus Document, however, describes a single census of those who reach adulthood, and the Rule of the Congregation says that, "at the age of twenty years he shall pass among them that are numbered." This accords with the minimum age mentioned in the Pentateuch. Liver suggested that the sect may have required the one-time payment when a man reached adulthood and his name was recorded for the first time in the census registers. The annual ceremony of entering the covenant and reviewing the registers was apparently not considered a "census" for those whose names were already recorded in the registers. Alternatively, the sect may have viewed the half-shekel regulation as a law that was to apply to the community of Israel only at the end of days.[56]

---

[53] Schiffman, "Ordinances and Rules," 147.

[54] Liver, "The Half-Shekel Offering," 191.

[55] For recent discussions see P. Richardson, "Why Turn the Tables? Jesus' Protest in the Temple Precincts," in E. H. Lovering (ed.), *Society for Biblical Literature 1992 Seminar Papers* (Atlanta: Scholars Press, 1992) 507-23; W. Horbury, "The Temple Tax," in E. Bammel and C. F. D. Moule (eds.), *Jesus and the Politics of His Day* (New York: Cambridge University Press, 1984) 265-86.

[56] Liver, "The Half-Shekel Offering," 196-98.

Hoards consisting mostly if not entirely of Tyrian tetradrachmas have been found at a number of sites in Palestine in contexts dating to the first century BCE.[57] By the middle of the first century CE, according to Kadman, "there was only one purpose for which the exclusive use of Tyrian shekels was prescribed: the Temple-Dues of half a Shekel, which every male Jew of 20 years of age and above had to pay yearly to the Temple at Jerusalem."[58] Ariel, however, has cautioned that: "From the finds in Jerusalem (mostly in hoards), there is every reason to believe that Tyrian shekels would have been current in Jerusalem–even without the Temple-tax."[59] He has noted that the absence of Roman coins in hoards in Jerusalem before 70 CE suggests that they did not become dominant until later. Ariel's observations regarding Jerusalem probably apply equally to Qumran, which was also a Judaean site occupied by Jews. It is possible, therefore, that the hoard at Qumran has no connection with the Temple tax, and simply represents a collection of the common type of valuable silver coinage that circulated in Judaea in the first century BCE. In this case, the hoard should be understood as representing the collected wealth of the community at the end of Period Ib (ca. 9/8 BCE), whose members were required to give up their private property and earnings when accepted into the sect.[60]

If, however, this hoard represents the collected wealth and private property of the members of the community, we might expect it to contain a mixture of coin types. Although Tyrian tetradrachmas were the dominant type of silver coinage circulating in first century BCE Palestine, the hoard contained none of the common bronze issues of the Hasmoneans. But such homogeneity is characteristic of many other Palestinian hoards of this period, which consist entirely of either silver or bronze coins.[61] This homogeneity usually reflects the circumstances of burial. Grierson has distinguished four classes

---

[57] See Ariel, "A Survey of Coin Finds," 308-18; M. Thompson, O. Mørkholm, and C. M. Kraay, *An Inventory of Greek Coin Hoards* (New York: American Numismatic Society, 1973) 221-24.

[58] L. Kadman, "Temple Dues and Currency in Ancient Palestine in the Light of Recently Discovered Coin-Hoards," *INJ* 1 (1962) 10.

[59] Ariel, "A Survey of Coin Finds," 284.

[60] See, for example, J. C. VanderKam, *The Dead Sea Scrolls Today* (Grand Rapids, MI: Eerdmans, 1994) 82-84.

[61] See Thompson, Mørkholm, and Kraay, *Inventory*, 222-24.

of hoards: accidental losses, emergency hoards, savings hoards, and abandoned hoards.[62] One of the differences between emergency hoards and savings hoards, which are the relevant classes to this discussion, is that the latter are more selective; that is, they contain not only high value (as opposed to low value) coins, but also better (unworn) specimens of such coins. In addition, because emergency hoards were withdrawn from circulation at the time they were deposited, they usually reflect the proportions of types of coins current at that moment. Savings hoards, on the other hand, often cover a considerable span of years.[63]

Thus, the hoard at Qumran, like many of the contemporary hoards from Palestine, fits the profile of a savings hoard (though it was apparently buried before the destruction of the site at the end of Period Ib). Ordinarily, such hoards represent the savings of their owners, accumulated over a period of years. This could apply to the hoard at Qumran only if we assume that it does not represent all of the property and earnings of the members of the community, which must have included at least some bronze coins and perhaps other types of silver issues. In fact, the hoard did contain a few coins that were not Tyrian tetradrachmas: "With a few exceptions, it includes only Tyrian coins, and these are almost exclusively tetradrachmae."[64]

Nevertheless, the overwhelming number of Tyrian tetradrachmas in this hoard may reflect a deliberate selection of the coins contributed by the members of the sect. This brings us back to the matter of the Temple tax. De Vaux noted that, "The later one proceeds in the period the more frequently all the various issues are represented, and the larger the number of new types."[64] Since a typical savings hoard reflects the resources of the owner from year to year,[65] those joining the sect must have been growing steadily either in wealth or in numbers over time. I believe that the composition and character of the hoard are best understood in connection with the sect's interpretation of the Temple tax as a one-time payment made when a man reached adulthood and his name was

---

[62] P. Grierson, *Numismatics* (New York: Oxford University, 1975) 130.

[63] Grierson, *Numismatics*, 133-35; J. F. Wilson, "The Gold Hoard," in V. Tzaferis, *Excavations at Capernaum, Volume I, 1978-1982* (Winona Lake, IN: Eisenbrauns, 1989) 157.

[64] De Vaux, *Archaeology and the Dead Sea Scrolls*, 34.

[65] See Grierson, *Numismatics*, 135; Wilson, "The Gold Hoard," 157.

recorded for the first time in the census registers. The steady growth in the number of new types in the hoard may thus reflect an increase in the number of new members over time, each of whom was required to make this one-time payment when joining the sect or reaching adulthood. The number of coins in the hoard may therefore provide an indication of how many members had joined the community at Qumran before its destruction in ca. 9/8 BCE

10. FUTURE PROSPECTS

The publication of the material from de Vaux's excavations now lags far behind the publication of the Dead Sea Scrolls, and unlike the scrolls, remains inaccessible to scholars and the general public. Therefore, much of what has been presented here is speculative. Only the final publication of all of the material from the excavations will make it possible to undertake more definitive studies and resolve some of the controversies surrounding the archaeology of Qumran.

SELECT BIBLIOGRAPHY

Ariel, D. T. "A Survey of Coin Finds in Jerusalem (Until the End of Byzantine Period)," *LA* 32 (1982) 273-326.

Avigad, N. *Discovering Jerusalem* (Nashville: Thomas Nelson, 1983).

Bar-Adon P. "Another Settlement of the Judean Desert Sect at ʿEn el-Ghuweir on the Shores of the Dead Sea," *BASOR* 227 (1977) 1-25.

Bar-Nathan, R. *The Pottery of Jericho in the Hasmonean Period and the Time of Herod, and the Problem of the Transition from Hasmonean Pottery Types to Pottery Types of the Time of Herod* (unpublished Ph.D. diss., Jerusalem: The Hebrew University, Institute of Archaeology, late 1980's [Hebrew]).

Baumgarten, A. I. "The Temple Scroll, Toilet Practices, and the Essenes," *Jewish History* 10 (1996) 9-20.

Berlin, A. M. "Between Large Forces: Palestine in the Hellenistic Period," *BA* 60 (1997) 2-51.

Broshi, M. "The Archaeology of Qumran," in D. Dimant and U. Rappaport (eds.), *The Dead Sea Scrolls, Forty Years of Research* (STDJ 10; Leiden: Brill, 1992).

Cahill J., K. Reinhard, D. Tarler and P. Warnock. "Scientists Examine Remains of Ancient Bathroom," *BAR* 17/3 (1991) 64-69.

Cook, E. "What was Qumran? A Ritual Purification Center," *BAR* 22/6 (1996) 39, 48-51, 73-75.

Cotton, H., O. Lernau and Y. Goren. "Fish sauces from Herodian Masada," *JRA* 9 (1996) 223-38.

Crown, A. and L. Cansdale. "Qumran—Was It an Essene Settlement?" *BAR* 20 (1994) 24-36, 73-78.

Delcroix G. and J.-L. Huot. "Les fours dits 'de potier' dans l'Orient ancien," *Syria* 49 (1972) 35-75.

Donceel-Voûte, P. "Les ruines de Qumran réinterprétées," *Archeologia* 298 (1994) 24-35.

Eshel H. and Z. Greenhut, "Ḥiam el-Sagha, A Cemetery of the Qumran Type, Judean Desert," *RB* 100-2 (1993) 252-59.

Golb, N. "Khirbet Qumran and the Manuscript Finds of the Judaean Wilderness," in Wise et al. (eds.), *Methods of Investigation of the Dead Sea Scrolls* 51-72.

—. *Who Wrote the Dead Sea Scrolls?* (New York: Simon and Schuster, 1995).

Grierson, P. *Numismatics* (New York: Oxford University, 1975).

Hachlili, R. "Burial Practices at Qumran," *RevQ* 62 (1993) 247-64.

Hamilton, R. W. "Mafjar, Khirbet el-," in E. Stern (ed.), *The New Encyclopedia of Archaeological Excavations in the Holy Land* (New York: Simon and Schuster, 1993) 923.

Hodge, A. T. *Roman Aqueducts and Water Supply* (London: Duckworth, 1992).

Horton, F. L. "A Sixth-Century Bath in Caesarea's Suburbs and the Transformation of Bathing Culture in Late Antiquity," in A. Raban & K. G. Holum (eds.), *Caesarea Maritima, A Retrospective after Two Millennia* (Leiden: Brill) 183.

Humbert, J.-B. "L'espace sacré à Qumrân," *RB* 101-2 (1994) 161-214.

Humbert, J.-B. and A. Chambon, *Fouilles de Khirbet Qumrân et de Aïn Feshkha I* (Göttingen: Vandenhoeck and Ruprecht, 1994).

Kadman, L. "Temple Dues and Currency in Ancient Palestine in the Light of Recently Discovered Coin-Hoards," *INJ* 1 (1962) 10.

Kapera, Z. J. "Some Remarks on the Qumran Cemetery," in Wise et al. (eds.), *Methods of Investigation of the Dead Sea Scrolls*, 97-113.

Laperrousaz, E.-M. "Does the Temple Scroll Date from the First or Second Century BCE?," in G. J. Brooke (ed.), *Temple Scroll Studies* (JSPSup 7; Sheffield: Sheffield Academic Press, 1989) 91-97.

Liver, J. "The Half-Shekel Offering in Biblical and Post-Biblical Literature," *HTR* 56 (1963) 173-98. Ariel, "A Survey of Coin Finds," 308-18.

Magness, J. "A Villa at Khirbet Qumran?" *RevQ* 63 (1994) 397-419.

—. "What was Qumran? Not a Country Villa," *BAR* 22/6 (1996) 38-47, 72-73

—. "The Community at Qumran in Light of Its Pottery," in Wise et al. (eds.), *Methods of Investigation of the Dead Sea Scrolls*, 39-50.

—. "The Chronology of Qumran, Ein Feshkha, and Ein el-Ghuweir," *The Qumran Chronicle* 8 (1997) 7-21.

—. "The Chronology of the Settlement at Qumran in the Herodian Period," *DSD* 2 (1995) 161-214.

Neudecker, R. *Die Pracht der Latrine, Zum Wandel öffentlicher Bedürfnisanstalten in der kaiserzeitlichen Stadt* (Munich: Friedrich Pfeil, 1994).

Patrich, J. "Khirbet Qumran in Light of New Archaeological Explorations in the Qumran Caves," in Wise et al. (eds.), *Methods of Investigation of the Dead Sea Scrolls*, 73-95.

Reich, R. "A Note on the Function of Room 30 ("the Scriptorium") at Khirbet Qumran," *JJS* 46 (1995) 157-60.
—. "The Great Miqveh Debate," *BAR* 19/2 (1993) 52-53.
Schiffman, L. H. "Ordinances and Rules," in J. H. Charlesworth (ed.), *The Dead Sea Scrolls. Hebrew, Aramaic, and Greek Texts with English Translations.* Vol. 1, *Rule of the Community and Related Documents* (Tübingen: Mohr-Siebeck; Louisville: John Knox, 1994) 145-75.
Scobie, A. "Slums, Sanitation, and Mortality in the Roman World," *Klio* 68 (1986) 409-17.
Steckoll, S. H. "Preliminary Excavation Report in the Qumran Cemetery," *RevQ* 23 (1968) 323-36.
Thompson, M., O. Mørkholm and C. M. Kraay, *An Inventory of Greek Coin Hoards* (New York: American Numismatic Society, 1973) 221-24.
VanderKam, J. C. *The Dead Sea Scrolls Today* (Grand Rapids, MI: Eerdmans, 1994) 82-84.
Vaux, R. de. "Fouilles au Khirbet Qumrân, Rapport préliminaire," *RB* 60 (1953) 83-106.
—. "Fouilles au Khirbet Qumrân, Rapport préliminaire sur la deuxième campagne," *RB* 61 (1954) 206-36.
—. "La poterie," in D. Barthelemy and J. T. Milik, *Qumran Cave 1* (DJD 1; Oxford: Clarendon Press, 1955) 8-13.
—. "Fouilles de Khirbet Qumrân, Rapport préliminaire sur les 3e, 4e, et 5e campagnes," *RB* 63 (1956) 533-77.
—. "Fouilles de Feshkha," *RB* 66 (1959) 225-55.
—. "Archéologie," in M. Baillet, J. T. Milik and R. de Vaux, *Les "Petites Grottes" de Qumran* (DJD 3; Oxford: Clarendon Press, 1962) 3-36.
—. *Archaeology and the Dead Sea Scrolls* (London: Oxford University Press, 1973).
—. "Le matériel archéologique. La poterie," in R. de Vaux and J. T. Milik, *Qumrân Grotte 4.2* (DJD 6; Oxford: Clarendon Press, 1977) 15-20.
—. "Une hachette Essenienne?," *VT* 9 (1956) 399-407.
Wilson J. F. "The Gold Hoard," in V. Tzaferis, *Excavations at Capernaum, Volume I, 1978-1982* (Winona Lake, IN: Eisenbrauns, 1989) 157.
Wise, M. O., N. Golb, J. J. Collins and D. G. Pardee (eds.). *Methods of Investigation of the Dead Sea Scrolls and the Khirbet Qumran Site, Present Realities and Future Prospects* (ANYAS 722; New York: New York Academy of Sciences, 1994).
Wood B. G. "To Dip or Sprinkle? The Qumran Cisterns in Perspective," *BASOR* 256 (1984) 45-60.
Yadin Y. *The Temple Scroll* (New York: Random House, 1985).

THE DEAD SEA SCROLLS AND THE BIBLICAL TEXT

EUGENE ULRICH

The past fifty years have witnessed a dramatic, unprecedented crescendo in both manuscript evidence for the biblical text and refined understanding of the history of the biblical text. Until the middle of this century our knowledge was based on the Masoretic Text (MT or 𝔐), the Samaritan Pentateuch (SP or 𝔪), the Septuagint (LXX or 𝔊), and the other versions. The oldest complete Hebrew manuscript of the Bible available was Codex Leningradensis, copied in 1008/9. There were, of course, other medieval codices; for example, Codex Cairensis, which held only the Former and Latter Prophets, was copied in 895/6, but a facsimile edition was not available until 1971. Similarly, the Aleppo Codex (ca. 925), which was preserved by a Jewish community in Syria but nearly lost in an anti-Jewish attack in 1948, emerging three-fourths extant with the loss of most of the Torah (up to Deut 28:26) and several late books, also lacked a published facsimile edition until 1976.[1] The oldest nearly complete Greek manuscript of the Bible available was Codex Vaticanus, copied in the fourth century, thus antedating the Hebrew codices by half a millennium, but still half a millennium later than the original Greek translation. Only a single Hebrew fragment of a biblical text from antiquity was extant: the Nash papyrus, dating from the middle of the second century BCE and containing a form of the Decalogue and the shema͑.

That was not a large supply of evidence for serious textual inquiry. There were numerous Masoretic manuscripts, but M. Goshen-Gottstein showed them to be almost exclusively witnesses to the medieval Masoretic tradition.[2] The Samaritan Pentateuch, rediscovered

---

[1] See E. Tov, *Textual Criticism of the Hebrew Bible* (Assen and Maastricht: Van Gorcum; Minneapolis: Fortress, 1992) 46-47, and E. Würthwein, *The Text of the Old Testament* (2nd ed.; Grand Rapids: Eerdmans, 1995) 35-38.

[2] M. Goshen-Gottstein, "Hebrew Biblical Manuscripts: Their History and Their Place in the HUBP Edition," *Biblica* 48 (1967) 243-90 [repr. in F. M. Cross and S. Talmon (eds.), *Qumran and the History of the Biblical Text* (Cambridge, MA: Harvard University, 1975) 42-89].

in 1616, was not taken seriously as a viable, religiously useful witness to the Hebrew text in antiquity. And the Septuagint suffered a reputation as a paraphrase when it differed noticeably from the MT.

The discovery of the scrolls from the Judaean Desert provided a vast amount of new data that would revolutionize our understanding of the biblical text in antiquity, but on the other hand the scrolls were tantalizingly fragmentary. Moreover, scholars naturally tended either to analyze the new data according to the old categories or, worse, to marginalize the important new evidence, possibly because it threatened long-held views. Since approximately 1960, however, most have accorded the new knowledge gained from the biblical scrolls the significance it deserves.[3]

1. PREVIOUS THEORIES ON THE HISTORY OF THE TEXT

The history of scholarship dealing with the history of the text of the Hebrew Bible is complex and, for lack of space, must be confined to the four major views of Cross, Talmon, Tov, and Ulrich.[4]

In 1947, the first two biblical scrolls were found: an intact scroll of the complete book of Isaiah (1QIsa^a), and a generous portion of fragments from a second scroll of Isaiah (1QIsa^b). The former was published immediately by M. Burrows, though there were understandably—since we had virtually no Hebrew manuscripts from this period, and thus no developed study of palaeography—some incorrect transcriptions. Its text was basically similar to the traditional *textus receptus* of Isaiah, though there were numerous individual textual variants and the orthography was noticeably

---

[3] This was due partly to two works: J. T. Milik's *Dix ans de Découvertes dans le Désert de Juda* (Paris: Cerf, 1957, translated by J. Strugnell, *Ten Years of Discovery in the Wilderness of Judaea* [SBT; London: SCM, 1959]); and F. M. Cross, *The Ancient Library of Qumran* (1st ed.; London: Epworth, 1958).

[4] For recent surveys, see E. Tov, "A Modern Textual Outlook Based on the Qumran Scrolls," *HUCA* 53 (1982) 11-27; E. Ulrich, "Horizons of Old Testament Textual Research at the Thirtieth Anniversary of Qumran Cave 4," *CBQ* 46 (1984) 613-36; idem, "Pluriformity in the Biblical Text, Text Groups, and Questions on Canon," in J. Trebolle Barrera and L. Vegas Montaner (eds.), *The Madrid Qumran Congress: Proceedings of the International Congress on the Dead Sea Scrolls, Madrid, 18-21 March 1991* (STDJ 11; 2 vols.; Leiden: Brill, 1992) 23-41; E. Tov, *Textual Criticism*, 14-17, 155-63, 180-97; E. Ulrich, "Multiple Literary Editions: Reflections toward a Theory of the History of the Biblical Text," in D.W. Parry and S.D. Ricks (eds.), *Current Research and Technological Developments on the Dead Sea Scrolls: Conference on the Texts from the Judean Desert, Jerusalem, 30 April 1995* (STDJ 20; Leiden: Brill, 1996) 78-105.

different. In contrast, the latter, published quickly by E. Sukenik exhibited a text and orthography quite close to those preserved in the MT of Isaiah.[5] But Cave 1 offered fragments of other biblical texts as well, and, before these were published in 1955, Cave 4 had been discovered, holding ca. 130 fragmentary biblical manuscripts. Eventually eleven caves were found in the area of Qumran plus other caves southward along the shore of the Dead Sea, yielding a total of over 220 biblical manuscripts, most with only a few fragments each.

In the wake of the publication of exciting new scrolls such as 4QpaleoExod^m and 4QNum^b, which showed dramatic alignment with the SP, and 4QDeut^q, 4QSam^a, and 4QJer^b, which showed dramatic correspondences with the LXX, W. F. Albright sketched the idea of a theory of local texts originating in Babylon, Palestine, and Egypt.[6] F. M. Cross developed this theory in greater detail, and for a number of years it stood alone as offering the clearest light available on the mass of new discoveries.[7]

Cross's theory and the multiple examples he presents to support it are too complex to present in full here. He succinctly states it thus:

> Three textual families appear to have developed slowly between the fifth and first centuries BC, in Palestine, in Egypt, and in a third locality, presumably Babylon. The Palestinian family is characterized by conflation, glosses, synoptic additions and other evidences of intense scribal activity, and can be defined as "expansionistic." The Egyptian text-type is often but not always a full text.... The Egyptian and Palestinian families are closely related.... The Babylonian text-type when extant is a short text. Thus far it is known only in the Pentateuch and Former Prophets.[8]

---

[5] The text is not quite so close to the MT as Sukenik had presented it; some uncertain letters were restored on the basis of the MT, but they are not always so. Yet other fragments of 1QIsa^b were recovered in the official excavations of Cave 1 and were published by D. Barthélemy in D. Barthélemy and J. T. Milik (eds.), *Qumran Cave 1* (DJD 1; Oxford: Clarendon Press, 1955) 66-68 + pl. XII.

[6] W. F. Albright, "New Light on Early Recensions of the Hebrew Bible," *BASOR* 140 (1955) 27-33. For the publication details of these MSS see below.

[7] F. M. Cross, "The History of the Biblical Text in the Light of Discoveries in the Judaean Desert," *HTR* 57 (1964) 281-99; and idem, "The Evolution of a Theory of Local Texts," R. A. Kraft (ed.), *1972 Proceedings: IOSCS and Pseudepigrapha* (Missoula, MT: Scholars Press, 1972) 108-26 (repr. in F. M. Cross and S. Talmon [eds.], *Qumran and the History of the Biblical Text* [Cambridge, MA: Harvard University Press, 1975] 306-20).

[8] Cross, "The Contribution of the Qumrân Discoveries to the Study of the Biblical Text," *IEJ* 16 (1966) 81-95, esp. 86 [repr. in Cross and Talmon, *Qumran and the History*, 278-92, esp. 283].

A different perspective was presented by S. Talmon, who surveyed the vast array of variation in the biblical scrolls. He did not see the neat "text-types" or "families" that Cross and others had been seeing, but rather opened our eyes to different directions, both textual and sociological. Textually, Talmon erased the false line between authors and copyists:

> [I]n the Qumran material coalesce the phase of creative authoring of biblical literature with the ancillary phase of text transmission ... in ancient Hebrew literature no hard and fast lines can be drawn between authors' conventions of style and tradents' and copyists' rules of reproduction and transmission.[9]

Sociologically, he also correctly taught us that the MT, the SP and the LXX were simply salvaged out of a much larger variety of text forms because the Rabbis, the Samaritans, and the Christians each preserved their own particular collection of texts, while the other rival forms of the texts perished with the groups that held them sacred.[10]

E. Tov also did not see the neat "text-types" or "families" that Cross and others had been seeing, and at first stated that they "must be regarded as reflecting three *texts* rather than text-types."[11] I then wrote that "Tov may turn out to be too reductionist in denying discernible text-types,"[12] and he currently recognizes two types of textual groupings: texts that show variant literary editions of a given book, and texts that are aligned with the MT, SP, LXX, or none (see below).[13]

I have proposed an alternate model for understanding the history of the biblical text. At a conference arranged by Talmon in 1988, I proposed a theory of successive literary editions as a model for tracing and classifying the development of the biblical text of the various books, and have been trying to refine the model during the

---

[9] S. Talmon, "The Textual Study of the Bible—A New Outlook," in Cross and Talmon (eds.), *Qumran and the History*, 321-400, esp. 380-81.

[10] S. Talmon, "The Old Testament Text," in P. R. Ackroyd and C. F. Evans (eds.), *The Cambridge History of the Bible. 1. From the Beginnings to Jerome* (Cambridge: Cambridge University Press, 1970) 159-99 [repr. in Cross and Talmon (eds.), *Qumran and the History*, 1-41, esp. 40].

[11] Tov, *The Text-Critical Use of the Septuagint in Biblical Research* (Jerusalem: Simor, 1981) 274.

[12] Ulrich, "Horizons," 624.

[13] Tov, *Textual Criticism*, 313-49 and 114-17.

intervening years.¹⁴ The heart of the theory is that the main lines in the picture of the history of the biblical text are formed by the deliberate activity of a series of creative scribes who, one after another in different eras for different reasons, produced the new literary editions of the books (or passages) of the Bible. A preliminary and twofold step for clearing the ground to be able to discern these variant literary editions is: (1) the removal of any purely orthographic differences, on the conviction that the specific orthographic profile of a manuscript is seldom related to any particular edition of that work; and (2) the temporary removal of individual textual variants that do not seem related to the *pattern of variants* by which an author or tradent or scribe systematically reworked an existing edition of a work into a revised edition.

> The fundamental principle guiding this proposal is that the Scriptures, from shadowy beginnings until the final, perhaps abrupt, freezing point of the Masoretic tradition, arose and evolved through a process of organic development. The major lines of that development are characterized by the intentional, creative work of authors or tradents who produced new, revised editions of the traditional form of a book or passage.¹⁵

New *Zeitgeisten* or events, new problems or possibilities, were probably the catalysts for such new editions. This happened repeatedly for virtually all books of the Bible, from the earliest formulations of their sources, until the threats to the continued life of Judaism itself—the Roman destruction and the Christian crisis in the late first or early second century CE—probably brought the process of development to an abrupt cutoff.

Before we attempt a critique of these four models, it will prove helpful first to review, with these models in mind, the evidence provided by the biblical scrolls.

2. THE EVIDENCE OF THE BIBLICAL MANUSCRIPTS

The biblical manuscripts which feature most prominently in discussions of the Dead Sea Scrolls and the biblical text are usually

---

¹⁴ See various aspects of this theory developed in Ulrich, "The Canonical Process, Textual Criticism, and Latter Stages in the Composition of the Bible," in M. Fishbane and E. Tov (eds.), *"Shaʿarei Talmon." Studies in the Bible, Qumran, and the Ancient Near East Presented to Shemaryahu Talmon* (Winona Lake, IN: Eisenbrauns, 1992) 267-91, idem, "Pluriformity" 23-41; and idem, "Multiple Literary Editions," 78-105.

¹⁵ Ulrich, "Multiple Literary Editions," 89.

divided according to their patterns of agreement into three categories—MT, SP, and LXX—or by Tov even into five categories: "texts produced by a school of Qumran scribes, proto-Masoretic and pre-Samaritan texts, texts close to the Hebrew *Vorlage* of the LXX, and non-aligned texts which are not exclusively close to any one of these groups."[16] According to this set of classifications, Tov and others might present the following list:[17]

Table 1: Grouping of MSS according to Text-Types

Q Practice	Proto-MT	Pre-Samaritan	Close to 𝔊	Non-aligned
1QIsa^a	1QIsa^b	4QpaleoExod^m	4QDeut^q	4QDeut^{b, c, h}
4QSam^c	4QJer^{a, c}	4QNum^b	4QSam^a	4QIsa^c
4QIsa^c	4QEzra		4QJer^{b, d}	4QDan^a

This type of categorization may be helpful for handy reference, but I suggest that it is not the most fitting manner of classifying and thinking about the texts and that it entails several problems. Some of the manuscripts (e.g. 4QNum^b, 4QIsa^c) could be classified in more than one category, and most slip over into a different category at least for certain readings. More importantly, the "Qumran scribal practice" is probably not confined to or characteristic of Qumran,[18] but it is more likely that, as E. Y. Kutscher wrote in the early 1980's concerning 1QIsa^a, "many of those points in which the Scroll differs linguistically from the Masoretic Isaiah represent characteristics of the literary Hebrew of the last centuries of the first millennium

---

[16] See E. Tov, *Textual Criticism*, 191; see also 114-17.

[17] E. Tov, *Textual Criticism*, 114-16.

[18] See E. Ulrich, "Multiple Literary Editions," 93-96. It appears that we simply have not yet sculpted a sufficiently precise vocabulary, for Tov (*Textual Criticism*, 108) acknowledges that it "must be conceded that the term *Qumran practice* ... is somewhat misleading, but no better term suggests itself. In many ways it was *a* Palestinian scribal system, but it would be equally, if not more, misleading, to call these texts Palestinian, since the use of such terminology would imply that there are no other Palestinian texts" [emphasis his]. Perhaps the problem is with the word "system": analysis shows there to be no consistent system of orthography in many books of the MT or in many of the scrolls. There are tendencies and ranges of permissible variation, but no system. From this perspective, scrolls found at Qumran that were presumably copied in Palestine represent an array of samples of scribal practices in use in Jerusalem and the wider country during the late Second Temple period and, insofar as some texts were copied without any change over centuries, even during the early Second Temple period.

BCE."[19] The manuscripts were *found* at Qumran, but they were certainly not composed there, and the majority were probably not copied there. Both the large number of scribal hands involved and the lack of any kind of uniformity in manuscript preparation point to the texts having been copied in general Palestine and imported to Qumran. Finally, neither the MT, the SP, nor the LXX is a text-type or even "a text"—they are collections of texts, differing from book to book. Thus, they should not constitute "text-types" to which others either conform or stand "non-aligned." Tov has very helpfully brought to scholarly awareness that the Qumran texts have "taught us no longer to posit MT at the center of our textual thinking."[20] We should move to the next stage and reshape our thinking about the MT, the SP and the LXX, so that we do not start with the later categories and fit the earlier data anachronistically into them; rather we should follow the evolution of the biblical text and form our categories in accordance with the historical reality of each period.

Thus, I would propose that we use the category of successive literary editions as the grid for classifying the various texts:

Table 2: Grouping of MSS according to Editions

Edition[21]

$n+1$	𝔊-Exod	𝔐-Num	4QJosh^a, Josephus	𝔊-Jer	𝔐-Dan	𝔐-Pss
$n+2$	𝔐-Exod	4QNum^b	[SamPent, OL]	𝔐-Jer	𝔊-Dan	11QPs^a
$n+3$	4QpaleoExod^m		𝔊-Josh			
$n+4$	SamPent-Exod		𝔐-Josh			

Since, however, the conclusions should logically follow the presentation of the data, I will first review some of the more richly instructive manuscripts and then discuss the resulting theory. I will mention here, so that the reader may follow, that it is helpful to

---

[19] E. Y. Kutscher, *A History of the Hebrew Language* (Jerusalem: Magnes Press, 1982) 95.

[20] E. Tov, "Hebrew Biblical Manuscripts from the Judaean Desert: Their Contribution to Textual Criticism," *JJS* 39 (1988) 5-37, esp. 7.

[21] The "$n+1$" type of designation for successive editions of a text assumes that there has been a series of editions during the composition of the text which constitutes its growth leading up to the first extant witness to a given book; see E. Ulrich, "The Community of Israel and the Composition of the Scriptures," in C. A. Evans and S. Talmon (eds.), *The Quest for Context and Meaning: Studies in Intertextuality in Honor of James A. Sanders* (BIS 28; Leiden: Brill, 1997) 327-42.

distinguish between three usually intermingled but unrelated aspects of the texts: differences in orthography, individual textual variants, and systematic patterns of variants which constitute variant literary editions (such as 𝕲-Jer versus 𝔐-Jer).

2.1 The Torah

4QpaleoExod^m: In 1955 Patrick Skehan published a group of fragments from 4QpaleoExod^m which contained parts of Exodus 32.[22] At that point he described the character of its text as "in the Samaritan Recension" but a few years later revised his conclusion because he had learned that, although the scroll contained most of the expansions exhibited by the Samaritan text of Exodus, "it did not contain the addition to the Ten Commandments after Exod 20:17, referring to the unhewn altar on Mt. Gerizim."[23] Skehan thus isolated a pair of what we can term variant literary editions of the Book of Exodus. The MT presents one version of the text, and the Samaritan version had already provided us with an intentionally-developed revised edition of that text. This was clearly based on the same edition of the text that the MT attests, but had systematically expanded it with other biblical texts, i.e. harmonizations drawn from other parts of Exodus and Deuteronomy and inserted at appropriate places. Skehan's contribution here was to show that the edition which had been attributed as a whole to the Samaritans was in fact a regular Jewish edition; the Samaritans simply took one of the available variant Jewish editions and added two small, specifically Samaritan points.[24]

Judith Sanderson, who collaborated with me on the completion of Skehan's edition of this scroll and published an excellent analysis of

---

[22] P. W. Skehan, "Exodus in the Samaritan Recension from Qumran," *JBL* 74 (1955) 435-440. In the early days the manuscript was designated 4QExod^α and was on occasion confusingly cited as 4QExod^a. The full publication is in P. W. Skehan, E. Ulrich and J. E. Sanderson, *Qumran Cave 4.IV: Palaeo-Hebrew and Greek Biblical Manuscripts* (DJD 9; Oxford: Clarendon Press, 1992) 53-130.

[23] P. W. Skehan, "Qumran and the Present State of Old Testament Text Studies: The Masoretic Text," *JBL* 78 (1959) 21-25, esp. 22.

[24] The two specific changes marking the Samaritan Torah are the commandment to build an altar at Shechem (after Exod 20:17), and the intermittent use of the perfect בחר "has chosen" [Shechem] in contrast to the future יבחר "will choose" [Jerusalem] to designate the central shrine.

its textual character,[25] noted that the OG of Exodus witnesses to an earlier form of the text than MT for a least eight individual readings, but they were sporadic and in her view were insufficient to constitute yet another literary edition.[26] Anneli Aejmelaeus subsequently studied Exodus 35–40, where the MT and OG texts display large-scale variation, and concluded that the *Vorlage* of the OG edition is an earlier edition of that section, relative to the subsequently developed edition preserved in the MT.[27]

Thus, there are four stages preserved in the development of the text of Exodus: the OG has one edition of 35–40 which the MT superseded; the entire book as in the MT was expanded systematically by one or more Jewish scribes into a form very close to the SP; and the Samaritans used the latter as their base text into which they inserted their two minor specific confessional changes.

4QNum^b: Nathan Jastram published an extensive scroll of Numbers which similarly exhibits the expanded edition of that book which served as the basis for the SP.[28] The scroll preserves more than 200 variants vis-à-vis the MT, in a pattern which amply justifies the prefatory note above concerning the distinct levels of orthography, individual variants, and variant editions. At the macro-level, the scroll is clearly aligned with the SP with regard to the majority of major harmonistic expansions, and thus it is a secondary, later edition based upon the edition attested in the MT but intentionally systematically developed. At the level of individual textual variants, the scroll agrees now with the SP, now with the LXX, now with the MT, although occasionally it uniquely adds a clarifying word or phrase beyond other witnesses; and once it adds a large expansion that is not in the SP though it is of the same type as

---

[25] J. E. Sanderson, *An Exodus Scroll from Qumran: 4QpaleoExod^m and the Samaritan Tradition* (HSS 30; Atlanta: Scholars, 1986).

[26] J. E. Sanderson, "The Old Greek of Exodus in the Light of 4QpaleoExod^m," *Textus* 14 (1988) 87-104.

[27] A. Aejmelaeus, "Septuagintal Translation Techniques—A Solution to the Problem of the Tabernacle Account," in G. J. Brooke and B. Lindars (eds.), *Septuagint, Scrolls and Cognate Writings (Manchester 1990)* (SBLSCS 33; Atlanta: Scholars Press, 1992) 381-402 [repr. in her *On the Trail of Septuagint Translators: Collected Essays* (Kampen: Kok Pharos, 1993) 116-30].

[28] See N. Jastram, "29. 4QNum^b," in E. Ulrich, F. M. Cross et al. (eds.), *Qumran Cave 4.VII: Genesis to Numbers* (DJD 12; Oxford: Clarendon Press, 1994) 205-67.

the other large expansions. Finally, the orthography is consistently full, with forms such as כול, לוא, and ויואמר.²⁹

4QRP: Finally, the proposal can be made that 4Q364–367, published in DJD 13 under the title "Reworked Pentateuch," constitute simply a variant literary edition of the Torah.³⁰ The editors of this collection state that the:

> text presented here probably contained the complete Pentateuch, reworked by the author of 4QRP.... This composition contained a running text of the Pentateuch interspersed with exegetical additions and omissions. The greater part of the preserved fragments follows the biblical text closely, but many small ... elements are added, while other elements are omitted, or, in other cases, their sequence altered.³¹

All of the additions are typically biblical; they are the types of variants one sees in Deuteronomy versus Exodus. In the light of the evidence provided by the larger collection of biblical scrolls from Qumran, it can be recognized that small additions, omissions, and rearrangements are *characteristic* of the biblical text throughout its history up to the second century CE, and that these are *hallmarks* of the biblical text, not disqualifiers.³² More work needs to be done before a final conclusion can be confidently reached, but it is possible that 4Q364–367 preserve yet a third variant literary edition of the Pentateuch, alongside the MT and the second Jewish variant edition that was at home in Second Temple Judaism and used by the Samaritans as the textual basis for their form of the Pentateuch. Indeed it should be noted that many of the readings in 4Q364–367 differing from the traditional MT Pentateuch agree with the Samaritan or, rather, with that other ancient Jewish Pentateuch which was taken up by the Samaritans. E. Tov and S. White write:

---

29 Jastram, "29. 4QNumᵇ," in *Qumran Cave 4.VII* (DJD 12) 212-13.

30 E. Tov and S. White, "364-367. 4QReworked Pentateuchᵇ⁻ᵉ," in H. Attridge et al. (eds.), in consultation with J. VanderKam, *Qumran Cave 4.VIII: Parabiblical Texts, Part 1* (DJD 13; Oxford: Clarendon Press, 1994) 187-351. Another manuscript, 4Q158, should also be classified as a copy of this work; see J. M. Allegro, "158. Biblical Paraphrase: Genesis, Exodus," in *Qumrân Cave 4.I (4Q158–4Q186)* (DJD 5; Oxford: Clarendon Press, 1968) 1-6 + pl. I.

31 Tov and White, "4QReworked Pentateuch" (DJD 13), 187, 191.

32 The editors' nuance, however, should be noted ("4QReworked Pentateuch" [DJD 13], 192): "While the exegetical character of 4QRP is easily recognized..., there are various borderline cases on which no clear opinion can be voiced as to whether the difference between 4QRP and the other textual witnesses [of the Bible] is exegetical [i.e. parabiblical] or textual [i.e. biblical]."

Summarizing the textual status of 4Q364, one notes its close agreement with 𝔐 in two major details which hitherto have been considered characteristic of 𝔐.... At the same time, 4Q364 does not disagree with 𝔐 in any major details.... The textual affiliations of 4Q365 are less clear..., [but the] summary of the relation between 4Q365 and 𝔐 is thus very similar to that between 4Q364 and 𝔐.[33]

2.2 The Former and Latter Prophets

4QJosh[a]: The oldest extant manuscript of Joshua provides evidence of an earlier literary version of the story, with a different sequence of events, than that in the MT or the LXX. As usual, the evidence is not complete, but Joshua apparently builds the first altar in the newly entered Promised Land, not on Mt. Ebal (as in the MT and the preserved LXX MSS) but at Gilgal, immediately after leading the people across the Jordan. This order turns out to be a more natural and logical sequence, with good claim to being the earlier form of the story which was later changed for polemical reasons. Moreover, a text like 4QJosh[a] seems to have constituted the biblical text which was used by the earliest independent witness, the late first-century historian Josephus.[34] The place of the erection of this altar is problematic in the MT, since it does not occur until the end of chapter 8, where Joshua strangely leads the people twenty miles north into enemy territory, builds the altar, and then returns, immediately abandoning the position. The earlier form, as found in 4QJosh[a], was probably secondarily changed by the Samaritans with the purpose of situating that important altar at their sacred site of worship, Mount Gerizim.[35] Thirdly the Judaeans, due to religious polemics, changed the name of the mountain from Gerizim to Ebal, despite the anomaly that was created. The scroll's fragmentary state offers only one other patch of evidence that it differed significantly

---

[33] "4QReworked Pentateuch," 193-94.

[34] See E. Ulrich, "47. 4QJosh[a]," in E. Ulrich, F. M. Cross, et al. (eds.), *Qumran Cave 4.IX: Deuteronomy, Joshua, Judges, Kings* (DJD 14; Oxford: Clarendon Press, 1995) 143-52, and "4QJoshua[a] and Joshua's First Altar in the Promised Land," in G. J. Brooke (ed.), *New Qumran Texts and Studies: Proceedings of the First Meeting of the International Organization for Qumran Studies, Paris 1992* (STDJ 15; Leiden: Brill, 1994) 89-104 + pls. IV-VI.

[35] "Gerizim" (where MT has the opposing "Ebal") is in fact the reading at Deut 27:4 attested by the SP and by the OL (which undoubtedly reflects an ancient Greek reading, thus providing double testimony). Deut 27:4 records the command which Joshua fulfills in the construction of this altar.

from the MT and the LXX, but it has long been suspected that the LXX presents an earlier, shorter form of the text than does gthe MT, which has now been demonstrated by L. Mazor.[36] Thus, again we can sketch four successive phases of the text of Joshua, though all may not be successive complete editions.

4QSam^a: It is still premature to give a final characterization of the text of Samuel, but there is a sufficiently large quantity and wide spectrum of types of variation in the text to challenge the textual critic to a strenuous workout. Only a tantalizing sampling may be offered here.

First, the David–Goliath story is a clear example of two different editions of a biblical narrative.[37] Some ancient scribe took a traditional form of the story of David and Goliath and intentionally interwove into it another account of Davidic traditions, thereby creating a significantly different edition of the text in quantity and in content. An earlier edition of the text with its own integrity and its own specific viewpoint is still found in the witnesses to the OG, and a second, later, harmonized edition is now found in the MT. The edition embedded in the MT has intentionally expanded the narrative with identifiably different types of material and different David-traditions.[38]

Two additional studies suggest further passages with contrasting editions, but space does not permit detailed discussion here. S. Walters has argued that the MT and LXX^B in 1 Samuel 1 constitute two different editions of Samuel's birth narrative.[39] Just as this article was going to press, E. Tov's 1997 article "Different Editions

---

[36] See, e.g. S. Holmes, *Joshua: The Hebrew and Greek Texts* (Cambridge: Cambridge University Press, 1914), and L. Mazor, "The Septuagint Translation of the Book of Joshua," *BIOSCS* 27 (1994) 29-38.

[37] For the detailed characteristics of the two editions, see D. Barthélemy, D. W. Gooding, J. Lust and E. Tov, *The Story of David and Goliath: Textual and Literary Criticism: Papers of a Joint Research Venture* (OBO 73; Fribourg, Suisse: Éditions Universitaires; Göttingen: Vandenhoeck und Ruprecht, 1986). Tov and Lust successfully argue complementary views, while the positions of Barthélemy and Gooding do not seem persuasive.

[38] Lust (*Story of David and Goliath*, 13-14) convincingly labels the content of the earlier, shorter edition as "heroic epic" material, and the supplemental content as "romantic epic" material.

[39] Stanley D. Walters, "Hannah and Anna: The Greek and Hebrew Texts of 1 Samuel 1," *JBL* 107 (1988) 385-412.

of the Song of Hannah and of Its Narrative Framework" appeared in print.[40]

4QJer[b, d]: Two textual traditions for the Book of Jeremiah were found at Qumran, although admittedly the evidence is small and fragmentary. Nonetheless, the OG has long since been recognized as preserving a shorter, earlier edition of the entire book, and 4QJer[b, d] provide fragmentary witness in Hebrew to that edition.[41] In contrast, the longer, later, rearranged edition preserved in the MT is documented in yet two other scrolls, 4QJer[a, c].

1QDan[a, b], 4QDan[a–e], 6QDan:[42] Eight manuscripts of the Book of Daniel have been identified at Qumran. Once again, one can distinguish the three aspects of orthography, individual textual variants, and variant editions of the book. Seven of these manuscripts align themselves with the shorter edition as found in the MT; 4QDan[e] is too fragmentary for classification. But as in other books above, the OG presents a variant edition of the book, this time a later edition characterized by large expansions, including the story of Suzanna, Bel and the Dragon, and the Prayer of the Three Youths. Moreover, in chapters 4–6 both the MT and the OG apparently preserve alternate secondary editions, i.e. they each expand with different material in different directions beyond an earlier common edition which no longer survives.[43] At the level of individual textual

---

[40] E. Tov, "Different Editions of the Song of Hannah and of Its Narrative Framework," in M. Cogan, B. L. Eichler and J. H. Tigay (eds.), *Tehillah le-Moshe: Biblical and Judaic Studies in Honor of Moshe Greenberg* (Winona Lake, IN: Eisenbrauns, 1997) 149-70.

[41] See E. Tov, "70-72b. 4QJer[a-e]," in E. Ulrich, et al. (eds.), *Qumran Cave 4.X: The Prophets* (DJD 15; Oxford: Clarendon Press, 1997) 145-207; and "The Literary History of the Book of Jeremiah in the Light of Its Textual History," in J. H. Tigay (ed.), *Empirical Models for Biblical Criticism* (Philadelphia: University of Pennsylvania, 1985) 213-37.

[42] The Book of Daniel was considered as a prophetic book by Jews and Christians alike in antiquity, only later being relegated by the Rabbis to the Writings; see E. Ulrich, "The Bible in the Making: The Scriptures at Qumran," in E. Ulrich and J. VanderKam (eds.), *The Community of the Renewed Covenant: The Notre Dame Symposium on the Dead Sea Scrolls* (CJA 10; Notre Dame, IN: University of Notre Dame Press, 1994) 77-93, esp. 81-82.

[43] See D. O. Wenthe, "The Old Greek Translation of Daniel 1-6" (Ph.D. diss., Notre Dame: University of Notre Dame, 1991), which demonstrates that the edition of the book in the MT is the earliest complete one available, but not the first edition of the biblical Book of Daniel, and that the MT and LXX exhibit variant editions.

variants, 4QDan^a and 4QDan^b at times agree with each other and 𝕲^O against 𝔐 𝕲^{θ'}, while at the level of orthography 4QDan^a and 𝔐 regularly agree with each other against the fuller spellings of 4QDan^b.[44]

2.3 Other Books of Our Ancestors[45]

11QPs^a:[46] This beautiful and generously preserved scroll from Cave 11 is considered by many scholars, especially in the past few decades, as nonbiblical. James Sanders, its editor, was in the minority in considering it biblical.[47] Others rather considered it a secondary "liturgical" scroll, denying its biblical status for some or all of the following reasons: (1) It presents the biblical psalms in an *order* that differs repeatedly from that of the MT. (2) It has *additional* psalms not found in the MT. (3) Even within the biblical Psalm 145 an *antiphon* is repeatedly added in contrast with the MT. (4) It includes a *prose* composition, "David's Compositions," among the Psalms. (5) The *tetragrammaton* is written in the Palaeo-Hebrew script, not in the normal Jewish script used for the remainder of the scroll.

None of those arguments, however, hold as valid in light of what the biblical scrolls have taught us, and Peter Flint has persuasively argued for the acceptance of 11QPs^a as an alternate edition of the Psalter in ancient Judaism.[48] Of course, 11QPs^a is a liturgical scroll,

---

[44] E. Ulrich, "Orthography and Text in 4QDan^a and 4QDan^b and in the Received Masoretic Text," in H. W. Attridge, J. J. Collins and T. H. Tobin (eds.), *Of Scribes and Scrolls: Studies on the Hebrew Bible, Intertestamental Judaism, and Christian Origins presented to John Strugnell on the Occasion of His Sixtieth Birthday* (CTSRR 5; Lanham, MD: University Press of America, 1990) 29-42.

[45] This category is taken from the Prologue to the *Wisdom of Ben Sira*, as historically contemporary with the Qumran scrolls. It is also as undefined as I think the category was in the late Second Temple period—containing some of those books which now form the *Ketubim*, plus others, but not over-interpreted to match exactly that subsequently delimited category.

[46] The Psalter, though explicitly claimed as given "through prophecy" to David in 11QPs^a 27:11, and though interpreted prophetically both at Qumran and in the NT, is here listed not among the Prophets but among "the other books." This is because some sources from around the end of the Second Temple period list it separately: see 4QMMT C 10 and Luke 24:44 (contrast Luke 16:16).

[47] See J. A. Sanders, *The Psalms Scroll of Qumrân Cave 11* [11QPs^a] (DJD 4; Oxford: Clarendon Press, 1965).

[48] P. W. Flint, *The Dead Sea Psalms Scrolls and the Book of Psalms* (STDJ 17; Leiden: Brill, 1997), esp. 202-27.

but so is the MT Psalter by its very nature. Moreover, all of the above features are contained either in the MT at other places or in other manuscripts which are undeniably biblical: (1) Both the LXX and the MT of Jeremiah are legitimate forms of the biblical book, and the MT is a secondarily revised edition of the book as found in the LXX, and it presents major blocks of the book in a variant order. (2) The Greek and especially Syriac Psalters include some of these "non-canonical" psalms that were clearly originally Hebrew psalms, even if not eventually accepted into the MT edition of the Psalter. (3) The antiphon "Blessed be the LORD and blessed be his name forever and ever" is totally derived from verse 1 of Psalm 145, and it is systematically repeated in the identical manner in which the antiphon "For his faithfulness endures for ever" is repeated in Psalm 136 in the MT. (4) The prose composition, called "David's Compositions," includes an explicit claim to scriptural status for the Psalter and may have earlier been positioned not *within* the collection but at the *end* of the collection, functioning as a quasi-colophon with the claim for scriptural status.[49] (5) The use of the Palaeo-Hebrew script for divine name in a text principally written in the Jewish script had earlier been considered an indication that the text was not biblical. However, as with the previous points, while

---

[49] The passage states that David composed all his psalms "through prophecy that was given to him from before the Most High" (Sanders, *Psalms Scroll* [DJD 4] 48 + pl. XVI), and it is through "prophecy" that the Psalter makes the transition from being the human hymnbook of the Temple to being God's word as Scripture (i.e. an integral part of "the Law and the Prophets"). With regard to sequence, this passage follows "the Last Words of David" (also found in 2 Sam 23:1-7), which panegyrizes "the man raised on high, the anointed of the God of Jacob, the sweet singer (?) of Israel" (23:1), and then claims, "The spirit of the Lord speaks through me; his word is upon my tongue" (23:2). In turn, "the Last Words of David" follows Psalms 149 and 150 and the closing "Hymn to the Creator." Thus, it is plausible that at an earlier stage this form of the Psalter concluded with the sequence: Psalms 149, 150, and the "Hymn to the Creator" (appropriate as a concluding psalm). Sometime later, a few more related passages were added (as happened at the end of other books such as Samuel, Isaiah, Amos, etc.): namely, "the Last Words of David" with the claim that "The spirit of the Lord speaks through me," plus "David's Compositions" with the assertion that all these psalms "he spoke through prophecy" from God. Then at yet a later stage, Psalms 140 and 134 would have been added. At the last stage, Psalm 151 was appended as a fitting Davidic finale to the collection in 11QPs[a], just as a version of the same Psalm provides a finale to the Greek Psalter.

that view was understandable in light of the early evidence, it should be laid to rest now that a number of biblical scrolls have attested the practice.[50]

Jubilees, Enoch, Tobit, Sirach: Copies of a number of "the other books of our ancestors"—which, together with "the Law and the Prophets" offered Israel "many great teachings" (Prologue to Sirach)—were also found in the Judaean Desert. Not considered among "the Law and the Prophets," the individual works probably had various rankings by different groups relative to their status as sacred and/or authoritative books. But there is strong reason to think that especially Jubilees and Enoch held a high ranking.

The Book of Jubilees, as James VanderKam says, "blatantly advertises itself as divine revelation"; this may explain why fifteen or possibly sixteen copies were found, rivaling the books of the Torah in frequency, and may also explain why it is quoted as an authoritative work in CD 16:2-3 (and possibly also in 4Q228).[51] Even more copies, perhaps as high as twenty, survive from the several parts of 1 Enoch; although quotations from this book have not been documented at Qumran, the New Testament quotes 1 Enoch 1:9, in the Epistle of Jude 14–15.[52] Moreover, 1 Enoch was translated into Greek, small fragments of which É. Puech recently identified among the remains of Cave 7.[53] Cave 4 held five manuscripts of Tobit, four in Aramaic and one in Hebrew, while the Hebrew text of Sirach is attested in manuscripts from Masada and Qumran Cave 2, as well as the Cairo Geniza.

Job, Proverbs, the Megillot, Ezra, Chronicles: In contrast to works such as Jubilees and Enoch, these "other books" are represented by one, two, or at most four copies from the Judaean Desert, although there is an extensive Targum of Job from Cave 11 plus a few fragments of the Targum also from Cave 4.

---

[50] See Ulrich, "Multiple Literary Editions," 101-104, including Plates I–II.

[51] J. VanderKam, *The Dead Sea Scrolls Today* (Grand Rapids: Eerdmans, 1994) 153-54.

[52] VanderKam, *Dead Sea Scrolls*, 155-6. In addition to Jubilees and 1 Enoch, VanderKam points to the Temple Scroll as also possibly understood as a revealed text, inasmuch as it is presented "as the direct speech of God to Moses on Mount Sinai" (156).

[53] É. Puech, "Notes sur les fragments grecs du manuscript 7Q4 = 1 Hénoch 103 et 105," *RB* 103-104 (1996) 592-600.

In sum, the abundant and multifaceted evidence provided by the biblical scrolls from the Judaean Desert has revolutionized our knowledge and understanding both of the text and textual history of the Hebrew Bible and of the canonical process.

3. CRITIQUE OF THE THEORIES

Virtually all of the biblical manuscripts have been published since the earlier theories discussed above were first formulated, and it is no surprise that there have been advances. Each has made its contribution and each has, or will have, some aspects that must be revised. The theory has more or less kept pace with the data, given the expected time-lag required to incorporate and process the new data.

Cross's local text theory was important both because it laid out numerous significant readings and because it stimulated the scholarly world to begin thinking about the issue and working toward a gradual solution. It is not broadly seen today as a fully satisfactory approach to describe the evidence. In 1991 I noted that our main source of evidence—the Qumran biblical scrolls—appears to invalidate the local text theory inasmuch as, at Qumran, "a single locality, we have a wide variety of quite diverse texts and text types in what was a rather strong-minded and single-minded group; and this situation apparently spanned two centuries."[54] Still at the general level, I also suggested that it was likely that there were differing ideological groups or parties in each locality, and thus probably different texts in each locality. At the detailed level, if the OG of Jeremiah had been translated from an Egyptian text in the second century BCE, why are 4QJer[b,d] found in Palestine a century or so later, alongside Palestinian texts such as 4QJer[a,c]?

Does the locality teach us much? There appears to be no causal link between a locality and the characteristics of the text-type; e.g. the OG of Jeremiah (earlier, shorter) and the OG of Daniel (later, longer) stand in opposite relationships vis-à-vis the MT. One might also wonder whether the local text theory is predicated on the questionable assumption that the MT, the SP and the LXX constitute three "text-types." Again, Talmon seems to be correct that there were multiple textual forms in antiquity, not just three. Those three

---

[54] Ulrich, "Pluriformity," 26-27.

collections of texts, insofar as they pose as textual categories are "resulting" categories, rather than "causal" categories. In other words, they are three collections that happened to survive in the end, but it is doubtful that they are text-types because they were produced by three distinct localities.

Tov notes that the "principal argument in favor [of Cross's view] ... is an abstract and logical one..., [but] there is no possibility of verifying the details of this theory."[55] He finds that the textual characterization is too general, that "the Hebrew *Vorlage* of 𝔊 does not reflect any proven Egyptian characteristics," and that 4QJer[b,d] as well as the "mixture of ... all three local textual groups" at Qumran "actually contradicts the logic of the theory of local families."[56] Just as Talmon did, Tov cogently argues that this tripartite view is based on the limited witnesses we had before the discovery of the scrolls; this tripartite view is not the proper stance, and these are not the proper categories or labels. Just as we may see more clearly if we learn "no longer to posit MT at the center of our textual thinking,"[57] so too we may see more clearly if we no longer use the MT, the SP and the LXX as if they were the three dominant categories for text-types in antiquity.

Where Cross's insight raised the question of the origins of different text-types, Talmon's focused on the final moment—that, after centuries of development and pluriformity of texts, only he MT, the SP and the LXX survived because the Rabbis, the Samaritans, and the Christians were the only groups that survived.

But just as there seems to be no causal link between locality and text-type, neither does there appear to be a causal link between religious group and text-type. Except for the three specifically Samaritan beliefs noted above,[58] the text was kept free of partisan variants; apparently none of the parties viewed the text as a legitimate battleground for controversial claims of one group against another. The sharper focus, however, contributed by Talmon's insight did lead to some newly articulated advances: the Samaritans chose a script (the ancient "Palaeo-Hebrew" script), while the Rabbis chose the contemporary Jewish script; and the Christians chose a

---

[55] Tov, *Textual Criticism*, 186.
[56] Tov, *Textual Criticism*, 186-87.
[57] Tov, "Hebrew Biblical Manuscripts," 7.
[58] Cf. notes 24 and 35.

language (Greek, for the mission to the Gentiles), while the Rabbis and Samaritans held to the traditional Hebrew. But these choices did not extend to text-type. If one were tempted to project more broadly the set of connections—that 4QpaleoExod^m exhibits the same script, orthography, and text-type as the SP—one should be sobered by the fact that neither 4QpaleoGen-Exod^l nor 4QpaleoDeut^r seem to share the same text-type or orthography as the SP.

Tov presents a "new description" of the textual development of the Hebrew Bible,[59] many of the aspects of which have been presented throughout these pages. His *Textual Criticism* is the most richly illuminating comprehensive description of the text of the Hebrew Bible. There is, of course, room for advances and refinement. Despite his decentralization of the MT, and his "Modern Textual Outlook,"[60] he continues to use he MT, the SP and the LXX as text-type categories (as noted in Table 1).[61] This does have the advantage of clear, handy labeling (although, since he MT, the SP and the LXX are different from book to book, only a specialist would know the significance of the labels). The disadvantage is that it gives the impression both (1) that MT, SP, and LXX were known textual categories in the Second Temple period, and (2) that critical comparison of parallel text-types was an activity in the period. In my view both impressions are inaccurate or at least (except for the SP) probably anachronistic.

His other two categories ("non-aligned" and "Qumran practice") also present problems. If he MT, the SP and the LXX were not text-types, why should they function as standards according to which other, older texts are compared for alignment or non-alignment? Are they not the wrong labels? And is not the stance anachronistic? With respect to "the Qumran practice," it has already been noted that Tov himself acknowledges that it "must be conceded that the term *Qumran practice ...* is somewhat misleading," and that it "was *a* Palestinian scribal system...."[62] But on the preceding page he says: "It appears that the texts belonging to this group were copied by the Qumran covenanters themselves."[63]

---

[59] Tov, *Textual Criticism*, 187-98, esp. 160-63.
[60] See note 4 above.
[61] In section 2 above.
[62] Tov, *Textual Criticism*, 108; emphasis his.
[63] Tov, *Textual Criticism*, 107.

The advantage I see in the "successive literary editions" theory is that it attempts to analyze the manuscript evidence in its historical context and chronological development and does not judge ancient evidence from the Second Temple period by the standard of the later MT. It attempts to derive the categories from within the textual evidence, as opposed to imposing the later categories derived from the three mixed text-collections that simply, from a historical perspective, happened to survive the two failed revolts against the Romans. It attempts through the category labels and descriptive vocabulary to describe the cause and rationale and significance of the variant editions, matching labels with causes.

To my knowledge, there has not yet appeared a critique of my "successive literary editions" theory.[64] I fully expect, of course, that such will appear in due time; that theory is by no means fully worked out yet, and we can all look forward to refinement and correction in this endeavor. Cross did state that:

> Any reconstruction of the history of the biblical text before the establishment of the traditional text in the first century A.D., must comprehend this evidence: the plurality of text-types, the limited number of distinct textual families, and the homogeneity of each of these textual families over several centuries of time.[65]

Whereas he had concluded that these data require us "to recognize the existence of local texts which developed in the main centers of Jewish life in the Persian and Hellenistic age,"[66] I would agree with his first statement and suggest that the "successive literary editions" theory does comprehend those three factors. But I would suggest that local texts do not constitute the only possible configuration for explaining the data.

Now that the publication of the biblical scrolls is approaching completion, a wider spectrum of views may emerge which may

---

[64] A. S. van der Woude judiciously argues to balance the perspective I share regarding the "proto-Masoretic" text, its degree of centrality prior to the Roman destruction, and the canonization process. See his "Tracing the Evolution of the Hebrew Bible," *BR* 11/1 (Feb. 1995) 42-45; and "Pluriformity and Uniformity: Reflections on the Transmission of the Text of the Old Testament," in J. N. Bremmer and F. García Martínez (eds.), *Sacred History and Sacred Texts in Early Judaism: A Symposium in Honour of A. S. van der Woude* (Kampen: Kok Pharos, 1992) 151-69.

[65] Cross, "Contribution of the Qumran Discoveries," 282.

[66] Cross, "Contribution of the Qumran Discoveries," 282.

illumine perspectives or aspects that do not yet even occur to us. The biblical scrolls were an unimagined and unforeseeable gift. They have already revolutionized our knowledge of the text of the Bible and the history of the biblical text. As we turn from looking at these past fifty years to the next fifty, we can look with confidence in expectation of gaining a yet richer, more accurate, and more comprehensive understanding both of the scrolls and of the biblical text.

SELECT BIBLIOGRAPHY

Aejmelaeus, A. "Septuagintal Translation Techniques—A Solution to the Problem of the Tabernacle Account," in G. J. Brooke and B. Lindars (eds.), *Septuagint, Scrolls and Cognate Writings (Manchester 1990)* (SBLSCS 33; Atlanta: Scholars Press, 1992) 381-402 [repr. in her *On the Trail of Septuagint Translators: Collected Essays* (Kampen: Kok Pharos, 1993) 116-30].

Albright, W. F. "New Light on Early Recensions of the Hebrew Bible," *BASOR* 140 (1955) 27-33.

Cross, F. M. *The Ancient Library of Qumran* (1st ed., London: Epworth, 1958; 3rd ed., Minneapolis: Fortress, 1995).

—. "The History of the Biblical Text in the Light of Discoveries in the Judaean Desert," *HTR* 57 (1964) 281-99.

—. "The Evolution of a Theory of Local Texts," in F. M. Cross and S. Talmon (eds.), *Qumran and the History of the Biblical Text* (Cambridge, MA: Harvard University Press, 1975) 306-20. First published in R. A. Kraft (ed.), *1972 Proceedings: IOSCS and Pseudepigrapha* (Missoula, MT: Scholars Press, 1972) 108-26.

—. "The Contribution of the Qumrân Discoveries to the Study of the Biblical Text," *IEJ* 16 (1966) 81-95 [repr. in *Qumran and the History*, 278-92].

Goshen-Gottstein, M. "Hebrew Biblical Manuscripts: Their History and Their Place in the HUBP Edition," *Biblica* 48 (1967) 243-90 [repr. in *Qumran and the History*, 42-89].

Kutscher, E. Y. *A History of the Hebrew Language* (Jerusalem: Magnes Press, 1982).

Milik, J. T. *Dix ans de Découvertes dans le Désert de Juda* (Paris: Cerf, 1957, translated by J. Strugnell, *Ten Years of Discovery in the Wilderness of Judaea* [SBT; London: SCM, 1959]).

Sanderson, J. E. *An Exodus Scroll from Qumran: 4QpaleoExod^m and the Samaritan Tradition* (HSS 30; Atlanta: Scholars, 1986).

—. "The Old Greek of Exodus in the Light of 4QpaleoExod^m," *Textus* 14 (1988) 87-104.

Skehan, P. W. "Exodus in the Samaritan Recension from Qumran," *JBL* 74 (1955) 435-40.

Talmon, S. "The Textual Study of the Bible—A New Outlook," in Cross and Talmon (eds.), *Qumran and the History*, 321–400.

—. "The Old Testament Text," in P. R. Ackroyd and C. F. Evans (eds.), *The Cambridge History of the Bible. 1. From the Beginnings to Jerome* (Cambridge: Cambridge University Press, 1970) 159–99 [repr. in Cross and Talmon (eds.), *Qumran and the History*, 1-41].

Tov, E. *Textual Criticism of the Hebrew Bible* (Assen and Maastricht: Van Gorcum; Minneapolis: Fortress, 1992).

—. "A Modern Textual Outlook Based on the Qumran Scrolls," *HUCA* 53 (1982) 11–27.

—. *The Text-Critical Use of the Septuagint in Biblical Research* (Jerusalem: Simor, 1981; 2nd ed., 1997).

—. "Hebrew Biblical Manuscripts from the Judaean Desert: Their Contribution to Textual Criticism," *JJS* 39 (1988) 5–37.

Ulrich, E. "Horizons of Old Testament Textual Research at the Thirtieth Anniversary of Qumran Cave 4," *CBQ* 46 (1984) 613-36.

—. "Pluriformity in the Biblical Text, Text Groups, and Questions of Canon," in J. Trebolle Barrera and L. Vegas Montaner (eds.), *The Madrid Qumran Congress: Proceedings of the International Congress on the Dead Sea Scrolls, Madrid, 18-21 March 1991* (STDJ 11; 2 vols.; Leiden: Brill, 1992) 23-41.

—. "Multiple Literary Editions: Reflections toward a Theory of the History of the Biblical Text," in D. W. Parry and S. D. Ricks (eds.), *Current Research and Technological Developments on the Dead Sea Scrolls: Conference on the Texts from the Judean Desert, Jerusalem, 30 April 1995* (STDJ 20; Leiden: Brill, 1996) 78-105.

—. "The Canonical Process, Textual Criticism, and Latter Stages in the Composition of the Bible," in M. Fishbane and E. Tov (eds.), *"Shaʿarei Talmon." Studies in the Bible, Qumran, and the Ancient Near East Presented to Shemaryahu Talmon* (Winona Lake, IN: Eisenbrauns, 1992) 267–91.

—. "The Community of Israel and the Composition of the Scriptures," in C. A. Evans and S. Talmon (eds.), *The Quest for Context and Meaning: Studies in Intertextuality in Honor of James A. Sanders* (BibInt 28; Leiden: Brill, 1997) 327–42.

Würthwein, E. *The Text of the Old Testament* (2nd ed.; Grand Rapids: Eerdmans, 1995).

THE DEAD SEA SCROLLS AND THE GREEK BIBLE

LEONARD J. GREENSPOON

This article deals with two separate, but related, ways in which the Dead Sea Scrolls shed light on the ancient Greek translation that is generally referred to as the "Septuagint." In the introductory paragraphs that follow we present an overview of the relevant manuscripts, pose questions concerning their interpretation and importance, and offer some definitions that will prove useful as we move to more detailed discussion and analysis.

1. THE GREEK MANUSCRIPTS

Most people, even some scholars, assume that all of the Dead Sea Scrolls were found in the same general location and are written in the same language: Hebrew or, to a lesser extent, Aramaic. In fact, several important biblical manuscripts discovered in the environs of the Dead Sea are written in Greek. These include a half dozen or so from the site of Qumran itself and another, highly significant text from Nahal Hever to the south. Although the number of these Greek manuscripts is very small in comparison with those written in Hebrew, they raise an interesting question: Who wrote them? Who read them? How were they used? What do they say about bi- or multilingualism at Qumran in particular, and throughout Palestine in general?

To speak of these as biblical manuscripts in this context identifies them in some way with the Septuagint. In general, the Septuagint or LXX refers to Greek translations or revisions of Old Testament books originally that were composed in Hebrew; but in addition, the term encompasses some original Greek material. It is useful to designate the original translation of each book or group of books as the "Old Greek" (hereafter OG)[1] and to consider that there was considerable scribal and revisional activity separating these

---

[1] On the use of terms such as "OG" and "LXX," see L. G. Greenspoon, "The Use and Abuse of the Term 'LXX' and Related Terminology in Recent Scholarship," *BIOSCS* 20 (1987) 21-29.

"autographs" from the great uncial manuscripts of the fourth and fifth centuries CE that provide us with our earliest witnesses to the complete Old Testament. The Greek biblical manuscripts from the Dead Sea, which were copied quite early in the period from autograph to uncial, are of great importance in allowing scholars to reconstruct some key moments in the textual history of at least some parts of the LXX.[2]

In summary then, the presence of these Greek manuscripts—though few in number—raises extremely interesting questions concerning the use of the Greek language in Palestine and the textual history of the Septuagint.

2. CONNECTIONS WITH THE SEPTUAGINT

Connections between the Scrolls and the Septuagint are not limited to manuscripts in the Greek language. A larger number of Hebrew biblical manuscripts are also relevant, although the nature of their impotance is somewhat disputed. Most clearly relevant are Hebrew manuscripts that represent to a substantial degree the probable *Vorlage* of the Old Greek. Prior to the discovery of these scrolls, it was fairly common to assert that the Greek translators worked with a Hebrew text that was essentially the same as our received or Masoretic Text. According to this view, differences between the MT and the OG were due primarily to interpretative and other activities on the part of the translators themselves. But when some biblical scrolls were found to have a text that looked very much like the Hebrew text the OG translators would have been reading, this view largely fell out of favor. This is not to say that we can identify any scroll *in toto* with the Hebrew *Vorlage* (underlying text) of a given book or block of material. Nonetheless, the discovery of such Hebrew manuscripts lays to rest many facile assumptions about textual "manipulation" on the part of the Greek translators.

We hasten to add that it is no easy task to retrovert even the most straightforward Greek text into Hebrew. Yet when due caution is exercised, it becomes clear that there are some biblical scrolls in Hebrew belonging to the same tradition that the Old Greek translators utilized in their work. Significant OG–DSS agreements (which generally arise in secondary, rather than original, readings)

---

[2] For recent work on all aspects of the Septuagint, see C. Dogniez, *Bibliography of the Septuagint: 1970-1993* (VTSup 60; Leiden: Brill, 1995).

are sporadically found in other Hebrew manuscripts as well. The extent and significance of such agreements are more problematic, but point us to another area where interest in the Septuagint and the Scrolls intersect. Finally, it seems clearly possible to learn something about LXX textual developments even from those Hebrew scrolls that seem to reveal little—if any direct—connections with the Greek Bible.

3. SPECIFIC SCROLLS AND THEIR IMPORTANCE

We turn now to a discussion of individual scrolls. In what follows we do not aim primarily at total coverage or original interpretations, but rather at presenting the reader with a fair picture of the scholarly *status quaestionis*—consensus, disagreements, and future prospects. We do not feel compelled to conceal our own opinions, but intend them to complement rather than mask the views of others. Additionally, we will make constant reference to major bibliographical resources, and wish to ensure that readers have access as directly as possible to the ancient documents themselves.

Seven Greek manuscripts are directly relevant to our discussion. Four of these—containing verses from Leviticus, Numbers, and Deuteronomy—were unearthed in Qumran Cave 4, which was also the final resting place for the vast majority of biblical fragments that were written in Hebrew. In addition to a series of preliminary publications, these Greek texts recently received their official public presentation in DJD 9 (1992).[3] Exactly three decades earlier two small fragments, from Exodus and the Letter of Jeremiah, appeared in DJD 3.[4] These texts were located in Qumran Cave 7, home to several other controversial Greek manuscripts that have been identified by some with portions of the New Testament. But the most famous of the Greek Dead Sea Scrolls comes not from Qumran but from Naḥal Ḥever, further to the south. Initially published and analyzed by D. Barthélemy,[5] this scroll contains fairly extensive portions from the Minor Prophets and is now available as volume 8

---

[3] P. W. Skehan, E. Ulrich and J. E. Sanderson, *Qumrân Cave 4.IV: Palaeo-Hebrew and Greek Biblical Manuscripts* (DJD 9; Oxford: Clarendon Press, 1992).

[4] M. Baillet, J. T. Milik and R. de Vaux, *Les "Petites Grottes" de Qumrân. 1.Textes* (DJD 3.1: Oxford: Clarendon Press, 1962).

[5] D. Barthélemy, "Redécouverte d'un chaînon manquant de l'histoire de la LXX," *RB* 60 (1953) 18-29.

in the DJD series.[6] The two Greek fragments from Cave 7, as well as one of the Leviticus fragments from Cave 4, are written on papyrus; the remainder are on leather.

When we compare these Greek texts with biblical manuscripts in Hebrew and with what is known about the community that presumably used and preserved them, it is no surprise that the Pentateuch figures so prominently in the extant material. According to one estimate, some 40% (82 out of 202) of the Hebrew biblical Scrolls from Qumran are Pentateuchal.[7] Yet it is rather surprising to note the relative absence of Psalms and prophetic texts, especially from the major prophets, among the Greek fragments. In this respect the contrast with Hebrew biblical manuscripts is startling: among the Qumran manuscrips, 36 are from the Psalter; another 33 are from the Major Prophets (Isaiah 21; Jeremiah and Ezekiel, 6 each. This number is still higher [by eight] if the book of Daniel figured among the prophets at Qumran).[8] There is no obvious hypothesis to explain these data; happenstance immediately suggests itself and, at this point in the inquiry, is as likely an explanation as any.

4. THE MINOR PROPHETS SCROLL

In any discussion of the Greek biblical material, pride of place belongs to the Minor Prophets Scroll, not because it is the earliest Greek biblical fragment, but because it has clearly been the most influential. Since it was first brought to scholarly attention by Barthélemy in 1953, this manuscript has had an extraordinary—one might say, with only slight exaggeration, a revolutionary—impact on Septuagint studies. The extant fragments of this scroll (or possibly scrolls) contain verses from the following books of the Twelve: Jonah, Micah, Nahum, Habakkuk, Zephaniah, and Zechariah. It is interesting to note that this sequence of books follows the order that is found in the MT, not that of the LXX.

As Barthélemy recognized early on (even long before all of the fragments had been pieced together and analyzed), the text of this

---

[6] E. Tov, with the collaboration of R. A. Kraft, *The Greek Minor Prophets Scroll from Naḥal Ḥever(8ḤevXIIgr): The Seiyâl Collection I* (DJD 8; Oxford: Clarendon Press, 1990).

[7] J. C. VanderKam, *The Dead Sea Scrolls Today* (Grand Rapids, MI: Eerdmans, 1994) 30-31.

[8] VanderKam, *Dead Sea Scrolls Today*, 30-31.

scroll is not the Old Greek or earliest translation of the Minor Prophets, but rather a revision of the OG in the direction of an evolving Hebrew text similar to—but not identical with—the received or Masoretic Text. The reviser(s) responsible for these changes made use of a distinctive vocabulary that is marked by a number of lexical equivalents, including the eponymous characteristic of וגם/גם being translated by the Greek words καίγε; the entire edition has thus come to be known as the *kaige* revision.[9] In his earliest publication Barthélemy designated this reviser as R; its connection with the larger kaige enterprise came later.

It is now widely accepted that Barthélemy had correctly interpreted the Minor Prophets Scroll as a representative of a hitherto "missing link" ("un chaînon manquant") in the history of the transmission of the Septuagint. He dated this manuscript to the mid-first century CE and believed that it reflected particular characteristics of contemporary rabbinic exegesis (hence, for Barthélemy, this was a "recension rabbinique"). Palaeographer P. J. Parsons re-examined this dating in DJD 8, and came to the conclusion—which is now generally accepted—that the Minor Prophets Scroll was earlier, being written in the last half of the first century BCE.[10] This earlier date precludes Barthélemy's attempts to link R or kaige with rabbinic techniques that developed only later.

Barthélemy was far more successful in his characterization of the Minor Prophets Scroll and its congeners as "devanciers d'Aquila," for many of the characteristics initiated and sporadically applied in these texts came to fruition, often with painful literalness, in the second century CE recension that is identified with Aquila. Moreover, Barthélemy's lack of success in connecting R with a particular rabbi was somewhat compensated for by his noting its many similarities with the Greek recension that is associated with Theodotion. Although historical Theodotion is to be located in the second century CE and the Minor Prophets Scroll clearly predates him by more than two centuries, Barthélemy's insights allow us to isolate an early layer of "Theodotion" that can properly be termed "proto-Theodotion."

The value and validity of Barthélemy's achievement have in general stood the test of further scholarly scrutiny and have been the

---

[9] D. Barthélemy, *Les Devanciers d'Aquila* (VTSup 10; Leiden: Brill, 1963).

[10] P. J. Parsons, "The Scripts and Their Date," in Tov, *Greek Minor Prophets Scroll*, 19-26.

subject of numerous dissertations, monographs, and articles. In the process it is inevitable that scholars have come to nuance some of his global statements and to question the unitary quality of what now appears to be a more fragmented and fragmentary effort. But there is can be no doubt that in the Minor Prophets Scroll we have conclusive evidence of Jewish Septuagintal revision of the in the pre-Christian era.[11]

5. THE GREEK SCROLLS FROM QUMRAN

The other Greek fragments from the Dead Sea both confirm and expand upon the nature of this revisional activity. At the same time, they provide salutary reminders that a given manuscript must be read diachronically as well as synchronically—that is to say that even a text marked by revision may also contain old, even original readings that are not witnessed elsewhere.

After briefly describing the contents, date, and other salient features of the remaining Dead Sea Scrolls of the Greek Bible, we will discuss two in some detail, in order to highlight major features that were mentioned in the previous paragraph. As already mentioned, M. Baillet published the Greek biblical texts from Cave 7 in 1962. The first of these is pap7QLXXExod, which consists of two fragments that cover Exod 28:4-7. Important features that were mentioned by Baillet include the date: "On pourrait dater la copie des environs de 100 av. J.-C.," and textual affinity: "Le texte est en général plus proche du TM que de la LXX et rencontre plusieurs fois les minuscules c et m de l'éd. de Brooke-McLean."[12] The second manuscript is pap7QLXXEpJer, from the same date as the preceding and containing vv 43 and 44 of the Letter. In line 3-5 Baillet detects "une variante de la Lucianique et du syriaque."[13]

We next list the four scrolls from Cave 4 in the canonical order of their contents: 4QLXXLeviticus[a] covers Lev 26:2-16; pap4QLXX Leviticus[b] comprises 31 identified fragments containing several dozen verses from the first five chapters of the book, as well as another 66 unidentified pieces; 4QLXXNumbers consists of 23 fragments that contain verses from the third and fourth chapters; and

---

[11] L. J. Greenspoon, "Recensions, Revisions, Rabbinics: Dominique Barthélemy and Early Developments in the Greek Traditions," *Textus* 15 (1990) 153-67.

[12] Baillet, Milik and de Vaux, *Les "Petites Grottes,"* 142.

[13] Baillet, Milik and de Vaux, *Les "Petites Grottes,"* 143.

4QLXXDeuteronomy, with one identifiable fragment and four other pieces ("presumably also from Deuteronomy"),[14] presents Deut 11:4.

P. J. Parsons, who provided the now generally accepted earlier date for the Minor Prophets Scroll (see above), also subjected the Cave 4 Greek material to careful palaeographical analysis. Given the fragmentary nature of most of this material and the lack of firmly dated comparative texts, Parsons urges us to take his conclusions with "a double pinch of salt."[15] Yet such laudable tentativeness should not deter us from attaching a high degree of confidence to Parsons' statements. For 4QLXXLeviticus[a],

> the general impression is of a script earlier than that of the Greek Minor Prophets Scroll (... dated about the later first century BCE ...), unlikely to be later than the first century BCE ... or much earlier.[16]

Scripts like that of pap4QLXXLeviticus[b] "may belong to the first century BCE... But they may extend well into the first century CE... This example has a slightly old-fashioned look...and could reasonably be assigned to the first century BCE."[17] In Parsons' judgment, 4QLXXNumbers is similar palaeographically to the Leviticus papyrus discussed just above: "This too could be of late Ptolemaic date; but the early Roman period cannot be excluded."[18] Finally, he concludes that 4QLXXDeuteronomy is:

> written in an informal hand with some ligatures. The overall impression is of a script rather earlier than the others of this find... But it should be emphasized that, with so small a sample, the dating must be more than usually uncertain.[19]

5.1 4QLXXNumbers

For more detailed comments, we turn first to the Numbers manuscript, which received its preliminary publication and discussion in the mid-70s by Patrick Skehan. As the sub-title of his work

---

[14] Skehan et al., *Qumrân Cave 4.IV* (DJD 9) 195. On these scrolls see also E. Ulrich, "The Greek Manuscripts of the Pentateuch from Qumrân, Including Newly-Identified Fragments of Deuteronomy (4QLXXDeut)," in Albert Pietersma et al. (eds.), *De Septuaginta: Studies in Honour of John William Wevers* (Mississauga, ON: Benben, 1984) 71-82.

[15] Parsons, "Greek Biblical Manuscripts," 7.

[16] Parsons, "Greek Biblical Manuscripts," 10.

[17] Parsons, "Greek Biblical Manuscripts," 10-11.

[18] Parsons, "Greek Biblical Manuscripts," 11.

[19] Parsons, "Greek Biblical Manuscripts," 12.

indicates, at that time Skehan understood 4QLXXNumbers to represent "a Pre-Christian reworking of the Septuagint." In other words, the American scholar believed that the scroll represented:

> a reworking of the OG of this portion of the book of Numbers to make it conform both in quantity and in diction to a Hebrew text that is nearly indistinguishable...from that of MT. The manner of this reworking corresponds to that of the kaige, or proto-Theodotionic recension. Nevertheless, there are indications ... that the reviser here cannot be identified with the kaige reviser of LXX Samuel and Kings.[20]

Some twenty years earlier, Skehan had not thought of this text in terms of such a revision.[21] His second analysis was partly confirmed and partly modified by John Wevers, who concluded that 4QLXX Numbers does indeed represent a revision in part influenced by the Hebrew text, but it is not particularly Hebraizing. In fact, Wevers concluded, it is not typically *kaige* or proto-Theodotionic in character, but tends towards a clearer and more exact Greek than that in LXX Numbers.[22] What is striking here is the isolation of a text that shows clear signs of revision from an older (the Old?) Greek towards a Hebrew text that generally corresponds to our MT, but at the same time lacks features that are characteristic of texts identified with *kaige*-Theodotion. A few years later, Walter Bodine located what we might term "parallel activity" in the book of Judges:

> The great majority of the sixth-column readings[23]...representing revision from the OG are unrelated either to the *kaige* characteristics specifically or to the *kaige* text generally.[24]

There is no real reason to limit such revision to any particular book or block of material in the Greek Old Testament. Such findings provide concrete documentation for a phenomenon whose existence should intuitively have been felt by scholars: The fact that some

---

[20] P. W. Skehan, "4QLXXNum: A Pre-Christian Reworking of the Septuagint," *HTR* 70 (1977) 39-40.

[21] P. W. Skehan, "The Qumran Manuscripts and Textual Criticism" in *Volume du Congrès Strasbourg 1956* (VTSup 4; Leiden: Brill, 1957) 148-60, esp. 155-57.

[22] J. W. Wevers, "An Early Revision of the Septuagint of Numbers," *Eretz-Israel* 16 (1982) 235*-239,* esp. 238.*

[23] The "Sixth Column" of Origen's monumental work, the Hexapla, usually contained Theodotion's recension of the Old Greek.

[24] W. R. Bodine, "*Kaige* and Other Recensional Developments in the Greek Text of Judges," *BIOSCS* 13 (1980) 49-50.

(many?) early readers were concerned that their Greek text differed from the Hebrew text then in use, and thus sought to "correct" this Greek on the basis of a Hebrew text like our MT, does not mean that: (a) all revisers were primarily interested in "lapses" in their Greek vis-à-vis the Hebrew; or (b) all Hebrew texts serving as directional points of revision were necessarily moving in the direction of the MT (see below). We have rather been granted a window—only partially opened and probably rather narrow at that—into what was probably a vast array of revising and re-writing in the pre-Christian and early Christian eras.

5.2 4QLXXLeviticus[a]

For Eugene Ulrich, the evidence "suggests that, in contrast to the Göttingen edition which is distilled from the later manuscript tradition, '4QLXXNum, just as 4QLXXLeviticus[a]..., presents the superior witness to the Old Greek translation.'"[25] It is to this Leviticus scroll that we now turn. When investigators first looked carefully at the text of 4QLXXLeviticus[a], they were confronted with seven readings that are not found elsewhere in Greek witnesses to the book "and three others attested by only one or two manuscripts."[26] The Qumran scroll contains five additional, more widely attested variants from the text of Leviticus as established by John Wevers in his Göttingen edition. In Ulrich's judgment:

> None of these variants are errors. All are sensible readings, constituting an alternate text or translation... All the readings in 4QLXXLeviticus[a] can be seen as adequate, free ways of translating the MT or possibly as more literal translations of a slightly variant Hebrew text.[27]

Ulrich observes that Wevers excluded all of these Qumran readings from his text, on the grounds that they are secondary, finding the original wording instead in Greek manuscripts that more closely approximate (if not actually equivalent to) the Masoretic Text.

In our opinion, there is force to Ulrich's arguments in favor of the originality of these Qumran readings as constituting the Old Greek

---

[25] Skehan et al., *Qumrân Cave 4.IV* (DJD 9) 189. Here Ulrich is quoting from an earlier work of his: "The Septuagint Manuscripts from Qumran: a Reappraisal of Their Value," in George J. Brooke and Barnabas Lindars (eds.), *Septuagint, Scrolls and Cognate Writings* (SCS 33; Atlanta: Scholars Press, 1992) 49-80, esp. 76.

[26] Skehan et al., *Qumrân Cave 4.IV* (DJD 9) 163.

[27] Ulrich, "Septuagint Manuscripts," 74-75.

text and as accurate reflections of a Hebrew *Vorlage* at variance with the MT: "It can be argued...that 4QLXXLeviticus[a] penetrates further behind the other witnesses to provide a more authentic witness to the Old Greek translation."[28] Such arguments demand that we take seriously the fidelity of Old Greek translators to their Hebrew text, while not denying some elements of interpretation on their part.

> It is from this perspective—that Greek texts must be evaluated in the light of the possibility that they represent a faithful translation of an ancient Hebrew text at variance with the Masoretic *textus receptus*—that I propose a reassessment of the value of the variants of the LXX MSS from Qumran... One must treat the elasticity of the Hebrew text with caution, to be sure, but one also must not underrate the variation in the Hebrew text abundantly demonstrated by the Qumran MSS and the versions. To underrate it will cause distortion in the understanding of the LXX and the forces behind its translation and transmission.[29]

At the very least, we must allow (in Ulrich's words) for the "stratified" nature of almost all biblical manuscripts, in this instance especially those in Greek:

> It must constantly be borne in mind that all texts are quite stratified—they contain many original readings, a certain number of unique errors, a certain number of errors inherited from parent texts, usually some intentional expansions or clarifications, and often some revisions (whether fresh or inherited) for a variety of purposes. It is perfectly logical, therefore, to maintain that the same text is original in one reading and secondary in the very next reading.[30]

In passing, we may note that the same holds true for manuscripts in the Lucianic (Antiochene) tradition. These manuscripts contain—sometimes right next to each other or at least in close proximity—hexaplaric readings[31] that clearly date to the period after Origen, revisions that are non- and probably pre-Origenic, and uniquely preserved original text.

5.3 Two More Greek Scrolls from Qumran

DJD 9 contains two further Greek manuscripts that may be categorized as "parabiblical": 4QUnidentified gr and pap4QPara Exodus gr. Parsons assigns the former to a date in "the first century BCE or

---

[28] Skehan et al., *Qumrân Cave 4.IV* (DJD 9) 163.
[29] Ulrich, "Septuagint Manuscripts," 65, 69.
[30] Ulrich, "Septuagint Manuscripts," 51.
[31] On "hexaplaric readings," see n.23 above.

possibly the early first century CE";[32] the second also appears to have been "written in the first century BCE or the earlier first century CE."[33] The designation of 4QUnidentified gr as "biblical" in any sense can, of course, be questioned, and the specific connection of the latter with the book of Exodus—although not without some justification—seems to exclude the possibility of a genre (or genres) that makes creative (and/or theological) use of biblical characters and events in settings far removed from the original. Therefore (for example) there is value in Devorah Dimant's suggestion that this papyrus possibly displays, albeit in highly fragmented form, "an apocalyptic work which involves both a review of history in 'the former times' and revelations and moral teaching for the present or future."[34]

6. THE SIGNIFICANCE OF THE GREEK SCROLLS

It is somewhat surprising that relatively little has been written on the implications of these Greek biblical texts for our understanding of the Qumran community and of the wider Palestinian context in which they were found and, presumably, were produced and used. A few preliminary remarks may be in order: (a) Although it might be possible to argue that material from Cave 7 was somehow or other peripheral, the same cannot be said for the texts from the central Cave 4.[35] (b) While Parsons is admirably and correctly tentative in his dating, given the paucity of comparative material, it is clear that even within relatively wide ranges these Greek texts come from the same time period as most of the biblical scrolls and most of the sectarian material (both Hebrew and Aramaic). (c) As observed by Eugene Ulrich and others, there is evidence that these Greek texts were on the whole carefully written, at least sporadically "corrected," and preserved with some care. To be especially noted are Ulrich's comments concerning 4QLXXLeviticus[a], pap4QLXX

---

[32] Parsons, "Greek Biblical Manuscripts," 12.

[33] Parsons, "Greek Biblical Manuscripts," 13.

[34] For Dimant's comment, see Skehan et al., *Qumrân Cave 4.IV* (DJD 9) 224. On the papyrus, see more fully E. Ulrich, "A Greek Paraphrase of Exodus on Papyrus from Qumran Cave 4," in D. Fraenkel et al. (eds.), *Studien zur Septuaginta—Robert Hanhart* (Göttingen: Vandenhoeck and Ruprecht, 1990) 287-98.

[35] 137 of the more than 200 Hebrew biblical manuscripts were unearthed from this cave (cf. J. VanderKam, *Dead Sea Scrolls Today*, 31).

Leviticus[b], and 4QLXXNumbers.[36] All of this leads to the reasonable conclusion that these extant Greek biblical texts were of considerable importance to someone, and bear witness to a much wider activity about whose extent we can only now speculate.

When it comes to more detailed analysis, A. R. C. Leaney has led the way. In the midst of a survey of Jewish literature either written in or translated early into Greek, he reminds us of a point of singular importance in any effort to assess the significance of Greek biblical texts at Qumran:

> Authors...who wrote in Greek either about or from within Judaism were related to "Hellenism" in a great variety of ways. While some entertained a lively interest in Hellenistic ideas, to write in Greek was perfectly consistent with a desire to maintain or reassert the Jewish claim to be unique and inviolable people of God.[37]

With specific reference to Qumran, Leaney adds: "It is hazardous indeed to try to guess their [i.e. Greek-speaking Jews at Qumran] quantity in relation to the rest...and it is better to rest content with the obvious fact that habitual readers of scriptures in Greek were among the members of the sect."[38]

More tendentious—yet no less worthy of consideration—are Leaney's considerations of "some characteristics of these [Dead Sea] Greek manuscripts which may illustrate their strict orthodoxy by their variation from the vocabulary of the main Septuagintal tradition."[39] Although Leaney fails, in our opinion, to give sufficient attention to the possibility of alternate Hebrew *Vorlagen*, he is undoubtedly correct in his main conclusions:

---

[36] On 4QLXXLeviticus[a]: "There are no clear errors on the extant manuscript, though the original scribe corrected a minor lapse..." On pap4QLXXLeviticus[b]: "The scribe made, or copied, very few errors... There is no evidence of corrections or supralinear insertions by the original scribe. But in frg. 20 [line] 7 there is a correction by a later hand..." On 4QLXXNumbers: "The scribe has made or transmitted only two possible scribal errors in the extant fragments...and has made only two (or perhaps three) corrections..." (cf. Skehan et al., *Qumrân Cave 4.IV* [DJD 9] 161, 168 and 188, respectively).

[37] A. R. C. Leaney, "Greek Manuscripts from the Judaean Desert," in J. K. Elliott (ed.), *Studies in New Testament Language and Text* (Leiden: Brill, 1976) 283-300, esp. 289.

[38] Leaney, "Greek Manuscripts," 291.

[39] Leaney, "Greek Manuscripts," 296.

Such evidence—admittedly little enough—which is afforded by the Greek manuscripts from the desert of Judah is consistent with Jewish scribes copying for Jews sensitive to the demands of their own traditions, Jews for whom use of the Greek language did not mean Hellenization in the sense of complacent acceptance of a place for their religion among other world outlooks of the time, but was consistent with a return to the fierce exclusiveness which was the very reason for the existence of the Qumran sect.[40]

We should perhaps add one further, admittedly speculative, comment: It is likely that the Qumran Greek readers (and speakers?) were always a numerical, perhaps even "power" minority, and it is probable that at least some at Qumran were not completely convinced of the validity of transmitting the divine word in a "foreign" language. This raises the possibility that there never were large numbers of Greek biblical manuscripts at Qumran or that—with the exception of Pentateuchal texts—some felt free to dispose of "the Septuagint" in ways that have left few, if any, traces.

More than one specialist in the textual criticism of the Hebrew Bible has remarked that there is more value in a scrap of ancient Hebrew than in dozens of complete manuscripts in Greek or in any of the other Versions. Although there is much to be said for an appropriate emphasis on Hebrew evidence for the Hebrew Bible, exclusive reliance on such data, to the virtual exclusion of the Versions, seems excessive and counterproductive. While admitting that there are all sorts of problems in (for example) determining the Hebrew *Vorlage* for almost any Greek word or phrase, we remain committed both to the validity of responsible retroversion and to the trustworthiness of the results thereby obtained.

7. THE VALIDITY OF RETROVERSION

The second main section of this paper raises these same issues of retroversion and reliability—but in reverse order. No one, of course, questions the value of Greek biblical manuscripts for the study of the Greek Bible. However, when we turn to the potentially far more abundant Hebrew evidence, all sorts of caveats appear, and rightly so. But, as in the case of the Hebrew Bible, awareness of such difficulties should not blind us to the very real possibilities that are uniquely opened by responsible investigation of admittedly complex material.

---

[40] Leaney, "Greek Manuscripts," 298.

Emanuel Tov has written extensively on questions relating to retroversion. To our knowledge, he is the only scholar to have devoted a full-length monograph to this issue in connection with the LXX: *The Text-Critical Use of the Septuagint in Biblical Research*, which was published in 1981 and extensively revised in 1997.[41] Although the Scrolls do not figure as centrally in this study as in the later works of Tov, many of his general insights retain their value when applied specifically to the Qumran material.

For present purposes it is sufficient perhaps simply to list some of the sub-headings in Part 1[42] of Tov's 1981 monograph, which include: "Criteria for retroversion" (Greek-Hebrew equivalents, intuition, textual probability, linguistic plausibility, and external support); "The Reconstruction of Elements not Indicated in the *Vorlage* of the Translators" (vocalization, word-divisions, and sense-divisions); and "Variants, Variants/Non-Variants, and Pseudo-Variants."

It should be clear, even from a cursory examination of these headings, that there is a subjective element in almost all retroversion. Recognition of this element does not invalidate every effort to reconstruct the Hebrew *Vorlage* of the Greek; the application of caution and good sense serves the researcher well in this endeavor as in so many others. Nonetheless, as Tov notes, such efforts have "too often deteriorated into an uncontrolled game."[43] One of the chief goals of his monograph was to provide some criteria or general guidelines for achieving sensible retroversion. It is a credit to Tov that his many reasonable observations have had in general a salutary effect on subsequent work in this field; it is to the discredit of others that they have not applied these observations with sufficient attention or rigor.

At about the same time Tov was working on the above monograph, he participated in a conference on the Hebrew and Greek texts of the book of Samuel. His contribution to that

---

[41] E. Tov, *The Text-Critical Use of the Septuagint in Biblical Research* (JBS 3; Jerusalem: Simor, 1981). The 2nd edition recently appeared as vol. 8 in the JBS series as the present essay was nearing completion; thus the references to Tov's book that follow are to the first edition.

[42] Part 1 is titled: "The Reconstruction of the Hebrew Underlying the LXX: Possibilities and Impossibilities."

[43] Tov, *Text-Critical Use*, 98.

symposium is contained in a chapter titled "Determining the Relationship between the Qumran Scrolls and the LXX: Some Methodological Issues."[44] It is worth reproducing his list of six issues that render "problematical... almost all aspects of comparing the LXX with the Qumran scrolls":[45]

1. The *reconstruction* of the *Vorlage* of the LXX is tentative.
2. Only *fragments* have been preserved of the Qumran scrolls.
3. The hitherto published *statistics* of the relationship between the LXX and the scrolls are *incomplete*.
4. Different *types of readings* common to the LXX and the scrolls must be distinguished.
5. Agreements in readings common to the scrolls, the LXX, *and* additional sources are less persuasive than agreements shared only by the scrolls and the LXX.
6. The generally accepted view of the *relationship* between the scrolls, the LXX and MT, and in particular the use of the term *text-type*, must be revised.

We have already noted some key aspects relating to Tov's first point. Here we should add one additional variable: namely, the degree and type of literalness and/or freedom that a translator exhibits in rendering his Hebrew text into Greek. Only after a modern scholar has thoroughly and convincingly demonstrated the methods by which the ancient Greek translator rendered his Hebrew text (i.e. his "translation technique") can we evaluate the soundness of suggestions in regard to retroversion. And when it is found that the ancient translator handled his *Vorlage* quite freely, only the most tentatively proposed speculation may legitimately be put forward.

Several factors have combined to ameliorate—but not yet eliminate—the problems that Tov highlights in points two and three. Almost all of the relevant biblical scrolls are now in the public domain or are scheduled for publication soon. But, as Tov notes, even the fullest publication of the scrolls will not resolve the difficulty caused by the fact that, with very few exceptions, the extant biblical texts are fragmentary. In terms of the relative (in)completeness of statistic analyses, it is indeed the case that many

---

[44] E. Tov, "Determining the Relationship between the Qumran Scrolls and the LXX: Some Methodological Issues," in idem (ed.), *The Hebrew and Greek Texts of Samuel* (Jerusalem: Academon, 1980) 45-67.

[45] Tov, "Qumran Scrolls and the LXX," 46.

earlier studies highlighted select areas of agreement between (e.g.) a Cave 4 biblical manuscript and the LXX, without giving equal attention to disagreements or even other patterns of agreement. Subsequent studies have tended to be more "evenhanded," thanks in large part to critical remarks by Tov and others.

The same holds true for Tov's fourth and fifth points. Original readings (when these can be confidently determined) that are held in common by two sources—4Q and the LXX, for example—are not nearly as important in text-critical terms as are secondary readings shared by the same two sources. Moreover, not all secondary readings are equally useful in establishing a close connection between two sources: in particular, uniquely shared variants are far more valuable in this case than widely attested ones.

All of these observations concerning the Septuagint come into play when we attempt to determine the relationship between a given Hebrew scroll and a Greek translation of biblical material, and when we assess the work of others in this area. There is one additional factor that Tov has introduced, and it is to this that we now turn.

8. GROUPS OR "TYPES" OF BIBLICAL TEXTS

When, in the late 1940s and early 1950s, the first group of scholars began to analyze the biblical texts that emerged from the caves at Qumran and elsewhere along the shore of the Dead Sea, they typically sought to place each manuscript into a known "text-type": the MT, LXX or Samaritan Pentateuch for the first five books of the Old Testament; and the MT and LXX for the remainder. This tendency to place new finds into familiar categories was not unique to the Scrolls; in fact, it can be documented in fields as far removed as fossil research. In such cases, be it in the sciences or the humanities, the next generation of scholars comes to recognize the fallacy of limiting possibilities to what was previously known rather than allowing the new discoveries to expand the number of "slots" that can be filled. Tov has led the way for Scrolls "revisionists" in arguing that the textual affiliations or relationships manifest among the Dead Sea biblical scrolls defy any easy categorization. In fact, so Tov argues, we should be looking more closely at individual texts rather than seeking necessarily to refurbish existing families or to carve out new ones.

After several decades of close analysis, Tov now distinguishes five groups among which he distributes the Hebrew biblical texts from

Qumran: (1) Texts written in the "Qumran practice," comprising about 20% of the relevant material; (2) The 60% of Qumran biblical texts which may be classified as "Proto-Masoretic"; (3) Pre-Samaritan texts, together with those of the following group, which account for some 5% of Qumran biblical documents; (4) A small group of manuscripts which Tov assigns to the category of "texts close to the presumed Hebrew source of the LXX"; and (5) The remaining 15% which Tov categorizes as "non-aligned."[46]

For present purposes, it is of course the fourth grouping that demands the most attention. It should first be observed how carefully Tov has nuanced his categorization of these texts (e.g. "close to, but not identical"; the "presumed, but not definite Hebrew source"). Each of these nuances is welcomed, as is the nuanced way in which he distributes texts into what might be termed three or four sub-groups within this category: Although no text has been found in Qumran that is identical or almost identical with the presumed Hebrew source of the LXX, a few texts are very close to the LXX: for instance, 4QJer^b and 4QJer^d bear a strong resemblance to the LXX in characteristic details, with regard both to the arrangement of the verses and to their shorter text. Similarly close to the LXX, although not to the same extent, are 4QLev^d and 4QDeut^q. Several agreements with the LXX and with the Lucianic tradition are evidenced in 4QSam^a and agreements with the LXX are also found in 4QDeut$^{c, h, j}$. However, these manuscripts actually belong to Tov's fifth group (the non-aligned texts). Other texts containing a relatively small number of individual readings that are identical with the Hebrew parent of the LXX should not be included in this group.[47]

Even if we disagree with Tov on the placement of one or another text in a given sub-grouping, we cannot but applaud his efforts to depict clearly several degrees of closeness—or (when viewed another way) separation—in texts that had too often been bunched together in previous listings. Before turning to specific Qumran manuscripts, including some that are not mentioned here by Tov, we should consider carefully his arguments against considering these scrolls as a "group" (although he himself actually used the term earlier):

---

[46] E. Tov, *Textual Criticism of the Hebrew Bible* (Minneapolis: Fortress, 1992) 114-16.

[47] Tov, *Textual Criticism*, 115.

They should not be considered a group... They represent individual copies that in the putative stemma of the biblical texts happened to be close to the Hebrew text from which the LXX was translated. Since the *Vorlage* of the OG was a single copy of the biblical text, and not a family, recension, or revision, the recognition of Hebrew scrolls that were close to the *Vorlage* of the OG is of limited importance for our understanding of the textual procedure.[48]

9. RELATIONSHIP OF VARIOUS TEXTS TO THE LXX

Rather than following Tov by moving from Hebrew manuscripts with the strongest to those with the least resemblance to the LXX, we will discuss individual scrolls in their canonical order.[49] We hope that this approach will impress readers as being neutral, thus allowing them more easily to make up their own minds.

James R. Davila calls attention to two interesting readings from the same verse (Gen 1:9) in two different Genesis manuscripts: 4QGen[h], which he dates to 50-25 BCE, and 4QGen[k], which was copied some half a century later (ca. 1-30 CE). The first confirms that the LXX reading συναγωγήν does indeed reflect a *Vorlage* with מקוה (where the MT reads מקום). The second reading likewise points to a Hebrew *Vorlage* for the LXX, but in this case a text that is longer than the MT. In Davila's judgment, the latter case represents the original reading, while the former contains a secondary variant. Both examples of 4QLXX agreement are distinctive to these two witnesses.[50] Unfortunately, the relevant Qumran fragments are tiny, so no one would wish to build any case for textual affiliation on so slight a foundation. But Davila's conclusions lead rather in another direction, serving to confirm earlier remarks by Ulrich that were based on his analysis of Greek texts (Here, of course, Davila begins with texts in Hebrew):

---

[48] Tov, *Textual Criticism*, 116. See also his comments in idem, "The Contribution of the Qumran Scrolls to the Understanding of the LXX," in Brooke and Lindars (eds.), *Septuagint, Scrolls and Cognate Writings*, 11-47, esp. 41-43.

[49] For additional examples and other approaches to some of the material discussed below, note especially the essays collected in Brooke and Lindars (eds.), *Septuagint, Scrolls and Cognate Writings*.

[50] J. R. Davila, "New Qumran Readings for Genesis One," in Harold W. Attridge et al. (eds.), *Of Scribes and Scrolls* (Lanham, MD: University Press of America, 1990) 3-11, esp. 9-11.

The most important general implication of the new Qumran material presented in this study is that we must take the LXX of Genesis very seriously as a source for a Hebrew tradition alternate to the MT. We have strong reason to believe that the translators of Genesis treated their Vorlage with respect and rendered the Hebrew text before them into Greek with great care and minimal interpretation. A judicious use of the LXX, with careful retroversion, gives the textual critic access to many variant Hebrew readings, some of which are original.[51]

Judith Sanderson gave the following title to her *Textus* article of 1988: "The Old Greek of Exodus in the Light of 4QpaleoExod^m."[52] While at first glance this title appears unexceptional, it raises an interesting question when we note, with Sanderson, that 4QpaleoExod^m "is the only manuscript of Exodus found at Qumran that represents the type of text preserved by the Samaritan community."[53] That being the case, what can this scroll tell us about the Old Greek? Quite a bit, at least in the careful analysis presented by Sanderson, who uses the additional data provided by this Cave 4 text, along with the MT and the Samaritan Pentateuch, to answer questions about the nature of the LXX text for Exodus and its affiliation. First, she calculates that the LXX preserves preferable readings in 58% of the variants, and secondary readings in the remaining 42% of cases where preferability can be determined. For Sanderson, these results render the LXX the second best text for those portions of Exodus that are preserved in the scroll. By comparison, the MT is judged the best text and 4QpaleoExod^m as third best, with the Samaritan Exodus trailing with "the largest percentage of secondary readings of the four."[54] As a further refinement, Sanderson uses her data to investigate the commonly-held assessment of OG Exodus as "expansionist." She concludes that while it "deserves its reputation of being expansionist in many places, it also deserves to gain a reputation of being shorter in other places, sometimes uniquely so."[55] Echoing the sentiments of Ulrich and Davila, Sanderson also finds that this OG translator exhibited a high degree of fidelity to his Hebrew *Vorlage*:

---

[51] Davila, "New Qumran Readings," 11.

[52] J. E. Sanderson, "The Old Greek of Exodus in the Light of 4QpaleoExod^m," *Textus* 14 (1988) 87-104.

[53] Sanderson, "Old Greek of Exodus," 88; see also Tov, *Textual Criticism*, 97-100, who places this among his very few pre-Samaritan texts (p. 115).

[54] Sanderson, "Old Greek of Exodus," 97.

[55] Sanderson, "Old Greek of Exodus," 97.

> Careful study of the book of Exodus shows that in general the translator seems to have taken pains to render his Hebrew *Vorlage* with a high degree of precision... [This] faithful translational technique suggests strongly that the differences between the LXX on the one hand and the other witnesses to the book of Exodus on the other hand are to be attributed for the most part not to the translator, but to the Hebrew scribes in the period of transmission of the *Vorlage* of the translation.[56]

Making further use of the combined evidence of these four sources, Sanderson proposes a reconstruction of the early history of the book of Exodus. With respect to the OG of this book, she summarizes her conclusions in the following way:

> The basic agreement among the four witnesses suggests that all go back to a common or at least similar origin. The preferable readings preserved in the LXX and the fact that it is the most unlike the other three suggest that the Hebrew tradition behind the LXX was the first to break off from the traditions behind the others. It then underwent a period of expansionism different from that experienced by 4Qpaleo Exod^m and the Samaritan text, receiving a host of minor expansions, perhaps by a succession of scribes.[57]

A very different relationship between the LXX and a Hebrew biblical scroll from Qumran is revealed when we look at 4QDeut^q. As noted above, Tov placed this manuscript, along with 4QLev^d, in what we might term his second tier of "texts close to the presumed Hebrew source of the LXX."[58] In terms of its contents, "this manuscript, surviving only in a few fragments with text from Deut 32:37-43 and 32:9-10(?), perhaps originally contained only the Song of Moses (Deut 32:1-43)..."[59] In terms of its connection with the LXX (and the Hebrew *Vorlage* of the LXX), Ulrich writes:

> Though not identical to the LXX, 4QDeut^q shares several unique readings with the Septuagint version of Deuteronomy and bears witness to the existence of the variant Hebrew *Vorlage* used by the Septuagint translator, at least for this section of Deuteronomy... 4QDeut^q and the LXX agree in seven readings against the MT, including all of the significant readings..."[60]

---

[56] Sanderson, "Old Greek of Exodus," 98-99.

[57] Sanderson, "Old Greek of Exodus," 103-04.

[58] Tov, *Textual Criticism*, 115.

[59] P. Skehan and E. Ulrich, "4QDeut^q", in Ulrich et al. (eds.), *Qumran Cave 4.IX: Deuteronomy, Joshua, Judges, Kings* (DJD 14; Oxford: Clarendon Press, 1995) 137-42, esp. 137.

[60] Skehan and Ulrich, "4QDeut^q," 138. See also Tov, "Contribution," 29-30.

Among such agreements, we may point to two individual words in Deut 32:43, where 4QDeut^q displays in its text precisely the words we would expect to find in the Hebrew *Vorlage* of the OG: שמים and בניו (MT: גוים and עבדיו). According to Ulrich, it is a "complicated... question whether the longer form of the poem found in 4QDeut^q and the LXX or the shorter form found in the MT is preferable..."[61]

Tov places three other Deuteronomy manuscripts from Cave 4, along with 4QSam^a, in a sort of hybrid sub-category. These exhibit some agreements with the LXX, but "actually belong to group 5 [the non-aligned texts]."[62] As representative of these Deuteronomy texts, we look briefly at 4QDeut^c, which was edited for DJD 14 by Sidnie White Crawford. She dates this manuscript to the period between 150 and 100 BCE,[63] and describes it as:

> the largest Deuteronomy manuscript from Cave 4... It has the greatest amount of text from the most number of chapters, and consists of 55 identifiable fragments, and eleven which have not yet been identified.[64]

With respect to textual affiliations, Crawford writes: "It can be said with assurance that 4QDeut^c is not a manuscript of the Samaritan tradition...but follows the text of the MT and the LXX."[65] Such a characterization places this manuscript in one of Tov's two sub-groupings of non-aligned texts: "Usually the employment of the term *non-aligned* merely implies that the texts under consideration follow an inconsistent pattern of agreements and disagreements with the MT, the Samaritan Pentateuch, and the LXX..."[66] Among its representative agreements with the OG, we may signal: בו כל at 16:8 (which is not found in the MT), לך at 26:19 (likewise absent in the MT), and ו]אמרו[at 27:26 (where MT reads the singular).

10. THE TEXTS OF SAMUEL AND JEREMIAH

We turn now to the two books that have elicited the most extensive discussion with respect to connections between Qumran biblical

---

[61] Skehan and Ulrich, "4QDeut^q," 138.

[62] Tov, *Textual Criticism*, 115.

[63] S. W. Crawford, "4QDeut^g," in E. Ulrich et al. (eds.), *Qumran Cave 4.IX* (DJD 14) 15.

[64] Crawford, "4QDeut^g," 15.

[65] Crawford, "4QDeut^g," 17.

[66] Tov, *Textual Criticism*, 116.

scrolls in Hebrew and the reconstructed Hebrew *Vorlage* of the OG, Samuel and Jeremiah. In a recent formulation of Tov's opinion, as we saw above, these reputedly close connections are of vastly different degrees of validity: "4QJer$^{b, d}$ bear a strong resemblance to the LXX... Several agreements with the LXX and the Lucianic tradition are evidenced in 4QSam^a," but this is actually a non-aligned text (Tov's group 5).[67]

Because of the "mixed" nature of the Greek evidence for Samuel, it was a happy coincidence when scholars uncovered relatively extensive fragments of this book in the early phases of Scrolls research.[68] When Tov reviewed the evidence in the late 1970s, he cautioned against uncritical acceptance of scholarship that insisted on "the Septuagintal character" of the Samuel scrolls:

> The existence of a relatively large number of "LXX readings" in 4QSam^a cannot be denied... However, the explanation of these readings remains a matter of dispute... and they should be put in their proper perspective. In particular, the agreements of the scrolls with the LXX should be balanced off by disagreements between these sources. At the same time, we notice a relatively large number of unique readings in the scrolls. Both factors preclude the assumption of a close connection between the scrolls and the LXX.[69] The practice of caution, as well as its preaching, is surely in order here. At the same time, it should not deter us from determining either that there is a unique relationship between 4QSam^a and the recension identified with Lucian or that the close DSS–LXX relationship denied to Samuel may be found elsewhere.

The "elsewhere" for a close Scrolls–OG relationship is to be located, in the opinion of just about all researchers, in the Jeremiah texts that were referred to above: 4QJer^b and 4QJer^d.[70] Few would dispute Tov's reasonable conclusion that, in terms of distinctive features such as length of the book and arrangement of verses, "it seems very likely that the OG was translated from a Hebrew text which was very close to these two Qumran texts."[71]

---

[67] Tov, *Textual Criticism*, 115.

[68] On this see E. Ulrich, *The Qumran Text of Samuel and Josephus* (HSM 10; Missoula, MT: Scholars Press, 1978).

[69] Tov, "Qumran Scrolls and the LXX," 62. See also idem, "Contribution," 30-33.

[70] See the still valuable J. G. Janzen, *Studies in the Text of Jeremiah* (HSM 6; Cambridge, MA: Harvard University Press, 1973).

[71] Tov, *Textual Criticism*, 320; cf. idem, "Contribution," 28-29.

11. OTHER TYPES OF EVIDENCE

Up to this point, we have discussed or at least referred to the vast majority of Hebrew manuscripts that have been judged relevant to our topic. There are two other types of evidence that merit consideration as well. The first consists of a few interlinear corrections that are said to agree with the LXX; in this case—as should be obvious—the biblical text being corrected stands at some distance from the LXX itself. The second line of argumentation finds evidence of agreement with the LXX in "biblical paraphrases" that have beeen found at Qumran.

In the same DJD volume in which Baillet published the two Greek biblical manuscripts from Cave 7, Milik published some Hebrew scrolls from Cave 5. Among these are several fragments of Deuteronomy, containing verses from chapters 7–9, and now designated 5QDeut. For our purposes, the text itself is not nearly so important as the four interlinear corrections that are witnessed by this manuscript. As described and evaluated by Milik, these corrections are closely reflective of the Hebrew *Vorlage* of the OG for this section of Deuteronomy:

> Au-dessus des lignes figurent quatre additions... Elles témoignent d'une revision du texte, qui paraît très systématique, faite sur un manuscript identique à l'archétype hébreu de la Septante. Trois cas... présentent entièrement les additions de la LXX...[72]

Tov has cast considerable doubt on this analysis, however. His position, which we accept, is as follows: "Supposed correction towards the LXX as suggested by Milik is unlikely... It seems that the corrections in this text only coincidentally agree with the LXX in two or possibly three instances."[73] As in other cases that we have discussed, a negative assessment in a particular circumstance does not rule out positive evidence elsewhere. Thus, it is possible to locate correction toward the LXX in (for example) 4QJos^b.[74] But no one

---

[72] J. T. Milik in Baillet, Milik and de Vaux, *Les "Petites Grottes"* (DJD 3) 179.

[73] E. Tov, "The Textual Base of the Corrections in the Biblical Texts Found at Qumran," in Dimant and Rappaport (eds.), *The Dead Sea Scrolls: Forty Years of Research*, 299-314, esp. 307-08.

[74] On this see L. J. Greenspoon, "The Qumran Fragments of Joshua: Which Puzzle are They Part of and Where Do They Fit?," in Brooke and Lindars (eds.), *Septuagint, Scrolls and Cognate Writings*, 166-67.

would argue, as Milik had for Deut, that such a phenomenon is anything other than sporadic.

Sporadic, but nonetheless interesting, is the evidence from paraphrases collected by Alexander Rofé.[75] He begins by pointing to two examples from the book of Joshua that had been noted earlier:

> I believe to have detected one such instance in Josh. 24:28-33 where the LXX is corroborated by a historical reference contained in the Damascus Document (= CD). Another case in the book of Joshua, in which the LXX to 6:26 is sustained by 4QTestimonia, has recently been highlighted...[76]

Rofé then goes on to "point out four more instances, all in the book of Deuteronomy [19:18; 19:14; 29:18-20; and 17:14-20], in which LXX deviations from the MT are fully confirmed by paraphrases in Qumranic non-biblical texts."[77] Other examples from Joshua and elsewhere may be cited as well.

The force of Rofé's argument does not depend on the relative strength or weakness of individual cases. Rather, he has succeeded in reminding us to cast our nets as widely as possible when seeking to explore in all its ramifications the relationship between the Scrolls and the Septuagint. And with these examples we conclude our discussion.

12. CONCLUSION

Through this article we have attempted to acquaint the interested reader with the variety of material that must be contended with in determining the relationship—or rather, the many different sorts of relationships—that exist between the Dead Sea Scrolls and the Septuagint. It has became clear, we hope, that it is simply insufficient to consult only those scrolls that were written in Greek. Nor can we limit ourselves to materials that we (or its authors) would label as "biblical." Beyond the question of which manuscripts to look at is the thorny, but fascinating, issue of interpretation. We have made a sincere effort to present, as impartially as possible, major points of view. At the same time, where we are partial to one opinion over another, we have not hid this fact from our readers.

---

[75] A. Rofé, Alexander. "Qumran Paraphrases, the Greek Deuteronomy and the Late History of the Biblical נשיא," *Textus* 14 (1988) 163-74.

[76] Rofé, "Qumran Paraphrases," 163.

[77] Rofé, "Qumran Paraphrases," 164, with discussion of examples on the pages that follow.

Finally, we are led to ask a different type of question: What does it all mean? Why does it matter? Let the answer to these queries and the final words of this article be those of Barnabas Lindars, who was an organizer of the International Symposium held at Manchester in 1990. Together with George Brooke, he edited the "Proceedings" volume that appeared shortly after his death. In his Introduction to the volume, Lindars wrote:

> Those who wish to use the Septuagint as a tool in biblical studies need to do so with caution on the basis of good information and study in depth. This must now include a proper appreciation of the information that can be gleaned from the Dead Sea Scrolls. Those who undertake such study will find that the Septuagint presents fascinating and challenging issues, which make it an absorbing field of study in its own right.[78]

SELECT BIBLIOGRAPHY

Baillet, M., J. T. Milik and R. de Vaux. *Les "Petites Grottes" de Qumrân. 1.Textes* (DJD 3: Oxford: Clarendon Press, 1962).

Barthélemy, D. "Un archétype commun au pré-**M**, au **G**, et à 1QpHab?," in R. Gryson (ed.), *Philologia Sacra* (Freiburg: Herder, 1993) 150-77.

—. *Les devanciers d'Aquila. Première publication intégrale du texte des fragments du Dodécaprophéon* (VTSup 10: Leiden: Brill, 1963).

—. "Redécouverte d'un chaînon manquant de l'histoire de la LXX," *RB* 60 (1953) 18-29.

Bodine, W. R. "*Kaige* and Other Recensional Developments in the Greek Text of Judges," *BIOSCS* 13 (1980) 45-57.

Brooke, G. J. and B. Lindars (eds.). *Septuagint, Scrolls and Cognate Writings: Papers Presented to the International Symposium on the Septuagint and Its Relations to the Dead Sea Scrolls and Other Writings [Manchester, 1990]* (SCS 33; Atlanta: Scholars Press, 1992).

Davila, J. R. "New Qumran Readings for Genesis One," in H. W. Attridge et al. (eds.), *Of Scribes and Scrolls* (Lanham, MD: University Press of America, 1990) 3-11.

Dimant, D. and U. Rappaport (eds.). *The Dead Sea Scrolls: Forty Years of Research* (STDJ 10; Leiden: Brill) 315-324.

Dogniez, C. *Bibliography of the Septuagint: 1970-1993* (VTS 60; Leiden: Brill, 1995).

Greenspoon, L. J. "Recensions, Revisions, Rabbinics: Dominique Barthélemy and Early Developments in the Greek Traditions," *Textus* 15 (1990) 153-67.

---

[78] B. Lindars in Brooke and Lindars (eds), *Septuagint, Scrolls and Cognate Writings*, 6-7.

—. "The Use and Abuse of the Term 'LXX' and Related Terminology in Recent Scholarship," *BIOSCS* 20 (1987) 21-29.

—. "The Qumran Fragments of Joshua: Which Puzzle are They Part of and Where Do They Fit?," in Brooke and Lindars (eds.), *Septuagint, Scrolls and Cognate Writings*, 159-94. [see under Brooke and Lindars]

Janzen, J. G. *Studies in the Text of Jeremiah* (HSM 6; Cambridge, MA: Harvard University Press, 1973).

Klein, R. W. *Textual Criticism of the Old Testament: From the Septuagint to Qumran* (Philadelphia: Fortress, 1974).

Leaney, A. R. C. "Greek Manuscripts from the Judaean Desert," in J. K. Elliott (ed.), *Studies in New Testament Language and Text* (Leiden: Brill, 1976) 283-300.

Orlinsky, H. M. "Qumran and the Present State of Old Testament Text Studies: The Septuagint Text," *JBL* 78 (1959) 26-33.

Rofé, A. "Qumran Paraphrases, the Greek Deuteronomy and the Late History of the Biblical נשיא," *Textus* 14 (1988) 163-74.

Sanderson, J. E. "The Old Greek of Exodus in the Light of 4QpaleoExod^m," *Textus* 14 (1988) 87-104.

Skehan, P. W. "4QLXXNum: A Pre-Christian Reworking of the Septuagint," *HTR* 70 (1977) 39-50.

Skehan, P. W., E. Ulrich and J. E. Sanderson. *Qumran Cave 4.IV: Palaeo-Hebrew and Greek Biblical Manuscripts* (DJD 9; Oxford: Clarendon, 1992).

Skehan, P. W. "The Qumran Manuscripts and Textual Criticism," in *Volume du Congrès Strasbourg 1956* (VTSup 4; Leiden: Brill, 1957) 148-160.

Tov, E. "Determining the Relationship between the Qumran Scrolls and the LXX: Some Methodological Issues," in E. Tov (ed.), *The Hebrew and Greek Texts of Samuel* (Jerusalem: Academon, 1980) 45-67.

—. *The Text-Critical Use of the Septuagint in Biblical Research* (JBS 3; Jerusalem: Simor, 1981).

—. "The Contribution of the Qumran Scrolls to the Understanding of the LXX," in Brooke and Lindars (eds.), *Septuagint, Scrolls and Cognate Writings*, 11-47. [see under Brooke and Lindars]

—. "The Textual Base of the Corrections in the Biblical Texts Found at Qumran," in Dimant and Rappaport (eds.), *The Dead Sea Scrolls: Forty Years of Research*, 299-314. [see under Dimant and Rappaport]

—. *Textual Criticism of the Hebrew Bible* (Minneapolis: Fortress, 1992).

—. *The Text-Critical Use of the Septuagint in Biblical Research* (2nd ed., JBS 8; Jerusalem: Simor, 1997).

Tov, E., with the Collaboration of R. A. Kraft. *The Greek Minor Prophets Scroll from Naḥal Ḥever (8ḤevXIIgr): The Seiyâl Collection I* (DJD 8; Oxford: Clarendon Press, 1990).

Ulrich, E. *The Qumran Text of Samuel and Josephus* (HSM 10; Missoula, MT: Scholars Press, 1978).

—. "The Greek Manuscripts of the Pentateuch from Qumrân, Including Newly-Identified Fragments of Deuteronomy (4QLXXDeut)," in A. Pietersma et al. (eds.), *De Septuaginta: Studies in Honour of John William Wevers* (Mississauga, ON: Benben, 1984) 71-82.

—. "A Greek Paraphrase of Exodus on Papyrus from Qumran Cave 4," in D. Fraenkel et al. (eds.), *Studien zur Septuaginta—Robert Hanhart* (Göttingen: Vandenhoeck and Ruprecht, 1990) 287-98.

—. "The Septuagint Manuscripts from Qumran: a Reappraisal of Their Value," in Brooke and Lindars (eds.) *Septuagint, Scrolls and Cognate Writings*, 49-80. [see under Brooke and Lindars]

Ulrich, E. et al. (eds.). *Qumran Cave 4.IX: Deuteronomy, Joshua, Judges, Kings* (DJD 14; Oxford: Clarendon Press, 1995).

VanderKam, J. C. *The Dead Sea Scrolls Today* (Grand Rapids, MI: Eerdmans, 1994).

Van der Kooij, A. "The Old Greek of Isaiah in Relation to the Qumran Texts of Isaiah: Some General Comments," in Brooke and Lindars (eds.), *Septuagint, Scrolls and Cognate Writings*, 195-213. [see under Brooke and Lindars]

Wevers, J. Wm. "An Early Revision of the Septuagint of Numbers," *Eretz-Israel* 16 (1982) 235*-239.*

PENTATEUCHAL INTERPRETATION AT QUMRAN

MOSHE J. BERNSTEIN

The list of documents found at Qumran which, in some sense or other, can be considered to contain interpretation of the Pentateuch includes more than fifty items, some of which exist in more than one copy. Pentateuchal interpretation at Qumran thus presents, unsurprisingly, a far more complex picture than that relating to any other biblical book or group of books. This is due, on the one hand, to the greater significance which the Torah possessed for the authors of the Dead Sea Scrolls compared with the books which we now know as the Prophets and Hagiographa, and to the very scope and generic variety of the material in the Torah, on the other. The ensuing discussion will offer a survey of a variety of Qumran texts which interpret the Pentateuch in different ways, and then present detailed analysis of three significant interpretive texts of different types. Needless to say, not all of the documents which fall under this rubric can be included in this limited approach.

1. WHAT IS "PENTATEUCHAL INTERPRETATION"?

How is "pentateuchal interpretation" to be defined? The focus of this survey is broadly on the works which interpret the books which make up the Pentateuch in the Hebrew Bible, and not on the particular type or technique of exegesis they employ in reading those books. Furthermore, we must recall that ancient biblical interpretation, including that found in the Dead Sea Scrolls, should not be measured by the standards of the modern biblical commentary. The modern commentator's goal is often to elucidate, by "objectively" employing the many tools (linguistic, historical, archaeological and literary) which have been developed over the last couple of centuries, the meaning of the biblical text by discerning what that text might have meant to its original audience. There is frequently an attempt today, even in biblical commentaries which are written from a particular confessional or theological perspective, to separate the detached and unprejudiced perception of the biblical text from comments on what it might mean to members of a particular faith community. As far as we can tell, no such attempt was made by the ancient interpreter; therefore, in order to gain a full picture of biblical interpretation in an ancient context, we must examine, in addition to works which might pass muster as biblical interpretation in the twentieth century, texts which use scripture to convey an ideological, doctrinal or theological message. To survey Qumran interpretation of the Pentateuch properly, we must examine what we, from a stance quite different from that of the ancient interpreters, perceive as eisegesis in addition to the exegesis which is more akin to the interpretation of the modern scholar.

Qumran biblical interpretation, in addition to being unlike modern interpretation by virtue of its obvious tendentiousness, also employs a much broader generic range to express that interpretation. We must therefore cast our net rather widely in order to capture the fullest picture of pentateuchal interpretation at Qumran. The works which we must include in our survey, therefore, must range from some of the so-called Reworked Pentateuch texts (whose rearrangements of biblical pericopes constitute a rudimentary form of biblical commentary) to works which resemble the modern commentary, to works which comment implicitly on the Pentateuch in the course of their presentation of legal or narrative themes from the Pentateuch, and finally, to works which employ pentateuchal material in the course of hortatory or sapiential presentations.[1] The absence of clear-cut generic categories in antiquity and the concomitant blurring of distinction at the borders between apparent genres can lead at times to some ambiguity regarding just which works are scriptural commentaries.

Thus the Genesis Apocryphon, written in Aramaic, and the Temple Scroll, written in Hebrew (to choose one narrative and one

---

[1] The question of the "canon" at Qumran thus also plays a role in our consideration of pentateuchal interpretation. Is it necessary for the Pentateuch to be considered "canonical" before we can speak of it as being the object of interpretation? Therefore, if the so-called "Re-worked Pentateuch" texts are not intended by their authors to be "biblical" documents, then we can assuredly include them in the category of pentateuchal interpretation. If, however, as is held by some scholars, the authors of RP believed that what they were composing was "Scripture," then the status of those texts as pentateuchal interpretation requires further investigation. Some of the works which we shall consider will doubtless remain in "gray areas" from the perspective of canon.

legal example of the rewritten Bible genre), and the so-called Genesis commentaries (4Q252-254) obviously belong in our survey, but what about the book of *Jubilees*? Should we consider it to be a work of biblical interpretation, or does its "near-canonical" status at Qumran exclude it from the category under consideration? And what of Enoch? In the case of that pseudepigraphical book, its connection with the material in the Hebrew Bible is fairly tenuous for most of the work, even though it is clear that a "scriptural" passage underlies its fundamental premise.[2]

The manifestations or forms of biblical commentary at Qumran are quite varied, and the interpretation of the Pentateuch is no exception. Our understanding of the nature of interpretation is, however, affected somewhat by the names which the early editors of the Qumran documents gave to some of the texts of very fragmentary nature, often names which imply greater content or range than they actually exhibit. In addition to full-fledged "rewritten Bible," whose shape resembles that of the Bible itself and whose exegetical or interpretive remarks must occasionally be teased out of the rewritten text, there are shorter pieces belonging to the same genre, but with less range or scope. Also explaining or employing the Pentateuch, at times for interpretive purposes but at times with other goals, are "commentaries," "paraphrases," "admonitions," "exposition," and others. The proliferation of names for these various biblically-oriented works is, in fact, one of the barriers to forming an accurate portrait of Qumran exegesis.

2. PENTATEUCHAL INTERPRETATION IN ANTIQUITY AS UNDERSTOOD BEFORE THE QUMRAN DISCOVERIES

The contribution of the Qumran texts to the history of pentateuchal interpretation in antiquity is difficult be overestimate. Before the discovery of the Qumran scrolls, what we knew of pentateuchal interpretation was limited to such works as Josephus'

---

[2] We shall actually not discuss the Aramaic fragments of *1 Enoch* and related literature because the biblical interpretation in them is minimal compared to the overall scope of the work. For a brief discussion of our theme in conjunction with Enoch, see J. C. VanderKam, "Biblical Interpretation in *1 Enoch* and *Jubilees*," in J. H. Charlesworth and C. A. Evans (eds.), *The Pseudepigrapha and Early Biblical Interpretation* (JSPSup 14; Sheffield: Sheffield Academic Press, 1993) 98-117.

Jewish Antiquities, Philo's allegorical material, early Christian exegesis, rabbinic midrash, and the then rarely-studied *Jubilees* and Pseudo-Philo.[3] The apparent scholarly neglect of the discipline of early Jewish biblical interpretation, the first half of the twentieth century, just before the Qumran discoveries, was thus due in part to the paucity of available material and in part to a failure to recognize that a variety of generic forms which might be subsumed under this rubric, which when integrated, constitute one of the most intellectually vibrant domains of ancient Jewish endeavor. Those two concomitant phenomena prevented the recognition of the major role which biblical interpretation, defined loosely, played in Judaism in its various manifestations during this crucial era. Indeed, the works which constituted the corpus of early Jewish biblical interpretation were scattered over centuries and among languages, and derived from diverse forms of Judaism.

Until recently we lacked any textual material in its original language for many of these works, including such apocryphal and pseudepigraphical texts as Ben Sira, Jubilees and Enoch. The tendency to define or group these texts in arbitrary or artificial collections, such as the Apocrypha (rather than according to literary category) and according to hypothetical source groups (Pharisee, Sadducee or the like), also hindered the emphasis on biblical interpretation as a category in and of itself worthy of investigation. Under the constraints of prevailing historiographical currents, there was little intrinsic interest in the period of the Second Temple except as the ground from which rabbinic Judaism and early Christianity sprang. The early treatments of post-biblical Jewish literature sought therefore merely to bridge the historical gap between Jewish literature of the *Tanakh* and the *Mishnah*, or between the two testaments which compose Christian Scripture. The systematic study of Jewish literature in antiquity, a significant portion of which constitutes early Jewish biblical interpretation, seems not to have piqued academic interest. One of the major effects of Qumran finds, therefore, was to extend and expand scholarly awareness of the scope

---

[3] We omit from our list inner-biblical interpretation, although it, too, did not make a mark on scholarly consciousness until comparatively recent times. See especially, M. Fishbane, *Biblical Interpretation in Ancient Israel* (Oxford: Clarendon Press, 1985).

of texts which interpret Scripture, particularly the Pentateuch, and to awaken inquiry into them as a discipline with intrinsic value.

3. PREVIOUS RESEARCH ON PENTATEUCHAL INTERPRETATION AT QUMRAN

Despite the fact that the Qumran texts have been subject to scholarly scrutiny for a half century now, there is not yet any survey or synthesis of that biblical interpretation at Qumran which is, strictly speaking, pentateuchal. The history of scholarship on biblical interpretation at Qumran focused, in its early years, on the hitherto unattested genre of the *pesharim* and, to a lesser degree, on the interpretation of Scripture which is implied in such sectarian works as CD and 1QS. This was due largely to the failure of the early editors of the Qumran texts to publish the works which contain the best and most diverse examples of works which focus on pentateuchal exegesis. The most notable exception was the publication by Israeli scholars of the five most readable columns of 1QapGen, the so-called "Genesis Apocryphon," in 1956.[4] As scholars recognized its profound significance as one of the earliest interpretive documents of Jewish antiquity, they began immediately to study its relationship to midrashic and targumic literature on the one hand, and to the book of Jubilees and other related literature on the other.[5]

The other major work of pentateuchal interpretation to have been published before the 1980's was, of course, the magisterial edition of the Temple Scroll (11QT) published by Yadin in 1977 in a Hebrew edition and then again in English in 1983. Already in this *editio princeps*, Yadin devoted a good deal of space to the relationship of

---

[4] N. Avigad and Y. Yadin, *A Genesis Apocryphon: A Scroll from the Wilderness of Judaea* (Jerusalem: Magnes Press and Heikhal Ha-Sefer, 1956). The "final" publication may be said to have continued through 1995 with the publication of the readable portions of all of the other columns by a group of scholars headed by Jonas Greenfield and Elisha Qimron, employing photographic and computer imaging techniques which were not available when the scroll was first opened. See J. C. Greenfield and E. Qimron, "The Genesis Apocryphon Col. XII," *Abr-N. Sup* 3 (1992) 70-77 and M. Morgenstern et al., "The Hitherto Unpublished Columns of the Genesis Apocryphon," *Abr-Nah* 33 (1995) 30-52.

[5] The edition of the Apocryphon by J. A. Fitzmyer (*The Genesis Apocryphon of Qumran Cave I: A Commentary* [2nd ed., Rome: Biblical Institute Press, 1971]) remains standard. For bibliography through the time of publication, see pp. 42-46.

the text to its presumed biblical *Vorlage* and began to set out the legal exegetical principles which appeared to be operative in the scroll.[6] But there was still no context for discussion of pentateuchal interpretation at Qumran other than the broader one of pentateuchal interpretation in antiquity, for there was simply not enough Qumran material in public circulation to make the effort worthwhile.

In the 1980's and early 1990's, with the acceleration of the appearance of the still-unpublished documents, many fragmentary documents which involve pentateuchal interpretation came to the attention of scholars. Of considerably greater variety than the texts which had been published in the early days, they include commentaries, paraphrases and admonitions based on the Pentateuch which show the genuine diversity of Qumran pentateuchal interpretive texts. We shall see that some of the exempla of biblical interpretation in the Qumran library derive from the sectarian ideology which characterizes many of the non-biblical scrolls, but also that some of them may be read as more neutral representatives of the practice of biblical exegesis in the late Second Temple era.

4. THE SCOPE OF BIBLICAL INTERPRETATION AT QUMRAN

When we turn to the question of the scope of the works which contain pentateuchal interpretation, we observe that the surviving texts from Qumran do not, with the possible exception of the Reworked Pentateuch, provide us with explication of more than one book of the Pentateuch at a time, and, as a rule, cover only small segments of the books to which they do refer. This fact cannot be attributable merely to the fragmentary remains of the Qumran documents, because in the surviving texts certain passages (such as the Flood and the Akedah) appear to be treated over and over, frequently enough that the fortunes of preservation may not be blamed for the lack of the other material.

4.1 Works Encompassing the Whole Pentateuch

The Reworked Pentateuch (4Q364-367) texts stand on the

---

[6] Y. Yadin, *The Temple Scroll* (3 vols., Jerusalem: Israel Exploration Society-Hebrew University of Jerusalem-Shrine of the Book, 1983). Further significant work on the exegesis of the Temple Scroll has been carried out by J. M. Baumgarten, J. Milgrom and L. H. Schiffman.

unclearly marked border between biblical texts and biblical interpretation.[7] If 4Q364-367 represent a late stage in the development of the biblical text, it is a phase wherein the writer of the text feels "allowed" to rearrange segments of the text for the sake of clarity, to introduce interpretive comments, and even to add new material. The goal of the writer of such a biblical text combines the copying or transmission of the text with its interpretation. If, on the other hand, we assume that the writers of these texts did not intend them to be "Scripture," then we might see in their purported scope which covers the entire Pentateuch, an attempt to "interpret" the entire Pentateuch in this broad rewriting. But the very breadth of the rewriting, coupled with the fact that the amount of interpretation achieved is proportionately small, reduces the significance which we might have expected of such far-ranging "commentaries."

The significance of the Reworked Pentateuch texts may lie in the realm of the history of biblical interpretation, wherein they represent first steps toward the commentary genre, rather than in the actual contents of their interpretation or exegesis, which is in fact comparatively meager. There are several passages which are often alluded to in discussions of the Reworked Pentateuch texts, the additional narrative material in Rebecca's farewell to Jacob in 4Q364 3 ii and the "song of Miriam" in 4Q365 6a ii-c, and the additional legal material in the introduction of the wood and oil festivals in 4Q365 23. If, however, we examine the total remains of these manuscripts, those kinds of substantial additions to the biblical text are the exception rather than the rule.

---

[7] Published by E. Tov and S. White (Crawford) in H. Attridge et al. (eds.), *Qumran Cave 4.VIII: Parabiblical Texts, Part 1* (DJD 13; Oxford: Clarendon Press, 1994) 187-351. There is another text which Tov and White consider to belong to this problematical work, 4Q158, published by J. Allegro, *Qumrân Cave 4.I (4Q158-186)* (DJD 5; Oxford: Clarendon Press, 196) 1-2, under the title "Biblical Paraphrase." I am not convinced that all of the RP manuscripts represent the same text, and am even more certain that 4Q158 belongs to a more exegetical genre than 4Q364-67 and that it furnishes one of the few surviving Qumran exegetical works which focus on Exodus. See the treatment by M. Segal, "Biblical Exegesis in 4Q158: Techniques and Genre," forthcoming in *Textus*, and "4QReworked Pentateuch or 4QPentateuch?", in Lawrence H. Schiffman, Emanuel Tov and James C. VanderKam (eds.), *The Dead Sea Scrolls-Fifty Years After Their Discovery, An International Congress, The Israel Museum, Jerusalem, July 20-25, 1997* (Jerusalem: Israel Exploration Society [forthcoming]).

Much more common are attempts to juxtapose passages which belong together thematically or to harmonize the occurrences of material which is repeated in more than one place in the Pentateuch with each other, an aspect of biblical interpretation which has already been recognized on the textual level from the Samaritan Pentateuch. Thus 4Q365 28 omits the laws of the ordeal of the wife suspected of adultery, of the Nazirite, and the priestly blessing, etc. (Num 5-6), so that the narrative flows smoothly from the appointment of the Levites (Num 4:47) to the setting up of the Tabernacle (Num 7:1). 4Q366 4 i combines two texts about Sukkot, joining the description of the special sacrifices of the day found in Num 29 with the rules for the festival found in Deut 16:13-14. The editors suggest that this combination may have even been followed by the account of Sukkot (Lev 23) and the extra festivals of 4Q365 23, although such a proposal must be considered highly speculative.[8] 4Q364 23a-b i harmonizes the account of Deuteronomy 2:8 with that of Num 20:17-18, adding to Deuteronomy the Numbers account of the exchange between the Israelites and the king of Edom as the Samaritan Pentateuch does by adding Deut 2:2-6 after Num 20:13.[9]

4.2 Works Encompassing Genesis

Jubilees

Having been thus far disappointed in our search for overall pentateuchal interpretation at Qumran, we turn to works which interpret substantial segments of the Pentateuch. Once again, our best representative is a work whose identification as commentary might be questioned, the book of *Jubilees*. Like the Reworked Pentateuch texts, *Jubilees* has an ambiguous status at Qumran. It rewrites Genesis and a bit of Exodus, on the basis of the canonical Pentateuch. At the same time, it seems itself to have had significant status at Qumran, based both on the number of manuscripts which survive and the fact that it is cited in other texts as authoritative.[10] But since

---

[8] Tov and White, in Attridge et al. (eds.), *Qumran Cave 4.VIII* (DJD 13), 341.

[9] See Tov and White, in Attridge et al. (eds.), *Qumran Cave 4.VIII* (DJD 13), 220-21.

[10] See J. C. VanderKam, "The Jubilees Fragments from Qumran Cave 4," in J. Trebolle Barrera and L. Vegas Montaner (eds.), *The Madrid Qumran Congress: Proceedings of the International Congress on the Dead Sea Scrolls, Madrid, 18-21*

the degree of the rewriting in *Jubilees* involves far more substantial issues than that in almost all of the Reworked Pentateuch material, its status as an interpretive text is far less questionable.

Once again the intention of the author may be relevant: was the goal of the author of *Jubilees* to interpret the book of Genesis or to replace it? Parts of *Jubilees* seem to rewrite Genesis for the purpose of clarifying it or of choosing among various understandings of the biblical text, while other, often halakhic, sections are superimposed on the narrative framework of Genesis externally and can in no way be regarded as interpretation of that pentateuchal book.[11] If we focus not on the supplements to Genesis, but on the ways in which *Jubilees* explains the biblical book, we can constructively speak of the later work interpreting the earlier one.[12]

Genesis Apocryphon

There is one other Qumran text which, like *Jubilees*, exhibits a significant amount of breadth as *Jubilees* does in the extent of its coverage of Genesis, and that is, of course, the Genesis Apocryphon (1QapGen). The opening of this work is missing and the scroll breaks off in the middle of a sentence at the end of a sheet at the bottom of column 22. The material in the preserved sections is parallel to that in Genesis 5-15, but there is no way to be certain how much further into Genesis (or beyond) the narrative extended.[13] The

---

March 1991 (2 vols., STDJ 11; Leiden: Brill, 1992) 635-48 and his publication of the texts in Attridge et al. (eds.), *Qumran Cave 4.VIII* (DJD 13), 1-185.

[11] One might consider those passages in *Jubilees* which deal with halakhic material from Exodus-Deuteronomy as interpretation of those texts, and such an approach might offer a profitable path of investigation.

[12] For discussions of biblical interpretation in *Jubilees*, see VanderKam, "Biblical Interpretation in *1 Enoch* and *Jubilees*," 117-25, and, more extensively, J. Endres, *Biblical Interpretation in the Book of Jubilees* (Washington, DC: Catholic Biblical Association, 1987).

[13] M. Morgenstern ("A New Clue to the Length of the Genesis Apocryphon," *JJS* 47 [1996] 345-47) has noted that the surviving sheets containing columns 5-22 are marked with the consecutive letters of the Hebrew alphabet, *pe, qop* and *ṣade*. He inferred that, since *pe* is the seventeenth letter of the Hebrew alphabet there must have been fifteen or sixteen sheets preceding the one on which column 1 is preserved. This would provide for a loss at the beginning of the Apocryphon of more than seventy columns, a length greater than that of any surviving Qumran manuscript. This suggestion, however, has yet to be evaluated thoroughly, and, at

stories of Enoch, Lamech, Noah and Abraham are expanded in this treatment which is generally characterized as another, albeit limited, example of "rewritten Bible." We shall return to the Apocryphon in detail as an example of pentateuchal interpretation later in this essay.

5. INTERPRETIVE WORKS OF NARROW SCOPE

5.1 Works Focusing on Parts of Genesis

The focus on Genesis in *Jubilees* and the Genesis Apocryphon, to the exclusion of almost the whole rest of the Pentateuch, is actually quite characteristic of Qumran biblical interpretation overall. Whatever the reason may be, it is the first book of the Pentateuch which attracts most of the attention of the Qumran interpreters, and, beyond that, it is the first portions of Genesis which attract most of that attention.[14] If we examine the fullest range of Qumran texts which interpret or refer to incidents from Genesis, it will become clear that the authors of the texts found at Qumran are interested primarily in the antediluvian period and the patriarchal period through Abraham, particularly through the *Akedah*. The few stories about Isaac in the Pentateuch, and the much larger Jacob and Joseph cycles seem to have made much less of an impact upon them, at least in terms of the literary remains which we possess. We shall see this most clearly as we survey the more narrowly focused remains of Qumran biblical interpretation.

There is a group of fragmentary texts labeled "pseudo-Jubilees" (4Q225-227) which seem to focus on Genesis.[15] 4Q225 retells portions of Genesis, in a fashion similar to *Jubilees*, but unlike *Jubilees*, it is selective, skipping large amounts of the narrative. But by doing so, the author presents us with juxtapositions which are significant. Thus in 4Q225 2 i God's promise to Abraham regarding his descendants (Gen 15) and the birth of Isaac (Gen 21) are juxtaposed, and are followed immediately by the story of the *Akedah* (Gen 22),

---

present, must be considered unproven.

[14] For a more detailed preliminary analysis of the texts discussed in this section, see M. J. Bernstein "Contours of Genesis Interpretation at Qumran: Contents, Context and Nomenclature" in J. L. Kugel (ed.), *Midrash Before the Rabbis* (Cambridge, MA: Harvard University Press [in press]).

[15] This text was published by J. C. VanderKam in H. Attridge et al. (eds.), *Qumran Cave 4.VIII* (DJD 13), 171-75.

all within a space of five lines. The *Akedah* story, on the other hand, is considerably elaborated with "Prince Mastemah" (שר המשטמה), a malevolent angelic figure known already from *Jubilees*, apparently acting as the stimulus for Abraham's test. As Isaac lies bound on the altar, the holy angels weep and the angels of M[astemah?] rejoice in the hope that Abraham will fail. When he passes the test, the text stresses the faithfulness of Abraham. This theme and a brief list of the succeeding generations, Isaac, Jacob and Levi, appear in both 4Q225 and 4Q226, although it cannot be shown that the two of them represent the same work. References to "jubilees of years," to Enoch, and to "the Watchers" in 4Q227 would seem to indicate an interest in calendar/chronology and in the antediluvian period, both of which are to be expected at Qumran, but we have no sense of context for this material. The surviving fragments of these texts exhibit very limited scope, and direct us to anticipate exegetical texts of less than grand scale.

The same can be said of the so-called Genesis Commentaries (4Q252-254a),[16] and we shall devote a fuller discussion to 4Q252 later. Although there is no verse from Genesis explicitly quoted in 4Q253, we find references to "the ark" and possibly to Noah, perhaps involving Noah's sacrificing after the flood.[17] 4Q254 cites Gen 9:24-25 which also appears in 4Q252, and seems to cite and interpret parts of Jacob's blessing from Gen 49, a section which also is found in 4Q252, although there is no overlap between the manuscripts. Some of the other material in this manuscript seems unrelated to Genesis, referring to the "two sons of oil" of Zech 4:14, and the work does not lend itself easily to generic classification. 4Q254a (formerly part of 4Q254) is identified as an independent document by G. Brooke, and also contains references to the ark and the story of the flood.

---

[16] Published by G. J. Brooke as "4Q Commentaries on Genesis A-D," in G. Brooke et al. (eds.), *Qumran Cave 4.XVII: Parabiblical Texts, Part 3* (DJD 22; Oxford: Clarendon Press, 1996) 185-236.

[17] For the a broad discussion of the various treatments of Noah and the flood story at Qumran, see M. J. Bernstein, "Noah and the Flood at Qumran," in E. Ulrich and D. Parry (eds.), *The Provo International Conference on the Dead Sea Scrolls: New Texts, Reformulated Issues and Technological Innovations* (STDJ 30; Leiden: Brill [in press]).

Even more limited in scope, but also focusing on the flood story, are 4Q370 ("An Admonition Based on the Flood"), and 4Q422 ("4QParaphrase of Genesis and Exodus").[18] 4Q370 summarizes the deluge, focusing on the flood generation as ingrates who have not appreciated God's gifts. The flood and God's subsequent promise not to bring another one are described very briefly. There are no references to the Watchers, to the ark or to Noah, as the story is told very compactly with a focus on disobedience and punishment. 4Q422 also summarizes the story in very brief compass, with no room for the chronology of the flood which we shall see in 4Q252, and there may not even have been room to describe the building of the ark within the fragmentary remains. Like 4Q370, 4Q422 seems to employ the material from Genesis in a hortatory fashion, relating God's deliverance of Noah and the subsequent covenant. In both works, God's actions seem to be the focus of the author's attention.

Two other texts deserve brief remarks before we leave Genesis: 4Q464 and 4Q180-181.[19] The former is an extremely fragmentary document which is distinguished by having a scope beyond that of most of the Genesis texts we are discussing. It has fragments dealing with Noah and Abraham, further demonstrating the interests of this literature in the flood and in the *Akedah*, but it also lists a series of events in the Jacob narrative, and seems to have references to Joseph as well. It is the patriarchs, and not Noah and his predecessors, who occupy the lion's share of the fragments, and we appear to have here a work of somewhat broader scope than we might have expected on the basis of the evidence we have examined.

4Q180 is a more clearly sectarian commentary than the others we have seen, employing characteristic "Qumran terminology" such as

---

[18] Published by C. A. Newsom in M. Broshi et al. (eds.), *Qumran Cave 4.XIV: Parabiblical Texts, Part 2* (DJD 19; Oxford: Clarendon Press, 1995) 85-97 and T. Elgvin, in Attridge et al. (eds.), *Qumran Cave 4.VIII* (DJD 13), 417-28, respectively. The first column of 4Q422 deals with the Genesis story of creation and man's disobedience, a theme which is also found in at Qumran a non-commentary, non-narrative text, 4QDibreHammeʾorot (4Q504 8+9 1-22).

[19] Published by M. E. Stone and E. Eshel, "An Exposition on the Patriarchs," in Broshi et al. (eds.), *Qumran Cave 4.XIV* (DJD 19) 215-30, and by J. Allegro with the first named "Ages of Creation" and the second untitled, in *Qumrân Cave 4.I* (DJD 5) 77-80, respectively. On the latter text, see D. Dimant, "The 'Pesher on the Periods' (4Q180) and 4Q181," *Israel Oriental Studies* 9 (1979) 77-102.

פשר ("interpretation"), סרך ("rule"), and קץ ("period"). Its purpose seems to be to utilize the book of Genesis in a sectarian fashion, not to retell or interpret it. There seems to be a strong chronological interest in the fragments, which do not take the biblical story down past the *Akedah*, two features which no longer surprise us. Furthermore, interspersed within this material which appears to be narrative is a large number of theological expansions, typical of Qumran in both language and content. This is the type of work which is liable to frustrate any attempt to analyze it thoroughly absent the discovery of further fragments.

5.2 Works Focusing on the Pentateuch Outside of Genesis

There is little Qumran biblical interpretation which deals with the pentateuchal narrative outside of Genesis. The stories of Exodus and the desert wanderings of the Israelites do not play a significant role in the Qumran scrolls, just as they do not in other Jewish writings of the Second Temple period. Beyond the Exodus segment of 4Q422 (Genesis-Exodus Paraphrase) we do not find exegetical or interpretive works belonging to the narrative segments of the biblical books from Exodus to Deuteronomy.[20] This text is the third column of the work discussed above whose first two columns dealt with creation and man's sin, and Noah and the flood. The Exodus column contains references to the midwives of Exodus 1 and children being thrown into the Nile. There follows immediately an allusion to Moses and a poetic listing of nine of the ten plagues, basically following the order of Exodus, but apparently omitting boils and moving darkness to the sixth position like Psalm 105. There is no way to know how the text continued after the list of plagues. The known contents of 4Q422 make it very difficult to categorize since the principles of its selectivity are completely unknown. What holds together the stories of creation, the flood and the exodus? There is a good deal of textual material in these columns which indicate an attempt to interpret the biblical text, but the selectivity of the text reveals that goal of the composition must be seen as more than that and a wisdom context for 4Q422 has been very plausibly suggested.

There are other fragmentary works which touch on the period

---

[20] Published by E. Tov, in Attridge et al. (eds.), *Qumran Cave 4.VIII* (DJD 13), 429-34.

between the exodus and the conquest, such as 4Q374, which seems to allude to Pharaoh and the entry into the land, whose context and function, however, are inaccessible, and some of the so-called Moses Apocrypha (4Q375-76) which seem to be pseudepigraphic legal, rather than narrative, texts.[21] Other texts not yet officially published, such as 4Q368 (Apocryphal Pentateuch) and 4Q377 (Apocryphal Moses) contain rewritten biblical narrative as well as other, perhaps supplementary, material which appears not to be legal in nature.[22] These texts will demand further study when they all appear in print.

6. PENTATEUCHAL LEGAL EXEGESIS

Most of the surviving biblical interpretation associated with Exodus-Deuteronomy is concerned with legal issues. In many legal texts the understanding reflected of biblical laws is clearly rooted in the way in which the Qumran author read Scripture. But outside of the Temple Scroll whose organization and contents are related to those of the Pentateuch, it is much more difficult than in the case of the interpretation of narrative to determine whether any particular aspect of biblical law attracted Qumran interpretation.

The most substantial example of legal pentateuchal interpretation at Qumran, and, indeed the longest extant scroll surviving in the caves, is 11QT (Temple Scroll). On the one hand, it clearly belongs to the broad genre "rewritten Bible," although it differs from virtually all other examples of the type by being almost exclusively legal. Thus *Jubilees*, pseudo-Philo's *Liber Antiquitatum Biblicarum*, and the Genesis Apocryphon are fundamentally narratives, while the Reworked Pentateuch texts from Qumran and Josephus *Jewish Antiquities* 1-11 are combinations of both legal and narrative

---

[21] 4Q374 was published by C. A. Newsom (pp. 99-110), and 4Q375-76 by J. Strugnell (pp. 111-36) in Broshi et al., *Qumran Cave 4.XIV* (DJD 19).

[22] For preliminary publication of these texts, see B. Z. Wacholder and M. G. Abegg (eds.), *A Preliminary Edition of the Dead Sea Scrolls. The Hebrew and Aramaic Texts from Cave Four: Fascicle Three*, based on a reconstruction of the original transcriptions of J. T. Milik and J. Strugnell (Washington, DC: Biblical Archaeology Society, 1995) 135-39 and 164-66, respectively. Other apparent Moses "apocrypha," such as 1Q22 "Dires de Moïse," and 2Q22 "un apocryphe de Moïse (?)" will need to be taken into consideration in drawing a full portrait of this material.

material.[23] Modeled on the Bible in its style and composition, and with large sections, which in the Pentateuch are spoken by Moses, placed in the mouth of God as speaker, the Temple Scroll interprets the laws of the Pentateuch as it paraphrases, rewrites, and rearranges them. Because it covers a far fuller range of legal matters than any other Qumran text, its content and methodology will be discussed in greater detail below.

4QMiqṣat Maʿaśe ha-Torah (4Q394-399), the so-called "Halakhic Letter," is not as thoroughly scripturally based as is the Temple Scroll. Its listing of halakhot, with few scriptural citations as support for them, is not what we might have expected from the bibliocentric Qumran milieu. Nevertheless, MMT is employing Scripture, but in a rather different way from other Qumran legal material.[24] The author of MMT is heavily influenced by scriptural vocabulary and employs biblical language in composing his work, both in the legal Section B and the hortatory Section C, as defined by the editors. Thus C 31-32, "it shall be reckoned for you as righteousness (צדקה) when you do that which is upright and good before Him, so that it be good for you and for Israel," is based on a combination of Deut 6:18, "you shall do that which is upright and good in the eyes of the LORD so that it be good for you," the only passage in the Hebrew Bible which shares with 4QMMT the word order "upright and good," and either Gen 15:6 "he believed in the Lord and He reckoned it for him as righteousness," or Ps 106:31 "it was reckoned for him as righteousness."

---

[23] The legal material in *Jubilees* and the Apocryphon is completely subservient to the narrative from a literary perspective, as a comparison between those works and the Reworked Pentateuch or Josephus will demonstrate.

[24] Immediately upon the publication of 4QMMT in E. Qimron and J. Strugnell (eds.), *Qumran Cave 4.V: Miqṣat Maʿaśe Ha-Torah* (DJD 10; Oxford: Clarendon Press, 1995), two complementary articles appeared on this theme: M. J. Bernstein, "The Employment and Interpretation of Scripture in 4QMMT: Preliminary Observations," in J. Kampen and M. J. Bernstein (eds.), *Reading 4QMMT: New Perspectives on Qumran Law and History* (SBL Symposium Series 2; Atlanta: Scholars Press, 1996) 29-51, and G. J. Brooke, "The Explicit Presentation of Scripture in 4QMMT," in M. J. Bernstein, F. García Martínez and J. Kampen (eds.), *Legal Texts and Legal Issues: Second Meeting of the IOQS, Cambridge 1995. Published in Honor of Joseph M. Baumgarten* (STDJ 23; Leiden: Brill, 1997) 67-88.

Whenever MMT uses scriptural formulation in composing a law, we might characterize it as implicit interpretation of the Pentateuch. Even though there is no citation formula and the verse is not actually quoted, the modeling of the law on the scriptural original is sufficient to indicate the relationship between them.[25] Thus when MMT writes "regarding the planting of fruit trees, that which is planted in the land of Israel belongs like firstfruits to the priests; and the tithe of cattle and sheep belongs to the priests" (B 62-64), it is clear that these laws are based on Lev 19:23-24 and 27:32, respectively, where the biblical text says these gifts are "sanctified to the Lord," and the Qumran exegesis assigns such sancta to the priests. In a few cases, scriptural references are introduced by the word כותב ("written"), which in Qumran as well as in rabbinic literature usually introduces a citation. What is striking is that in MMT this is not always followed by a direct citation, and Qimron actually asserts that "In MMT it never introduces biblical verses."[26] I have argued that it can introduce either citations or paraphrases of the biblical text, while Brooke suggests more subtly that the word "is nearly always associated with scripture explicitly or in summary form."[27] What we have in 4QMMT is a very flexible way of referring to the biblical text as supporting the list of laws which are at the center of this document.

In the final section of MMT as well, where the language on the whole appears to become more biblical than in the legal section, we find phraseology based on passages in the book of Deuteronomy integrated into the exhortation.[28] The references to the misfortunes predicted for the "end of days" are taking place (or have taken place) in contemporary times. Both the language and the tone of the final section, wherein the author of the "letter" encourages his addressee to repent and to follow the author's interpretation of the laws, rely heavily on deuteronomic theology with its prediction of Israel's

---

[25] This is very different from the rewriting of biblical laws in the Temple Scroll where, despite the editorial changes, the text still reads like Scripture; in these instances of MMT it does not.

[26] Qimron and Strugnell, *Qumran Cave 4.V* (DJD 10), 40-41.

[27] Bernstein, "4QMMT," 39; Brooke, "4QMMT," 71.

[28] Brooke ("4QMMT") 84, notes correctly that, by contrast, Section B is dominated by Leviticus and Numbers.

ultimate repentance after it has acknowledged the error of its ways.

The Damascus Document or Zadokite Fragment (CD) interprets and employs pentateuchal passages in both of its hypothetical divisions, the Admonition and the Law.[29] Opposition to divorce (4:21-5:2) is grounded in two narrative passages, "male and female he created them" (Gen 1:27), and "they went into the ark two by two" (Gen 7:9), coupled with the interpretation of Deut 17:17 "he shall not multiply wives for himself," as meaning that *even* the king may not take many wives. The laws of consanguinity operate for both males and females, so that uncle-niece marriage is to be prohibited on the same grounds as aunt-nephew marriage (Lev 18:13; CD 5:7-10). These passages occur not in the "Laws," but in the "Admonition." In the "Laws," some of the newly-published material furnishes interesting examples of pentateuchal exegesis. The prohibition against defrauding (Lev 25:14) is interpreted to mean that the seller must disclose defects in his wares to the buyer (4Q271 3 4-6), and the failure to disclose the faults in a prospective bride to the potential groom (*ibid.* 7-10) is characterized as "leading the blind astray from the road" (Deut 27:18).

Laws of reproof are presented as interpretation of Lev 19:17-18 (CD 9:2-8), and the Sabbath code—while not pentateuchally based in its details—is framed by citations of Deut 5:12, "observe the Sabbath day to make it holy," and Lev 23:38 "apart from your Sabbaths." The laws of repayment or restitution (CD 9:13-16) are modeled on biblical formulations, even though we do not see direct quotation. While the laws of CD are not presented like those of 4QMMT or those of 11QTemple, each with its unique relationship to the

---

[29] Since the publication by J. M. Baumgarten of the Cave 4 texts (*Qumran Cave 4.XIII: The Damascus Document [4Q266-273]* [DJD 18; Oxford: Clarendon Press, 1996]), it has become less easy to dismember this document into its alleged components. It is therefore perhaps unfortunate that J. G. Campbell (*The Use of Scripture in the Damascus Document 1-8, 19-20* [BZAW 228; Berlin, New York: De Gruyter, 1995]) chose to treat only the Admonition material in his comprehensive study. One of the ways in which we will be able to ascertain the degree of coherence between Laws and Admonition is by comparing the scriptural interpretation in the two parts. The present survey focuses on the legal exegesis of CD, although the famous "well-metaphor" of CD 6:3-10 (based on Numb 21:18 and the "messianic" interpretation of Num 24:17, the star out of Jacob) in CD 7:19-21 must at least be mentioned in passing.

Pentateuch, we can observe enough connections between some of the laws and the biblical text to realize that the ultimate framework for the legal code is pentateuchal.

7. THREE TYPES OF INTERPRETIVE TEXTS: A DETAILED ANALYSIS

7.1 Genesis Apocryphon: A Rewritten Biblical Narrative

The Genesis Apocryphon rewrites the book of Genesis from chapters 5 to 15, from the birth of Noah through the beginning of Abram's vision after his defeat of the four kings. Within those boundaries, we find various modes of rewriting the Bible, ranging from an at times fairly close translation of the Hebrew into Aramaic, a virtual *targum*, to the supplementation of the biblical text with new data based on a real or perceived exegetical demand, to the introduction of completely new material, without any overt reason for its introduction. It should be noted that much of the time we can underline or bracket the biblical material around which the author of the Apocryphon has built his narrative, in the case of the Abram story even more than in the Noah section. The Hebrew original of parts of both dialogue and narrative is visible in Aramaic garb. Even when the expansion is substantial, as in the detailed extrabiblical description of Abram's traversing the land, we find biblical virtual quotations.

It has recently become apparent that the Apocryphon is very likely not a work composed as a whole *ab initio*, but consists of parts, probably deriving from other, pre-existing works. Thus, at the end of column 5, following the recently deciphered words, "the book of the words of Noah," the narrative shifts from a story about Noah, where the first person narrative was spoken by his father Lamech, to a first person narrative by Noah. Later on in the Noah section, there are portions in which a narrator tells the story about Noah in the third person, and the Abraham section contains both first and third person narration about him. Many scholars have pointed to these markers as evidence for the composite nature of the Apocryphon.[30]

The Genesis Apocryphon is one of the classic examples which helped provoked the delineation of the genre "rewritten Bible."

---

[30] See in particular R. C. Steiner, "The Heading of the *Book of the Words of Noah* on a Fragment of the Genesis Apocryphon," *DSD* 2 (1995) 66-71.

While following the biblical story, it supplements the narrative with such details as (apparently) the remarkable appearance of Noah at birth which causes alarm to his father Lamech who believes that his wife Batenosh has been unfaithful to him with one of the Watchers, those wayward angels who populate so much of Second Temple Jewish literature.[31] When Batenosh protests her innocence, Lamech sets off to find out from his father Methuselah and, ultimately, his grandfather Enoch, what the nature of this unusual child is to be. The narrative contained in column 2 and its fragmentary successors tells a tale which is found elsewhere in the literature of this era (*1 Enoch* and other fragmentary Qumran texts such as 1Q19), but for which there is no overt stimulus in the biblical text. It belongs to the type of traditional or free compositions which are introduced into the biblical narrative to flesh out or enliven the story. According to our loose definition, however, it falls into the category of biblical interpretation.

Columns 10-12 apparently expand the biblical narrative of Noah's activity after the flood (Gen 8:4, 20–9:20) with surviving references to Noah's atoning for the earth with his sacrifice, and to his later fulfilling the biblical injunction against drinking wine from a vineyard during the first four years of its production. God's words to him "do not fear, Noah; I am with you and your children," (11:15) are reminiscent of God's words to Abram (Gen 15:1), "do not fear Abram, for I am your shield" whose translation in the Apocryphon begins with the words, "do not fear; I am with you." Likewise, the passage as a whole, describing Noah walking "on the earth through its length and breadth" (11:11) is also reminiscent of God's command to Abram (Gen 13:17) to "arise and walk in the land, through its length and its breadth," which the Apocryphon renders, "arise, walk, go, and see how great its length and how great its breadth" (21:13-14). The employment of phrases from the Abram story in the Noah material probably points to a kind of association between the biblical figures in the mind of the interpreter, with Noah depicted as a more significant link in patriarchal tradition than he is held to be in later Judaism.

The Apocryphon's parallel to the biblical story of Noah breaks off

---

[31] For the possibility of relating the Noah material in the Apocryphon to the other texts referring to Noah at Qumran, see Bernstein, "Noah and the Flood."

in column 12, and we cannot know how, for example, it handled the incident of Noah's drunkenness. The following columns (13-15) contain unparalleled extrabiblical accounts of Noah's visions and their interpretations. Their content is unlikely to be directly related to the biblical interpretation of the text. When the narrative returns to the biblical account, columns 16-17 describe the division of the earth among Noah's sons, narrating this in greater detail than the Pentateuch, and in parallel to the presentation *Jubilees* 8-9. The geographical interests of the Apocryphon can be observed here as well as in the detailed itinerary of Abram's trip through the land in column 21.

Since column 18 does not survive, we do not possess the transition between the Noah and Abram sections of the scroll, and the Abram material begins with him and Sarai traveling south (12:9) prior to their entry into Egypt to escape the famine in Canaan.[32] The tale is told by Abram in the first person, and we immediately see the exegetical artistry of the author at work. We read of a dream which Abram had wherein there were a palm tree and a cedar tree, and the cedar tree was going to be cut down, but was saved by the intercession of the palm tree. Relating the dream to Sarai, he realizes that this is an omen signaling how they must deal with their impending visit to Egypt, and Abram then asks Sarai to identify him as her brother so that he may live (19:14-20). It is quite evident that the insertion of this extrabiblical incident into the narrative is not merely decorative, but is employed to resolve a difficulty in the text which we might describe as theological. The text of Genesis does not explain why Abram suggested the deception to Sarai upon entry to Egypt. Surely the patriarch would not lie with no cause, and the Apocryphon furnishes the reason for his actions. The dream, it appears, also functions to suggest to Abram the nature of the plan, with its focus on the relationship between the cedar (Abram) and the palm (Sarai).

It is not only the introduction to the story which is expanded by

---

[32] We should have liked to know whether there was a marker which delineated the shift from the Noah source to the beginning of the Abraham one, like the words כתב מלי נוח ("the book of the words of Noah") at the end of column 5, or whether there was no explicit indication of demarcation between them as in the move from the first person Abraham story to the third person account in column 21.

the Apocryphon; the whole episode, which in the Bible is included in the eleven verses of Gen 12:10-20, covers a column and a half from 19:14 to 20:32 in the Qumran version. The terse dialogue of Genesis is developed at length in the Apocryphon which also elaborates its retelling of the biblical narrative with additional details which do not necessarily respond to difficulties in the biblical text. There is an elaborate, detailed and explicit description of Sarai's beauty, probably an expansion of "the nobles of Pharaoh saw her, and praised her to Pharaoh" (Gen 12:15). This, too, is typical of the style of rewritten Bible. Abram's prayer in response to Sarai's abduction (20:10-16), while not a response to a specific textual stimulus, is likewise an appropriate extrabiblical insertion by the author of the Apocryphon.

The final extant portion of the Apocryphon relates the story of the wars of the four and five kings of Genesis 14. Here it is likely that another source begins to be used by the author of the Apocryphon, as Abram no longer narrates the story in the first person (21:23ff). In this section, as well, we find the narrative more closely bound to the biblical original, as the passages which are translations of the biblical text increase in number and density. But we find examples of exegesis in the rewriting here too. Genesis 14:1-3, "In the days of Amraphel king of Shinar...they warred against Bera, king of Sodom....They all came together to the valley of Siddim which is the Dead Sea" is background to the ensuing narrative and does not describe a war prior to the rebellion of Gen 14:5. For the author of the Apocryphon, however, those verses are not introductory, but describe events earlier in history. He inserts the words "Before those days" at the beginning of the sentence, treating the Hebrew עשו מלחמה, "they made war" as a pluperfect, "they had made war," thus making the opening verses not redundant as they speak, in this reading, about a conflict prior to the one described in the rest of chapter 14. This sort of reading maximizes the information which can be teased out of the biblical text, and is quite characteristic of the ancient reader. The tithe which Abram gives to Melchizedek is not "of everything" (Gen 14:20), but of all the property of the king of Elam and his allies (22:17).

One of the ways in which a work of rewritten Bible accomplishes its interpretation of the biblical text is through various types of rearrangement of material, and the Genesis Apocryphon is no exception.[33] The birth of Noah's grandchildren is described in quotations or paraphrases from Gen 10:1b, 11:10, 10:22, and 10:6, but is located in the Apocryphon's equivalent of Genesis 9, while Gen 9:18-19 are omitted. The goal appears to be the telling of the biblical story without the parenthetical introduction of Canaan as Ham's son and with a smoother introduction to the family celebration of the fruits of the vineyard of which we read in 12:13-19. When Abram leaves Egypt, he takes with him, in addition to great wealth, Hagar (20:32); her introduction to the narrative at this point is obviously intended to explain her presence later on (in the lost section of the manuscript) as Sarai's "Egyptian maidservant." A slight deviation from the biblical narrative in the description of the defeat of the kings of Sodom and Gomorrah has only the king of Gomorrah falling into the pit while the king of Sodom fled (21:32-33) rather than both of them suffering the same indignity. This change seems to be made in order to explain how later in the narrative (Gen 14;17; Genesis Apocryphon 22:12) the king of Sodom alone comes out to meet Abraham.

Related to rearrangement as a technique is harmonization, and there are two sorts which we find at work in the Apocryphon. One simply involves the employment in one biblical story of language which echoes another, often unconsciously, without regard for content. In the Apocryphon's retelling of the story of Abram and Sarai in Egypt, language like "he was unable to approach her" (20:17), and "tell the king to send his wife away from him to her husband, so that he may pray over him and live" (20:23) utilizes expressions which, in the Bible, are not found in Genesis 12 where the story of Sarai and Pharaoh is told, but in Genesis 20 (verses 4 and 7, respectively), where the story of Sarah and Abimelech is narrated. One wife-sister story furnishes, probably on an unconscious level, vocabulary for the other in the method of the Apocryphon.

The other type of harmonization which the Apocryphon exhibits is a well-known exegetical feature of texts such as the Samaritan Pentateuch and the reworked Pentateuch texts from Qumran, the

---

[33] For discussion beyond the examples cited here, see M. J. Bernstein, "Rearrangement, Anticipation and Harmonization as Exegetical Features in the Genesis Apocryphon," *DSD* 3 (1996) 37-57.

retrojection to a location early in the narrative passages of which, appearing later in the biblical text, allude to a statement or incident which occurred earlier but which appear to have been omitted from the earlier part of the story.[34] The Apocryphon, in an unparalleled treatment, has Abram address Sarai with the words "this be the whole kindness which you shall do with me, wherever we are, say regarding me that 'he is my brother'" (19:19-20). Gen 20:13 records that Abraham tells Abimelech that he had said to Sarah at the time of their initial wanderings "wherever we arrive, say that he is my brother." Although the biblical text does not indicate where Abram made this request, the Apocryphon, in order to confirm the truth of Abraham's words later, inserts them here at the appropriate passage.

7.2 Genesis Commentary A—Selective Interpretation

A very different kind of interpretive document is 4Q252, the first and best-preserved of the "Genesis Commentaries."[35] Fragments of six columns (perhaps all it ever contained) survive, with virtually all of column 1 and substantial portions of column 2 remaining. But the contents of even the far less well-preserved segments of columns 3-6 can be detected, and what is obvious is that this text represents some sort of "commentary" which offers remarks, comments or syntheses on a variety of unconnected passages in Genesis. Not all of the comments are of the same literary nature, with some resembling "rewritten Bible," others apparently composed of biblical lemma plus explanatory addition, and still others consisting of interpretive

---

[34] There are many examples of such treatment in the Samaritan Pentateuch; see Bernstein, "Re-arrangement," 52-54 and E. Tov, *Textual Criticism of the Hebrew Bible* (Minneapolis: Fortress, 1992) 86-88. Both the Samaritan Pentateuch and Reworked Pentateuch (4Q364 4b-e ii 21-26) insert an account of the dream in which an angel speaks with Jacob prior to the incident where he tells his wives about that dream (Gen 31:10).

[35] The interpretive nature of 4Q252 was the subject of a productive debate between George J. Brooke and myself. See his articles, "The Genre of 4Q252: From Poetry to Pesher," *DSD* 1 (1994) 160-79; and "The Thematic Content of 4Q252," *JQR* 85 (1994-95) 33-59, and "4Q252 as Early Jewish Commentary," *RevQ* 17 (1996) [J. T. Milik Festschrift], 385-401. Contrast my treatments, "4Q252: From Re-Written Bible to Biblical Commentary," *JJS* 45 (1994) 1-27; and "4Q252: Method and Context, Genre and Sources. A Response to George J. Brooke," *JQR* 85 (1994-95) 61-79.

comment alone. What is very striking about this commentary is that only parts can be said to owe their existence to tendentious or ideological rationales, and that it seems to represent both one of the earliest examples of selective biblical commentary from antiquity and at the same time the earliest attempt to resolve exegetical dilemmas in the biblical text other than through the means of full-scale "rewritten bible."[36]

The scope of 4Q252 is Genesis from chapter 6 to chapter 49, but it is discontinuous; we observe material deriving from Genesis 6, 7, 8, 9, 11, 15, 16?, 18, 22, 28, 35, and 49. Even granting the scanty remains of the columns after 2, it is clear that one of most striking features of the document on the whole is its selectivity. This must exclude it from being "rewritten Bible" in any ordinary fashion. In our ensuing discussion, we shall focus on the parts of 4Q252 which can be reconstructed with the greatest confidence, but shall point out certain difficulties in our overall approach which arise from the apparent contents of some of the more damaged segments.

Although almost the whole first column and part of the second deal, in painstaking detail, with the chronology of the biblical flood story, the opening lines of 4Q252 focus on what appears to be a less significant chronological issue, the identification of the 120 years of Gen 6:3, "his days shall be one hundred and twenty years."[37] Locating the divine statement in the 480th year of Noah's life, the commentary interprets "their days shall be fixed at one hundred twenty years until the time of the waters of the flood" (4Q252 1-2 i 2-3). This reading of the verse is unexceptional and is shared by a variety of other early Jewish exegetical sources, despite the fact that it implies the lack of strict chronological sequence in the biblical text, since in Gen 5:32 Noah has already been described as five hundred years old. The other reading attested for this verse in antiquity, that the life-span of humankind will be limited to one

---

[36] The formulation of this argument is dependent largely on my articles referred to in the previous note, although I should be inclined to modify some of my position in light of Brooke's remarks in the Milik Festschrift.

[37] G. J. Brooke has argued cogently, on the basis of physical evidence that the first column, despite seeming to begin mid-sentence, was indeed the first of the scroll ("4QCommentary on Genesis A," in G. Brooke et al. [eds.], *Qumran Cave 4. XVII* [DJD 22] 186-87).

hundred twenty years in the future, is not accepted by this interpreter, despite the fact that it poses no internal chronological problem within the biblical text.

The detailed chronology of the flood which 4Q252 presents in 1-2 i 3 through 1+3 ii 5 is meant to delineate the specific days of the week and month on which the events described in the biblical flood narrative took place. The basic presentation describes virtually nothing except the chronology; it is the only aspect of the story in which the author seems to be interested. The destruction of all living things on the face of the earth seems to him of much less significance than the implicit observation that no event in the narrative took place on the sabbath and that Noah's stay in the ark was a perfect 364-day year (1+3 ii 3). Granted the calendrical interests of the Qumran group and their concerns, like that of *Jubilees*, for the observance of biblical law by even pre-Sinaitic figures, we can read this longest individual segment of 4Q252 as an attempt to explicate the biblical text in a straightforward sense, on the one hand, while stressing certain Qumranic values, on the other.[38]

There is one other chronological passage in 4Q252 at the end of column 2 where, if my reconstruction is correct, our document dates Abram's leaving Ur Kasdim with his father Terah to Abram's seventieth year, with his departure to Canaan taking place five years later and Terah's death sixty years after Abram had left Haran. The author of 4Q252 stresses the non-sequential nature of the biblical narrative by highlighting it and by explaining to the reader how to follow the sequence of events in the Bible. The way this is done is by rewriting the text in a clearer fashion. But the same rewriting also may be intended to resolve a more global pentateuchal chronological crux, by allowing us to calculate the 430 years of Israelite servitude in Egypt (Exod 12:40-41), counting from Abraham's leaving his home in Ur Kasdim, to be the same as the 400 years predicted to Abraham in Gen 15:13. The biblical text does not record any events in Abraham's life in his seventieth year, so this Genesis commentary

---

[38] The calendaric portion of 4Q252 has received probably more discussion than the rest of the text because of the importance which calendar played at Qumran in so many other ways. But the authors of the texts found at Qumran were certainly capable of treating the Noah material as something more than a calendar. See Bernstein, "Noah and the Flood at Qumran."

comes to the rescue with its creative chronology.[39]

It is not only chronology, however, which interests 4Q252. At 1+3 ii 4-6 it responds to the fairly obvious question of why Noah cursed Canaan, Ham's son, rather than Ham who had been the one to offend him. The answer furnished, in this case employing the lemma + comment form, is that God has blessed Noah's sons and therefore Noah could not curse Ham.[40] The text continues with what I take to be a comment on Gen 9:25, "and may he dwell in the tents of Shem" making the subject of the verb God who will dwell in "the land which He gave to Abraham His friend." Once again the ambiguity of the biblical original, where the verb could refer either to God or to Japheth, has been clarified.[41]

The nature of 4Q252 as a document whose stance is apart from that of the Hebrew Bible (i.e. that it cannot be considered "rewritten Bible") is perhaps confirmed by the opening words of column 3, "as it is written," a common Qumran idiom employed to introduce biblical citations within interpretive documents. Unfortunately, it is impossible to reconstruct what follows as all that survives of the column are the first and last word or two on each line. Finally, beginning in column 4 line 3, 4Q252 concludes with a section headed with the words "Blessings of Jacob." The only substantial extant material comes from the blessings of Reuben in column 4 and of

---

[39] For a more detailed discussion of the arithmetic in this section, see Bernstein, "From Re-written Bible to Biblical Commentary," 12-14 and nn. 41-45.

[40] The same question and answer are to be found in Genesis Rabbah 36:7 in the name of Rabbi Judah (2nd century CE).

[41] I have presented the interpretation of 4Q252 as a primarily exegetical document to this point according to my analysis in the articles referred to above. Brooke ("4Q252 as Early Jewish Commentary," 387) has argued that this approach does not focus sufficiently on that which might hold the disparate comments on the passages in Genesis together, and that it "underplays both whether the exegetical answers presented in the text may have some characteristic distinctiveness and whether there might be some overall purpose in the work beyond that of the clarification of exegetical difficulties." He further observes correctly (pg. 388) that my approach omits the treatment of as significant a story as the Aqedah (Gen 22) in 4Q252. Both of these criticisms are well-taken. I chose to describe and analyze those portions of 4Q252 which presented consecutive text, and it is possible that, were we to possess more of the fragmentary portions, my conclusions would need to be modified and extended.

Judah in column 5. The former, although it employs the characteristic Qumran exegetical term פשרו ("its interpretation"), seems merely to link the derogatory remarks directed at Reuben by his father to the incident with Bilhah in Gen 35:22. The exegesis is in no way unusual or characteristically Qumranic. The latter, on the other hand, interprets Gen 49:10 with "a ruler shall not depart from the tribe of Judah while Israel has dominion, and one shall not be cut off from sitting on David's throne." The מחקק of the biblical verse is "the covenant of the kingdom, and the [thou]sands of Israel are the 'standards'[42] until the arrival of the righteous messiah, scion of David for to him and his seed was given the covenant of the kingdom of his people for eternal generations." The following fragmentary line contains a familiar idiom, אנשי היחד, "the men of the community." Here we recognize ourselves as being in a thoroughly Qumranic milieu; the exegesis is eschatological and messianic, and the terminology is recognizable as shared by other interpretive documents among the scrolls.

7.3 11QTemple—A Different Kind of Rewritten Bible

The Temple Scroll is a very unusual form of rewritten Bible. This single scroll, defective at the beginning, which seems to have been compiled from a variety of sources and virtually all of whose content is legal. Beginning with the Sinaitic covenant in Exodus 34, it moves to the construction of the tabernacle in Exodus 35, and proceeds through many of the laws of the Torah. Certain laws correspond quite literally with laws in the Pentateuch, some are modifications and revisions of pentateuchal material, while yet others are free compositions of the author or a non-pentateuchal source. The status intended by the author of this text, whether as a "new" book of the Bible or as a non-biblical but authoritative lawbook, has been debated by scholars. For our purpose, however, we are not concerned with the status of the scroll in the mind of its author, whether as biblical text or biblical commentary, for in either case it reflects interpretations of what we recognize as the Hebrew Bible, particularly the book of Deuteronomy. By transposing many of the elements

---

[42] Brooke et al. (eds.), *Qumran Cave 4.XVII* (DJD 22), 205, writes that "from computer enhanced images, the *dalet* is certain," and the word must be read as a form of דגל as in the Samaritan Pentateuch, not רגל as in MT and probably LXX.

of Deuteronomy from commandments delivered by Moses to commandments delivered by God, the Temple Scroll asserts that much more of the Pentateuch derives directly from God than the Pentateuch itself does.

Because the Temple Scroll is such an extensive work, this survey of its interpretive method will focus on the first section of the part of the scroll often referred to as the "Deuteronomic Paraphrase" (columns 51:11-56:21).[43] We shall examine the compositional and exegetical techniques through which the pentateuchal original has been arranged and revised in order to produce the new legal text. In this section, as is frequent in the scroll, references to God in the third person are altered to the first person.

Deut 16:18-17:1 contains the command to appoint judges by tribes, followed by the prohibitions against perversion of justice, showing favoritism and taking bribes. The scroll adds to the biblical material a further reason against bribery which "causes great guilt and defiles the house with the sin of iniquity," but then adds to the end of passage (51:16-18) a death penalty for accepting bribes, "and the man who takes a bribe and perverts righteous justice shall be put to death, and you shall not fear him (ולא תגורו ממנו) to put him to death." This seemingly unscriptural penalty is based, according to Y. Yadin, on the author's exegesis of Deut 1:17 "you shall not show favoritism in judgment, but listen to small and great alike; you shall not fear any man (לא תגורו מפני איש), for judgment is God's." That verse also deals with the laws of fair justice, and is implied here according to the method of the scroll which gathers material dealing with the same topic into one place. Since in its only other pentateuchal occurrence (Deut 18:22) [ו]לא תגור is coupled with the death penalty for the false prophet, the exegetical approach of the scroll infers that the language implies the death penalty for accepting bribes as well.[44] This kind of linking of passages based on shared language resembles the rabbinic hermeneutic principle of *gezerah shavah*.

Where the biblical text continues in Deut 16:21-22 with a prohibition against planting sacred trees near the altar and setting up

---

[43] Cf. L. H. Schiffman, "The Deuteronomic Paraphrase of the *Temple Scroll*," *RevQ* 15 (1992) 543-67; and M. O. Wise, *A Critical Study of the Temple Scroll from Qumran Cave 11* (SAOC 49; Chicago: Oriental Institute, 1990).

[44] Yadin, *Temple Scroll*, 2.229.

sacred pillars, the scroll takes the opportunity to merge into one place those prohibitions, as well as the laws of Lev 26:1 against setting up figured stones to bow down upon. The formulation is "you may not do in your land that which the nations do," followed by a list of their practices, and then a series of prohibitions against carrying out those practices. Vermes characterizes this as "grouping and collating parallel texts."[45]

The single biblical verse Deut 17:1, prohibiting the sacrifice of blemished animals because it is an abomination, becomes in the scroll the springboard for a series of laws about slaughtering, including the prohibitions against the sacrifice of pregnant animals, against slaughtering mother and young on the same day, and against "smiting the mother with the children" (52:3-7).[46] The first prohibition is not explicitly scriptural, but derives from an interpretation of scriptural passages. The animal's pregnant state presumably makes it "blemished," and, furthermore, there is a prohibition against slaughtering mother and child on the same day (Lev 22:28), a law which presumably would be violated by the killing of a pregnant animal and its fetus. Finally, there is a prohibition against taking a mother bird with its fledglings (Deut 22:6), which the author of the scroll modifies (under the influence of Gen 32:12) to a prohibition against smiting the mother with the children. The thematic juxtaposition of these laws creates a rationale for the one amongst them which is not found in the biblical text.

The subject of animal slaughter becomes the focus of the scroll's attention for the rest of column 52 and a good deal of column 53. The laws about the slaughtering of first-born animals (Deut 15:19-23) are introduced, following the biblical text fairly closely, but adding, after the equivalent of the end of the final verse "you shall pour it out [the blood] like water," the words "and cover it with dust" which derive from Lev 17:13. Vermes calls this kind of incorporation of details from one law into another a "harmonizing

---

[45] G. Vermes, "Bible Interpretation at Qumran," *Eretz Israel* 20 (1989) 185*.

[46] On the series of laws regarding slaughtering animals in this and the following column, see L. H. Schiffman, "Sacral and Non-Sacral Slaughter According to the Temple Scroll," in D. Dimant and L. H. Schiffman (eds.), *Time to Prepare the Way in the Wilderness: Papers on the Qumran Scrolls by Fellows of the Institute for Advanced Studies of the Hebrew University, Jerusalem, 1989-1990* (STDJ 10; Leiden: Brill, 1995) 69-84, to which some of the ensuing discussion is indebted.

expansion."[47] Such terminology appears to be literary rather than legal and does not emphasize the fact that the author of the law in the scroll seems to create a kind of *gezerah shavah* between texts which use the term "pour out the blood," and to apply the details of one passage to the next as a result.

The Pentateuch contains a variety of passages about the permissibility or prohibition of animal slaughter, some of which appear to be mutually exclusive. One of the goals of the author of the Temple Scroll was to harmonize and reconcile such difficulties. The grouping of laws regarding slaughter proceeds to a rule prohibiting slaughter of pure animals within three days of the Temple, a rule which combines elements and language from Deut 17:1 ("You shall not slaughter to the Lord your God"), from Lev 17:3 ("ox or sheep or goat"), as well as from Deut 12:5-7 which stresses the requirement to sacrifice at a central location. Schiffman points out that the juxtapositions indicate "a halakhic midrash according to which the author (or his source) determined that Deut 12:5-7 deals with the prohibition of Leviticus 17, that of non-sacral slaughter."[48] The Temple Scroll proceeds to create out of these and other passages a system which prohibited non-sacral slaughter within a three-day distance of the Temple, which permitted the slaughter of blemished animals outside thirty stadia from it, and the prohibition against eating within Jerusalem any flesh which was not slaughtered in the Temple. All of these laws reflect a specific legal understanding of the various passages on slaughter within the Pentateuch, as well as the interpretations of specific words and phrases which are based on other pentateuchal laws that do not pertain to animal slaughter.[49]

Finally, it is worth observing a broader compositional principle at work a little bit later in this section of the Temple Scroll. The passage at the beginning of column 53 is modeled on the laws of slaughter in Deut 12:20-25. The next verse in Deuteronomy proceeds to the commandment to bring holy things and vowed offerings "to the place which the Lord has chosen." The Temple Scroll concludes

---

[47] G. Vermes, "Bible Interpretation," 186*.

[48] Schiffman, "Slaughter," 76.

[49] This brief summary can only hint at the complexity of the creative exegesis and composition of the scroll in this section. For a much more complete treatment, see Schiffman, "Slaughter."

its rewriting of that verse with "You shall slaughter there before me as you have dedicated or vowed with your mouth," a rewriting of Deut 23:24 ("as you have vowed to the Lord your God an offering which you have spoken with your mouth"). This prepares a transition to the subject of vows, beginning with Deut 23:22-24 which is rewritten in 11QT 53:11-14. At that point, the author proceeds to the lengthy pericope on the laws of vows in Numbers 30:3ff.

Having completed the section on vows, the author of the scroll (54:5-7) returns to Deut 13:1, indicating again that the framework of his composition in this passage was Deut 12. The laws of the idolatrous prophet, the enticer to idolatry and idolatrous city follow (54:8-55:14), and then the case of the individual idolater (55:15-21), bringing the composition back to Deut 17:2ff., the point from which the collections of laws on animal slaughter were initiated. We thus see how the principle of collecting laws on like themes together with the maintenance of a framework based on the biblical original combine to assist the composer of the Temple Scroll in creating a coherent structure for the work.

SELECT BIBLIOGRAPHY

Bernstein, M. J. "Contours of Genesis Interpretation at Qumran: Contents, Context and Nomenclature" in J. L. Kugel (ed.), *Midrash Before the Rabbis* (Cambridge, MA: Harvard University Press [in press]).

—. "4Q252: From Re-Written Bible to Biblical Commentary," *JJS* 45 (1994) 1-27.

—. "4Q252: Method and Context, Genre and Sources. A Response to George J. Brooke," *JQR* 85 (1994-95) 61-79.

—. "The Employment and Interpretation of Scripture in 4QMMT: Preliminary Observations," in J. Kampen and M. J. Bernstein (eds.), *Reading 4QMMT: New Perspectives on Qumran Law and History* (SBL Symposium Series 2; Atlanta: Scholars, 1996) 29-51.

—. "Noah and the Flood at Qumran," in E. Ulrich and D. Parry (eds.), *The Provo International Conference on the Dead Sea Scrolls: New Texts, Reformulated Issues and Technological Innovations* (STDJ 30; Leiden: Brill [in press]).

—. "Re-arrangement, Anticipation and Harmonization as Exegetical Features in the Genesis Apocryphon," *DSD* 3 (1996) 37-57.

Brin, G. "Concerning Some Uses of the Bible in the Temple Scroll," *RevQ* 12 (1987) 519-28.

Brooke, G. J. "The Genre of 4Q252: From Poetry to Pesher," *DSD* 1 (1994) 160-79

—. "The Thematic Content of 4Q252," *JQR* 85 (1994-95) 33-59

—. "4Q252 as Early Jewish Commentary," *RevQ* 17 (1996) [J. T. Milik Festschrift], 385-401.

—. "The Explicit Presentation of Scripture in 4QMMT," in M. J. Bernstein, F. García Martínez and J. Kampen (eds.), *Legal Texts and Legal Issues: Second Meeting of the IOQS, Cambridge 1995. Published in Honor of Joseph M. Baumgarten* (STDJ 23; Leiden: Brill, 1997) 67-88.

Campbell, J. G. *The Use of Scripture in the Damascus Document 1-8, 19-20* (BZAW 228; Berlin, New York: De Gruyter, 1995).

Eshel, E. "Hermeneutical Approaches to Genesis in the Dead Sea Scrolls," in J. Frishman and L. Van Rompay (eds.), *The Book of Genesis in Jewish and Oriental Christian Interpretation: A Collection of Essays* (Traditio Exegetica Graeca 5; Leuven: Peeters, 1997) 1-12.

Fishbane, M. "Use, Authority and Interpretation of Mikra at Qumran," in M. J. Mulder (ed.), *Mikra: Text, Translation, Reading, and Interpretation of the Hebrew Bible in Ancient Judaism and Early Christianity* (CRINT 2.1; Assen: Van Gorcum; Minneapolis: Fortress, 1990) 339-77

Fitzmyer, J. A. *The Genesis Apocryphon of Qumran Cave I: A Commentary* (2nd ed., Rome: Biblical Institute Press, 1971).

Greenfield, J. C. and E. Qimron. "The Genesis Apocryphon Col. XII," *Abr-N. Sup* 3 (1992) 70-77.

Milgrom, J. "The Qumran Cult: Its Exegetical Principles," in G. J. Brooke (ed.), *Temple Scroll Studies* (JSPSup 7; Sheffield: JSOT Press, 1989) 165-80.

—. "The Scriptural Foundations and Deviations in the Laws of Purity of the Temple Scroll," in L. H. Schiffman (ed.), *Archaeology and History in the Dead Sea Scrolls* (Sheffield: JSOT Press, 1990) 83-99.

M. Morgenstern et al. "The Hitherto Unpublished Columns of the Genesis Apocryphon," *Abr-Nahrain* 33 (1995) 30-52.

Schiffman, L. H. "The Deuteronomic Paraphrase of the *Temple Scroll*," *RevQ* 15 (1992) 543-67

Segal, M. "Biblical Exegesis in 4Q158: Techniques and Genre," *Textus* (1998 [forthcoming]).

Slomovic, E. "Toward an Understanding of the Exegesis in the Dead Sea Scrolls," *RevQ* 7 (1969-71) 3-15.

Swanson, D. D. *The Temple Scroll and the Bible: The Methodology of 11QT* (STDJ 14; Leiden: Brill, 1995).

Tov, E. "Biblical Texts as Reworked in Some Qumran Manuscripts with Special Attention to 4QRP and 4QParaGen-Exod," in E. Ulrich and J. VanderKam (eds.), *Community of the Renewed Covenant: The Notre Dame Symposium on the Dead Sea Scrolls* (CJA 10; Notre Dame: University of Notre Dame Press, 1994) 111-34.

Vermes, G. "Bible Interpretation at Qumran," *Eretz Israel* 20 (1989) 184*-91*.

—. "Biblical Proof-texts in Qumran Literature," *JSS* 34 (1989) 493-508.

BIBLICAL LAW AT QUMRAN

HANNAH K. HARRINGTON

An area of growing importance in Dead Sea Scrolls research is that of law—in particular, law that is derived from or is in some way linked to the biblical text. Later rabbinic sages called this *halakhah* and considered it binding on all Israel. Since biblical law was considered the divine blueprint for behavior, the study of it has been at the center of Jewish scholarship throughout history. While there is often room in the academy for differences of opinion, some points of law, especially those centering around the Temple and its cultic calendar, created schisms among Jews which were irreconcilable. Thus the study of law in the sectarian Dead Sea Scrolls is critical to the identification of the religious background of the authors vis-à-vis other Jewish systems in the Second Temple period.[1] This essay will (1) survey the research that has been done on the subject over the last several decades; (2) examine the contents of several legal documents from Qumran; and (3) offer some conclusions and explore the directions in which this branch of Dead Sea Scrolls scholarship is now turning.

1. HISTORY OF RESEARCH

Research on biblical law in the Scrolls has led to various interpretations regarding the religious identity of their authors. When Solomon Schechter first discovered the Damascus Document in a Cairo genizah in 1910, he thought he had uncovered an ancient Zadokite sect related to the Karaites.[2] He also noted that the laws of these 7th century "Zadokites" were very similar to the ones found in the genizah, e.g. prohibition of marriage to nieces, certain divorce laws and a unique sectarian calendar. Adolf Büchler, however, did

---

[1] Here the term "sectarian" refers to those works found at Qumran which were authored by Jews who had separated themselves to a large degree, both theologically and physically, from the current priestly establishment in Jerusalem.

[2] S. Schechter, *Fragments of a Zadokite Work* (Documents of Jewish Sectaries 1; Cambridge: Cambridge University Press, 1910 [repr. New York: Ktav, 1970]).

not accept the presumed antiquity of the original Damascus Document but identified the author as a medieval Karaite. In 1922, Louis Ginzberg reviewed Schechter's findings; emphasizing the consonance between this document and Pharisaic (rather than Zadokite) law, he explained away the dissonant views as later interpolations.[3]

With the discovery in 1947 of the Dead Sea Scrolls, whose antiquity could not be disputed, Schechter's early view that the document originated from a Jewish sect during the time of the Second Temple was vindicated. Saul Lieberman focused on the stages of purity that are required for initiation into the sect according to the Community Rule; comparing them with the purity laws of the *haberim*,[4] he concluded that the underlying concerns were very similar. Lieberman also noticed that certain views that are ascribed by the Sages of the Mishnah to heterodoxy are the very views adopted in some of the Scrolls, and ascribed to the Essenes by Josephus. Most notable among these is the blessing over the sun, the use of "El" as opposed to the Tetragrammaton when swearing, and the excessive filtering of wine and vinegar for purity reasons. Nevertheless, Chaim Rabin followed on from Lieberman's work only to reach the same conclusion set forth earlier by Ginzberg: that the sect was a branch of the Pharisees, or "hyper-Pharisees," if you will.[5]

On the other hand, there was an expectation among some scholars that the sectarians would turn out to be a proto-Christian group since they subscribed to many of the beliefs found in the New Testament.[6]

---

[3] L. Ginzberg, *An Unknown Jewish Sect* (Moreshet 1; New York: Ktav, 1976 (based on his privately published volume *Eine unbekannte Jüdische Sekte* [New York, 1922]).

[4] S. Lieberman, "Light on the Cave Scrolls from Rabbinic Sources," *PAAJR* 20 (1951) 395-404; idem, "The Discipline in the So-called Dead Sea Manual of Discipline," *JBL* 71 (1952) 199-206. For an analysis of the stages of purity at Qumran in comparison with those of the *haberim*, see also J. Licht, מגילת הסרכים [*The Rule Scroll—A Scroll from the Wilderness of Judaea—1QS, 1Sa, 1QSb: Text, Introduction and Commentary*] (Jerusalem: Bialik Institute, 1965).

[5] C. Rabin, *Qumran Studies* (London: Oxford University Press, 1957).

[6] Y. Sussman, "The History of the Halakha and the Dead Sea Scrolls: Preliminary Talmudic Observations on *Miqṣat Maʿaśe ha-Torah* (4QMMT)," Appendix 1 in E. Qimron and J. Strugnell, *Qumran Cave 4.V: Miqṣat Maʿaśe Ha-Torah* (DJD 10; Oxford: Clarendon Press, 1994) 179-200, esp. 184 (originally published as חקר תולדות ההלכה ומגילות מדבר יהודה: הרהורים תלמודיים ראשונים לאור "מגילת "מקצת מעשי התורה, *Tarbiz* 59 [1989-90] 11-76).

Such "spiritual" ideas as the community's self-consciousness constituting a holy Temple that obviated the need for animal sacrifices, immersion as part of the atonement process, God's mercy versus human degeneracy, and an apocalyptic messianism seemed to place the sectarians at the other end of the spectrum from the "legalistic" orientation of the Pharisees.

In the wake of the discovery of the Temple Scroll and its publication by Yigael Yadin in 1977,[7] as well as the more recent publication of 4QMMT (*Miqṣat Maʿaśe ha-Torah* or "Some Precepts of the Torah"),[8] attention again turned to the legal material in the Scrolls. These texts provide clear evidence that the sectarians were not apocalypticists who had spiritualized Jewish law, but that the Temple and its cult were at the heart of their belief system. Their secession from the priestly estabishment was due to its alleged corruption, a situation the sect believed would soon be reversed by the Messiah. Both the Temple Scroll and MMT espouse a sectarian cultic system which was even stricter than that of their opponents. In fact, MMT pleads with its addressees not to relax the standards of purity which should be kept in the sanctuary and in Jerusalem. Since the laws of the Temple Scroll and MMT are very similar in type, construction and concerns to the laws of the early Rabbis, the expertise of rabbinic scholars was enlisted to provide a clearer undertanding of these texts. It was increasingly obvious that the sectarian authors could not be identified with a Christian sect.

It soon became apparent that the laws which are set forth in the Temple Scroll, MMT and other recently transcribed scrolls exhibit a certain consistent stance which the Mishnah ascribes to the Sadducees.[9] While several scholars have discussed this Sadducean slant

---

[7] Y. Yadin, *Megillat ha-Miqdash* (3 vols.; Jerusalem: Israel Exploration Society, 1977).

[8] Qimron and Strugnell, *Qumran Cave 4.V* (DJD 10).

[9] Three of the foremost "Sadducean" laws are: (a) The insistence that a person is not pure until after sunset on the day of purification. According to several Qumran texts, and contrary to the Mishnah, only those who have immersed from impurity and upon whom the sun has set are pure even for non-sacral activities (for full discussion of this rule, cf. L. H. Schiffman, "Pharisaic and Sadducean Halakhah in Light of the Dead Sea Scrolls. The Case of Tevul Yom," *DSD* 1 [1994] 285-99). (b) The law that an impure water stream can convey impurity upwards to the container from which it was poured. (c) Bones, hides and nails of unclean animals are just as defiling as their flesh.

of many of the laws, Lawrence Schiffman has gone one step further by concluding that the sectarians, at least in the beginning of the Hasmonean period, were an early group of pious Sadducees.[10]

The Sadducean identification is being challenged, nevertheless, due to the parallels between the Qumran texts and the description of the Essenes by Josephus, Philo and Pliny. Joseph Baumgarten has insisted that even from a legal point of view there are several unique links between the Qumran texts and the first century descriptions of the Essenes which cannot be ignored.[11] Todd Beall has noted 27 points of agreement between the Qumran texts and Josephus' Essenes, together with another 21 probable parallels.[12] Apparently, the sectarians shared points of agreement with both the Sadducees of the Mishnah as well as with the Essenes described by Josephus, Pliny and Philo.

Most recently, scholars have again focused on legal material found in the Scrolls because of the publication of many heretofore unknown fragments of the Damascus Document. Almost all of this new material sets forth interpretations of biblical law, many of which were already known from other Qumran texts. These fragments increase the length of the document considerably and reveal that some two thirds of the original text was on issues of Jewish law. In addition, many fragments of other works that were found in Cave 4 contain important exegetical material.

2. EXAMINATION OF THE TEXTS

The texts that are examined in the following paragraphs focus on biblical rules which are considered binding upon all Israel. Aside

---

[10] Cf. J. M. Baumgarten, "The Pharisaic-Sadducean Controversies about Purity, and the Qumran Texts," *JJS* 31 (1980) 157-70; Y. Sussman, "History of the Halakha," 187-92; L. H. Schiffman, "The Sadducean Origins of the Dead Sea Scrolls Sect," in H. Shanks (ed.), *Understanding the Dead Sea Scrolls* (New York: Biblical Archaeology Society, 1992) 35-49, esp. 44-45; idem, "New Halakhic Texts from Qumran," *HS* 34 (1993) 21-33, esp. 24.

[11] J. M. Baumgarten, "Sadducean Elements in Qumran Law," in E. Ulrich and J. C. VanderKam (eds.), *The Community of the Renewed Covenant: The Notre Dame Symposium on the Dead Sea Scrolls*, (CJA 10; Notre Dame: University of Notre Dame Press, 1994) 29-31; J. C. VanderKam, "The People of the Dead Sea Scrolls: Essenes or Sadducees?," in H. Shanks (ed.), *Understanding the Dead Sea Scrolls*, 52-58.

[12] T. Beall, *Josephus' Description of the Essenes Illustrated by the Dead Sea Scrolls* (SNTSMS 58; Cambridge: Cambridge University Press, 1988).

from the Damascus Document, most of these texts are small fragments that have just recently come to light. Although other Qumran documents discuss Jewish law in passing, the following are largely devoted to the subject:

Damascus Document (CD) A+B, 4Q266-273; 5Q12, 6Q15
Some Precepts of the Torah (MMT) 4Q394-99
Ritual Purity Laws Concerning Liquids 4Q274
The Ashes of the Red Heifer 4Q276-77
Ritual Purity Laws Concerning Menstruation 4Q278
Laws for Purification 4Q284
Laws about Gleaning 4Q284a
Ordinances 4Q159, 4Q513-14
Serekh Damascus 4Q265
4QHalakha[a] 4Q251

These texts can be roughly classified into four groups: the Damascus Document; Some Precepts of the Torah (MMT); the Ṭohorot ("Purities") texts (4Q274-284a); and Related Texts (4Q159, 4Q513-14, 4Q265). Although the Temple Scroll (11Q19) is of a different genre and its sectarian origin is debatable, it accords dramatically with many of the sectarian interpretations and will be included in the discussions below. It will also be helpful to compare the Pharisaic positions on various laws in order to clarify the issues at stake.

2.1 The Damascus Document

The largest of the texts listed above is the Damascus Document, also known as the Zadokite Fragments. The work is a sort of legal treatise in two parts. The first section, the "Admonition," details the pre-history of the author's group which saw itself as the "remnant" of Israel spoken of by the prophets—in other words, the true Israel to which belong the blessings of the future age. The second section, the "Laws," is twice as long as the Admonition and sets forth various matters of Jewish law.

The laws of the Damascus Document are formulated both in exegetical and apodictic forms. That is to say, some laws are provided a basis in Scripture, such as the citation of a verse or simply the formula אשר אמר, while others are not. However, most of the time laws are formulated apodictically, i.e. without any explicit Scriptural support. Nevertheless, as is often the case in the Mishnah, sometimes the law is clearly based on Scripture even though no passages are actually cited.[13]

Law in the Damascus Document was considered the product of "progressive revelation," to use Baumgarten's terminology.[14] The canon was still an open-ended collection; there was a clear consciousness of "holy books," but the sectarian interpretations were so vital to correct understanding that they were often presented as part and parcel of divine law.

The Damascus Document is a sort of anthology of law on various biblical topics, including regulations concerning priests, gentiles, the Sabbath, agricultural gifts, oaths, diet, ritual purity, and marriage. Some of the fragments found in Cave 4 date back to the first half of the first century BCE; suprisingly enough, these agree for the most part with the medieval Genizah text. Unlike the Community Rule (1QS), which is an organizational document for the sect which lived at Qumran, the laws of the Damascus Document are considered by the author as applicable to all Jews wherever they might live in the land of Israel. Marrying and raising families throughout the land of Israel, adherents maintained their own property and income (CD 14:12-13). The Qumran Community may well be an offshoot of the group which produced the Damascus Document, perhaps a more rigorous subset which shunned marriage and family life for a certain period of time in order to devote themselves to holier tasks.[15]

Sectarian emphases come through the text strongly even though the document is not presented in a polemical style. The Admonition accuses those who "sought smooth things" (דרשו בחלקות) and "chose delusions and sought out loopholes ... and caused the covenant to be broken and the statute to be violated" (CD 1:18-20). This may be sarcasm directed against the Pharisees who derived their halakhah from Scripture, with an agenda to alleviate its difficulties if possible.

---

[13] J. M. Baumgarten, *Qumran Cave 4.XIII: The Damascus Document (4Q266-273)* (DJD 18; Oxford: Clarendon Press, 1996) 131. See also L. H. Schiffman, *Sectarian Law in the Dead Sea Scrolls: Courts, Testimony and the Penal Code* (Chico, CA: Scholars Press, 1983), who probes the exegetical basis of numerous apodictic laws from Qumran.

[14] Baumgarten, *Qumran Cave 4.XIII* (DJD 18) 16.

[15] S. Talmon, "The Community of the Renewed Covenant: Between Judaism and Christianity," in Ulrich and VanderKam (eds.), *Community of the Renewed Covenant*, 3-24, esp. 8-9.

The Priests

The author's brand of exegesis favors the priests throughout.[16] For example, Leviticus reads, "And he [the leper] is to be shaved except for the diseased area" (Lev 13:33). The Damascus Document adds a phrase to the beginning of this verse: "And the priest shall order...," underlining the authority of the priest (4Q266 6 i 9). Another example concerns lost articles. The illegality of finding and withholding a lost article from its owner is addressed in Lev 5:21-26, but the text has no instruction for a case in which the owner is unavailable. Num 5:6-8 discusses restitution in cases of unlawful gain, stating that when the wronged party can no longer be found, restitution must go to the priest. From the amalgamation of these two verses, the Qumran exegete concludes that all property for which no owner can be found must be given to the priests (CD 9:13-16).[17]

Gentiles

At the other end of the spectrum, gentiles were to be avoided, and Jews were especially enjoined not to spend the Sabbath among them (CD 11:14). The Damascus Document also restricts selling animals, agriculture and servants to gentiles (CD 12:11), for the author is concerned that gentiles might use animals and produce belonging to Jews for idolatrous sacrifices. Conversely, any metals which gentiles had used for idolatry were permanently forbidden for Jewish use (4Q269 8:1-3; as opposed to *m. ʿAboda Zara* 3:2 where the Rabbis "nullify" idolatrous metals, especially if the images are broken).[18] Of course, those who disagreed with the author, even though they may be Jewish, were considered false Israelites and as much outsiders as were non-Jews.

---

[16] Cf. also many non-exegetical laws. Orders had to come from the mouth of a priest (CD 13:2-7), and priests were the ones to read the Torah publically (4Q266 frg. 5 ii). By the same token, penalties on priests were severe; those who had travelled to pagan lands were excluded from serving in the sanctuary and from eating priestly food (4Q266); cf. J. M. Baumgarten, "The Disqualifications of Priests in 4Q Fragments of the 'Damascus Document,' a Specimen of the Recovery of Pre-Rabbinic Halakha," in J. T. Barrera and L. V. Montaner (eds.), *The Madrid Qumran Congress: Proceedings of the International Congress on the Dead Sea Scrolls Madrid 18-21 March 1991* (2 vols., STDJ 11; Leiden: Brill; Madrid: Universidad Complutense, 1992) 503-13, esp. 509.

[17] Cf. Schiffman, *Sectarian Law in the Dead Sea Scrolls*, 116-17.

[18] J. Baumgarten, *Qumran Cave 4.XIII* (DJD 18) 131.

The Sabbath

Sabbath laws form a large part of the document. The Torah rules that Israelites must "Guard the Sabbath day to make it holy" (Deut 5:12). To this end, the Damascus Document, like the Rabbis, marks the beginning of the Sabbath well before sundown (CD 10:14-17; cf. 4Q270 frg. 6 v 2-3; b. Yoma 81b). In keeping with the Torah's rule, "Let no man go out of his place on the seventh day" (Exod 16:29), strict limits were set on the distance a person could walk outside the town (1,000 cubits) or graze an animal (2,000 cubits); cf. CD 10:21; 11:5-6; cf. 1QM 7:7. To protect the Torah's ban on work during the Sabbath (Deut 5:14), the sectarians forbade handling certain tools on that day, even to save a life (CD 11:17). An animal which fell into a ditch had to be left there, and newborn animals could not be assisted in delivery on the Sabbath (CD 11:13-14; cf. the rabbinic law allowing one to help an animal climb out of a ditch on its own as well as to assist the mother in delivering her young, b. Šabbat 128b).[19] It is thus clear that the sectarians followed a very literal, constricted reading of Scripture.

Unlike the later Tannaim, the sectarians enlist verses from the Prophets as well as the Torah for their laws. On the Sabbath, for example, a man shall not "talk disgraceful and empty talk...he shall not talk about the work and the task to be done the next morning" (CD 10:17-19; cf. 1QS 7:9). This passage seems to be influenced by Isa 58:13, where the community is enjoined not to "do your own ways, nor find your own pleasure, nor speak you own words" on the Sabbath.[20] Another example comes from Jeremiah: "Bear no burden on the sabbath day, nor bring it in by the gates of Jerusalem; neither carry forth a burden out of your houses on the sabbath day, neither do any work" (Jer 17:21-22). According to the Damascus Document, not even an infant, stone, or piece of dust could be carried on the Sabbath (CD 11:7-11; cf. R. Nathan's lenience on this in b. Šabbat 141b). These laws accord with Josephus' statement that the Essenes would not carry any vessel on the Sabbath (*Jewish War* 2 §147).

---

[19] Cf. also Matt 12:11, where it is assumed that the average Jew would certainly get his animal out of a ditch on the Sabbath.

[20] J. M. Baumgarten and D. R. Schwartz, "Damascus Document (CD)," in J. Charlesworth (ed.), *The Dead Sea Scrolls: Hebrew, Aramaic, and Greek Texts with English Translations*, Vol. 2. *Damascus Document, War Scroll, and Related Documents* (Tübingen: Mohr-Siebeck; Louisville: Westminster John Knox, 1995) 4-58, esp. 47.

Agricultural Laws

Agricultural laws form a large part of the Damascus Document, including the laws of *Orlah* ("the fruit of four-year old trees"), *Leqeṭ* ("gleanings"), *Maʿaser* ("tithes"), and *Ḥallah* (the "dough offering"). There is an underlying concern that Jews donate the appropriate contributions to the priests. These laws deal with the ambiguity of Scripture as to the recipients and amounts of the gifts. Comparison with rabbinic rules reveals marked differences in interpretation. For example, the fruit of four-year old trees is designated "holy" in Scripture, but the recipient is not stated (Lev 19:24). Like several other Qumran texts, the Damascus Document requires this fruit to be given to the priests like the holy firstfruits of other crops (4Q251; 4Q266 6 iv; 4Q270; 4QMMT B 62-63; cf. Neh 10:37). The Rabbis, by contrast, regard this fruit like the second tithe which all Israelites eat together in purity in Jerusalem, and so they do not give it to the priests (*Sipre Num.* 6[9]). The Damascus Document requires priestly tithes to be separated even by the poor who subsisted only from gleanings (4Q270 3 ii 18) *Ḥallah*, the bread contribution to the priests, was considered an annual offering of the bread. It is identified with the two loaves offered at the sanctuary on the festival of Shavuot as a firstfruit of the grain harvest (4Q270 2:19-20; cf. Lev 23:17; as opposed to *m. Ḥalla* 3:1 where *ḥallah* is separated from every kneading).

Dietary Laws

Laws relating to food and eating derive from a very strict interpretation of Scripture. The prohibited "swarmers" of Leviticus 11 are interpreted to include even small organisms, such as bee larvae or any sea creature (CD 12:11-13). According to the Torah, animals must be properly slaughtered so as to drain the blood (Lev 17:13-14). But according to the Damascus Document, even fish had to be ritually slaughtered and the blood drained (CD 12:13-14). Locusts had to be intentionally killed either by fire or hot water (CD 12:13-15), probably—as in Karaite law—in order to avoid transgression of the Levitical rule that forbids eating creatures which have died naturally (CD 12:14-15; cf. Lev 17:15).[21]

Oaths and Public Reproof

Sometimes the Damascus Document seeks to substantiate its own

---

[21] Baumgarten and Schwartz, "Damascus Document (CD)," 53.

sectarian laws with Scripture. To forbid the taking of oaths outside a sectarian court-setting, the author decrees: "Let not your hand help you," a citation not found in the Bible (although Baumgarten says it may be inferred from 1 Sam 25:25, 31, 33). The author of the Damascus Document uses this "citation" presumably to forbid raising one's hand in an oath without authorization from a judge. Similarly, the group required public reproof in the presence of witnesses before a criminal was condemned on the "basis" of Lev 19:17-18: "You shall not hate your brother in your heart: you shall in any wise rebuke your neighbor, and not suffer sin upon him. You shall not take vengeance nor keep a grudge against the sons of your people" (CD 9:2-8). These are examples of forced exegesis on the part of the author for the purpose of lending support to the sect's practices.

Skin Diseases

Laws regarding those who bear impurity in Leviticus 12-15 are prominent in the Damascus Document. Several of the Cave 4 fragments discuss leprosy, i.e. various skin diseases. Like the Rabbis, the author considers a leper a sinner on whom God has sent a plague (cf. *t. Negaʿim* 6:7; *b. Berakot* 5b). This notion is implicit in the Bible where examples of leprosy as the result of a curse abound.[22] The Qumran author explicitly connects leprosy and sin by attributing the disease to an evil spirit which interferes with the flow of blood (4Q266 2-3): "...the sp[irit] enters [and takes] hold of the artery, (making) the blood [recede up]wards and downwards ..."

The Zab

In addition, the *zab* (i.e. a man with an abnormal seminal flow) is regarded as a sinner by the Damascus Document (4Q266, 4Q272). Indeed, the disease is used in the Bible as a curse for wrongdoing and requires an atoning sacrifice for purification after healing (Lev 15:14-15; 2 Sam 3:29). The Damascus Document associates the affliction with "lascivious thoughts."[23] This is in marked contrast to the explanations of rabbinic sages, which limit the definition to a great degree and state that if the condition resulted from sexual

---

[22] Cf. Lev 14:34; Num 12:9-11; 2 Kgs 5:27; 2 Chr 26:23. Note also the atoning sacrifices which the leper must bring for purification (Lev 14:19-20).

[23] J. M. Baumgarten, "Zab Impurity in Qumran and Rabbinic Law," *JJS* 45 (1994) 273-77. See also 4Q512 col. 5, where a person being purified from *nega ha-nidda* aks forgiveness from hidden faults. This phrase, however, probably does not denote menstruation but may refer generally to the "plague of impurity."

fantasies it was not considered the biblical disease (*m. Zabim* 2:2). This tendency of the Rabbis towards alleviation was probably due to the hopelessness of remedying the situation, especially after the destruction of the Temple (which had been necessary for the concluding sacrifice following the *zab*'s purification for the week).

Female Impurity

Menstrual impurity was a big concern among the sectarians. In the Admonition, priests are rebuked for having sexual intercourse with menstruants, thereby polluting the sanctuary (CD 5:7; cf. 4Q266 6 ii 2). This attitude is strongly supported by Scripture. Leviticus rules, "And if one has sexual intercourse with her [a menstruant] and her impurity is on him, he will be impure seven days" (Lev 15:24); and Ezekiel lists such behavior together with murder and incest (Ezek 22:10). The exact relationship between sin and impurity, however, is not defined by the sect. J. Baumgarten's rendering of 4Q266 6 ii 2 suggests that—according to the sect—menstruation itself was in some way tainted with sin: "One who has sexual intercourse with her [a menstruant] will bear the [s]in of her impurity on him and be impure seven days."[24]

The laws of the *zabah* provide a fine opportunity for comparison of the exegetical methods of the sectarians vis-à-vis the Rabbis. Leviticus defines a *zabah* as "a woman who has a discharge of blood for many days at a time other than her monthly period, or has a discharge that continues longer than her period" (Lev 15:25). In accordance with the "many days" of the first clause, the Rabbis require three successive days of abnormal bleeding before designating a woman a *zabah* (*Sipra Mesora Zabim* par. 5:9). By contrast, the sectarians are concerned with the more stringent second clause, and thus define the *zabah* as a woman who discharges any amount of blood outside the seven-day menstrual period (4Q266 6 ii 2-4).

According to Scripture, two periods of impurity apply to the woman who has just given birth: first, a 7- or 14-day period[25] of severe impurity equivalent to menstruation, and then a 33- or 66-day period of lesser impurity. The Damascus Document insists that during even the lesser impurity period the mother may not nurse her

---

[24] Baumgarten, *Qumran Cave 4.XIII* (DJD 18) 56. But compare Ezek 18:6, which includes sexual intercourse with menstruants in a list of transgressions.

[25] Depending on the sex of the child.

infant, evidently because her milk would convey impurity to the child (4Q266 6 ii 11).[26]

Impurity from Corpses

It is of no surprise that the contaminating power of impurity from corpses was understood to the greatest degree. All wood, stones and dust within the house of the dead could transmit impurity if moistened with oil (CD 12:15-17). The author also regards all *kelim*[27] within the house of the dead as subject to impurity. Numbers states that everyone in such a house is impure along with every *keli* ("vessel") without a lid (Num 19:14-15). The rabbinic interpretation understands *keli* to refer only to those items that are listed in Lev 11:32: earthenware, leather, and fabric "with which any work is done." Hence these items must form complete, usable vessels (*m. Kelim* 2:1; *Sipre Num.* 126[162]). But according to the Damascus Document, the *keli* also includes "any vessel, nail, or peg in a wall," thus reflecting a far more stringent code (CD 12:17-18).

Immersion

Immersion pools had to be of requisite size, i.e. enough "to cover a man," in order to be effective. One that was not large enough was defined as a "vessel" (CD 10:11-13; cf. Lev 15:16, which commands a man to wash "all his body" after sexual intercourse). The distinction between a vessel that is susceptible to impurity and an immersion pool that is insusceptible is easily derived from Lev 11:36ff., where vessels of various kinds are all contaminated by the carcasses which fall into them, but a fountain or pit "wherein there is plenty of water" is immune to impurity. The Mishnah recognizes this same distinction and clarifies it at length in Tractate *Miqva'ot*. In addition, bearers of impurity were not considered totally pure until the sun had set on the day of their immersion (4Q266 9 ii 1-4). This contrasts with the rabbinic allowance for the *tebul yom*, the one who has been immersed but is still waiting for sunset, to function in every way as a pure individual except with regard to holy things.

Marriage Laws

These laws must be understood within the context of the sectarians' impurity system. Judging from the many laws regulating it, marriage was the norm for the group behind the Damascus Document.

---

[26] Baumgarten, *Qumran Cave 4.XIII* (DJD 18) 56.

[27] I.e. items that were susceptible to impurity.

Nevertheless, there is mention of a holier "camp," possibly at Qumran, where the residents do not live in a married state. This opposition to marriage is due to the impurity resulting from sexual intercourse, which is in direct conflict with the holiness of the sanctuary. Since some of the sectarians desired to recreate this holiness within a closed community, they abstained from conjugal relations. The Damascus Document also prohibits sexual intercourse in Jerusalem, the "City of the Temple" (CD 12:1-2), but in other cities it was allowed, apparently only for purposes of procreation. No sexual intercourse was permitted during pregnancy, probably because no child could result from it.[28] Moreover, the text forbids "*zenut* with one's wife," which is somewhat unclear but probably prohibits intercourse for mere pleasure rather than for procreation (4Q270 7 i 13).[29]

More Laws Relating to Women and Marriage

Other laws relating to women and to marriage are of interest. As in the Mishnah, a suspected adulteress was to be brought to an ordeal at the Temple only when someone had witnessed her together with the man in question (4Q270 1-4; *m. Sota* 1:1).[30] If she declares she was raped, she is not subjected to the ordeal. The words "And she was not seized" from Num 5:13 are not interpreted (as is often done) as "And she was not caught [in the act]," but rather as "And she was not raped"—thus allowing for humane treatment of rape victims (4Q270 4:2-3; cf. *Sipre Num.* 7 [12]). The author forbids polygamy in CD 4:20-5:2, citing "male and female he created them" (Gen 1:27), the collection of the animal species into the ark "two by two" (Gen 7:9), and the order for the king "not to multiply wives" (Deut 17:17). He conspicuously omits any discussion of the many examples and laws of polygamy to be found throughout the Bible (cf. Deut 21:13).[31] Unlike the Rabbis, the Damascus Document forbids

---

[28] According to J. M. Baumgarten, it may also be due to the "fear that coital pressure during pregnancy might lead to bleeding, thus making intercourse illicit" ("A Fragment on Fetal Life and Pregnancy in 4Q270," in D. P. Wright, et al. [eds.], *Pomegranates and Golden Bells: Studies in Biblical, Jewish and Near Eastern Ritual, Law, and Literature in Honor of Jacob Milgrom* [Winona Lake, IN: Eisenbrauns, 1995], 448).

[29] Baumgarten, *Qumran Cave 4.XIII* (DJD 18) 165.

[30] Baumgarten, *Qumran Cave 4.XIII* (DJD 18) 153.

[31] Baumgarten, *Qumran Cave 4.XIII* (DJD 18) 12.

marriage with one's niece, since it seems to be implied in the biblical prohibition against marriage with one's aunt (CD 5:8-11; cf. Lev 18:12-13).

2.2 Some Precepts of the Torah (MMT)

Another major corpus of biblical law at Qumran is the group of fragments of a text entitled *Miqṣat Maʿaśe ha-Torah* ("Some Precepts of the Torah"), or simply "MMT" (References that follow are to the composite text transcribed by E. Qimron and J. Strugnell).[32] This treatise, which appears to have been sent to the establishment at Jerusalem, argues for Jewish temple and purity procedures to be carried out in accordance with the ideas of the author, who is clearly a representative of a priestly faction. This faction may have later evolved into the Qumran sect under the Teacher of Righteousness.[33] The author pleads to his addressees not to give in to certain others, who would seek to conduct the cult according to a different calendar and a lower code of ritual purity.

A Focus on Holy Things

Unlike the broader scope of topics that appear in the Damascus Document, the laws of MMT are narrowly focused on priestly matters concerning the Temple and ritual purity. What is striking about these laws is their resemblance to other legal texts that have been found at Qumran. Furthermore, many of its topics and even terms remind the reader of the Mishnah.[34] Nevertheless, the position of the author is usually more stringent than that of the later Rabbis and contains many Sadducean views.[35]

The author appears to base his laws on Scripture: "We have [written] to you so that you may study (carefully) the book of Moses and the books of the Prophets and (the writings of) David..." (C 10). The idea is that only the writer's interpretation of biblical law is correct—although it is admittedly hidden from a mere surface

---

[32] E. Qimron and J. Strugnell, *Qumran Cave 4.V* (DJD 10); see n.6 above.

[33] J. Strugnell, "MMT: Second Thoughts on a Forthcoming Edition," in Ulrich and VanderKam (eds.), *Community of the Renewed Covenant*, 57-73, esp. 72.

[34] Y. Sussmann, "History of the Halakha," 186.

[35] L. H. Schiffman, "The Place of MMT in the Corpus of Qumran Manuscripts," in J. Kampen and M. Bernstein (eds.), *Reading 4QMMT: New Perspectives on Qumran Law and History* (SBLSym 2; Atlanta: Scholars Press, 1994) 81-98, esp. 97-98.

reading, and requires careful study.³⁶ Nevertheless, as occurs in the Damascus Document, some passages seem removed from the Torah and the interpretation is somewhat forced.³⁷

Jerusalem

The key to understanding the laws of MMT is recognition of its expansive definition of holy area and personnel. According to MMT the entire city of Jerusalem is the "camp of holiness":

> Jerusalem is the camp of holiness and is the place which he has chosen from among all the tribes of Israel. For Jerusalem is the capital of the camps of Israel. (B 60-62).

The sectarians derive Jerusalem's superior status from Deuteronomy, which often refers to the special "place (מקום) which the LORD your God shall choose" (cf. Deut 12:11). The writer of MMT sets forth his hierarchy of holy space as follows: "And we are of the opinion that the sanctuary [is the 'Tent of Meeting'] and that Jerusalem is the 'camp,' and that 'outside the camp' [is outside Jerusalem], that is, the encampment of their settlements" (B 29-31). From these passages it becomes clear that the writer equates Jerusalem with the "camp," i.e. the holy wilderness camp of Numbers. His respondent evidently disagrees and probably limits the application of holiness to the sanctuary only.

MMT's emphasis on the sacred status of Jerusalem is also reflected in other Qumran texts. The Messianic Rule and the Temple Scroll both require at least a three-day purification for impure persons before entering into the sacred assembly or the holy city, respectively (1QSa 1:25-26; 11Q19 45:7-12). As occurs in MMT, the Temple Scroll and the War Scroll ban the physically impaired from Jerusalem and the holy War Camp, respectively (11Q19 45:12-14; 1QM 7:3-5; MMT B 42-57). Both the Temple Scroll and the Damascus Document prohibit sexual intercourse within Jerusalem (11Q19 45:11-12; CD 12:1-2). Hides used in Jerusalem must be from animals that have been slaughtered as sacrifices within the city, according to both the Temple Scroll and MMT (11Q19 51:1-6; 4QMMT B 21-26).³⁸

---

[36] Qimron and Strugnell, *Qumran Cave 4.V* (DJD 10), 132-33 n.22.

[37] M. Bernstein, "The Employment and Interpretation of Scripture in 4QMMT: Preliminary Observations" in Kampen and Bernstein (eds.), *Reading MMT*, 29-51.

[38] Josephus refers to an Essene gate in Jerusalem as *Bethso* (Βηθσώ) which may be *Beit Tso'ah* (בית צואה), the "place of excrement" (*Jewish War* 5 §144-45).

The distinction of Jerusalem vis-à-vis other cities is thoroughly biblical. The prophets already mark Jerusalem as the "holy city" (Isa 52:1; Joel 4:17). Indeed, Deuteronomy emphasizes that the tithes of Israel, which must be pure, are to be eaten within the boundaries of the chosen city (Deut 14:23 and 26:1-15). The Rabbis, too, regard the city of Jerusalem as at a higher level of purity (*m*. Roš Haššana 4:1-2; *m. Kelim* 1:8); but the difference between the Scrolls and the rabbinic position lies in to what degree Jerusalem is to be set apart from other cities.

Holiness of the Priests

In line with the expansive category of holy area, the sanctity of holy personnel is maximal. According to the reconstruction of MMT by Qimron and Strugnell, not just the High Priest but all priests are called קדש קדשים ("most holy"): "They (Israel) are holy, and the sons of Aaron are [most holy]" (B 79). So whereas Scripture regards the priests as "holy," MMT refers to them as "most holy" and the Israelites as "holy." A practical result of this view concerns marriage. The Torah states that only the high priest is required to marry a woman "from his own kin" (Lev 21:14). MMT, however, extends this ruling to all priests and insists that they marry only women from priestly families (B 75-82).[39]

This expansive definition of holy persons concurs with other Qumran scrolls (1QS 8:5-10; 9:6; cf. 4Q381 76:7).[40] The Community Rule refers to "ranks" in the "community of holiness," and describes two specific groups: A house of holiness consisting of Israelites and a most holy congregation consisting of Aaron (1QS 8:5-6; 9:2-6). The idea that the priests comprise the congregation of Aaron at the most holy level, and Israelites are a holy community of perfection, appears to be a hallmark of Qumran law.[41]

In the light of MMT's expansive application of holiness, its other laws become understandable. To ensure the holiness of Jerusalem and

---

The understanding is that the Essenes did not defecate in Jerusalem but perhaps went through this gate to relieve themselves at a place outside of the city wall.

[39] Qimron and Strugnell, *Qumran Cave 4.V* (DJD 10) 172.

[40] Qimron and Strugnell, *Qumran Cave 4.V* (DJD 10) 173, state that *qodesh qodashim* (קדש קדשים) in the Dead Sea Scrolls refers to priests or angels.

[41] Although not the rabbinic interpretation, this concept can nevertheless be derived from Exod 19:6, Lev 11:44 and 1 Chr 23:13 (cf. Qimron and Strugnell, *Qumran Cave 4.V* [DJD 10] 173).

its cult, dogs are banned from the city, holy food must not remain overnight, the purity of liquids must be maintained so that water containers are not retroactively contaminated, and physically impaired persons are excluded from "the purity of the Temple" lest they defile it.

An Expanded Definition of Holiness

Just how many of these laws were inherited and how many were exegeted by the group is hard to determine. Nevertheless, when one examines the relevant Scriptural passages on these subjects it is clear that the author, like the writer of the Damascus Document, has a systematic agenda: to require the maximal purity standard which can be derived from the text. As in the Damascus Document, laws from various Scriptures are combined to create the most rigorous standard. Jacob Milgrom refers to this unique exegetical trait as "homogenization."[42]

MMT shares many particular interpretations of biblical law with various Qumran documents. These include: the prohibition to slaughter pregnant animals because it violates the Torah's prohibition to take the mother animal and her young in the same day (4Q270 2 ii 15; 11Q19 52:5-7; MMT B 30-33; cf. Lev 22:28; Deut 22:6-7); the requirement for an impure person to wait for sunset on the day of purification in order to participate within society (4Q266 9 ii 4; 4Q276-77; 11Q19 51:2-5; MMT B 13-17); unique requirements regarding peace offerings (11Q19 20:11-13; MMT B 62-63); and apportionment of fourth-year produce and animal tithes to the priest (4Q251 3:7-9; 4Q266 6 iv; 4Q270; 11Q19 60:2-4; MMT B 62-63).[43]

Gentiles

Like the Damascus Document,[44] MMT has strong rules against gentiles. According to Deuteronomy, certain classes of people may not "enter the congregation of the LORD" (Deut 23:2-4), a phrase which for MMT forbids non-Israelites from marrying Israelites or to enter the sanctuary (MMT B 39-49; cf. 4Q174 1:3-4). The food of gentiles was excluded entirely from the community: "No one should

---

[42] J. Milgrom, "The Qumran Cult: Its Exegetical Principles" in G. J. Brooke (ed.), *Temple Scroll Studies* (JSPSup 7; Sheffield: JSOT Press, 1989) 165-80.

[43] See full discussion in L. H. Schiffman, "*Miqṣat Maʿaśe ha-Torah* and the Temple Scroll," *RevQ* 14 (1990) 435-57, esp. 436-38; 448-51.

[44] See section 2.1 above.

eat any of the new wheat grains of the gentiles" (B 4-5). Sacrifices brought by gentiles are especially repulsive: "And concerning the sacrifice of the gentiles: we are of the opinion that they sacrifice to the ... that is like (a woman) who whored with him" (B 8-9). This is in contrast to the rabbinic position, which does accept sacrifices from gentiles although the subject was controversial in the Second Temple period (*m. Zebah.* 4:5; cf. Josephus, *Jewish War* 2 §§409–410).

2.3 The Ṭohorot Texts (4Q274-284a)

Our third group of texts, several Cave 4 fragments numbering between 4Q274-284a, are sometimes given the common rubric, *Ṭohorot*, or "Purities," since they all deal with some aspect of ritual purity. J. T. Milik was the first to work on these texts and he labeled them "Règle de la pureté."[45] They have also been termed with alphabetic sigla, e.g. Ṭohorot A (4Q274) and Ṭohorot B (4Q276-77).

All of these texts interpret biblical laws of ritual purification and contamination. One of the more significant among them, 4Q274 has been explicated by both Jacob Milgrom and Joseph Baumgarten.[46] While it is well known that the purity of the food at Qumran was guarded and all who ate of it had to immerse, 4Q274 reveals that even impure persons, who would continue in their impurity or purification for an extended period, had to immerse themselves in water if they contracted any further impurity. They would, of course, still be barred from the communal meal and have to eat separately but they would not be allowed to eat at all unless they had bathed.[47]

---

[45] J. T. Milik, "Milkî-ṣedeq et Milkî-rešaʿ dans les anciens écrits juifs et chrétiens," *JJS* 23 (1972), 129.

[46] J. M. Baumgarten, "Zab Impurity" 112-19; J. Milgrom, "4QṬohorotª: An Unpublished Qumran Text on Purities" in D. Dimant and L. H. Schiffman (eds.), *Time to Prepare the Way in the Wilderness: Papers on the Qumran Scrolls* (STDJ 16; Leiden: Brill, 1994) 59-68.

[47] Cf. 4Q514, which was initially thought to allow the *tebul yom* to participate in the life of the community. But J. Milgrom has demonstrated that 4Q514 is demanding what 4Q274 states explicitly: an impure person too must bathe before eating. Even though this will not make him pure, it will give him access to ordinary food ("The Purification Rule," in J. Charlesworth [ed.], *The Dead Sea Scrolls. Hebrew, Aramaic, and Greek Texts with English Translations*, Vol. 1. *Rule of the Community and Related Documents* [Tübingen: Mohr-Siebeck; Louisville: Westminster John Knox, 1994] 177-79, esp. 177; cf. also idem, "4QṬohorotª," *Time to Prepare the Way in the Wilderness*, 67-68).

Is there an exegetical base for these laws? Perhaps, although it seems to be after the fact. In their effort to require maximal purity at Qumran, it seems that these sectarians combined the purification rules addressed to all Israel in Leviticus 11-15 with the purity required to eat sacrificial portions in Lev 7:19-21. From this "homogenization" came the requirement that all Israelites (even those who are hopelessly impure) bathe before eating any food. This ruling is not without parallel. The Pharisees, too, bathed before eating, although probably not those who were isolated with extended, severe impurities (Luke 11:38).[48]

Liquids

The potency of liquids as conveyors of impurity is treated in two other 4QTohorot texts: 4Q284a and Fragment 3 of 4Q274.[49] According to these texts, crops which in any way became wet—even by rain—become susceptible to impurity thus requiring all those who harvest them to be in a state of ritual purity. Agricultural laws played an important role because food for the communal meals had to be pure from the time of harvesting to the point of consumption. Liquids were especially important since they conveyed impurity. For instance, the juice of grapes or olives in the harvesters' baskets would naturally ooze out and thus potentially transmit impurity from the harvester or other source to the produce. Thus, all harvesters had to perform their gleaning in a state of purity.

The original Scriptural basis for this issue must be Lev 11:38 where it is stated that if water *yutan* "is put" on seed and a carcass falls on it, the seed becomes impure. Thus, liquid conveys impurity to produce. According to the 4QTohorot texts, however, the possibility of impurity being conveyed to the fruit began already when the harvesters gathered the fruit into their baskets. Some juice would no doubt ooze out in the process and, according to the sectarians, convey any impurity with which it might come in contact.

A similar concern over the purity of liquids is attested in other documents from Qumran.[50] As we have seen already in the

---

[48] Cf. also H. K. Harrington, "Did the Pharisees Eat Ordinary Food in a State of Purity?" *JSJ* 26 (1995) 42-54.

[49] J. M. Baumgarten, "Liquids and Susceptibility to Defilement in New 4Q Texts" *JQR* 85 (1994) 109-23.

[50] J. M. Baumgarten, "The Essene Avoidance of Oil and the Laws of Purity" *RevQ* 6 (1967) 183-93.

Damascus Document, oil stains in the house of the dead had to be removed so that corpse impurity would not spread (CD 12:15-17). The Temple Scroll insists that all liquid, even water stains, in such a house becomes impure and must be removed (11Q19 49:8-11). It is well known that access to communal drinks was granted to the novitiate at Qumran only after 2-3 years of probation (1QS 6:20; 7:20; cf. Josephus, *Jewish War* 2 §123).

In the rabbinic system, too, liquids were the conveyors of impurity *par excellence*; however, the interpretation of Lev 11:36ff is not as stringent as among the sectarians. On the basis of the word *yutan*, "is put," the Rabbis insisted that there must be intentional and desired putting of the water on the seed by permission of the owner in order for it to become susceptible to impurity (*m. Makhširin* 1:1; 3:6; *b. Qiddušin* 59b). The issue of purity of the harvest was also important to the Sages, since they quarantined the workers of the olive presses while they pressed the oil (*m. Ṭoharot* 9-10). However, it is only at this stage, when liquid was pressed from the fruit, that impurity was allowed to become an issue.

Status of the Purer Person

Another principle which comes into relief in these texts is the difference in status of an ordinary person and one who has decided to live at a higher standard of purity (cf. the distinction between camps in the Damascus Document). Like the Temple Scroll, 4Q274 suggests that a purer person will not eat the contents of even a sealed vessel in the house of the dead (4Q274 3; 11Q19 49:8).[51]

The Rite of the Red Cow

Ṭohorot texts 4Q276-277 discuss the rite of the red cow, which was burned to produce ashes to be mixed with water and sprinkled on corpse contaminated items for purification (Num 19:17-21). The Pharisees and Sadducees of the Mishnah argued over the correct standard of purity for those who participated in the rite. The Sadducees, who did not regard a purifying person pure until sunset, would not let any such person participate. The Pharisees, who subscribed to the *tebul yom* concept discussed above, would intentionally make the participants impure so that they would immerse, and, to the dismay of the Sadducees, be in this intermediate status when they performed the rituals. This insistence on full purification before

---

[51] Baumgarten, "Liquids and Susceptibility to Defilement," 98.

functioning within society in any way surfaces in several Qumran texts (cf. also 4Q266 9 ii 1-4; MMT B 13-17; 11Q19 51:2-5).

Sprinkling

In addition, there seems to be a disagreement over who should be involved in the sprinkling. According to the Mishnah, the Rabbis allowed young boys, pure from any sexual emissions, to sprinkle the corpse-contaminated (*m. Para* 3). In the Ṭohorot texts, however, the author insists that only a mature priest be allowed this privilege.[52]

2.4 *Related Texts (4Q159, 4Q513-14, 4Q265, 4Q251)*

Texts that are related to those discussed above include the Ordinances (4Q159, 4Q513-514) the Serekh Damascus (4Q265), and 4QHalakhah[a] (4Q251), where the same types of issues and sectarian interpretation are present. Ordinances A (4Q159) provides a good example of the "homogenization" technique discussed above with regard to laws for gleaning. Deut 23:25 states that one may eat a neighbor's produce while in his field. The sectarians combine this verse with Deut 24:22 and 15:15, which allow the poor to collect gleanings from the threshing floor and winepress. The result is that only the poor may pick up gleanings in the field and/or from the threshing-floor and winepress. But the Qumran scroll adds "whoever is in (the people of) I[sra]el who does not have (something to eat), may eat of it." This ruling thus restricts a person from taking advantage of farmers by eating sizeable amounts of produce without payment while on their property.

Other issues surface in Ordinances A (4Q159). The author regards the half-shekel tax on every adult male (Exod 30:12-15) to be a one-time payment when a man reaches the age of twenty.[53] In addition, the biblical law not to wear a garment designed for the opposite sex is quoted using three plural terms for the "garment." Apparently, the sect wanted to emphasize that all garments of the opposite sex were forbidden, not just the overgarments that were visible.[54] In accordance with the Torah, it is stressed that a man who falsely accuses his

---

[52] J. M. Baumgarten, "The Red Cow Purification Rites in Qumran Texts," *JJS* 46 (1995) 112-19.

[53] The Rabbis required this tax to be paid every year in order to support the public offerings of the Temple.

[54] L. H. Schiffman, "Ordinances and Rules," in Charlesworth (ed.), *Dead Sea Scrolls* (Vol. 1) 145-75, esp. 155.

wife of non-virginity is fined and never allowed to divorce her (Deut 22:18-19).

4Q513, or Ordinances B, adds further biblical interpretations. Illicit sexual relations include the marriage of the daughters of priests with non-Jews (cf. 4QMMT B 75-82); according to the author, neither these women nor their families are allowed to eat of priestly contributions or even touch any other pure food. Furthermore, the mixture of ordinary food with priestly food results in *avon zimmah*, the "sin of immorality" (4Q513 11:3). Other laws that are recorded include the concern of oil transmitting impurity (cf. CD 12:16; 11Q19 49:8-11), the prohibition on using an immersion pool which is too shallow (cf. CD 10:11-13), and some fragmentary purity laws. As is evident in other Qumran texts, ritual purity was highly-valued.

The Serekh Damascus (4Q265), while primarily discussing community rules, is of interst here with regard to the Sabbath. According to the Serekh, on the Sabbath dirty or even dusty clothes were not allowed to be worn, and carrying vessels or food was forbidden (4Q265 2 i 2-8). These restrictions remind the reader of the ban in the Damascus Document on carrying even a stone or piece of dust on the Sabbath (CD 11:7-11). Most interesting in the Serekh Damascus is the notion that an animal which had fallen into water could not be retrieved on the Sabbath; nevertheless, a person in the same situation should be helped to safety by throwing him one end of a garment and lifting him up out of the water (4Q265 2 i 5-7). This is significant in the light of CD 11:17 which strictly forbids handling certain tools, even to save a life. Lawrence Schiffman regards these texts as complementary in that both allow saving human life on the Sabbath, as long as normal work tools are not employed.[55]

4QHalakhah[a] (4Q251) contains fragments of biblical law as well. Typical Pentateuch laws, such as those penalizing the owner of a goring ox and various incest regulations, are included. As in the texts discussed above, the priestly right to fourth-year fruit and other disputed holy gifts is emphasized (4Q251 3:7-9; cf. 4Q266 6 iv; 4Q270; 4QMMT B 62-63; 11Q19 60:2-4). An especially interesting law is the disallowance of grain, wine or oil until their firstfruits have been separated at the festivals:

---

[55] L. H. Schiffman, "New Halakhic Texts from Qumran," *Hebrew Studies* 34 (1993) 21-33, esp. 29.

> No-one is to eat the new wheat... until the day of the bread from the first- fruits arrives... (4Q251 2:5-6).

Each crop had to be first offered to God by giving a certain amount to the priests on the designated festival day before the rest of the crop could be released for human consumption. This reminds the reader of the firstfruit festivals of grain, wine, and oil as outlined in the Temple Scroll (11Q19 43:3ff).

3. CONCLUSIONS AND NEW DIRECTIONS

From the survey above it is remarkable how much consonance there is between the legal texts found at Qumran. Allowing for a community at Qumran which shunned the married life and private ownership of property (at least for a season), as opposed to those of the sect living in private homes all over Palestine, differences in interpretation of biblical law among the various Scrolls are minor.

Let us summarize some of the underlying legal issues. Although there may not be complete agreement between them, certain concerns recur throughout the texts: (a) protection of the holiness of the Temple and its city; (b) proper contributions for the priests; (c) the potency and contagion of impurity (especially as conveyed by liquids), which is sometimes linked to sin; (d) maximal purifications and adequate immersion pools; (e) a celibate ideal that restricts sexual intercourse and prohibits polygamy as well as niece marriages; (f) the purity of priestly marriages; (g) proper ritual slaughter of animals; and (h) repudiation of gentiles. In all of these areas, a fairly consistent sectarian interpretation is championed.

The result of this agreement is to bring into relief a cultic system that is opposed to the established practice in Jerusalem from which these sectarians departed. The Jerusalemite priests regarded holiness at the level described by these laws as above and beyond the demands of the Torah. Both sides agreed that priests were the main officiants at the sanctuary, that Jews should contribute certain gifts to them, and that all Israel should maintain a certain purity code. The point at issue here was one of degree: there was serious disagreement on how far sacred space should extend, how holy personnel were to be supported, and how holiness should be effected in the daily life of Israel.

Many of the above sectarian principles come into sharper relief when one compares them to the Pharisaic legal system which is detailed in early rabbinic literature. Since we know that the rabbinic position on many of these laws is more flexible and often matches exactly what the sectarians were trying to reform, we assume that much of the Pharisaic *halakhah* existed at the time of the writers of these Scrolls. The Pharisees' primary goal was to enable the populace to participate in religious life as much as possible, alleviating the law as much as possible and extending holiness to all Israel.[56] This was clearly contrary to the thinking of the sectarians who wished to increase holiness standards and limit them to a priestly community which could ensure their observance.

On the other hand, many beliefs and practices that are discussed in the texts are not polemics, but common Second Temple practice.[57] One new direction of legal research in the Scrolls is interested in identifying the concepts and practices which the Scrolls' writers assume to be the case and about which they do not argue. Philip Davies points out that "sects magnify certain characteristics of the parent society, illuminating its fissures but also indicating it basic undeniable presuppositions."[58] Further examination of these "presuppositions" can teach us more about Second Temple practice and perhaps illuminate religious customs of the late biblical period, providing information about the post-exilic cult as far back as the time of Haggai and Zechariah. As Baumgarten says: "There is a large, very significant body of halakha which apparently was not limited to any of the three groups, but represents the common traditional law of the Second Temple period."[59] Qumran legal texts thus continue to be closely analyzed in light of parallels from biblical and post-biblical literature of the Second Temple.

The nature of exegesis at Qumran continues to intrigue scholars. Of interest is the particular style of exegesis found in the Qumran texts, in particular the methods that are used to incorporate various

---

[56] I. Knohl, "Post-Biblical Sectarianism and the Priestly Schools of the Pentateuch: The Issue of Popular Participation in the Temple Cult on Festivals" in J. T. Barrera and L. V. Montaner (eds.), *The Madrid Qumran Congress*, 601-09; H. K. Harrington, *The Impurity Systems of Qumran and the Rabbis* (Atlanta: Scholars Press, 1993), 264.

[57] Y. Sussmann, "History of the Halakha," 186; cf. also M. Weinfeld, "Prayer and Liturgical Practice in the Qumran Sect," in D. Dimant and U. Rappaport (eds.), *The Dead Sea Scrolls: Forty Years of Research* (STDJ 10; Leiden, Brill: 1992) 241-58, who notes religious practices such as tefillin, minyan, and ritual prayers at Qumran.

[58] P. R. Davies, "Who Can Join the 'Damscus Covenant'?" *JJS* 46 (1995) 142.

[59] Baumgarten, "Disqualifications of Priests," 513.

sectarian laws into the biblical text for authority.[60] In addition, the agenda behind the laws continues to be explored. While the priestly bias is apparent, are there other special interests which the writers defend? Do they promote a certain type of jurisprudence?[61]

The value of this material to rabbinic studies cannot be overestimated. Many elements in rabbinic texts that had heretofore been considered late or influenced by Christianity now appear in documents whose antiquity and Jewish character cannot be doubted. The Qumran legal texts provide an important link between the biblical period and the later exegesis of the Rabbis.

In addition, many areas of Qumran law have direct import for New Testament scholars. Associations that are made in the Scrolls between sin and impurity in both atonement and baptism processes should shed light on similar practices in the New Testament. Moreover, the issue of celibacy as a mark of greater holiness, which is prominent in the Qumran Scrolls but nowhere stated in the Hebrew Bible, is pursued in the Gospels and in the writings of Paul.

SELECT BIBLIOGRAPHY

Baumgarten J. M. *Qumran Cave 4.XIII: The Damascus Document* (DJD 18; Oxford: Clarendon Press, 1996).

Charlesworth J. (ed.). *The Dead Sea Scrolls: Hebrew, Aramaic, and Greek Texts with English Translations, I.Rule of the Community and Related Documents* (Tubingen: J.C.B. Mohr, 1994); *II.Damascus Document, War Scroll and Related Documents* (1995).

Kampen J. and M. Bernstein (eds.). *Reading 4QMMT: New Perspectives on Qumran Law and History* (Atlanta: Scholars Press, 1996).

Milgrom J. "The Qumran Cult: Its Exegetical Principles" in G. J. Brooke (ed.), *Temple Scroll Studies,* (JSPSup 7; Sheffield: JSOT Press, 1989) 165-80.

Qimron E. and J.Strugnell, *Qumran Cave 4.V: Miqṣat Maʿaśe Ha-Torah* (DJD 10; Oxford: Clarendon Press, 1994).

Schiffman L. H. "Miqṣat Maʿaśe ha-Torah and the Temple Scroll," *RevQ* 55 (1990) 435-58.

—. *Sectarian Law in the Dead Sea Scrolls: Courts, Testimony and the Penal Code* (Chico, CA: Scholars Press, 1983).

---

[60] L. H. Schiffman, "The Temple Scroll and the Nature of Its Law; the Status of the Question," in Ulrich and VanderKam (eds.), *Community of the Renewed Covenant*, 37-55.

[61] Cf. D. R. Schwartz, "Law and Truth: On Qumran-Sadducean and Rabbinic Views of Law," in Dimant and Rappaport (eds.), *Forty Years of Research*, 229-40.

Y. Sussman, "The History of the Halakha and the Dead Sea Scrolls: Preliminary Talmudic Observations on *Miqṣat Maʿaśe Ha-Torah* (4QMMT)," Appendix 1 in E. Qimron and J. Strugnell, *Qumran Cave 4.V: Miqṣat Maʿaśe Ha-Torah* (DJD 10; Oxford: Clarendon Press, 1994) 179-200, esp. 184 (originally published as חקר תולדות ההלכה ומגילות מדבר יהודה: הרהורים תלמודיים ראשונים לאור "מגילת מקצת מעשי התורה", *Tarbiz* 59 [1989-90] 11-76).

Ulrich E. and J. C. VanderKam (eds.). *The Community of the Renewed Covenant* (CJA 10; Notre Dame, IN: University of Notre Dame Press, 1994).

CONSTITUTIONAL RULES AT QUMRAN

SARIANNA METSO

1. INTRODUCTION

Fifty years after the discovery of the Dead Sea Scrolls, we are now moving into a new era in research on the Qumran rule texts. During the past twenty years, while waiting for the Cave 4 material of The Damascus Document (CD) and the Community Rule (1QS) to be published, there was little discussion on the rules. Although there were some reports on additional fragmentary rule texts, it was almost exclusively the manuscripts 1QS and CD^{a,b} which were referred to as the Essene rules. The Cave 4 material of both the Damascus Document and the Community Rule has now become available,[1] but more investigation on the new material is needed before it is possible to form a synthesis. The investigation has barely begun, but already it does not seem plausible to me that simple supplementation of the old theories regarding both the textual development of the various documents and the history of the community in light of the new material is sufficient. A re-evaluation at a deeper level is necessary, and it needs to be asked whether the earlier theories stand the test of the new evidence. The textual basis

---

[1] J. M. Baumgarten and M. T. Davis (eds.), "Cave IV, V, VI Fragments Related to the Damascus Document (4Q266-273 = 4QD^{a-h}, 5Q12 = 5QD, 6Q15 = 6QD)," in J. H. Charlesworth *et al.* (eds.), *The Dead Sea Scrolls. Hebrew, Aramaic and Greek Texts with English Translation*. Vol. 2: *Damascus Document, War Scroll, and Related Documents* (Tübingen: Mohr-Siebeck; Louisville: John Knox, 1995) 59-79; J. M. Baumgarten, with Jozef T. Milik, Stephen Pfann and Ada Yardeni, *Qumran Cave 4.XIII: The Damascus Document (4Q266-273)* (DJD 18; Oxford: Clarendon Press, 1996); E. Qimron and J. H. Charlesworth, with an Appendix by F. M. Cross, "Cave IV Fragments (4Q255-264 = 4QS MSS A-J)," in Charlesworth *et al.* (eds.), *The Dead Sea Scrolls. Hebrew, Aramaic, and Greek Texts with English Translations*. Vol. 1: *Rule of the Community and Related Documents* (Tübingen: Mohr-Siebeck; Louisville: John Knox, 1994) 53-103; C. Martone, *La "Regola della Comunité." Edizione critica* (Quaderni di Henoch 8; Torino: Silvio Zamorani Editore, 1995); S. Metso, *The Textual Development of the Qumran Community Rule* (STDJ 21; Leiden: Brill, 1997).

of the individual documents needs to be known before posing the question as to the function of the rule texts in the Essene movement or attempting a reconstruction of the history of the community on the basis of the rule texts, and quite obviously there is a lot to be done in this area. Therefore, many of the views presented in this article can only be the beginning of a synthesis.

The editors of the present volume divided the Essene rules into two groups: halakhic and constitutional. From the practical point of view the division is understandable, but methodologically it is not without problems. If we take as our starting point the simple assumption that a text is "constitutional" if it lays out the basic principles of the community's life, the community's own rules, but is 'halakhic' if it deals with different aspects of the religious life, such as purity, we are faced with the problem that the majority of the rule texts found at Qumran include regulations belonging to both categories. If the division is made on the basis of the relationship of the regulations to the Bible, so that the "halakhic" regulations are supposed to have been derived from scriptural exegesis, whereas the "constitutional" rules lack a scriptural background, there is an a priori assumption that the community would have made a distinction between its own regulations and the regulations of the Bible. Words describing the self-understanding of the community, such as the community as the covenant or the temple, seem rather to indicate that the community considered its whole existence as holy and as an atonement of sins. There is a possibility, of course, that the rules indeed fall into two different categories. Initially, however, the question is to be kept open.

In the past questions regarding the history of the Qumran community and that of the larger Essene movement have played a central role in the study of the rule texts. Influenced by Josephus' reports on the Essenes, something of a consensus was formed fairly early among Qumran scholars that the Community Rule describes the life of the Qumran Community specifically, whereas the Damascus Document was addressed to the members of the larger Essene movement. The view that the Essene movement may have included groups differing in their practices and ideas, may be correct; but with the availability of new material consisting both of additional copies of earlier published manuscripts as well as of previously unknown documents, we should aim at a sharper picture. Not only contents but also methodology need re-examination. In light of the new evidence, we should re-test not only earlier hypotheses and results, but also the way or the method that the Qumran rule texts have been used in the reconstruction of the history of the Qumran community. In what follows my focus will be on the pluriformity of the legal material found at Qumran, and I shall attempt to outline both the differences and the similarities included in the manuscripts.

In my opinion, in the present situation of research it is no longer possible to reckon only with the community behind the Damascus Document on the one hand and the community behind the Community Rule on the other hand. Many of the recently published Cave 4 documents that were previously unknown do not seem to represent clearly either one group or the other. Moreover, the Cave 4 copies of the Damascus Document and the Community Rule have confirmed the view that they are composite documents with complex redactional histories. The composite nature of the texts needs to be taken seriously when different documents are compared with one another. Instead of comparing the whole documents, we ought rather to pay attention first to separate sections. Before the historical questions can be put to the manuscripts, their textual similarities and differences need to be considered, for the history of redaction provides the key to the history of the communities. It is possible and even likely that there were contacts between the different groups responsible for various sections. They may have used common sources and borrowed material from each other. Quite naturally, the manuscripts found at Qumran functioned as whole documents, and individual sections may have gained new focuses in their new contexts. But if the purpose of study is to reach to the historical reality of the groups behind the texts, a more detailed analysis is needed, viz., analysis of the compositional history of the text rather than considering only the latest redactional stage.

2. EARLIER RESEARCH

2.1 The Community Rule

The Community Rule has often been seen as an Essene rule text *par excellence*. Soon after the publication of 1QS already scholars began to make isolated remarks about the non-uniformity of the document,[2] but the theory which came to exercise the strongest

---

[2] *Editio princeps*: M. Burrows with J. C. Trever and W. H. Brownlee, *The Dead Sea Scrolls of St. Mark's Monastery. Vol. II, Fasc. 2. Plates and*

influence on the interpretation of 1QS was not presented until 1969. Using the hypothesis of E. F. Sutcliffe that 1QS 8–9 represents the earliest material of the Community Rule,[3] J. Murphy-O'Connor argued that there was a three-stage development from the nucleus or "Manifesto" formed by 1QS 8:1-16 and 9:3–10:8. The redactional stages, in his view, corresponded to the archaeological phases of Khirbet Qumran.[4] The theory of a Manifesto is widely accepted among scholars, but many have doubted the possibility of dividing the text into four clearly defined redactional stages and, especially, of connecting them with the archaeological periods of Khirbet Qumran.[5] Murphy-O'Connor's theory was developed and modified in the 1970s and 1980s in publications by various scholars,[6] but no one presented a serious alternative.

The hesitancy shown by scholars in the last decade to develop new theories about the redaction of the Community Rule is at least partly explained by the fact the DJD edition of the *Serekh* material has not

---

Transcription of the Manual of Discipline (New Haven: The American Schools of Oriental Research, 1951); A. Dupont-Sommer, *Nouveaux apercus sur les manuscrits de la mer Morte* (Paris: Maisonneuve, 1953) 90; P. Wernberg-Møller, *The Manual of Discipline Translated and Annotated with an Introduction* (STDJ 1; Leiden: Brill, 1957) 56 n.49; K.-G. Kuhn, "Der gegenwärtige Stand der Erforschung der in Palästina neu gefundenen hebräischen Handschriften," *TLZ* 85 (1960) 649-58, esp. 652; J. Maier, *Die Texte vom Toten Meer, I-II* (München and Basel: E. Reinhardt, 1960) 1.21.

[3] E. F. Sutcliffe, "The First Fifteen Members of the Qumran Community. A Note on 1QS 8:1 ff.," *JSS* 4 (1959) 134-38.

[4] J. Murphy-O'Connor, "La genèse littéraire de la Règle de la Communauté," *RB* 76 (1969) 528-49.

[5] See, for example, M. Delcor, "Qumran. La Règle de la Communauté," *DBSup* (Paris: Letouzey et Ané, 1979) 9.851-57, esp. 852-54; D. Dimant, "Qumran Sectarian Literature," in M. Stone (ed.), *Jewish Writings of the Second Temple Period. Apocrypha, Pseudepigrapha, Qumran Sectarian Writings, Philo* (CRINT 2; Assen: Van Gorcum; Philadelphia; Fortress Press, 1984) 483-550, esp. 495-96 and n.77; M. A. Knibb, *The Qumran Community* (CCJC 2; Cambridge: Cambridge University Press, 1987) 77-8.

[6] J. Pouilly, *La Règle de la Communauté. Son evolution littéraire* (Cahiers RB 17; Paris: Gabalda 1976); É. Puech, "Recension: J. Pouillly, La Règle de la Communauté de Qumran. Son evolution littéraire," *RevQ* 10 (1979) 103-11; C. Dohmen, "Zur Gründung der Gemeinde von Qumran (1QS VIII-IX)," *RevQ* 11 (1982) 81-96; P. Arata Mantovani, "La stratificazione letteraria della Regola della Communita': A propositio di uno studio recente," *Henoch* 5 (1983) 69-91.

yet appeared. Before 1992, when the Brill microfiche edition became available,[7] scholars were dependent on a list of 4QS variants published by J. T. Milik in connection with a book review in 1960.[8] A fragment of the Community Rule found in Cave 5 was published by Milik in 1962,[9] but because of its small size it was of little use. G. Vermes, who together with P. S. Alexander has been entrusted with the preparation of the edition of 4QS^{a-j} for the DJD series, published an article in 1991 about the 4QS^{b,d} parallels to 1QS 5.[10] In the same year E. Qimron published two columns of the manuscript 4QS^d, providing parallels to 1QS 8:24–9:10 and 9:15–10:2.[11] In the Princeton Dead Sea Scrolls volume that was published in 1994 Qimron provided transcriptions of almost all the fragments of the Community Rule found in Cave 4. C. Martone's edition of the Cave 4 material of the Community Rule appeared in 1995, and transcriptions of the 4QS fragments are also included in my study of the redaction history of the work.[12]

2.2 The Rule of the Congregation

Two other works, the Rule of Congregation (1QSa) and Blessings (1QSb), were copied on the same scroll as 1QS. D. Barthélemy, the editor of 1QSa, noted the differences included in the manuscript in comparison with 1QS: the group about which the text speaks is named עדה, not יחד, and unlike in the Community Rule, women and children are mentioned, too. Barthélemy considered 1QSa as a rule for Israel which has been mobilized for an eschatological war, and Milik argued that the latter part of the document, 1QSa 2:11-22,

---

[7] E. Tov, with S. Pfann (eds.), *The Dead Sea Scrolls on Microfiche. A Comprehensive Facsimile Edition of the Texts from the Judaean Desert* (Leiden: Brill and IDC, 1993).

[8] J. T. Milik, "Texte des variantes des dix manuscrits de la Règle de la Communauté trouvés dans la Grotte 4. Recension de P.Wernberg-Møller, *The Manual of Discipline*," *RB* 67 (1960) 410-16.

[9] J. T. Milik, "Textes de la Grotte 5Q," in M. Baillet, J. T. Milik, R. de Vaux (eds.), *Les 'Petites Grottes' de Qumran. Textes* (DJD 3; Oxford: Clarendon Press, 1962) 167-97 + pls. XXXVI–LXII, esp. 180-81 + pl. XXXVIII.

[10] G. Vermes, "Preliminary Remarks on Unpublished Fragments of the Community Rule from Qumran Cave 4," *JJS* 42 (1991) 250-55.

[11] E. Qimron, "Manuscript D of the Rule of the Community from Qumran Cave IV: Preliminary Publication of Columns 7-8," *Tarbiz* 60 (1991) 434-43 (Hebrew).

[12] For Qimron, Martone and Metso, see n.1 above.

formed a description of an eschatological banquet.[13] L. H. Schiffman's interpretation of the document presented in his monograph of 1989 is in line with Barthélemy's and Milik's views, but while Schiffman considers 1QSa as a messianic document, he also emphasizes that 1QSa has the same theological and doctrinal basis as 1QS. Schiffman considers the Rule of the Congregation to be a messianic mirror of the community described in the Community Rule; the community attempted to create messianic conditions for its life even before the beginning of the eschatological era. In Schiffman's opinion, the regulations that are included in the Rule of the Congregation found actualization in the life of the community itself.[14]

Recently, the discussion about the Rule of the Congregation has been rekindled. A. Steudel discussed the term אחרית הימים in her article of 1993 and argued that at Qumran the term, while having an eschatological aspect, signified the era in which the community was presently living. Thus, the title of the Rule of the Congregation would not refer to a period of time which was still in the future, but to a time that had already begun.[15] H. Stegemann uses Steudel's observation in support of his theory that the Rule of the Congregation is the oldest of all Essene rule texts. In his view, the Rule of the Congregation was created prior to the Damascus Document and the material of 1QS 5-9, and was meant specifically for the cultic assemblies of the community.[16] C. Hempel also finds early material in the document. She considers the Rule of the Congregation to be a composite document, with 1QSa 1:6-2:11a as early Essene communal legislation which only at a later stage was placed in an eschatological frame. She argues that the picture of the community behind that section corresponds to the one emerging from the communal rules of the Damascus Document. She further points out that the introductory section of the Rule of the

---

[13] D. Barthélemy and J. T. Milik, *Qumran Cave 1* (DJD 1; Oxford: Clarendon Press, 1955) 107-30, esp. 108 and 121.

[14] L. H. Schiffman, *The Eschatological Community of the Dead Sea Scrolls: A Study of the Rule of the Congregation* (SBLMS 38; Atlanta: Scholars Press, 1989).

[15] A. Steudel, "אחרית הימים in the Texts from Qumran," *RevQ* 16 (1993-94) 225-46.

[16] H. Stegemann, "Some Remarks to 1QSa, 1QSb, and to Qumran Messianism," *RevQ* 17 (1996) 479-505.

Congregation (1QSa 1:1-3) displays terminologial affinities with the Community Rule, especially with 1QS 5:1-3.[17]

2.3 *The Scroll of 1QS, 1QSa and 1QSb*

One area of scholarly interest has been the reason why the separate works 1QS, 1QSa, and 1QSb were copied in the same scroll. Unfortunately, the title written on the verso of the handle sheet is not wholly preserved. The words סר[ך היחד ומן] can be read. Milik thought the words סר[ך] היחד referred to the material of the Community Rule (1QS 1–11), and ומן] started the part of the title that referred to the rest of the material of the scroll, i.e., to 1QSa and 1QSb, which are often seen as the two appendices of 1QS.[18] Stegemann, however, is of the opinion that the scroll contained not three, but four works: The words סרך היחד, which are the same as in 1QS 1:1, would refer only to columns 1QS 1–4, and 1QS 5 would commence a new, separate work reaching as far as 1QS 11 (the third and the fourth works would be formed by 1QSa and 1QSb). Stegemann describes the scroll as a *Schriftensammlung*, and the term is indeed pertinent to the way in which scholars have regarded the nature of the scroll (irrespective of how many works the scroll is thought to have contained).[19] More attention has been paid to the differences between the works than to their possible similarities: The *Gattung* of 1QSb is different from that of 1QS and 1QSa; 1QSa describes an eschatological community, whereas 1QS describes the community that lived at Qumran. The question has even been raised whether the community that created 1QS was the same as the community behind 1QSa.[20]

P. Alexander, however, thinks that he has found the link connecting the works in the *Serekh* scroll. He holds that the hymn (or hymns) of 1QS 10–11 were not for public use but were sung by the *maskil*, perhaps in the yearly festival of the renewal of the covenant. The *maskil* is also the one to whom the text of the

---

[17] C. Hempel, "The Earthly Essene Nucleus of 1QSa," *DSD* 3 (1996) 253-69.

[18] J. T. Milik, "Annexes à la Règle de la Communauté," in *Qumran Cave I* (DJD 1) 107-30 + pls. XXII–XXIX, esp. 107 + pl. XXII.

[19] H. Stegemann, *Die Essener, Qumran, Johannes der Täufer und Jesus. Ein Sachbuch* (Freiburg: Herder, 1993) 152-59; idem, "Some Remarks to 1QSa, 1QSb, and to Qumran Messianism," 479-505, esp. 481-83.

[20] See P. R. Davies, "Communities in the Qumran Scrolls," *Proceedings of the Irish Biblical Association* 17 (1994) 55-68, esp. 63.

Blessings (1QSb) was addressed; it was his duty to bless the God-fearing, the priests, and the prince of the congregation. In Alexander's view the liturgy was not yet used in the current community, but it was to be inaugurated at the beginning of the eschatological era. The perspective of 1QSb, he emphasizes, is eschatological, as is that of 1QSa, and its focus on the tasks of the *maskil* connects the work with the final column of 1QS.[21] It may be pointed out that no additional copies of 1QSa and 1QSb have been found at Qumran, whereas the number of manuscripts of the Community Rule totals twelve. The material reconstruction of the Cave 4 manuscripts of the Community Rule indicates that no standard collection of texts existed, such that any other scroll would have included the Rule of the Congregation and the Blessings together with the Community Rule. In fact, there seems to have been considerable variation as to which works or sections of works could have been copied on the same scroll. On the recto of 4QS[a], for example, there is a text of the Pseudo-Hodayot, and instead of the final psalm included in 1QS 10–11, the manuscript 4QS[e] has the calendrical text 4QOtot. The phenomenon is, of course, at least partly to be explained through the redaction processes which most texts underwent, but sometimes the choices by scribes appear to have been somewhat accidental.[22]

2.4 The Damascus Document

Most of the research on the Damascus Document has been based on the two medieval manuscripts of this work (CD[a, b]) found in the Cairo Geniza.[23] Ten copies were found at Qumran: eight manuscripts from Cave 4 and one each from Caves 5 and 6. Milik published a preliminary report on the Cave 4 manuscripts in 1957,[24] and Milik

---

[21] P. S. Alexander, "The Redaction History of Serekh Ha-Yaḥad: A Proposal," *RevQ* 17 (1996) 437-56, esp. 441-42.

[22] Metso, *The Textual Development*, 18-68 and 151.

[23] S. Schechter, *Documents of Jewish Sectaries*, Vol. I. *Fragments of a Zadokite Work* (Cambridge, 1910; repr. New York: Ktav, 1970); S. Zeitlin, *The Zadokite Documents. Facsimile of the Manuscripts in the Cairo Genizah Collection in the Possession of the University Library, Cambridge, England* (JQRM 1; Philadelphia: Dropsie College, 1952).

[24] J. T. Milik, *Ten Years of Discovery in the Wilderness of Judaea* (SBT 26; London: SCM, 1959) 38. The original French publication was *Dix ans de découvertes dans le Désert de Juda* (Paris: Cerf, 1957).

and Baillet published those from Caves 5 and 6 in DJD 3 in 1962.[25] On the basis of the combined Qumran evidence, Milik suggested the following reconstruction as the order of the original document: (1) an opening section, which is not preserved in the Geniza manuscripts; (2) material parallel to CD 1–8; (3) a section consisting of mainly halakhic material, which has been preserved fragmentarily only in the Qumran manuscripts; (4) material parallel to CD 15–16; (5) material parallel to CD 9–14; and (6) a final section extant only in the Cave 4 copies, which consists of a penal code and an expulsion liturgy to be used at the renewal of the covenant.[26] With the publication of all the Cave 4 manuscripts by J. Baumgarten in the DJD edition in 1996, the discussion of the full material can begin.[27] Until recently, two topics have been particularly prominent in the study of the Damascus Document: questions regarding the halakhah and regarding the history of the community. I shall not deal with these topics here, however, since there are separate articles devoted to them in these two volumes on the Scrolls after fifty years.[28] Instead, I shall briefly discuss the textual studies on the Damascus Document and compare it with other rule texts found at Qumran.

Of the two parts of the Damascus Document, the Admonition (CD 1–8 + 19–20) and the Laws (CD 9–16), the analysis of the former has clearly dominated the discussion about the document. Most scholars consider the Admonition to be literarily incoherent,[29] yet their views as to how the section was put together vary considerably. Philip Davies' assessment of the different trends found in the study of the Admonition is very illuminating: "Some consider it a fragment of a larger work (Dupont-Sommer), others as a collection of smaller units worked together (Maier), some as a number of coherent documents built up in a more or less systematic way around a core (Murphy-O'Connor) or a basic document heavily interpolated

---

[25] J. T. Milik, "Document de Damas (5Q12)," in Baillet, Milik and de Vaux (eds.), *Les 'Petites Grottes' de Qumran. Textes* (DJD 3) 181; M. Baillet, in idem, "Document de Damas (6Q15)," 128-31.

[26] Milik, *Ten Years of Discovery*, 151-2, n.3.

[27] See n.1 above.

[28] See the articles by H. Harrington in this Volume and by J. VanderKam in Volume 2.

[29] L. Rost is the one scholar who suggested that the Admonition is literally coherent, *Die Damaskusschrift neu bearbeitet* (Kleine Texte 167; Berlin: De Gruyter, 1933) 1.

(Rabinowitz and, to a large extent, Stegemann)."[30] For our purposes, however—i.e. for considering the Damascus Document as a rule text—the large section consisting of laws is more interesting. The material of the section appears very heterogeneous. Some of the laws were likely grouped together even before their insertion in the document, and very probably the material underwent editorial modification in its present context as well. Although it is at some places unclear whether the latest redactor actually intended the laws to be grouped in the way suggested below,[31] the following thematic entities can be discerned within the legal sections: regulations for entry into the covenant (15:1–16:16), internal laws of conduct (9:1–10:10a), rites to be observed in the community (10:10b–12:18), community organization (12:19–14:19), penal code (14:20-22).[32] As mentioned above, the manuscripts from Cave 4 contain additional laws which correspond to nothing in the Cairo Geniza manuscripts.[33]

2.5 The Relationship Between 1QS and CD

The Damascus Document shares many features with the Community Rule in vocabulary, themes, and theological ideas, but there are clear dissimilarities, too: The Damascus Document has long sections describing the history of the community, but the Community Rule shows no particular interest in the events of the community's past. There is nothing comparable to the Doctrine of the Two Spirits

---

[30] P. R. Davies, *The Damascus Covenant. An Interpretation of the "Damascus Document"* (JSOTSup 25; Sheffield: JSOT Press, 1983) 48.

[31] In CD 10:10 the scribe has not indicated in any way (e.g. by using an interval) that there would be a beginning of a new section.

[32] See J. A. Fitzmyer's "Prolegomenon" to Schechter, *Documents of Jewish Sectaries*, 9-35, esp. 18-19.

[33] Baumgarten and Schwarts have listed the following eight additional segments included in the Cave 4 material: (a). Introduction to the laws, a catalogue of transgressions ending with an appeal to those who know to choose between the paths of life and perdition. (b). The priests and their communal role, rules about priestly disqualification. (c). The ordeal (before the priests) of the wife suspected of adultery (Num 5:11-31). (d). Diagnosis (by the priests) of skin diseases. (e). Impurity resulting from fluxes and childbirth. (f). The law of fraud (Lev. 25:14) applied to the arrangement of marriages. (g). Levitical laws pertaining to harvest. (h) Impurity of metals used in pagan cults [segments I-W have parallel in CD]; X. A ritual for expulsion from the Community at the time of the annual renewal of the covenant in the third month. Baumgarten and Schwartz, "Damascus Document (CD)," in Charlesworth et al. (eds.), *The Dead Sea Scrolls*, 2.4-57, esp. 5.

(1QS 3:13–4:26) in the Damascus Document. Puzzling differences occur in the thematically parallel sections found in both 1QS and CD. For example, the novitiate for membership in the community is longer according to the Community Rule than according to the Damascus Document; and in 1QS it is the *rabbim*, but in CD it is the *mebaqqer*, who approves candidates for membership. The differences in the organizational terminology may be the most difficult to explain: (1) *mebaqqer* and *rabbim* occur as organizational functionaries in both, but the tasks attributed to them differ; (2) 1QS knows a community official called *paqid*, whereas in CD there is no mention of him (the verb פקד is used in CD, however); (3) *maskil*, who is frequently mentioned in 1QS, does not appear in CD at all;[34] (4) *yahad* is the term with which the community refers to itself in 1QS, but it does not occur in CD; instead, the term used there is *mahaneh*; (5) CD mentions women and children, whereas there is no mention of them in 1QS.

The differences between the two documents have often been explained using sociological and historical factors. That is, 1QS was viewed as written for the community centered at Qumran, whereas CD was aimed at the larger Essene membership in the towns. But there are differences even within these approaches. Baumgarten, for example, maintains that the community living at Qumran was celibate,[35] but Schiffman thinks that most members were either not yet married or already married before they came to the community but had (at least temporarily) left their families.[36] Dimant, on the other hand, begins with a historical differentiation. She considers the possibility that CD, at an early stage, pertained to a community in which marriage was the normal practice, whereas 1QS pertained to a subsequent stage in which celibacy had become the ideal.[37] In contrast, Stegemann does not consider the absence of women and

---

[34] It may be noted, however, that there is one occurrence of the term in the Cave 4 material, in 4QD^a 9 iii, 15.

[35] J. M. Baumgarten, "The Qumran-Essene Restraints on Marriage," in L. H. Schiffman (ed.), *Archaeology and History in the Dead Sea Scrolls. The New York University Conference in Memory of Yigael Yadin* (JSPSup 8; Sheffield: JSOT Press, 1990) 13-24.

[36] L. H. Schiffman, *Sectarian Law in the Dead Sea Scrolls. Courts, Testimony and the Penal Code* (BJS 33; Chico, CA: Scholars Press, 1983) 12-13.

[37] Dimant, "Qumran Sectarian Literature," 503.

children in the community to be a problem. He thinks that the rules regulating marriage as well as purity, Sabbath, cultic calendar, tithes, etc., had already been established in the pre-Essene period and needed no explicit repetition. Although Stegemann holds that much pre-Essene material has been included in the Damascus Document, he thinks that in its present form it is the latest of the Essene rule texts.[38]

When comparing the Community Rule and the Damascus Document there has also been discussion about how the rules originated that were included in the documents. Schiffman takes as his starting point that the doctrine of oral transmission of law, and more generally the concept of oral law, were absent at Qumran. According to him the Qumranic legal traditions originated only from scriptural exegesis.[39] P. Davies and M. Weinfeld have criticized his views from different angles. Davies emphasizes the differences between the two rules. He thinks that the Damascus Document indeed, with one or two exceptions, is based on scriptural exegesis, whereas the laws recorded in the Community Rule have not been presented as, or were not intended to be understood as, derived from scriptural exegesis. From this Davies concludes that the group behind the Damascus Document must have been different from that behind the Community Rule.[40] Moshe Weinfeld's criticism of Schiffman's views stems from his observation that the rules regulating the community organization and admission of new members are very similar to those found in Hellenistic and Roman religious groups. He argues that we must distinguish between rules sanctified by the Torah and those arising only within the community itself: the laws of Torah belong to the realm of the covenant between God and Israel, whereas community regulations concern social organization, the members of which were bound by a voluntary commitment to the rules approved by the group. Weinfeld does not subscribe to Schiffman's conclusion that, if a member of the community did not obey an order given by a

---

[38] H. Stegemann, *Die Essener, Qumran, Johannes der Täufer und Jesus*, 156 and 165.

[39] L. H. Schiffman, *The Halakhah at Qumran* (SJLA 16; Leiden: Brill, 1975) 19-20.

[40] P. R. Davies, "Halakhah at Qumran," in P. R. Davies and R. T. White (eds.), *A Tribute to Geza Vermes. Essays on Jewish and Christian Literature and History* (JSOTSup 100; Sheffield: JSOT Press, 1990) 37-50, esp. 43-49.

superior, by rejecting a communal rule he ultimately was rejecting a divine commandment.[41]

3. THE EVIDENCE FROM CAVE 4

The analysis of the material from Cave 4 is still in an early stage, but the results that have been achieved already offer promise of a lively discussion in the near future. Both the additional copies of those rule documents previously known and the texts that have only recently become known have not only opened a possibility of testing and modifying earlier theories but have also posed many new questions not raised before. In the following, I shall first consider the material of the Community Rule and the Damascus Document, and then comment on the rule fragments that have recently become accessible.

3.1 The Community Rule

Milik expressed a preliminary view that 4QS[b, d] represented an earlier form of the text than 1QS.[42] Geza Vermes' tentative estimate pointed in the same direction when he published transcriptions of the parallels to 1QS 5 in 4QS[b, d]. Vermes paid special attention to a variant between 1QS 5:2-3 and 4QS[b] frg. 5 line 3 = 4QS[d] 1 i line 2 referring to the authority of the community. The words על פי הרבים in 4QS[b, d] have been replaced by a longer formulation in 1QS: על פי בני צדוק הכוהנים שומרי הברית ועל פי רוב אנשי היחד המחזקים בברית על פיהם יצא תכון הגורל. Whereas Vermes speaks of two different traditions,[43] C. Hempel has developed the idea further, speaking of a Zadokite recension, the marks of which she detects also in the text of 1QSa which is part of the same scroll as 1QS.[44] R. Kugler discusses another variant concerning בני הצדק/בני הצדוק in 1QS 9:1/4QS[e] 1 iii 10, arguing that the form in 1QS typifies a later recension which indicates that the Zadokite priests had not always had a prominent

---

[41] M. Weinfeld, *The Organizational Pattern and the Penal Code of the Qumran Sect. A Comparison with Guilds and Religious Associations of the Hellenistic-Roman Period* (NTOA 2; Göttingen: Vandenhoeck & Ruprecht, 1986) 71-76.

[42] J. T. Milik, "Numérotation des feuilles des rouleaux dans le scriptorium de Qumran (Planches X et XI)," *Sem* 27 (1977) 75-81, esp. 78.

[43] G. Vermes, "Preliminary Remarks," 255: "At a preliminary guess, it can already be surmised that 1QS is more likely to be an expanded edition of the Cave 4 texts rather than 4QS an abridgement of 1QS."

[44] C. Hempel, "The Earthly Essene Nucleus of 1QSa," *DSD* 3 (1996) 253-69.

role in the community but gained that position only at a later stage. In his view the Zadokites, however, remained obedient to the superior *maskil*.[45]

P. Alexander thinks that the order in which the manuscripts were copied holds the key to the order in which the different recensions were created. 1QS, which contains a longer version, is generally dated earlier than 4QS[b, d]. Alexander considers it more likely that the version of 4QS[b, d] would be a result of secondary omissions than that 1QS was an expansion of 4QS[b, d], as Milik and Vermes think. Alexander explains the variant in 1QS 5:2-3 // 4QS[b] frg. 5 line 3 = 4QS[d] 1 i line 2 in such a way that 1QS reflects an early stage in the history of the community when the Zadokites held a leading position, whereas 4QS[b, d] belong to a later stage when their position had weakened. Alexander also discusses the large section 1QS 8:15–9:11 which is lacking in 4QS[e]. He thinks that the omission was intentional, after the redactor observed contradictions and repetitions in that section. In relation to 4QS[b,d], Alexander maintains that 4QS[e] represents the latest redactional stage. Thus, his suggestion of the order of the MSS is 1QS (the oldest), 4QS[d], and 4QS[e] (the youngest).[46]

In my literary- and redaction-critical analysis of the Cave 4 manuscripts (4QS[a–j]) I attempted to present a comprehensive treatment of all the *Serekh* variants. In my opinion, the version of 4QS[b, d] on the one hand and the version of 4QS[e] on the other hand have preserved forms of the text earlier than that of 1QS. Comparison between 4QS[b, d] and 1QS reveals a redaction, the purpose of which was to provide scriptural legitimization for the rules of the community and to strengthen its self-understanding as the true keeper of the covenant and the law. The editorial changes that can be observed by comparing 1QS and 4QS[e] aim at bringing the text up to date. Thus, 4QS[b, d] and 4QS[e] represent two lines of tradition which derive from a yet earlier version, a version which (1) presumably did not include the material parallel to 1QS 1–4; (2) commenced with 1QS 5 and was addressed to the *maskil*; (3) lacked scriptural quotations and additions aimed at strengthening the community's self-understanding; (4) did not include the section

---

[45] R. Kugler, "A Note on 1QS 9:14: The Sons of Righteousness or the Sons of Zadok," *DSD* 3 (1996) 315-20.

[46] Alexander, "The Redaction History," 437-56.

parallel to 1QS 8:15–9:11; and (5) lacked the final psalm found in 1QS 10–11 but possibly included the calendric text Otot instead. Derived from that earliest version were 4QS[b, d] on the one hand, with its addition of the final psalm, and 4QS[e] on the other, with its addition of the scriptural quotations and other supplements aimed at strengthening the community's self-understanding. The manuscript 1QS is a combination of both lines of tradition as in 4QS[b, d] and 4QS[e], and thus includes both the scriptural quotations and other additions, as well as the final psalm. The latest stage of redaction is to be seen in the revisions and additions made secondarily by the scribal corrector in 1QS 7–8.[47]

I did not extend my study to cover questions regarding the history of the community. Although I do not wish to exclude the possibility of learning about the events of the community's history through a comparison of the manuscripts, I do not find it compelling to presume a conflict between different groups of the community behind the variant concerning the sons of Zadok in 1QS 5:2-3. In my view, the redaction in 1QS 5 was primarily theological. The variant speaks about the sons of Zadok and the men of the community, i.e. the priests and the laymen. The *rabbim*, who appear in 4QS[b, d] instead, also consisted of priests and laymen (cf. 1QS 6:8-9). The substitute wording in 1QS is heavily loaded with theological vocabulary: "The sons of Zadok, the priests who keep the covenant, and the multitude of the men of the community who hold fast to the covenant; on their word the decision shall be taken." If the motivation for replacing הרבים is considered to be above all theological, it is in line with other redactional changes occurring in the section.

One of the main results of my study of the redaction history of the Community Rule was that the need to find a scriptural legitimation for the regulations of the community arose only at a later stage, presumably in a situation in which the community's strict rules had been questioned. Thus, the process appears to have been the reverse of what has been often presumed, at least in some cases. The laws regulating especially "matter of fact" details of the community life seem not to have emerged as a result of scriptural exegesis, but scriptural quotations or allusions were added because of the need to justify the rules already in effect. Though some of the rules did come from scriptural exegesis, the scriptural sources were not always

---

[47] Metso, *The Textual Development*, esp. 143-49.

explicitly quoted. The section in 1QS 6:8-13 dealing with the session of the *rabbim* provides quite a detailed picture of a situation in which community legislation was created. What draws attention is that the Torah or written rules are not referred to at all. Whenever the community authority is discussed in the Community Rule, the decisions are said to be made on the basis of the word of the *rabbim* (על פי הרבים) or, as in 9:7, on the word of the sons of Aaron. The hypothesis, however, that the community would have made a distinction between its own rules and the regulations of the Torah does not seem plausible. The fact that in the redactional process of the Community Rule scriptural quotations were added as proof-texts for the community regulations speaks rather for the assumption that ultimately the community regarded its own regulations as resting on biblical authority. The formula "for thus it is written" (כיא כן כתוב or כאשר כתוב) is a clear indication of this. From the point of view of a modern reader, the connection between a regulation and a citation supporting it may be artificial. The community, however, considered its laws to be in accordance with the Torah.

3.2 The Damascus Document

J. Baumgarten writes in the introduction to his edition of 4QD that approximately 47 percent of the Cave 4 material is parallel to the Cairo Geniza manuscripts, and that in the parallel sections the readings in the Cave 4 material coincide well with the A manuscript. According to Baumgarten, the material includes only about thirty significant variants. However, the amount of legal material is considerably larger in the Cave 4 manuscripts than in the Cairo manuscripts. Moreover, there are three sections with no parallel at all in the Cairo manuscripts: a hortatory preface, a list of wrongdoers, and a liturgy of expulsion. Baumgarten does not attempt to provide any comprehensive or definitive reconstruction of the original document. He is largely relying on Milik's view of the order of the sections;[48] he remarks, however, that H. Stegemann, who is preparing a material reconstruction of the Damascus Document manuscripts, would rather place the list of wrongdoers at the end of the legal section, whereas Milik places it before the laws. Although the Cave 4 manuscripts are generally comparable to each other, Baumgarten points out that some laws are absent from certain

---

[48] For Milik's view, see section 2.4 above.

manuscripts. For example, the rule in CD 11:14-15, which forbids spending Sabbath in the proximity of pagans, is included in 4Q271 (5 i, line 9), but is lacking in the parallel section of 4Q270 (6 v).[49]

Although it is possible to compare thematically parallel passages between 1QS and CD (rules for admission of new members, for example) there are no identical passages between them. The Cave 4 version, however, of the Damascus Document (witnessed by both 4Q266/4QD[a] and 4Q270/4QD[e]) includes a section of a penal code which is clearly based on the same text as the one in 1QS 7. Although the text in 1QS contains a few regulations that are absent from the parallel sections of 4QD[a,e], the order of the shared regulations is the same. Either the writers of the Community Rule and those of the Damascus Document used the same source, or the sections are directly dependent on each other. The transgressions are in most cases expressed in an identical way; the differences, when they occur, are mainly orthographic and morphological. The punishments, however, tend to differ in an interesting way: Unlike in the Community Rule, many of the punishments in 4QD sections consist of two parts, of punishment (נענש) and exclusion (הובדל). In most cases the length of the punishment in 1QS corresponds to that of the exclusion in D. Baumgarten comments on these sections in the following way: "It thus appears that the penal code, which in the Community Rule seems to reflect the discipline of an all male order, was capable of being also applied to a society in which both men and women took part in communal life."[50] Baumgarten does not consider the implications of his observation for the methodology of the study of the rule texts: If various groups may have used common sources and borrowed material from each other, how can the groups behind the manuscripts be identified and categorized? If large parts of the material included in various manuscripts are borrowed and modified, what is the criterion that enables us to assign whole manuscripts to particular groups (e.g. a celibate community versus a

---

[49] Baumgarten, *The Damascus Document* (DJD 18) 1-22.

[50] Idem, *The Damascus Document* (DJD 18) 8. As this volume was going to press, the following penetrating and insightful article by Charlotte Hempel appeared: "The Penal Code Reconsidered," in M. Bernstein, F. García Martínez and J. Kampen (eds.), *Legal Texts and Legal Issues: Proceedings of the Second Meeting of the International Organization For Qumran Studies, Cambridge 1995, Published in Honour of Joseph M. Baumgarten* (STDJ 23; Leiden: Brill, 1997) 337-48.

community in which marriage was a common practice)? The case of the penal codes in S and D, in my view, shows clearly that the composite nature of the documents needs to be taken into account. Rather than on whole documents, the analysis should be concentrated on separate passages.

3.3 Serek Damascus

The manuscript 4Q265 provides an example similar to the penal codes mentioned above. The name of the manuscript, Serek Damascus, describes well the nature of the document: 4Q265 contains features from both the Community Rule and the Damascus Document. Serek Damascus will be edited by J. Baumgarten in the DJD series, and he has discussed the manuscript in his article of 1992.[51] Serek Damascus includes rules that are typical for the Damascus Document (e.g. Sabbath regulations), and like the Damascus Document, 4Q265 mentions women and children. On the other hand, 4Q265 lists transgressions which occur in the Community Rule, such as complaining against those ranked higher in the community, lying about a neighbor, insulting or betraying a neighbor, falling asleep in the community meeting and guffawing stupidly. A double punishment consisting of punishment and exclusion which occurs in 4Q266 (4QD^a) and 4Q270 (4QD^e) is also met in 4Q265. Whereas in the Community Rule and the Damascus Document the exact nature of the punishment is often unclear, 4Q265 mentions explicitly that the punishment means cutting the food ration.[52] Apparently in the lost parts of 4Q265 biblical quotations were used as proof-texts to justify the regulations that are listed in the manuscript, because the introductory formulas כאשר כתוב and כאשר כתוב בספר which occur in 1QS and CD are also found in 4Q265 (cf. 1QS 5:17; 8:14; CD 7:10, 19). The organizational terminology used in Serek Damascus is also close to that of 1QS and CD:

---

[51] J. M. Baumgarten, "The Cave 4 Versions of the Qumran Penal Code," *JJS* 43 (1992) 268-76. Milik appears to have presumed a third group in addition to those behind the Damascus Document and the Community Rule, for he speaks of "tertiaries" in connection with 4Q265. See his *Ten Years of Discovery*, 90.

[52] The content of the punishment is clear only in 1QS 6:25, where it means—as in 4QSD—cutting the food ration. It remains unclear whether the meaning of נענש is the same also later in the text where the verb is used alone without any further definitions. The reader of the Damascus Document is faced with the same problem, for the content of the punishment is clarified in none of the occurrences of the verb.

מושב הרב[ים (4QSD 1 ii, line 1, cf. 1QS 6:8, 11; 7:10, 13);

עצת ה[יח]ד (4QSD 1 ii, line 3; cf. (for example) 1QS 5:7; 6:3, 10, 14, 16; 7:2, 22, 24; 8:1, 5);

הרבים (4QSD 1 ii, line 5; cf. (for example) 1QS 6:1, 17; 7:21; 8:19; CD 13:7; and 14:7, 12);

המבקר אשר על מושב הרבים / המבקר על היחד / הא[י]ש המבקר על הרבים (4QSD 1 ii, lines 4, 68; cf. 1QS 6:12; CD 15:8).

3.4 Decrees

The manuscript 4Q477 also represents the organizational terminology characteristic of the Essenes. Esther Eshel published the manuscript in 1992 under the name "Rebukes by the Overseer" (תוכחות המבקר), dating it to the Herodian period.[53] The text of the document does not explictly say, however, that the rebuke would be carried out by the *mebaqqer*, but the manuscript (frg. 2 especially) follows the pattern "And they rebuke X son of Y" + an allusion to the man's sin. The assumption that the one responsible for the rebuking would be the *mebaqqer*, is based on the descriptions of his tasks occurring in other Qumran manuscripts, esp. in CD 9:16-20 (see also 4Q266 4QD[a] 18 v, line 16). Stephen Reed argues that although the parallel texts do indicate that it was the *mebaqqer*, whose task it was to compile the kind of lists of transgressions as the one in 4Q477, a more accurate name for the text would be "List of rebukes made by the *community*."[54] The manuscript is unique at Qumran as it has preserved the names of two community members, Hananiah Notos and Hananiah ben Shimon.

The rule of rebuke is based on Lev 19:17, but Eshel has pointed out that there are two significant passages dealing with rebukes in the manuscripts of the community: 1QS 5:25–6:1 and CD 9:2-4.[55]

---

[53] E. Eshel, "4Q477: The Rebukes by the Overseer," *JJS* 45 (1994) 111-22. According to Eshel "the text preserves remnants of a legal record, compiled by the sect's Overseer (מבקר), of those members who were rebuked after committing a sin. It appears that, although it is an official written text, it was probably read out in public by the Overseer" (111).

[54] S. A. Reed, "Genre, Setting and Title of 4Q477," *JJS* 46 (1995) 147-48.

[55] 1QS 5:25–6:1: "They shall reprove one another in tr[uth], humility, and kindly love towards man. Let no man speak to his neighbour in anger or in complaint or with a [stiff] neck [or in a jealou]s spirit of wickedness, and let him not hate him [...] of his heart. But let him reprove him on the same day lest he incur guilt because of him. And let no man bring a matter against his neighbour before the many except after reproof before witnesses" (translation by M. A. Knibb, *The*

According to them, rebuking a neighbor forms a preliminary stage of a judicial process.[56] The section 1QS 5:25–6:1 also indicates that lists of the kind in 4Q477 were used in the members' yearly inspection and ranking. It is worth noting that the transgressions mentioned in 4Q477 are of a moral rather than a cultic nature and that many of them are listed in 1QS (doing evil, being short-tempered, being haughty in spirit, loving one's relatives and therefore failing to rebuke them, disturbing the spirit of the יחד, and choosing a good life.) A feature that links 4Q477 to CD is the use of the term מחנה: 4Q477 frg. 2 lines 1 and 3 refer to מחני הרבים. The term מחנה does not occur in 1QS at all, whereas it is very common in CD. The term הרבים is used both in 1QS and CD, but the combination מחני הרבים is attested in 4Q477 only.

3.5 The Manuscripts 4Q275 and 4Q279

In the preliminary concordance (printed from a card index) 4Q275 and 4Q279 appear under the sigla 4QS^x and 4QS^y; it seems that Milik had already noticed the similarities between these manuscripts and the Community Rule. Neither 4Q275 nor 4Q279 has been published yet, although Milik discussed one of the fragments (frg. 3) of 4Q275 in an article in 1972, in which he compared it with 4Q280 (4QBer^f/4QMaledictions).[57] Milik named 4Q275 "4QTeharot B," and in the Microfiche Companion Volume it is listed as "Tohorot B a." The name of 4Q279 in the Companion Volume includes the question mark "Tohorot D a?"[58] The preparation of their edition was entrusted to J. Baumgarten, but when he and I concluded that 4Q275 and 4Q279 do not actually belong to the group of Tohorot

---

Qumran Community, 113). CD 9:2-4: "And what it says: *Lev 19:18* 'Do not avenge yourself or bear resentment against the sons of your people:' everyone of those who entered the covenant who brings an accusation against his fellow, unless it is with reproach before witnesses, or who brings it when he is angry, or he tells it to his elders so that they despise him, he is 'the one who avenges himself and bears resentment'" (translation by F. García Martínez, *The Dead Sea Scrolls Translated. The Qumran Texts in English* [Leiden: Brill, 1994] 40).

[56] The practice of rebuking has been treated at length by L. H. Schiffman in his *Sectarian Law in the Dead Sea Scrolls. Courts, Testimony and the Penal Codes* (BJS 33; Chico, CA: Scholars Press, 1983) 89-109.

[57] J. T. Milik, "Milkî-ṣedeq et Milkî-rešaʿ dans les anciens écrits juifs et chrétiens," *JJS* 22 (1972) 95-144, esp. 129-30.

[58] E. Tov, with S. Pfann (eds.), *The Dead Sea Scrolls on Microfiche. Companion Volume*, 39.

manuscripts, they were handed over to G. Vermes and P. Alexander. Now 4Q275 has been renamed "Communal Ceremony" or "Order of Initiation," while 4Q279 has been renamed "Order of Assembly."[59]

The vocabulary of 4Q275 resembles that of columns 1–4 of 1QS and is particularly similar to the liturgy of the renewal of the covenant (1QS 2:18–3:12), although due to the fragmentary state of the text, it is difficult to form a picture of the line of thought. Possibly the manuscript provides a liturgy for a new member's joining the community. (1) The words בחודש השלישׁי [are preserved in the manuscript, and the text speaks about registering a member, testing and rebuking him; blessings and curses were apparently also included. The Damascus Document manuscript 4Q270 (4QD^e) 7 ii, line 11 also speaks about gathering the members in the third month, referring presumably to the renewal of the covenant. Similarly, the liturgy in the Community Rule implies that the new members were accepted during the renewal of the covenant. (2) The term נחלה ("inheritance") is mentioned twice in the preserved parts of 4Q275. In the Community Rule it is used in the sense that everyone is assigned a lot under the dominion of either the prince of light or the prince of darkness. (3) As to the organizational functionaries, the elders (הזקנים) and the *mebaqqer* (המבקר) are mentioned. The members are referred to by the name קריאי השם, which has a parallel in CD 4:3-4 (בחירי ישראל קריאי השם).

Only one fragment of 4Q279 is large enough for determining the nature of the document, and it appears to present a kind of rule for a community assembly. The word הגורל occurs three times in the fragment, once in the wording יצא הגור]ל. Some ordinal numbers are preserved, presumably indicating a hierarchical order, and ranked

---

[59] 4Q275 and 4Q279 are the the two lower manuscripts on Rockefeller Museum plate 679 and on PAM photograph 43.315. Both manuscripts are poorly preserved. Of 4Q275, there are only three fragments extant, each preserving part of the upper margin and parts of 7-8 lines. The fragments are very similar in shape; most likely they were close to each other in the original scroll, possibly from three consecutive layers. Of 4Q279 there are only five fragments extant, the largest containing text from five lines and a lower margin. The other four fragments contain only isolated words and letters. One of the fragments on the plate (frg. 5) has been put together from three small pieces, but the join between the two lower pieces does not seem correct. The piece on the right may not belong to the same manuscript: the hand appears very light compared to that of the other fragments, and the line spacing does not match that of the piece on the left.

groups of the community are termed לכה[נים בני אהרון] and גר[ים (the small fragment preserves only these two). Similar rules with an emphasis on the hierarchical order of different groups of the community are to be found, e.g. in CD 14:3-6 and 1QS 2:19-25 and 6:8-9. The section in CD 14:3-6 may provide a key for the interpretation of the fragment: "Rule of the session of all the camps. All shall be enlisted by their names: the priests first, the levites second, the children of Israel third, and the proselyte fourth; and they shall be inscribed by their [na]mes, each one after his brother; the priests first, the levites second, the children of Israel third and the proselyte fourth." Perhaps the text of 4Q279 should be reconstructed accordingly so that the four groups discussed would be כוהנים בני אהרון, לויים, בני ישראל, and גרים.

3.6 The Manuscript 5Q13

Although 5Q13 was published under the name "Une règle de la secte" by Milik in DJD 3, the *Gattung* is not self-evidently that of a rule. The most extensively-preserved fragments (1 and 2) form rather a hymn or prayer, in which God is addressed in the second person and his deeds in Israel's history are recounted. Fragment 4, however, does have similarities with the Community Rule: line 1 reads "He shall stand before the *mebaqqer*," the next two lines cite 1QS 3:4-5, and line 4 has wording which coincides with 1QS 2:19.[60] One Cave 4 manuscript of the Community Rule may provide an interesting parallel to the case of 5Q13. 4QS^h has three fragments preserved, but only one (frg. 1) finds a parallel in 1QS. The text in the other two cannot be identified. Fragment 1 contains a parallel to 1QS 3:4-5, which is the same phrase as that in 5Q13, and like 5Q13, the two unidentified fragments in 4QS^h bear characteristics of a hymn. Thus, a question arises of whether 4QS^h is a copy of the Community Rule at all, or another example of a work simply citing it.

4. CONCLUSION

The present article covers only some of the rule texts found at Qumran, and, in order to build a synthesis, the manuscripts discussed

---

[60] I should like to take this opportunity to make a correction on p. 66 of my book *The Textual Development*. There I reproduced Milik's transcription of fragment 4 of 5Q13, but accidentally omitted the word בשנה from line 4. The correct reading of the line is: [ה]אלה יעשו שנה בשנה ב[ול ימי].

by Hannah Harrington in this volume should also be taken into consideration. On the basis of the material dealt with here, however, the following questions may be brought forth for future discussion:

(a) What is the function of the rule texts in the Qumran community and the wider Essene movement? Quite naturally, this question has been widely discussed in connection with the debate about the relationship between 1QS and CD. In addition to the differences between the two documents, the issue is complicated by the fact that there are discrepancies even within single documents. At least three basic solutions have emerged so far: the manuscripts were effective successively, i.e. in the course of time one rule document (or part of it) was replaced by another (Stegemann);[61] the manuscripts or sections of manuscripts were addressed to different groups (Sanders and Baumgarten);[62] the manuscripts describe not a real but fictive community (Davies).[63] The Cave 4 material of the Community Rule adds a new component for the discussion, for it seems that the community continued copying earlier versions of the text even when new versions were already available. Thus, the question arises, in what sense or whether the so-called rule texts could have functioned as prescriptive rules.[64]

(b) How should we explain differences in the organizational terminology? While it does not seem easy to fit together the organizational terms occurring in the previously known documents, the new material only compounds the confusion. Should we think that the use of different organizational terms indicates the existence of different types of groups? Or is it possible that a single group or functionary had several names in use simultaneously? Or was the use

---

[61] Stegemann, *Die Essener, Qumran, Johannes der Täufer und Jesus*, 152-67, esp. 164-67.

[62] E. P. Sanders, *Paul and Palestinian Judaism. A Comparison of Patterns of Religion* (London: SCM, 1977) 323-25; J.M. Baumgarten, *The Damascus Document* (DJD 18) 8.

[63] P. R. Davies, "Redaction and Sectarianism in the Qumran Scrolls," in F. García Martínez, A. Holhorst and C. J. Labuschagne (eds.), *The Scriptures and the Scrolls. Studies in Honour of A. S. van der Woude on the Occasion of His 65th Birthday* (VTSup 49; Leiden: Brill, 1992) 152-63.

[64] For further discussion, see my article "In Search of the *Sitz im Leben* of the Community Rule," in D. Parry and E. Ulrich (eds.), *Proceedings of the 1996 International Dead Sea Scrolls Conference, 15-17 July, 1996, Provo, Utah* (STDJ 30; Leiden: Brill [forthcoming]).

of different terms successive, so that terms could have changed even though the structure of the community (or communities) would have remained the same? Interestingly, many of the previously unknown texts are not clearly close to either the Damascus Document or the Community Rule in their terminology, but seem to represent a kind of combination of the two. Clearly the organizational terminology will provide fruitful material for the analysis of the sociological nature of the Essene movement.

(c) What is the relationship between the community rules and the biblical laws? The question as to how the community regulations emerged has already been a subject of lively discussion. Some of the rules have a clear background in biblical legislation. Often this background is stated explicitly through a direct scriptural quotation, but in some cases the quote is only implicit although the rule has clearly emerged as a result of scriptural exegesis. One group of rules, however, lacks a background in the Bible: many of the rules deal with the basic principles of the community's everyday life. The Cave 4 versions of the Community Rule highlight examples of cases in which community rules were justified by secondarily adding quotations of scripture, possibly in a situation in which the community's strict rules had been questioned.

(d) Methodologically, how do the rule texts function as a tool for the reconstruction of the community's history? Many of the redaction-critical theories related to the rule texts aim at creating links between the stages of textual growth and the stages of historical development of the Essene movement and the Qumran community. The plurality of the various rule texts found at Qumran, on the one hand, and the fact that older versions of the documents continued to be copied even when new versions were available, on the other hand, warn us against placing an equal-sign between the picture painted by a document and the historical reality behind it. Whereas literary- and redaction-critical analysis of a document can provide some indication about the comparative age of a rule or practice, linking a rule or practice with an actual historical period of time is far more difficult. It is particularly problematic when pieces of information provided by different manuscripts are combined in an attempt at historical reconstruction. The interplay between redactional and historical analysis will undoubtedly continue to play an important role in the discussion about the Qumran community.

SELECT BIBLIOGRAPHY

Alexander, P. S. "The Redaction History of Serekh Ha-Yaḥad. A Proposal," *RevQ* 17 (1996) 437-56.

Baillet, M. "Document de Damas (6Q15)," in M. Baillet, J. T. Milik and R. de Vaux, *Les 'Petites Grottes' de Qumran. Textes* (DJD 3.1; Oxford: Clarendon Press, 1962) 128-31.

Barthélemy, D. "Règle de la Congrégation," in D. Barthélemy and J. T. Milik, *Qumran Cave 1* (DJD 1; Oxford: Clarendon Press, 1955) 107-18.

Baumgarten, J. M. "The Cave 4 Versions of the Qumran Penal Code," *JJS* 43 (1992) 268-76.

—. with J. T. Milik, S. Pfann and A. Yardeni. *Qumran Cave 4.XIII: The Damascus Document (4Q266-273)* (DJD 18; Oxford: Clarendon Press, 1996).

Burrows, M. with J. C. Trever and W. H. Brownlee. *The Dead Sea Scrolls of St. Mark's Monastery. Vol. II, Fasc. 2. Plates and Transcription of the Manual of Discipline* (New Haven: The American Schools of Oriental Research, 1951).

Davies, P. R. *The Damascus Covenant. An Interpretation of the "Damascus Document"* (JSOTSup 25; Sheffield: JSOT Press, 1983).

Eshel, E. "4Q477: The Rebukes by the Overseer," *JJS* 45 (1994) 111-22.

Hempel, C. "The Penal Code Reconsidered," in M. Bernstein, F. García Martínez and J. Kampen (eds.), *Legal Texts and Legal Issues: Proceedings of the Second Meeting of the International Organization For Qumran Studies, Cambridge 1995, Published in Honour of Joseph M. Baumgarten* (STDJ 23; Leiden: Brill, 1997) 337-48.

Metso, S. *The Textual Development of the Qumran Community Rule* (STDJ 21; Leiden: Brill, 1997).

Milik, J. T. "13. Une règle de la secte," in M. Baillet, J. T. Milik, R. de Vaux (eds.), *Les 'Petites Grottes' de Qumran. Textes* (DJD 3; Oxford: Clarendon Press, 1962) 181-3 + pls. XXXIX–XL.

Murphy-O'Connor, J. "La genèse littéraire de la Règle de la Communauté," *RB* 76 (1969) 528-49.

Qimron, E. and J. H. Charlesworth, with an Appendix by F. M. Cross. "Cave IV Fragments (4Q255-264 = 4QS MSS A-J)," in Charlesworth et al. (eds.), *The Dead Sea Scrolls. Hebrew, Aramaic, and Greek Texts with English Translations. Vol. 1: Rule of the Community and Related Documents* (Tübingen: Mohr-Siebeck; Louisville: John Knox, 1994) 53-103.

Schechter, S. *Documents of Jewish Sectaries*, Vol. I. *Fragments of a Zadokite Work* (Cambridge, 1910; repr. New York: Ktav, 1970).

Schiffman, L. H. *The Eschatological Community of the Dead Sea Scrolls: A Study of the Rule of the Congregation* (SBLMS 38; Atlanta: Scholars Press, 1989).

Vermes, G. "Preliminary Remarks on Unpublished Fragments of the Community Rule from Qumran Cave 4," *JJS* 42 (1991) 250-55.

Weinfeld, M. *The Organizational Pattern and the Penal Code of the Qumran Sect* (NTOA 2; Göttingen: Vandenhoeck & Ruprecht, 1986).

THE DIVERSE ASPECTS OF WISDOM
IN THE QUMRAN TEXTS

JOHN I. KAMPEN

In the field of Qumran studies, where an established consensus on many subjects has either broken down or has been rightly and often wrongly under attack in recent years, the exploration of the topic of wisdom has been relatively uneventful. There are several reasons for this. When the first Qumran scrolls were discovered, the topic of wisdom in the Hebrew Scriptures was not considered as important as it is today. This field of research, however, has expanded considerably since 1947. Since there were no texts among those first major scrolls resembling the sapiential literature of the Hebrew Scriptures, researchers turned their attention to topics that seemed more significant for studying the new material from the Judaean Desert.

Since this particular area of research was simply not considered very important, no significant synthesis was attempted nor any consensus established. For this and other reasons, the fragments of sapiential material—which are currently still being published—have only begun to receive significant attention in the present decade. The analysis of this material is still rather preliminary, and attempts to integrate the insights that have been gained from its study are even more primitive. At this point, however, a survey of available work may be instructive for future research. There is a particular set of issues which require discussion and resolution, as well as an engaging collection of texts to be encountered by scholars.

1. HISTORY OF RESEARCH PRIOR TO 1990

1.1 Beginnings

When James Sanders published the large Psalms Scroll from Cave 11, he noted that "no work has been done, to my knowledge, on Wisdom thinking generally in Qumran literature."[1] He did not find this particularly surprising, since elsewhere he had stated that "the

---

[1] J. A. Sanders, *The Psalms Scroll of Qumran Cave 11 (11QPs^a)* (DJD 4; Oxford: Clarendon Press, 1965) 69 n.1.

Sapiential is not a Qumran characteristic."[2] While Sanders did note the presence of wisdom vocabulary in other documents such as 1QS and 1QH, he likened their context to usage in the canonical Psalms. Such claims reflect the evaluation of the majority of scholars of Qumran literature with respect to the question of wisdom at the end of the first two decades of research.

A study of wisdom in the literature from the Qumran library must take cognizance of two different types of texts. The first, based on the definition implied by Sanders, points to compositions which resemble the wisdom literature of the Hebrew Scriptures. Compositions from this same literary tradition that are found within the literature of early Judaism, including the Apocrypha and Pseudepigrapha,[3] must also be taken into consideration. But in order to get a full picture of the understanding of wisdom in the compositions of the Qumran library, we must also examine other works: i.e. those making extensive use of a wide array of Hebrew terms that are synonymous with, and incorporate, wisdom and knowledge, but which do not fit into this specific Hebrew literary tradition on the basis of either form or content.

Early examinations of the Qumran texts that were initially identified in 1947 already recognized the presence of wisdom terminology. The first surveys of this material note the extensive presence of terminology related to knowledge in some of these texts; in 1950, for instance, M. Burrows wrote:

> "Knowledge" is one of the prominent words of DCD and it is used primarily with reference to the divine law.[4]

Using דעת as the key term along with its cognates, W. D. Davies divided the material from the major scrolls from Cave 1 that deal with the question of "knowledge" into six categories: (a) where it means intelligent discernment; (b) passages associated with the Law; (c) where there is an expressed or implied secret knowledge; (d) where it is concerned with the interpretation of events or has an

---

[2] Attributed to Sanders in J. E. Worrell, "Concepts of Wisdom in the Dead Sea Scrolls," (Ph.D. diss., Claremont, CA; Claremont Graduate School, 1968) 115.

[3] For example, Ben Sira.

[4] M. Burrows, "The Discipline Manual of the Judaean Covenanters," *OTS* 8 (1950) 156-92, esp. 168-71 (quote from p. 168); cf. A. Dupont-Sommer, *The Dead Sea Scrolls: A Preliminary Survey* (Oxford: Blackwell, 1950) 42, 65 n.1. "DCD" refers to the Damascus Document and is now abbreviated as "CD."

eschatological significance; (e) where knowledge of an intimate or personal kind is suggested; and (f) where knowledge is mediated.[5] Rejecting any connection with gnosticism, he pointed to eschatology and ethics as features that distinguish the Qumran materials from the perspectives of this other movement. In his classification, Davies also highlighted a connection between knowledge and law:

> [They] seem to have placed a greater emphasis upon the concept of knowledge, whatever its exact connotation, than the more strictly Jewish circles, whose literature across the centuries is preserved in the Old Testament.[6]

Clearly he recognized the importance of "knowledge" for the sectarian authors of these Cave 1 documents.

1.2 Wisdom and Gnosticism

One of the major questions, already noted by Davies, which interested many early researchers was the relationship of these new materials to Gnosticism, in view of their extensive use of wisdom terminology. According to K. Schubert, 1QS 3:13–4:26 is the oldest Gnostic text that is presently available.[7] K. G. Kuhn, on the other hand, argued that a "gnostic" understanding of knowledge lies behind these texts; thus Qumran represents a Gnostic pattern of thought, but this is not encased in Gnostic mythology in the documents themselves.[8] On the basis of the Qumran materials Kuhn argued for a distinction between the "knowledge" of the Hellenistic mystery religions and of Gnosticism, an understanding of which was now impacted by the Qumran documents.[9]

This issue was not driven primarily by the recently-discovered Nag Hammadi materials, but rather by theories which discerned a Gnostic influence in the New Testament documents, which Davies referred to as "Hellenistic Gnosticism."[10] The major purpose of

---

[5] W. D. Davies, "'Knowledge' in the Dead Sea Scrolls and Matthew 11:25-30," *HTR* 46 (1953) 113-39.

[6] Davies, "'Knowledge' in the Dead Sea Scrolls," 135.

[7] K. Schubert, "Der gegenwärtige Stand der Erforschung der in Palästina neu gefundenen hebräischen Handschriften, 25. Der Sektkanon von En Feshcha und die Anfänge der jüdischen Gnosis," *TLZ* 78 (1953) 495-506, esp. 502.

[8] K. G. Kuhn, "Die in Palästina gefundenen hebräischen Texte und das Neue Testament," *ZTK* 47 (1950) 192-211, esp. 203-205.

[9] K. G. Kuhn, "Die Sektenschrift und die iranische Religion," *ZTK* 49 (1952) 296-316.

[10] Davies, "'Knowledge' in the Dead Sea Scrolls," 113.

Davies' study of "knowledge" was to compare it with the *gnosis* of the Hellenistic mysteries. He notes similarities between each group's sense of being "chosen," and also a secret knowledge which each claimed was related to revelation.[11] After surveying the results of this analysis he concluded:

> Although there are passages which suggest that the sect was possibly, and even probably, concerned with cosmological speculations such as were native to the *Maʿaseh Bereshit*, ... the DSS is mainly concerned with the interpretation of the works of God in history, and especially with events conceived as belonging to the period of the End, that is, with the "mysteries" of the prophecies of the Old Testament.[12]

The other significant feature which set the knowledge of the Dead Sea Scrolls apart was its connection with the law, which Davies interpreted as an ethical nuance, "which is not always a mark of Hellenistic *gnosis*."[13] Friederich Nötscher differentiates the "knowledge" of the scrolls from Gnosticism by its "practical" purpose, in other words that it serves an ethical and religious purpose rather than an intellectual one (which we might term cosmological or speculative).[14] When Helmer Ringgren produced his theology of Qumran, based upon that first decade of research, he argued:

> Knowledge in Qumran as in Gnosticism can be described as man's knowledge of himself and his nature as revealed by God, and also knowledge of God as Savior and of the way to salvation. But salvation in Qumran is not as it is in Gnosticism an ascent to the divine and deification, but it is salvation under the conditions of earthly life. And the dualism of the Qumran congregation is not a metaphysical-cosmic dualism but a religious-ethical dualism. Thus it becomes rather a question of definition as to whether the Essenes in Qumran should be called Gnostics or not. ... Viewed from a historical point of view, perhaps it should be a question of a preliminary stage of Gnosticism, a proto- or para-Gnosticism.[15]

The recognition of the ethical and religious dimensions of the dualism present in the Qumran documents was an attempt to

---

[11] Davies, "'Knowledge' in the Dead Sea Scrolls," 131-32.

[12] Davies, "'Knowledge' in the Dead Sea Scrolls," 133-34. These similarities are also denied by Burrows, "Discipline Manual," 168.

[13] Davies, "'Knowledge' in the Dead Sea Scrolls," 135.

[14] F. Nötscher, *Zur theologischen Terminologie der Qumran-Texte* (BBB 10; Bonn: Hanstein, 1956) 39-40.

[15] H. Ringgren, *The Faith of Qumran: Theology of the Dead Sea Scrolls* (expanded edition; New York: Crossroad, 1995 [1961]), 250-51, esp. 111-12 on Gnosticism.

differentiate it from Gnosticism. The lack of emphasis on cosmic or metaphysical aspects reflects a failure to understand the relationship of some of this material to the dimensions of apocalyptic thought, our understanding of which had not yet seen the full impact of the Qumran discoveries.

1.3 Wisdom, Apocalypticism and Dualism

One of the dominant perspectives to impact upon research concerning wisdom at Qumran and which provides a second reason for interest in the subject was the viewpoint of Gerhard von Rad concerning the origins of apocalypticism.[16] Arguing that the apocalyptic conception of history and time had its origin in wisdom circles, von Rad attributed this to a recognition that there is a very ancient interest among wisdom circles in the identification of the appropriate times. When this interest is placed on a more decisive theological footing in the biblical materials—an emphasis which is paralleled in the later Egyptian wisdom texts—we find in works such as Qoheleth and Sirach a sudden increase in the use of the term עת, which is related to "time" and the "times." The emphasis has now shifted from knowing the correct behavior at the appropriate time to dealing with the issues people face when "the times" pose threats and challenges. For von Rad, the determinism of the apocalyptic worldview is a development out of this conception which emerged in wisdom circles. Such interest in history, whose integration into wisdom materials is reflected within the Hebrew Scriptures, has advanced to a deterministic perspective which is dominated by the question of the end of history. It is still the wise man, however, who knows how to read the times, but now from an apocalyptic perspective.

An important attempt to evaluate the perspectives of von Rad utilizing the Qumran evidence is the study by Benedikt Otzen.[17] In his analysis of the dualism in 1QS 3:13-4:26, with reference to similar lists in the Testaments of the Twelve Patriarchs, Otzen notes that the list of virtues and vices in col. 4 has its best parallels from

---

[16] G. von Rad, *Old Testament Theology* (2 vols., New York: Harper & Row, 1965) 2.301-308; idem, *Wisdom in Israel* (Nashville: Abingdon, 1972) 263-83.

[17] B. Otzen, "Old Testament Wisdom Literature and Dualistic Thinking in Late Judaism," in *Congress Volume: Edinburgh 1974* (VTSup 28; Leiden: Brill, 1975) 146-157.

the Hebrew Scriptures in Proverbs 1-9.[18] It is within these wisdom traditions that he finds the basis of the urge to divide humankind and the world into two spheres, the domains of good and evil. This division, which lies behind the catalogues and lists he cites, has its origin in the desire for order which is the driving-force of wisdom thinking. However, Otzen sees evidence of such wisdom influence only in what he terms "cosmic-ethical dualism," and finds it absent from the "psychological-ethical" and "eschatological" types. This helpful distinction continues to appear in a number of studies and bears further investigation.

James Sanders began asking questions about wisdom in the Scrolls because of the presence of wisdom vocabulary in cols. 18 and 24 of 11QPs^a, which contain Psalms 154 and 155.[19] Pointing to the "poetic personification" of wisdom in col. 18, he points out that this emphasis exceeds anything that was previously known in Qumran literature or in the canonical psalter. However, while noting the presence of wisdom vocabulary in 1QS and 1QH, Sanders failed to see this as significant. In fact, it was his understanding of the lack of wisdom material at Qumran that provided the basis for him to classify these psalms as proto-Essenian or Hasidic.[20]

Following the initial identification of wisdom themes in the large Psalms Scroll, in 1978 W. Lowndes Lipscomb (in conjunction with Sanders) summarized the state of research on the question of wisdom.[21] He noted that while the major Cave 1 texts make abundant use of wisdom terminology, they are not sapiential texts:

> The object of wisdom at Qumran was the revealed mysteries of God's predestined plan of salvation, knowledge of sectarian doctrine, for example... The search for knowledge gained through consistent personal experience of the divine world order found in wisdom texts does not appear in the Essene documents.[22]

---

[18] Otzen (pp. 151-56) attributes the original insight to P. Wernberg-Møller and A. R. C. Leaney.

[19] Which were previously known in Syriac.

[20] Sanders, *The Psalms Scroll* (DJD 4), 70.

[21] W. L. Lipscomb with J. A. Sanders, "Wisdom at Qumran," in J. G. Gammie, W. A. Brueggemann, W. L. Humphreys and J. M. Ward (eds.), *Israelite Wisdom: Theological and Literary Essays in Honor of Samuel Terrien* (Missoula, MT: Scholars Press, 1978) 277-285.

[22] Lipscomb and Sanders, "Wisdom," 278.

While accepting the view which finds the origin of ethical dualism in wisdom literature, Lipscomb was unable to explain its cosmic and psychological aspects in the same way. He even distinguished the ethical dualism in the form found at Qumran, with its divinely-predestined truth, from wisdom perspectives where a dualism is based on "humanity's own experience of the divine world order... There are no true wisdom texts among the scrolls of undisputed Essene authorship."[23] Listing evidence from 11QPs^a and 4Q184 Lipscomb claimed that the only true wisdom texts are those of unknown (i.e. non-Essene) authorship. For him, as well as Sanders, the wisdom vocabulary and expressions of the sectarian compositions were superimposed upon the apocalyptic fabric of Qumran thought. Lipscomb concluded that in the absence of a consistent method for determining wisdom influence, and since the relationship between apocalpytic and wisdom had not been adequately clarified, there was little more to be said about "wisdom influence" upon the sectarian texts.

In actuality, Lipscomb's article summarizes an extensive literature on the nature of the dualism found at Qumran, with 1QS 3:13-4:26 as the focal point of the discussion. The major issue under debate is the question of its nature and origin, with Hebrew wisdom literature as one of the major contenders. Commentators such as P. Wernberg-Møller, who stressed the psychological dimension of this dualism, relied upon its connection with wisdom literature to distinguish it from the cosmological interests attributed to Zoroastrianism.[24] In his presidential address to the Society of Biblical Literature in 1962, Herbert G. May challenged the viewpoint of Wernberg-Møller and Treves, arguing that the creation context of the passage in the Community Rule points to its cosmic and cosmological reference-points.[25] He then documented the presence of these cosmic conceptions within the Hebrew Scriptures, noting particularly the personification or hypostatization of wisdom as the first of God's creation in Prov 8:22-31, as well as other associations it had with cosmogony.

---

[23] Lipscomb and Sanders, "Wisdom," 278.

[24] P. Wernberg-Møller, "A Reconsideration of the Two Spirits in the Rule of the Community (1QSerek III,13–IV,26)," *RevQ* 3 (1961) 413-441. Note also M. Treves, "The Two Spirits of the Rule of the Community," *RevQ* 3 (1961) 449-452.

[25] H. G. May, "Cosmological Reference in the Qumran Doctrine of the Two Spirits and in Old Testament Imagery," *JBL* 82 (1963) 1-14.

May also pointed to the prophets and psalms to document the presence of the mythopoeic conception of time, space and events.

J. Licht connected the "knowledge" of 1QS 3:15 and 4:25-26 with predestination (in his estimation one of the three major themes of this section), but without discussing the question of origin.[26] A similar perspective was advanced by B. Sharvit who argued that the righteous man "or ideal sectarian" in 1QS 4:2-14 is the one who possesses wisdom. This emphasis arises from biblical wisdom and postbiblical texts, rather than either gnostic or Greek influence.[27] A considerable advance in the discussion was initiated by John Gammie: documenting the varieties of dualism available in the literature up to that time, he argued that the ethical dualism known already in the biblical wisdom literature is both internalized into a psychological dualism and externalized into a cosmic dualism within the Qumran materials.[28] Such early scholarly literature demonstrates to what extent this basic expression of Qumran dualism forms the centerpiece for the debates concerning the nature of wisdom within the Qumran compositions that are primarily attributed to Cave 1.

The Hebrew text of Ben Sira and the Cave 2 fragments of this work were to occasion related research. While noting the considerable difference in its orientation from 1QS 3:13–4:26, Paul Winter argued for a connection with Sirach 33:7-15.[29] M. Lehmann also postulated a variety of points of contact in the philosophy of the two compositions.[30]

1.4 Wisdom in the Damascus Document

The interpretation of wisdom in the Qumran texts receives a more complex treatment in the literary-critical work of Albert-Marie Denis.[31] Based on similarities in vocabulary—particularly with regard

---

[26] J. Licht, "An Analysis of the Treatise on the Two Spirits in DSD," *Scripta Hierosolymitana* 4 (1958) 88-99.

[27] B. Sharvit, "The Virtue of Wisdom in the Image of the Righteous Man in 1QS," *Beth Mikra* 19 (1974) 526-30.

[28] J. G. Gammie, "Spatial and Ethical Dualism in Jewish Wisdom and Apocalyptic Literature," *JBL* 93 (1974) 356-85.

[29] P. Winter, "Ben Sira and the Teaching of 'Two Ways,'" *VT* 5 (1955) 315-18.

[30] M. R. Lehmann, "Ben-Sira and the Qumran Literature," *RevQ* 3 (1961) 103-16.

[31] A.-M. Denis, *Les thèmes de connaisance dans le Document de Damas* (Studia Hellenistica 15; Louvain: Publications universitaires, 1967).

to wisdom—in the first three admonitions of the work comprising CD 1:1-4:6a, Denis regards them as forming a redactional unity.[32] The type of knowledge found here in CD is a *pénétration*, a keen insight into the deeds of God (בינו במעשי אל); it provides a clear vision of events that are imminently eschatological and those have already been inaugurated by the establishment of the assembly of the definitive covenant. In the midst of the universal apostay of the rebels, God intervened to raise up a remnant of the faithful, and then raised up a teacher of righteousness who ידע ("knows") and mediates knowledge to those who hold fast to the covenant. These are the only ones who are able to perceive and understand the נסתרות ("hidden things"), those works of God which are about to be performed, including the punishment of the impious. In this first section the work of God is a secret (רז) which is revealed (גלה) to those who "know justice." Influenced by the vocabulary of the book of Daniel, they announce the divine judgment on those impious who are in rebellion against God, the apostates of history.

In the second section (CD 4:6b–6:11), attention is directed to the new covenant with a focus upon teaching and instruction rather than understanding.[33] There is now a shift in the meaning of some wisdom terminology: for instance, "instruction" becomes more central. The final section (7:4–8:21; 19–20) is composite. Its oldest portion (7:13–8:13) speaks of the faults of those who did not understand (הבינו) and were led astray, an occurrence that is already predicted in 1:8. Other themes include the "men of knowledge" (20:5), who are to rebuke in accordance with the law (כפי מדרש התורה). Philip Davies' summary of Denis' contribution is worth noting:

> His study reminds us of the extent to which the "Damascus covenant" was an *esoteric* one, whose members belonged not by virture of obedience to manifest laws, but of insight into sectarian, "hidden" interpretations of that law. The covenant community comprised those who "understood," and understood because God chose them. The saving "knowledge" is a gift of divine grace. It is in this area that election operates.[34]

This comment of Davies applies most clearly to those sections which Denis considered the earliest, and hence is a comment on the origins

---

[32] Denis, *Thèmes de connaisance*, 5-82.

[33] Denis, *Thèmes de connaissnce*, 83-130.

[34] P. R. Davies, *The Damascus Covenant: An Interpretation of the "Damascus Document"* (JSOTSup 25; Sheffield: JSOT Press, 1983) 35-36.

of the community. It may be a significant insight into the history of the use of conceptions of wisdom at Qumran.

1.5 A "Sapiential Milieu"

An important attempt at a synthesis in the context of historical development was the dissertation of James Worrell.[35] In the first section, he proposed that the wisdom tradition in the Hebrew Scriptures led to the creation of a sapiential milieu which was not a formal group or sect, but an understanding of life that existed in antiquity. This milieu became more influential during the post-exilic and Hellenistic periods, and was instrumental in establishing a vernacular used in subsequent creative endeavors for the following centuries.[36] For Worrell, Qumran represents one of those endeavors. Combining the evidence from Josephus and Philo with the use of the terms עצה or סוד, both of which (in his view) can mean "counsel" or "council," he defined Qumran as a "wisdom community."[37] After thoroughly surveying all of the relevant terms and the texts in which they appear, Worrell concluded that at Qumran wisdom had been adapted for sectarian purposes. The pertinent compositions were authored by sages rooted in the "sapiential milieu," who utilized the wisdom tradition to advance sectarian values in a polemical format. This suggested for Worrell that the dualism of these texts was ultimately subordinated, so that it was of an ethical rather than a cosmological nature.[38] He attributed the relative absence of the term חכמה in these compositions to the sectarian opposition to the hermeneutical authorities of the day—the Pharisees.[39]

There are several legitimate critiques of this study. W. Lipscomb, for instance, critiques it for lacking a clear methodology.[40] Worrell's generalizations concerning the significance of the "sapiential milieu" for post-biblical Judaism are overstated, and he certainly draws more historical conclusions than can seemingly be justified on the basis of linguistic analysis. S. Tanzer's explanation for the relative absence of the term חכמה is preferable, when she argues that it is the particu-

---

[35] J. E. Worrell, "Concepts of Wisdom."
[36] Worrell, "Concepts of Wisdom," 107-09.
[37] Worrell, "Concepts of Wisdom," 123-50.
[38] Worrell, "Concepts of Wisdom," 400-10.
[39] Worrell, "Concepts of Wisdom," 119, 406.
[40] W. Lipscomb, "Wisdom at Qumran," 281 n.2.

larization of the character of wisdom at Qumran which accounts for the eclipse.[41] Worrell's argument also strains the evidence concerning the Pharisees prior to the Common Era. Nevertheless, his dissertation was the best available collection of the texts and evidence concerning the topic prior to the new examinations of the question during the last decade.

1.6 The Question of Hellenistic Influence

The topic of wisdom does not lack mention in the magisterial volumes of Martin Hengel, who attributed great significance to the Essene movement, particularly with regard to the development of Jewish theology during the Second Temple era.[42] He related the use of wisdom terminology in compositions such as 1QS, 1QH, 1QM and CD to an increase in the level of abstraction which accompanied the Hebrew encounter with the Greek world. The presence of terms such as הווה and נהיה attest to an attempt to relate the Jewish belief in creation to the Greek concepts of being and becoming. For Hengel, this "Essene" interest reflects a development that was already evident in the "late" wisdom literature such as Koheleth and Ben Sira. He noted, of course, that this interest in creation does not relate to any notion of a hypostatized mediator figure, but rather pointed to the "sovereign, perfect knowledge possessed by God himself," which in these texts was related to the idea of predestination. The concept of predestination in *"the course of history and the fate of the individual is new,"* while building on earlier developments.[43]

The grouping of concepts such as knowledge, insight and wisdom, along with their verbal equivalents, was an attempt to describe the "knowledge about the deeper connections in creation and history," which the wise man knows because God has revealed the mysteries of knowledge to him.[44] In addition to the secret nature of this knowledge, Hengel also pointed to its dualistic features. While he is correct in emphasizing the impact of the Hellenistic world on Jewish life during this period, his thesis concerning the level of abstraction may

---

[41] S. Tanzer, "The Sages at Qumran: Wisdom in the *Hodayot*" (Ph.D. diss., Cambridge, MA: Harvard University, 1987) 179.

[42] M. Hengel, *Judaism and Hellenism: Studies in Their Encounter in Palestine during the Early Hellenistic Period* (2 vols., Philadelphia: Fortress Press, 1974) 1.218-47.

[43] Hengel, *Judaism and Hellenism*, 1.219 (italics are his).

[44] Hengel, *Judaism and Hellenism*, 1.222.

not be the best explanation for such ideological developments, which grew out of the stresses and strains of colonial life during the latter portion of the Hellenistic reign and the Roman Imperial period.

1.7 Wisdom in the Hodayot

Immediately prior to the dramatic developments in Qumran studies in the 1990's, Sarah Tanzer completed a more disciplined study by focusing upon the Hodayot.[45] Applying the literary-criticial method to the study of this text, Tanzer concluded that wisdom elements were confined to those portions of the Hodayot which are categorized as the Hymns of the Community, and are for the most part absent from the Hymns of the Teacher.[46] Those Hymns of the Teacher which betray some wisdom presence are all hybrids, where the wisdom elements are found in portions corresponding to material adapted from the Hymns of the Community. A further classification suggests that the wisdom elements are strongest in Hymns which Tanzer suggests are distinguished by an emphasis on *Niedrigkeitsdoxologie* and on the revealed word of God. These focus on the lowliness of the human, as contrasted with the righteousness of God, and are characterized by the form of rhetorical questions—a feature that is familiar from certain biblical wisdom compositions. The most prevalent themes among these pieces are creation and predestination, with widespread reference to God's covenant. Less well-attested—due to the fragmentary nature of the text—are the Deuteronomic Hodayot, which also betray evidence of wisdom themes.

In both types of Community Hymns, Tanzer identifies three characteristics of this knowledge which are pertinent to our topic: (a) All knowledge and understanding come from God alone. (b) Knowledge is available only to those to whom God chooses to reveal it—i.e. this is knowledge revealed only to a select group. (c) Responding to this knowledge is a key to salvation for man, who is otherwise limited by his own base inclinations. Knowledge thus provides a link between righteous God and lowly man.[47]

On the contrary, within the Hymns of the Teacher knowledge is limited to a focus "on the psalmist as the repository and interpreter of God's mysteries and/or secret knowledge,"[48] which appears to fit

---

[45] Tanzer, "Sages at Qumran."
[46] Note the summary chapter in Tanzer, "Sages at Qumran," 136-60.
[47] Tanzer, "Sages at Qumran," 154.
[48] Tanzer, "Sages at Qumran," 154.

well with the apocalyptic tone of these hymns.[49] Tanzer's dissertation is a good summary of the first forty years of research, and an example of the possibilities resulting from the careful methodological treatment of a specific text. There are only small hints, however, of the dramatic changes that were to follow in the study of this topic.

2. WISDOM TEXTS PUBLISHED PRIOR TO 1990

Since the significance of the wisdom tradition at Qumran only came to be fully-appreciated with the new publications after 1990, wisdom texts that were previously available did not receive sufficient attention. Now that 1Q26 (manuscript f of "Sapiential Work A") and 1Q27 ("Mysteries") have been identified as portions of compositions more widely-attested among the Cave 4 fragments, it seems appropriate to discuss these in the third part of this essay.[50]

2.1 The Wiles of the Wicked Woman (4Q184)

Two wisdom texts from Cave 4, which were already published in 1968, find new significance in light of the recent publications. These are 4Q184 ("Wiles of the Wicked Woman") and 4Q185 (a sapiential work).[51] It is in these two texts that we find the primary treatment of the biblical figures of Lady Wisdom and Dame Folly at Qumran.[52] The wanton woman who leads the simple astray with her sexuality is familiar from Prov 2:16-19; 5:1-23; 6:23-26; 7:1-27; and 9:13-18. In 4Q184, however, this female figure appears to have more cosmic significance than the seductress of Proverbs:

> Foundations of darkness...darkness of night ... her clothes are shadows of twilight, and her ornaments are plagues of corruption ... depths of the pit, her lodgings are beds of darkness... Amid everlasting fire is her inheritance, not among those who shine brightly.[53]

---

[49] Tanzer, "Sages at Qumran," 139-40.

[50] See sections 3.1 and 3.2.

[51] J. M. Allegro, *Qumrân Cave 4:1 [4Q158-4Q186]* (DJD 5; Oxford: Clarendon Press, 1968), 82-87; J. Strugnell, "Notes en marge du Volume V des 'Discoveries in the Judaean Desert of Jordan,'" *RevQ* 7 (1970) 163-276, esp. 263-73; D. J. Harrington, *Wisdom Texts from Qumran* (The Dead Sea Scrolls; London: Routledge, 1996) 31-39.

[52] S. White Crawford, "Lady Wisdom and Dame Folly at Qumran" (Paper presented at the Annual Meeting of the Society of Biblical Literature, Philadelphia, 1995), where she also discusses 4Q525 ("Wisdom Text with Beatitudes").

This portrayal of Dame Folly appears to place her closer to the context of the dualistic, cosmological struggle between good and evil that is portrayed in texts such as 1QS 3-4 or which is represented in the sectarian history of CD 3-5 (dealing with the nets of Belial).[54] Also of significance is the observation that the potential victims of the wanton woman in Proverbs are the simple and unwise—whereas in 4Q184 it is the righteous who may be led astray.[55]

2.2 Sapiential Work (4Q185)

In 4Q185 Lady Wisdom finds personification similar to that in Proverbs 1-9 and Ben Sira:

> Seek her and find her and hold fast to her and get her as an inheritance. With her is length of days and fatness of bone and joy of heart. Her youth will multiply mercies for him and salvation[...]. Happy is the man who does it and does not play tricks against her, nor with [a spirit] of deceit seeks her, nor holds fast to her with flatteries. As she is given to his fathers, so he will inherit her...[56]

T. Tobin has analyzed the manner in which this composition continues the style of the wisdom instruction or admonition that is so familiar from Proverbs and Ben Sira. However, he identifies examples of where this text moves beyond what can be found in the other two, which were compatible with viewpoints expressed in sectarian compositions found at Qumran.[57] Tobin also observes that the term גבורה ("mighty wisdom") appears in the biblical text only at Prov 8:14, but is used rather frequently in this sense at Qumran.[58] Of greater significance is the role played by angels in the judgment of humans. While moving beyond the biblical wisdom tradition, however, the presence of angels is not unique to Qumran. These developments will require further discussion and research.

---

[53] The translation is from Harrington, *Wisdom Texts*, 31-32.

[54] R. D. Moore, "Personification of the Seduction of Evil: 'The Wiles of the Wicked Woman,'" *RevQ* 10 (1981) 505-519; Crawford, "Lady Wisdom," 5.

[55] Harrington, *Wisdom Texts*, 34.

[56] 4Q185 1-2 ii lines 11-14. See also Thomas Tobin, "4Q185 and Jewish Wisdom Literature," in H. W. Attridge, J. J. Collins and T. H. Tobin (eds.), *Of Scribes and Scrolls: Studies on the Hebrew Bible, Intertestamental Judaism, and Christian Origins, presented to John Strugnell on the Occasion of His Sixtieth Birthday* (CTSRR 5; Lanham, MD: University Press of America, 1990) 145-52.

[57] Tobin, "4Q185," 150-52.

[58] This observation is attributed to Strugnell, "Notes en marge," 270.

2.3 Psalm 154 (in 11QPs^a)

Also to be considered are several compositions found in 11QPs^a, the large Psalms Scroll.[59] Psalm 154 in col. 18 (previously known in Syriac) merits particular attention.[60] Unfortunately, as a result of damage to the leather, portions of this piece—which J. Sanders dubs a "sapiential hymn"—have to be reconstructed from the Syriac. The theme of wisdom is introduced in line 3 with the declaration: "To make known the glory of the Lord is wisdom given, and for recounting his many deeds is she given to man." As S. Tanzer notes, the purpose of the psalm is to exhort the righteous to bind their souls together in the praise of God.[61] Wisdom elements in the composition are thus tied to that purpose of exhortation. She agrees with J. Magne's hypothesis that here a wisdom psalm has been combined with one of invitation in order to produce an exhortation to teaching.[62] In this case, wisdom is the result of revelation.

Sanders demonstrates that three distinct groups are to be found in the content of Psalm 154. One group is referred to as the רבים ("many"), טובים ("good"), תמימים ("perfect"), חסידים ("pious"),[63] and other similar terms. These are called to proclaim the glory of God—through the wisdom which they have received—to another group referred to as the "senseless" and "foolish," so that the latter will not be drawn into the circles of a third group, the "wicked."[64] While there is no direct compositional evidence for tying this psalm to a sectarian group, it would have been very much at home in such circles.[65] Other works of a similar nature are to be found in 11QPs^a.

2.4 Hymn to the Creator (in 11QPs^a)

Another work of a sapiential nature, the "Hymn to the Creator," is found in 11QPs^a col. 26:9-15.[66] The significance of this hymn for

---

[59] See section 1.1 above.
[60] Sanders, *The Psalms Scroll* (DJD 4), 64-70.
[61] Tanzer, "Sages at Qumran," 168.
[62] J. Magne, "Le Psaume 154," *RevQ* 9 (1977) 95-102.
[63] I argue elsewhere that this is not a reference to the חסידים of 1 Macc 2:42, 7:14 and 2 Macc 14:6 (J. Kampen, *The Hasideans and the Origin of Pharisaism: A Study in 1 and 2 Maccabees* [SCS 24; Atlanta: Scholars Press, 1988] 14-16).
[64] Sanders, *The Psalms Scroll* (DJD 4), 68-69.
[65] 4QMMT appears to deal with three similar groups; cf. E. Qimron and J. Strugnell, *Qumran Cave 4.V: Miqṣat Ma'aśe Ha-Torah* (DJD 10; Oxford: Clarendon Press, 1994), 110-11, 205.
[66] Sanders, *The Psalms Scroll* (DJD 4), 89-91.

our topic is the manner in which it explicitly links wisdom terminology with the act of creation. Also of interest is its treatment of דעת ("knowledge") as synonymous with חכמה.[67] David's Compositions, the prose summary towards the end of 11QPs[a] (col. 27:2-11), lists him as a "wise man (חכם) and a light like the light of the sun and literate (סופר)."[68] This sage is credited with the composition of 4,050 works, and—somewhat suggestive of other aspects of the wisdom tradition at Qumran—"he spoke all these things through prophecy." In other words, David's compositions are the result of revelation.

2.5 Sirach 51 (in 11QPs[a])

A final composition from 11QPs[a] that deserves attention is a portion of the text of Sirach 51:13-30, an autobiographical poem on the search for wisdom (cols. 21:11–22:1).[69] While the Hebrew text is capable of a more erotic interpretation than the Greek, those differences should not be overemphasized.[70] In both texts the male begins a quest in his youth for Lady Wisdom, a figure already familiar to us from Proverbs 8, Wisdom of Solomon 7, 4Q185 and elsewhere.[71] In this acrostic poem, Wisdom lets herself be found and in so doing takes over his life. Whether this section is part of Ben Sira or a later addition will remain a point of debate.[72]

3. NEW TEXTS AND RECENT RESEARCH

Research on wisdom at Qumran has been dramatically transformed through the study of several fragmentary texts from Cave 4. While synthetic treatments of this material are not yet available, research has rather focused upon the publication and study of specific texts. In 1996 Daniel Harrington published a volume which summarizes these texts and some of the issues involved in their study.[73] The present article offers a description and discussion of the relevant texts.

---

[67] Tanzer, "Sages at Qumran," 176; Harrington, *Wisdom Texts*, 25-26.

[68] Sanders, *The Psalms Scroll* (DJD 4), 91-93; Tanzer, "Sages at Qumran," 176; Harrington, *Wisdom Texts*, 176.

[69] Sanders, *The Psalms Scroll* (DJD 4), 79-85.

[70] Harrington, *Wisdom Texts*, 28-30; J. L. Crenshaw, "Sirach," *The New Interpreter's Bible* (Nashville: Abingdon, 1997) 5.867.

[71] Tanzer, "Sages at Qumran," 168-69.

[72] Harrington, *Wisdom Texts*, 28; Crenshaw, "Sirach," 5.867.

[73] Harrington, *Wisdom Texts*. Since most of the texts dealt with in this essay are discussed in his book, references will not always be noted.

3.1 Sapiential Work A (1Q26, 4Q415-418, 4Q423)

The most extensive composition is "Sapiential Work A," which recently appeared in the official DJD series[74] but has already been widely discussed due to its importance for research on the topic of wisdom.[75] Since we possess fragments of six or seven extant copies, it is more widely attested than most of the other texts to be considered: 1Q26, 4Q415-418, 4Q423.[76] On the very limited evidence of 4Q416 frg. 1, D. Harrington proposes that the work's preface or introduction set it within a cosmic and eschatological framework.[77] This column consists of phrases such as "season by season," "the host of the Heavens he has established," and "luminaries for their portents, and signs for their festivals." The eschatological aspect is very evident in these lines:

> In heaven he shall pronounce judgement upon the work of wickedness, but all his faithful children will be accepted with favor by Him... and every spirit of flesh will be laid utterly bare but the sons of Heaven shall rejoice in the day when it (i.e. wickedness) is judged. And all iniquity shall come to an end until the epoch of destruction will be finished.[78]

---

[74] A Steudel, "4QSapiential-Didactic Work A," in T. Elgvin et al. (eds.), *Qumran Cave 4.XV: Sapiential Texts, Part 1* (DJD 20; Oxford: Clarendon Press, 1997) 163-67 + pl. VIX.

[75] D. J. Harrington, "Wisdom at Qumran," in E. Ulrich and J. VanderKam (eds.), *The Community of the Renewed Covenant: The Notre Dame Symposium on the Dead Sea Scrolls* (CJA 10; Notre Dame: University of Notre Dame Press, 1994) 137-152; T. Elgvin, "Wisdom, Revelation, and Eschatology in an early Essene Writing," SBLSP (1995) 440-463. See also the notes to the following discussion. A copy of the text is included in B. Z. Wacholder and M. G. Abegg, *A Preliminary Edition of the Unpublished Dead Sea Scrolls: The Hebrew and Aramaic Texts from Cave Four* (4 vols., Washington: Biblical Archaeology Society, 1991-1996) 2.44-154, 166-73. For translations see F. Garcia Martinez, *The Dead Sea Scrolls Translated: The Qumran Texts in English* (Leiden: Brill, 1994) 383-93; and M. Wise, M. Abegg, Jr. and E. Cook, *The Dead Sea Scrolls: A New Translation* (San Francisco: HarperCollins, 1996) 378-90 (The latter collection seems to include some extra manuscripts beyond this one composition).

[76] T. Elgvin has suggested that 4Q418 contains two copies of the work: "Admonition Texts from Qumran Cave 4," in M. O. Wise, N. Golb, J. J. Collins and D. G. Pardee (eds.), *Methods of Investigation of the Dead Sea Scrolls and the Khirbet Qumran Site: Present Realities and Future Prospects* (ANYAS 722; New York: New York Academy of Sciences, 1994) 179-96, esp. 180.

[77] Harrington, *Wisdom Texts*, 41.

[78] Harrington, *Wisdom Texts*, 41.

While the placement of this fragment at the beginning of the composition has been questioned, its value for understanding the ideology of the work is important.[79] The cosmological aspect is also apparent, suggesting a speculative interest in questions concerning the nature and origin of the heavens and the earth. The cosmological theme recurs elsewhere, which demonstrates its importance in this document. In 4Q417 2 i 8-9 we read in translation:

> For the God of knowledge is the foundation of truth, and by the *raz nihyeh* [רז נהיה] He has laid out its foundation, and its deeds He has prepared with [...] wisdom, and with all cunning He has fashioned it. And the domain of its deeds [...] He expounded for their understanding every deed so that he could walk in the inclination of his understanding. And He expounded for hu[mankind...], and in purity of understanding were made known the secrets of his plan together with how he should walk perfect[ly in all his wo]rks. These things investigate always, and gain understanding [about a]ll their outcomes. And then you will know the glory of His might together with His marvellous mysteries and His mighty acts.[80]

It is important to note that most of the remaining extant contents of Sapiential Work A do not offer further expositions of eschatological mysteries, but instead practical advice for daily life. This includes issues such as a sensitivity to the embarassment of another, the necessity of paying back loans or surety bonds quickly, maintaining integrity in the service of others, the avoidance of selling your soul or yourself for money or possessions (even if you are in poverty), not boasting about your poverty, not violating a trust of money or property and not using poverty as an excuse for avoiding study. There are also injunctions concerning the honor due to one's father and mother, and the importance of living in harmony with one's wife.[81] Such instruction suggests a document similar in purpose to that of Ben Sira, which also demonstrates a continuity with the biblical wisdom tradition rooted in experiences of daily living (often referred to as "secular" wisdom). In similar fashion, we see that at its heart the wisdom undergirding this composition is that which was inherent in creation. Eschatology, therefore, is only one of the subjects to be covered within this larger theme. The number of copies of the work attest to its popularity among the Qumran community.

---

[79] T. Elgvin, "The Reconstruction of Sapiential Work A," *RevQ* 16 (1995) 559-580, esp. 566 n.20.

[80] Harrington, *Wisdom Texts*, 53.

[81] Harrington, *Wisdom Texts*, 43-45.

What, then, is the secret, the *raz nihyeh* that is highlighted throughout this and some of the other documents from Qumran with a wisdom connection. It is this *raz nihyeh* which the reader is enjoined to meditate upon by day and by night.[82] While there is a temptation to highlight its eschatological dimension, this element may not represent its core.[83] Typical of the kind of phrases in which it occurs is 4Q416 2 iii 14: "Study the *raz nihyeh*, and understand all the ways of truth, and all the roots of iniquity you shall contemplate." There is nothing in this phrase which requires an eschatological interpretation; in fact, a phrase in 4Q418 2 i 18 seems to imply that the roots of iniquity have their origin in creation: "Gaze in the *raz nihyeh*, and know the inheritance of everything that lives." In the light of such evidence, the viewpoint of Lawrence Schiffman is to be preferred:

> *Raz* refers to the mysteries of creation, that is the natural order of things, and to the mysteries of the divine role in the historical processes. The source of these mysteries is divine wisdom.[84]

This leads Schiffman to translate רז נהיה as "mystery of that which was coming into being," as opposed to the Milik-Strugnell-Harrington phrase, "mystery that is to be/come." A similar viewpoint is advanced in the book of Mysteries and some other texts.

3.2 Mysteries (1Q27, 4Q299 and 4Q300)

Fragments of three manuscripts of the text entitled "Mysteries" are now available (1Q27, 4Q299 and 4Q300).[85] The name is indicative

---

[82] 4Q417 2 i line 6.

[83] See T. Elgvin, "Admonition Texts," 189-91; idem, "Wisdom, Revelation, and Eschatology," 450-51; D. J. Harrington, "The *Raz Nihyeh* in a Qumran Wisdom Text (1Q26, 4Q415-418, 423)," *RevQ* 17 (1966) 549-53. I am indebted to Ben Zion Wacholder for his suggestion to re-examine this question. His own preference is "mystery of being" (B. Z. Wacholder and M. G. Abegg, *Preliminary Edition*, 2.xii-xiv. This is similar is the phrase "mystery of existence," as used by F. García Martínez, *Dead Sea Scrolls Translated*, 383-94).

[84] L. H. Schiffman, *Reclaiming the Dead Sea Scrolls: The History of Judaism, The Background of Christianity, The Lost Library of Qumran* (Jerusalem and Philadelphia: Jewish Publication Society, 1994) 206-7.

[85] L. H. Schiffman, "4QMysteries: A Preliminary Translation," in *Proceedings of the Eleventh World Congress of Jewish Studies, Division A* (Jerusalem: World Union of Jewish Studies, 1994) 199-206; idem, "4QMysteries[b], A Preliminary Edition," *RevQ* 16 (1993) 203-223; idem, "4QMysteries[a]: A Preliminary Edition

of the frequency with which רז is found throughout the work and provides one tie, among others, to Sapiential Work A. In this document the purpose of wisdom is explained:

> that they would know (the difference) between good and evil, (that they would understand the) mysteries of transgression (with) all their wisdom.[86]

Regrettably, humankind has ignored this wisdom: "But they did not know the *raz nihyeh*, and the former things they did not consider, nor did they know what was to come upon them. And so they did not save their lives from the *raz nihyeh*."[87] This is followed by a description of God's plan for the end of time and the signs of that era, including those which point to its impending arrival; this interest in eschatology is more extensive than in Sapiential Work A. But the work still makes it clear that wisdom was rooted in the order of creation. The problem is that this divine wisdom is sealed and only available to the righteous, the portion of humankind which God permits to see and understand it. In continuity with the biblical tradition and Sapiential Work A, the book of Mysteries goes on to regard extensive moral advice as wisdom, even if it is not as universally available.[88] In this text, then, we continue to see wisdom's foundation in creation and the emphasis on practical moral advice. But eschatological interests and the selective nature of wisdom's availability are more prominent here than in Sapiential Work A.

3.3 Ways of Righteousness (4Q420–421)

An important composition for understanding the varieties of connection between wisdom and Qumran sectarianism is 4Q420–421 (manuscripts a and b of the "Ways of Righteousness"), published in a

---

and Translation," in Z. Zevit, S. Gitin and M. Sokoloff (eds.), *Solving Riddles and Untying Knots: Biblical, Epigraphic, and Semitic Studies in Honor of Jonas C. Greenfield* (Winona Lake, IN: Eisenbrauns, 1995) 207-60. The text 4Q301 (Mysteries[c]) was classified as part of this same composition by J. T. Milik, but Schiffman expresses reservations about this identification ("4QMysteries[b]," 203; "4QMysteries[a]," 207). The text of 4QMysteries is also available in Wacholder and Abegg, *Preliminary Edition*, 2.1-34. Translations can be found in García Martínez, *Dead Sea Scrolls Translated*, 400-401; and Wise, Abegg and Cook, *Dead Sea Scrolls*, 174-77.

[86] 1Q27(Mysteries) 1 i lines 2-3 = 4Q300(Mysteries[b]) 3 lines 2-3; Schiffman, *Reclaiming the Dead Sea Scrolls*, 207.

[87] 1Q27 1 i lines 3-4; Schiffman, *Reclaiming the Dead Sea Scrolls*, 207.

[88] Schiffman, *Reclaiming the Dead Sea Scrolls*, 207-10.

preliminary edition by Torlief Elgvin.[89] The fragments of this possibly composite work suggest three sections, some of which may be based on different sources. The first deals with the organization of the יחד, including the injunction that "[he shall bring all] his [wi]sdom and knowledge and understanding and good things [into the Community (יחד) of God]."[90] The second section contains a series of wisdom sayings, frequently in the form of proverbs, in which the righteous man is exhorted to "bear the yoke of wisdom (עול חכמה)."[91] The third section deals with matters of temple service, with emphasis on issues of purity. Fragmentary references to categories of persons who are prohibited from entering the temple court and from eating in the temple suggest parallels to 11QT and 4QMMT, as well as issues such as the "pure food" discussed in texts attributed to the יחד. Even though this may be a composite text, the interrelationship of sectarian organization and sapiential material found in a single sapiential literary form is significant. Despite its fragmentary condition, this document provides the most significant link between the explicitly "sectarian" texts from Qumran and those compositions which most resemble the sapiential biblical texts in form and content.

3.4 Wisdom Text with Beatitudes (4Q525)

An important text which connects with some New Testament literature is 4Q525 ("Wisdom Text with Beatitudes").[92] Frg. 2, col. 2 contains portions of five macarisms (or beatitudes) which in some ways bear similarities to those of Matt 5:3-12 and Luke 6:20-23. Of

---

[89] T. Elgvin, "Wisdom in the *Yaḥad*: 4QWays of Righteousness," *RevQ* 17 (1996) 205-232. For the text, see Wacholder and Abegg, *Preliminary Edition*, 2.159-65.

[90] 4Q421 1a i lines 2-3; Elgvin, "Wisdom in the *Yaḥad*," 209-10.

[91] 4Q421 1 ii lines 9-10; Elgvin, "Wisdom in the *Yaḥad*," 212-13.

[92] Puech, "Un Hymne essénien en partie retrouvé et les Béatitudes: 1QH V 12–VI 18 (= col. XIII–XIV 7) et 4QBéat.," *RevQ* 13 (1988) 59-88; G. J. Brooke, "The Wisdom of Matthew's Beatitudes (4QBéat and Mt. 5:3-12)," *Scripture Bulletin* 19/2 (1989) 35-41; Puech, "4Q525 et les péricopes des Béatitudes en Ben Sira et Matthieu," *RB* 98 (1991) 80-106; B. Viviano, "Eight Beatitudes at Qumran and in Matthew: A New Publication from Cave Four," *SEÅ* 58 (1993) 71-84. The text can also be found in Wacholder and Abegg, *Preliminary Edition*, 2.185-203. Translations are available in García Martínez, *Dead Sea Scrolls Translated*, 395-98; and Wise, Abegg and Cook, *Dead Sea Scrolls*, 423-26.

course, both 4Q525 and the NT texts represent the development of a tradition already evident in the Hebrew Bible, mostly in the wisdom literature, and also found in other post-biblical Jewish literature.[93] The macarisms in 4Q525 consider the attainment of חכמה to be the source of blessing. The wisdom discussed in these lines is to be practiced since the person who has attained it "walks in the law of the Most High." Wisdom is thus equated with Torah.[94]

In frg. 14 the מבין ("the one who understands") is exhorted "to listen to me." As in frgs. 2 and 4, where the third person singular feminine suffix could designate either חכמה or Torah, the personal pronoun here seems to equate the two, as also occurs in Sirach. Evidence of the more developed dualism that is characteristic of literature from Qumran and other apocalyptic works is apparent in frg. 15, with its references to "eternal fire," the "venom of serpents," "darkness," "flames of death" and "flaming brimstone," apparently with regard to those who "do not attain the paths of life." Finally, the dualistic viewpoint of the text is evident in the mention of Mastemah in frg. 19.

3.5 Sapiential Work (4Q424)

4Q424 is the number of yet another sapiential work,[95] which contains instructions concerning the treatment of various types of persons. In particular, the text itemizes which persons should be avoided, spelling out the reasons in each specific case. Many of these instructions concern legal and business relationships. However, issues of a moral nature appear in frg. 3, where the term חכמה, which is considered more characteristic of biblical wisdom, occurs three times. Also present in the last line of the preserved text is the term בני צדק ("sons of righteousness"), which has sometimes been considered indicative of the Qumran sectarians or a group within that movement. These indications point to this same body of literature which was viewed with particular favor by the Qumran community; however, it should not be considered a sectarian composition, even if it is demonstrated to be clearly post-biblical.

---

[93] Extensive citations are listed in R. Collins, "Beatitudes," *ABD* 1.629-31.

[94] Fragment 4 incorporates a similar equation.

[95] For the text, see Wacholder and Abegg, *Preliminary Edition*, 2.174-76. Translations appear in García Martínez, *Dead Sea Scrolls Translated*, 393-94; and Wise, Abegg and Cook, *Dead Sea Scrolls*, 393-94.

3.6 Hymn of Knowledge (4Q413)

Only one fragment survives from a sapiential work (4Q413) which Daniel Harrington has entitled the "Hymn of Knowledge," since the first word in the fragment is מזמור ("hymn" or "psalm").[96] The form of the preserved material—with its references to wisdom and understanding—places it closer to other wisdom texts discussed in this section of the present article, than to liturgical or worship material. As was the case in a number of the texts just discussed, we also find here allusions that are closer to the sectarian texts: "He made great his inheritance in the knowledge of his truth, and according to his loathing of all evil..." The fragment concludes with a reference to the revelation of God, which Elgvin suggests is the beginning of the phrase, "as God opened the ears of those who understand to the Mystery of Being,"[97] a phrase which is characteristic of Sapiential Work A but not other compositions.

3.7 Words of the Sage to the Sons of Dawn (4Q298)

4Q298 ("Words of the Sage to the Sons of Dawn") is one of the few documents from Qumran that was written in a cryptic script. The term חכמה is not found in the extant fragments, but the necessity to "understand" is emphasized, since "those who seek truth... and those who know have pursued these things and have turned..."[98] This text is addressed to the "sons of dawn," who could well be initiates that have not yet become full members of the sect, when they would be termed "sons of light." The contents are introduced as the words of the משכיל, the person who is referred to elsewhere in the Qumran wisdom literature,[99] but also presumably the spiritual and intellectual leader whose role is described in sectarian compositions.[100] These and other allusions indicate that 4Q298 is a wisdom composition of sectarian origin (i.e. that is was composed within the sect).

---

[96] Harrington, *Wisdom Texts*, 64-65. The text appears in Wacholder and Abegg, *Preliminary Edition*, 2.43; and translations in García Martínez, *Dead Sea Scrolls Translated*, 382-83; Wise, Abegg and Cook, *Dead Sea Scrolls*, 380.

[97] T. Elgvin, "Admonition Texts," 183.

[98] S. Pfann, "4Q298: The Maskil's Address to All Sons of Dawn," *JQR* 85 (1994) 205-235, esp. 227. See also M. Kister, "Commentary to 4Q298," *JQR* 85 (1994) 237-249. Translations can be found in García Martínez, *Dead Sea Scrolls Translated*, 382; and Wise, Abegg and Cook, *Dead Sea Scrolls*, 294-95.

[99] Notably in "Sapiential Work A" and the "Ways of Righteousness."

[100] 1QS, 1QSb, 1QH and CD, as well as in Cave 4 fragments of these works.

3.8 Admonition Based on the Flood (4Q370)

Wisdom admonitions that are coupled with eschatological interests characterise the extant fragment of 4Q370 ("Admonition Based on the Flood").[101] While the first column seems to follow the biblical account of the flood, the second mentions terms such as guilt, transgression and evil—even after the rainbow and the covenant. Alluding to the Hymn to the Creator,[102] the first lines of 4Q370 appear to cite col. 26:13-15 of the large Psalms Scroll (11QPs^a) and to paraphrase other sections of it. The connection between wisdom and the Hymn to the Creator is substantiated by the reference in col. 26:14 (of 11QPs^a), where the claim is made: "Blessed... is he who establishes the world with his wisdom."[103]

There are sufficient affinities with 4Q185, another admonition text, to postulate a literary relationship between the two, even though it is difficult to determine in which direction the dependence may lie.[104] While we find no evidence of distinctly sectarian terminology in the extant text of 4Q370, its relationship to some other sapiential writings with eschatological interests makes it similar to several of the Qumran texts that have been discussed in this article.

3.9 Praise of God and Parable of the Tree (4Q302–302a)

In 4Q302–302a ("Praise of God and Parable of the Tree") the חכמים ("wise men") are enjoined to discern a parable. Written on papyrus, this text was originally classified as a sapiential work by J. T. Milik and designated "SapA" in the *Preliminary Concordance*; it is not to be confused with "Sapiential Work A" which was discussed above.[105] These fragments are considered by Bilhah Nitzan to

---

[101] See M. Broshi et al. (eds.), *Qumran Cave 4.XIV: Parabiblical Texts, Part 2* (DJD 19; Oxford: Clarendon Press, 1995) 85-87 + pl. XII; and C. A. Newsom, "4Q370: An Admonition Based on the Flood," *RevQ* 13 (1988) 23-43. On this text, see also J. J. Collins, "Wisdom, Apocalypticism and Generic Compatibility," in L. J. Perdue, B. B. Scott and W. J. Wiseman (eds.), *In Search of Wisdom: Essays in Memory of John G. Gammie* (Louisville, KY: Westminster/John Knox, 1993) 165-185, esp. 180 n.46. The Hebrew text is available in Wacholder and Abegg, *Preliminary Edition*, 2.237-39. Translations appear in García Martínez, *Dead Sea Scrolls Translated*, 224-25; and Wise, Abegg and Cook, *Dead Sea Scrolls*, 330-31.

[102] See section 2.4 above, and Newsom, "4Q370," 30.

[103] Sanders, *The Psalms Scroll* (DJD 4), 90.

[104] In addition to Newsom ("4Q370," 39-41), see Tobin, "4Q185," 149.

[105] Section 3.1 above.

represent distinct chapters of the same composition, rather than two separate treatises.[106]

This rare appearance of a parable in post-biblical Jewish literature outside of the New Testament is significant for studying the history of the genre. It appears to be in the biblical tradition of parables about trees (Ezek 19:10-14; Ps 80:9-17; and Dan 4:7-14, 17-18).[107] Nowhere is the term משל to be found in these fragments; while its use sometimes denotes popular sayings or proverbs in the Hebrew Bible (1 Sam 10:12; 24:13; and Ezek 12:22-23; 16:44; 18:2-3), the limited extant material in the fragments does not offer any significant connection with the sapiential material that has been discussed above. Nevertheless, the admonition to the addressee ("Discern this, O wise men") suggests that this text may be part of the wisdom tradition in the Qumran corpus.

3.10 Other Compositions

A number of works attested by very limited fragmentary evidence have been designated sapiential works, but further classification has so far not been possible. These include: 4Q307–4Q308; 4Q408;[108] 4Q410–4Q412;[109] 4Q425–4Q426;[110] 4Q472–476;[111] 4Q486–487;[112]

---

[106] B. Nitzan, "4Q302/302A (Sap. A): Pap. Praise of God and Parable of the Tree, A Preliminary Edition," *RevQ* 17 (1996) 151-173, esp. 152. The text also appears in Wacholder and Abegg, *Preliminary Edition*, 2.228-31; and a translation in Wise, Abegg and Cook, *Dead Sea Scrolls*, 295-96.

[107] Nitzan, "4Q302/302A," 160.

[108] Wise, Abegg and Cook, *Dead Sea Scrolls*, 377.

[109] Wacholder and Abegg, *Preliminary Edition*, 2.40-42; Wise, Abegg and Cook, *Dead Sea Scrolls*, 379-80.

[110] Wacholder and Abegg, *Preliminary Edition*, 2.177-84.

[111] This group of scrolls is listed in this manner by Harrington, *Wisdom Texts*, 73. For the texts of 4Q474 and 4Q476, see Wacholder and Abegg, *Preliminary Edition*, 3.362 and 2.297, respectively. 4Q473 ("The Two Ways") is also referred to as a "Sapiential Work" in some listings (e.g. E. Tov, "The Unpublished Qumran Texts from Caves 4 and 11," *BA* 55 [1992] 94-104). The text is given in Wacholder and Abegg, *Preliminary Edition*, 3.361; and a translation in Wise, Abegg and Cook, *Dead Sea Scrolls*, 405. It is difficult to determine much about this text due to its fragmentary nature, but one might speculate on similarities to 4Q420–421 ("Ways of Righteousness"), a wisdom text that was discussed above (see section 3.3).

[112] M. Baillet, *Qumrân Grotte 4:III [4Q482-4Q520]* (DJD 7; Oxford: Clarendon Press, 1968), 4-10.

and 4Q498 ("Sapiential Hymn").[113] Although 4Q419 has been labelled "Sapiential Work B," Daniel Harrington has rightly called into question its relationship to the wisdom tradition.[114] Frg. 1 speaks of the משפטים which were delivered via the hand of Moses and then passed on to the priests; the readers are also enjoined to avoid abomination. This appears to reflect the language of the legal literature, and is reminiscent of Deuteronomy in particular, rather than actual wisdom concerns. Nevertheless, the incomplete and fragmentary nature of the extant text makes it difficult to reach any firm conclusion.

4. IMPLICATIONS FOR FUTURE STUDY

This survey of the wisdom literature that became available after 1990 provides evidence of a tradition that was previously unrecognised in Qumran scholarship. The hints of wisdom material available prior to this time were understandably viewed as aberrations and of limited significance. The literature that was summarized above points to a new wisdom tradition which was not simply an imitation of biblical material, nor an expansion of the sectarian use of wisdom vocabulary that was noted early on in the study of Qumran materials. The connections between many of these texts provide strong evidence of another significant wisdom tradition in Second Temple Judaism, the study of which is only in its infancy.

This brings us back to the sectarian literature which occupied those first scholars of this ancient library. We now have a much better explanation for the preponderance of terms concerning knowledge and wisdom which are distributed freely throughout those scrolls. Furthermore, we find in both 1QS and 1QH works that are admittedly dominated by dualism and eschatology, and an interest in creation, the times and the celestial bodies. In fact, the dualism and eschatology found in these texts are rooted in creation and the cosmos. But now the time of speculative wisdom has ended; wisdom has rather been placed in the service of the sect. These developments will only be more fully understood with further discussion and research.

The work of Armin Lange is one attempt to trace an intellectual history of the wisdom traditions within the compositions found in the

---

[113] Baillet, *Qumrân Grotte 4:III* (DJD 7), 73-74.
[114] Harrington, *Wisdom Texts*, 73.

Qumran caves.[115] Starting from the premise of wisdom's interest in questions of order, he traces the manner in which "the sapiential idea of an ethical and social order according to which God created the world and ordered human life" developed in those documents which can be demonstrated to have an interest in this question.[116] In 4QSapiential Work A, Lange finds "a pre-existent, hidden, sapiential order of the world, dualistic in character."[117] In the 4QMysteries manuscripts we see that the full realization of this pre-existent order of the world will be in the eschaton.[118] The Teaching of the Two Spirits (1QS 3:13–4:26) is within the same sapiential tradition—but here the eschatological triumph over wickedness is necessary for the knowledge of the pre-existent dualistic order of the world to be revealed. Thus for Lange, wisdom is on its way to apocalypticism in this important text.[119]

These ideas find a sectarian expression in 1QH, where the idea of a pre-existent order inscribed on the heavenly tablets prior to creation serves to authenticate the glory of God, in contrast to the lowliness of the human being. This theology is used to justify the form of dualism which is developed in the sectarian documents, and is then employed to deal with the problem of a reality "which had not lived up to the *yaḥad*'s theological hopes and eschatological expectations."[120] Such doctrines developed out of sapiential circles and—when utilized in a different historical context—were pushed to their logical conclusions. Lange has provided us with one explanation for the enduring presence of wisdom vocabulary in this later literature.

John Collins has also examined the question of wisdom and apocalypticism. In a re-evaluation of the von Rad question, he notes that Ben Sira and Qumran share a common perception of the role of

---

[115] A. Lange, *Weisheit und Prädestination. Weisheitliche Urordnung und Prädestination in den Textfunden von Qumran* (STDJ 18; Leiden, Brill, 1995; idem, "Wisdom and Predestination in the Dead Sea Scrolls," *DSD* 2 (1995) 340-354.

[116] Lange, "Wisdom and Predestination," 340.

[117] Lange, "Wisdom and Predestination," 343.

[118] Lange, "Wisdom and Predestination," 345.

[119] Lange ("Wisdom and Predestination," 348) points out that here wisdom is "designated as knowledge of the Most High and the wisdom of the Sons of Heaven." The reader should note that he considers this section of 1QS to be an independent text ("Wisdom and Predestination," 346 n.18).

[120] Lange, "Wisdom and Predestination," 354.

Torah which is different from apocalypticism.[121] Collins also argues that, while both share an ethical and psychological dualism, on this topic texts such as 1QS 3:13–4:26 contain a metaphysical perspective which is absent from Ben Sira.[122] Noting that documents such as Sapiential Work A are also found at Qumran, he goes on to observe that "wisdom" is not to be confined to any single world-view; thus Qumran demonstrates that traditional wisdom instruction could be adapted to an apocalyptic world-view.[123] Further research is required to demonstrate the finer and more specific aspects of this adaptation in these Qumran texts, as well their interrelationships.

In view of these issues, a subject that has found only preliminary treatment in the literature so far achieves greater prominence. Attempts must be made to understand the propagators of this wisdom as well as the texts which recorded it. Recent studies concerning the nature of the persons entrusted with wisdom and its impartation in these texts has focused on the figure of the משכיל, the one who "shall instruct all the sons of light and shall teach them…" (1QS 3:13).[124] This line introduces 1QS 3:13–4:26, one of the crucial passages concerning the subject of dualism and wisdom that was discussed above.[125] The "sage," who as teacher again receives emphasis in 1QS 9:12–10:5, is:

> concerned with the formation of the community, both through his admission and regulation of members and through his instruction in the knowledge that the community shares in common, yet that separates it from outsiders.[126]

This knowledge is related to the Torah, and to the particular practices based on the community's interpretation of it: "He shall conceal the teaching of the Law from men of falsehood, but shall

---

[121] J. J. Collins, "Wisdom, Apocalypticism and the Dead Sea Scrolls," in his *Seers, Sybils and Sages in Hellenistic-Roman Judaism* (JSJSup 54; Leiden: Brill, 1997) 369-83, esp. 371.

[122] "Wisdom, Apocalypticism and the Dead Sea Scrolls," 382.

[123] J. J. Collins, "Wisdom, Apocalypticism and Generic Compatibility," 165-185, esp. 179-81; this material also appears in idem, *Seers, Sybills and Sages*, 385-404.

[124] C. A. Newsom, "The Sage in the Literature of Qumran: The Functions of the Maskil," in J. G. Gammie and L. G. Perdue (eds.), *The Sage in Israel and the Ancient Near East* (Winona Lake, IN: Eisenbrauns, 1990) 373-382, esp. 374.

[125] See section 1.3.

[126] Newsom, "The Sage," 375.

impart true knowledge and righteous judgment to those who have chosen the Way."[127]

This same figure is the subject of 4Q510-511 ("Songs of the Sage[a, b]").[128] Here the משכיל, writing in the first person, is the one who "makes known (משמיע) the splendor of his beauty, in order to frighten and ter[rify] all the spirits of the angels of destruction...."[129] Newsom notes the manner in which the sage refers to the divine gift of knowledge which he has received.[130] In this case, however, the "sage" has the further role to keep the "spirits of the angels of destruction" at bay.[131] For him, this knowledge is the source of the authority and power necessary to gain victory within the dualistic struggle in which the יחד ("community") is engaged. As noted by Newsom this figure—based on a title already found in Psalms—also constitutes the heading (למשכיל) for each composition in the Songs of the Sabbath Sacrifice (4Q400-407). While not considering this work a sectarian composition, she regards it as influential within the literature which did originate from the life of the community, as is demonstrated by the literary dependence of 4Q510-511 upon it.[132] Thus a figure who was initially not connected with the wisdom materials becomes integrated into that tradition by way of the very particular ideological developments to be found in the growth of that movement. A question beyond the scope of the present article would be an analysis of this development from the standpoint of the liturgical history of the group involved.

The observations of George Nickelsburg concerning connections between certain strands in the Enochic compositions and the Qumran

---

[127] 1QS 9:17-18.

[128] M. Baillet, *Qumrân Grotte 4:III* (DJD 7) 215-62; B. Nitzan, "Hymns from Qumran—4Q510-4Q511," in D. Dimant and U. Rappaport (eds.), *The Dead Sea Scrolls: Forty Years of Research* (STDJ 10; Leiden: Brill; Jerusalem: Magnes Press and Yad Izhak Ben-Zvi, 1992) 53-63.

[129] 4Q510 1 lines 4-5 (translation by Newsom, "The Sage," 381, from which this discussion of 4Q510-511 is drawn). See also S. Tanzer, "Sages at Qumran," 165-67.

[130] She cites 4Q511 18 ii lines 7-9 as an example.

[131] See also Nitzan, "Hymns from Qumran," 55.

[132] C. A. Newsom, "'Sectually Explicit' Literature from Qumran," in W. H. Propp, B. Halpern and D. N. Freedman (eds.),*The Hebrew Bible and Its Interpreters* (Winona Lake, IN: Eisenbrauns, 1990) 167-87, esp. 180-81; idem, "The Sage," 381.

texts[133] become most relevant in light of this discussion of a wisdom figure within the life of a community, as described by its literature. While his work does not deal with wisdom literature as such, it is of significance for our topic due to his attempt at identifying similarities in the social construction of the groups associated with this literature. Similar questions must be addressed concerning the relationship between a composition such as Sapiential Work A and some of the explicitly sectarian texts which make extensive use of wisdom terminology (notably 1QS and 1QH). Armin Lange's dissertation represents one attempt to address this issue. Included in the Groningen hypothesis is one more attempt to account for these kinds of data, even though F. García Martínez and A. S. van der Woude are not specifically interested in wisdom.[134] In addition, the early essay on this subject by Carol Newsom posed the question from a sociological standpoint.[135] Because of the particular variety of wisdom texts from Qumran that have recently been published, important material is now available for case-studies concerning issues of sociological classification and historical development. This work, however, is still in its infancy.

Additional basic classification-work may also be required for these texts. In the mid-1970's the study of apocalyptic literature began to make significant groundbreaking advances, following some rudimentary efforts at description and classification.[136] The diversity of wisdom literature and terminology among the Qumran texts may require us to re-examine this issue with regard to other Second Temple literature as well. Questions and procedures of description

---

[133] G. W. E. Nickelsburg, "The Epistle of Enoch and the Qumran Literature," *JJS* 33 (1982) 333-348; idem, "Social Aspects of Palestinian Jewish Apocalypticism," in D. Hellholm (ed.), *Apocalypticism in the Mediterranean World and the Near East* (Tübingen: Mohr-Siebeck, 1983) 641-654; idem, "1 Enoch and Qumran Origins: The State of the Question and Some Prospects for Answers," SBLSP (1986) 341-360.

[134] F. García Martínez and A. S. van der Woude, "A 'Groningen' Hypothesis of Qumran Origins and Early History," *RevQ* 14 (1989-1990) 521-41; F. García Martínez, "Qumran Origins and Early History: A Groningen Hypothesis," *Folia Orientalia* 25 (1988) 113-36.

[135] Newsom, "'Sectually Explicit' Literature."

[136] This effort is represented in J. J. Collins (ed.) *Apocalypse: The Morphology of a Genre* (*Semeia* 14; Missoula, MT: Scholars Press, 1979).

and classification may be important prior to addressing the issues that were raised in the previous paragraph.

The evidence from Qumran again compels us to reconsider the relationship between wisdom and apocalypticism.[137] I am reminded of the new ground that was broken by Michael Stone with respect to the development of apocalypticism in his 1976 article on the "lists of revealed things."[138] In that piece and subsequent ones, Stone's work led to the recognitition that apocalypticism did not originate with, nor needs be dominated by, eschatology.[139] The place of eschatology with respect to the classification of wisdom literature at Qumran is in considerable debate, and is an issue that certainly requires further examination. But at this point, it is abundantly clear that the texts from Qumran which are now available force us to re-examine our understanding of wisdom at Qumran and in Second Temple Judaism.

SELECT BIBLIOGRAPHY

Baumgarten, J. M. "On the Nature of the Seductress in 4Q184," *RevQ* 15 (1991) 133-43.

Brooke, G. J. "The Wisdom of Matthew's Beatitudes (4QBéat and Mt. 5:3-12)," *Scripture Bulletin* 19/2 (1989) 35-41.

Collins, J. J. *Seers, Sybils and Sages in Hellenistic-Roman Judaism* (JSJSup 54; Leiden: Brill, 1997).

—. "Wisdom, Apocalypticism and Generic Compatibility," in L. J. Perdue, B. B. Scott and W. J. Wiseman (eds.), *In Search of Wisdom: Essays in Memory of John G. Gammie* (Louisville: Westminster/John Knox, 1993) 165-185.

Davies, W. D. "'Knowledge' in the Dead Sea Scrolls and Matthew 11:25-30," *HTR* 46 (1953) 113-39.

Denis, A-M. *Les thèmes de connaisance dans le Document de Damas* (Studia Hellenistica 15; Louvain: Publications universitaires, 1967).

Deutsch, C. M. *Lady Wisdom, Jesus, and the Sages: Metaphor and Social Context in Matthew's Gospel* (Valley Forge, PA: Trinity Press International, 1996).

Elgvin, T. "Admonition Texts from Qumran Cave 4," in M. O. Wise, N. Golb, J. J. Collins and D. G. Pardee (eds.), *Methods of Investigation of the Dead Sea*

---

[137] In his recent collection of essays (*Seers, Sybils and Sages*), John Collins devotes a number of chapters to this subject.

[138] M. E. Stone, "Lists of Revealed Things in the Apocalyptic Literature," in F. M. Cross, W. E. Lemke and P. D. Miller, Jr. (eds.), *Magnalia Dei: The Mighty Acts of God* (Garden City, NY: Doubleday, 1976) 414-52.

[139] M. E. Stone, *Scriptures, Sects and Visions: A Profile of Judaism from Ezra to the Jewish Revolts* (Philadelphia: Fortress, 1980).

Scrolls and the Khirbet Qumran Site: Present Realities and Future Prospects. (ANYAS 722; New York: New York Academy of Sciences, 1994) 179-96.

—. "The Reconstruction of Sapiential Work A," *RevQ* 16 (1995) 559-80.

—. "Wisdom in the *Yaḥad*: 4QWays of Righteousness," *RevQ* 17 (1996) 205-32.

—. "Wisdom, Revelation, and Eschatology in an early Essene Writing," SBLSP (1995) 440-63.

Gammie, J. G. "Spatial and Ethical Dualism in Jewish Wisdom and Apocalyptic Literature," *JBL* 93 (1974) 356-85.

Gordis, R. "The Knowledge of Good and Evil in the Old Testament and the Qumran Scrolls," *JBL* 76 (1957) 123-38.

Harrington, D. J. "The *Raz Nihyeh* in a Qumran Wisdom Text (1Q26, 4Q415-418, 423)," *RevQ* 17 (1996) 549-53.

—. *Wisdom Texts from Qumran* (The Dead Sea Scrolls; London: Routledge, 1996).

—. "Wisdom at Qumran," in E. Ulrich and J. VanderKam (eds.), *The Community of the Renewed Covenant: The Notre Dame Symposium on the Dead Sea Scrolls* (CJA 10; Notre Dame: University of Notre Dame Press, 1994) 137-52.

Lange, A. *Weisheit und Prädestination. Weisheitliche Urordnung und Prädestination in den Textfunden von Qumran* (STDJ 18; Leiden: Brill, 1995).

—. "Wisdom and Predestination in the Dead Sea Scrolls," *DSD* 2 (1995) 340-54.

Lehmann, M. R. "Ben-Sira and the Qumran Literature," *RevQ* 3 (1961) 103-16.

Lipscomb, W. L. with J. A. Sanders. "Wisdom at Qumran," in J. G. Gammie, W. A. Brueggemann, W. L. Humphreys and J. M. Ward (eds.), *Israelite Wisdom: Theological and Literary Essays in Honor of Samuel Terrien.* (Missoula, MT: Scholars Press, 1978) 277-85.

Martínez, F. G. and A. S. van der Woude. "A 'Groningen' Hypothesis of Qumran Origins and Early History," *RevQ* 14 (1989-1990) 521-41.

Martínez, F. G. "Qumran Origins and Early History: A Groningen Hypothesis," *Folia Orientalia* 25 (1988) 113-36.

May, H. G. "Cosmological Reference in the Qumran Doctrine of the Two Spirits and in Old Testament Imagery," *JBL* 82 (1963) 1-14.

Moore, R. D. "Personification of the Seduction of Evil: 'The Wiles of the Wicked Woman'," *RevQ* 10 (1981) 505-19.

Newsom, C. A. "The Sage in the Literature of Qumran: The Functions of the Maskil," in J. G. Gammie and L. G. Perdue (eds.), *The Sage in Israel and the Ancient Near East* (Winona Lake, IN: Eisenbrauns, 1990) 373-82.

—. "4Q370: An Admonition Based on the Flood," *RevQ* 13 (1988) 23-43.

Nitzan, B. "Hymns from Qumran—4Q510-4Q511," in D. Dimant and U. Rappaport (eds.), *The Dead Sea Scrolls: Forty Years of Research.* (STDJ 10; Leiden: Brill; Jerusalem: Magnes Press and Yad Izhak Ben-Zvi, 1992) 53-63.

—. "4Q302/302A (Sap. A): Pap. Praise of God and Parable of the Tree, A Preliminary Edition," *RevQ* 17 (1996) 151-73.

Nötscher, F. *Zur Theologischen Terminologie der Qumran-Texte.* (BBB 10; Bonn: Hanstein, 1956).

Otzen, B. "Old Testament Wisdom Literature and Dualistic Thinking in Late Judaism," in *Congress Volume: Edinburgh 1974.* (VTSupp 28; Leiden: Brill, 1975) 146-57.

Pfann, S. "4Q298: The Maskil's Address to All Sons of Dawn," *JQR* 85 (1994) 205-235.

Puech, É. "4Q525 et les péricopes des Béatitudes en Ben Sira et Matthieu," *RB* 98 (1991) 80-106.

—. "Un Hymne essénien en partie retrouvé et les Béatitudes: 1QH V 12–VI 18 (= col. XIII-XIV 7) et 4QBéat," *RevQ* 13 (1988) 59-88.

Ringgren, H. *The Faith of Qumran: Theology of the Dead Sea Scrolls.* (Expanded ed., New York: Crossroad, 1995 [1961]).

Sanders, J. A. *The Psalms Scroll of Qumran Cave 11 [11QPs^a]* (DJD 4. Oxford: Clarendon Press, 1965).

Schiffman, L. H. "4QMysteries[a]: A Preliminary Edition and Translation," in Z. Zevit, S. Gitin and M. Sokoloff (eds.), *Solving Riddles and Untying Knots: Biblical, Epigraphic, and Semitic Studies in Honor of Jonas C. Greenfield* (Winona Lake, IN: Eisenbrauns, 1995) 207-60.

—. "4QMysteries[b], A Preliminary Edition," *RevQ* 16 (1993) 203-23.

Sharvit, B. "The Virtue of Wisdom in the Image of the Righteous Man in 1QS," *Beth Mikra* 19 (1974) 526-30.

Tanzer, S. "The Sages at Qumran: Wisdom in the Hodayot," (Ph.D. diss., Cambridge, MA: Harvard University, 1987).

Tobin, T. H. "4Q185 and Jewish Wisdom Literature," in H. W. Attridge, J. J. Collins and T. H. Tobin (eds.), *Of Scribes and Scrolls: Studies on the Hebrew Bible, Intertestamental Judaism, and Christian Origins, presented to John Strugnell on the occasion of His Sixtieth Birthday* (CTSRR 5; Lanham, MD: University Press of America, 1990) 145-52.

Winter, P. "Ben Sira and the Teaching of 'Two Ways'," *VT* 5 (1955) 315-18.

Worrell, J. E. "Concepts of Wisdom in the Dead Sea Scrolls," (Ph.D. diss, Claremont, CA: Claremont Graduate School, 1968).

HYMNS AND PRAYERS IN THE DEAD SEA SCROLLS

ESTHER G. CHAZON

Fifty years after their initial discovery, the Dead Sea Scrolls present scholars with more than two hundred hymns and prayers, most of which were previously unknown. These are found in prayer collections or are embedded in works that are as diverse in character as pseudepigraphic writings and sectarian rules. Together with nearly forty manuscripts containing copies or portions of some 125 biblical psalms,[1] these texts are a treasure-trove for the study of religious practice and spirituality as well as for the study of many other disciplines, ranging from biblical criticism and interpretation to mysticism and magic.

The current state of research on this important corpus is assessed below. An initial review of watersheds in previous research is followed by a careful examination of the latest developments in the field, which also points toward directions for future investigation. The final section provides a comprehensive, descriptive catalogue of the various texts. Special attention will be paid throughout to the broader implications of research in this whole field.

1. THE FIRST 35 YEARS (1947–1982)

As early as 1959, Shemaryahu Talmon was able to envision the extent to which the Qumran sect developed a regular practice of prayer at fixed times of the day and year.[2] In that early period, when relatively few texts were available, Talmon based his theory largely on the sociological analogy between the Qumran community's renunciation of the Temple cult and the cessation of that cult which was forced upon all Jews when the Second Temple was destroyed in 70 CE. According to this analogy, like the Rabbis would later do in

---

[1] For this total, see P. W. Flint, *The Dead Sea Psalms Scrolls and the Book of Psalms* (STDJ 17; Leiden: Brill, 1997) 48.

[2] S. Talmon, "מחזור הסרכות של כת מדבר יהודה" ["The Order of Prayers of the Sect from the Judaean Desert"], *Tarbiz* 29 (1959) 1-20; "The 'Manual of Benedictions' of the Sect of the Judaean Desert," *RevQ* 2 (1960) 475-500.

the post-destruction era, the sect instituted fixed prayer ("worship of the heart") as a substitute for sacrificial worship. Indeed, the use of sacrificial language to characterize prayer like "an offering of the lips" (1QS 9:5) and the commitment to daily and festive praise expressed in the sect's writings (e.g. 1QS 10:1-17) lend credence to this part of Talmon's theory with the result that prayer's function at Qumran as a substitute for sacrifice is indeed widely recognized by scholars.[3]

Talmon devoted the bulk of his pioneering study to the reconstruction of a "Manual of Benedictions," portions of which he saw scattered among scrolls that had already been published.[4] Based primarily on what he termed the "Psalm of Appointed Times" and the "Psalm of Benedictions" (1QS 9:26-11:15),[5] Talmon posited that the "Manual of Benedictions" contained a list of daily and yearly prayer times followed by the actual texts of the prayers to be recited at those times. He accordingly viewed the "Psalm of Benedictions" as a paraphrase of the sect's daily prayers, noting their affinities with the later, standard Jewish liturgy (especially the *Qedušat Yoṣer*, the *Shema* and the *Amidah*).[6] In an expanded version of his original article, Talmon concluded that "despite the enormous breadth of common ground, no definite historical interdependence can be established between the emergence of institutionalized prayer at Qumran and the early prayer of the normative Jewish community."[7]

---

[3] For an early assessment of this function see J. Baumgarten, "Sacrifice and Worship Among the Jewish Sectarians of the Dead Sea (Qumran) Scrolls," *HTR* 46 (1953) 141-59.

[4] Talmon ("Manual of Benedictions," 499-500) conjectured that the War Scroll gives the sectarian title of the "Manual" as the "[B]ook of the Manual of Appointed Times" (‏[ס]פר סרך עתו‎]).

[5] The hymn at the end of 1QS does not appear in all of the Cave 4 manuscripts of the Community Rule and is now considered a later addition (see section 2 below, "Research in the 1990's").

[6] This tendency to draw parallels with later Jewish liturgy has been vigorously pursued over the years, notably by M. Weinfeld as in his "Prayer and Liturgical Practice in the Qumran Sect," in D. Dimant and U. Rappaport (eds.), *The Dead Sea Scrolls: Forty Years of Research* (STDJ 10; Leiden: Brill; Jerusalem: Magnes Press and Yad Ben-Zvi, 1992) 241-58.

[7] S. Talmon, "The Emergence of Institutionalized Prayer in Israel in the Light of the Qumran Literature," in M. Delcor (ed.), *Qumrân. Sa piété, sa théologie et son milieu* (BETL 46; Paris-Gembloux: Duculot, Leuven: Leuven University Press,

Nearly thirty years and scores of publications later, no prayerbook or "Manual of Benedictions" such as that proposed by Talmon has come to light, nor should such a find any longer be anticipated. Rather than a "Manual" which like later prayer-books[8] sets forth the complete order of daily and holiday prayers in a calendric arrangement, the Scrolls collate these kinds of prayers according to different criteria. One important criterion was to incorporate in a single collection prayers similar in form and content that were designated for the same type of occasion. A fine example is 4Q503, known as the Daily Prayers. These very brief evening and morning blessings for the days of the month surely did not constitute the entire daily liturgy but must have been said together with additional prayers that are recorded in other scrolls.[9] Indeed, Talmon's basic theory that the Qumran sect instituted fixed prayer was essentially corroborated and nuanced by the subsequent publication of such liturgical collections.

2. THE NEXT SEVEN YEARS (1982-1989)

The surge in publication of prayer texts that began just fifteen years ago marks the second stage of research in this field. 1982 saw the publication of the seventh volume in the definitive series "Discoveries in the Judaean Desert," and was followed three years later with the complete publication of the Songs of the Sabbath Sacrifice.[10] The appearance of these new texts changed our picture of

---

1978) 283. Talmon combined both articles under a similar title in his collected studies, *The World of Qumran from Within* (Leiden: Brill; Jerusalem: Magnes Press, 1989) 200-43.

[8] The earliest Jewish prayerbooks date from about the ninth century CE. For a history and summary of the data, see S. C. Reif, *Judaism and Hebrew Prayer: New Persectives on Jewish Liturgical History* (Cambridge: Cambridge University Press, 1993) 122-52.

[9] For this observation see also L. Schiffman, "The Dead Sea Scrolls and the Early History of Jewish Liturgy," in L. I. Levine (ed.), *The Synagogue in Late Antiquity* (Philadelphia: ASOR, 1987) 39. Other daily prayers which may have been said at the same time include the morning and evening blessings in 4Q408, the prayers for the days of the week in the Words of the Luminaries (4QDibHam), and the daily prayers that are alluded to in 1QS 9:26-10:17. The relationship between 4Q503 and 4Q408 is treated in section 3 below ("Research in the 1990's").

[10] For bibliography, see below.

the corpus of prayers from Qumran in several important ways, since the magnitude of this corpus, the variety of material, and the prominence of liturgical works now became apparent for the first time.

The few texts that were available in the 1950's were distinctively sectarian and, aside from the annual covenant ceremony, were either individual hymns (the Hodayot and the hymn which concludes 1QS) or prayers for the eschatological era (in the War Scroll and 1QSb).[11] This impression did not essentially change during the next two decades which really only saw one major publication in this area, the large Cave 11 Psalms Scroll, whose function as a liturgical collection has not been sufficiently recognized.[12]

The impact of texts that had been partially published in the 1960's, such as the Songs of the Sabbath Sacrifice[13] and the Words of the Luminaries, was felt only when they were fully published in the 1980's[14] along with another five major liturgical documents that

---

[11] This impression of the corpus was continued by the later publication of another eschatological blessing (A. S. van der Woude, "Eine neuer Segensspruch aus Qumran [11QBer]," in S. Wagner [ed.], *Bibel und Qumran* [Festschrift H. Bardtke; Berlin: Evangelische Hauptbibelgesellschaft, 1968] 253-58); and more eschatological texts and parts of another version (4QBerakhot) of the covenant ceremony (J. T. Milik, "Milkî-ṣedeq et Milkî-rešaʿ dans les anciens écrits juifs et chrétiens," *JJS* 23 [1972] 95–144). An exception is the copy of the Festival Prayers (1Q34-34 *bis*) that was published in D. Barthélemy and J. T. Milik, *Qumran Cave I* (DJD 1; Oxford: Clarendon Press, 1955) 136, 152-55. This small, fragmentary manuscript did not attract much attention until other copies from Cave 4 appeared in DJD 7 in 1982 (see below); Talmon, however, took this text into consideration for reconstructing his proposed Manual of Benedictions.

[12] J. A. Sanders, *The Psalms Scroll of Qumran Cave 11 (11QPsª)* (DJD 4; Oxford: Clarendon Press, 1965). Sanders considers the Psalms Scroll (11QPsª) an edition of the canonical Psalter. See now P. Flint, *Dead Sea Psalms Scrolls*, 202-27, for a similar assessment based on the newly-available data and a review of the debate over the canon versus liturgy question. On 11QPsª as a liturgical collection see S. Talmon, "Pisqah Beʾemsaʿ Pasuq and 11QPsª," *Textus* 5 (1966) 11-21; and M. H. Goshen-Gottstein, "The Psalms Scroll (11QPsª). A Problem of Canon and Text," *Textus* 5 (1966) 22-33; P. W. Skehan, "A Liturgical Complex in 11QPsª," *CBQ* 34 (1973) 195-205; and idem, "Qumran and Old Testament Criticism," in M. Delcor (ed.), *Qumrân. Sa piété*, 163-72.

[13] J. Strugnell, "The Angelic Liturgy at Qumran-4Q Šerek Šîrot ʿOlat Haššabbat," in *Congress Volume* (VTSup 7; Leiden: Brill, 1960) 318-45;

[14] See M. Baillet, "Un recueil liturgique de Qumran, grotte 4: 'Les paroles des luminaires'," *RB* 68 (1961) 195-250; C. Newsom, *Songs of the Sabbath Sacrifice:*

appeared in DJD 7.[15] It now became clear that the corpus did not primarily consist of hymns for private devotion and eschatological speculation that had been written by members of the sect, but was rather much more varied. The corpus was now seen to encompass prayers of different types that served different functions, from matrimonial celebration (4Q502)[16] and blessings during ritual purification (4Q512), to protection against demons (4Q510-511)[17] and an experience of the heavenly realm (Songs of the Sabbath Sacrifice).[18] Moreover, liturgies for fixed prayer-times which display striking parallels with later Jewish liturgical forms were now seen to figure prominently in the corpus. The publication of subsequent texts in the 1990's has enriched, but not essentially altered, this new and complex picture.

While appreciation of such common liturgical material spawned some informative, if limited, comparative studies,[19] of greater potential significance was the concomitant recognition that many of

---

A Critical Edition (HSS 27; Atlanta: Scholars Press, 1985). One other major collection published in the 1980's is worth noting, although it is evidently not a liturgical collection: E. Schuller, *Non-Canonical Psalms from Qumran: A Pseudepigraphic Collection* (HSS 28; Atlanta: Scholars Press, 1986).

[15] M. Baillet, *Qumrân Grotte 4.III (4Q482–4Q520)* (DJD 7; Oxford: Clarendon Press, 1982) 81-286.

[16] J. Baumgarten has suggested that 4Q502 was a "golden age ritual" rather than a marriage ritual ("4Q502, Marriage or Golden Age Ritual?," *JJS* 34 [1983] 125-35). The text bears directly on the question of the status of women in the community.

[17] This text's appearance in DJD 7 provided a broader framework for understanding the prophylactic apocryphal hymns of 11QPsAp[a] that were first published in 1971 by J. P. M. van der Ploeg ("Un petit rouleau de psaumes apocryphes," in G. Jeremias, H.-W. Kuhn, H. Stegemann (eds.), *Tradition und Glaube* (Festscrift K.G. Kuhn, Göttingen: Vandenhoeck and Ruprecht, 1971), 128-39 + pls. II–VII. See now E. Puech, "11QPsAp[a]: Un Rituel d'exorcismes. Essai de reconstruction," *RevQ* 55 (1990) 377-408.

[18] Newsom, *Songs of the Sabbath Sacrifice*, 17-19, 59-72. For a different opinion see J. Maier, "Shîrê ʿÔlat hash-Shabbat. Some Observations on their Calendric Implications and on their Syle," in J. Trebolle Barrera and L. Vegas Montaner (eds.), *Proceedings of the International Congress on the Dead Sea Scrolls, Madrid. 18–21 March 1991* (2 vols., STDJ 11; Leiden: Brill; Madrid: Universidad Complutense, 1992) 552-53.

[19] Examples are Weinfeld, "Liturgical Practice;" Schiffman, "Early History;" J. Maier, "Zu Kult und Liturgie der Qumran- gemeinde," *RevQ* 14 (1989/90) 543-86.

the prayers (and other texts) which were being published were not distinctively sectarian in character and were probably not Qumranic in origin. The late 1980's thus ushered in several ground-breaking methodological studies devoted to the establishment of criteria for distinguishing between Qumranic and non-Qumranic texts, and to categorizing and classifying works of different provenance.[20] At stake in this endeavor is no less than the recovery of authentic traditions shared by different Jewish groups during the Second Temple period. This is because the Scrolls—to the extent that they preserve imported, non-Qumranic works amassed by the Qumran covenanters—provide direct evidence of Jewish religious practice, belief and literature outside the confines of that sectarian community.

Unfortunately, this new research on the provenance of different documents found at Qumran was not incorporated into the first monograph on Qumran prayer, which was completed by Bilhah Nitzan in 1989 (Hebrew) and published in English in 1994.[21] Closer attention to recent assessments of the non-Qumranic origin of certain texts would have enabled Nitzan to substantiate better her theory that texts found among the Scrolls drew upon a contemporary tradition of prayer alongside the cult, and thus bear witness to the existence of fixed prayer in Second Temple Judaism.[22] Nitzan regards the similarities to rabbinic prayer in these documents as reflecting the transitional stage in a developmental process that proceeded from spontaneous biblical prayer to fixed rabbinic prayer.[23] In this respect

---

[20] See E. G. Chazon, "Is Divrei ha-meʾorot a Sectarian Prayer," in Dimant and Rappaport (eds.), *Forty Years of Research*, 3-17; C. A. Newsom, "'Sectually Explicit' Literature from Qumran," in W. H. Propp, B. Halpern and D. N. Freedman (eds.), *The Hebrew Bible and Its Modern Interpreters* (Winona Lake, IN: Eisenbrauns, 1990) 167-87; D. Dimant, "The Qumran Manuscripts: Contents and Significance," in D. Dimant and L. H. Schiffman (eds.), *Time to Prepare the Way in the Wilderness* (STDJ 16; Leiden: Brill, 1995) 23-58.

[21] B. Nitzan, "התפילה והשירה הדתית מקומראן בזיקתן למקרא" ["Biblical Influence in Qumran Prayer and Religious Poetry"], (Ph.D diss., Tel Aviv: Tel Aviv University, 1989); idem, *Qumran Prayer and Religious Poetry* (STDJ 12; Leiden: Brill, 1994).

[22] For my review, see E. Chazon, on "*Qumran Prayer and Religious Poetry* by Bilhah Nitzan," *DSD* 2 (1995) 361-65.

[23] For this historical model of gradual development see the seminal work by J. Heinemann, *Prayer in the Talmud* (Studia Judaica 9; Berlin and New York: de Gruyter, 1977). The different approaches to the origins and institutionalization of Jewish liturgy are discussed in section 4 below: "From the Present to the Future."

she differs from S. Talmon, who some years earlier described the institutionalization of prayer at Qumran as an isolated phenomenon in the Second Temple period, and essentially unrelated to the parallel phenomenon in rabbinic Judaism. Nitzan's emphasis on fixed prayer and the inclusion of material on magical and mystical poetry in her study betrays an indebtedness to both DJD 7 and the full text of the Songs of the Sabbath Sacrifice, as she readily acknowledged in her preface. Her important study, which is so heavily influenced by the scrolls publications of the 1980's but does not yet incorporate the new material or developments of the 1990's, may be viewed as the culmination of the second stage of research in this field.

3. RESEARCH IN THE 1990's

Since the beginning of the present decade, more than a score of new prayer texts have been published and this number will increase as the remaining material is edited, hopefully by the turn of the millennium. Several of the most recent publications introduce new prayer types: apocryphal Barki Nafshi hymns (4Q435-438), magic formulas (4Q560), and a ritual for the expulsion of recalcitrate Community members (4QD^a).[24] Newly published political prayers that were directed against the Samaritans (4Q371-2)[25] and for King

---

[24] For a description of the Barki Nafshi hymns and a sample of their contents see M. Weinfeld, "Grace after Meals in Qumran," *JBL* 111 (1992) 427-40 and D. Seely, "The 'Circumcised Heart' in 4Q434 Barki Nafshi," *RevQ* 17 (1996) 527-35. The Aramaic magic text of 4Q560 (D. L. Penny and M. O. Wise, "By the Power of Beelzebub: An Aramaic Incantation Formula from Qumran [4Q560]," *JBL* 113 [1994] 627-50) differs in form and content from the prophylactic Hebrew hymns in the Songs of the Sage (4Q510-511) and in 4Q444 (E. Chazon, "New Liturgical Manuscripts from Qumran," in *Proceedings of the Eleventh World Congress of Jewish Studies, Division A, The Bible and its World* [Jerusalem: World Union of Jewish Studies, 1994] 87-94). The expulsion ritual in the Damascus Document (4Q266 11, lines 5-14) has its counterpart in the annual covenant renewal ceremony (1QS cols. 1-2) but, rather than cursing the sons of darkness and those who insincerely enter the covenant, it has the priest recite a blessing which states that God curses those who transgress.

[25] E. Schuller, "4Q372 1: A Text about Joseph," *RevQ* 14 (1989-90) 349-76, idem, "The Psalm of 4Q372 Within the Context of Second Temple Prayer," *CBQ* 54 (1992) 67-79; H. Eshel, "תפילת יוסף מקומראן והמקדש השומרוני בהר גריזים" ["The Prayer of Joseph, A Papyrus from Masada and the Samaritan Temple on Mt.Gerizim"], *Zion* 56 (1991) 125-36.

Jonathan (= Alexander Jannaeus)[26] have far-reaching implications for the sect's history and its relations with other Jewish groups, as well as for the nature of its prayer corpus. Besides such representatives of new genres, additional texts have considerably enriched the categories that were previously known to scholars. For instance, the number of pseudepigraphic prayers has grown considerably with the proliferation of "parabiblical texts,"[27] while a few important additions to the liturgies for fixed prayer times reflect the latest developments in the field that will be considered below (at the end of this section).

One of the most significant advancements in recent Dead Sea Scrolls' scholarship has been that of tracing the literary history of long-known sectarian writings such as the Hodayot, the War Scroll and the Community Rule, all three of which are rich repositories of hymns and prayers. Eileen Schuller's research on the Cave 4 Hodayot manuscripts reveals that different Hodayot collections circulated at Qumran, some of which apparently had only "Hymns of the Teacher" (4QH^c), others only "Hymns of the Community"

---

[26] E. Eshel, H. Eshel, A. Yardeni, "A Qumran Composition Containing Part of Ps. 154 and a Prayer for the Welfare of King Jonathan and his Kingdom," *IEJ* 42 (1992) 295-324. For the argument that this is a prayer against the king see now E. Main, "For King Jonathan or Against Him: On the Use of the Bible in 4Q448," in M. E. Stone and E. G. Chazon (eds.), *Biblical Perspectives: Early Use and Interpretation of the Bible in Light of the Dead Sea Scrolls* (STDJ 28; Leiden: Brill [forthcoming]).

[27] In addition to the prayers in previously known works that are also preserved at Qumran such as 1 Enoch, Jubilees and Tobit, "parabiblical texts" contain many new pseudepigraphic prayers. Some examples are: the Prayer of Joseph (see n.24 above); the Song of Miriam in 4QReworked Pentateuch^c 6a ii + 6c and a prayer attributed to Enosh (4Q369 1 i 1-7) which were published in J. VanderKam (ed.), *Qumran Cave 4.VIII: Parabiblical Texts, Part 1* (DJD 13; Oxford: Clarendon Press, 1994) 353-62; the prayer of Levi in the Aramaic Levi Document (4QLevi^b ar, frg. 1) and several prayers in 4QApocryphon of Joshua$^{a, b}$ that appeared in J. VanderKam (ed.), *Qumran Cave 4.XVII: Parabiblical Texts, Part 3* (DJD 22; Oxford: Clarendon Press, 1996) 25-36, 241-63; the prayers of Noah and Abraham in the Genesis Apocryphon 6-12, 20 (see J. C. Greenfield and E. Qimron, "The Genesis Apocryphon Col. XII," in T. Muraoka (ed.), *Studies in Qumran Aramaic* (AbrNSup 3; Louvain: Peeters, [1992]) 70-77; M. Morgenstern, E. Qimron and D. Sivan, "The Hitherto Unpublished Columns of the Genesis Apocryphon," *AbrN* 33 [1995] 30-53; and N. Avigad and Y. Yadin, *A Genesis Apocryphon* [Jerusalem: Magnes Press and Heikhal Ha-Sefer, 1956] 43, XX).

(4QH^a), while still others included both types of hymns (1QH^a, 4QH^b).[28] These divergent collections, together with the two new hymns that were recovered in the Cave 4 manuscripts—a Teacher Hymn in 4QH^b frg. 7 with parallels to the festival liturgy (4Q507 frg. 1), and a Community Hymn in 4QH^a frg. 7 with pronounced liturgical elements—are rekindling the debate over both the function of the Hodayot and the relationship between the different types of Hodayot material.[29] Moreover, the recognition that the "new" hymn in 4QH^a 7 also occurs in two other texts (4Q471b and 4Q491) which were formerly, but are no longer, associated with the War Scroll[30] suggests that the Hodayot—like the War Scroll and other composite works—reused originally independent sources such as eschatological hymns.[31] Other newly published texts, such as the hymn describing eschatological blessings in the Messianic Apocalypse (4Q521 2) and the eschatological hymn in 4Q457, also fit this emerging picture.[32]

---

[28] E. Schuller, "Prayer, Hymnic and Liturgical Texts from Qumran," in E. Ulrich and J. VanderKam (eds.), *The Community of the Renewed Covenant* (CJA 10; Notre Dame: University of Notre Dame, 1993) 153-55, 166-69; idem, "The Cave Four Hodayot Manuscripts: A Preliminary Description," *JQR* 85 (1994) 137-50.

[29] E. Schuller, "A Hymn from a Cave Four Hodayot Manuscript: 4Q427 7 i+ii," *JBL* 112 (1993) 605-28; idem, "A Thanksgiving Hymn from 4QHodayot^b (4Q428 7)," *RevQ* 16 (1995) 527-55.

[30] Schuller, "A Hymn from a Cave Four Hodayot Manuscript," 625-27; M. G. Abegg, "4Q471: A Case of Mistaken Identity?," in J. C. Reeves and J. Kampen (eds.), *Pursuing the Text* (Festshrift B. Z. Wacholder; JSOTSup 184; Sheffield: Sheffield Academic Press, 1994) 136-38, 141; and E. Eshel, "4Q471^b: A Self-Glorification Hymn," *RevQ* 17 (1996) 175-77.

[31] Schuller, "A Hymn from a Cave Four Hodayot Manuscript," 625-28; "Four Hodayot Manuscripts." On the relationship between these three versions of the hymn see also J. J. Collins and D. Dimant, "A Thrice-Told Hymn: A Response to Eileen Schuller," *JQR* 85 (1994) 151-55; D. Dimant, "A Synoptic Comparison of Parallel Sections in 4Q427 7, 4Q491 11 and 4Q471B," *JQR* 85 (1994) 157-61; and the two articles by E. Eshel, "4Q471^b" and "The Identification of the 'Speaker' of the Self-Glorification Hymn," in D. W. Parry and E. Ulrich (eds.), *The Provo International Conference on the Dead Sea Scrolls: New Texts, Reformulated Issues, and Technological Innovations* (STDJ 30; Leiden: Brill [in press]).

[32] É. Puech, "Une apocalypse messianique (4Q521)," *RevQ* 15 (1992) 475-95, 514-15; E. Chazon, "457.4QEschatological Hymn," which will appear in M. Broshi et al. (eds.), *Poetical and Liturgical Texts, Part 2* (DJD 29; Oxford: Clarendon Press [forthcoming]).

The interrelationship between the Scrolls' literary history and the history of Qumran religious practice is well illustrated by the two different covenant liturgies found in the Community Rule (1QS, 4QS$^{b, c}$) and in 4QBerakhot. The stemma of the Community Rule's redactional history recently drawn by Sarianna Metso shows that the opening sections on covenant renewal and the two spirits in 1QS, as well as its concluding hymn, were not originally part of the Rule.[33] Even a glance at the covenant renewal section in cols. 1-2 of 1QS makes it evident that the ceremonial liturgy has not been reproduced in its entirety and that redactional activity has taken place. One clear example is the summary description of the opening blessing to God found in 1:18-20: "When they enter the covenant, the priests and the levites bless the God of salvation and all his true works, and all those entering the covenant say after them, 'Amen, Amen.'" The reworking in 1QS and its parallels (4QS$^{b, c}$) means that the actual liturgical source(s) used by the redactor may have originally been closer to the form of the liturgy in 4QBerakhot; therefore, the possibility of a single archetype cannot be ruled out.

On the other hand, judging by the material that has been transmitted, the differences between the texts are too substantial to be explained simply as stemming from two versions of the same liturgy. For example, in the Community Rule the opening blessing on God's salvation mentioned above is followed immediately by the recounting of God's righteousness, mighty deeds and mercies as contrasted with Israel's sins (1QS 1:21-23, cf. Nehemiah 9). The message, mood and religious experience conveyed there differ markedly from those effected by 4QBerakhot's opening blessings with their numinous descriptions of the heavenly Temple, merkabah, angels, divine attributes, mysteries and cosmology.[34] The formulations of the curses against Belial's lot are also quite different.[35] These striking

---

[33] S. Metso, *The Textual Development of the Qumran Community Rule* (STDJ 21; Leiden: Brill, 1997) 143-49.

[34] B. Nitzan, "4QBerakhot (4Q286-290): A Preliminary Report," in G. J. Brooke (ed.), *New Qumran Texts and Studies* (STDJ 15; Leiden: Brill, 1994) 53-71; idem, "4QBerakhot^{a-e} (4Q286–290): A Covenantal Ceremony in the Light of Related Texts," *RevQ* 16 (1995) 487-506.

[35] For the curses in 4QBerakhot (4QBer^a 7 ii//4QBer^b 6) and parallels in 4Q280 and the War Scroll, see Milik, "Milkî-ṣedeq et Milkî-rešaʿ," 127-37 and B. Nitzan, "4QBerakhot^{a-e} (4Q286–290)," 489-90, 493-96. 4QBerakhot does not have (or

differences between 4QBerakhot and the Community Rule point to the existence of two separate covenantal liturgies.

One wonders which came first and what prompted the creation of different liturgies for the same ceremony. Nitzan has argued, partly on the basis of the Herodian manuscripts of 4QBerakhot, that its form is the later one.[36] One can certainly understand the impetus for introducing such an inspiring piece at a later stage in the history of the Community. However, the Herodian date of the 4QBerakhot manuscripts does not necessarily mean their form of the liturgy is later than that in 1QS, since relative manuscript dates are not a criterion for priority of composition. Indeed, Metso has shown that older forms of the Rule without the covenant liturgy continued to be copied well into the Herodian period, long after the full form of 1QS was available. The implications are thus clear: just as the Community continued to copy and transmit more than one Rule, so too it seems to have copied and transmitted more than one form of its covenant liturgy. The question of just how these two different texts were used in the life of the Community thus remains open, thereby complicating further the historical reconstruction of religious practice at Qumran.[37]

As new scrolls have been published, scholarly awareness of this phenomenon of different prayers for the same occasion continues to grow. Besides the two covenant liturgies we now have, for example: Ritual Purity[a] (4Q414) which overlaps with, but is not identical to, the Purification Ritual of 4Q512;[38] the hymnic incantation of 4Q444 which is linguistically and functionally similar to the Songs of the

---

has not preserved) the blessing to God's lot; were it in this text, it would have come at the bottom of 4Q286 7 i, which is now lost.

[36] Nitzan, "4QBerakhot (4Q286-290)," 54, 71 and idem, "The Benediction Texts from Qumran," in Lawrence H. Schiffman, Emanuel Tov and James C. VanderKam (eds.), *The Dead Sea Scrolls-Fifty Years After Their Discovery, An International Congress, The Israel Museum, Jerusalem, July 20-25, 1997* (Jerusalem: Israel Exploration Society [forthcoming]).

[37] Metso concludes that "the relation between a written document (the Community Rule) and actual life in an Essene community has so far been conceived in too direct and simplistic a manner" (*Textual Development*, 148-49).

[38] E. Eshel, "4Q414 Fragment 2: Purification of a Corpse Contaminated Person," in M. J. Bernstein and J. Kampen (eds.), *Legal Texts and Legal Issues* (STDJ 23; Leiden: Brill, 1996).

Sage (4Q510-511) but is not the same text;[39] the hymn in 4Q409 calling for praise on the festivals, which contrasts sharply with the Festival Prayers of 1Q34-34*bis* and 4Q507-509;[40] and the morning and evening blessings of 4Q408 which attest the same practice as the Daily Prayers of 4Q503, but constitute a different liturgical text.[41]

The last of these examples well illustrates both the promise and the challenge which the Scrolls hold for the synchronic reconstruction of liturgical practice at Qumran and in Second Temple Judaism, as well as for the diachronic study of Jewish liturgy. What is the relationship between these two sets of morning and evening blessings? To what extent were these two liturgies, surviving only in one manuscript each, recited by the Qumran community during the course of its 200-year history? And, if they were of non-Qumranic origin, to what extent do they represent liturgical practice outside of Qumran? Were these short blessings said together with other daily prayers such as those for the days of the week in the "Words of the Luminaries" (דברי המארות), whose title implies recital at the hour when the luminaries interchange? Was there any correlation between the Sabbath prayers in the daily and weekly liturgies of 4Q503, the Words of the Luminaries, and the Songs of the Sabbath Sacrifice? Can we discern a relationship between the festival liturgies in the scrolls mentioned above and the blessings for the festival days which fell in the month-long liturgical cycle described in 4Q503? How did the different modes of prayer with the angels which are reflected in the standard joint praise for the daily renewal of creation, on the one hand,[42] and in the heightened experience of communion with the angels, on the other,[43] function together in the religious life of the

---

[39] E. Chazon, "New Liturgical Manuscripts from Qumran," 87-94. The full text will be published in M. Broshi et al. (eds.), *Qumran Cave 4.XX* (DJD 29 [forthcoming]).

[40] E. Qimron, "Times for Praising God: A Fragment of a Scroll from Qumran (4Q409)," *JQR* 90 (1990) 341-47. On the different festival calendars as a criterion for provenance see Newsom, "'Sectually Explicit' Literature," 177-78.

[41] A. Steudel, "4Q408: A Liturgy on Morning and Evening Prayer, Preliminary Edition," *RevQ* 16 (1994) 313-34. The texts are compared in E. Chazon, "The Function of the Qumran Prayer Texts," in Schiffman, Tov and VanderKam (eds.), *The Dead Sea Scrolls-Fifty Years After;* see also later in this section.

[42] In 4Q503 and 4Q408.

[43] In the Songs of the Sabbath Sacrifice.

Qumran Community? And how did they function in that of other Jewish groups in Second Temple Judaism who may have used these liturgies?[44]

Admittedly, not all of the questions posed above will be answered with any degree of certainty now or even in the future. But the availability of virtually all the Dead Sea Scrolls material does facilitate a broader comparative analysis and puts us in a better position to grapple with these questions. For example, real progress can now be made in addressing the first two questions that were posed concerning the relationship between 4Q503 and 4Q408, and the extent to which they represent liturgical practice. A close comparison between these two texts reveals their similarity in form, content, and function: both include communal blessings for the daily renewal of light and darkness, which mention the luminaries' praise and are said in the morning and evening. However, differences in detail, including the blessing formula and order in which the morning and evening are mentioned, indicate that these are two different liturgies for the same liturgical occasion which were probably not recited concurrently.[45]

On the other hand, 4Q503 and 4Q408 do serve as two contemporary, independent witnesses to a similar liturgical practice of blessing God for the daily renewal of the luminaries at the hour when that renewal takes place.[46] Furthermore, continuity with

---

[44] The Masada manuscript of the Songs of the Sabbath Sacrifice points to their usage outside of Qumran. On their non-Qumranic origin see Newsom, "'Sectually Explicit' Literature," 179-85. For the possible non-Qumranic origin of 4Q408 and 4Q503 see Steudel, "4Q408: A Liturgy on Morning and Evening Prayer," 333-34; J. Baumgarten, "4Q503 (Daily prayers) and the Lunar Calendar," *RevQ* 12 (1986) 399-406; E. Chazon, "Prayers from Qumran and Their Historical Implications," *DSD* 1 (1994) 282 n.68. On human praise with the angels in these texts see Newsom, *Songs of the Sabbath Sacrific*, 17-21; E. Chazon, "On the Special Character of Sabbath Prayer: New Data from Qumran," *Journal of Jewish Music and Liturgy* 15 (1992-93) 1-21 and "The Function of the Qumran Prayer Texts."

[45] Steudel, "4Q408: A Liturgy on Morning and Evening Prayer," 332; and Chazon, "The Function of the Qumran Prayer Texts."

[46] For the suggestion that the prayers for the days of the week in the Words of the Luminaries were recited at this hour see above in this section. Sectarian texts such as 1QS 10:1-3 and 4Q502 27 refer to prayer that was said twice a day at these hours (cf. the emphasis on sunrise in the Hymn to the Creator in 11QPs[a] and in Josephus' description of the Essenes in the Jewish War 2 §128). See Chazon, "The Function of the Qumran Prayer Texts."

rabbinic prayer and a shared liturgical tradition are indicated by the striking parallels in content, language, form and function between 4Q503 and the statutory Blessing on the Luminaries, which also blesses God every evening and morning for the daily renewal of the heavenly lights, describing the angelic praise at least in the morning prayer. Thus, although we cannot know to what extent the texts of 4Q503 and 4Q408 were used by the Qumran community or by its contemporaries,[47] we can be reasonably sure that daily prayers of this type were said by different Jewish groups in the late Second Temple period and were considered important enough to be incorporated into the liturgy that was institutionalized by the Rabbis in the aftermath of the destruction of the Second Temple in 70 CE.

4. FROM THE PRESENT TO THE FUTURE

During the last five years of research on the hymns and prayers in the Dead Sea Scrolls, the corpus has been well delineated and signficant progress has been made in assessing the Qumranic or non-Qumranic provenance of most of the material. A new awareness of the literary history of individual works and of the relationship between various works in the corpus has also emerged. Various recensions of single hymns, diverse collections of the Hodayot hymns, and alternate liturgical texts for the same occasion have been uncovered. The great number of prayer texts that are now available to us, coupled with the assessment that much of this material is non-Qumranic in origin, has enabled scholars to trace more accurately the common threads of a shared liturgical tradition in Second Temple Judaism and its continuity with rabbinic prayer. Moreover, the liturgical texts that have been published in the last fifteen years provide our first solid examples of fixed public prayer in non-sectarian circles during the Second Temple period.[48] These data have important implications for the debate over the character of the institutionalization of Jewish prayer accomplished by the Rabbis at Yavneh following the destruction of the Second Temple in 70 CE.[49]

---

[47] For the non-Qumranic provenance of these texts see above, n. 44. On the significance of multiple copies of a document versus a single copy see Newsom, "'Sectually Explicit' Literature from Qumran," 169-75.

[48] Chazon, "Prayers from Qumran and Their Historical Implications," 281-84.

[49] There is considerable debate over whether the Rabbis created and fixed the liturgy at Yavneh (ca. 90 CE) as a response to the destruction of the Second Temple

Tracing the development of Jewish liturgy in its formative stages as well as the historical reconstruction of liturgical practice at Qumran and in Second Temple Judaism will remain difficult challenges for the future. The relationship between the prayers within the Qumran corpus will need further investigation, as will the relationship between the Qumran prayers and those preserved in other Second Temple period works, rabbinic literature, early Christian sources, and the first Jewish prayerbooks from medieval times. While the vast growth of the published corpus and the development of advanced methodologies have added layers of complexity to certain issues, they have also begun to produce a richer and more accurate picture of religious practices in Second Temple Judaism—and together with it a better understanding of the background against which rabbinic Judaism and early Christianity emerged.

5. CATALOGUE OF HYMNS AND PRAYERS IN THE SCROLLS[50]

The Dead Sea Scrolls preserve more than 300 psalms, hymns and prayers. Virtually all of these were discovered at Qumran, while only a handful are from other sites in the Judaean Desert.[51] The corpus of this literature may be divided into seven major categories: (1) Liturgies for fixed prayer times; (2) Ceremonial liturgies; (3) Eschatological prayers; (4) Magical incantations; (5) Psalmic collections; (6) Hodayot (or thanksgiving) hymns; and (7) Prayers embedded in narratives. Prayers in the last group were written in Hebrew or Aramaic, depending on the language of the larger work in which they are incorporated. All the texts in the other six categories are in Hebrew. In the catalogue that follows, major works from each category are described is some detail, while other texts are mentioned more briefly.

(thus E. Fleischer, "לקדמוניות תפילות החובה בישראל" ["On the Beginnings of Obligatory Jewish Prayer"], *Tarbiz* 59 [1991] 397-441; or whether the liturgy emerged gradually during the Second Temple period with the destruction giving an impetus to the institutionalizaion that was begun, but not completed, at Yavneh (thus J. Heinemann, *Prayer in the Talmud*).

[50] A similar catalogue appears in my article on "Psalms, Hymns and Prayers" in L. H. Schiffman and J. C. VanderKam (eds.), *The Encyclopedia of the Dead Sea Scrolls* (New York: Oxford University Press [forthcoming]).

[51] The Masada finds included two Psalms manuscripts, a copy of the Songs of the Sabbath Sacrifice, and a prayer mentioning Mt. Gerizim. Another Psalms scroll and two prayers from the Bar Kokhba period were found at Naḥal Ḥever.

5.1 Liturgies for Fixed Prayer Times

The Qumran corpus preserves several collections of communal prayers for recitation at fixed times of the day, week and year. Each collection contains prayers that are similar in form, content and liturgical function. These liturgical collections differ from other communal prayers whose time of recitation is not explicitly stated (for example, the communal confessions in 4Q393, 4Q501 [4QLamentation] and 4Q481c [4QPrayer for Mercy]).

Daily Prayers (4Q503). These are evening and morning blessings for each day of the month. They praise God for the renewal of the heavenly lights at sunset and sunrise, and with each daily change in the moon's phases. Praise in unison with heavenly beings is also mentioned. This liturgy is similar to the to the *Qedušat Yoṣer* in the rabbinic *Blessing on the Lights*. References to a festival in the middle of the month indicate that the liturgy is for Nisan or Tishrei. On Sabbaths, special themes (notably rest, delight, holiness, election) are added. 4Q503 is written in a Hasmonean hand (c. 100-75) and may be non-Qumranic in origin. 4Q408 is another liturgy of morning and evening blessings which praises God's creation and daily renewal of light and darkness.

Words of the Luminaries (4Q504-506). These are prayers for the days of the week, ending with the Sabbath. All six weekday prayers open with a historical review and then petition for physical deliverance (Tuesday, Wednesday, Friday) or spiritual fortitude: knowledge of the Law, turning from sin and forgiveness (Sunday, Thursday; the Monday petition is unfortunately lost). Each petition is followed by a concluding blessing and "Amen, Amen" response. The Sabbath prayer consists of doxological hymns. The title דברי המארות ("Words of the Luminaries") is written on the back of the oldest copy, 4Q504 (ca. 150 BCE) and seems to refer to its liturgical function as a daily prayer (with מארות as a term for "day," cf. Gen 1:14). The early date of 4Q504 indicates this liturgy was probably composed before the Qumran settlement was founded.

Songs of the Sabbath Sacrifice (4Q400-407, 11Q17, Mas1k).[52] These are songs by a sage (*maskil*) for the first thirteen Sabbaths of the year. The dating of these Sabbaths presumes a solar calendar of 364 days. This is an earthly liturgy in which human worshippers

---

[52] See Newsom, *Songs of the Sabbath Sacrifice.*

invite the angels to praise God and describe angelic worship in the heavenly Temple. Song 12 portrays the divine chariot-throne (*merkabah*) with its attendant angels, while the angelic high priests are depicted offering sacrifices in the final song. Possible functions of these songs are: as a substitute for the earthly sacrifice; liturgical accompaniment to the angelic offering; communion with the angels; and experiencing the heavenly Temple. Nine copies from Qumran (late Hasmonean to late Herodian periods) indicate that this liturgy was of great importance for that community; however, the discovery of a copy at Masada suggests a non-sectarian origin or use.

Festival Prayers (1Q34-34bis, 4Q507-509). These are prayers for the annual festivals beginning with the New Year in Tishrei (a calendric arrangement that may well indicate non-Qumranic origin). Each prayer opens with the words "Remember, Lord," then formulates reminiscences and petitions that are connected with the special aspects of the festival, and concludes with a blessing and "Amen, Amen" response (for this form see also the Words of the Luminaries). The Prayer for the Day of Atonement[53] thus opens with a petition asking God to remember the time of his compassion, refers to the divine law establishing this day as "an appointed time of fasting," and includes a confession of sin. This liturgy differs in calendric arrangement, form and content from the hymn in 4Q409 that calls for praise on the festivals.

5.2 Ceremonial Liturgies

The Qumran sect held numerous communal ceremonies on fixed occasions as well as on an *ad hoc* basis, as circumstances required (for example, ritual purification). Liturgies that were comprised mainly of blessings and/or curses accompanied such ceremonies.

Covenant Renewal Ceremony, Rule of the Community (1QS 1-2). The Community Rule enjoins all members to participate in an annual ceremony in which they reaffirm their commitment to the divine commandments. This ceremony apparently was held on the Festival of Shebuot (Weeks and Oaths or Covenants).[54] The heart of the ceremony is the blessing of God's lot by the priests and the curse of Belial's lot by the Levites (for the content, compare the priestly blessing in Num 6:22-27). The ceremony is modeled upon the

---

[53] The title is preserved.

[54] See Jubilees 6 and below, "Expulsion Ceremony."

covenant made in Moab and the recitation of blessings and curses on Mt. Gerizim and Mt. Ebal (cf. Deuteronomy 27-29, Josh 8:30-35). Unlike the biblical model, the sectarian blessings are extended only to the Qumran Covenanters (i.e. God's lot) while the curses automatically attach to their opponents (Belial's lot). It is interesting to note that this covenant renewal ceremony is not found in all versions of the Community Rule. 4QBerakhot contains a different covenant renewal liturgy which opens with praise of the *merkabah*-throne, heavenly abode, angels and divine mysteries—rather than the review of divine salvation and confession of Israel's sins as in 1QS 1:16-2:1.

Expulsion Ceremony, Damascus Document (4Q266 11, lines 5-14). A ritual for the expulsion of those who reject the Community's laws follows the penal code in the last section of the Damascus Document. The priest recites a blessing which praises God for choosing "our forefathers" while causing the other nations to "stray in chaos." The blessing states that God curses those who transgress, but no curse occurs in the expulsion ritual per se. The text does mention the curse pronounced in the third month in what appears to be a reference to the annual covenant ceremony held on the Shebuot festival.[55] The expulsion ritual may have been conducted on the same occasion.

Ritual of Marriage (4Q502). This is a ritual for a public ceremony that was held on a joyous occasion. The entire assembly, as well as certain individuals, recite blessings in which they offer praise and thanks, particularly for human fertility. The text mentions men and women of different ages (young, mature, old). References to human seed, fruit of the womb, men and women in their prime, and a married couple (perhaps Adam and Eve) prompted the designation "Ritual of Marriage." It has also been proposed that this is a Golden Age Ritual, based on the blessings for longevity and the prominence of elders.[56] Although the precise function of this text is not certain, it clearly challenges conventional views of the Qumran community as an all-male, celibate order. The work's sectarian origin is confirmed by the fact that it quotes from the Rule of the Community.

Ritual of Purification (4Q512). This sectarian text is written on the back of the Daily Prayers (4Q503). It gives instructions and blessings for ritual purification from different types of impurities (sexual

---

[55] See above on the "Covenant Renewal Ceremony."

[56] Thus J. Baumgarten, "Marriage or Golden Age Ritual?," 125-35.

impurity, leprosy, corpse contamination) and on holy days. The blessings connect the cleansing of the body during ritual immersion with spiritual cleansing through repentance and atonement (since impurity is apparently associated with sin). Both confession of sin and thanksgiving for purification are prominent themes. A related text is Ritual Purity^a (4Q414), which overlaps with 4Q512, but is not identical to it.

5.3 Eschatological Prayers

The Qumran sectarians prepared themselves for the eschaton ("end of days"), which they believed was imminent. Their preparations included setting forth prayers to be recited during the final war and ensuing messianic era. The Qumran corpus also contains prayers that are not eschatological in function, but which request or depict messianic redemption (e.g. the Apostrophe to Zion in 11QPs^a, the hymn in 4Q457, and the hymnic description of eschatological blessings in 4Q521, frg. 2).

War Scroll (1QM, 4QM$^{a, b, e}$). This operative plan for the eschatological war between the sons of light and the sons of darkness prescribes prayers for several stages of the campaign. The prayer before battle (1QM 10:8–12:18; 18:5–19:8) appeals to prophecies of salvation and divine deliverance of Israel in the past, while petitioning God to crush the nations and redeem his elect, holy people in the upcoming battle. Immediately after the battle the priests, levites, and elders are to bless God and his angels, curse Belial and all evil spirits, and offer praise for the victory of the sons of light over the forces of darkness (1QM 13:1–14:1; compare 19:9-12). Upon their return to the camp, the troops are to recite a hymn and, after cleansing themselves the next morning, they are supposed to return to the place of arrayal for a thanksgiving ceremony (1QM 14:2–15:2; the parallel passage in the second part of the War Scroll has not survived but it probably included a thanksgiving ceremony for the final victory over the Kittim).[57] The War Scroll appears to have utilized older and originally independent prayers.

War Rule (4Q285) and 11QBerakhot. The overlapping portion of these scrolls is a blessing for Israel and the angels which reflects the sect's belief in its communion with angels. This blessing for rain,

---

[57] See below, "War Rule (4Q285) and 11QBerakhot."

produce and physical well-being is based on deuteronomic covenant blessings and curses (Deut 11:14; 28:12, 21-22; 31:20), with the biblical priestly blessing (Num 6:24) supplying the opening framework. Parallels between the War Rule and the War Scroll suggest this blessing was to be said by the high priest during the final stages of the eschatological war, and may come from the concluding section of the War Scroll, which unfortunately is now lost.

Rule of the Blessings (1QS^b). This rule contains blessings to be recited by a sage (*maskil*) for all "upholders of the covenant" as well as for dignitaries. Persons mentioned are Zadokite priests, the Prince of the Congregation, and probably an eschatological high priest. The priestly blessing in Num 6:24-26 serves as a paradigm for all the blessings, except the last which is based on Isa 11:1-5 and so identifies the one being blessed (the Prince of the Congregation) with the Davidic Messiah. This eschatological blessing ceremony, which lacks curses since evil would already have been expunged, was apparently designed to supplant the covenant renewal ceremony that is prescribed in the Rule of the Community (1QS^b and 1QS^a—comprising the Rule of the Congregation for "the end of days"—are appended to 1QS, the Rule of the Community).

5.4 Magical Incantations

The Qumran corpus also contains hymns to God which were used to dispel demons and thus functioned as incantations. These may be contrasted with magical formulae, which address the demons exclusively and are therefore not classed as prayers.

Songs of the Sage (4Q510-511). These are doxological hymns to be pronounced by a sage (*maskil*) in order "to frighten and terrify" evil spirits. The hymns qualify as incantations on the basis of this prophylactic function, as well as their form and content, including the citation of Psalm 91 and naming of demons.[58] These pieces are distinctive, however, (1) in their address to God rather than to the demons; (2) in their use of hymnic praise as words of power; and (3) in their communal dimension as protection for all sons of light and, possibly, as a liturgy for a public ceremony.[59] The terminology

---

[58] The demons are related to the Fallen Angels of Gen 6:1-5.

[59] Note the calls to praise and the concluding blessing with its "Amen, Amen" response.

and ideas (dualism, determinism, eschatology, "dominion of Wickedness," "sons of light" and the Yaḥad) are all indicators of Qumranic authorship. The short text in 4Q444 opens with a similar hymn, but then contains curse formulae.

11QApocryphal Psalms^a. This prophylactic ritual consists of three apocrphyal psalms followed by Psalm 91. The first psalm refers to demons, an oath and perhaps adjuration. The second praises God but also refers to demons, their judgment and banishment to the underworld. The third psalm purports to be an incantation addressed to Belial, which also announces his imprisonment in Sheol. The formula "Amen, Amen, Selah" closes each psalm. All of these psalms appear to be attributed to David and may well be the "four songs for making music over the stricken" (שיר לנגן על הפגועים ארבעה) that are mentioned in the list of David's Compositions in 11QPs^a.[60]

Magic Formula (4Q560). This Aramaic text names male and female demons, lists illnesses that are caused by demon-possession, and adjures the demon(s) by addressing them directly. Although not formally a prayer, it is included in order to highlight the distinctiveness of the other incantations from Qumran, all of which are hymns written in Hebrew, as well as to show the connection between ancient Near Eastern traditions and later Palestinian Jewish magic.

5.5 Psalmic Collections

Thirty-six scrolls containing biblical psalms have been preserved at Qumran.[61] At least seven of these (4QPs$^{a, b, d, e, k, n, q}$) differ from the Masoretic text in the order of the psalms preserved and may represent different recensions of the biblical psalter or secondary arrangements for various purposes. Of four more scrolls which juxtapose both biblical and apocryphal psalms, 11QApPs^a is a prophylactic ritual,[62] while the great Psalms Scroll (11QPs^a) appears to be a liturgical arrangement.[63] 11QPs^b contains the same arrangement as 11QPs^a, while 4QPs^f has one biblical and one apocryphal psalm[64] in common with it. There are also several psalmic

---

[60] In col. 27, line 10. See section 1 above, and compare the similar rabbinic term שיר של פגועים for Psalm 91 in *b. Šebuʿot* 15b; *y. ʿErubin* 10, 26c.

[61] For a recent listing, see Flint, *Dead Sea Psalms Scrolls*, 31-43.

[62] See above section 5.4, "Magical Incantations."

[63] Cf. the following paragraph.

[64] I.e. Psalm 109 and the Apostrophe to Zion, respectively.

collections without any biblical psalms: for example, the apocryphal Barki Nafshi hymns (4Q435-438), the Non-Canonical Psalms (4Q380-381) and 4Q448,[65] a scroll containing a partial quotation of Psalm 154 and a prayer for King Jonathan, who may be identified with Alexander Jannaeus (103-76 BCE).[66] None of these extra-biblical psalms bears distinctive marks of Qumranic authorship.

The Great Psalms Scroll (11QPs^a). This is the best preserved and most famous of all the psalmic collections from Qumran. Column 27 (lines 2-11) includes an important prose insert known as "David's Compositions," which serves to attribute the entire collection to David himself:

(2) And David, the son of Jesse, was wise, and a light like the light of the sun, and literate,
(3) and discerning and perfect in all his ways before God and men. And the LORD gave
(4) him a discerning and enlightened spirit. And he wrote
(5) 3,600 psalms; and songs to sing before the altar over the whole-burnt
(6) perpetual offering every day, for all the days of the year, 364;
(7) and for the offering of the Sabbaths, 52 songs; and for the offering of the New
(8) Moons and for all the Solemn Assemblies and for the Day of Atonement, 30 songs.
(9) And all the songs that he spoke were 446, and songs
(10) for making music over the stricken, 4. And the total was 4,050.
(11) All these he composed through prophecy which was given him from before the Most High.[67]

There are ample indications in this manuscript that the psalms were arranged for liturgical purposes (note especially the refrain added to Psalm 145). About forty biblical psalms are interspersed with seven others not found in the Hebrew Bible, four of which are attested elsewhere: Sir 51:13-30; Psalm 151 (in the Septuagint); and Psalms 154, 155 (in Syriac). The three previously unknown psalms are: Plea for Deliverance, Apostrophe to Zion and Hymn to the Creator.[68] The

---

[65] See E. Schuller, *Non-Canonical Psalms from Qumran*.

[66] See E. Eshel, H. Eshel and Yardeni, "A Qumran Composition Containing Part of Ps. 154," 295-324.

[67] Translation by J. Sanders, *The Dead Sea Psalms Scroll* (Ithaca, NY: Cornell University Press, 1967) 87.

[68] While the "Catena" in column 16 may in fact be a new composition, it more likely forms a longer ending to Psalm 136 in this manuscript (cf. Flint, *Dead Sea Psalms Scrolls*, 40, 91).

Plea for Deliverance is an individual thanksgiving for salvation from imminent death which incorporates a tripartate petition for forgiveness, knowledge, and protection from Satan and the evil inclination.[69] The Apostrophe to Zion is an acrostic poem addressed to Zion (cf. Isaiah 54, 60, 62), which assures Zion that she is remembered and that the prayers for her redemption and prophecies of her future glory[70] will be fulfilled.[71] The Hymn to the Creator praises God for his creation of light and darkness and heaven and earth, stressing God's creation with knowledge, and the granting of knowledge to the angels who then sing out their praise. It has been likened to the *Qedušat Yoṣer* in the rabbinic *Blessing on the Lights*.[72]

5.6 Hodayot Hymns

The *Hodayot* are thanksgiving hymns which often open with the characteristic formula "I thank you, Lord" (אודכה אדוני).[73] The speaker offers thanks for his election by God's grace and for his endowment with the divine gifts of speech and knowledge. Characteristic Qumranic terminology and ideas are employed throughout these pieces. Two types of hymns have been recognized in the *Hodayot* collections: Hymns of the Teacher and Hymns of the Community (see below). Comparison between the eight *Hodayot* manuscripts (1QH[a, b] and 4QH[a–f]) indicates that different types of collections circulated at Qumran. Some of these were longer, and others shorter; some apparently contained only Hymns of the Teacher (e.g. 4QH[c]), others only Hymns of the Community (e.g. 4QH[a]), while still others included both types (1QH[a], 4QH[b]). These divergent collections shed new light on the ongoing debate over the function of these hymns in private devotion or public liturgy.

Hymns of the Teacher. These occur in 1QH[b], 4QH[b, c, d, f] and en bloc in the middle of the large Hodayot scroll from Cave 1 (1QH[a]).[74]

---

[69] Much of the Plea is also in preserved in 11QPs[b].

[70] Note especially Isa 66:10-11.

[71] 4QPs[f] preserves most, and 11QPs[b] just a few words, of the Apostrophe.

[72] See section 3 above, on 4Q503.

[73] Cf. E. Schuller, "The Cave Four Hodayot Manuscripts," 137-50.

[74] Cols. 10–19 in the reconstructed scroll, or 2–9 in the edition of E. L. Sukenik, *The Dead Sea Scrolls of the Hebrew University* (Jerusalem: Magnes Press and The Hebrew University, 1955).

The Hymns of the Teacher give expression to the personal encounters, thoughts and feelings that were experienced by a leading member of the Qumran community, who has sometimes been identified with the Teacher of Righteousness. The main themes are his own suffering, persecution, and mockery by his enemies as well as being tested in the crucible, reliance on divine salvation, justice and annihilation of evil. The speaker thanks God repeatedly for protecting him from the "men of Belial," for saving his soul from the "snares of the Pit," and for granting him the gift of knowledge and the task of "enlightening the Many" (i.e. the Qumran community).

Hymns of the Community. These are found at the beginning and end of 1QH[a] as well as in 4QH[a, b, e]. The Hymns of the Community introduce "we" language and stress less personal themes: the human condition, communal affiliation, congregational praise and communion with angels. They make use of the opening blessing formula "Blessed are you, Lord" (ברוך אתה אדוני) more often than the highly personal "I thank you, Lord" (אודכה אדוני) which typifies the Hymns of the Teacher. They also express thanks for personal salvation, election and spiritual gifts (especially knowledge) which constitute an essential component of the *Hodayot* hymns.

5.7 Prayers Embedded in Narratives

Prayers that have been pseudepigraphically attributed to figures of great antiquity are often incorporated in the narrative framework of a "para-biblical" work (i.e. a nonbiblical work based in some way upon a biblical text). These literary prayers bear a resemblance to prayers that were in actual use and reflect current religious practice. Besides the prayers in previously known works such as 1 Enoch, Jubilees, and Tobit, the Qumran corpus brings to light much new material of this type, including: Levi's prayer in the Aramaic Levi Document; Joseph's prayer in the apocrypon named after him (see below); the prayers of Noah and Abraham in the Genesis Apocryphon (cols. 6–12, 20); a prayer attributed to Enosh (4Q369 1 i, lines 1-7); the Song of Miriam in Reworked Pentateuch[c] (frgs. 6a ii + 6c); and several prayers in the Psalms of Joshua (4Q378, 379 *passim*).

Aramaic Levi[b] (frg. 1, lines 5-18). The Aramaic Levi Document (ca. late third century BCE) preserves a prayer attributed to Levi that is also found in one manuscript of the Greek Testaments of the Twelve Patriarchs. The Greek manuscript juxtaposes the prayer with Levi's report that he grieved over human unrighteousness and prayed to be saved (TLevi 2:3-4; see also 4:2). However, the context may be different in Aramaic Levi where the prayer is preceded by Levi's purification. Here Levi petitions God for spiritual support: for the wisdom, knowledge and strength (cf. Isa 11:2) to do God's bidding, for protection from every satan and evil, for purification of his heart from every impurity. Levi also asks that he be drawn near to God in order to serve him, particularly as teacher and judge (cf. Deut 33:10). This piece displays the features of two related prayer-types: the tripartate petitions for knowledge, repentance and forgiveness;[75] and apotropaic prayers which counterpose pleas for protection from evil and sin with requests for knowledge and purification.[76] Also to be noted are Levi's posture in prayer (lifting his eyes to heaven and stretching forth his hands) and his silent prayer following his verbal one.

Apocryphon of Joseph (4Q372 1,4Q371). This Hebrew text (second century BCE) polemicizes against the Samaritans' claim to be descended from Joseph and against their Temple on Mt. Gerizim.[77] The first part (4Q372 1, lines 1-15) is a historical review in the Sin-Exile-Return pattern which culminates with a critique of those who make "a high place upon a high mountain" and "revile against the tent of Zion." It stresses that Joseph, who is identified here with the Northern Tribes, is still in exile among foreigners. Joseph's prayer is then introduced (lines 15-16). Joseph pleads for deliverance from the hand of the nations, decries the hostile people who are dwelling on the land, and expresses confidence that they will be destroyed (lines 16-22). As is typical of individual laments, Joseph's prayer ends with a promise to worship God as well as to teach his laws to sinners (lines 23-31). Two features of significance to both Jewish and Christian liturgical history are the invocation to God as "my father,"[78] and the expanded list of divine epithets.[79]

---

[75] See Psalms 51 and 155; 4Q504 4, lines 6-15; 1-2 ii, lines 7-18; *b. Berakhot* 29a; and *b. Megillah* 17b.

[76] Cf. the Plea for Deliverance in 11QPs^a (19:13-16); Matt 6:13; and *b. Berakhot* 16b, 60b.

[77] Cf. Schuller, "4Q372 1: A Text about Joseph," 349-76; idem, "The Psalm of 4Q372," 67-79.

[78] Cf. Sir 23:1, 4; 3 Macc 6:3, 8; Matt 6:9; Mark 14:36; and Luke 11:2.

[79] See Ps 99:3; the Hymn to the Creator; the non-canonical psalm in 4Q381 frgs. 76–77, line 14; *b. Berakhot* 33b; and the *Amidah* prayer.

6. EPILOGUE: FUTURE PUBLICATIONS

Two forthcoming volumes in the series "Discoveries in the Judaean Desert" will be devoted to poetical and liturgical texts.[80] A third volume will contain a full publication of all the Psalms manuscripts from Cave 4.[81] Additional DJD volumes containing new parabiblical, sapiential and miscellaneous texts from Caves 4 and 11, as well as from other Judaean Desert sites, will also include some prayers. Complete listings of the Scrolls are available in the *Companion Volume to the Microfiche Collection*[82] and in the *Dead Sea Scrolls Catalogue*.[83]

SELECT BIBLIOGRAPHY

Baillet, M. *Qumran Grotte 4.III (4Q482-4Q520)* (DJD 7; Oxford: Clarendon Press, 1982).

Chazon, E. G. "The Function of the Qumran Prayer Texts," in L. H. Schiffman, E. Tov and J. C. VanderKam (eds.), *The Dead Sea Scrolls-Fifty Years After Their Discovery, An International Congress, The Israel Museum, Jerusalem, July 20-25, 1997* (Jerusalem: Israel Exploration Society [forthcoming]).

—. תעודה ליטורגית מקומראן והשלכותיה: דברי המארות (Ph.D. diss., Jerusalem: Hebrew University, 1991). To be published as *The Words of the Luminaries: A Liturgical Document from Qumran and Its Implications (4QDibHam)* (STDJ series; Leiden: Brill [forthcoming]).

—. "Prayers from Qumran and Their Historical Implications," *DSD* 1 (1994) 265-84.

—. "On the Special Character of Sabbath Prayer: New Data from Qumran," *Journal of Jewish Music and Liturgy* 15 (1992-93) 1-21.

Eshel, E., H. Eshel and A. Yardeni. "A Qumran Composition Containing Part of Ps. 154 and a Prayer for the Welfare of King Jonathan and His Kingdom," *IEJ* 42 (1992) 295-324.

---

[80] E. Eshel et al. (eds.), *Qumran Cave 4.VI: Poetical and Liturgical Texts, Part I* (DJD 11; Oxford: Clarendon Press, [forthcoming]); and M. Broshi et al. (eds.), *Qumran Cave 4.XX* (DJD 29 [forthcoming]).

[81] E. Ulrich et al. (eds.), *Qumran Cave 4.XI: Psalms to Chronicles* (DJD 16; Oxford: Clarendon Press [forthcoming])

[82] E. Tov, with S. J. Pfann (eds.), *The Dead Sea Scrolls on Microfiche. A Comprehensive Facsimile Edition of the Texts from the Judaean Desert, Companion Volume* (Leiden: Brill and IDC, 1993).

[83] S. A. Reed, with M. J. Lundberg and M. J. Phelps (eds.), *The Dead Sea Scrolls Catalogue: Documents, Photographs and Museum Inventory Numbers* (SBLRBS 32; Atlanta: Scholars Press, 1994).

Falk, D. F. *Daily, Festival, and Sabbath Prayers from Qumran* (STDJ 27; Leiden: Brill, 1997).

Flint, P. W. *The Dead Sea Psalms Scrolls and the Book of Psalms* (STDJ 17; Leiden: Brill, 1997).

Maier, J. "Zu Kult und Liturgie der Qumrangemeinde," *RevQ* 14 (1989-90) 543-86.

Newsom, C. A. "'Sectually Explicit' Literature from Qumran," in W. H. Propp, B. Halpern and D. N. Freedman (eds.), *The Hebrew Bible and Its Modern Interpreters* (Winona Lake, IN: Eisenbrauns, 1990) 167-87.

—. *Songs of the Sabbath Sacrifice: A Critical Edition* (HSS 27; Atlanta: Scholars Press, 1985).

Nitzan, B. "4QBerakhot (4Q286-290): A Preliminary Report," in G. J. Brooke (ed.), *New Qumran Texts and Studies* (STDJ 15; Leiden: Brill, 1994) 53-71.

—. *Qumran Prayer and Religious Poetry*. (STDJ 12; Leiden: Brill, 1994).

Sanders, J. A. *The Psalms Scroll of Qumran Cave 11 (11QPs^a)* (DJD 4; Oxford: Clarendon Press, 1965.)

—. *The Dead Sea Psalms Scroll* (Ithaca, NY: Cornell University Press, 1967).

Schuller, E. "The Cave Four Hodayot Manuscripts: A Preliminary Description," *JQR* 85 (1994) 137-50.

—. *Non-Canonical Psalms from Qumran: A Pseudepigraphic Collection* (HSS 28; Atlanta: Scholars Press, 1986).

—. "Prayer, Hymnic and Liturgical Texts from Qumran," in E. Ulrich and J. C. VanderKam (eds.), *The Community of the Renewed Covenant* (CJA 10; Notre Dame: University of Notre Dame Press, 1993) 153-71.

—. "The Psalm of 4Q372 Within the Context of Second Temple Prayer," *CBQ* 54 (1992) 67-79.

Stone, M. E. and J. C. Greenfield. "The Prayer of Levi," *JBL* 112 (1993) 247-66.

Talmon, S. "The Emergence of Institutionalized Prayer in Israel in the Light of the Qumran Literature," in his *The World of Qumran from Within: Collected Essays* (Leiden: Brill; Jerusalem: Magnes Press, 1989) 200-43.

PARABIBLICAL PROPHETIC NARRATIVES

GEORGE J. BROOKE

There are a large number of compositions amongst the manuscripts found in the Qumran caves which may loosely be categorized as "Rewritten Bible."[1] This chapter is an attempt to discuss in one place most of the rewritten Bible texts from Qumran which relate to the biblical prophets. In the scrolls from Qumran interest in prophecy and the prophets is widespread.[2] This interest is not confined to the prophets who have left books, the so-called "literary prophets," but also embraces a range of other prophetic figures, including Moses and David.[3]

It is curious that amongst this wide range of manuscripts no composition has yet been identified clearly as a rewritten form of either the Book of Isaiah or of any of the Twelve Minor Prophets. Moreover, nor are there any narrative biographies to be linked with these prophets, even though some scholars have suggested that works such as the *Ascension of Isaiah* have characteristics which are to be found amongst the sectarian compositions that were discovered at

---

[1] Preliminary and principal editions of most of the texts cited in this chapter are given in the footnotes and concluding bibliography. English translations of many of the fragments, sometimes with valuable suggestions for readings and restorations can be found in F. García Martínez, *The Dead Sea Scrolls Translated: The Qumran Texts in English* (2nd ed., Leiden: Brill; Grand Rapids: Eerdmans, 1996); G. Vermes, *The Complete Dead Sea Scrolls in English* (5th ed., London: Allen Lane/Penguin, 1997); M. Wise, M. Abegg, E. Cook, *The Dead Sea Scrolls: A New Translation* (San Francisco: HarperCollins, 1996). A German translation, again sometimes with valuable suggestions for the better understanding of some fragments, can be found in J. Maier, *Die Qumran-Essener: Die Texte vom Toten Meer* (UTB 1862-63; München: Ernst Reinhardt, 1995).

[2] See the contribution by J. Bowley, "Prophecy in the Dead Sea Scrolls," in Vol. 2 of this Fiftieth Anniversary collection.

[3] Since pesher may only be applied to partially or completely unfulfilled prophecies or promises, other figures might be included in the list such as as Jacob whose blessings receive pesher in 4Q252 4:3-6:4.

Qumran.[4] Conversely, for the literary prophets, the genre of pesher is applied only to Isaiah and several of the Twelve Minor Prophets; there are no (and maybe never were any) pesharim devoted to Jeremiah or Ezekiel, though extracts from both are used in a secondary and supportive fashion in various exegetical passages in the scrolls.

Given the interest in prophets and prophecy in the scrolls,[5] it need be no surprise to encounter the view that some in the sectarian movement saw themselves as standing in the line of the prophets as inspired by God to disclose all the mysteries of his servants the prophets (cf. 1QpHab 7:4-5) and to understand the story of their own experiences as an unfolding of the events predicted by their prophetic forebears.

1. MOSES

Together with his other roles, Moses is understood as a prophet. Exod 20:21 as cited in 4Q175 1-8[6] makes this plain: in the eschatological expectation of some sectarians one day God will raise up for them a prophet like Moses. That Moses is described as "anointed" (4Q377 2 ii, line 5) is best understood in terms of his prophetic role too.[7]

There are several sets of fragments from the Qumran caves which have been variously associated with Moses. Some are narratives in which Moses figures in the third person; some are rewritten forms of parts of the Law, or historical overviews, given to Moses to repeat or being spoken by him directly. Not all this material can be

---

[4] See, for example, D. Flusser, "The Apocryphal Book of *Ascensio Isaiae* and the Dead Sea Sect," *IEJ* 3 (1953) 30-47; repr. in idem, *Judaism and the Origins of Christianity* (Jerusalem: Magnes Press, 1988) 3-20; M. Philonenko, "Le *Martyre d'Ésaïe* et l'histoire de la secte de Qumrân," in idem (ed.), *Pseudépigraphes de l'Ancien Testament et manuscrits de la mer morte* (Cahiers de la *RHPR* 41; Paris: Presses universitaires de France, 1967) 1-10.

[5] Cf. Josephus' accounts of the Essenes: *J.W.* 1 §78-80; 2 §113; 2 §159; *Ant.* 15 §373-78.

[6] 4Q175 1-8 cites Exod 20:21 in a form similar to that found in the Samaritan Pentateuch (= MT Deut 5:28-29 and 18:18-19).

[7] If pesher is given only to texts that are deemed prophetic in some way, then Moses may be counted a prophet on the basis of 4Q159 frg. 5 in which it seems as if a variant form of Lev 16:1 is interpreted through pesher.

shown to be based on the view that Moses was a prophet, but to appreciate something of the range of pseudo-Moses texts, it is worth listing the principal compositions: 1QWords of Moses (1Q22),[8] The Liturgy of the Three Tongues of Fire (1Q29; 4Q376),[9] 2QApocryphon of Moses (2Q20),[10] 4QDiscourse on the Exodus/ Conquest Tradition (4Q374),[11] 4QApocryphon of Moses[a] (4Q375),[12] 4QApocryphon of Moses[b]? (4Q376),[13] 4QApocryphon of Moses[c] (4Q377),[14] and five copies of a Pseudo-Moses text (4QPseudo-Moses[a] [4Q385a]; 4QPseudo-Moses[b] [4Q387a]; 4QPseudo-Moses[c] [4Q388a]; 4QPseudo-Moses[d] [4Q389]; 4QPseudo-Moses[e] [4Q390]).[15]

---

[8] J. T. Milik, "Dires de Moïse," in D. Barthélemy and J. T. Milik (eds.), *Qumran Cave I* (DJD 1; Oxford: Clarendon Press, 1955) 91-97.

[9] J. T. Milik, 'Liturgie de 'trois langues de feu'," in Barthélemy and Milik (eds.), *Qumran Cave I* (DJD 1), 130-32; J. Strugnell, "Moses-Pseudepigrapha at Qumran: 4Q375, 4Q376, and similar works," in L. H. Schiffman (ed.), *Archaeology and History in the Dead Sea Sect: the New York Conference in Memory of Yigael Yadin* (JSPSup 8; Sheffield: JSOT Press, 1990) 221-56; J. Strugnell, "376. 4QApocryphon of Moses[b]?," in M. Broshi et al. (eds.), *Qumran Cave 4.XIV: Parabiblical Texts, Part 2* (DJD 19; Oxford: Clarendon Press, 1995) 121-36, esp. 131-36 on "Moses the Pseudepigrapher at Qumran."

[10] M. Baillet, "Un apocryphe de Moïse?," in M. Baillet et al. (eds.), *Les "Petites Grottes" de Qumrân* (DJD 3; Oxford: Clarendon Press, 1962) 79-81.

[11] Sometimes called "4QApocryphon of Moses A"; cf. C. A. Newsom, "4Q374: A Discourse on the Exodus/Conquest Tradition," in D. Dimant and U. Rappaport (eds.), *The Dead Sea Scrolls: Forty Years of Research* (STDJ 10; Leiden: Brill, 1992) 40-52; C. A. Newsom, "374. Discourse on the Exodus/Conquest Tradition," in Broshi et al. (eds.), *Qumran Cave 4.XIV* (DJD 19), 99-110.

[12] Sometimes called "4QApocryphon of Moses B"; cf. J. Strugnell, "Moses-Pseudepigrapha at Qumran: 4Q375, 4Q376, and similar works," in Schiffman (ed.), *Archaeology and History in the Dead Sea Sect*, 221-56; J. Strugnell, "375. 4QApocryphon of Moses[a]," in Broshi et al. (eds.), *Qumran Cave 4.XIV* (DJD 19) 111-19.

[13] The same composition as 1Q29.

[14] Available to date only in the edition by B.-Z. Wacholder and M. Abegg (which was based on the *Preliminary Concordance*), *A Preliminary Edition of the Unpublished Dead Sea Scrolls: The Hebrew and Aramaic Texts from Cave Four* (Washington: Biblical Archaeology Society, 1995) 3.164-66. Frg. 2, col. 2 is translated by M. Wise in Wise, Abegg and Cook, *The Dead Sea Scrolls*, 338; and by G. Vermes, *The Complete Dead Sea Scrolls in English*, 542.

[15] For preliminary details of these see D. Dimant, "New Light from Qumran on the Jewish Pseudepigrapha—4Q390," in J. Trebolle Barrera and L. Vegas Montaner (eds.), *The Madrid Qumran Congress: Proceedings of the International*

In addition some other compositions, such as the whole range of Jubilees manuscripts[16] and the copies of the Temple Scroll,[17] can be readily associated with Moses and can be understood as looking forward from his time to the present experiences and future hopes of their authors and traditors.

In particular it may be important that it is Moses, perhaps as a prophet, who is entrusted with charging Israel to distinguish between true and false prophets (4Q375). The application of such distinctions may be seen in the list of false prophets (4Q339):[18] Balaam (Num 22-24), the Old Man from Bethel (1 Kgs 13:11-31), Zedekiah (1 Kgs 22:1-28), Ahab and Zedekiah (Jer 29:21-24), Shemaiah (Jer 29:24-32), Hananiah (Jer 28). In their principal edition the editors of 4Q339 restore and read the last on the list as "[Hananiah son of Az]ur, [a prophet from Gib]eon" (4Q339 frgs. 8–9); but in their contribution to the Greenfield *Festschrift* they follow the suggestion that was made independently by Elisha Qimron and Alexander

---

Congress on the Dead Sea Scrolls, Madrid 18-21 March 1991 (STDJ 11; Leiden: Brill, 1992) 405-48. See also M. Knibb, "A Note on 4Q372 and 4Q390," in F. García Martínez et al. (eds.) *The Scriptures and the Scrolls: Studies in Honour of A.S. van der Woude on the Occasion of his 65th Birthday* (VTSup 49; Leiden: Brill, 1992) 170-77.

[16] See esp. J. C. VanderKam, *Textual and Historical Studies in the Book of Jubilees* (HSM 14; Missoula: Scholars Press, 1977); J. C. VanderKam and J. T. Milik, "Jubilees," in Attridge et al. (eds.), *Qumran Cave 4.VIII* (DJD 13) 1-185.

[17] See esp. É. Puech, "4Q524: le premier exemplair du Rouleau du Temple," in M. Bernstein, F. García Martínez and J. Kampen (eds.), *Legal Texts and Legal Issues: Proceedings of the Second Meeting of the International Organization for Qumran Studies, Published in Honour of Joseph M. Baumgarten* (STDJ 23; Leiden: Brill, 1997) 19-64; E. Tov and S. White, "365a. 4QTemple?," in Attridge et al. (eds.), *Qumran Cave 4.VIII* (DJD 13) 319-33; Y. Yadin, *The Temple Scroll* (Jerusalem: Israel Exploration Society, Institute of Archaeology, Shrine of the Book, 1983); E. Qimron, *The Temple Scroll: A Critical Edition with Extensive Reconstructions* (Beer-Sheva: Ben-Gurion University Press; Jerusalem: Israel Exploration Society, 1996); F. García Martínez, "11QTemple[b]: A Preliminary Publication," in Trebolle Barrera and Vegas Montaner (eds.), *The Madrid Qumran Congress*, 363-91.

[18] M. Broshi and A. Yardeni, "On *netinim* and False Prophets," in Z. Zevit, S. Gitin, M. Sokoloff (eds.), *Solving Riddles and Untying Knots: Biblical, Epigraphic, and Semitic Studies in Honor of Jonas C. Greenfield* (Winona Lake, IN: Eisenbrauns, 1995) 29-37; M. Broshi and A. Yardeni, "339. 4QList of False Prophets ar," in Broshi et al. (eds.), *Qumran Cave 4.XIV* (DJD 19) 77-79.

Rofé[19] of restoring the last line as "[And Yohanan son of Sim]eon," a reference to John Hyrcanus I, who was known for his prophetic abilities (Josephus, *Jewish War* 1 §68-69; *Antiquities* 13 §300), but who could well have been despised by those responsible for writing and passing on this list.

2. DAVID[20]

Known in the New Testament as a prophet (Acts 2:29-31), David is described in a similar way in 11QPs^a: "And David, son of Jesse, was wise, a luminary like the light of the sun, literate, discerning, and perfect in all his ways before God and men... All these he spoke through prophecy (נבואה) which was given him from before the Most High" (11QPs^a 27:2-3, 11). Indeed, from the way in which some Psalms are given interpretation through pesher (4QpPs^a; 4QpPs^b; 4Q174 3:14-4:3), just as were Isaiah and some of the Twelve, so the Psalms were viewed as prophecy.[21]

In light of this we may suggest that several compositions associated with David are in some sense parabiblical prophetic narratives, even if the biographical material is presented in poetic form. There are four parabiblical narrative compositions concerning David: both 2QApocryphon of David? (2Q22)[22] and 4QApocryphon of Joseph^c (4Q373)[23] are autobiographical poetic narratives retelling and

---

[19] E. Qimron, "On the Interpretation of the List of False Prophets," *Tarbiz* 63 (1994) 273-75 [Hebrew]; A. Rofé, "The List of False Prophets from Qumran: Two Riddles and Their Solutions," *Ha'aretz* 13 April, 1994) 11 [Hebrew]. Their proposal is also followed by M. Wise in Wise, Abegg and Cook, *The Dead Sea Scrolls*, 323-25.

[20] On David in the scrolls see E. Jucci, "Davide a Qumran," *Ricerche Storico Bibliche* 7 (1995) 157-73; C.A. Evans, "David in the Dead Sea Scrolls," in S.E. Porter and C.A. Evans (eds.), *The Scrolls and the Scriptures: Qumran Fifty Years After* (JSPSup 26; Sheffield: Sheffield Academic Press, 1997) 183-97.

[21] See, for example, W. H. Brownlee, *The Meaning of the Qumran Scrolls for the Bible with Special Attention to the Book of Isaiah* (New York: Oxford University Press, 1964) 69-71; D. N. Freedman, "Pottery, Poetry, and Prophecy: An Essay on Biblical Poetry," *JBL* 96 (1977) 21-22.

[22] M. Baillet, "Un apocryphe de David(?)," in Baillet et al. (eds.), *Les "Petites Grottes" de Qumrân* (DJD 3), 81-82.

[23] E. Schuller, "A Preliminary Study of 4Q373 and Some Related(?) Fragments," in Trebolle Barrera and Vegas Montaner (eds.), *The Madrid Qumran Congress*, 515-30.

embellishing the biblical story of David and Goliath; parts of 6QApocryphon of Samuel-Kings (6Q9)[24] may be concerned with the same episode; within 11QPs^a Psalm 151 (col. 28:3-14)[25] is a first person description of the anointing of David. In addition, it is likely that 11QApPs^a[26] should be understood as a collection of Davidic psalms put together for very particular magical purposes which depended on identifying with the status and role of David in some way.

3. ELIJAH

The paucity of copies of the Books of Kings and of Ezra-Nehemiah and Chronicles in the Qumran caves is seldom pointed out. It seems, however, as if those responsible for the collection of manuscripts in the caves had little time for studying these history books; for them, apparently little of value could ever come from a palace. And yet, much in the Books of Kings is narrative about prophets, both true and false. The cycles of stories concerning Elijah and Elisha are extensive. Thus it need come as no surprise to learn that some compositions found at Qumran seem to concern the prophets who feature in the historical works.

The fragments from the first half of the first century BCE assigned to 4Qpap paraKings et al. (4Q382)[27] probably belong to more than one manuscript. Nevertheless, several of the fragments represent a narrative retelling of some of the Elijah stories: frgs. 1-5 concern Ahab, Jezebel and Obadiah, frgs. 9 and 11 allude to the opening of the story of the succession of Elisha (2 Kgs 2:1-4), frg. 30 may reflect the episode in 1 Kgs 19 of Elijah's anointing of Hazael, Jehu

---

[24] M. Baillet, "Un apocryphe de Samuel-Rois," in Baillet et al. (eds.), *Les "Petites Grottes" de Qumrân* (DJD 3), 119-23. Frg. 22 mentions David, and several other fragments can be linked with events involving him.

[25] See J. A. Sanders, *The Psalms Scroll of Qumrân Cave 11 (11QPs^a)* (DJD 4; Oxford: Clarendon Press, 1965).

[26] J. P. M. van der Ploeg, "Le Psaume xci dans une recension de Qumrân," *RB* 72 (1965) 210-17; idem, "Un petit rouleau de psaumes apocryphes (11QPsAp^a)," in G. Jeremias, H.-W. Kuhn, H. Stegemann (eds.), *Tradition und Glaube: Festgabe für Karl Georg Kuhn* (Göttingen: Vandenhoeck & Ruprecht, 1971) 128-39; É. Puech, "Les deux derniers Psaumes davidiques du rituel d'exorcisme, 11QPsAp^a IV 4–V 14," in Dimant and Rappaport (eds.), *The Dead Sea Scrolls: Forty Years of Research*, 64-89.

[27] S. Olyan, "382. 4Qpap paraKings et al.," in Attridge et al. (eds.), *Qumran Cave 4.VIII* (DJD 13), 363-416.

and Elisha, and frg. 40 features either Elijah or Elisha. Not enough remains in any of these fragments to disclose the purpose of this retelling of the prophetic cycle, beyond that there was an ongoing interest in Elijah.

As some form of narrative text, mention should also be made of the so-called "Messianic Apocalypse" (4Q521).[28] The beginning of the principal surviving passage (frgs. 2 ii and 4) mentions an anointed figure whom heaven and earth will obey and contains an exhortation addressed to those who seek the Lord that they should strengthen themselves in his service. The justification for such exhortation follows. Based on Psalm 146 the future activity of God is made plain: amongst other things, "he will heal the wounded, give life to the dead and preach good news to the poor." Since 4Q521 2 iii, line 2 contains a clear allusion to Elijah, it is appropriate that the anointed figure of the previous column should be understood as *Elijah redivivus* and the text understood to be describing how God will act through him, as he had done through Elijah in the past, including raising the dead.[29]

4. ELISHA

As for Elijah, so for Elisha. Three fragments in a late Hasmonean hand have been allocated to what has been designated an Apocryphon of Elisha (4Q481a).[30] Frg. 1 is too small for comment. Frg. 2 is slightly more substantial. The name of Elisha is preserved in line 3 and J. Trebolle Barrera has suitably restored the name in lines 2 and

---

[28] É. Puech ("Une Apocalypse messianique [4Q521]," *RevQ* 15 [1992] 475-519) dates this manuscript copy to the first quarter of the first century BCE; cf. also J. J. Collins, "The Works of the Messiah," *DSD* 1 (1994) 98-112, esp. 102-6 on Elijah.

[29] On the return of Elijah see also the fragment of 4Q558 (4QpapVision[b] ar) published by É. Puech, *La croyance des Esséniens en la vie future: immortalité, résurrection, vie éternelle? Histoire d'une croyance dans le Judaïsme ancien* (EB 22; Paris: Gabalda, 1993) 676-77: לכן אשלח לאליה קד[ם, "I will send you Elijah befo[re..."

[30] J. Trebolle Barrera, "Histoire du texte des livres historiques et histoire de la composition et de la rédaction deutéronomistes avec une publication préliminaire de 4Q481a, 'Apocryphe d'Élisée'," in J. A. Emerton (ed.), *Congress Volume, Paris 1992* (VTSup 61; Leiden: Brill, 1995) 327-42; idem, "481a. 4QApocryphe d'Élisée," in G. J. Brooke et al. (eds.), *Qumran Cave 4.XVII: Parabiblical Texts, Part 3* (DJD 22; Oxford: Clarendon Press, 1996) 305-9.

4. In addition he has been able to show convincingly that with minor variations lines 3–6 contained a version of 2 Kgs 2:14-16, the verses in which the company of prophets (בני הנביאים) recognize that the spirit of Elijah rests on Elisha. Not enough text is preserved on frg. 3 to enable its location in the Elisha cycle, but it seems to refer to a lament of some kind and may suggest that poetic or liturgical materials were added to the prophetic narrative, perhaps to encourage the audience to identify with the prophet himself.

4Qpap paraKings et al. (4Q382)[31] also contains some material which relates to Elisha. Frgs. 9 and 11 allude to the opening of the story of the succession of Elisha (2 Kgs 2:1-4), frg. 30 may reflect the episode in 1 Kings 19 of Elijah's anointing of Elisha, and frg. 40 may feature Elisha. Unfortunately, not enough text remains in any of these fragments to disclose the purpose of this retelling of the prophetic cycle.

5. JEREMIAH[32]

The most obvious parabiblical material in the scrolls found at Qumran which concerns Jeremiah is to be found in the fragments variously assigned to 4Q383–389. For 4Q385–390 D. Dimant is of the opinion that there are three distinct works: Pseudo-Ezekiel, Pseudo-Moses and a Jeremiah Apocryphon. Jeremiah is named in at least five fragments.[33] Dimant has described the Jeremiah materials as belonging to five manuscripts, Apocryphon of Jeremiah A–E;[34]

---

[31] See above, n. 27.

[32] For an overview of the Jeremiah apocryphal texts in the context of the use of Jeremiah at Qumran see G.J. Brooke, "The Book of Jeremiah and its Reception in the Qumran Scrolls," in A.H.W. Curtis and T. Römer (eds.), *The Book of Jeremiah and its Reception* (BETL 128; Leuven: University Press and Peeters, 1997) 183-205.

[33] 4Q385 16 i 2, 6, 8; ii 3, 4, 6; 4Q385 25 1; 4Q385 39 2; 4Q387 15 2; and 4Q389 3 5.

[34] D. Dimant, "An Apocryphon of Jeremiah from Cave 4 (4Q385 B = 4Q385 16)," in G.J. Brooke with F. García Martínez (eds.), *New Qumran Texts and Studies: Proceedings of the First Meeting of the IOQS, Paris 1992* (STDJ 15; Leiden: Brill, 1994) 12. ApocrJer A = 4Q383; ApocrJer B = 4Q384; ApocrJer C = 4Q385 16, 28 (listed as frag. 25 in the *Preliminary Concordance*); ApocrJer D = 4Q387 9, 10, 11, 15, 16?; ApocrJer E = 4Q389 6, 15?, 16. B. Z. Wacholder and M. Abegg have presented the texts as allocated to manuscripts by J. Strugnell and

though she has implied that this is a single composition, it is preferable to use upper case letters for their technical designation to indicate that these five manuscripts may contain different compositions.[35] Also in this category of apocryphal Jeremiah texts belong 4Q470, the fragment mentioning Zedekiah, and 7Q2, the fragment of the Greek Epistle of Jeremiah, and possibly some other fragmentary manuscripts.

5.1 4QApocryphon of Jeremiah A (4Q383)

Three small fragments belong to this manuscript.[36] The largest has parts of five lines. Dimant has described this manuscript as containing a discourse by Jeremiah, including the phrase ואני ירמיה, "And I, Jeremiah" (4Q383 1, line 2). The same line continues א[בכ]ה בם with which Dimant has compared *Par. Jer.* 2:10 ("Therefore they both remained in the altar-area weeping"); 3:20 ("and they both sat down and wept"); 4:6 ("while Jeremiah was still weeping"); and 7:32 ("wailing and weeping").[37] "The same tradition is reflected in the common view that Lamentations was composed by Jeremiah (attested by the title of the Septuagint Greek translation)."[38]

5.2 4QpapApocryphon of Jeremiah B? (4Q384) [39]

This papyrus manuscript in a Herodian hand has been edited by M. Smith. It is extant in 27 small fragments which provide very little context. The name תחפנס can be read in frg. 7, line 2; the same name occurs in 4Q385 16 ii 1 (cf. Jer 2:16; 43:7-9; 44:1; 46:14). Other significant phrases are כאשר כתוב "as it is written" (frg. 8 2), implying that something is about to be quoted; אל השבים "to the returnees" (frg. 20 3) which reflects the use of the same root in

---

as represented in the *Preliminary Concordance*; see Wacholder and Abegg, *A Preliminary Edition*, 3.221-66

[35] The same applies to 4Qpap Apocryphon of Jeremiah B? in DJD 19 (see n.39 below).

[36] In the middle of PAM 44.189; as described in S. Reed and M. J. Lundberg with M. Phelps, *The Dead Sea Scrolls Catalogue: Documents, Photographs and Museum Inventory Numbers* (SBLRBS 32; Atlanta: Scholars Press, 1994) 397.

[37] Text and translation in R. A. Kraft and A.-E. Purintun, *Paraleipomena Jeremiou* (SBLTT 1; Missoula, MT: Society of Biblical Literature, 1972).

[38] D. Dimant, "An Apocryphon of Jeremiah," 23.

[39] M. Smith, "384. 4QpapApocryphon of Jeremiah B?" in Broshi et al. (eds.), *Qumran Cave 4.XIV* (DJD 19) 137-52.

many places in the so-called sectarian scrolls, especially in relation to returning from the exile (CD 4:2; 6:5; 8:16). Smith has proposed reading בספר מ[חלקות העת]ים in frg. 9, line 2, as a possible reconstruction based on CD 16:3 in which the term may refer to the *Book of Jubilees* or some similar writing.[40] Because of this, Smith is unsure whether all the fragments of 4Q384 should be taken together as belonging to a single manuscript. However, 4Q384 9:4 refers to a "covenant," and since CD 8:20-21 can be understood to associate Jeremiah with the new covenant in the land of Damascus, perhaps 4Q384 frg. 9 should be understood as part of the Jeremiah apocryphon which may have referred to a work like *Jubilees,* just as occurs in CD 16:3-4. If correct, this would suggest the mid-second century BCE as the earliest date for the composition of this apocryphon.

5.3 4QApocryphon of Jeremiah C (4Q385b) [41]

Two fragments have been definitely assigned to this late Hasmonean or early Herodian manuscript.[42] The principal fragment of this manuscript has been edited in detail by D. Dimant. The text runs as follows:

Col. i

2   ... and] Jeremiah the prophet [went] from before Yahweh
3   to go with the] captives who were led captive from the land of Jerusalem and came [to]
4   ] ... king of Babylon, when Nebuzaradan, the Chief Cook, smote
5   ] ... and he took the vessels of the House of God, the priests
6   ] and the children of Israel and brought them to Babylon. And Jeremiah the prophet went
7   ... and he reached...unto] the river and he commanded them what they should do in the land of [their] captivity
8   ... to listen to] the voice of Jeremiah concerning the words which God had commanded him

---

[40] The term מחלקות nowhere occurs in Jeremiah, but it is frequent in 1 and 2 Chronicles.

[41] D. Dimant ("An Apocryphon of Jeremiah," 11-30) has assigned two fragments from 4Q385 to this Jeremiah Apocryphon. What she labels frg. 28 is almost certainly to be understood as frg. 25 according to the enumeration of the *Preliminary Concordance,* since the name Jeremiah occurs: frg. 28 (i.e. 25) reads: 1. יר[מיהו הנב]יא; 2.]ויתן כ ○[. Note that the name Jeremiah is in the longer form.

[42] 4Q385 frgs. 16 and 28; cf. Dimant, "New Light from Qumran on the Jewish Pseudepigrapha," 412.

9   ... so that] they should keep the covenant of the God of their fathers in the land
10 of their captivity...and should not d]o as they had done, they themselves and their kings and their priests
11 and their princes]...[they de]file[d the na]me of God... [

Col. ii

1   In Tahpanes wh[ich is in the land of Egypt...]
2   and they told him: "Inquire [of G]od [on our behalf" ...And the word of Yahweh came to Jeremiah: "Inquire]
3   on their behalf, Jeremi[ah], of me as Go[d] inquire on their behalf[
4   supplication and prayer." And Jeremiah was lamenting...[laments]
5   ov]er Jerusalem. *vacat* [And the word of Yahweh came to]
6   Jeremiah in the land of Tahpanes, which is in the land of Egy[pt thus: "Go to
7   the children of Israel and to the children of Judah and Benjamin[and tell them as follows]:
8   'Every day study my statutes and ke[ep] my commandments [and do not go]
9   after the i[d]ols of the gentiles, [after] which [your fathers and your kings] we[nt, for]
10 they will not sa[ve] y[ou   ] not ['   ]"[43]

This two-column fragment draws on Jeremiah 40-44, though 1:4-6 recalls the biblical story of the fall of Jerusalem as in Jer 52:12-13. For the name Nebuzaradan this fragment follows the spelling of 4QJer^d over against the Masoretic Text. Column 1 seems to be concerned chiefly with Jeremiah's relations with the deportees to Babylon, whereas column 2 is clearly about his relations with the Jews in Egypt. The narrative behind the passage implies that Jeremiah accompanied the deportees to the river, probably the Euphrates, then presumably returned to Mizpah to witness the assassination of Gedaliah before being involved in the flight to Egypt. Tahpanes is the scene of the events described in Jer 43:8-44:30.

Dimant has made the striking observation about this passage that all of its non-biblical elements can be found in other non-Qumranic works. The Epistle of Jeremiah and 2 Macc 2:1-4 recall how Jeremiah exhorted the deportees, not simply accompanied them (Jer 40:1). The *Paraleipomena of Jeremiah* and *2 Baruch* locate this activity clearly in Babylon. And *Pesikta Rabbati* records how Jeremiah made the journey with the deportees only so far as the river Euphrates. Since 2 Macc 2:1 and 4 refer to an actual source

---

[43] D. Dimant, "An Apocryphon of Jeremiah," 14-17.

document, it is tempting to see there a reference to some such written tradition as is found now in this Jeremiah Apocryphon.

Another intriguing feature to which Dimant has drawn attention is the tendency in these sources to portray Jeremiah in terms like Moses. In 1:7 Jeremiah's setting at the river is analogous to that of Moses in the Plains of Moab near the Jordan (Numbers 33-36; Deuteronomy 1, 29-31). In 1:8 the phraseology is very similar to that of Exod 19:7 in relation to Moses. More generally, like Moses, Jeremiah here is the one who issues commands on God's behalf. Both Moses' prophetic status and the Mosaic status of Jeremiah may have been of particular interest to the Qumranic traditors of this material.

5.4 4QApocryphon of Jeremiah D (4Q387b)[44]

For physical reasons D. Dimant has associated four or five small fragments, which were once considered part of 4Q387 proper, with this manuscript: 4Q387 frgs. 9, 10, 11, 15, 16?[45] The fragments are legible on PAM 43.501. It is fragment 15 which most clearly suggests an association of these pieces with Jeremiah. Line 2, the most complete line of the fragment, reads שמ[עו לדברי ירמי]ה.[46] This phrase occurs nowhere in MT Jeremiah, but in a way similar to 4Q385 frg. 16 it implies that like Moses Jeremiah is to be listened to and obeyed.

5.5 4QApocryphon of Jeremiah E (4Q389a)

Dimant has assigned 4Q389 frgs. 6, 15(?), and 16 to a fifth Jeremiah Apocryphon manuscript.[47] Frg. 16 contains וי[אמר ברוך עמ]; as she has pointed out,[48] ברוך could be either the proper name Baruch or a participle; if the former, it may be a reference to Jeremiah's scribe and so indicate that the fragment belongs to a Jeremianic text. The most obvious piece of 4Q389 to be associated

---

[44] Not yet published in any edited form.

[45] D. Dimant, "An Apocryphon of Jeremiah," 12. The third fascicle of Wacholder and Abegg's *Preliminary Edition* only includes the five large fragments of 4Q387, and is thus of no use in determining the content of this Jeremiah Apocryphon.

[46] In the *Preliminary Concordance* this fragment is labelled as Sl 22 (= 4Q385) 39, but Dimant clearly understands it to be part of 4Q387 ("New Light from Qumran on the Jewish Pseudepigrapha" 2.412, n.24).

[47] For frg. 6, in which Nebuchadrezzar is probably mentioned twice, see Wacholder and Abegg, *Preliminary Edition*, 3.262.

[48] "New Light from Qumran on the Jewish Pseudepigrapha," 2.413, n.25.

with this prophet is labelled as fragment 3 in the *Preliminary Concordance*,[49] but as fragment 6 by Dimant. It reads as follows:

2   ...] in the land... [
3   ...] and they will seek concerning th[eir children
4   ...] all the remnant in the land of E[gypt
5   ... and Je]remiah son of Hilkiah [went] from the land of Egyp[t
6   ... six]ty/thir]ty[50] six years from the exile of Israel, after the events
7   ... when I]srael was at the river Sour (סור). In the presence of... [[51]

The most detailed comments on this fragment were offered by Dimant in Paris in 1992.[52] There is no overlap between the texts of 4Q385 16 and 4Q389 6, yet they deal with the same stage of Jeremiah's career in a similar narrative style. In itself 4Q389 6 speaks of the exile and of Jeremiah's role in Egypt. The fragment speaks of the river Sour. This is probably the same as the river Soud referred to in 1 Bar 1:4; at some point there has been dalet/reš confusion.[53] In light of this Qumran evidence scholars should refrain from emending the name in 1 Baruch.

5.6 4QText Mentioning Zedekiah (4Q470) [54]

Three tantalizing fragments have now been assigned to this manuscript (early Herodian period), which takes its name after the principal one which mentions Zedekiah. Frg. 1 reads as follows:

---

[49] And also in Wacholder and Abegg, *Preliminary Edition*, 3.261. The text as presented in Wacholder and Abegg is followed here without their proposed restorations and with the exception of one reading in line 6; cf. PAM 43.495.

[50] Dimant has proposed reading ארבעים, but Wacholder and Abegg have reckoned that a ש is legible, so have read either ששים or שלושים.

[51] An English translation of this fragment is also available in F. García Martínez, *The Dead Sea Scrolls Translated*, 285, where it is wrongly labelled as fragment 1 of 4QApocryphon of Jeremiah D (4Q387b).

[52] D. Dimant, "An Apocryphon of Jeremiah"; the comments were offered in the as yet unpublished part of her presentation at the first meeting of the International Organization for Qumran Studies, Paris 1992. The published form of the paper in the Proceedings of the meeting did not include this fragment of 4Q389a.

[53] As proposed by Dimant, "An Apocryphon of Jeremiah," 20, n.18.

[54] See E. Larson, "4Q470 and the Angelic Rehabilitation of King Zedekiah," *DSD* 1 (1994) 210-28; E. Larson, L. H. Schiffman and J. Strugnell, "4Q470, Preliminary Publication of a Fragment Mentioning Zedekiah," *RevQ* 16 (1994) 335-50; E. Larson, L. H. Schiffman and J. Strugnell, "470. 4QText Mentioning Zedekiah," in Broshi et al. (eds.), *Qumran Cave 4.XIV* (DJD 19) 235-44.

1]...[
2]... Michael[
3]... Zedekiah [shall en]ter, on [th]at day, into a/the co[ven]ant
4]... to perform and to cause the performance of all the law
5 at] that time M[ich]ael shall say to Zedekiah
6] I will make with you [a cove]na[nt]before the congregation
7 to d]o and...[   ]...[

The fragment seems to describe the making of a covenant between God and Zedekiah through the agency of the archangel Michael. This covenant involves both the observing of the law and the encouragement of others to do the same. Because some elements in the content of this fragment echo phrases in some sections of Jeremiah, Larson considers that the composition may be some kind of Pseudo-Jeremiah text.[55] Such is made more likely by the presence of Michael in another Jeremiah apocryphon in Coptic, Arabic and Karshuni;[56] there Michael interacts with Nebuchadnezzar rather than Zedekiah.

The key interpretative issue in the fragment is the identification of Zedekiah. Larson concludes justifiably that the most likely candidate is the king of Judah of that name. Zedekiah the king is not uniformly described as one who did evil in the sight of the Lord (2 Kgs 24:19; Jer 52:2; 2 Chron 36:12),[57] and so might be deemed worthy by some to receive a covenant. Though the setting for this fragment may be the covenant mentioned in Jer 34:8-22, or even the new covenant of Jer 31:31-34 and 32:40, it seems most likely that Jer 23:5-8 and 33:14-26 provide the best backdrop for the passage. In Jeremiah 22 the three kings Jehoahaz, Jehoiakim and Jehoiachin are all denounced, but not Zedekiah. Rather, through wordplay on his name, Zedekiah is associated with a divine promise (Jer 23:5-6). Jer 33:15 even speaks of what will happen "in those days and at that time" (cf. frg. 1, lines 3 and 5).

---

[55] On palaeographic grounds Larson has resisted assigning the fragments of 4Q470 to one or other of the Jeremiah Apocryphons described above.

[56] See K.-H. Kuhn, "A Coptic Jeremiah Apocryphon," *Le Muséon* 83 (1970) 95-135, 291-350.

[57] Larson notes amongst other things that Zedekiah is accused explicitly in LXX Jer 45:9, but not in MT Jer 38:9 (a later mollification?), that Josephus notes he had a sense of justice (*Ant.* 10 §120), and that a positive characterisation appears in *b. ʿArak.* 17a; *b. Sanh.* 103a; *b. Šabb.* 149b.

5.7 papEpistle of Jeremiah gr (7Q2) [58]

All the manuscripts from cave 7 are in Greek. It may be that they should be treated as a deposit independent of the rest of the Qumran collection,[59] but the way in which access to the cave depends on traversing the terrace on which are the community buildings suggests that this cave too was an integral part of the library. The letters preserved belong to verses 43-44. The Epistle of Jeremiah is a condemnation of idolatry.

5.8 papProphetic Text (4Q485) [60]

Five small fragments are assigned to this mid-first century BCE papyrus manuscript; they are presented by their editor in order of size. Frg. 1 may possibly contain an allusion to Jer 30:18, "I am going to restore the fortunes of the tents of Jacob." Frg. 2 may allude to Jer 7:6, "to your own hurt" (לרע לכם). No continuous running text of Jeremiah can be restored, but it is possible that the manuscript contained some rewritten form of Jeremiah.

6. EZEKIEL[61]

Though there are no pesharim devoted to providing interpretations of Ezekiel, passages from the prophet feature in a variety of ways in the sectarian compositions found at Qumran. So, for example, some sections of the book seem to be determinative of how the sectarian movement viewed its history (CD 1:5-6 uses the 390 from Ezek 4:5), and its identity as made up of priests and Levites (CD 3:21-4:1 uses Ezek 44:15 in an adapted form) chosen and marked out by God (CD

---

[58] M. Baillet, "Lettre de Jérémie," in Baillet et al. (eds.), *Les "Petites Grottes" de Qumrân* (DJD 3), 143. The identification was made by P. Benoit and M. Boismard.

[59] As is implied by D. Dimant in her recent analysis (in which she excludes Cave 7 from her overall discussion): "The Qumran Manuscripts: Contents and Significance," in D. Dimant and L. H. Schiffman (eds.), *Time to Prepare the Way in the Wilderness: Papers on the Qumran Scrolls by Fellows of the Institute for Advanced Studies of the Hebrew University, Jerusalem, 1989-1990* (STDJ 16; Leiden: Brill, 1995) 23-58.

[60] M. Baillet, *Qumrân Grotte 4,III (4Q482-4Q520)* (DJD 7; Oxford: Clarendon Press, 1982) 4.

[61] For an overview of most of the Ezekiel materials from Qumran see G. J. Brooke, "Ezekiel in Some Qumran and New Testament Texts," in Trebolle Barrera and Vegas Montaner (eds.), *The Madrid Qumran Congress*, 317-37.

19:12 uses Ezek 9:4). The New Jerusalem ideology is also dependent in some respects on Ezekiel 40-48, as is also the presentation of some aspects of the temple in the Temple Scroll.

As with Jeremiah, so there are several sets of fragments which are a rewritten form of Ezekiel in several copies. These are to be found amongst the fragments originally assigned to 4Q385-388 and 4Q391. D. Dimant—to whom the principal edition of most of the fragments has been assigned—considers there to be three separate compositions, Pseudo-Ezekiel, Pseudo-Moses, and a Jeremiah Apocryphon.[62] As for the Jeremiah Apocryphon, in the comments which follow I have attempted to be guided by Dimant's insights. Strugnell and Dimant have commented that the subject-matter of Pseudo-Ezekiel is based on the prophecies of canonical Ezekiel and "from the dialogue between God and the prophet it appears that the narrative is pseudepigraphically situated in the time of Ezekiel; it therefore refers in the past to events that occurred before Ezekiel's time, and in the future to events after the prophet's time."[63]

6.1 4QPseudo-Ezekiel^a (4Q385) [64]

Originally assigned forty-eight fragments, this mid-first century BCE manuscript may now only be extant in eight (frgs. 1-5, 6+24 and 12) because D. Dimant has assigned several fragments to other manuscripts.[65] The order of the fragments is difficult to determine and so their numbering may be misleading. H. Stegemann, for one, has calculated that 4Q385 2 represents the last preserved column of 4Q385, whereas frg. 3 came from some four columns before that.[66]

---

[62] In working from the *Preliminary Concordance*, B. Z. Wacholder and M. Abegg (*Preliminary Edition*, 3.xvi-xviii) are less certain that there are three compositions. They reckon that mention of the River Chebar, which in the Bible occurs exclusively in Ezekiel, binds many of the fragments together in the way that J. Strugnell originally proposed.

[63] See J. Strugnell and D. Dimant, "4QSecond Ezekiel (4Q385)," *RevQ* 13 (1988) 48.

[64] Apart from the individual fragments and phrases which Dimant and Strugnell have published in a preliminary form, most of the fragments of Pseudo-Ezekiel are most readily accessible (on the basis of the *Preliminary Concordance*) in Wacholder and Abegg, *Preliminary Edition*, 3.228-63.

[65] For the allocation of fragments to the various copies of Pseudo-Ezekiel see Dimant, "New Light from Qumran on the Jewish Pseudepigrapha," 409.

[66] See Strugnell and Dimant, "4QSecond Ezekiel (4Q385)," 45-46, n.1a.

If that allocation is correct, the placing of the dry bones vision at the climactic end of the composition may be highly significant.

Ezekiel is explicitly mentioned in 4Q385 1:1, 3, 4, and 4:5. Frg. 1 is a retelling of the oracle of Ezek 30:2-9 depicting the detruction of Egypt, together with Put, Cush and others. Frg. 2, together with its parallels in other manuscripts, was first made known by J. Strugnell and D. Dimant in 1988.[67] Lines 1-4 of the fragment contain the end of a dialogue between the prophet and God concerning the reward of the pious. Then there follows a section in which God issues three commands to prophesy, concerning the dry bones (cf. Ezek 37:4-5), sinews (cf. Ezek 37:6), and breath (cf. Ezek 37:9), so that a large crowd is restored to bless the Lord of hosts. The last two lines of the fragment contain a question from the prophet concerning the timing of events, and part of the divine answer which refers cryptically to a tree which bends and straightens up. É. Puech has proposed that this tree should most suitably be understood in light of Ezek 17:22-24, the so-called allegory of the cedar, as referring to the restoration of the people of God.[68] Although it is very unlikely that Pseudo-Ezekiel as now known from these fragmentary manuscripts is the same as the *Ezekiel Apocryphon*, extracts from which are known from several Church Fathers,[69] phrases from the part of the composition represented in 4Q385 frg. 2 have been detected in the *Apocalypse of Peter* 4, 7-9[70] and the *Epistle of Barnabas* 12:1, 4:3.[71] Frg. 3 speaks of the proximity of the time when Israel will enter into its inheritance. God then addresses Ezekiel directly declaring that he controls the days and the years. Dimant and Strugnell have drawn

---

[67] Strugnell and Dimant, "4QSecond Ezekiel (4Q385)," 45-58.

[68] É. Puech, "L'image de l'arbre en 4QDeutéro-Ézéchiel," *RevQ* 16 (1993-95) 437-40. In particular Puech argues convincingly against the proposals of M. Philonenko that the tree should be understood as the tree of life of Isa 65:22 (LXX) and that such a tradition explains some of the imagery of the Dura-Europos Synagogue: see, M. Philonenko, "Un arbre se courbera et se redressera (4Q385 2 9-10)," *RHPR* 73 (1993) 401-404; idem, "De Qoumrân à Doura-Europos: la vision des ossements desséchés (Ézéchiel 37,1-4)," *RHPR* 74 (1994) 1-12.

[69] See especially M. R. James, "The Apocryphal Ezekiel," *JTS* 15 (1914) 236-43; J. R. Mueller, *The Five Fragments of the* Apocryphon of Ezekiel: *A Critical Study* (JSPSup 5; Sheffield: Sheffield Academic Press, 1994).

[70] R. J. Bauckham, "A Quotation from *4QSecond Ezekiel* in the *Apocalypse of Peter*," *RevQ* 15 (1991-92) 437-45.

[71] M. Kister, "Barnabas 12:1; 4:3 and 4QSecond Ezekiel," *RB* 97 (1990) 63-67.

attention to the way in which similar concerns can be found in 4 Ezra 4:33-37.[72]

The first four lines of frg. 4 are poorly preserved; they may have contained the end of a divine speech addressed to Ezekiel and some other material which was designed to set the scene for the throne vision that follows.[73] In the rewriting of the throne chariot vision,[74] whilst Ezekiel 1 remains the base or controlling text, there appear to be identifiable elements of the parallel visionary description of Ezekiel 10, so that a degree of harmonization between the two accounts has taken place. The passages of Ezekiel are not simply repeated, but clarified: there is explicit mention of the chariot and the description is concerned directly with the four living creatures, not their likenesses. In addition, some other scriptural passages such as Isa 6:1-2 may have been used to elucidate the vision of Ezekiel 1.

6.2 4QPseudo-Ezekiel^b (4Q386)

This manuscript is extant in only a single large fragment with remains of three columns. Column 1 contains extensive overlaps with other copies of the composition: 4Q386 1 i, lines 1–9 overlaps with 4Q385 2 2-8 and 4Q386 1 i, lines 1–5 with 4Q388 8 4-7. Because of these overlaps, 4Q386 col. 1 can be extensively restored.

Column 1:1-4 contains the end of a dialogue between the prophet and God concerning the reward of the pious. Then, as in the copy of the text in 4Q385 col. 2, God commands the prophet concerning the dry bones, sinews and breath, so that a large crowd is restored to bless the Lord of hosts. In column 2 the prophet is asked to consider the land of Israel; noting its desolation, he asks God when restoration will take place. The divine reply informs the prophet that a son of Belial will plot to oppress the people, and though he will defile many, his dominion will not be established; in fact the wicked[75] will be slain in Memphis, whence the people will go out. Maybe this is a development of the tradition in Ezek 30:13-19 in which the destruction of all Egypt at the hand of the king of Babylon is depicted. The

---

[72] "4QSecond Ezekiel (4Q385)," 56-57, esp. 57, n.18.

[73] For details on these lines, see Brooke, "Ezekiel in Some Qumran and New Testament Texts," 323-25.

[74] See esp. D. Dimant and J. Strugnell, "The Merkabah Vision in Second Ezekiel (4Q385 4)," *RevQ* 14 (1989) 331-48.

[75] The term is singular and so may refer to the son of Belial; or, it may refer to the wicked in Memphis corporately.

few words which survive in column 3 concern the poor who will be brought to Babylon, though Babylon is a mere tool in God's hands; the image of Babylon as a cup echoes Jer 51:7, but there is plenty in Ezekiel to allow for the portrayal of Babylon as a divine pawn.

6.3 4QPseudo-Ezekiel^c (4Q387)

The current situation in the analysis of 4Q387 is complicated. PAM 43.493 contains images of two fragments originally assigned to 4Q387. Based on the *Preliminary Concordance* B.Z. Wacholder and M. Abegg number these as fragments 1 and 2. Though frg. 1 may contain some phraseology similar to Ezek 8:12 and 9:9 and frg. 2 overlaps with 4Q385 41 2-4, D. Dimant views both fragments as part of 4Q387a (4QPsMos^b). Depending upon how the pieces are considered suitably juxtaposed, PAM 43.501 contains images of 15 fragments. Only the three largest are transcribed by Wacholder and Abegg; frg. 3 and its overlaps are ascribed to 4Q387a (4QPsMos^b), 4Q385a (4QPsMos^a) and 4Q389 (4QPsMos^d), respectively.

Left with 4QPsEzek^c is the *Preliminary Concordance's* frg. 4 which seems to contain a close paraphrase of Ezek 13:11-13 (the tirade against false prophets). Dimant only ascribes to 4QPsEzek^c three other fragments which she labels frgs. 5, 7, and 8;[76] however, she also ascribes apparently the same frg. 5 to 4QPsMos^b.[77]

6.4 4QPseudo-Ezekiel^d (4Q388)

On the basis of its overlaps with 4Q385 2 and 4Q386 1 i, 4Q388 8 clearly seems to belong to yet a third copy of the part of the composition which speaks of the vision of the dry bones. Dimant suggests cautiously that two other fragments originally assigned to this manuscript may still belong, the very small frgs. 5 and 7, neither of which contain any obvious allusion to the text of Ezekiel.

6.5 4QpapPseudo-Ezekiel^e (4Q391)

D. Dimant has declared that "most of the fragments of 4Q391 belong, perhaps, to a fifth copy" of Pseudo-Ezekiel.[78] The principal

---

[76] D. Dimant ("New Light on the Jewish Pseudepigrapha—4Q390," 409) seems to confuse 4Q387 and 4Q388. She suggests that 4Q387 frg. 8 overlaps 4Q385 2 and 4Q386 1 i, but it is actally 4Q388 8 which contains those overlaps. None of the small fragments at the bottom of PAM 43.501 overlaps with 4Q385 2.

[77] "New Light on the Jewish Pseudepigrapha—4Q390," 409, 412.

[78] "New Light on the Jewish Pseudepigrapha—4Q390," 409.

edition of the seventy-eight fragments assigned to this manuscript has been published by M. Smith.[79] He has noted that the principal reasons for connecting 4Q391 with the other copies of Pseudo-Ezekiel include its narrative style with frequent first-person speeches presumably by Ezekiel,[80] some dialogue between God and the prophet (frg. 36), and some vocabulary which evokes the book of Ezekiel,[81] or the other copies of Pseudo-Ezekiel.[82]

Two other features of the manuscript are also worth mentioning. Compared with the other copies of Pseudo-Ezekiel, which do not seem to go beyond Ezekiel 37, frg. 65 of 4Q391 contains a measurement which corresponds with the width of the gate as described in Ezek 40:11 and the word גבוה ("height," line 7) belongs to Ezekiel's technical vocabulary (cf. Ezek 40:42; 41:8, 22). 4Q391 65 8 contains the word המשפש ("postern"),[83] of which the Aramaic counterpart occurs in 5Q15 1 i, line 8, one of the manuscripts containing the New Jerusalem text. Since that composition depends in part on Ezekiel 40-48, the use of this same term in 4Q391 in the context of measurements confirms the association of at least frg. 65 with Ezekiel 40-48. Another intriguing feature of 4Q391 is the use of four dots to represent the tetragrammaton.[84]

7. DANIEL

At least in the sectarian texts from Qumran Daniel was clearly recognized as a prophet. 4Q174 4:3 speaks of "that which is written in the book of Daniel the prophet."

Compared with the prophets discussed so far, the non-canonical materials from the Qumran caves which can be associated with Daniel are distinctive even if only because all of them are written in

---

[79] "391. 4QpapPseudo-Ezekiel^e," in Broshi et al. (eds.), *Qumran Cave 4.XIV* (DJD 19) 153-93.

[80] Frgs. 15, 20, 36, 39(?), 40 41, 51, 52, 55, 65, 67.

[81] כבוד (frg. 62, line 2); כרב (frg. 16 2); כבר (frg. 65 4), the river which occurs exclusively in Ezekiel in the Bible.

[82] Egypt (frg. 1, line 2; 4Q385 24 4); Abaddon (frg. 25 4; 4Q385 24, lines 2, 5-6); קרא בשמך (frg. 62 3; cf. 4Q385 2 2; 42 3; 4Q387 2 5).

[83] See the discussion of this term in F. García Martínez, *Qumran and Apocalyptic* (STDJ 9; Leiden: Brill, 1992) 188-89.

[84] Cf. 1QIsa^a 33:7^cor; 1QS 8:14; 4QSam^c 1, line 3, frg. 9, frg. 10; 4Q175 lines 1 and 19; 4Q176 1-2 i 6, 7, 9; ii 3; 10 6, 8, 10; 4Q462 1 7, 12.

Aramaic. Five or six Aramaic manuscripts can be associated with the Book of Daniel.[85]

7.1 4QPrayer of Nabonidus ar (4Q242) [86]

The so-called "Prayer of Nabonidus" (4Q242) has been known since 1956 when Milik published most of it.[87] With allowance for a margin of error, the manuscript dates from the second quarter of the first century BCE . The first fully extant line of the principal column begins with the title: "The words of the p[ra]yer which Nabonidus, king of [Baby]lon, [the great]king, prayed." The text continues with a narrative in the first person which provides the setting and reason for the prayer; nothing of the prayer itself has survived. Much of the debate in reading and restoring the text has centered on how far apart frgs. 1 and 2 should be placed. In describing how a sick person is restored to health through the appropriate acknowledgment of God, the story has affinity with some wisdom tales,[88] and in providing a hostile view of idolatry, it is a wisdom text with a polemic that asserts the sovereignty of God even over Gentiles.

Two further matters of interpretation have especially exercised scholars. The first concerns the relationship of the text both to Babylonian sources and also to Daniel 4. Nabonidus was the last king of Babylon (556-39 BCE). According to the Nabonidus Chronicle, for ten years he absented himself from Babylon and resided at Teima in Arabia; other sources strongly suggest this was because of opposition from the priests of Babylon. Whilst 4Q242 agrees with the Babylonian sources that it was Nabonidus who was in exile at

---

[85] F. García Martínez (*Qumran and Apocalyptic*, 149-60) has provided a survey of many of the later apocryphal texts associated with Daniel, none of which corresponds directly with the Qumran Aramaic texts linked to Daniel.

[86] The principal edition is by J. J. Collins, "242. 4QPrayer of Nabonidus ar," in G. Brooke et al. (eds.), *Qumran Cave 4.XVII* (DJD 22) 83-93. The bibliography on 4Q242 is extensive; to begin with see the list under "Previous discussion" in Collins' edition and the studies indexed for 4Q242 in F. García Martínez and D. W. Parry, *A Bibliography of the Finds in the Desert of Judah 1970-1995* (STDJ 19; Leiden: Brill, 1996) 521.

[87] J. T. Milik, "'Prière de nabonide' et autres écrits d'un cycle de Daniel: fragments araméens de Qumrân," *RB* 63 (1956) 407-15.

[88] See, for example, M. Delcor, "Le Testament de Job, la prière de Nabonide et les traditions targoumiques," *Religion d'Israël et Proche Orient Ancien: des Phéniciens aux Esséniens* (Leiden: Brill, 1976) 201-18.

Teima, in other respects it is closer to Daniel 4. As in 4Q242, in Daniel 4 the story of Nebuchadnezzar's madness is recounted largely in the first person, the Babylonian king is exiled for seven years (not ten), and the story features a Jewish intermediary. It thus seems as if actual historical circumstances involving Nabonidus have been recast by the author of Daniel 4; we may conclude that 4Q242 stands midway between the Babylonian traditions and Daniel 4, sharing features with both.

The second matter of debate concerns the role and function of the Jew. The key phrases are to be found at the beginning of line 4: וחטאי שבק לה גזר והוא יהדי מ[ן][89] The end of the previous line is not extant, though very probably God was mentioned there, and yet a scholarly consensus has emerged which prefers to understand God as the subject of שבק. This avoids the somewhat problematic proposal that the Jew of line 4 is able to pardon sins. The first three words of line 4 can then be taken together, "and as for my sin, he (God) remitted it."[90] This understanding then leaves גזר as the subject of what follows. What is a גזר? Despite the arguments put forward by A. Dupont-Sommer for the meaning "exorcist,"[91] since the root meaning is "cut," it is preferable to opt for some such translation as "diviner" (cf. Dan 2:27; 4:4; 5:7, 11). Thus this line in the king's narration of his circumstances may most suitably be understood as implying that it was God who forgave the king his sins and that the diviner, a Jew, had a role in encouraging the king to acknowledge and pray to God, so that his having been forgiven could become a reality in his being healed.

---

[89] It is preferable to read גזר with most scholars, despite the suggestion that גיר would make for an easier or preferable contextual reading; see A. Lange and M. Sieker, "Gattung und Quellenwert des Gebets des Nabonid," in H. J. Fabry et al. (eds.), *Qumranstudien: Vorträge und Beiträge der Teilnehmer des Qumranseminars auf dem internationalen Treffen der SBL, Münster, 25.-26. Juli 1993* (SIJD 4; Göttingen: Vandenhoeck & Ruprecht, 1996) 24. גיר is never written with *yod* in other scrolls from Qumran.

[90] As proposed by (amongst others) A. S. van der Woude, "Bemerkungen zum Gebet des Nabonid," in M. Delcor (ed.), *Qumrân: sa piété, sa théologie et son milieu* (BETL 46; Paris-Gembloux: Duculot, 1978) 124-25; P. Grelot, "La prière de Nabonide (4QOrNab)," *RevQ* 9 (1977-78) 483-95; F. M. Cross, "Fragments of the Prayer of Nabonidus," *IEJ* 34 (1984) 260-64.

[91] A. Dupont-Sommer, "Exorcismes et guérisons dans les écrits de Qoumrân," in *Congress Volume: Oxford, 1959* (VTSup 7; Leiden: Brill, 1960) 256-8.

7.2 4QPseudo-Daniel^{a-c} ar (4Q243-245) [92]

Three fragmentary manuscripts in Aramaic which mention Daniel have been labelled Pseudo-Daniel. Two of them (4Q243 and 4Q244) overlap and so contain various parts of the same composition; the third (4Q245) seems closely related and is suitably associated with the other two.[93]

4Q243 consists of forty small fragments in a Herodian hand; the largest contains but a few words from five lines. Fourteen small framents are assigned to the Herodian manuscript 4Q244; its frg. 12 overlaps with 4Q243 frg. 13. Partly at the suggestion of others, the editors of these two manuscripts have proposed that the composition reflected in them comprises two parts, a court setting and then a review of history. The several fragments mentioning Daniel (4Q243 1, line 1; 2 1; 5 1; and 6 3; 4Q244 4 2; 4Q245 1 i 3), one of which also mentions Belshazzar (4Q243 2:2), are plausibly ascribed to the description of the court setting which, amongst other matters, seems to contain a dialogue between Daniel and the king. The historical review can be divided into four eras: the primaeval history (Enoch, Noah, Mount Lubar, the tower), from the patriarchs to the exile (Abraham?, Egypt, four hundred years, crossing the Jordan, Qahat, Phinehas, Abishua, Nebuchadnezzar, the Chaldaeans), the Hellenistic era (Balakros), and the eschatological period which the author presumably envisages as initiated in his own time. It is difficult to suggest when this eschatological period might begin, and thus to propose when this Pseudo-Daniel text might have been composed.[94] 4Q243 frg. 28 provides the most likely evidence for associating both 4Q243 and 4Q244 with 4Q245: the fragment seems to refer to Qahat, Phinehas and Abishua who are mentioned in the priestly genealogy of 1 Chron 5:27-6:15 (Eng. 6:1-30).

4Q245 is extant in only four Herodian fragments, of which frg. 2 seems to describe eschatological matters, including the destruction of

---

[92] The principal edition is by J. J. Collins and P. W. Flint, "Pseudo-Daniel," in Brooke et al. (eds.), *Qumran Cave 4.XVII* (DJD 22), 95-164.

[93] On 4Q243 and 4Q244, see J. J. Collins, "*Pseudo-Daniel* Revisited," *RevQ* 17 (1996) 111-35; and on 4Q245 see P. W. Flint, "4QPseudo-Daniel ar^c (4Q245) and the Restoration of the Priesthood," *RevQ* 17 (1996) 137-50.

[94] F. García Martínez (*Qumran and Apocalyptic*, 147) has reckoned that the composition post-dates Daniel itself, but he does not offer any reasons why this should be so.

wickedness, in which the Hasmonean house may be implicated. Daniel is mentioned in frg. 1: apparently he has a book in which are written firstly the names of the priests or high priests from Levi to the time of Jonathan and Simon,[95] then the names of the kings from David onwards. Since Simon is to be identified with Jonathan Maccabee's successor, it is clear that the date of composition of this text must be after 142 BCE.

7.3 4QDaniel Apocryphon ar (4Q246) [96]

This composition is extant on a single fragment whose hand is dated to the last half of the first century BCE. The ends of the nine lines of column one are extant and the whole of column two. Though the seer is not named in what remains, the text resembles the apocalyptic section of the Book of Daniel. It seems as if the seer has come before a king to interpret his vision. The interpretation speaks of wars involving Assyria and Egypt and the coming of an ultimate ruler who will be called, or call himself, Son of God and Son of the Most High. During his rule there will be much violence. Finally the people of God will arise and all will rest from the sword; here are phrases such as "its kingdom is an everlasting kingdom" (ii, line 5) and "his sovereignty will be an everlasting sovereignty" (ii, line 9) which are especially reminiscent of Dan 3:33; 7:27; 4:31 and 7:14.

Puech has identified four interrelated issues that perplex the text's interpreters. First, there is the need to decide if the violence depicted has an actual historical referent or is purely eschatological. For actual history, the mention of Egypt and Assyria might be understood as reflecting events during the Seleucid and Ptolemaic period, as J. T. Milik originally proposed. For an eschatological scenario, the same pair are understood archetypically in light of their

---

[95] Cf. P. W. Flint, "The Daniel Tradition at Qumran," in Craig A. Evans and Peter W. Flint (eds.), *Eschatology, Messianism, and the Dead Sea Scrolls* (SDSRL 1; Grand Rapids: Eerdmans, 1997) 41–60, esp. 51-55.

[96] The principal edition is by É. Puech, "246. 4QApocryphe de Daniel ar," in Brooke et al. (eds.), *Qumran Cave 4.XVII* (DJD 22) 165-84; see also É. Puech, "Fragment d'une apocalypse en araméen (4Q246 = pseudoDan^d) et le 'Royaume de Dieu'," *RB* 99 (1992) 98-131; idem, "Notes sur le fragment d'apocalypse 4Q246-'le fils de Dieu'," *RB* 101 (1994) 533-58. The bibliography on 4Q246 is extensive; to begin with, see the list under "Publication préliminaire" in Puech's edition (and p. 165, n.1) and the studies indexed for 4Q242 in García Martínez and Parry, *A Bibliography...1970-1995*, 521.

use in 1QM 1:2-4[97] as participants in the last battles. If the author's own historical experiences are understood as the first stages of the eschaton, then there may be veracity in both views.

More problematic is the identification of the Son of God or Son of the Most High. Those who suggest that the battles depicted are real, also understand the figure behind these titles as an actual king. In his first pronouncement on the text, J. T. Milik proposed that this figure was Alexander Balas;[98] Puech has allowed for this possibility or preferably that the text may refer to Antiochus Epiphanes.[99] More scholars have tended towards understanding the text eschatologically and have then been faced with the challenge as to whether the Son of God should be viewed as good or bad, as heavenly or earthly. There have been proposals that this figure is the messiah,[100] the antichrist,[101] or the archangel Michael or Melchizedek,[102] or some

---

[97] It has often been recognized that the War Scroll itself is to some extent an elaboration of themes which occur in the Book of Daniel; see, for example, A. Mertens, *Das Buch Daniel im Lichte der Texte vom Toten Meer* (Stuttgart: Echter Verlag, 1971).

[98] Reported in J. A. Fitzmyer, "The Contribution of Qumran Aramaic to the Study of the New Testament," *NTS* 20 (1973-74) 382-407; reprinted in idem, *A Wandering Aramean: Collected Aramaic Essays* (SBLMS 25; Missoula, MT: Scholars Press, 1979) 85-113.

[99] É. Puech, "Notes sur le fragment d'apocalypse 4Q246" *RB* 101 (1994) 533-58; idem, "246. 4QApocryphe de Daniel ar," 183-84.

[100] Cf. Luke 1:32-35. See J. J. Collins, *The Scepter and the Star: The Messiahs of the Dead Sea Scrolls and Other Ancient Literature* (New York: Doubleday, 1995) 154-72; F. M. Cross, "Notes on the Doctrine of the Two Messiahs at Qumran and the Extracanonical Daniel Apocalypse (4Q246)," in D. W. Parry and S. D. Ricks (eds.), *Current Research and Technological Developments on the Dead Sea Scrolls: Conference on the Texts from the Judean Desert, Jerusalem, 30 April 1995* (STDJ 20; Leiden: Brill, 1996) 1-13; and as an option, É. Puech, "246. 4QApocryphe de Daniel ar," 180-183. Collins suggests in particular that 4Q246 presents the Son of the Most High as an interpretation of the Son of Man in Daniel 7.

[101] D. Flusser, "The Hubris of the Antichrist in a Fragment from Qumran," *Immanuel* 10 (1980) 31-37; reprinted in idem, *Judaism and the Origins of Christianity* (Jerusalem: Magnes, 1988) 207-13.

[102] F. García Martínez, "4Q246: ¿Tipo del Anticristo o Libertador escatológico?," in V. Collado and E. Zurro Rodriguez (eds.), *El misterio de la Palabra: Homenaje a L. Alonso Schökel* (Madrid: Ediciones Cristiandad, 1983) 229-44; reprinted in idem, *Qumran and Apocalyptic*, 162-79.

future king of Israel;[103] in addition, in light of the corporate understanding of the Son of Man in Daniel 7, it has been suggested that the Son of God should be viewed as the symbolic representative of the people of God, mentioned in the second half of column two.[104]

Thirdly, in column two the third-person singular masculine suffix occurs several times. It is not clear whether its referent is the Son of God figure or the people of God. If the Son of God is understood both positively and corporately, then the roles of the representative figure and the people of God merge, but if he is viewed individualistically, then his roles are outlined distinctively in 4Q246 ii 5-9.

Lastly, there is the question of who is speaking and to whom. Although it is possible to imagine that the seer is before the divine throne, most scholars have considered him to be in the presence of a gentile king, as is often the setting in the Book of Daniel. Indeed, it is this similarity of setting together with certain phrases which suggests that the seer of this fragment might even be Daniel himself.

7.4 4QDaniel Susanna(?) ar (4Q551)

Amongst the additions to Daniel in the Greek traditions is the story of Susanna in which Daniel features as a young man. In 1981 J.T. Milik proposed that 4Q551, 4QDanSuz(?) ar, might be an Aramaic counterpart to the story of Susanna.[105] Only enough text is preserved on the three late first century BCE fragments to discern that a figure whose family line is given seems to be a judge and seems to play a significant role at a regular meeting of the court.

7.5 4QFour Kingdoms ar (4Q552, 4Q553) [106]

The remains of two very fragmentary manuscripts contain a further para-Danielic composition. 4Q552 and 4Q553 seem to

---

[103] J. A. Fitzmyer, "4Q246: The 'Son of God' Document from Qumran," *Bib* 74 (1993) 153-74.

[104] Suggested by M. Hengel, *The Son of God* (Philadelphia: Fortress Press, 1976) 44-45; and worked out in detail by A. Steudel, "The Eternal Reign of the People of God-Collective Expectations in Qumran Texts (4Q246 and 1QM)," *RevQ* 17 (1996) 507-25.

[105] J. T. Milik, "Daniel et Susanne à Qumrân," in M. Carrez, J. Doré and P. Grelot (eds.), *De la Tôrah au Messie: Mélanges Henri Cazelles* (Paris: Desclée, 1981) 337-59.

[106] Preliminary edition in K. Beyer, *Die aramäischen Texte vom Toten Meer: Ergänzungsband* (Göttingen: Vandenhoeck & Ruprecht, 1994) 108-109.

present a seer's narrative of his vision of an angel and four trees. At the command of the angel the seer seems to interrogate the trees one by one. Enough text survives for only one tree's identification as Babel to become plain. On that basis it is likely that the text is a metaphorical reworking of the story of the four empires in Daniel 7-8. God is called Most High as in Dan 7:18, 22, 25, 27.

7.6 4QpapApocalypse ar (4Q489) [107]

Eight small fragments in a first century CE hand are assigned to this papyrus manuscript which contains an Aramaic text. Frg. 1 contains either וחזותה or והזיתה twice, with which can be compared Dan 2:41; 4:8, 17. Only partial words survive in other fragments.

8. CONCLUSION

The list of compositions contained in this survey could easily be extended through the inclusion of several other manuscripts which are extant only in a single or small sets of fragments and which have not yet been fully assessed in light of this large range of parabiblical material which can be associated with one prophet or another.[108] Nevertheless this survey of parabiblical prophetic narratives is extensive enough to show that in the late Second Temple period there was extensive reflection on the lives, deeds and sayings of various biblical prophetic figures, both the literary prophets and others.

Several points are especially to be noted. First, the range of compositions discussed here shows that the range of genres within both the former and latter prophets was fully exploited during the Second Temple period. Some traditions about prophetic figures were presented as narratives with the prophet described in the third person, some traditions are presented in poetry, some were dialogues between the prophet and God, and some were speeches of admonition or comfort addressed to Israel (often envisaged as in exile).

Secondly, all these parabiblical prophetic narratives relate to the scriptural texts concerning these prophetic figures in a variety of

---

[107] M. Baillet, *Qumrân Grotte 4,III (4Q482-4Q520)* (DJD 7) 10-11.

[108] Amongst manuscripts that could be added to this survey are the so-called "Apocryphal Prophecy" (6Q12), a single fragment which has some phraseology reminiscent of parts of Jeremiah and which speaks of jubilees; and the seven fragments of 4QNarrative C (4Q462), of which the principal piece describes the future restoration to Jerusalem of the exiled people.

ways. With respect to Moses, David, Elijah, Elisha, Jeremiah and Ezekiel, it seems that predominantly these compositions are dependent in various ways on the biblical text. Nevertheless, it is also clear that there are non-biblical elements to be found throughout this corpus, some of which emerge in later texts preserved amongst the better known apocrypha and pseudepigrapha. The range of Aramaic Danielic material is particularly instructive. Some items may best be considered as source material which was adapted for the Book of Daniel, some is parallel material which never became part of the Book, some is secondary and dependent on the biblical Book. On the basis of such a range of compositions, perhaps we should reconsider how all of the prophetic books came to be the way they are. They were not produced in a vacuum, nor always had pride of place. In their various forms they were the particular crystallizations of a set of traditions at certain times for certain purposes.

Thirdly, there is nothing in any of the literature discussed here which is especially sectarian. The sectarian interpretation of the prophets seems to have been reserved for the pesharim or for the secondary use of particular prophetic passages in compositions of an altogether different kind. In those compositions the sectarians were able to identify their own experiences as the actualizations of prophetic utterances understood as predictions. But all the non-sectarian compositions mentioned in this chapter show that many Jews in the Second Temple period had an intense interest in the prophets of old and sought to identify themselves as the heirs of what God had promised through them.

Yet, fourthly, despite all these compositions being non-sectarian, almost every text mentioned in this chapter is preserved on a manuscript which is from either the first century BCE or shortly afterwards. The actual manuscript copies of these compositions are all contemporary with the occupation of the Qumran site by the movement that seems to have been responsible for putting the manuscripts in the caves. Indeed, that most of them come from Cave 4, the community's working library, suggests that there was an active and ongoing interest in these compositions throughout the community's existence. Some may have been copied at Qumran, others brought there from elsewhere. Altogether, however, the presence and use of these compositions in the Qumran community need to be taken into account when their relationship to authoritative texts is discussed. Although none of these parabiblical prophetic narratives ever seems to be cited as an authority in any of the sectarian documents, unlike the works of the literary prophets themselves, clearly the scriptural narratives about the prophets from Moses to Daniel were not enough to satisfy the members' need to relate to the prophetic traditions of old. Indeed, that several copies of some of these compositions were present in the Qumran caves strongly suggests that they were not collected merely out of antiquarian interest.

SELECT BIBLIOGRAPHY

Bauckham, R. J. "A Quotation from *4QSecond Ezekiel* in the *Apocalypse of Peter*,"*RevQ* 15 (1991-92) 437-45.

Brooke, G. J. "Ezekiel in Some Qumran and New Testament Texts," in Trebolle Barrera and Vegas Montaner (eds.), *The Madrid Qumran Congress*, 317-37.

—. "The Book of Jeremiah and its Reception in the Qumran Scrolls," in A. H. W. Curtis and T. Römer (eds.), *The Book of Jeremiah and Its Reception* (BETL 128; Leuven: University Press/Peeters, 1997) 183-205.

Broshi, M. and A. Yardeni. "On the Netinim and the False Prophets," in Z. Zevit et al. (eds.), *Solving Riddles and Untying Knots: Biblical, Epigraphic, and Semitic Studies in Honor of Jonas C. Greenfield* (Winona Lake, IN: Eisenbrauns, 1995) 29-37 [Hebrew].

Collins, J. J. *The Scepter and the Star: The Messiahs of the Dead Sea Scrolls and Other Ancient Literature* (New York: Doubleday, 1995).

—. "*Pseudo-Daniel* Revisited,"*RevQ* 17 (1996) 111-35.

Cross, F. M. "Fragments of the Prayer of Nabonidus," *IEJ* 34 (1984) 260-64.

—. "Notes on the Doctrine of the Two Messiahs at Qumran and the Extracanonical *Daniel Apocalypse (4Q246)*," in D. W. Parry and S. D. Ricks (eds.), *Current Research and Technological Developments on the Dead Sea Scrolls: Conference on the Texts from the Judaean Desert, Jerusalem, 30 April 1995* (STDJ 20; Leiden: Brill, 1996) 1-13.

Delcor, M. "Le Testament de Job, la prière de Nabonide et les traditions targoumiques," in his *Religion d'Israël et Proche Orient Ancien: des Phéniciens aux Esséniens* (Leiden: Brill, 1976) 201-18.

Dimant, D. "New Light from Qumran on the Jewish Pseudepigrapha: 4Q390," in Trebolle Barrera and Vegas Montaner (eds.), *The Madrid Qumran Congress*, 405-48.

—. "The Apocalyptic Interpretation of Ezekiel at Qumran," in I. Grunewald et al. (eds.), *Messiah and Christos: Studies in the Jewish Origins of Christianity Presented to David Flusser* (Tübingen: Mohr-Siebeck, 1992) 31-51.

—. "An Apocryphon of Jeremiah from Cave 4 (4Q385^B=4Q385 16)," in G. J. Brooke et al. (eds.), *New Qumran Texts and Studies: Proceedings of the First*

Meeting of the International Organization for Qumran Studies, Paris 1992 (STDJ 15; Leiden: Brill, 1994) 11-31.

—. "ציטטה מנחום ג-חי בקטע 4Q385–6," ["A Quotation from Nahum 3:8-10 in 4Q385–6"], in S. Japhet; (ed.), "מקומראן" המקרא בראי מפרשיו ספר זיכרון לשרה קמין [*The Bible in the Light of Its Interpreters: Sarah Kamin Memorial Volume*] (Jerusalem: Magnes Press, 1994) 31-37.

Dimant, D, and J. Strugnell. "The Merkabah Vision in Second Ezekiel (4Q385 4)," *RevQ* 14 (1989) 331-48.

Dupont-Sommer, A. "Exorcismes et guérisons dans les écrits de Qoumrân," in *Congress Volume: Oxford, 1959* (VTSup 7; Leiden: Brill, 1960) 246-61.

Fitzmyer, J. A. "4Q246: The 'Son of God' Document from Qumran," *Bib* 74 (1993) 153-74.

Flint, P. W. "4QPseudo-Daniel ar[c] (4Q245) and the Restoration of the Priesthood," *RevQ* 17 (1996) 137-50.

—. "The Daniel Tradition at Qumran," in Craig A. Evans and Peter W. Flint (eds.), *Eschatology, Messianism, and the Dead Sea Scrolls* (SDSRL 1; Grand Rapids: Eerdmans, 1997) 41–60.

Flusser, D. "The Hubris of the Antichrist in a Fragment from Qumran," *Immanuel* 10 (1980) 31-37.

Fohrer, G. "4QOrNab, 11QTgJob und die Hioblegende," *ZAW* 75 (1963) 93-97.

Freedman, D. N. "The Prayer of Nabonidus," *BASOR* 145 (1957) 31-32.

García Martínez, F. "4QSecond Ezequiel y las Tradiciones Apocalípticas," in J. Carreira das Nuevas et al. (eds.), *III Simposio Bíblico Español* (Valencia: Fundación Bíblica Española, 1987) 477-88.

—. "Tradiciones apocalípticas en Qumrán: 4QSecond Ezekiel," in A. Viviano (ed.), *Biblische und judaistische Studien: Festschrift für Paolo Sacchi* (Frankfurt: Lang, 1990) 303-21.

—. *Qumran and Apocalyptic: Studies on the Aramaic Texts from Qumran* (STDJ 9; Leiden: Brill, 1992).

Grelot, P. "La prière de Nabonide (4QOrNab)," *RevQ* 9 (1977-78) 483-95.

Kister, M. "Barnabas 12:1; 4:3 and 4QSecond Ezekiel," *RB* 97 (1990) 63-67.

Kister, M. and E. Qimron. "Observations on *4QSecond Ezekiel (4Q385 2-3)*," *RevQ* 15 (1991-92) 595-602.

Lange, A. and M. Sieker. "Gattung und Quellenwert des Gebets des Nabonid," in H. J. Fabry et al. (eds.), *Qumranstudien: Vorträge und Beiträge der Teilnehmer des Qumranseminars auf dem internationalen Treffen der SBL, Münster, 25.-26. Juli 1993* (SIJD 4; Göttingen: Vandenhoeck & Ruprecht, 1996) 3-34.

Larson, E., L. H. Schiffman, and J. Strugnell. "*4Q470*, Preliminary Publication of a Fragment Mentioning Zedekiah," *RevQ* 16 (1993-95) 335-49.

Mertens, A. *Das Buch Daniel im Lichte der Texte vom Toten Meer* (SBM 12; Stuttgart: Echter, 1971).

Meyer, R. *Das Gebet des Nabonid: Eine in den Qumran-Handschriften wiederentdeckte Weisheitserzählung* (Berlin: Akademie, 1962).
Milik, J. T. "'Prière de nabonide' et autres écrits d'un cycle de Daniel: fragments araméens de Qumrân," *RB* 63 (1956) 407-15.
Philonenko, M. "Un arbre se coubera et se redressera (4Q385:2 9-10)," *RHPR* 73 (1993) 401-404.
—. "De Qoumrân à Doura-Europos: la vision des ossements desséchés (Ézéchiel 37,1-4)," *RHPR* 74 (1994) 1-12.
Puech, É. "Fragment d'une apocalypse en araméen (4Q246 = pseudoDan^d) et le 'Royaume de Dieu'," *RB* 99 (1992) 98-131.
—. "Notes sur le fragment d'apocalypse 4Q246-'le fils de Dieu'," *RB* 101 (1994) 533-58.
—. "L'image de l'arbre en 4QDeutéro-Ezéchiel (*4Q385* 2, 9-10)," *RevQ* 16 (1993-95) 429-40.
Steudel, A. "The Eternal Reign of the People of God-Collective Expectations in Qumran Texts (*4Q246* and *1QM*)," *RevQ* 17 (1996) 507-25.
Strugnell, J. "Moses-Pseudepigrapha at Qumran: 4Q375, 4Q376, and Similar Works," in L. H. Schiffman (ed.), *Archaeology and History in the Dead Sea Scrolls: The New York Conference in Memory of Yigael Yadin* (JSPSup 8; Sheffield: Sheffield Academic Press, 1990) 221-56.
Strugnell, J. and D. Dimant. "4QSecond Ezekiel (4Q385)," *RevQ* 13 (1988) 45-58.
Trebolle Barrera, J. "Histoire du texte des livres historiques et histoire de la composition et de la rédaction deutéronomistes avec une publication préliminaire de 4Q481a, 'Apocryphe d'Élisée'," in J. A. Emerton (ed.), *Congress Volume, Paris 1992* (VTSup 61; Leiden: Brill, 1995) 327-42.
Trebolle Barrera. J. and L. Vegas Montaner (eds.). *The Madrid Qumran Congress: Proceedings of the International Congress on the Dead Sea Scrolls, Madrid 18-21 March 1991* (STDJ 11; Leiden: Brill, 1992).
Woude, A.S. van der. "Bemerkungen zum Gebet des Nabonid," in M. Delcor (ed.), *Qumrân: sa piété, sa théologie et son milieu* (BETL 46; Paris-Gembloux: Duculot, 1978) 121-29.

THE COPPER SCROLL

AL WOLTERS

The Copper Scroll (3Q15) has been called "the most difficult of all the Qumran texts,"[1] and is in many ways also the most puzzling and intriguing. It consists of a list of hidden treasures, inscribed in Hebrew on thin copper sheets. The text breaks down into sixty-four sections, each typically describing a hiding-place and the treasure to be found there. The hiding-places that are listed appear to be mainly in and around Jerusalem, and the treasure described is enormous, consisting of many tons of silver and gold, as well as other valuables. Many of these treasures are cultic items, and may well have a connection with the temple in Jerusalem.

The Copper Scroll was discovered in Cave 3 (about 2 kilometers north of Qumran) on March 20, 1952, by archaeologists working under the joint auspices of the American School of Oriental Research, the École Biblique et Archéologique Française de Jérusalem, and the Palestine Archaeological Museum. Since 1956, the Copper Scroll has been housed in the Archaeological Museum of Amman, Jordan.

1. DISTINCTIVE FEATURES

The Copper Scroll stands out from all the other Dead Sea Scrolls in several distinctive ways.

1.1 Writing material

Whereas the other texts are written on parchment or papyrus, the Copper Scroll is inscribed on copper sheets. The original scroll consisted of three copper sheets that had been riveted together, but it was discovered in two rolled-up pieces. Apparently one of these three sheets had become detached before the scroll was rolled up and hidden. The metal is of exceptional purity (99% copper) and thinness (about 1 millimeter), and must have have been very costly. We may

---

[1] Klaus Beyer, *Die aramäischen Texte vom Toten Meer. Ergänzungsband* (Göttingen: Vandenhoeck & Ruprecht, 1994) 224-33, esp. 224.

conclude that 3Q15 is a replica of a standard parchment scroll because of the size of the sheets (roughly 30 by 80 cm each), as well as the manner in which they were attached to each other and inscribed in columns. It is unclear why copper was chosen as the medium on which this text was inscribed; the choice may have been dictated by considerations of durability or ritual purity.

The uniqueness of the writing material had two important consequences. First, the text of the Copper Scroll was not so much "written" by a trained scribe as "engraved" by one or more metalworkers, who may themselves have been illiterate. The letters of the text appear to have been hammered into the copper with a punch (each letter requiring several blows), with the result that they show through on the reverse side of the thin copper. Second, during the period of almost two thousand years that the scroll lay hidden, the copper was completely oxidized. This means not only that some parts of the scroll were completely destroyed by corrosion, but also that its two rolled-up pieces could not be unrolled without destroying them.

1.2 The Script

The palaeographical analysis of the Copper Scroll is complicated by the fact that the engraver or engravers were themselves probably illiterate, copying from a *Vorlage*. As a result, the shape of the writing looks rough and unpracticed, and many look-alike letters of the Hebrew alphabet are not distinguished at all, notably *bet* and *kap*, *dalet* and *reš*, *he* and *ḥet*, *waw* and *yod*. Despite these irregularities, it is possible to classify the script of the Copper Scroll as a "vulgar semiformal" variety of the late Herodian script. There are some indications that the *Vorlage* used cursive forms, and that the hands of different engravers are discernible in the writing of the scroll. Because so many graphically similar letters are confused in the script of the Copper Scroll, it is often difficult to establish the correct reading of a word, even for words where all the letters have been preserved intact. For example, the last four letters of line 3 of Column II are usually read as רובד ("landing" or "ledge"), but J. T. Milik reads them as דביר, a putative variant of דְּבִיר ("recess"). In fact, this four-letter sequence of characters could in principle represent sixteen permutations—quite a number of which spell possible Hebrew words.

1.3 Orthography

The Copper Scroll has its own brand of Hebrew spelling, which conforms to neither the "Qumran orthography" that is characteristic of many of the literary Dead Sea Scrolls, nor to any other standard orthography. Some notable features are the use of *ʾalep* instead of *he* to represent a final long –āh (e.g. חומא, "wall," in col. 2:10), the use of *samek* instead of *śin* (e.g. עסר, "ten" in 2:9), and the occasional dropping of gutturals (e.g. מרב for מערב, "west," in 12:1).

1.4 Subject-Matter

Whereas almost all the other Dead Sea Scrolls contain material that can be broadly classified as "religious" or "literary," the Copper Scroll appears to be an administrative document which simply enumerates, in a dry bookkeeping style, a series of physical locations and the valuables that are hidden there. In connection with its bookkeeping character, it should be noted that the Copper Scroll is one of the very few *autographs* among the Dead Sea Scrolls. Almost all the others, heterogeneous though they may be, appear to be copies of works belonging to a religious or literary canon.

1.5 Language

The Copper Scroll is written in an early form of Mishnaic Hebrew, and thus constitutes an invaluable linguistic link between Late Biblical Hebrew and the language of the Mishnah. Its affinity with Mishnaic Hebrew can be demonstrated in the areas of morphology (e.g. ין- instead of ים- as the regular masculine plural ending), of syntax (e.g. the frequent use of שֶׁל to indicate the genitival relationship), and of vocabulary (some fifty items illustrate words or usages that are characteristic of Mishnaic Hebrew). Another feature which it shares with Mishnaic Hebrew—and which sets it off from the literary Hebrew of the other scrolls—is the frequent use of Greek loanwords (e.g. פרסטלין for περιστύλιον, "peristyle," in 1:7). The language of the Copper Scroll, therefore, constitutes important evidence that there was a form of Hebrew used around the turn of the era that already had clearly Mishnaic features, and that this Hebrew differed significantly from the classical language used in literary works. Linguistically speaking, the closest analogue to the Copper Scroll among the Dead Sea Scrolls is 4QMMT, although the latter still differs in important respects from Mishnaic Hebrew (e.g. the absence of ין- and שֶׁל).

1.6 Literary Structure

Although the Copper Scroll is not "literary" in the sense of belonging to *belles lettres*, its content is organized in accordance with a very specific structure. In an unvarying pattern, the sixty-four sections present material in the following order:

    (a) A designation of a hiding place ("Place")
    (b) A further specification of the hiding place ("Specification")
    (c) A command to dig or measure ("Command")
    (d) A distance expressed in cubits ("Distance")
    (e) A treasure description ("Treasure")
    (f) Additional comments ("Comments")
    (g) Greek letters ("Greek")

Each of these standard components has stereotypical features of its own. For example, the second component regularly begins with ש plus a preposition, and the fourth typically consists of the word אמות ("cubits"), followed by a number written out in full. Although no section includes all seven components, a section is always filled in the order indicated. As a result, the text as a whole reads very much like a bookkeeper's ledger (cf. the accompanying chart: "The Text of the Copper Scroll Arranged in Columns").[2]

1.7 Greek Letters

The seventh component consists of two or three Greek letters,[3] and is found in only seven of the sixty-four sections, all of them in the first four columns. Although various theories have been offered to explain the presence of these Greek letters, they remain an enigma. It may be significant that they may in each case be the beginning of a Greek proper name.

2. MAKING THE TEXT AVAILABLE

Another way in which the Copper Scroll is unique is the manner in which it was initially opened for reading, and its text was subsequently published.

2.1 Opening the Scroll

Following their discovery in 1952, the two rolled-up pieces of the scroll remained unopened for three and a half years; they could not be unrolled, since the oxidized copper crumbled to the touch. During

---

[2] The Chart appears at the end of this article.
[3] For example, in sections 1 and 6.

this time, scientists searched in vain for a way to reconstitute the original copper, so that the scroll could be unrolled in the usual way. In the end, the two pieces were successively brought to Manchester in 1955 and 1956, where they were opened by being coated on the outside with an adhesive, and then cut into narrow strips by means of a small circular saw. After cleaning, the concave side of the resulting 23 curved segments of oxidized copper revealed the inscribed text. This delicate operation was successfully carried out by H. Wright Baker at the Manchester College of Science and Technology, who was advised and assisted by John Allegro of the University of Manchester, a member of the international team of scholars entrusted with the publication of the Dead Sea Scrolls. Allegro had arranged for the Copper Scroll to be brought from Jerusalem to Manchester, and was the first to transcribe and translate the Hebrew text as it became legible.

2.2 Publishing the Text

Although black-and-white photographs of the Copper Scroll segments have been published in DJD 3,[4] these are virtually illegible, both because the indented letters do not stand out visually from the surrounding oxidized and corroded copper, and because the curvature of the segments makes reading difficult. In the absence of legible photographs, the text of the Copper Scroll has been made available in the form of handdrawn facsimiles, of which three have been published. The first was prepared by the Jordanian artist Muhanna Durra, who copied directly from the twenty-three segments housed in Amman. This is the text that was published by Allegro in his 1960 book on the Copper Scroll.[5]

The second facsimile is that prepared by Wright Baker in Manchester, which was published in DJD 3 in 1962.[6] This was based on various photographs of each segment (which were taken from different angles), and was checked against the original, but without a knowledge of Hebrew. The third facsimile is a revision of the

---

[4] M. Baillet, J. T. Milik and R. de Vaux (eds.), *Les 'Petites Grottes' de Qumran. Textes* (DJD 3; Oxford: Clarendon Press, 1962) plates XLVI–XLVII, XLIX–LXXI.

[5] J. M. Allegro, *The Treasure of the Copper Scroll* (Garden City, NY: Doubleday, 1960).

[6] See Baillet, Milik, de Vaux (eds.), *Les 'Petites Grottes' de Qumran. Planches* (DJD 3) pl. XLV.

second, carried out by the expert Hebraist J. T. Milik, who also had an opportunity to consult the original in Amman. Milik's facsimile, which may be considered the most authoritative of the three, was also published in DJD 3.[7] However, the many divergences between the three published facsimiles still introduce a significant element of uncertainty in any detailed textual study of the Copper Scroll.

Given this situation, it is highly desirable that a reliable reproduction of the Copper Scroll text be made available as the basis for further scholarly study. Such a reliable reproduction was due to be published in 1997, as one of the results of the highly sophisticated restoration work on the Copper Scroll that was completed by the Electricité de France in 1996. Also awaiting publication are the new color photographs of the scroll which were taken by Bruce and Kenneth Zuckerman in 1988. Since the material of the scroll has suffered further deterioration since the time it was first opened in the mid-1950's, it is also important to recover the hundreds of photographs of the copper segments taken in Manchester at that time.

3. MAJOR ISSUES OF INTERPRETATION

Apart from many differences concerning questions of exegetical detail, scholarship on the Copper Scroll has been divided over three major issues which affect the overall interpretation of this enigmatic document.

3.1 Dating

Although F. M. Cross dated the script of the Copper Scroll to the period 25-75 CE in his paleographical excursus in DJD 3,[8] some scholars have rather relied on the later paleographical dating proposed by W. F. Albright in 1960, namely 70-135 CE. Depending on the dating chosen, it is thus possible to associate the Copper Scroll either with the First Jewish Revolt of 66-70, or the Second Jewish Revolt of 132-135—or the period in between.

The archeological evidence with respect to the dating question has also been interpreted in two different ways. If the Copper Scroll was deposited in Cave 3 at the same time as the fragmentary manuscripts

---

[7] See Baillet, Milik, de Vaux (eds.), *Les 'Petites Grottes' de Qumran. Textes* (DJD 3) pls XLVIII–LXX.

[8] Baillet, Milik, de Vaux (eds.), *Les 'Petites Grottes' de Qumran. Textes* (DJD 3) 217-21.

and broken pottery which were also discovered there, it must be dated to the time around 68 CE. According to William Reed, who reported on the discovery of the Copper Scroll in 1954,[9] it is "certain that the rolls were placed on the floor of the cave prior to 70 A.D." This has become the accepted view of most scholars. However, some have argued that the archeological evidence does not exclude the possibility that the Copper Scroll might have been deposited later—and therefore had nothing to do with the other artifacts in Cave 3.

3.2 Authenticity

From the moment that the text of the Copper Scroll first became known, there has been scholarly disagreement about its authenticity. Could the enormous amounts of gold and silver, some of it buried at a depth of 17 cubits (about 9.3 meters), really be seriously viewed as real treasure that was actually hidden in antiquity? Milik, followed by a number of other scholars, argued that they could not, and that the Copper Scroll therefore represents a kind of folklore, comparable to other legendary accounts of hidden treasure. The opposing viewpoint was taken by Allegro and others, who argued that a fictional account would not have been so laboriously inscribed on such expensive material, nor composed in such a dry bookkeeping style. Advocates of the latter view account for the high numbers in the scroll in different ways: either as historically plausible at face value, or as in fact representing smaller amounts. Most recent studies of the Copper Scroll have adopted the second, realistic view, partly because the legendary interpretation may originally have been influenced by political considerations, as well as a desire to discourage treasure-hunters.

3.3 Relation to the Other Scrolls

If the documents found in the caves near Qumran all belonged to the "library" of a quasi-monastic group residing at Qumran, then the Copper Scroll can reasonably be regarded as a product of that same community, and should be interpreted in this light. However, because the Copper Scroll is so distinctive in many respects, it has been argued that it was a later deposit which has no historical connection with the other scrolls found in the vicinity. Alternatively, if the

---

[9] "The Qumrân Caves Expedition of March, 1952", *BASOR* 135 (1954) 8-13, esp. 10.

Qumran scrolls are a heterogeneous collection emanating from Jerusalem, then the Copper Scroll may be of the same date as the other scrolls, but with no essential connection to them.

4. THE MAJOR THEORIES

Because of the varied answers which students of the Copper Scroll have offered on the questions of its date, its authenticity, and its relation to the other scrolls, a number of distinct theories of interpretation have emerged. The following six proposals may be classified under two main headings.[10]

4.1 Four Theories Assuming Authenticity

(a) The treasure is authentic, and belonged to the Qumran community before 70 CE. This view was defended in the 1950's by André Dupont-Sommer,[11] and more recently by Bargil Pixner (1983)[12] and Stephen Goranson (1992).[13]

(b) The treasure is authentic, and belonged to the temple in Jerusalem prior to 70 CE. Prominent defenders of this view in the 1950's and 1960's were Cecil Roth,[14] Karl Heinrich Rengstorf,[15] John Allegro[16] and Godfrey Driver.[17] This theory was revived in 1980 by Norman Golb,[18] who has since been followed on this point

---

[10] See Al Wolters, "History and the Copper Scroll," in M. O. Wise et al. (ed.), *Methods of Investigation of the Dead Sea Scrolls and the Khirbet Qumran Site: Present Realities and Future Prospects* (Annals of the New York Academy of Sciences 722; New York: New York Academy of Sciences, 1994) 285-98, esp. 285-92.

[11] A. Dupont-Sommer, "Les rouleaux de cuivre trouvés à Qoumrân," *Revue de l'histoire des religions* 151 (1957) 22-36, esp. 27-36.

[12] B. Pixner, "Unravelling the Copper Scroll Code: A Study of the Topography of 3Q15," *RevQ* 11 (1983) 323-58, esp. 331-40.

[13] S. Goranson, "Sectarianism, Geography, and the Copper Scroll," *JJS* 43 (1992) 282-87, esp. 282.

[14] C. Roth, *The Historical Background of the Dead Sea Scrolls* (Oxford: Blackwell, 1958) 44-45, 67.

[15] K. H. Rengstorf, *Hirbet Qumran und die Bibliothek vom Toten Meer* (Studia Delitzschiana 5; Stuttgart: Kohlhammer, 1960) 26-28.

[16] J. M. Allegro, *The Treasure of the Copper Scroll*.

[17] G. R. Driver, *The Judaean Scrolls. The Problem and a Solution* (Oxford: Blackwell, 1965) 30-36.

[18] "The Problem of the Origin and Identification of the Dead Sea Scrolls," *Proceedings of the American Philosophical Society* 124 (Feb. 1980) 1-24, esp. 5-8.

by many scholars, including David Wilmot (1984),[19] P. Kyle McCarter, (1992),[20] Michael Wise (1994),[21] Al Wolters (1994),[22] and Judah Lefkovits (1997).[23]

(c) The treasure is authentic, and belonged to the Jewish rebels under Bar Kochba around 135 CE. This interpretation was put forward independently in the early 1960's, by the French scholar Ernest-Marie Laperrousaz and the Israeli scholar Ben-Zion Luria,[24] but they have had no followers.

(d) The treasure is authentic, and represents undelivered temple contributions following the destruction of the temple in 70 CE. This is the theory of Manfred Lehmann,[25] who believes the Copper Scroll can be dated to the period 70 to 90-92 CE.

4.2 Two Theories Assuming the Copper Scroll to be Legendary

(e) The treasure is legendary, and was part of the folklore of the Qumran community before 70 CE. This was the view of a number of scholars in the 1950's, including Frank M. Cross,[26] L. Silberman[27]

---

[19] D. Wilmot, "The Copper Scroll of Qumran (3Q15), and the Graeco-Roman Temple Inventories" (Abstract), in *AAR/SBL Abstracts* (Atlanta: Scholars Press, 1984) 214.

[20] See P. K. McCarter, Jr., "The Copper Scroll Treasure as an Accumulation of Religious Offerings," in M. O. Wise et al. (eds), *Methods of Investigation of the Dead Sea Scrolls and the Khirbet Qumran Site: Present Realities and Future Prospects* (ANYAS 722; New York: New York Academy of Sciences, 1994) 133-48.

[21] M. O. Wise, "The Copper Scroll," *Parabola. The Magazine of Myth and Tradition* 19 (1994) 44-52.

[22] A. Wolters, "History and the Copper Scroll," in Wise et al. (eds.), *Methods of Investigation of the Dead Sea Scrolls*, 285-98.

[23] J. K. Lefkovits, *The Copper Scroll--3Q15: A Reevaluation: A New Reading, Translation, and Commentary* (Leiden: Brill, 1997).

[24] E-M. Laperrousaz, "Remarques sur l'origine des rouleaux de cuivre découverts dans la grotte 3 de Qumran," *Revue de l'histoire des religions* 159 (1961) 157-72; B-Z. Luria, מגלת הנחשת ממדבר יהודה [*The Copper Scroll from the Desert of Judah*] (Jerusalem: Kiryath Sepher, 1963).

[25] M. R. Lehmann, "Identification of the Copper Scroll Based on its Technical Terms," *RevQ* 5 (1964) 97-105.

[26] F. M. Cross, Jr., "Excursus on the Palaeographical Dating of the Copper Document," in Baillet, Milik and de Vaux (eds.), *Les 'Petites Grottes' de Qumran. Textes* (DJD 3; Oxford: Clarendon, 1962) 217-21.

[27] L. H. Silberman, "A Note on the Copper Scroll," *VT* 10 (1960) 77-79.

and Sigmund Mowinckel.[28] Prior to 1959 it was also held by J. T. Milik[29] and Roland de Vaux.[30]

(f) The treasure is legendary, and was part of Jewish folklore around 100 CE, when the Copper Scroll was deposited in Cave 3. This view, which J. T. Milik adopted in 1959, is reflected in his authoritative edition of the Copper Scroll in DJD 3 (1962). In the 1960's, Milik's position was adopted by de Vaux and Manuel Augusto Rodrigues,[31] but by virtually no one thereafter.

5. EVALUATION

In assessing the various theories, it should be borne in mind that the burden of proof rests on those who assign a post-68 CE date to the Copper Scroll. It may be true (although this has been disputed by Pixner) that the archaeological evidence does not rule out the possibility that the Copper Scroll was deposited in Cave 3 after the other Cave 3 finds had been deposited there. However, there is no positive indication that this was in fact the case. In the absence of evidence to the contrary, it is methodologically preferable to assume that the material remains found in Cave 3 were all deposited there at the same time, probably around 68 CE. In other words, there is an inherently implausible aspect to theories (c), (d) and (f).

Furthermore, it is difficult to imagine any document that is less like folklore than the Copper Scroll, with its dry catalogue of locations and valuables. Moreover, attempts to classify it in that category can be shown to have an identifiable political background.[32] Such considerations count heavily against theories (e) and (f).

The weight of the evidence, therefore, seems to point to the theories designated (a) and (b) above: that the treasure is authentic, and belonged prior to 70 CE to either the Qumran community or the Jerusalem temple. Almost all recent scholarship on the Copper Scroll

---

[28] Sigmund Mowinckel, "The Copper Scroll—An Apocryphon?" *JBL* 76 (1957) 261-65.

[29] J. T. Milik, "The Copper Document from Cave III, Qumran," *BA* 19 (1956) 60-64.

[30] R. de Vaux, "Un communiqué relatif aux rouleaux de cuivre," *CRAIBL* (1956) 224-25.

[31] M. A. Rodrigues, "Aspectos linguísticos do documento de cobre de Qumran (3Q15)," *Biblos. Revista da Faculdade de Letras, Universidade de Coimbra* 39 (1963) 329-423.

[32] Al Wolters, "Apocalyptic and the Copper Scroll," *JNES* 49 (1990) 483-95.

(with the notable exceptions of Laperrousaz and Lehmann) has moved in this direction.

Two further considerations tip the scales in favor of linking the Copper Scroll with the Jerusalem temple rather than the Qumran community. The first is the enormous size of the treasure, which (if taken at face value) could only have come from the vast wealth of the temple itself. The second is the incidence of cultic terminology in the scroll, which is much higher than was previously recognized. Many terms in the Copper Scroll, especially in the treasure descriptions, identify specifically temple-related items. Examples include: מעסר שני ("second tithe") in col. 1:10 and מנקיאות ("libation bowls") in 3:3.

If the treasure of the Copper Scroll is indeed part of the legendary wealth of the Second Temple, and if it was hidden shortly before the destruction of the temple in 70 CE, then the most likely historical context for the scroll and its treasure is the military conflict between the Romans and the Zealot-led Jewish forces in Jerusalem.

SELECT BIBLIOGRAPHY

Allegro, J. M. *The Treasure of the Copper Scroll* (Garden City, NY: Doubleday, 1960).

Beyer, K. *Die aramäischen Texte vom Toten Meer. Ergänzungsband* (Göttingen: Vandenhoeck & Ruprecht, 1994) 224-33 [contains a German translation of the Copper Scroll].

Brooke, G. J. and P. R. Davies. *Copper Scroll Studies: Papers Presented at the International Symposium on the Copper Scroll, Manchester, September 1996* (JSPSup series; Sheffield: Sheffield Acadenic Press, 1998).

Driver, G. R. *The Judaean Scrolls. The Problem and a Solution* (Oxford: Blackwell, 1965) 30-36.

Golb, N. "The Problem of the Origin and Identification of the Dead Sea Scrolls," *Proceedings of the American Philosophical Society* 124 (Feb. 1980) 1-24, esp. 5-8.

Greenfield, J. "The Small Caves of Qumran," *JAOS* 89 (1969) 128-41, esp. 135-41.

Lefkovits, J. K. *The Copper Scroll—3Q15: A Reevaluation: A New Reading, Translation, and Commentary* (Leiden: Brill, 1997).

Lehmann, M. R. "Identification of the Copper Scroll Based on its Technical Terms," *RevQ* 5 (1964) 97-105.

Luria, B-Z. מגלת הנחשת ממדבר יהודה [*The Copper Scroll from the Desert of Judah*] (Jerusalem: Kiryath Sepher, 1963).

McCarter, P. Kyle, Jr. "The Copper Scroll Treasure as an Accumulation of Religious Offerings," in M. O. Wise et al. (eds). *Methods of Investigation of the Dead Sea Scrolls and the Khirbet Qumran Site: Present Realities and Future Prospects* (ANYAS 722; New York: New York Academy of Sciences, 1994) 133-48.

Milik, J. T. "Le rouleau de cuivre provenant de la grotte 3Q (3Q15)," in M. Baillet, J. T. Milik and R. de Vaux (eds.), *Les 'petites grottes' de Qumrân* (DJD 3; Oxford: Clarendon Press, 1962) 200- 302.

Pixner, B. "Unravelling the Copper Scroll Code: A Study of the Topography of 3Q15," *RevQ* 11 (1983) 323-58.

Vaux, R. de. "Un communiqué relatif aux rouleaux de cuivre," *CRAIBL* (1956) 224-25.

Wilmot, D. "The Copper Scroll of Qumran (3Q15), and the Graeco-Roman Temple Inventories" (Abstract), in *AAR/SBL Abstracts* (Atlanta: Scholars Press, 1984) 214.

Wise, M. O. "The Copper Scroll," *Parabola. The Magazine of Myth and Tradition* 19 (1994) 44-52.

Wolters, A. "The Copper Scroll and the Vocabulary of Mishnaic Hebrew," *RevQ* 14 (1990) 483-95.

—. "Apocalyptic and the Copper Scroll," *JNES* 49 (1990) 483-95.

—. "Literary Analysis and the Copper Scroll," in Z. J. Kapera (ed.). *Intertestamental Essays in Honour of Józef Tadeusz Milik. Vol. 1* (Kracow: Enigma Press, 1992) 239-52.

—. "History and the Copper Scroll," in M. O. Wise et al. (eds.). *Methods of Investigation of the Dead Sea Scrolls and the Khirbet Qumran Site: Present Realities and Future Prospects* (Annals of the New York Academy of Sciences 722; New York: New York Academy of Sciences, 1994) 285-98.

—. *The Copper Scroll: Overview, Text and Translation* (Sheffield: Sheffield Academic Press, 1996).

—. "Paleography and Literary Structure as Guides to Reading the Copper Scroll," in George J. Brooke (ed.), *Proceedings of the International Symposium on the Copper Scroll held in Manchester, September 8-11, 1996* (Sheffield: Sheffield Academic Press [forthcoming]).

THE TEXT OF THE COPPER

Place	Specification	Command
1. In the ruins	which are in the Valley of Achor, under the steps which go eastward,	
2. In the sepulchre of Ben Rabbah the Third:		
3. In the big cistern	in the court of the peristyle, in a recess of its bottom which is plugged up with sediment, across from the upper opening:	
4. In the ruin-heap	of Koḥlit:	
5. In the plastered cistern	of Manos, on the way down to the left, three cubits high from the bottom:	
6. In the salt pit	which is under the steps:	
7. In the cave of the old Washer's Chamber,	on the third ledge:	
8. In the vault	which is in the court there is donated firewood, in the midst of which, in the recess:	
9. In the cistern	which is across from the Eastern Gate, at a distance of nineteen cubits:	
10.	And in the conduit leading into it:	
11. In the cistern	which is under the wall on the east, in the tooth of the cliff:	
12. In the pond	which is on the east of Koḥlit, in the northern corner,	dig
13. In the court of…,	under the southern corner,	

SCROLL ARRANGED IN COLUMNS

Distance	Treasure	Comments	Greek
forty rod-cubits:	a strongbox of silver and its vessels	—a weight of seventeen talents.	KEN
	100 ingots of gold.		
	nine hundred talents.		
	vessels of tribute of the master of nations, and ephods.	All of this belongs to the tribute and the seventh treasure, a second tithe rendered unclean. Its opening is in the edge of the aqueduct on the north, six cubits to the immersion bath.	ΧΑΓ
	forty talents of silver.		
	42 talents.		HN
	sixty-five ingots of gold.		ΘE
	vessels and seventy talents of silver.		
	in it there are vessels.		
	ten talents.		ΔΙ
	six jars of silver.	Its entrance is under the big threshold.	
four...cubits:	22 talents.		
nine cubits:	silver and gold vessels of tribute; basins, cups, bowls, flagons	—a total of six hundred and nine.	

THE TEXT OF THE COPPER

Place	Specification	Command
14.	Under the other corner, the eastern one,	dig
15. In the cavern	which is in Milḥam, on its north:	
16. In the tomb	which is in east Milḥam, on the north,	
17. In the big cistern	which is in the..., in the pillar on its north end:	
18. In the aqueduct which leads...	on your way in,	
19. Between the two tamarisk trees	which are in the Valley of Achon, in the middle of *nḥnyn*,	
20. In the red reservoir	which is on the edge of the (Wadi) ʿAṣla:	
21. In the eastern cavern	on the north of Koḥlit:	
22. In the cairn	of the Secacah Gorge,	dig
23. At the head of the aqueduct...	...Secacah, on the north, under the big stone	dig
24. In the crevice	which is in Secacah, on the east of Solomon's Reservoir:	
25. Above Solomon's Canal,	towards the big stoning heap, sixty cubits,	dig
26. In the tomb	which is in the Wadi Kippa, on the way in from Jericho to Secacah,	dig
27. In the cave of the pillar	—the one having the two openings and facing east—in the northern opening,	dig
28. In the cave	of the base belonging to the stoning heap, which faces eastward,	dig in the opening
29. In the Queen's Residence,	on the west side,	dig

SCROLL ARRANGED IN COLUMNS

Distance	Treasure	Comments	Greek
sixteen cubits:	40 talents of silver.		TP
	vessels of tribute, my garments.	Its entrance is under the western corner.	
three cubits under the defilement	13 talents.		
	14 talents.		ΣΚ
four cubits...	55 talents of silver.		
three cubits:	two cauldrons are there, full of silver.		
	two hundred talents of silver.		
	seventy talents of silver.		
... cubits:	12 talents of silver.		
three cubits:	7 talents of silver.		
	vessels of tribute.	And their document is beside them.	
three cubits:	23 talents of silver.		
seven cubits:	32 talents.		
three cubits.	A pitcher is there; in it there is one scroll; under it there are 42 talents.		
nine cubits:	21 talents.		
twelve cubits:	27 talents.		

THE TEXT OF THE COPPER

Place	Specification	Command
30. In the cairn	which is in the Pass of the High Priest	dig
31. In the aqueduct	of...the northern reservoir...on the four sides...	measure off
32. In the cave	which is next to the fountain opposite the end house,	dig
33. On (Mount) Duq,	under the eastern corner of the guardhouse,	dig
34. By the mouth of the water outlet	of the Koziba,	dig
35. In the aqueduct	which is on the road east of Bira, the rock which is east of ʾAḥud:	
36. In the Outer Gorge,	in the middle of the sheepfold, by the stone,	dig
37. In the cairn	of the mouth of the Pottery Ravine,	dig
38. In the fallow field	of the Shaveh facing west, on the south, in the vault facing north,	dig
39. In the irrigated parts	of the Shaveh, in the waterless region which is in it,	dig
40. In the columbarium	on the edge of the Natuf,	measure off from its edge
41. On the estate of the *šnyg*,	in the vault facing east,	dig
42. In the vaults of (Beth) Ḥoron,	on the side facing west, in a recess,	dig
43.	In its funnel:	
44. In the outflow of the waters	which are close to the edge of the drain, a wide space in front of them,	dig
45. In the cavern	which is on the north of the mouth of the ravine of Beth Tamar, in the arid region of Garpela:	

SCROLL ARRANGED IN COLUMNS

Distance	Treasure	Comments	Greek
...nine cubits:	22 talents.		
twenty cubits... seven:	four hundred talents.		
six cubits:	six jars of silver.		
seven cubits:	22 talents.		
three cubits:	60 talents of plundered loot, two talents of gold.		
	vessels of tribute, and my scrolls, and a bar of silver.		
seventeen cubits.	Under it there are 17 talents of silver and gold.		
three cubits:	4 talents.		
twenty-four cubits:	66 talents.		
twenty-one cubits:	70 talents of silver.		
thirteen cubits:	two tusks, and also seven rocks, four jars containing *statēr* coins.		
eight and a half cubits:	23 1/2 talents.		
sixteen cubits:	22 talents.		
	a mina of silver, a consecrated offering.		
seven cubits:	9 talents.		
		Everything in it is a consecrated offering.	

THE TEXT OF THE COPPER

Place	Specification	Command
46. In the columbarium	which is in the defile of Oboth...south, in the second upper room—the descent into it is from above:	
47. In the lime-plastered cistern of the conduits	which draw water from the Great Wadi, on its bottom:	
48. In the reservoir	which is in Beth Kerem, as you go in, to the left of it	
49. In the pool	of the Zered Gorge, in its side:	
50. Under Absalom's monument,	on the western side,	dig
51. In the pool of Privy	of Rachel, under the pipe:	
52. [In...]	in the four corners of Waheb:	
53. Under the southern corner of the Stoa,	in Zadok's Tomb, under the pillar of the exedra:	
54. In the 'Throne,'	the top of the cliff facing west, across from Zadok's Garden, under the great flagstone which is in its gutter:	
55. In the tomb	which is under the Knife:	
56. In the tomb of the common people:		
57. In Beth Eshdatain,	in the reservoir, on your way in toward it from its tanks:	

SCROLL ARRANGED IN COLUMNS

Distance	Treasure	Comments	Greek
	9 talents.		
	12 talents.		
ten notches:	sixty-two talents of silver.		
	the *ma'â* coins and a stone which has attached to itself two *ma'â* coins—that one is in the opening; three hundred talents of gold and twenty expiatory vessels.		
twelve notches:	80 talents.		
	17 talents.		
	vessels of tribute.	Their document is beside them.	
	vessels of Suaḥ's tribute, Seneh's tribute.	And their document is beside them.	
	consecrated offerings.		
	40 talents.		
	my pure things are in it; vessels of Az's tribute, Suaḥ's tribute.	Their document is beside them.	
	vessels of Leah's tribute, Sira's tribute	Their document is beside them.	

THE TEXT OF THE COPPER

Place	Specification	Command
58. In the entry-way of the...	of the western grave chamber, a little on...:	
59.	Under the black stone:	
60.	Under the threshold of the crypt:	
61. On Mount Gerizim,	under the step of the upper cavern:	
62. In the mouth of the spring	of Beth Sham:	
63. In the big drain	of the crypt:	
64. In the cavern of the Presence	on the north of Koḥlit—its opening is north, and tombs are at its mouth:	

SCROLL ARRANGED IN COLUMNS

Distance	Treasure	Comments	Greek
	...nine hundred...5 talents of gold, sixty talents.	Its entrance is on the west.	
	juglets.		
	42 talents.		
	one strongbox and all its vessels, and 60 talents of silver.		
	silver vessels and gold vessels of tribute, and silver	—a total of six hundred talents	
	vessels of the crypt chamber.	The total is a weight of 71 talents, twenty minas.	
	a duplicate of this document, and the interpretation, and 'their oils,' and the *prōtokollon* of the one and the other.		

THE HEBREW OF THE DEAD SEA SCROLLS

MARTIN G. ABEGG, JR.

There are more than 870 manuscripts which were found in the eleven caves in and above the marl terrace at the northwest corner of the Dead Sea. The corpus can be conveniently divided into "biblical" and "non-biblical" texts. The first category—texts with counterparts in the Hebrew Bible—accounts for 220 of the total. The non-biblical or "sectarian" manuscripts can be further subdivided for the sake of our current study: slightly more than 100 Aramaic texts and approximately 550 Hebrew manuscripts. It is this latter group that forms the basis of our study.[1]

1. THE CORPUS

There are seven Qumran manuscripts which by accident of preservation comprise a full third of the total sectarian corpus. They are *The Manual of Discipline* (1QS),[2] *The Rule of the Congregation*

---

[1] At the Annual Meeting of the Society of Biblical Literature (November, 1994) Dr. Roy Brown and I collaborated on a paper entitled, "A Time for Tagging? (For Everything There is a Season)." We demonstrated the benefits to research of a grammatically-tagged text which we had prepared as a module for the commercial search platform "Accordance" (Oak Tree Software). We have continued to work since that time and have added substantially to our data-base, which has been expanded from ten preliminarily-tagged manuscripts to include 66. This figure is only 12% of the corpus by manuscript count, but because we have chosen—in the main—the larger texts, the resultant module now represents 65% of the whole by word-count. With some noted exceptions, it is this group of tagged texts that forms the basis for the following discussion: CD, 1QS, 1QSa, 1QSb, 1QpHab, 1QM, 1QHª, 1Q22, 1Q27, 1Q29, 1Q34*bis*, 4Q159, 4Q169, 4Q171, 4Q175, 4Q251, 4Q252, 4Q253, 4Q254, 4Q254a, 4Q274, 4Q276, 4Q280, 4Q285, 4Q286, 4Q287, 4Q288, 4Q289, 4Q299, 4Q300, 4Q301, 4Q371, 4Q372, 4Q384, 4Q385, 4Q386, 4Q387, 4Q388, 4Q389, 4Q390, 4Q394, 4Q395, 4Q396, 4Q397, 4Q398, 4Q399, 4Q409, 4Q418, 4Q427, 4Q434, 4Q435, 4Q436, 4Q437, 4Q438, 4Q439, 4Q491, 4Q492, 4Q493, 4Q494, 4Q495, 4Q496, 4Q503, 4Q521, 4Q525, 11Q14, 11QT.

[2] E. Qimron and J. Charlesworth, "Rule of the Community (1QS)," in J. Charlesworth (ed.), *The Dead Sea Scrolls: Hebrew, Aramaic, and Greek Texts*

(1QSa),³ *Blessings* (1QSb),⁴ *The Pesher to Habakkuk* (1QpHab),⁵ *The War Scroll* (1QM),⁶ *The Thanksgiving Scroll* (1QHª),⁷ and *The Temple Scroll* (11QTª).⁸ In addition to these documents I have also included *The Damascus Document* (CD).⁹ Although it is clear that the two manuscripts discovered in a Cairo synagogue genizah in 1895 date to the Middle Ages, the discovery of older parallels from Cave 4 (4Q266-273) has underlined the general reliability of the text while at the same time highlighting its distinct orthographic (spelling) tradition. As this tradition occasionally surfaces in other more ancient manuscripts from the caves, I have considered CD in the following discussions. Sources for the remainder of the corpus are best determined through the catalogue published by S. Reed.¹⁰

With English Translations. Vol. 1, *Rule of the Community and Related Documents* (Tübingen: Mohr-Siebeck; Louisville: Westminster John Knox, 1994) 1-51.

³ J. Charlesworth and L. Stuckenbruck, "Rule of the Congregation (1QSa)," in Charlesworth (ed.), *The Dead Sea Scrolls* (Vol. 1), 108-17.

⁴ J. Charlesworth and L. Stuckenbruck, "Blessings (1QSb)," in Charlesworth (ed.), *The Dead Sea Scrolls* (Vol. 1), 119-31.

⁵ W. Brownlee, *The Midrash Pesher of Habakkuk* (SBLMS 24; Missoula, MT: Scholars Press, 1979), and B. Nitzan, מגילת פשר חבקוק: ממגילות מדבר יהודה (Jerusalem: Bialik Institute, 1986).

⁶ J. Duhaime, "War Scroll (1QM, 1Q33)," in Charlesworth (ed.), *The Dead Sea Scrolls* (Vol. 1), 80-141.

⁷ I have prepared a critical text of this manuscript based mainly on the study of É. Puech, "Quelques aspects de la restauration du Rouleau des Hymnes (1QH)," *JJS* 39 (1988) 38-55. Until Puech publishes a critical text based on his research, it is important to note that the order of columns and fragments have changed and thus will not correspond with any published Hebrew text; all English translations published since 1994 represent Puech's thesis. For those willing to work through the problems, the best Hebrew text is still that of E. L. Sukenik, *The Dead Sea Scrolls of the Hebrew University* (Jerusalem: Magnes Press and The Hebrew University, 1955).

⁸ Y. Yadin, *The Temple Scroll* (3 vols. and supplementary plates; Jerusalem: Israel Exploration Society, 1983).

⁹ E. Qimron, "The Text of CDC," in M. Broshi (ed.), *The Damascus Document Reconsidered* (Jerusalem: Israel Exploration Society–Shrine of the Book–Israel Museum, 1992); and J. M. Baumgarten, "Damascus Document (CD)," in Charlesworth (ed.), *The Dead Sea Scrolls* (Vol. 1), 4-57.

¹⁰ S. A. Reed, with M. J. Lundberg and M. J. Phelps (eds.), *The Dead Sea Scrolls Catalogue: Documents, Photographs and Museum Inventory Numbers* (SBLRBS 32; Atlanta: Scholars Press, 1994).

Grammatical studies concerning various aspects and particular texts are numerous. The most important for present consideration are the seminal works of E. Y. Kutscher[11] and his student E. Qimron.[12] As Qimron's *The Hebrew of the Dead Sea Scrolls* (hereafter *HDSS*) will most certainly continue to be the foundation from which much future work will build, I will frequently direct the reader to its pages for more complete or comparative findings. Given the nature of the task, the following treatment of linguistic features does not intend to be comprehensive. I have attempted to keep the student and teacher of Biblical Hebrew ("BH") in mind so that the discussions might be used in the classroom as an introduction to Qumran Hebrew ("QH"). Yet I trust that my own conclusions will provide benefit for the expert as well.

2. ORTHOGRAPHY

Consonants

The orthography of ś is occasionally at variance with BH. Forms normally written with שׂ are occasionally found with ס: וספות (1QM 5:12), בבסר (1QHª 45 6), מסיאים (4Q394 3-7 i 16; 4Q395 1 7), והסורף (4Q394 3-7 i 17), הנעסה (4Q396 1-2 iv 4), סלמותמה (11QTª 49:18). Corrections also exist which evidence an awareness of existing spelling conventions: הש{ס}רים (1QM 3:3), נ{ס}ˢגבה (1QHª 14:25), ת{ס}ˢיג (4Q418 126 ii 13). Alternately, שׂ is found written for ס: מאשו (1QpHab 1:11), יתשגנשגו (1QHª 16:9), מנשה (11QTª 54:12), ישיתכה (11QTª 54:19). Note the correction: ונ{ש}סכמה (11QTᵇ 14-15 7).

Although there is some confusion in the representation of gutturals which points to the lack of distinction or weakening of their pronunciation (*HDSS* §200.11), the vast majority of the misspellings concerns the confusion of א and ה or the elision of א. For א instead of ה see: באופיע (1QS 10:2), באמרות (1QS 6:26), הויא (4Q418 43 3). א for ה to indicate the final vowel *â* might have been influenced by the Aramaic determinative: התורא (1QSa 1:11), עשרא (1QSa

---

[11] E. Y. Kutscher, *The Language and Linguistic Background of the Isaiah Scroll* (STDJ 6; Leiden: Brill, 1974).

[12] E. Qimron, *The Hebrew of the Dead Sea Scrolls* (HSS 29; Atlanta: Scholars Press, 1986). This study is based on Qimron's much more comprehensive Ph.D. dissertation, דקדוק הלשון העברית של מגילות מדבר יהודה (Jerusalem: The Hebrew University, 1976).

2:22), חוכמא (4Q286 1 ii 6), [וה]קללא (4Q398 14-17 i 7). ה for א also occurs: הברכנו "I shall bless Him" (1QS 10:6), הבחרה "I shall choose" (1QS 10:12), הנשי (=אנשי, 1QS 8:13), הטמה (=הטמא, 4Q394 3-7 i 19). The א occasionally is elided: הרץ (=הארץ, 1QpHab 13:1), היש (=האיש, 4Q175 1:22), ונצה (=ונאצה, 4Q175 1:28), ופרי (=פארי, 1QM 7:11). א following a *shewa* is especially liable to elision: מודה (=מאודה, 1QS 10:16 *et al.*), במוזני (=מאוזני, 4Q418 127 6; 167 2), ורבעים (=וארבעים, 11QT[a] 40:10). See verbs III-*he* and III-ʾ*alep* for additional misspellings.

The letter ʾ*alep* is also frequently used as a digraph following the vowels *î, ô,* or *û* (*HDSS* §100.51, 52). The BH word כי "that, for" is the most frequent example of this phenomenon as it is often written כיא (240 times or 37% of all occurrences). The following examples are also found: מפיא (1QpHab 2:2), לפיא (4Q491 1-3 8; 20 2), אניא (4Q491 11 i 18), מיא (1QM 10:8, *et al.*). It is also found in instances of the first common singular pronominal suffix: ואפיא (1QS 10:19), ביא (4Q491 11 i 13, cf. 15, 16, 18), יגיד{ו}ניאʾ (4Q491 11 i 17). The vowel *ô* shows the digraph in a few cases of the third masculine singular pronominal suffix: לוא "to him" (1QS 6:27; 11QT[a] 56:19; 65:15; 66:10). The digraph א for *û* occurs with the verb: יכמוא "they yearn" (√כמה, 1QH[a] 14:21) and יאמינוא (1QpHab 2:6).

Vowels

The most notable characteristic of QH is the use of *waw* and *yod* to indicate vowels. The letter *waw* most regularly represents the *o/ō* and occasionally the *u/ū* of BH. Nearly 200 words could be used to illustrate this phenomenon; those listed in Table 1 below represent the most frequent. The partial list produced here is suggestive of a classification of manuscripts according to different scribal schools.[13] At one end of the spectrum is the highly defective CD with 4Q372 and 4Q418 close beside. At the other extreme are manuscripts such as 1QS, 1QSa, 1QSb, 1QpHab, 1Q22, 4Q491, and 4Q503 which are characterized by a *scriptio plena* or full approach to spellings. Although most documents from Qumran fall somewhere between these two extremes, generally they are nearer the *scriptio plena* end of the spectrum. See the description of the verb for further comments on the *plene* nature of QH.

---

[13] E. Tov, "The Orthography and Language of the Hebrew Scrolls Found at Qumran and the Origin of these Scrolls," *Textus* 13 (1986) 31-57.

TABLE 1: *Waw and Yod as Vowel Letters*

BH	QH	Meaning	Total #	% Plene	Defective MSS
אדני	אנוני	Lord	55	78%	4Q521
אלהים	אלוהים	God	89	76%	4Q171, 4Q372, 4Q385, 4Q387, 4Q388, 4Q389
את	אות	DO w/suffix	89	82%	1QM, 4Q299, 4Q372, 4Q387, 11Q14
זאת	זואת, זאות	this (f.)	61	77%	1Q34*bis*, 4Q252, 4Q418, 4Q521
חדש	חודש	month	76	95%	CD
חכמה	חוכמה	wisdom	41	32%	CD, 1QS, 4Q372, 4Q387
חק	חוק	statute	86	85%	4Q521
חשך	חושך	dark	55	98%	----
כהן	כוהן	priest	212	92%	CD, 4Q385, 4Q387
כח	כוח	strength	70	92%	4Q372, 11QT^a
כל	כול	all	1707	86%	CD,* 4Q300, 4Q372, 4Q398, 4Q521
לא	לוא	not	983	69%	CD, 1Q34*bis*, 4Q169, 4Q251, 4Q254, 4Q300, 4Q371, 4Q372, 4Q385, 4Q386, 4Q387, 4Q388, 4Q389, 4Q390, 4Q434
משה	מושה	Moses	36	56%	CD, 1QM, 4Q299, 4Q418
עון	עוון	iniquity	66	64%	CD, 4Q171, 4Q286, 4Q372, 4Q384, 4Q385, 4Q389, 4Q398
קדש	קודש	holy	289	90%	CD, 4Q251, 4Q388, 4Q394, 4Q396
ראש	רואש, ראוש	head	58	69%	CD, 1QM, 4Q169, 4Q372, 4Q394, 4Q396, 4Q418
שלש(ה)	שלוש(ה)	three	90	100%	

*With pronominal suffixes (5 times): כול

The letter *yod* is used to indicate the vowel *i* and less frequently *ē*. As examples, note the QH spellings of בנימין (BH: בִּנְיָמִן), דויד (BH: דָּוִד), רישון/ריאשון/ראישון (BH: רִאשׁוֹן), and שרירות (BH: שְׁרֵרוּת). The examples of *ē* tend to be exceptions rather than the rule: וראשית (4Q252 1 iv 4, BH: רֵאשִׁית), המ'אות (11QT^a 58:4, BH: מֵאוֹת); העיד (11QT^a 61:9, BH: עֵד), עידות (CD 3:15, BH: עֵדוֹת), ופירוש (CD 4:6, BH: פֵּרוּשׁ), and ריעיכה (11QT^a 54:20, BH: רֵעַ). It is of note in this regard that although *Hipʿil* forms of geminate verbs are regularly vocalized with *ē*, they are never written with the *yod* in QH. Nouns ending in *he* whose construct singular is vocalized with a *ṣere* are occasionally spelled with a *yod*, especially in 11QT^a: אשי ריח ניחוח (11QT^a 23:17; 28:02, 2, BH: אִשֶּׁה) and חזי התנופה (11QT^a 22:9, BH: חֲזֵה). For further discussion see *HDSS* §110.33, 34.

3. MORPHOLOGY: THE PRONOUN

Independent Personal Pronouns
First Person Singular

The form אני (86 times) is regular. Note the digraph אניא (4Q491 11 i 18). As Qimron has noted (*HDSS* §321.11), the longer form אנוכי (41 times) always refers to God: 1Q22 1:7 (+3); 4Q175 1:7; 4Q166 1 ii 1 (Hos 2:10); 4Q167 2 2 (Hos 5:14); 4Q216 1:12, 14; 4Q223-4 2 ii 3 (+2); 4Q252 1 iii 4; 4Q365 23 5; 4Q390 1 3; 11QT^a 29:7 (+22).

Second Person Singular

The second masculine singular form אתה (168 times) is normal with את extant only at 1QH^a 13:32. There are no occurrences of the second feminine singular pronoun.

Third Masculine Singular

The form הוא (199 times) is normal. The longer form, הואה (47 times) occurs regularly in 1QS (3:17 +11); 1QM (1:10 +3); 4Q301 (3 4 +6); 4Q491 (1-3 9 +2) and occasionally with הוא elsewhere. The normal feminine form, היא (56 times), is also countered with the longer form היאה (25 times): 1QS (8:7 +4); 1QM (1:11 +4) and elsewhere with היא.

First Person Plural

Two forms of the first person plural pronoun are used equally. Although rare in BH (Jer 42:6), אנו occurs 12 times in QH: 1QS

1:25; 1QM 13:7 (+3); 1Q34*bis* 2+1 6; 4Q491 8-10 10 (+1); and 4Q503 1-6 iii 20 (+3). The usual BH form, אנחנו (13 times), is also used: CD 20:29; 1QHᵃ 10 7; 4Q390 2 ii 5; and in manuscripts of the MMT: 4Q394 3-7 i 5 (+4); 4Q396 1-2 i 3 (+2); 4Q397 6-13 10 (+1); 4Q398 11-13 3 (+1); 4Q399 i 10.

Second Person Plural

The BH form אתם (11 times) is found: 1QM 17:4, 8; 4Q185 1:9; 4Q299 10 8; 66 3; 4Q396 1-2 iii 8; iv 9; 4Q397 14-21 8; 4Q418 69 ii 10, 14; 4Q491 11 ii 13; as well as the longer form אתמה (8 times): 1QM 10:3; 17:2; 4Q185 2:7; 4Q200 6 8; 4Q228 1 i 10; 4Q397 6-13 13; 11QTᵃ 48:7; 61:15. The feminine plural is not extant.

Third Person Plural

The two forms of the third masculine plural pronoun are found in approximately the same ratio as in BH: הם (55 times, 23 in CD) and המה (73 times, 13 in 11QTᵃ). The feminine plural הנה occurs but twice: 1QS 3:18 and 1QHᵃ 2 i 7.

Suffixed Personal Pronouns

Pronominal suffixes are common in QH and given the lack of vowel pointing, very few changes occur in the spelling of the forms to which they are joined. Normally (98 times), third person plural verbal forms ending in *waw* append the suffix directly following: ישכילוהו (1QSa 1:7). Occasionally (11 times, 9 in 1QS), however, the *waw* is no longer written: יכתובהו "they shall enroll him" (1QS 6:22), ידיחני "they drove me out" (1QHᵃ 12:8), וסקלהו "they shall stone it" (4Q251 4 3). There is one similar example of the masculine plural imperative, הגידנה (4Q427 7 i 17), and one instance of the first common singular perfect: צויתכה (11QTᵃ 54:17) which lacks a written *yod*.

The *Qal* of the strong verb (in the imperfect) with the suffixes evidences two forms; one according to the form וישמורכה (1QS 2:3, 8 times) but more often ידורשהו (1QS 6:14, 17 times). In addition, the *Qal* of the strong verb with suffixes shows a rare alteration in the normally *plene* nature of QH. In 22 of 47 cases (47%) of the imperfect and 7 of 8 cases (88%) of the *waw* consecutive the theme vowel is not written when a suffix is present. CD is always defective (3 and 4 occurrences respectively) whereas 1QS is always *plene* (6 imperfects). Most scrolls exhibit both forms: ישפטנו "he shall judge him" (1QpHab 10:5) but ישופטנו (1QpHab 12:5). No other part of the verb shows any consistent pattern of change in form in instances with the pronominal suffix.

First Person singular

The form י- (722 times) occurs with nouns, adjectives, participles, most infinitive constructs, all prepositions except מן and כ, the direct object marker את (only 4Q175 1:3), and the adverbial forms סביבותי (11QT^a 56:13) and מאחרי (11QT^a 56:19). The suffix occurs six times with the digraph ʾ*alep*: ואפיא (1QS 10:19), ביא (4Q491 11 i 13, 15, 16), לאי (4Q491 11 i 15), and ו[לבודריא (4Q491 11 i 18). The form ני- (136 times) occurs with verbs, the prepositions מן and כ, the interjection הנה, and six times with infinitive constructs: הגישני (1QH^a 6:13), לטהרני and ולהגישני (1QH^a 8:21), בכלו[תֹנִי (1Q22 2:8), לעבדני (4Q387 3 ii 1), and ללכודני (4Q437 2 i 2). The digraph ʾ*alep* occurs once with the longer form: יגו׳ד{ו}ניֹא (4Q491 11 i 17).

Second Person Singular

The most common second person masculine singular suffix is כה- (1298 times). The shorter form, ך- (330 times), is predominant in the early columns of 1QH^a (4-8), 1Q34*bis*, 4Q175, 4Q384-390, 4Q398, and 4Q434-439. The second feminine singular suffix (ך-) occurs eight times in 1QM 12:14 and 19:6. It also occurs in the lemmas from Nahum in 4Q169.

Third Person Singular

The third masculine singular pronominal suffix is generally expressed in three ways: ו- (1953), הו- (196), and נו- (86). ו- is used for singular forms of the perfect verb, infinitive constructs, participles, nouns, adjectives, all prepositions except מן and כ, the direct object marker את, and the adverbial form אחרי. The suffix הו- is used with forms of the perfect verb ending in a vowel (i.e., third common plural as well as III-*he* verbs in the third masculine singular), the imperfect (except first common singular), imperative, singular nouns which take their construct in ־י (אב, אח, רע), singular nouns from III-*he* roots (משנה), and the preposition כ. The suffix נו- is used with singular forms of the imperfect not ending in a vowel, the preposition מן, and the negative particle אין. Two additional forms of the third masculine singular suffix have been suggested. E. Qimron (*HDSS* §322.144) has proposed reading the Aramaic plural והי- in several instances where editors have traditionally read הו- oddly attached to plural or dual forms ending in *yod*. Examples are

ועיניהו (1QS 5:5, Qimron: ועינוהי, but see Job 24:23) and עליהו (1QpHab 12:11, Qimron: עלוהי). See also 1QS 5:11, 25; 6:13, 26; 8:8; 4Q175 21; and 4Q491 1-3 8. J. Baumgarten has noted the use of ה- for the third masculine singular suffix in 4Q266 2 ii 21 (אפה, "His wrath," CD 2:21, אפו); 5 ii 6; 8 i 2, 6; 8 ii 6.[14]

The third feminine singular pronominal suffix is most commonly ה- (430 times). It is used for all forms of the perfect verb, the imperfect (apart from the feminine plurals, which do not exist with suffixes), infinitive constructs, participles, nouns, adjectives, all prepositions except מן and כ, the direct object marker את, and the adverbial forms אחרי and סביב. The pronominal suffix -נה (31 times) is used with singular forms of the imperfect, once with the masculine plural imperative (הגִידֶנה, 4Q427 7 i 17), and the prepositions מן and כ (note כמוהה, 1QM 18:10).

First Person Plural

The first common plural suffix is -נו (165 times) and is found in all instances without variance.

Second Person Plural

The second masculine plural suffix is extant in both short -כם (108 times) and long -כמה (51 times, 33 in 11QT[a]) forms. Note the variant forms רחמיכהם (4Q427 7 ii 16) and אלוהיכהמה (11QT[a] 48:10). The second feminine plural suffix is not extant.

Third Person Plural

There are two forms of the third person masculine plural, each of which exhibits a long and short form. -ם (789 times) and -מה (224 times) are found with all parts of the verb except the masculine plural participle, all nouns and adjectives whose construct forms do not end in *yod*,[15] the negative particle אין, the direct object marker את, and the prepositions את, ב, בין, בעד and זולה. The forms -הם (474 times) and -המה (225 times) occur with nouns, adjectives, and masculine plural participles whose construct forms end in *yod*, adverbial forms אחרי and סביבותי, the relative pronoun -ש, and the

---

[14] J. M. Baumgarten, *Qumran Cave 4.XIII: The Damascus Document (4Q266-273)* (DJD 18; Oxford: Clarendon Press, 1996) 30.

[15] In approximately 30% (=46 times) of all instances of the third masculine plural suffix attached to forms ending with the feminine plural -ות, an appended י- precedes the suffix. This is probably an echo of the ending of the construct state in the masculine plural (GKC §91m).

propositions אֶל, בְּ, בֵּין, כְּ, לְ, מִן, עַל, and עִם. According to Qimron, ־וֹם (גבורתום, 1QS 1:21 and רוחום, 1QS 5:21; 9:14) is simply a phonological variant of ־ם (*HDSS* §322.18). ־מוֹ (11 times) is used only with the proposition לְ.

The third person feminine plural is ־ן (4 times), used as the masculine ־ם, and ־הן (8 times) which corresponds to ־הם. The form ־הון, corresponding to ־וֹם, is found only once: ועליהון (1QS 3:25).

4. MORPHOLOGY: THE NOUN

As Qimron has concluded, "Noun formation in the DSS is not significantly different from that in BH" (*HDSS* §330.1). As in BH there are numerous masculine nouns with feminine plurals. Examples of the most common in QH are אבות (אב, father), שמות (שם, name), דורות (דור, period, generation), עורות (עור, skin), גורלות (גורל, lot), and שופרות (שופר, horn). Conversely, there are many feminine nouns with masculine plural forms. Examples are שנים (שנה, year), ערים (עיר, city), עזים (עז, she-goat), פעמים (פעם, occurrence), אבנים (אבן, stone) and נשים (אשה, woman).

There is a notable expansion of the construct or bound form in QH for which traces are found in BH. *Genesius' Hebrew Grammar* ("GKC") suggests three possible means of making a plural expression of a bound form: 1) using the plural of the construct noun, בני אור "sons of light" (1QS 1:9, GKC §124p); 2) the plural of both nouns, מעשי תועבות "abhorrent deeds" (1QpHab 12:8, GKC §124q); or 3) less frequently, the plural of the genitive after a singular construct (GKC §124r), a structure which occurs in QH only when the genitive refers to individuals who have a member in common: פי כפירים, "mouths of young lions" (1QHa 13:9). As an extension of this third use is the singular construct with a compound genitive: וְרֹאשׁ־עֹרֵב וּזְאֵב, "the heads of Oreb and Zeeb" (Judg 7:25 and elsewhere in BH with יד: Ps 77:21, et al.). This "distributive" use is the likely explanation of Gen 14:10 as well, מֶלֶךְ־סְדֹם וַעֲמֹרָה, "the kings of Sodom and Gomorrah." Although rare in BH, this distributive construct is used with some frequency in QH.

- מות אלעזר ויהושע, "the deaths of Eleazar and Joshua" (CD 5:3-4, see Josh 24:33 and Judg 2:8)
- מבוא יום ולילה, "beginnings of day and night" (1QS 10:10)
- מוצא ערב ובוקר, "departures of evening and morning" 1QS 10:10
- שם ישראל ואהרן, "the names Israel and Aaron" (1QM 3:13-14; cf. 5:1. See also 1QS 6:6; 1QSa 2:18-19, 19-20; 4Q251 6 5; 11QTa 43:8-9).

These examples serve to establish a context for the expression משיח אהרן וישראל, "Messiahs of Aaron and Israel" (CD 12:23-13:1; 14:19; 19:11).[16] The instance of the plural at 1QS 9:11, עד בוא נביא ומשיחי אהרון וישראל, "until there come the Prophet and the Messiahs of Aaron and Israel," perhaps reflects a sense that the distributive construct would have seemed ambiguous after the singular "prophet."

5. MORPHOLOGY: THE VERB

Inflection of the Perfect

	Singular	Plural
3rd person masc.	——	ו——
3rd person fem.	ה——	unattested
2nd person masc.	־תה/־ת	־תם/־תמה
2nd person fem.	ת——	unattested
1st person	־תי	נו——

Third masculine singular: This is regular throughout; חקקא (1QS 10:1) is possibly in error for חקק אל, "God determined."

Third feminine singular. The ending -ה is regular throughout, with the possible exception of שזנת "that she played the harlot" (4Q394 3-7 i 12).

Second masculine singular. The longer form of the suffix (־תה) is the rule, accounting for nearly 96% of cases. The shorter form (־ת) occurs regularly in 4Q385 (ואמרת 4Q385 1 2), 4Q388 (וֹאָמרת[4Q388 8 7), and sporadically elsewhere: יצרת (1QHa 9:15), ובערת (11QTa 54:17) are examples.

Second feminine singular. Only in the quotation of Nah 3:5: וגלית (4Q169 3-4 ii 10) and והרא[י]תִ (4Q169 3-4 ii 11).

First person common singular: This form is always written with the *yod* with the exception of שמעת, "I have heard" (4Q175 1:1).

Second masculine plural. The longer form (־תמה) occurs in ונזכרתמה (1QM 10:7, a quote of Num 10:9), שמעתמה (4Q418 55:8) and regularly in 11QTa: והקרבתמה (11QTa 17:12 +17).

---

[16] I have here reversed my conclusion as reflected in "The Messiah at Qumran: Are We Still Seeing Double?" *DSD* 2 (1995) 129-30, and now agree with the conclusions of S. Talmon, "The Concepts of Māšîaḥ and Messianism in Early Judaism," in J. H. Charlesworth (ed.), *The Messiah: Developments in Earliest Judaism and Christianity* (Minneapolis: Fortress, 1992) 105 n.64.

Inflection of the Imperfect

	Singular	Plural
3rd person masc.	——י	י——ו
3rd person fem.	——ת	ת——נה
2nd person masc.	——ת	ת——ו
2nd person fem.	ת——י	unattested
1st person	א——	נ——

Second feminine singular. The only examples are found in the quotations of Nah 3:8a התיטיבי (4Q169 3-4 iii 8), and Nah 3:11a ותהי (4Q169 3-4 iv 5).

First common singular. The prefix (-א) is regular with the exception of הברכנו, "I shall bless Him" (1QS 10:6) and again הבחרה (1QS 10:12).

Third masculine plural. At least two instances of the energic *nun* occur: יטיפון (CD 4:20) and יריבון (4Q251 3 i 2).

Second masculine plural. Six instances of the so-called energic *nun* exist. all from 11QT^a: תתוצון (cols. 2:6, cf. 2:7; 54:14 *tris*, 15).

Jussive/Vetitive

The shortening of the imperfect which occurs in certain environments in BH in all forms of the *Hipʿil* and in the *Qal* of the verbs II-*waw/yod*, and in all conjugations of the verbs III-*he* continues somewhat altered in QH. It is of note that when the imperfect does not follow *waw* or the particle אל that there are only 8 shortened forms in over 600 instances. Examples include יהי (1QS 2:13), ימח (1QS 11:3), יעל (1QH^a 16:25), יכח (4Q372 18 2), יוסף (4Q418 137 2), and תוסף (4Q418 199 2). The fact that none of these cases has a demonstrably "jussive" sense, whereas ויהכין, "Let him order" (1QS 3:9) and וישוב, "let him return" (11QT^a 62:3) do, suggests that the short form of the imperfect has lost the sense of command in QH. However, for the vetitive after the negative אל the short form is common, occurring in 26 of 37 (70%) instances: אל יגל (4Q251 12 6). See the discussion of the *waw* consecutive for the most significant use of the "shortened form" of the imperfect.

Cohortative

The lengthening of the imperfect or cohortative is fairly common, comprising fully 35% of the singular first person forms and 65% of the plural. The singular is never hortatory and is most common in hymnic writings; 1QS column 10 and 1QH^a (+4Q427) account for 75% of the instances.[17] 11QT^a prefers the simple imperfect with the exception of ואקדשה (11QT^a 29:8) and אשים֯ (11QT^a 56:13). In the plural, apart from the combination נלכה ונעבודה, "let us go and serve" (11QT^a 54:10, 21; 55:4), there again seems little contextual information for distinguishing the use of the cohortative from the simple imperfect.

Waw Consecutive[18]

Given the fragmentary nature of the majority of the Qumran manuscripts and the non-narrative nature of most the corpus, it is often difficult to determine whether a prefixed form of the verb following a *waw* is a conjunctive imperfect *(wəyiqtol)* or a *waw consecutive (wayyiqtol)*. Overall, however, it has become clear that as in BH, QH has two ways of expressing a completed action: the perfect *(qatal)* and the *waw* consecutive *(wayyiqtol)*. The incompleted action is expressed by *waw* plus the perfect *(wəqatal)*, the simple imperfect *(yiqtol)*, and conjunctive imperfect *(wəyiqtol)*. The following table compares the frequency of these forms in BH and QH.[19]

	BH	QH
qatal	27%	24%
wəqatal	13%	16%
yiqtol	28%	46%
wayyiqtol	29%	8%
wəyiqtol	3%	6%

Two important conclusions can be drawn from this table. First, the forms determining incomplete action account for 44% of the verbal system in BH and 68% in QH. Conversely, while the completed aspect is 56% in BH it is only 32% in QH. The two corpora are distinct generically. In general the difference in the percentages can be accounted for by the lack of historical texts in the Qumran corpus.

---

[17] No cases from *lamed he* verbs have been included.

[18] M. Smith, *The Origins and Development of the* Waw-*Consecutive* (HSS 39; Atlanta: Scholars Press, 1991) 35-63.

[19] I have incorporated the chart published by B. Waltke and M. O'Connor, *An Introduction to Biblical Hebrew Syntax* (Winona Lake, IN: Eisenbrauns, 1990) 456; this was in turn based on the study by L. McFall, *The Enigma of the Hebrew Verbal System* (HTIBS 2; Sheffield: Almond, 1982) 104.

Second, the incomplete action shows the following makeup:
>BH: 29% wəqatal, 64% yiqtol, and 7% wəyiqtol.
>QH: 24% wəqatal, 68% yiqtol, and 8% wəyiqtol.

However, the completed aspect shows a distinct shift:
>BH: 48% qatal, and 52% wayyiqtol
>QH: 75% qatal, and 25% wayyiqtol

These data show that the *waw* consecutive seems to have lost ground to the simple perfect as a means of expressing completed action.

In BH, the *waw* consecutive in the *Hipʿil*, the *Qal* of the verbs II-*waw/yod*, and all conjugations of the verbs III-*he* exhibits a shortened form. Likewise in QH, 92 of 116 (79%) of these verbs are shortened. It is notable, however, that the first common singular of היה is not shortened in any of its occurrences (ואהיה, all in 1QHª: 10:8, 10, 14, 15; 11:7; 16:27; compare Judg 18:4 with 2 Sam 7:9). There are, nevertheless, a substantial number of short forms following *waw* which are to be understood as simple imperfects. The fragmentary nature of the text precludes a clear decision in each case, but this latter group may be as large as 20% of all short forms following *waw*: ויקם (1QS 5:8) and ותעש (1QM 11:9) are examples.

Inflection of the Imperative

	Singular	Plural
2nd person masc.	——	ו——
2nd person fem.	י——	נה——

All forms of the imperative are extant; the endings are regular according to BH. Examples of the long form of the masculine singular imperative with the final ־ה also occur: שמעה (1QM 10:3, see also 4Q525 14 2:18); קומה (1QM 12:10); רומה (1QM 14:16, 4Q491 8-10 13), and תנה (4Q389 4 2).

Infinitive

It is relatively common for the prefix *he* to be dropped in *Nipʿal*, *Hipʿil* and *Hithpaʿel* infinitive construct forms following the preprosition ל (*HDSS* §310.145). *Nipʿal*: ולדרש (CD 1:8) and לנצל (1QpHab 9:13); *Hipʿil*: ולסיע (CD 1:16, but see ו[להסיע, 4Q266 2 i 19), ולקריב (1QS 8:9), ולסתר (1QS 9:17), לכות (1QpHab 3:1), לשחית (1QpHab 4:13), לחריב (1QpHab 6:8), לוסיף (1QpHab 8:12), ולקים (1QpHab 10:10), לוגיע (1QpHab 10:11), ולכשילם (1QpHab 11:8), לוסיף] (1QpHab 11:15), ולחזיק (1QM 10:6), ולשיב (1QHª

20:20), לפיל (4Q171 1-10 ii 15), לשבית (4Q171 1-10 iv 14), לריע
(4Q285 8 2); לביא (4Q394 3-7 i 8), לקטיר (11QTª 33:15), לשכין
(11QTª 47:4; 56:5); *Hithpaʿel*: לתיסר (1QS 9:10), ולשתחות (1QpHab
12:13), and ולתהלך (1QHª 7:15). There are no cases of this
phenomenon in the *Hopʿal*.

6. THE STRONG VERB

Qal Imperfect

Second masculine plural: The so-called pausal form predominates.
All eleven extant forms are *plene*: תספורו (11QTª 21:14).

Third masculine plural: The pausal form again prevails, accounting for 89 of the 110 cases (81%). Of the 21 defective forms, five
appear in CD (6:14; 9:16; 12:2; 15:8; 20:32) against no *plene* forms.

The fact that 83% of all other inflections normally exhibiting the
theme vowel (i.e., not the second feminine singular) are *plene* argues
that these so-called pausal forms of the second masculine and third
masculine plural are regular for QH.

Qal Imperative

All instances of the masculine singular imperative are *plene*: זכור
(4Q398 14-17 ii 1). The imperative feminine singular is not extant.
As in the imperfect, the longer form of the masculine plural appears
to be regular: זכורו (1QM 17:2) and שמורו (1Q29 5-7 4). חדלו (1QS
5:17) is found in a quote from Isa 2:22. There are no feminine plural
imperatives among the strong verbs.

Qal Infinitive

The infinitive construct is overwhelmingly *plene*. Defective forms
are עמד (CD 6:10), בפקד (CD 7:9; 19:6), לעמד (CD 20:5), למשל
(1QpHab 5:13); ברדף (1QM 18:2), ולפתח (1QHª 23:13), ולזבח
(4Q372 1 24). The infinitive absolute is always *plene*, מכור (11QTª
48:6, see Deut 14:21).

With suffix ובעוברם (1QS 1:18), although the vocalizations
לתפושם (1QpHab 4:7) and ללכודני (4Q437 2 i 2) also occur. Note
that לפוקדם (CD 8:2) is vocalized ל[פ]קודם in 4QDª (4Q266 3 iii
24).[20] Of the few forms, only חפזי (1QHª 20:19), לעבדני (4Q387 3
ii 1), עזבי (4Q387 3 iii 5), and לעזרנו (4Q495 2 2) are found apart

---

[20] J. Baumgarten (*Qumran Cave 4.XIII* [DJD 18] 44) reads the *Hipʿil* form
ל[פ]קידם.

from the text of CD. It is of note that 4QD^a (4Q266 8 i 2) reveals a defective predecessor to עמדו and בדרשו (CD 15:11).[21]

Qal Participle

Slightly more than 10% of all forms are defective. Of the 31 defective forms, nine are found in CD (CD 4:4; 5:13; 9:10; 10:4 [לשׁוּפְטִי, 4Q270 6 iv 15]; 15:4; 19:2, 25; 20:21, 22; 35% of all participles in CD), and seven in 4Q372 (4Q372 1 13, 15, 19, 21, 27 bis; 3 10; 70% of all participles in 4Q372). As noted in the discussion of orthography,[22] these manuscripts show a marked tendency toward defective forms.

The more than 300 examples of the passive participle are all *plene*.

7. STATIVE VERBS

Stative forms can be recognized by the fact that they describe attributes (strong), mental (fear) or physical states (clothed), and by the consistent lack of ô in the imperfect of the Qal (Joüon-Muraoka §41 c). The following list is representative: אהב "to love," גבה "to be high," גבר "to be strong," דבק "to cling," זקן "to be old," חזק "to be strong," חסר "to be wanting," חפץ "to delight," טהר "to be clean," טמא "to be unclean," יכל "to be able," ירא "to fear," ישׁן "to sleep," כבד "to be heavy," לבשׁ "to be clothed," למד "to learn," מלא "to be full," נגשׁ "to approach," פחד "to fear," צדק "to be just," צמא "to be thirsty," קדשׁ "to be consecrated," קטן "to be small," קרב "to be near," רגז "to be agitated," רחק "to be far," רעב "to be hungry," שׂבע "to be sated," שׂנא "to hate," שׁכב "to be lying" (see ישׁכוב 1QS 7:10, but regularly ישׁכב 11QT^a 45:11), שׁכח "to forget," שׁלם "to be complete," and שׁפל "to be low" (see ישׁפול 1QS 2:23 but also תשׁפל 4Q169 3-4 iv 3). Although verbal adjectives are the rule for this group: וטמא (1QS 5:20), קרבים (1QM 10:3), and כבד (11QT^a 59:6), the common form of the participle is also used: לובשׁים (1QM 7:10).

Nip‘al

The *Nip‘al* is regular in QH apart from היעצל (4Q418 47 2) where the ē of the preformative is represented by the *yod*.

Pi‘el

The *Pi‘el* is regular in QH and never *plene*.

---

[21] See the discussion of orthography in section 2 above.

[22] In section 2 above.

Puʿal

Apart from גנב (CD 9:11), לקח (1QHª 20:27) and מרבע (11QTª 4:13) forms of the *Puʿal* are *plene*: יסופר (1QpHab 2:1).

Hipʿil

In the *Hipʿil* perfect, the *î* of the indicative is, as in BH, regular: for example, החליקו (1QHª 12:7).

The *î* is also regular in inflections of the imperfect. Apart from jussive forms following אל, exceptions are few: ויקשב (CD 20:18), ותכרת (1QHª 12:20), וֿאֿסתר (4Q390 1 10), ישמדו (4Q418 69 ii 8), תשכל (4Q418 184 3), and ויקטר (11QTª 23:16).

In the imperative, the masculine singular is lacking, but will likely conform to the BH (הַקְטֵל). The masculine plural is regular with *î*: for example, האזינו (4Q525 23 ii 2).

The infinitive construct is regularly *plene* (86%): ולהכרית (1QM 1:4). The most common environment for defective forms is following the negative particle אין: לאין השבת (1QHª 14:12 and 8 times elsewhere in 1QHª and 4Q427, *HDSS* §400.09). See also לאין השב (1QHª 11:27). Apart from this pattern there seems to be little evidence in the *Hipʿil* of the strong verb of "pseudo-infinitive-absolute" (defective) forms in environments not preceded by prepositions (*HDSS* §310.14): להמטר (1Q22 2:10), להבדל (1Q34*bis* 3 ii 6), להברך (1QS 6:5, 6), להשבת (1QHª 15:15), and ולסתר (1QS 9:17).

The form הפלא is likely a true infinitive absolute, used adverbially in the pattern of BH הַרְבֵּה. See בהפלא מודה, "by (His) wondrous might" (1QS 10:16). See further 1QM 18:10; 1QHª 12:28; 17:39; 10 8, 10; 19:15; 5 3; 4Q427 3 i 5; 4Q427 7 ii 16.

The participle is regular; the *î* is present in every form apart from the feminine singular (ending in *taw*): e.g. מכנעת (1QM 1:14).

Hopʿal

The only defective *Hopʿal* is הסגרו (CD 19:13). See the parallel passage with הוסגרו (CD 7:13)

Perfect third masculine singular והובדל (1QS 8:24; CD 9:21), third plural הוסגרו (CD 7:13), participle masculine singular מובדל (1QS 7:3, 11QTª 16:12); masculine plural מובדלים (11QTª 35:11, 13; 46:17).

Hithpaʿel

The form והתדשנו (4Q171 1-10 ii 10) is of note as all forms of the *Hithpaʿel* with a root beginning with *dalet* in the MT show assimilation of the *taw* and *dalet* (מְדַבֵּר, Num. 7:89) except one (מִתְדַּפְּקִים, Judg 19:22).

8. I-NUN VERBS

Qal

Although the hallmark of the I-*nun* verb is the assimilation of the initial *nun* to the following consonant in environs where the *nun* closes the first syllable, roots which are also II-guttural resist this change in both BH and QH: תנחל (4Q525 13 1:4; 14 ii 14), תנאץ (1QHa 12:12). The often idiosyncratic 4Q175 records the unassimilated forms ינצר (4Q175 1:17) and ינתן (4Q175 1:3) as well.

As in BH, the verb לקח exhibits forms in the *Qal* imperfect in keeping with the I-*nun* verbs; the imperfect יקח (4Q251 12 2 and elsewhere) and the infinitive construct form]בקחת (4Q159 5 4) are representative.

Nipʿal

In the perfect, the *nun* of the root normally assimilates, ונגש (1QM 16:13; 19:11), but see ננתנו (1QHa 10:37).

Hipʿil and Hopʿal

In all forms of the *Hipʿil* and *Hopʿal*, the *nun* regularly assimilates, הפיל (4Q418 81 5) and הוגשתי (1QHa 6:18).

9. I-ʾALEP VERBS

Qal

Of the five verbs in BH where the *ʾalep* regularly quiesces to a long *ô*, אבה "to be willing," and אפה "to bake," are lacking in the imperfect in QH. אבד "to perish," יובדו (4Q169 3-4 ii 9; 4Q171 1-10 ii 1; 1-10 iii 3, 4, 8; 1-10 iv 18; 4Q372 3 6) and ויאובדו[(4Q462 2 2) and אכל "to eat," תאוכל (1QHa 11:30), but more frequently תואכל (1QM 12:12; 19:4; 1QHa 16:30; 11QTa 52:11; 52:19 and elsewhere) are common. Defective forms of אכל do occur: יאכל (CD 10:22, 23; 4Q251 5 5; 7 2, 3; 4Q274 2 ii 5; 4Q396 1-2 i 3),]יאכלו (4Q251 11 2) and תאכל (4Q169 3-4 i 9; 11QTa 20:12). אמר "to say," אומר (1QS 10:11), יואמר (4Q159 2-4 8), but also יוֹמַר (4Q418 145 2). Defective forms of אמר also occur: יאמרו[(4Q385 3 2; 4Q386 1 ii 7; 4Q418 69 ii 13),]תאמר (4Q418 8 6; 9 13) and תאמרו (4Q418 69 ii 11). As in BH, אסף occasionally occurs in similar forms: וְתוֹסֶף (1QHª 13:14), and perhaps וִיסְפֵהוּ (1QpHab 5:14). The ʾalep has possibly quiesced in לסורים, "to the captives" (4Q439 1 i 5), alternately read סירים, "thorns."

10. I-WAW/YOD VERBS

Qal

In verbs originally I-*waw*, the *yod* regularly quiesces in the imperfect of the *Qal*: יֵשְׁבוּ (1QS 6:4), יִרְשׁוּ (4Q171 1-10 iii 11), יֵצְאוּ (4Q493 1 4). On one occasion, the resultant *ṣere* is indicated by an ʾ*alep:* יְ[אצאו (4Q491 1-3 9). Occasionally the *yod* is retained; commonly with יִרא (to fear), תִירְאוּ (1QM 10:3; 15:8 and elsewhere) and תִירא (11QTª 61:13). See also יִירְשׁוּ (4Q385 3 3), and יִיעֲפוּ (1QpHab 10:8, Hab. 2:13: יָעֵפוּ). The normal form of the infinitive construct is רשׁת (1QSa 2:18) but see לִירוֹשׁ (CD 1:7 and 4Q266 2 i 12).

The historical I-*yod* verbs are represented by the imperfect יֵיטַב (11QTª 53:7), although יִטַב (4Q175 1:4) and the consecutive וַיִּקֶץ (4Q252 1 ii 5) which lack the root *yod* are also found. The only infinitive construct, וְלִיצוֹר (4Q299 10 4), occurs in the expected form.

As in BH, the verb הלך acts as a I-*waw* verb. In the *Qal* imperfect the *he* (as if a *yod*) is elided and forms such as אֵלֵךְ (1QS 2:14), יֵלֵךְ (11QTª 62:3) occur. There are no *Hipʿil* or *Nipʿal* forms.

יכל is also present in the imperfect *Qal*; third feminine תוּכַל (4Q274 1 i 5) and third plural יוּכְלוּ (1QHª 22:2; 11QTª 20:11; 43:13 *bis*).

Nipʿal

I-*waw* verbs regularly reveal the original *waw* in all parts of the verb extant: perfect נוֹעַדְנוּ (1QHª 10 7), imperfect יִוָּדַע (1QHª 9:8), infinitive construct לְהִוָּחֵד (1QS 1:8), and participle הַנּוֹעָדִים (1QSa 2:2). Only the occurrence of the infinitive construct לְהִיָּעֵץ (CD 3:5) reveals any confusion with I-*yod*.

There are no I-*yod* verbs which occur in the *Nipʿal* in QH.

Piʿel and Puʿal

Piʿel and *Puʿal* are as the strong verb with I-*waw/yod* verbs.

Hipʿil

As in the *Nipʿal*, I-*waw* verbs regularly reveal the original *waw*: perfect וְהוֹצֵאתָה (11QTª 55:20), imperfect אוֹכִיחַ (1QS 10:11), imperative הוֹצֵא (4Q418 81 18), participle וּמוֹדִיעַ (4Q427 7 i 18), and infinitive לְהוֹדִיעַ (1QHª 9:29). The few forms which lack the *waw* might be considered defective: להחיד (1QHa 2 i 10), ויד‍יעהו (CD 9:17), התיר (CD 2:11, although this may be from נתר), להכיחי (4Q372 1 28) and ולהרותם (1QpHab 10:11).

The I-*yod* is well represented in the *Hipʿil* by יטב: perfect היטיבו (4Q175 1:2), imperfect תיטיבי (4Q169 3-4 iii 8), imperative היט]יב (1Q22 1:5), and infinitive absolute היטב (11QTa 55:5, 19). The forms תטיב יטיב "(I]f) you do well, He shall prosper you" (4Q525 8-9 6), and המטיב (1Q27 1 ii 4), are either from טוב or reflect the elision of the root *yod*. The same can be said for ויקיצו (1QpHab 8:14).

The third class (GKC §71) of I-*waw/yod* verbs, the *yod* assimilating to the following consonant, may be instanced in [יצ]יעו (4Q525 15 9).

Hithpaʿel

The *Hithpaʿel* is usually regular with I-*waw/yod* verbs: יתיצבו (1QM 2:4). Notice, however, the forms of ויתודו, ידה (CD 20:28) and והתודה (CD 15:4; 11QTa 26:11) as well as יסר; for example, התוסרו (CD 4:8).

11. GEMINATE VERBS

Qal

Geminate forms of the *Qal* perfect are represented by the third masculine singular, all of which are formed after the pattern of זמם (11QTa 61:10). חקקא (1QS 10:1) is possibly in error for חקק אל, "God determined." All instances of the second masculine singular have the separating vowel before the sufformative: חקותה (1QHa 21:12; 4Q427 5 3). As in BH, two forms exist for the third common plural, סבבום (1QHa 10:25), which in general is transitive, and שעו (1QHa 15:2), which is intransitive.

The imperfect is normally *plene* (69%), ירוק (1QS 7:13). As in BH, the roots חלל, חתת, מלל, צלל, and רכך are formed with the *pataḥ*: ירך (1QM 10:3). Against BH, the root תמם appears to follow this second pattern as it is defective in each of its nine occurrences: for instance, תתם (1QS 8:25), יתמו (1QM 14:7). The imperative of geminate verbs is *plene* where it occurs: ושול (1QM 12:10) and שול (4Q492 1 3).

The infinitive construct is regularly *plene*, תום (1QS 10:21). תם (CD 20:14) and זכו, "his being pure" (CD 10:3) are defective according to the scribal school reflected in CD.

Both active and passive participles are according to the strong verb and regularly *plene* (97%), זולל (11QT^a 64:5) and סוררת (CD 11:7 and 4Q271 5 i 3). The only defective forms are סררי (CD 2:6) and שממים (4Q372 1 11). מסי (1QM 10:6) is not a participle of מסס but the plural construct of the adjective מס, "melting." See סורירה (CD 1:13) for the spelling of MT סֹרֵרָה (Hos. 4:16).

Nip'al

The *Nip'al* is represented by the perfect נדמו (1QpHab 5:10), imperfect וימס (1QH^a 12:33; 16:32; 4 14; 11QT^a 62:4), infinitive construct בהמס (4Q427 6 3) and participle נמס (1QM 11:9; 14:6; 4Q491 8-10 3; 11 ii 15).

Pi'el

The *Pi'el* is as the strong verb and is represented by the verbs ארר, קלל, מדד, חקק, חלל, הלל, זקק, גשש, ברר, and רנן.

Pu'al

The *Pu'al* is represented by forms of the perfect שודדה (4Q169 3-4 iii 6) and זוקקה (4Q427 3 i 12), imperfect יהולל (1QH^a 19:24 and 4Q427 1 6), participles ומהולל (4Q503 40-41 ii 6), מזוקק (1QH^a 13:16), מרודד (1QM 8:5, 14), ממוזזים (1QM 5:5, 8), מזוקקי (1QH^a 6:3), and מקוללי (11QT^a 64:12, 4Q171 1-10 iii 9).

Po'el

The *Po'el* is extant in imperfects ויחוננכה (1QSb 2:26, see also 1QSb 1:5; 2:3, 27), ידולל (4Q525 15 3) and יסובבונ (1QH^a 13:35), infinitive construct להולל (1QH^a 12:17), and participles מחוקק (CD 6:4 [4Q267 2 10], 7, 9, see the defective form at 4Q252 1 v 2) and ומעונן (11QT^a 60:18).

Po'al

The *Poal* is present in only a few instances, all of which are participles: ומגולל (1QH^a 22:4), מחוקק (4Q417 2 i 15), and המגוללים (4Q525 21 6).

Pilpel

Instances of the *Pilpel* are the perfect וקרקר (CD 7:20, see also 1QM 11:6 and 4Q175 1:13); the imperfects יתעתעו (1QpHab 4:3), תששע (1QH^a 18:31, see also 1QH^a 17:32), ישעשע (4Q418 69 ii 12, also 1QSb 2:23) and]תקלקל (4Q385 1 4); the cohortative]אשתעשעה (1QH^a 18:16); and the infinitive construct]כשעשע[(1QH^a 15:21).

Hip'il

The *ē* of the second syllable in the *Hip'il* is never indicated with the *yod* in the extant forms of the perfect: for instance, הפרו (11QTª 59:8) and הצרה (1QHª 11:9). The separating vowel before consonantal sufformatives is usually written החתותני (1QHª 10:35) and הרעונו (1QM 11:4), but is defective in the form החתתה (1QHª 15:8).

As in the perfect, there are no sure examples of *plene* forms in the imperfect. יחל (4Q274 1 i 1) and יפרו (4Q390 2 i 6) are examples of typical forms. The only imperative is הרנינו (4Q427 7 i 14), which, as in BH, is formed according to the strong verb (see Ps 32:11).

The infinitive construct is regularly defective (90%), להרע (1QpHab 3:5). The forms לה[מים] (1QM 9:11) and ל[החיל (4Q251 1 6) are exceptions.

The three instances of the participle are all defective: והמרע (1Q27 1 ii 4), מרעים (4Q171 1-10 ii 2), and מפרים (4Q390 2 i 5).

Hop'al

The *Hop'al* is represented by the defective perfect form השם (1QHª 15:3; 21:5), defective imperfect יכתו (1QM 18:2), *plene* imperfects יוארו (CD 12:22) and יושדו (1QHª 5 6), and the participle מוסב (1QM 5:5).

Hithpa'el

The *Hithpa'el* is according to the strong verb and is represented by the roots חנן (1QHª 4:18; 20:4), חלל (4Q387 1 3), פלל (1QHª 4:18), and פרר (1QHª 3 5).

Hithpo'el

The *Hithpo'el* is extant in the perfects התגוללתי (1QHª 4:19), והתגולל (1QS 4:21), התגוללה (1QS 4:19), התגוללו (CD 3:17), imperfects ויתהולל (1QHª 18:33), ויתגוללו (CD 8:5; 19:17; 1QHª 14:22), ויתהוללו (1QHª 11:33), and infinitive construct להתהולל (1QHª 12:12). Note that התגללו (4Q416 1 11) and תתגדרו (11QTª 48:8) are probably defective *Hithpo'el*s rather than forms of the *Hithpa'el*.

Hithpalpel

The *Hithpalpel* is found in the imperfect forms אשתעשע (1QHª 17:13), תשתעשע (1QHª 17:8; 19:7), and יתערערו (4Q416 1 12).

12. II-WAW/YOD VERBS

Qal

The II-*waw/yod* verb is regular in the perfect in QH. Note, however, the odd case of the third common plural of בוא: שֶׁבָּאוּ (4Q398 11-13 3). The verbs גוע (CD 2:20), איב (often in participle), as in BH, are treated as strong verbs.

As in BH, the medial root letter becomes evident in the *Qal* imperfect. The imperfect is regularly *plene* (97%). Aside from the short forms following אַל and the *waw* consecutive, there are only nine defective forms: יבאו (CD 12:14); יבאו (CD 14:10, יבאוו 4Q266 10 i 3); יצדו (CD 16:15), [ו]ישם (1QSb 5:26), וירדמו (1QHa 16:9), בש]ו (4Q418 69 ii 8), יבא (4Q427 7 i 10), and וימת (11QTa 56:10; 64:8).

The imperative is *plene* throughout. However, the difficult form בֹאי (4Q169 5 3) should be noted.

The infinitive construct is *plene* throughout. The infinitive absolute shares the same form: ואור (1QM 1:8); וקול (1QpHab 3:6) and בוא (1QpHab 7:9) in the biblical lemma from Habakkuk.

The participle is regular throughout according to BH. The passive participle exists in regular forms: טוח (CD 11:9 and 4Q271 5 i 5) and פוח (1QS 7:14).

Nipʿal

The perfect of the II-*waw/yod* verbs is represented by the third masculine singular נימול (CD 16:6, see the Cave 4 counterpart: נמול, 4Q271 4 ii 7), and the third masculine plural forms נזורו (1QHa 12:19), and נכונו (CD 5:12; 1QHa 12:14; 1QHa 2 i 15).

The imperfect is likewise extant only in the third person forms: third masculine singular forms יכון (1Q34*bis* 3 ii 5; 4Q299 31 1), יאות (CD 20:7), and ילון (1QS 7:17 *bis*), third feminine singular תכון (1QHa 12:13, 31; 16:2; 1Q27 1 i 6; 4Q299 6 ii 16), and the third masculine plural יכונו (1QHa 12:22; 15:31; 4Q418 122 i 1; 172 3).

The *Nipʿal* participle is represented in the masculine singular by נכון (1QHa 12:6, *et al.*), the feminine singular נכונה (1QS 8:5) and נסוגה (1QS 8:12; 4Q525 4 2), the masculine plural והנבונים (1QSa 1:28; CD 6:2; 4Q266 3 ii 10; 4Q525 4 9; 4Q525 16 3) and the construct נמוגי (1QM 14:6; 4Q491 8-10 4), and the feminine plural נכונות (1QHa 21:8). The participle is always *plene*.

The infinitive construct is extant in להסוג (1QS 2:12).

Pi‛el

There are only three II-*waw/yod* forms that appear to follow the strong verb in the *Pi‛el*, וחיב (4Q276 1 2, as Dan 1:10), קימו (CD 20:12, as Esther 9:27, 31), and ומעור (11QT^a 51:13, cf. 2 Kgs 25:7 and elsewhere). See also]שׁוּעתי (1QpHab 1:1) in the lemma from Hab 1:1.

Pu‛al

There are no examples of the *Pu‛al* in the II-*waw/yod* verbs.

Polel

The *Polel* is *plene* throughout and is regularly characterized by the doubling of the third root radical, thus echoing the *Po‛el* of the geminate verbs. Both II-*waw* and II-*yod* forms are spelled the same. The perfect is represented in the first common singular כוננתי (1QH^a 47 3), second masculine singular כוננתה (4Q428 7 5), and third common plural ורוממו (1QM 14:4; 4Q427 7 i 15; 4Q491 16 5).

The imperfect being more common, the following instances are examples of existing forms: first common singular אשוחח (1QS 10:16), second masculine singular תנובב (11Q14 1-2 ii 9), third masculine singular יעורר (1QH^a 17:3), third feminine singular תנובב (11Q14 1-2 ii 9), first common plural נרוממה (1QM 14:13), and third masculine plural יעופפו (4Q525 15 5).

The imperative is extant in the masculine plural form ר[ו]ממו (4Q427 7 i 15).

The participle occurs in the masculine singular מקונן (4Q385 16 ii 4), masculine plural מרוממים (4Q503 11 v 3), and feminine plural ובמחוללות (4Q285 5 5). This last form is by context more likely a *Polel* of חול (to dance), echoing Exod 15:20, than a *Po‛al* of חלל (to pierce), reflecting Isa 53:5.

Polal

The only example of the *Polal* is ירוממ (4Q491 11 i 13). כונ[נו] reproduces Ps 37:23 (4Q171 1-10 iii 14).

Pilpel

The *Pilpel* is found in the following examples: imperfects, second masculine singular תכלכלני (1QH^a 17:34, see also 17:36; 4Q418 46 2), third masculine singular יכלכלם (1QS 3:17) and plural יתשגשגו (1QH^a 16:9), participle masculine plural מזעזיעכה (1QpHab 8:14) and מפצפצים (4Q372 1 11).

Hip'il

In all parts of the *Hip'il* both II-*waw* and II-*yod* verbs show identical forms. Apart from one instance, הבאתי (4Q389 2 6), the characteristic separating vowel found before consonantal endings in the perfect is regular in QH. Examples of existing forms of the perfect are: first person singular הביאׄתי (4Q438 3 3), second masculine singular האירותה (1QHª 17:27), third masculine singular הבין (1Q34*bis* 3 ii 3), third feminine singular הכׄינה (4Q491 11 i 10), second masculine plural והביאותמה (11QTª 18:13), and third common plural הבינו (4Q387 5 4). Note the *yod* for the *ṣere* in הׅיעירו (CD 8:17).

Examples of existing inflections of the imperfect are: first common singular אביא (1QHª 6:21), second masculine singular תבין (4Q418 77 3), third masculine singular ירים (4Q427 7 ii 10), third feminine singular תחיש (1QHª 14:29), first common plural נשיב (1QHª 10 3), second masculine plural תכׄינו (4Q418 46 1), and third masculine plural יזידו (11QTª 56:11). As in the *Qal*, the imperfect is regularly *plene* (98%). Aside from the short forms following אַל and the *waw* consecutive, there are only three defective forms: ויקם (1QS 5:8), ויכן (1QS 11:13), and ויאר (11Q14 1-2 ii 6). Notable is the retention of the *he* in ויהכין (1QS 3:9). Some scribal confusion is evident in יאנה (11QTª 53:20) for MT יָנִיא (Num 30:9).

The masculine singular imperative, as in BH, is according to the form הכן (1QS 11:16), while the plural is הרימו (1QHª 14:34). The feminine plural is not extant in BH but is evidenced in QH: והגלנה (1QM 12:13; 19:5)

The infinitive construct, להאיר (1QM 17:7 and elsewhere), and absolute, השב (11QTª 64:14), are present. The construct infinitive is normally *plene* (90%). It is notable that apart from ולהשב (1QS 8:6), להקם (1QS 8:10), להרע (4Q171 1-10 ii 2), הנף (11QTª 11:10), and the frequent הטל (1QM 8:15; 16:6; 17:12; 4Q491 13 5), the defective forms occur following the negatives לבלתי (הבן, 4Q525 7 ii 2), אין (הסר, 1QHª 11:27; 14:18); and לוא (הסר, 1QS 6:11; 9:20). For a similar pattern, see השבת in the discussion of the *Hip'il* of the strong verb. The infinitive absolute is extant in הנא (11QTª 53:20) and השב (11QTª 64:14).

The participle is extant in all of its forms except the feminine singular: masculine singular מבין (4Q418 81 15), masculine plural מריעים (1QM 8:12), and feminine plural מריעות (1QM 8:1). Without exception these forms are all *plene*.

Hopʿal

The *Hopʿal* of the II-*waw/yod* verb is *plene* throughout, with the perfect third masculine singular הוכן (4Q385 9 ii 3) and והומת (4Q251 4 3; 11QTª 61:2; 66:5), the third feminine singular והומתה (4Q159 2-4 9) and הושבה (CD 6:6), and the third plural הובאו (CD 6:11 and 4Q266 3 ii 17). The imperfect third masculine singular is יומת (4Q159 2-4 6; CD 12:4; 11QTª 35:5; 51:17; 54:15; 64:9) and the third masculine plural is יומתו (11QTª 35:7; 66:2). For participial forms, the masculine singular is מוטל (4Q372 1 10), הושבה (CD 6:6) and המוכן (CD 10:22), and masculine plural is מובאים (CD 11:3).

Hithpolel

The reflexive stem *Hithpolel* is common and nearly *plene* throughout; the only defective example is והתבנן (4Q398 11-13 6). Most likely reflecting a scribal error is the intermediate *yod* in the construct masculine plural participle ולמשתוחיחי (1QHª 17:9).

Hithpalpel

The only examples of *Hithpalpel* are found with the verb זוע (to shake). The expected metathesis is evident in the form יזדעזעו (1QS 8:8) but is lacking in תחזעזע (1QHª 14:27). The confusion concerning the forms of this word, see ת'ד{ז}עז (1QHª 15:9), is perhaps behind the meaningless יזד עזרע (1QS 11:4, for יזדעזע?).

13. II AND III-GUTTURALS

As in BH, the II and III-guttural verbs consistently lack the theme vowel in the imperfect and imperative of the *Qal*. Note the correction ישח{ו}קו (1QpHab 4:6, see Jer 5:7 Q אֶסְלַח, K אֶסְלוֹחַ). The doubtful reading יש[מוע (4Q491 1-3 13) should perhaps be corrected to יש[מיעו.

14. III-ʿALEP VERBS

There is some confusion with III-*he* verbs: יאנה from the root נוא, "to refuse" (11QTª 53:20), הִפָּלה[from פלא (4Q491 11 i 8), הנבה from נבא (4Q385 2 5), קורה for קרא (1QS 7:1), and perhaps ב[רִיתנו (1QM 13:9, see ברתנו, 4Q495 2 1) from ברא. Note the correction להפל{א}ה (1QpHab 7:8, see Joel 2:26).

There is the occasional quiescence of the *ʾalep*, יוצי (4Q159 2-4 8), וחוטי (1QpHab 10:2), often with the verb פלא, especially in the second masculine singular: הפלתה (1QM 14:9; 18:10; 1QHª 13:15; 15:34; 19:3; 2 i 16) and ברתנו (4Q495 2 1). See also the *Hipʿil* participle, masculine plural construct המפלי (4Q427 7 i 18) and לשת from נשא (1QHª 18:25).

Note the confusion in the representation of the infinitive construct of מלא: וּבִמְגֻלוֹאת (1QS 7:20); מִלֹּאת (1QS 6:17, 18, 21 *bis*; 8:26), מלואת (1QS 7:22), מילואת (1QSa 1:10, but see וּבמלוא, 1QSa 1:12)

15. III-*HE* VERBS

The regular forms of the III-*he* are as in BH. There are no roots such as תמה in which the *he* is original. There is some confusion with III-ʾ*alep*: והווא (1QS 11:4, 5, but see 1QS 3:15; 11:11), ו[הֹוֹדא (4Q409 1 i 11), בזא (4Q434 1 ii 2) and היֹא (4Q398 14-17 ii 1, 2).

The perfect is generally according to BH. Both הייתי (1QHª 10:11 and 6 times elsewhere) and היתי (11QTª 59:18) exist for the first singular. Likewise הייתה (1QSb 5:24 and 7 times elsewhere) and היתה (1QpHab 8:14, see 2 Sam 10:11) exist for the second masculine singular. See also חבתה (1QHª 13:11, 25) for חביתה.

The imperfect is likewise according to BH. The cohortative of the first person singular occurs, אחסיה (1QHª 17:29, see וְאֶהֱמָיָה, Ps 77:4). The third person masculine singular is regularly יהיה (78 times) but see יהייה (4Q252 1 ii 6). Note יחישו (1QM 8:11) for יחשו.

The infinitive construct is everywhere *plene* except ולרצת (1QS 8:3) for ולרצות. Note כגולו]ת (4Q300 3 5) for כגלות (1Q27 1 i 5) and קצוות (1QpHab 9:14) for קצות (1QpHab 10:2).

Qal

The participle in the *Qal* is regularly *plene* in 98 of 108 instances (91%). For examples of defective forms see ועשים (4Q372 1 12), ועשה (CD 20:21), עשה (1QM 11:7), הדמה (4Q491 11 i 16), and הרעה (CD 19:8). The same is true for verbs which are also II-*waw/yod*: note קוי (Q427 7 i 20), לוה (4Q171 1-10 iii 8), and שו[ה] (4Q417 1 ii 9).

Apart from CD 2:21 and 3:8 (עשיהם), the participle with suffixes is always *plene*. In singular masculine forms it is usual for pronominal suffixes to be attached directly to the form without the *he*: עושו (4Q299 2 ii 7, 8). Occasionally, however, the *he* appears to revert to the original *yod*: עושיו, "his Creator" (1QS 9:26) and עשיהם, "their creator" (CD 2:21; 3:8) and perhaps יוריהם, "their teacher" (CD 3:8). Actually, these are likely *plene* spellings of the ṣere. See the discussion under orthography. Note the feminine singular הוֹרִיתִי, "the one who bore me," (1QHa 17:30). See GKC §75v.

Note the lack of the *yod* in the passive participle וגלו (4Q175 1:11)

Nipʿal

The *Nipʿal* participle is as BH, but note the participle masculine singular form ונהייה (1QS 3:15).

Hipʿil

The root *he* occasionally apocopates in the *Hipʿil* imperative form הך (CD 19:8, cf. 2 Kgs 6:18); הרף (4Q171 1-10 ii 1, see Deut 9:14).

16. CARDINAL NUMBERS

	With the Masculine		With the Feminine	
	Abs.	Const.	Abs.	Const.
1.	אחד	אחד	אחת	אחת
2.	שנים	שני	שתים	שתי
3.	שלשה/שלושה	שלשת/שלושת	שלוש	שלוש[23]
4.	ארבעה	ארבעת	ארבע	ארבע
5.	חמשה	חמשת	חמש	חמש
6.	ששה	ששת	שש	שש
7.	שבעה	שבעת	שבע	שבע
8.	שמונה[24]	שמונת	שמונה	—
9.	תשעה	תשעת	תשע	תשע
10.	עשרה[25]	עשרת	עשר	עשר

The Numeral One

The numeral אחד (one), with its feminine אחת, always agrees with the substantive in gender and definiteness.

(a) Most frequently it occurs as an adjective (GKC §97a) and follows that which it modifies. When indefinite it often carries a force similar to an indefinite article:

שנה אחת   "one year" (1QS 6:25 and often)
שגגה אחת   "a single unintentional sin" (1QS 9:1)

---

[23] Written as שלש only at 3Q15 10 10 in construct with מאות ("hundred").

[24] שמנה is found only in a correction at frgs. 1 ii + 2 ii 7 of 4Q317, a text that was written in Cryptic A script.

[25] Written as עשרא at 1QSa 2:22.

This anarthrous use can also convey the sense of "the same":

 ביום אחד "the same day" (4Q396 1-2 i 2; 11QTᵃ 52:6)

When modifying a definite noun this numeral may convey the sense of "each":

 למערכה האחת "to each battle line" (1QM 5:4)
 החיה האחת "each being" (4Q385 4 7)

Definite usage frequently emphasizes the particular nature of what is being modified:

 הכוהן האחד "the one priest" (1QM 7:12)
 הכבש האחד "the one lamb" (11QTᵃ 13:11)

Occasionally the contrasted item is also mentioned:

 לעבר האחד...לעבר השני "on the one side...on the other" (1QM 6:9)

(b) Although rare, אחד is occasionally found in the construct:

 ואח[ד נ]שר ואחד עגל "on]e (face) of an eagle and one of a calf" (4Q385 4 9)

(c) The "ordinal" use of אחד in conjunction with יום (day) to indicate the first day of the month occurs in QH:

 יום א[חד לשנים עשר [החודש] "the f[irst] day [of the twelfth] month" (4Q252 1 i 19)

The first day of the week is also indicated in a like manner:

 יום אחד בשבת "on the first day of the week" (4Q252 1 i 13)

The Numeral Two

The numeral שנים (two), with its feminine form שתים, always agrees with the gender of its noun. The forms are used in four ways.

(a) The numeral is placed after the noun like an adjective:

 ושערים שנים "two gates" (1QM 9:14)
 וכוהנים שנים "two priests" (4Q159 2-4 4)

(b) Most commonly the numeral is in the construct state preceding the qualified word:

 שתי רוחות "two spirits" (1QS 3:18)
 שני אחיו "his two brothers" (4Q372 1 10)

(c) Occasionally the numeral is placed in apposition to the noun modified and precedes it in the absolute state:

 ושנים שערים "two gates" (11QTᵃ 33:10)
 שנים עדים "two witnesses" (11QTᵃ 61:7; 64:8)

(d) The ordinal use of the numeral שנים is not well attested in QH:

 ביום שנים "the second day" (4Q320 1 iii 14)

The Numerals Three–Ten

The curious characteristic of Hebrew numerals, the masculine nouns modified by feminine forms and feminine nouns by masculine forms, continues in QH. The substantive which is numbered is found without exception, as in BH, in the plural (GKC §134e).

(a) By far the most common use of the numbers 3-10 is in apposition before the substantives they modify:

עשרה אנשים   "ten men" (1QS 6:3)
וחמש שנים   "five years" (4Q252 1 ii 9)

(b) Less frequently in construct with the following substantive:

עשרת ימים   "ten days" (1QS 7:10)
ובעשר השנים   "during the ten years" (1QM 2:13)

(c) Occasionally in apposition following:

ימים ששה   "six days" (CD 14:21)
כהנים שלושה   "three priests" (4Q387 2 4)
וכבשים בני שנה שבעה "and seven yearling lambs" (11QT^a 17:14)

(d) Following the singular of יום (day) the numeral takes on the force of an ordinal.

יום חמשה רשרה   "the fifth day of the week (Thursday)" (4Q252 1 i 7)
ביום חמשה   "on the fifth day" (4Q503 37-38 12:13)

It is to be noted that the only occurrence of this pattern in the calendar texts is the doubtful phrase ביוֹם שנים ("on the second day," 4Q320 1 iii 14). Elsewhere in the calendars, however, the ordinals are used.

The Numerals Eleven–Nineteen

In the partial chart below, the forms of 14-19 continue according to the pattern established by thirteen. In the masculine the first element is with one exception (שני עשר) in apposition to עשר (ten). In the feminine the first element of 13-19 may be in the construct state. There are certain substantives which are found in the singular when used after these numbers: איש (man, 1QS 8:1, but cf. the reconstruction of 4Q252 1 iii 1-2), אמה (cubit, 1QM 4:15, 16), יום (day, 4Q252 1 ii 1; 11QT^a 27:10), נשכה (chamber, 11QT^a 42:5), and מעלה (step, 11QT^a 46:6-7). These patterns follow BH. Due to the compound nature, 11-19 are never in construct with the following substantive.

	With the Masculine	*With the Feminine*
11.	אחד עשר[26]	אחת עשרה[27]
	עשתי עשר	עשתי עשרה[28]
12.	שנים עשר[29]	שתים עשרה
	שני עשר[30]	
13.	שלשה עשר	שלש עשרה

(a) Normally the numbers 11-19 are in apposition preceding the substantive being modified:

שנים עשר איש "twelve men" (1QS 8:1)

ושתים עשרה מעלה "twelve steps" (11QT[a] 46:6-7)

(b) Occasionally they are in apposition following:

ראשים שנים עשר "twelve chiefs" (1QM 2:1)

כבשים בני שנה ארבעה עשר "fourteen yearling lambs" (11QT[a] 28:10)

(c) They are also used as ordinals"

בשבעה עשר בו "on the seventeenth of it (the month)" (4Q252 1 i 4)

ובחמשה עשר יום "and on the fifteenth day" (11QT[a] 27:10)

The Numerals Twenty to Ninety-Nine

As in BH, multiples of ten are plural forms of the units, except for עשרים (twenty) which is the plural of עשר (ten). The masculine plural form is used to modify both masculine and feminine substantives. Compounds are formed by the unit—which agrees in gender with the substantive being modified—followed by *waw* and the "ten."

(a) Most frequently they are in apposition before the substantive:

חמש ועשרים שנה "twenty-five years" (1QSa 1:12)

---

[26] According to the Masoretic tradition, this form is to be pointed עָשָׂר. This combination is found only in four instances, all of them in the calendrical texts: 4Q321a 1 ii 3; 4Q323 2 2; 4Q324 1 7; and 4Q324a 1 ii 4. The form עשתי עשר is preferred in QH.

[27] עֲשֶׂרֵה according to the Masoretic pointing. This combination is extant only in the reconstruction at 4Q159 1 ii 13.

[28] This form is found only at 1QM 4:16.

[29] Note שנים העשר האלה ("these twelve") in 4Q159 2-4 4, which echoes the construction of Josh 4:4 and 1 Kgs 19:19.

[30] The only occurrence of the masculine construct form is שני עשר העמודים ("twelve pillars") at 11QT[a] 34:15. The MT favors the absolute (86 times) over the construct (6 times) in both the masculine and feminine forms (absolute 34 times, construct 4 times).

(b) This pattern is occasionally reversed:

ראשי המשמרות ששה ועשרים "the twenty-six chiefs of the courses" (1QM 2:2)

(c) The use of ordinals is also extant:

יום עשרים וששה "the twenty-sixth day" (4Q252 1 i 6)

Hundreds

One hundred is מאה, two hundred is the dual form מאתים (1QM 6:9), while three to nine hundred are formed by prefacing the feminine construct form of the units to the plural form of מאה:

שלוש מאות "three hundred" (11QT^a 40:13)

The intermediate numbers can be formed by either beginning with the component expressing 1–99 (10 times) or with the component expressing the hundred (20 times).

ארבעה וששים ושלוש מאות "three hundred and sixty four" (11QPs^a 27:6-7)

שלוש מאות ששים וארבעה "three hundred and sixty four" (4Q252 1 ii 3)

Thousands

One thousand is אלף, two thousand is the dual form אלפים (1QM 7:7), while three to nine thousand are formed by prefacing the masculine construct form of the units to the plural form of אלף:

ששת אלפים "six thousand" (1QM 6:11)

For a compounds of hundreds and thousands, it is more common for the thousands to come first (5 times), but the reverse occurs as well (1 time).

שלושת אלפים ושש מאות "three thousand six hundred" (11QPs^a 27:5)

שש מאות וארבעת אלפים "four thousand six hundred" (1QM 6:10)

Higher numbers also exist.

שנים עשר אלף "twelve thousand" (11QT^a 57:6)

שמונה ועשרים אלף "twenty-eight thousand" (1QM 9:4)

לשש מא[ו]ת האלף "six hundred thousand" (4Q159 1 ii 8)

Ten Thousand is expressed by the term רבוא. It is not used in counting, however, but refers to a tribal division (1QM 3:16; 4:16; 12:4). The term רבבה found in BH does not occur in QH.

17. END NOTE

Drawing conclusions based on the grammar of QH, and thereby venturing into a meaningful discussion of QH syntax, is unfortunately beyond the scope of this study. Within the next decade the initial stages of publication will have been completed and those who are driven by a passion for Hebrew as a language will be able at last to refine preliminary conclusions. This will allow for a second stage of mending difficult readings in the editions, and of suggesting meaningful and grammatically suitable reconstructions. This process will of course continue until the אחרית (ה)ימים (1QSa 1:1)!

For most of us, however, grammatical study is not the end; rather it is the necessary means to the appreciation of that which Edward Cook has aptly termed "lost letters from home."[31] The rewards are undoubtedly promising and great.

SELECT BIBLIOGRAPHY

Goshen-Gottstein, M. H. "Studies in the Language of the Dead Sea Scrolls," in his *Text and Language in Bible and Qumran* (Tel Aviv: Orient Publishing House, 1960) 86-89.

—. "Linguistic Structure and Tradition in the Qumran Documents," in his *Text and Language in Bible and Qumran* (Tel Aviv: Orient Publishing House, 1960) 97-132.

Kesterson, J. C. *Tense Usage and Verbal Syntax in Selected Qumran Documents.* (Ph.D. diss., Washington, DC: Catholic University of America, 1984).

Kutscher, E. Y. "Hebrew Language, The Dead Sea Scrolls," *EncJud* (1971) 16.1583-90.

—. *The Language and Linguistic Background of the Isaiah Scroll.* (STDJ 6; Leiden: Brill, 1974).

—. הכתובות העבריות והארמיות בירושלים מימי הבית השני, in *Hebrew and Aramaic Studies* (Jerusalem: 1977) 27-35.

Morag, S. "Qumran Hebrew: Some Typological Observations," *VT* 38 (1988) 148-64.

Qimron, E. דקדוק הלשון העברית של מגילות מדבר יהודה (Ph.D. diss., Jerusalem: Hebrew University, 1976).

—. *The Hebrew of the Dead Sea Scrolls* (HSS 29. Atlanta: Scholars, 1986).

—. "Observations on the History of Early Hebrew (1000 B.C.E.-200 C.E.) in the Light of the Dead Sea Documents," in D. Dimant and U. Rappaport (eds.), *The Dead Sea Scrolls: Forty Years of Research* (STDJ 10; Leiden: Brill; Jerusalem: Magnes, 1992) 349-61.

Rabin, C. "The Historical Background of Qumran Hebrew," in Chaim Rabin and Yigael Yadin (eds.), *Scripta Hierosolymitana IV: Aspects of the Dead Sea Scrolls* (Jerusalem: Magnes, 1958) 144-61.

---

[31] M. Wise, M. Abegg, Jr., and E. Cook, *The Dead Sea Scrolls: A New Translation* (San Francisco: HarperSanFrancisco, 1996) 34.

Smith, M. S. *The Origins and Development of the Waw-Consecutive: Northwest Semitic Evidence from Ugarit to Qumran.* (Atlanta: Scholars Press, 1991).

Thorion-Vardi, T. "The Use of the Tenses in the Zadokite Documents," *RevQ* 12 (1985) 65-88.

Tov, E. "The Orthography and Language of the Hebrew Scrolls Found at Qumran and the Origin of these Scrolls," *Textus* 13 (1986) 31-57.

THE ARAMAIC OF THE DEAD SEA SCROLLS

EDWARD M. COOK

Among the Qumran documents there are over 100 Aramaic texts, which constitute the earliest examples—besides Biblical Aramaic (abbreviated as "BA")—of Jewish Aramaic. The Qumran Aramaic ("QA") found in these documents has provided a great impetus to the study of the Aramaic dialects.*

1. THE CORPUS

The largest and most significant texts are the Genesis Apocryphon (1QapGen), the translation (targum) of Job (11QtgJob), the Enoch literature (4Q201–212, 530–533, 1Q23, 2Q26, 6Q8), the Aramaic version of Tobit (4Q196–199), the New Jerusalem texts (1Q32, 2Q24, 5Q15, 4Q554–555, 11Q18), the Vision of Amram (4Q543–548), and the fragments of an early Aramaic Levi Document (1Q21, 4Q213–214, possibly also 4Q540–541).

Shorter texts include the Prayer of Nabonidus (4Q242), Pseudo-Daniel ar (4Q243–245), the "son of God" text (4Q246), a brontologion (4Q318), a list of false prophets (4Q339), the Words of Michael (4Q529), the "elect of God" text (4Q534), the Testament of Qahat (4Q542), a text mentioning Hur and Miriam (4Q549), a fragmentary narrative set in the Persian court (4Q550), the "four kingdoms" texts (4Q552–553), an incantation (4Q560), and a horoscope (4Q561). Many of the smaller fragmentary texts seem to bear some resemblance, as far as one can tell, to the testamentary or apocalyptic genres already well represented in the other literature: 1Q24, 1Q63–68, 3Q12–14, 5Q24, 6Q14, 6Q19, 6Q23, 6Q26, 6Q31, 4Q488–490, 4Q535–536 (which may belong with 4Q534), the Vision of Jacob (4Q537), Testament of Judah (4Q538), Testament of Joseph

---

* The following abbreviations should be noted in this chapter: *ATTM* = K. Beyer, *Die aramäischen Texte vom Toten Meer* (Göttingen: Vandenhoeck & Ruprecht, 1984); *ATTME* = K. Beyer, *ATTM Ergänzungsband* (Vandenhoeck & Ruprecht, 1994); *SQA* = T. Muraoka (ed.), *Studies in Qumran Aramaic* (Abr-Nahrain Supplement 3; Louvain: Peeters, 1992).

(4Q539), 4Q551, 4Q556–558, 4Q562–575. Some legal texts attributed to Cave 4 (4Q344–355) have not yet been published.[1]

The earliest studies concentrated on the first published Aramaic text, the Genesis Apocryphon (1QapGen), still the longest connected Aramaic document from Qumran. E. Y. Kutscher, in an influential study, attempted to place 1QapGen within the spectrum of Aramaic dialects.[2] His approach was imitated by Michael Sokoloff in later studies of the Targum of Job from Cave 11 (11QtgJob)[3] and the Enoch texts from Cave 4.[4] This quantitative approach catalogs differences and similarities in the linguistic features of the texts, assigns them a label of either "early" or "late," and constructs a relative chronology of composition based on the proportion of early and late features. The approach has not yielded unambiguous results and in recent times scholars have criticized it,[5] seeking instead a more nuanced analysis in dialect geography[6] or sociolinguistics.[7]

J. A. Fitzmyer suggested a new classification of the Aramaic dialects, partly in order to accommodate the new data from Qumran. First in his commentary on 1QapGen,[8] and then in a programmatic

---

[1] A list of the Aramaic texts from Cave 4 is provided by Stephen A. Reed, "Preliminary List of Aramaic Documents from Qumran Cave 4," *Comprehensive Aramaic Lexicon Newsletter* 9 (1992) 1-4. See now S. A. Reed, with M. J. Lundberg and M. J. Phelps (eds.), *The Dead Sea Scrolls Catalogue: Documents, Photographs and Museum Inventory Numbers* (SBLRBS 32; Atlanta: Scholars Press, 1994) esp. 80-2, 140-5; and E. Tov, with S. J. Pfann (eds.), *The Dead Sea Scrolls on Microfiche. A Comprehensive Facsimile Edition of the Texts from the Judaean Desert, Companion Volume* (Leiden: Brill and IDC, 1993) esp. 36, 47-8.

[2] E. Y. Kutscher, "The Language of the Genesis Apocryphon: A Preliminary Study," *Scripta Hierosolymitana* 4 (1957) 1-35.

[3] M. Sokoloff, *The Targum to Job from Qumran Cave XI* (Ramat-gan: Bar-Ilan University, 1974).

[4] M. Sokoloff, "Notes on the Aramaic Fragments of Enoch from Qumran Cave 4," *Maarav* 1 (1979) 197-224.

[5] Cf. Robert I. Vasholz, "An Additional Note on the 4QEnoch Fragments and 11QtgJob," *Maarav* 3 (1982) 115-18; E. M. Cook, "Remarks on the Testament of Kohath from Qumran Cave 4," *JJS* 44 (1993) 205-19.

[6] E. M. Cook, "Qumran Aramaic and Aramaic Dialectology," in T. Muraoka (ed.), *SQA*, 1-21.

[7] M. O. Wise, "Accidents and Accidence: A Scribal View of Linguistic Dating of the Aramaic Scrolls from Qumran," in T. Muraoka (ed.), *SQA*, 124-67.

[8] J. A. Fitzmyer, *The Genesis Apocryphon of Qumran Cave 1: A Commentary* (2nd ed., Rome: Biblical Institute, 1971) 22-23, n.60.

essay,[9] he proposed a fivefold division: (1) Old Aramaic ("OA"), (2) Imperial Aramaic ("IA"), (3) Middle Aramaic, (4) Late Aramaic, and (5) Modern Aramaic. It should be noted that Fitzmyer's divisions are based partly on chronological, and partly on dialectal, grounds. He placed QA in the Middle Aramaic phase.

The most massive and ambitious study of the QA material is Klaus Beyer's *Die aramäischen Texte vom Toten Meer*, which was recently supplemented with an extensive *Ergänzungsband*. Beyer's work is nothing less than a description of the evolution of the Aramaic dialects with QA at the center. Beyer clings to the old tripartite classification of the dialects as Old, Middle, and Late, and distinguishes a number of Old Aramaic dialects within the QA corpus, including Hasmonean, Jewish Old Palestinian, and Old Judean. It now seems, however, that Beyer is arguably guilty of multiplying dialects without cause, while Fitzmyer's periodization is gaining increasing acceptance.

Fitzmyer, Beyer, and others have stressed the importance of QA for the study of the Semitic background of the New Testament, since the Dead Sea Scrolls for the first time provide Aramaic texts contemporaneous, or nearly so, with the origins of Christianity.[10]

The following discussion of linguistic features cannot even pretend to be comprehensive. Only a few highlights can be touched on. No comprehensive grammar devoted to QA has been published, although Fitzmyer and Sokoloff have provided brief sketches of the grammar of particular texts.[11] Beyer's grammar includes, but is not devoted to, QA.[12] There is also no QA lexicon—again, Beyer's glossary is broader[13]—and no systematic study of the syntax.[14]

---

[9] "The Phases of the Aramaic Language," in *A Wandering Aramean: Collected Aramaic Essays* (Missoula, MT: Scholars Press, 1979) 57-84.

[10] See especially J. Fitzmyer, "The Contribution of Qumran Aramaic to the Study of the New Testament," in *A Wandering Aramean*, 85-113.

[11] J. Fitzmyer, "A Sketch of Qumran Aramaic," in *The Genesis Apocryphon*, 193-227; M. Sokoloff, "Morphology of the Aramaic of TG1," in *Targum to Job*, 173-89.

[12] K. Beyer, *ATTM*, 409-497; idem, *ATTME*, 277-99.

[13] But see now the valuable study by J. C. Greenfield and M. Sokoloff, "The Contribution of Qumran Aramaic to the Aramaic Vocabulary," in T. Muraoka (ed.), *SQA*, 78-98.

[14] The best partial treatment of QA syntax is T. Muraoka's "Notes on the Aramaic of the Genesis Apocryphon," *RevQ* 8 (1972-1974) 7-51.

2. ORTHOGRAPHY

Consonants

The orthography throughout represents the original Aramaic interdentals as having become dentals, as in BA.[15]

The orthography of etymological /ś/ wavers between שׂ and ס. It seems likely that the former was merely a historical spelling, the later a phonemic spelling. It is not possible to date manuscripts by their use of either spelling.

The letters אוהי are often used to signal the presence of vowels.

י may represent final or medial long /i/ or /e/.

ה may represent final long /a/ or /e/.

ו may represent final or medial long /o/ or /u/ or medial short /u/. The latter feature is an innovation with respect to OA and IA, and is also a feature of Qumran Hebrew.[16] Both QH and QA use the spelling כול, "all," which is rare in other corpora. For the spelling of etymological *qutl* -pattern nouns, see below.[17]

א may represent final long /a/ or /e/, or medial long /a/ after the letters ו/י. The latter is rare elsewhere, and generally serves to disambiguate homographs. Examples are: בניאן, 4Q566, line 12; עואן, 4Q560, col. 1:4; מריאם, 4Q549 1:8; הואת, 1QapGen 12:9; אוחידואן, 4Q541, frg. 2 i 7; דיאץ, 4Q542 1 i 11; and elsewhere. The development of א as a medial vowel letter is conditioned by the prior development of ו/י as vowel letters. If they were not ambiguous, there would be no need for medial א.

Only rarely, if at all, does א represent long /a/ after consonants other than ו/י. Examples are כלאן, 1QapGen 20:6, טב]לאל 4Q533 2:12, באתין, 4QJNª ar (4Q554) 1 ii 6.

Sometimes an א is added for graphic purposes after a long vowel or diphthong, as, for instance, תבוא, 11QtgJob 32:3; הווא, 4Q563 16; מנוא, 4Q539 2 3; ביא, 4QEnᶜ ar (4Q204) I vi 23;[18] כיא, 1Q32 14

---

[15] F. Rosenthal, *A Grammar of Biblical Aramaic* (PLO Neue Serie V; Wiesbaden: Harrassowitz, 1974) 14-5.

[16] E. Qimron, *The Hebrew of the Dead Sea Scrolls* (Atlanta, GA: Scholars Press, 1986), 17-8.

[17] For further exemplification, see Beyer, *ATTM*, 414-15; Fitzmyer, *Genesis Apocryphon*, 200.

[18] Note: for some of the Enochic material, the capitals "I" (etc.) denote groups of fragments that were assembled by J. T. Milik. Thus I vi 23 means fragment-group I, col. vi, line 23.

3; and often in the particle גוא. The same phenomenon is also found in Qumranic Hebrew.[19]

3. PHONOLOGICAL PROCESSES

Changes involving א

The glottal stop /ʔ/ (i.e ʾalep) has quiesced in certain environments. After *a and before another consonant, the segment becomes /e/: /-aʾC/ > /-eC/, as in (for example) ראש, "head," which in later Aramaic is written ריש. In QA, the word combines historical and phonemic spellings in the spelling ראיש (1QapGen 16:9, 17:11; 4Q213). Elsewhere the spelling ריש appears (4Q550ᵈ 2:8), as well as the historical ראש (4QEnᶜ ar [4Q204] 4 3). The change also occurs in the imperfects of I-ʾalep verbs (see below).

Sometimes when it begins a syllable after a vowelless consonant, /ʔ/ quiesces. Examples: סתא, plural of סאה, 11Q18 3 4-5; טמתכון, 4QEnᵃ ar (4Q201) I ii 13, from טמאה. See below concerning I-ʾalep verbs.

Sometimes א is inserted to separate vowels between morpheme boundaries, as in Qumran Hebrew.[20] Examples: גניאין, 4Q541 9 i 6; צבואין, 1QapGen 21:31; עניאין, 1QapGen 21:33; נכראין, 4QTQahat ar (4Q542) 1 i 5. This practice accounts for the spelling of forms like אחיאת, 4QEnᵈ ar (4Q204) I ii 5, 8; אתחזיאת, 1QapGen 12:3; אתב[נ]יאת, 1QapGen 19:9; אחזיאני, 5Q15 1 ii 6; תמניאת, 1QapGen 22:6; etc. In all of these forms the /ʔ/ comes between the morpheme boundary of long /i/ and /aC/. The ʾalep does not in these cases represent a long /a/.

Changes involving נ

Substitution of nasalization (נ-insertion) for gemination, as well as non-assimilation of נ, is found only in certain cases, e.g. always in the pronouns אנתה and אנתון, often in the imperfect of the verb ידע, often in the nouns א(נ)תה, "woman," and א(נ)פין, "face." Verbs with initial radical נ vary between assimilation and non-assimilation (see below). It is not certain that the נ was pronounced in such cases; in any case, the extent of the nasalization/non-assimilation is less than in IA or BA; for instance, the relevant forms of the verbs סלק and עלל do not exhibit nasalization as in BA.

---

[19] Qimron, *Hebrew of the Dead Sea Scrolls*, 21-22.

[20] Qimron, *Hebrew of the Dead Sea Scrolls*, 31-33.

Monophthongization

The primarily consonantal writing system makes it difficult to tell whether the diphthongs /ay/ and /aw/ had contracted to /e/ and /o/, respectively, since the monophthongs were generally indicated by the same letters. However, there is some evidence that /ay/ had contracted in the writings תרן ("two") for תרין (4QEnastr[b] ar [4Q209] 7 iii 4, 26 3) and לת ("there is not") for לא איתי/לית (4QEn[a] ar [4Q201] I ii 14).

Gutturals

There is no orthographic indication that the gutturals (ע ח) had weakened in QA. Indeed, in words containing two gutturals, both are preserved, in contrast to later Aramaic: עע, "wood" (4QTLevi[d, e] ar [4Q214] 2 2), later אע; חעך, "smile, laugh" (4Q543 3 4), later לעורע האך,· "towards" (1QapGen 22:13), later לאורע.[21]

4. MORPHOLOGY: THE PRONOUN

Independent Personal Pronouns

	Masculine	Feminine
Singular Forms		
First person	אנה	
Second	אנתה	[אנתי]
Third	הוא	היא
Plural Forms		
First person	אנחנא	
Second	אנתון	[אנתין]
Third	המון, אנון	אנין

First Person

Singular. אנה (the usual form), אנא (rare, only in 4QTQahat ar [4Q542]). The orthography is the same as in OA and IA; later Aramaic typically uses אנא.

Plural. אנחנא (usual), אנחנה (rare; only in 4QVisAmram[c] ar [4Q545] 1 ii 19). The more common orthography contrasts with OA אנחן and IA אנחנה. BA has forms with both final א- and final ה-. The later dialects use different forms altogether. [22]

---

[21] All of these roots, it should be noted, contain etymologically distinct gutturals; compare IA עק ("wood"); and Hebrew צחק ("laugh").

[22] For more on these orthographic forms, see E. M. Cook, "The Orthography

Second Person

Masculine singular. אנתה is the invariable form. This accords with the *Ketiv* forms in the Masoretic Text of BA. Only BA and QA use this form, while other dialects typically prefer את or אנת. (The medieval copyist of the *Words of Levi* from the Geniza used אנת).[23]

Masculine plural. אנתון is the more frequently attested spelling, but אנתן is found in 4QEn^a ar (4Q201) I ii 7,12. (The spelling אתון may occur in 4QEn^g ar [4Q212] 1 ii 25 or in 3Q14 5 3, but the contexts are fragmentary.)

Third Person

Masculine singular. The form is invariably הוא. The form הואה occurs in 4QEn^c ar (4Q204) V ii 30, a scribal Hebraism.[24]

Feminine singular. היא is the normal, and only attested, form.

Masculine plural. The Qumran texts have two forms for the masculine plural: אנון and המון. The latter is very rare, occurring three times in 11QtgJob (25:23, 28:2, 34:9) and twice in 4QPrNab ar (4Q242) cols. 1:8 and 2:1. It is a survival of the old independent pronoun that came to be used only as a direct object, as in BA.[25] The standard form in the Qumran documents is אנון. The initial א contrasts with the initial ה forms used in other dialects of the time.[26] Feminine אנין occurs only in 4QEn^a (4Q201) I iii 15.

Suffixed Personal Pronouns

	Masculine	Feminine
Singular Forms		
First person	–ִי, –ִנִי	
Second person	–ָךְ, –ֵכָה	–ִכִי
Third person	–ֵהּ, –וֹהִי	–ַהּ, –ַהָא
Plural Forms		
First person	–ַנָא, –ַנָה	
Second person	–ְכֹן, –ְכוּן	unattested
Third person	–ְהֹן, –ְהוּן	–ְהִין/–ְהֵן

---

of Final Unstressed Vowels in Old and Imperial Aramaic," *Maarav* 5 (1990) 53-67.

[23] It is therefore unlikely that אתה in 4Q246 1:2 is the masc. sing. pronoun, as has been suggested by É. Puech, J. J. Collins, J. A. Fitzmyer and others.

[24] S. E. Fassberg, "Hebraisms in the Aramaic Documents from Qumran," in T. Muraoka (ed.), *SQA*, esp. 51.

[25] F. Rosenthal, *Grammar of Biblical Aramaic*, 19 (§26).

[26] Cf. Cook, "Qumran Aramaic," 11.

First Person

Singular. The form י- functions as a possessive suffix on nouns ("mine"), while ני- functions as a pronominal object on verbs. *Plural.* The variation in the final *matres lectionis* א and ה corresponds to the same variation in the form of the independent personal pronouns (see above).

Second Person

Singular. The orthography of the masculine form -כה has been the subject of some discussion. While some hold that the suffix represents an authentically archaic Aramaic /-ka, -áka/,[27] others believe that it is a Hebraism.[28] The majority of the forms of this suffix are spelled without the *mater. Plural.* The usual form of the masculine suffix at Qumran is -כון, although -כן occurs in 4QEn[a] ar (4Q201), 4QTLevi[b] ar (4Q213a), and 4QVisAmram[a] ar (4Q543).[29]

Third Person

Singular. -ה is the invariable spelling of the masculine pronoun suffixed to a word ending in a consonant, while -הי occurs after a (long) vowel. On masculine plural nouns, the normal form is -והי, /-ohi/, as is standard in Western Aramaic.[30] (It has been claimed that אחוי in 1QapGen 21:34 is an anticipation of the later form -וי, but it is probably a scribal error. No other examples of -וי occur at Qumran.) Several examples of -והי occur in 1QIsa[a] as Aramaisms.[31] The feminine singular form -הא is subject to the same conflict of interpretations as the second person masculine -כה. Is it a reflex of

---

[27] Beyer, *ATTM,* 424, 449-50; and Cook, "Orthography of Final Unstressed Vowels," 60-61.

[28] Fassberg, "Hebraisms in Aramaic Documents," 51-53. E. Qimron ("The Pronominal Suffix -כה in Qumran Aramaic," in T. Muraoka [ed.], *SQA,* 119-123), hesitantly favors the view that this is an authentic Aramaic form.

[29] These spellings should not be considered "archaic," since similar spellings occur in the later texts from Murabbaʿât and the Naḥal Ḥever. They are simply the preferences of a particular scribe.

[30] Since the underlying segment is {ay + hi}, the surface form is surprising. The Eastern Aramaic dialects in fact all have reflexes of /-ayhi/. For a historical discussion of the /-ohi/ form, see Cook, "Orthography of Final Unstressed Vowels," 56-57.

[31] E. Y. Kutscher, הלשון והרקע הלשוני של מגילת ישעיהו השלמה ממגילות ים המלח (Jerusalem: Magnes Press and Hebrew University, 1959) 161.

earlier Aramaic /-ha/ or a Hebraism?[32] The more usual form is -ה.

Plural. The standard masculine form is -הון, although a few manuscripts use -הן (e.g. 4Q568 11 בעדניהן, 4Q246 2:2 מלכותהן, 4Q562 2 2 ידיהן, 4QEn[a] ar [4Q201] passim, etc.).[33] The usual form in OA and IA is -הם, but the final *nun* forms are already found in some IA texts.[34] The standard feminine form is also -הן, vocalized as /-hen/, but the *plene* form is attested, e.g. עמהין, 4QGiants[c] 1 4.

Demonstrative Pronouns

	"Near"	"Far"
Masculine singular	דנה, דן	דך
Feminine singular	הדא, דה, דא	unattested
Plural	אלין, אלן	unattested

Masculine Singular

דן ("this") occurs in QA for the first time in Jewish Aramaic, and is the standard form, although there are several occurrences of the older דנה, which is standard in BA, Nabatean and Palmyrene.[35] Later Jewish Aramaic differentiates between דין, used as the subject of a sentence, and הדין, used as an attributive adjective (except in the frozen expression יומא דין, "today"). QA uses דנה/דן for both functions.[36] דך ("that") occurs only in 4Q533 2 13.

Feminine Singular

The spelling דא ("this") is standard, דה being attested only in 4Q243 16 2 (*si vera lectio*). Like the masculine, the feminine pronouns later formally differentiate the functions by two forms, דא

---

[32] Fassberg, "Hebraisms in Aramaic Documents," 53-54. Fassberg states that –הא occurs only in 1QapGen (54), but a few instances have turned up in other texts: ל[אבוהא] in 4QTob[b] ar (4Q197) 4 ii 2; ב[עלהא] in 4Q549 (Hur and Miriam) 1 2; and נורהא in 4QTLev[c] ar (4Q541) 9 i 4. In addition, the few examples in the Genizah text of the *Words of Levi* (Cambridge MS, C 18, 19, F 17) should not be overlooked.

[33] Once again, the later Bar Kokhba letters also favor the defective spelling.

[34] Examples are provided in Beyer, *ATTM*, 450.

[35] Cf. Cook, "Qumran Aramaic," 10-11.

[36] There are possible early uses of the demonstrative with ה– in 4Q529 14 (הא דן) and 4Q544 2 2 (הדן). But since both examples occur before lacunae, they could be construed as the interrogative ה before the pronoun.

and הדא.³⁷ A "far" feminine demonstrative is not attested, but comparative evidence suggests it would have been דך or דכי. ³⁸

Plural

Two different spellings are used. The standard is אלין, but אילין occurs in several manuscripts (4QEnᵃ ar [4Q201], 4QEnᵇ ar [4Q202], 4QVisAmramᵃ ar [4Q543], 11QtgJob). It is not clear if the different spellings reflect different pronunciations; later vocalized texts of Jewish Aramaic attest variations between אִלֵּין and אִלַּיִן.³⁹ There are no attested forms of the "far" demonstrative, such as the BA form אלך.

Relative Pronoun

The standard form of the relative pronoun is די, although many examples of the proclitic ד- are found, even in the same manuscript. The archaic זי occurs in 4QEnᵉ ar (4Q206) IV ii 13, IV iii 16 and TLeviᶜ ar (4Q213b) 3 5; and frequently in the legal texts from Wadi Murabbaʿât.

Interrogative Pronouns

The interrogative "what?" was spelled either מא or מה, usually the former, although scribes were consistent within manuscripts.

The interrogative "who?" is always מן. An archaic form מנו occurs in 4QEnᵍ ar (4Q212) I v 17, 20, 22.⁴⁰

5. MORPHOLOGY: THE NOUN

	Masculine	Feminine
Singular Forms		
Absolute	——	–א/–ה
Construct	——	–ת
Determined	–א/–ה	–תא

---

³⁷ A single example of the latter may be attested in 1QapGen 2:6, but this should probably be construed as the interrogative particle prefixed to דא.

³⁸ Cf. S. Segert, *Altaramäische Grammatik* (Leipzig: Verlag Enzyklopädie, 1975) 176.

³⁹ See S. E. Fassberg, *A Grammar of the Palestinian Targum Fagments from the Cairo Genizah* (HSS 38; Atlanta: Scholars Press, 1990). In the Palestinian targum fragments, אלין is used pronominally, אליין attributively (with ה–). This distinction, however, does not obtain in QA.

⁴⁰ That this form is archaic and not a result of the crasis of מן and הוא is argued by Sokoloff, "Aramaic Fragments of Enoch," 223 n.124.

Plural forms

Absolute	─ִין	─ָאן/ן
Construct	─ֵי	─ָאת/ת
Determined	─ַיָּא	─ָאתָא/תָא

The inflection of the noun in QA presents no peculiarities. The masculine plural Hebrew ending -ִים appears sporadically in 1QapGen.[41] For the *plene* spelling of the feminine plurals, see the section on "Orthography."[42]

The absolute forms of masculine adjectives ending in ־ַי /ay/ have the endings ־ָיָא /aya/ for the singular, ־ָיֵא /aye/ for the plural, agreeing with the Ketiv forms in BA, and constrasting with the Qere forms ־ָאָה and ־ָאֵי. An exception is אמוראא, "Amorites" (1Qap Gen 21:21; contrast חוריא, "Horites," in 21:29).

The dual ending, if present, is not distinguishable in the orthography from the masculine plural forms.

Noun Formation

The process of noun formation in QA is like that of the other Aramaic dialects.[43] The following types are worthy of comment.

Nouns ending in ־ֹון. If the nouns ending in ־ֹון are all Hebraisms,[44] this ending (in contrast to indigenous Aramaic ־ָן) was not productive in QA. However, some "native" Aramaic words are found with the ending: note [ב]סֹ֗רון in 4QTLevi[a] ar (4Q213) 1 i 11; and גועלון in 4Q541 6 i 4.

Nouns originally *qutl-. Nouns originally monosyllabic and ending in a consonant cluster have undergone anaptyxis in the vocalized traditions of Aramaic. It is still unclear whether, or to what degree, anaptyxis had begun to operate in QA. The consonantal text preserves evidence only for originally **qutl-* forms. In some manuscripts **qutl-* can be written קוטל. (Examples include: קובל, 4Q201 I iii 20; קושט, 4Q204 I v 7; קודש, 4Q213a 3 8; 1QapGen אונס 20:11; קודם, 4QGiants[a] 9 2; סולת, 11Q18 3 3; פותי, 5Q15 1 ii

---

[41] Fassberg, "Hebraisms in Aramaic Documents," 55-56.

[42] I.e. section 2 above.

[43] Lists of noun patterns, together with examples, are given in Beyer, *ATTM*, 425-44; and idem, *ATTME*, 282-5.

[44] Fassberg, "Hebraisms in Aramaic Documents," 56-57, *pace* K. Beyer, *ATTM*, 442. The word נחשירון (4Q246 1:5) is the feminine plural of נחשירו; cf. E. M. Cook, "4Q246," *BBR* 5 (1995) 43-66.

12; עובע, 4Q544 1 3; etc.) Often, however, the spelling קטול appears. (Examples: קשוט, 4Q548 1 12; כתול, 2Q24 3 4; רגוז, 4Q204 I vi 5; אנוס, 4Q550a 1 8; תקוף, 4QGiants^c 1 3; etc.[45] Finally, a few spellings occur with ו written twice: קושוט, 4Q242 1 i 4, סודום, 1QapGen 21:32. All of these data taken together indicate that original *qutl- was realized as /qutul/ or /qotol/ in QA.[46]

6. MORPHOLOGY: THE VERB

Verbal Inflection

The principal parts of the verbal system are generally the same as in common Aramaic: the perfect, imperfect, imperative, infinitive, and participle.

Inflection of the Perfect

	Singular	Plural
3rd person masc.	——	–ו/–א
3rd person fem.	–ת	–א
2nd person masc.	–ת/–תא/–תה	–תן/–תון
2nd person fem.	–ת	unattested
1st person	–ת	–נא/–נה

Third Person. Later Palestinian Aramaic sometimes has the masculine plural ending ון-, and some have suggested the same ending can be found in QA אתון ("they came"), a form in 1QapGen 19:26 and 11QtgJob 2:2; 38:4. These readings are not certain, however, and it is likely that the ending in question is the participial -ין. More typical is the use of otiose -א on the masculine plural in forms like הווא (see above, under "Orthography").

Unlike IA, QA has a separate ending for the feminine plural: שלמא, 1QapGen 20:6; 22:28.

Second Person. The masculine singular ending is usually written defectively (-ת) but *plene* forms (-תה, -תא) occur, e.g. חזיתא, 4Q246 2:2; מללתא, 4Q552 4 11; עבדתה, 1QapGen 20:26; and אצלתה, 1QapGen 22:19. Again, the *plene* form may indicate that a final long vowel survived from earlier Aramaic, or it may be due

---

[45] Both spellings occur in the adverbial סוחר סחור, "around," in 5Q15 10 i 1.

[46] Cf. E. M. Cook, "Remarks on the Testament of Kohath," 208-209, *contra* T. Muraoka, "Segolate Nouns in Biblical and Other Aramaic Dialects," *JAOS* 96 (1976) 231-32.

instead to the influence of Hebrew.[47]

The masculine plural is normally written חון-, as in (for example) the forms חזיתון, 11QtgJob 11:2; אתיתון, 4Q196 14 ii 7; and הולכתון, 4QTQahat ar (4Q542) 1 i 12. The form שניתן occurs in 4QEn[a] ar (4Q201) I ii 12.

First Person. The plural form is always written *plene,* usually נא-, as in (for example) אתכנשנא, 1QapGen 12:16; הוינא, 4Q564 12; and עגננא, 4QGiants[a] 7 7. The spelling נה- is also found in 4QVis Amram[b] ar (4Q544) 1:6, הוינה.

Inflection of the Imperfect

	Singular	Plural
Third person masc.	י——	י——ון
Third person fem.	ת——	י——ן
Second person masc.	ת——	ת——ון
Second person fem.	ת——ין	ת——ן
First person	א——	נ——

Third person. The preformative -י is characteristic of Western Aramaic; Eastern Aramaic typically uses -ל or -נ in the imperfect third person forms.[48] QA uses -ל consistently in the masculine forms of the verb הוי, "to be," but nowhere else: להוא (4QZodiology and Brontology ar [4Q318] 2:8, 11QtgJob 29:4; 4QGiants[a] 7 6, etc.); להוה (4Q246 1:7; 4Q534 1:4; 4Q561 1:4, etc.); להוון (4Q318 2:8; 4QVisAmram[f][?] ar [4Q548] 1 10; 2Q24 2 5, etc.). The feminine uses preformative -י: for instance, יהוין in 4QVisAmram[f](?) ar (4Q548) 2 ii 6.

Jussive

Only QA among the Middle Aramaic dialects preserves a productive jussive form.[49] The paradigm is the same as the imperfect except that the jussive is indicated by final -ו in the masculine plural forms: יש[ב]חו, 4Q196 17 ii 7;[50] תקוצו (אל), 1QapGen 19:16; תמחלו (אל),

---

[47] Cook, "Orthography of Final Unstressed Vowels," 62-63; Fassberg, "Hebraisms in Aramaic Documents," 52.

[48] Cook, "Qumran Aramaic," 12-13.

[49] Kutscher, "Language of the Genesis Apocryphon," 5; Cook, "Qumran Aramaic," 12-13.

[50] This form could be an imperative: יש[ב]חו.

4Q213 1 i 13; and תתנו (אל), 4QTQahat ar (4Q542) 1 i 5.⁵¹

It is indicated by final ־י in the feminine singular: תדחלי (אל), 4QTob^b ar (4Q197) 4 i 2, 3; 5 8; תצפי (אל), 4Q197 4 i 3. For the form of the jussive in final-weak verbs, see below.

Since the form of the infinitive and participle differs by stem, they will be discussed in the context of stem formation.

Stems (Binyanim)

QA has a system of verbal formations (stems) very much like that of BA: the simple stem *(Peʿal)*, and two derived stems: the factitive/plurative stem *(Paʿel)*, and causative stem *(Aphʿel/Haphʿel)*. The *Peʿal* and the *Paʿel* have corresponding -את stems *(Itpeʿal and Itpeʿel)* that function as the passive voice; the *Peʿal* also has an internal passive *Peʿil* that appears only in the perfect tense. The *Aphʿel* has an internal passive, but its vocalization is uncertain. The *Aphʿel* also has an -את form *(Ittaphʿal)*.

Peʿal

In QA, the thematic vowel of the imperfect is usually a *u*-class vowel, to judge from the occasional *plene* writing: יפרוס in 11QtgJob 33:7; תקוב (< נקב) in 11QtgJob 35:5; אסמוך in 1QapGen 20:22; יפשור in 4QGiants^b 14; יפוק in 6Q14 1 4; ישכונן in 4Q542 (4QTQahat ar) 1 ii 3; etc. This is true even for some roots that in other dialects have *a*-class or *i*-class theme vowels: e.g. ישכון in 11QtgJob 33:9 (cf. Syriac ܢܫܟܒ); יפול in 4Q541 1 ii 2 (cf. BA יִפֵּל).

The infinitive had the pattern מקטל. There is no certain evidence as to the vocalization; the reading לְמִשְׁבֹּוֹק (1QapGen 19:15) is very tenuous, and לְמִשְׁבַּק is more likely.⁵²

Peʿil

In QA, the *Peʿil* perfect was apparently still productive, although in later Jewish Aramaic it was completely displaced by the *Itpeʿel*. Examples include פתיחו in 4QEn^e ar (4Q206) IV i 17; שכירו in 4Q206 IV ii 2; שביקת and קטילת in 1QapGen 20:10; דבירת in 1QapGen 20:11; and יהיבת in 2QJN ar (2Q24) 4 15.⁵³

---

⁵¹ A jussive followed by נה could occur in 1QapGen 20:25: יתיבו נה But the reading is uncertain, and could instead be the imperative אתיבו. The particle נא/נה is usually preceded by the imperative in QA.

⁵² *Contra* Kutscher, "Language of the Genesis Apocryphon," 9; and Fitzmyer, *Genesis Apocryphon*, 112.

⁵³ Further examples may be given.

Pa‛el Infinitive

The infinitive of the derived stems generally follows the formation of the infinitive in IA: קטלא, *Pa‛el*; אקטלא, *Aph‛el*; and אתקטלא, *Itpe‛el/Itpa‛al*.[54] But there are some cases of the infinitive with preformative *mem*, in the manner of later Western Aramaic: למחזיא (4QTQahat ar [4Q542] 1 ii 6), למעמרא (4QVisAmram[b] ar [4Q544] 1:1). The latter instance is particularly interesting, since the same text in another manuscript has the older form לעמרה (4QVis Amram[c] ar [4Q545] 1 ii 13).

Aph‛el/Haph‛el

There is a certain amount of variation in the causative stem between initial -א and -ה. This seems to have depended on the whim of the scribe. Some texts prefer the *Haph‛el* (such as 11QtgJob), others the *Aph‛el* (such as 1QapGen). Some texts combine both spellings, for instance 4QpapTob[a] ar (4Q196) has the forms החוי (3 1), אשלט (2 5), אשלטה (2 8), אתבת (2 10), וֹאַקרבו (2 11), [ת]הֹשכח (2 12), לאפטרותני (6 8), ה[ש]לִחו (14 ii 6), and מהודה (17 ii 3). In 4QTQahat ar (4Q542), a participle was originally written as *Aph‛el*, and then was changed to *Haph‛el* by a supralinear correction: מ^השלמא (1 ii 4). Overall, the *Aph‛el* appears much more often, and the *Haph‛el* forms that appear seem to be historical spellings.[55]

Aph‛el Passive

There appears to be an internal passive of the causative stem in QA, but its vocalization is unknown. K. Beyer suggests that it was אָקְטֶל or אָקְטֵל,[56] but אָקְטַל is more probable.[57] In QA it is attested only in the perfect.[58] There is also an external passive, the *Ittaph‛al*, that is attested twice: יתוספון (< יסף; 4Q541 9 ii 7) and יתאיית[א] (< אתי; 4QTob[c] ar [4Q198] 1 6).[59]

---

[54] Cook, "Qumran Aramaic," 11-12.

[55] Cook, "Qumran Aramaic," 13-14.

[56] Beyer, *ATTM*, 152, 467.

[57] Compare the Masoretic vocalization of Biblical Aramaic: הָקְטַל. See H. Bauer and P. Leander, *Grammatik des Biblisch-Aramäischen* (Hildesheim: Olms, 1981 [1927]) 115.

[58] Beyer, *ATTM*, 467.

[59] Another possible example is ואתהייתה in 4Q196 ii 13, but the form is strange and another reading is more likely; cf. M. Morgenstern, "Language and Literature in the Second Temple Period," *JJS* 48 (1997) 132.

Itpeʿel and Itpaʿal

The preformative of the "t"-stems varies between את- and הת-. The הת- form is not the earlier, as has occasionally been stated. The usual form in Old and Imperial Aramaic is את-; the הת- form appears in Jewish Aramaic texts under the influence of the Hebrew *Hithpaʿel*.[60] 11QtgJob usually has the הת- forms, while the other QA texts use primarily את- or a combination. For instance Enastr^c ar (4Q210) has [מותהון]השתּלֹ (1 ii 18) and לאתח[זיא] (1 iii 3), while (4Q550)[61] has both אשתכח (1 6) and השתכח(1 7), etc.

Other Stems

The stems called *Poʿlel* and *Itpoʿlel* are the equivalent of the *Paʿel* and *Itpaʿal* for verbal roots with a weak middle radical (see below). Some have suggested that the stems are indigenous to Aramaic,[62] but the only attestations in QA are in roots that also frequently appear in Hebrew in those stems (התרוממו, 11QtgJob 27:3; אתבוננא, 4Q204 I i 20; מתבונן, 4Q541 7 i 2; see also 4Q201 I ii 1, 10; 4Q212 I iii 22; 4Q553 1 ii 3; and 4Q541 3 i 4).

Quadriliteral roots may form derived stems. Such roots are generally borrowed by Aramaic from other languages. For example, שזיב (11QtgJob 14:6; 4QTob^b ar [4Q197] 4 ii 18) or שיצי (4QVis Amram^c ar [4Q545] 1 i 7; 11QJN ar [11Q18] 4:2) have been borrowed from Akkadian, while הימן (11QtgJob 15:1) and הולך (4QTQahat ar [4Q542] 1 i 12, ii 13) have been taken over from Hebrew. One quinquiliteral is attested: חלחלי (4Q560 col. 1:3, חלחלית, לחלח<לי>א).

7. WEAK VERBS

I-nun Verbs. Verbs whose first radical is *nun* sometime assimilate the *nun* when no vowel separates it from the following consonant, but not consistently.[63] Thus, for instance, 11QtgJob has ינפק (29:3) as well as יפק (31:2), 4QTQahat ar (4Q542) has תתנו (1 i 5) as well as תנתנון (1 i 10), and so forth. It is likely that the forms with *nun* are historical spellings derived from IA orthography.[64]

---

[60] Beyer, *ATTM*, 466.

[61] 4Q550 has erroneously been termed a "proto-Esther" text.

[62] Fassberg, "Hebraisms in Aramaic Documents," 61-62.

[63] Cf. M. Sokoloff, *Targum to Job*, 18 (comparing 11QtgJob to 1QapGen).

[64] Beyer, *ATTM*, 483-84.

I-ʾalep Verbs. It is common in later Aramaic that the ʾ*alep* in this class of verbs quiesces when it occurs immediately before or after another consonant with no vowel intervening. Although spellings without the ʾ*alep* are less frequent than those with it, they are not unusual. It seems likely that the pronunciations without ʾ*alep* were regular in speech and this sometimes affected spelling. Thus, 11QtgJob usually has the ʾ*alep* (e.g. תתאשד in 16:5, יאחדון in 16:8, תאמר in 26:9, and יאבדון in 27:7), but not consistently (יתון in 16:1, 2; and יבא in 32:8). 4Q551 has both ימרון (1 4) and יאמרו (1 5). 4Q541 sometimes has the ʾ*alep* (יאתה in 3 i 5, יאמרון in 9 i 5, and תתאבל in 24 ii 2), but sometimes not (יתזה in 9 i 4,[65] תתה in 17 i 2). Spellings of the imperfect of אתי without ʾ*alep* are virtually standard in QA (e.g. יתא in 4Q537 14, תתא in 4Q246 1:4, ייתא in 4Q545 1 i 18, and למתה in 4QEnastr[b] ar [4Q209] 7 ii 2).

II-w/y Verbs. The *Peʿal* active participle in this class replaces the weak middle radical with ʾ*alep*. This is in contrast with IA and the *Qere* of BA[66] which use *yod*, and in agreement with the BA *Ketiv*. Later Aramaic uses ʾ*alep* when a vowel follows, and *yod* when the vowel is reduced.[67] Examples include: ראם in 4Q205 II ii 2; קאם in 4Q552 (Four Kingdoms[a] ar) 1 ii 1, 2; תאבה in 4Q550[d] 1 6; זאעין in 1QapGen 1 7; דאנין in 4QVisAmram[b] ar (4Q544) 1:10. A possible exception is בֿיזין in 4QpapTob[a] ar (4Q196) 17 ii 15 (*si vera lectio*).

III-y Verbs. It is an open question whether QA preserves a difference in this class of verbs between the imperfect and the jussive. In OA and IA, the jussive singular forms ended in ־י, and the imperfects in ־ה. In QA, the imperfects end in א־ or ה־. There are few attestations of the singular jussive in the corpus, but two examples are of this class: יתחזי (אל), 4Q214 (TLevi[d]) 2 4, and תמחי (אל), 4Q541 24 ii 4.[68] Judging from these forms, the distinction seems to have survived in QA.

---

[65] M. Sokoloff (review of K. Beyer's *ATTME* in *DSD* 2 [1997] 221, 227) wishes to emend this form to ית<ח>זה, since the root אזי is otherwise unattested in this stem, and because the subject נור is feminine, not masculine. But נור can be masculine or feminine in Aramaic, and there is no obvious semantic or syntactical constraint preventing אזי from being used in the *Itpeʿel*. Moreover, for his first emendation to work Sokoloff must also improbably emend נור into נהור.

[66] Segert, *Altaramäische Grammatik*, 288-89.

[67] Beyer, *ATTM*, 487-89.

[68] Beyer's reading of the phrase is אל תמחולהי (*ATTME*, 80), which is highly unlikely. The proper reading is אל תמחי להן.

Geminate Verbs. The *Peʿal* participles of verbs such as עלל can take the "strong" forms עלל (4Q560 1:3) or עללין (11Q18 4:3), thus agreeing with the *Ketiv* of BA, but not with the *Qere* which has עלין. The *Qere*-type is also attested: note בזין in 1QapGen 21:28 and 22:4, but compare בזזין in 4QZodiology and Brontology ar (4Q318) 2:8.

8. THE VERBAL SYSTEM

J. A. Fitzmyer has described the verbal system of 1QapGen.[69] His description can be applied, *grosso modo*, to QA as a whole.

Perfect. The perfect expresses the narrative past, the past perfect, and the performative. For the latter, Fitzmyer cites: וכען קבלתך, "I hereby lodge my complaint against you" (1QapGen 20:14); now see also אומיתך רוחא, "I adjure you, O spirit" (4Q560 2:6).

Imperfect. The imperfect expresses the future. It may also express a general present: כל בתולן וכלאן די יעלן לגנון, "all the virgins and brides that enter the bridal canopy" (1QapGen 20:6), although this meaning is usually signified by the active participle.

When preceded by a *waw* and following an imperative or another imperfect, it may express purpose or result: ויצלה עלוהי ויחה, "and he will pray for him that he might be cured" (1QapGen 20:23); ויודענכון שמה רבא ותנדעונה, "and he will make his great name known to you that you may know him" (4QTQahat ar [4Q542] 1 ii 1-2); and אשתעי לי חלמך ואנדע, "tell me your dream so I may know it" (1QapGen 19:18). Sometimes the jussive form is used in this syntagm: [אמרי]...ואחי בטליכי, "[say] ... so I may live on your account" (1QapGen 19:34, and elsewhere).[70] It may also express a modal nuance, in positive expressions: אהך לי עד סיאפי ארעא, "I will go to the ends of the earth" (4Q568 1); and ימללון בתהלי[ן], "let them speak with psalms" in 4QpapTobᵃ ar (4Q196) 17 ii 7.

Preterite (waw-consecutive). The old Semitic preterite, which survives in biblical Hebrew in the *waw*-consecutive construction, existed in certain dialects of Old Aramaic. Whether it survived in QA is still an open question. S. Fassberg considers ויושע in 4Q243 16 2 as a *waw*-consecutive, noting that the root of the verb is borrowed from Hebrew.[71] Another suggested instance is in 1QapGen

---

[69] Fitzmyer, *Genesis Apocryphon*, 222-24.

[70] T. Muraoka, "Notes on the Aramaic of the Genesis Apocryphon," 28.

[71] Fassberg, "Hebraisms in Aramaic Documents," 67.

20:26-27: מָא עבדתה לי בדיל [שר]י וְתֵאמַר לי די אחתי היא, "what have you done to me because of [Sar]ah, and (=for) you said to me, She is my sister?" Although it does look like a preterite verb, the construction is awkward, and K. Beyer's reading of the lines is smoother: בדיל [מָא] הָוִית אמר לי די אחתי היא, "why did you keep saying to me, She is my sister?" But other undoubted imperfects are used in a preterite manner: ועמי תמלל ולי תאמר, "with me she spoke and to me she said" (1QapGen 2:13). Other instances may occur in 4Q551 4-5:

ויתכנשון כל אנש קרתא על ביתא וימרון לה הנפק[
א]להא ויאמרו [

These lines are clearly a rewriting of Judg 19:22 or Gen. 19:4-5.[72] But in what tense? Although the fragment could be from a prophecy drawing from these texts, the natural presumption is that the verbs are past tense, and therefore *waw*–consecutives. But the text is too fragmentary to be certain.[73]

Participles. The active participle is usually used to indicate ongoing action, either past, present, or future, depending on the intent of the speaker.

(1) *Past:* אזלין תריהֹ[ו]ן [כ]חדא, "the two of them went together," 4QTob[b] ar (4Q197) 4 i 11; והא תרין דאנין עלי, "two were debating about me" in 4QVisAmram[b] ar (4Q544) 1:11; [א]נפוהי חעכין, "his face was cheerful" in 4QVisAmram[a] ar (4Q543) 3 4; and elsewhere. The past signification is more often signified by the use of הוי, "to be," as an auxiliary: note חזה הוית, "I was watching" in 2QJN ar (2Q24) 4 17; שנין שבע מצלא הוית, "seven years I was praying" in 4QPrNab ar (4Q242) 1:7; and כולהון הוא ערקין, "all of them fled" in 1QapGen 22:9.[74]

(2) *Present:* כדי מדקין קלופיא אלן, "when they crush these barks" in 4QEn[c] ar (4Q204) I ii 7; עליא די אנתון דחלין ו[פ]לחין, "the Most High God that you revere and worship" in 4Q550[d] 1:1; as well as

---

[72] Beyer, *ATTM*, 224.

[73] The verbs are translated as future forms by K. Beyer (*ATTM*, 224); as presents by Johann Maier (*Die Qumran-Essener: Die Texte vom Toten Meer*, [München: Reinhardt, 1995] 2.729-30); and as past forms by F. García Martínez (*The Dead Sea Scrolls Translated: The Qumran Texts in English* [Leiden: Brill, 1994] 289).

[74] Further examples are available.

קרין לה תרע יוסף, "they call it the gate of Joseph" in 4QJN[a] ar (4Q554) 1 i 18.[75]

(3) *Future:* מן צפונא אתיה באישתא, "from the north evil will come" in 4Q550[f] 1; לעלמא אתה רגז, "wrath will come to the world" in 4Q246 1:3; etc. Here also the use of הוי as an auxiliary is more common: for example, להוון מכפר[י]ן, "they will make atonement" (2Q24 8 5); להוון בזזין, "they will despoil" in 4QZodiology and Brontology ar (4Q318) 2:8; and להוה לבש, "he will wear" in 11QJN ar (11Q18) 4:5.[76]

SELECT BIBLIOGRAPHY

Beyer, K. *Die aramäischen Texte vom Toten Meer* (Göttingen: Vandenhoeck & Ruprecht, 1984).

—. *Ergänzungsband* (Vandenhoeck & Ruprecht, 1994).

Cook, E. M. "The Orthography of Final Unstressed Vowels in Old and Imperial Aramaic," *Maarav* 5 (1990) 53-67.

—. "Remarks on the Testament of Kohath from Qumran Cave 4," *JJS* 44 (1993) 205-19.

Fitzmyer, J. A. *The Genesis Apocryphon of Qumran Cave 1: A Commentary* (2nd ed., Rome: Biblical Institute, 1971) 22-23, n.60.

—. "The Phases of the Aramaic Language," in *A Wandering Aramean: Collected Aramaic Essays* (Missoula, MT: Scholars Press, 1979) 57-84.

Kutscher, E. Y. "The Language of the Genesis Apocryphon: A Preliminary Study," *Scripta Hierosolymitana* 4 (1957) 1-35.

Muraoka, T. "Notes on the Aramaic of the Genesis Apocryphon," *RevQ* 8 (1972-1974) 7-51.

— (ed.). *Studies in Qumran Aramaic* (Abr-Nahrain Supplement 3; Louvain: Peeters, 1992).

Reed, S. A. "Preliminary List of Aramaic Documents from Qumran Cave 4," *Comprehensive Aramaic Lexicon Newsletter* 9 (1992) 1-4.

—. *The Targum to Job from Qumran Cave XI* (Ramat-gan: Bar-Ilan University, 1974).

"Notes on the Aramaic Fragments of Enoch from Qumran Cave 4," *Maarav* 1/2 (1979) 197-224.

Tov, E., with S. J. Pfann (eds.). *The Dead Sea Scrolls on Microfiche. A Comprehensive Facsimile Edition of the Texts from the Judaean Desert, Companion Volume* (Leiden: Brill and IDC, 1993).

---

[75] Further examples are available.

[76] Further examples are available.

PALAEOGRAPHY AND THE DEAD SEA SCROLLS

FRANK MOORE CROSS

The dating of ancient scripts or manuscripts is of little difficulty—given sufficient study and a good eye for form—if the palaeographer has ample materials for typological sequencing, and a series of documents with firm dates (i.e. dated by archaeological context, or by references in their contents from which a date can be inferred, or, best, when documents bear date formulae in a known chronology). Ancient Latin and Greek palaeography are highly developed disciplines thanks to the plethora of dated documents and a scholarly tradition of detailed analysis of several types of script. The typological development of the several styles of the Early Jewish scripts in the Hellenistic and Roman periods—the era of the Dead Sea Scrolls—has been less well known in the past owing to a relative paucity of well-dated scripts from Palestine. A further complication is the controversy that broke out over the palaeographical dating of the early finds, especially those of Cave 1 at Qumrân.

1. OVERVIEW OF SOURCES AND INSCRIPTIONS

In 1937, there was a sufficient number of documents and inscriptions in the Jewish scripts of the Hellenistic and Roman periods to enable W. F. Albright to publish a programmatic study which organized the basic typological outlines of the development of the late Aramaic script of the Persian chancellery (used throughout the Persian Empire), and the early Jewish formal hands which developed from it.[1] Indeed, at the beginning of the Hellenistic period when Greek replaced Aramaic as the *lingua franca*, local national scripts began to spring up and develop independently in many areas of the Near East of which the best known in the Western part of the empire were Nabataean, Palmyrene, and Judaean (or Jewish). The Jewish scripts which evolved into an independent tradition in Judaea are traditionally

---

[1] W. F. Albright, "A Biblical Fragment from the Maccabaean Age: The Nash Papyrus," *JBL* 56 (1937) 145–57.

called "Hebrew," qualified as "square" or "Assyrian" (i.e. Aramaic). The surviving, archaizing form of the Old Hebrew script that we term "Palaeo-Hebrew" was largely displaced for ordinary purposes by the Jewish descendent of the official Aramaic script of the fourth century BCE, that is, at the close of the Persian sway over Syria-Palestine. It is a distinct national script, not evolved directly from Old Hebrew, and clearly distinguishable from the Aramaic hand from which it *did* evolve in the course of the early third century BCE, with the end of Persian rule and the beginning of Hellenistic times. So we may best call it "Jewish"—the script that was at home in Judaea, and occasionally used by Jews in the Diaspora. The Palaeo-Hebrew script died away in the first and second centuries CE, totally displaced in the Jewish community, and surviving as a sacred script only in the remnant Samaritan community.

In the past half-century the field of early Jewish palaeography has grown rich in materials for typological analysis, and, as well, has furnished the palaeographer with a series of absolutely dated documents which provide pegs in the typological sequence, dividing up periods, and specifying the speed of changes in the scripts—the emergence of new forms and styles of script. The caves of the Wâdi Qumrân, emanating out from the community center on the Dead Sea, have yielded up some eight hundred documents on skin and papyrus (and in one instance, copper).[2] These range in date from the mid-third century BCE (Plate 9, lines 2 and 3) to the third quarter of the first century of the Common Era (Plate 10, lines 6–8).[3] These manuscripts and manuscript fragments exhibit a variety of scripts, predominantly early Jewish, including formal and cursive styles, more rarely Palaeo-

---

[2] For a catalogue of the documents from the Qumrân caves with bibliography, see S. A. Reed, M. J. Lundberg, with M. B. Phelps (eds.), *The Dead Sea Scrolls Catalogue: Documents, Photographs and Museum Inventory Numbers* (SBLRBS 32; Atlanta: Scholars Press, 1994), hereafter *Catalogue*. The manuscripts of Caves 1–3, 6-11 have all been published. The publication of Cave 4 materials is proceeding in the official series *Discoveries in the Judaean Desert* (Oxford: Clarendon Press, 1955–). At the time of writing, ten volumes of Cave 4 documents have been published in this series, beginning in 1968 and continuing into the present. For fuller bibliography of publications since 1970, see F. García Martínez and D. W. Parry, *A Bibliography of the Finds in the Desert of Judah 1970–95* (STDJ 19; Leiden: Brill, 1996), hereafter *García and Parry*.

[3] Plates 9–14 are found at the end of the volume.

Hebrew, and sporadically, Greek. There is even an esoteric manuscript (4Q186) that is written in a mixture of these three scripts.[4]

Only slightly less important than the Qumrân documents are the finds further south in the Judaean Desert: the documents of the caves of the Wâdi Murabbaʿât,[5] the Naḥal Ḥever,[6] the Naḥal Ṣeʾelim (Wâdi Ṣeiyâl), and other minor caves.[7] These date in large part to the first and second centuries CE, many of the documents containing date formulae that pin them to a specific day, month, and year. There are materials in Jewish scripts including the extreme cursive, as well as in Greek, Latin, and Nabataean.

The dating of documents of the Herodian Age (30 BCE–70 CE) is now capable of great refinement. The limits of the period are marked by materials bearing date formulae, or otherwise may be absolutely dated within narrow limits by archaeological context or historical content. For example, there are the inscriptions of the Tomb of Jason (before 31 BCE), the Tomb Inscription of Queen Helena (ca. 50 CE), and the funerary monument of the Benê Ḥezîr (end of the first century BCE).[8] Jerusalem and its environs have produced hundreds of inscribed ossuaries.[9] The ossuary inscriptions have regularly been attributed

---

[4] Published by J. Allegro in *Qumrân Cave 4.I* [4Q158–4Q186] (DJD 5; Oxford: Clarendon Press, 1968) 88-91 + pl. XXXI.

[5] The Murabbaʿât documents have been published in P. Benoit, J. T. Milik and R. de Vaux (eds.), *Les grottes de Murabbaʿât* (DJD 2; Oxford: Clarendon Press, 1961).

[6] Principal publications include Y. Yadin, *The Finds of the Bar Kokhba Period in the Cave of Letters* (JDS; Jerusalem: Israel Exploration Society, 1963); Naphtali Lewis, Yigael Yadin and Jonas C. Greenfield, *The Documents from the Period of Bar Kokhba in the Cave of Letters* (JDS; Jerusalem: Israel Exploration Society, the Hebrew University, Shrine of the Book, 1989); Emanuel Tov, with R. A. Kraft and P. J. Parsons, *The Greek Minor Prophets Scroll from the Naḥal Ḥever (8ḤevXIIgr)* (DJD 8; Oxford: Clarendon Press, 1990).

[7] See especially Ada Yardeni, תעודות 'נחל צאלים' [*Naḥal Ṣeʾelim' Documents*] (JDS; Jerusalem: Ben-Gurion University, the Israel Exploration Society, 1995). Further preliminary publications are listed in Reed et al., *Catalogue*, 263-79.

[8] See N. Avigad, "Aramaic Inscriptions in the Tomb of Jason," *IEJ* 17 (1967) 101-10; and É. Puech, "Inscriptions funéraire palestiniennes: tombeau de Jason et ossuaires," *RB* 90 (1983) 481-533.

[9] J.-B. Frey in his *Corpus Inscriptionum Judaicarum* II (Rome: Pontificio istututo di archeologia cristiana, 1952) lists more than 200 ossuary or funerary inscriptions. Among the more important of many recent discoveries are the rich finds of the "Dominus Flevit." See P. B. Bagatti and J. T. Milik (eds.), *Gli scavi*

to the last century before the destruction of the Temple, on historical as well as typological grounds, and this dating is solidly confirmed. Indeed, the ossuary scripts may now be used boldly in setting up typological series of formal, semicursive and cursive scripts of the Herodian era. We can demonstrate now that the scripts of these funerary inscriptions, several hundred in number—whether engravings, dipinti, or graffiti—correspond to formal or cursive styles used in leather and papyrus documents. Less important, no doubt, but worthy of mention, is the fact that in newer ossuary finds, careful descriptions of associated finds of pottery and lamps and coins have been published, even as our knowledge of common Roman pottery has been made more precise by the large and narrowly dated ceramic series from Ḥirbet Qumrân, and Masada, not to mention the recent excavations in Jerusalem.[10]

Particularly noteworthy is a recently discovered ostracon from Qumrân, evidently written in the sectarian community to judge from its content, and dated "in the second year...," presumably the second year of the First Jewish Revolt against Rome (67 CE).[11]

The excavations of Yigael Yadin at Masada have produced ostraca, papyri, and leather manuscripts deposited in *loci* that were sealed in the fall of the bastion to the Romans in 73 CE. These include biblical fragments, a Ben Sira scroll, and fragments of sectarian documents.[12]

---

del *"Dominus Flevit"* (Jerusalem: Tipographia dei PP. Franciscani, 1958) 70-109. For other recent ossuary finds, see the paper of Puech listed in the previous note.

[10] See Y. Yadin and J. Naveh, *Masada I: The Yigael Yadin Excavations 1963–1965, The Aramaic and Hebrew Ostraca and Jar Inscriptions* (Jerusalem: Israel Exploration Society and the Hebrew University, 1989) 6-67 + pls. I–LX; R. de Vaux, *Archaeology and the Dead Sea Scrolls* (Schweich Lectures 1959; London: Oxford University Press for the British Academy, 1973) esp. 3-45 + pl. XLII. On the abecedary from Level I (before 31 BCE), see R. de Vaux, "Fouilles au Khirbet Qumrân," *RB* 61 (1954) 229 + pl. Xa; and F. M. Cross, "The Oldest Manuscripts from Qumran," *JBL* 74 (1955) 147-72, esp. 147 n.2 (discussion of the abecedary's script). For synthetic studies of the pottery of this period, see Paul Lapp, *Palestinian Ceramic Chronology, 200 BC–AD 70* (New Haven, CT: American Schools of Oriental Research, 1961); and P. Kahane, "Pottery Types from the Jewish Ossuary-Tombs around Jerusalem," *IEJ* 2 (1952) 125-39, 176-82; ibidem, in *IEJ* 3 (1953) 48-54.

[11] See F. M. Cross and Esther Eshel, "Ostraca from Ḥirbet Qumrân," *IEJ* 47 (1997) 17-28.

[12] See especially, Yadin and Naveh, *Masada I*; Y. Yadin, *The Ben Sira Scroll from Masada* (Jerusalem: Israel Exploration Society, Shrine of the Book, 1965);

Until recently, the dating of documents in the Archaic or Proto-Jewish period (ca. 275-150 BCE) has been based largely on typological sequence, making use of some fourth- and third-century papyri from Egypt for comparison.[13] New discoveries in Palestine of dated documents stemming from the end of the fourth century and the beginning of the third century BCE are especially important for the dating of the beginning of the Archaic series. The Samaria Papyri from the Wâdi ed-Dâliyeh provide a series of legal contracts dated by the Persian kings mostly from the reigns of Artaxerxes III (359-338 BCE) and Darius III (338-331).[14] Historical and archaeological evidence combine to show that these Samaritan owners of the documents perished in an attack by troops of Alexander the Great in 331 BCE, providing a precise *terminus ad quem* for the abandonment of the papyri in the Dâliyeh cave.

A series of ostraca in Aramaic script from the end of the fourth and the beginning of the third centuries BCE stems from Idumaean circles living on the border of Judaea in the south, notably from Mareshah, Ḥirbet el-Qôm, and vicinity. A. Lemaire has recently published nearly two hundred Aramaic ostraca, many of which bear date formulae: the oldest from 362, and the latest from 331 BCE (the latter being the second year of Alexander the Great according to the Egyptian reckoning of his reign).[15] Another two hundred and one Aramaic ostraca stemming from the period between 361 and 311 BCE have been published by the Israeli scholars Israel Ephʿal and Joseph

---

C. Newsom, *Songs of the Sabbath Sacrifice: A Critical Edition* (HSS 27; Atlanta: Scholars Press, 1985) 167-84 (on the Masada Songs of the Sabbath Sacrifices); S. Talmon, קטעי כתבים עברים של עברים כתובים המצדה ["Fragments of Writings Written in Hebrew at Masada"], *EI* 20 (Y. Yadin Memorial Volume, 1989) 278-86; idem, קטעי מגילות ספר ויקרא המצדה ["Fragments of Two Leviticus Scrolls from Masada"], *EI* 24 (Festschrift A. Malamat, 1993), 99-110. For a list of other preliminary publications of Masada documents, see Reed et al., *Catalogue*, 185-216.

[13] See F. M. Cross, "The Development of the Jewish Scripts," in G. Ernest Wright (ed.), *The Bible and the Ancient Near East: Essays in Honor of W. F. Albright* (Garden City, NY: Doubleday, 1961) 133-202, esp. 140-45 (hereafter abbreviated *DJS*).

[14] F. M. Cross, "The Scripts of the Dâliyeh Papyri," in P. and N. Lapp (eds.), *Discoveries in the Wâdī ed-Dâliyeh* (AASOR 41; Cambridge, MA: American Schools of Oriental Research, 1974) 25-27 + Chart of Scripts, pl. LIX.

[15] A. Lemaire, *Nouvelles inscriptions araméennes d'Idumée au Musée d'Israël* (Supplément 3 à Transeuphratène; Paris: Gabalda, 1996).

Naveh.[16] A cave in Ketep Yeriḥo (the "Mount of Temptation") has produced a well-preserved papyrus of the beginning of the third century, dated by associated materials in the find spot as well as typology.[17] Lawrence Geraty has published an ostracon from Ḥirbet el-Qôm, a receipt for money paid, dated in the sixth year (of Ptolemy Philadelphus).[18]

A marriage contract from Mareshah bears the date 176 BCE, the 136th year of the Seleucid Era. Its semicursive script is virtually identical with that of the Nash Papyrus[19] (see Plate 11, lines 1 and 2).

In the present state of palaeographical study, therefore, we are enabled to draw a typological line of developments of several script styles. These appear in scores if not hundreds of documents, inscribed on a variety of materials, their evolution pegged by a series of absolute dates at intervals in the early Hellenistic period, in the Hasmonaean, and in the Herodian Ages—and indeed, through the subsequent era between the two Jewish Revolts against Rome.

The Palaeo-Hebrew scripts, found for the most part in Pentateuchal manuscripts from Qumrân, are more difficult to date, the script evolving very slowly. When these were initially found at Qumrân, there was some confusion about their date. However, the appearance of Palaeo-Hebrew inscriptions on late fourth century bullae, and on inscriptions and coins from the ruins of the city on the slopes of Mount Gerizim (which was destroyed by John Hyrcanus in 128 BCE), has aided in clarifying the chronology.[20] In the late Persian, Early

---

[16] I. Ephʿal and J. Naveh, *Aramaic Ostraca from the Fourth Century BC from Idumaea* (Jerusalem: Magnes Press, Hebrew University and the Israel Exploration Society, 1997).

[17] H. Eshel and H. Misgav, "A Fourth Century B.C.E. Document from Ketef Yeriḥo," *IEJ* 38 (1988) 158-76 + pls. XXV–XXVI. See the revised dating of the papyrus in H. Eshel and B. Zissu, "Ketef Yeriḥo, 1993," *IEJ* 45 (1995) 292-95; and Esther Eshel, "Some Paleographic Success Stories," *BAR* 23/2 (1997) 48-49.

[18] L. T. Geraty, "The Khirbet el-Kom Bilingual Ostracon," *BASOR* 212 (1975) 55-61.

[19] Amos Kloner and Esther Eshel, "An Aramaic Ostracon of an Edomite Marriage Contract from Maresha, Dated 176 B.C.E.," *IEJ* 46 (1996) 1-22; cf. E. Eshel, "Paleographic Success Stories," 48-49.

[20] For the excavations in the city on Mount Gerizim, and samples of Palaeo-Hebrew inscriptions, cf. Y. Magen, עיר מבוצרת מן התקופה ההלניסטית בהר גריזים ["A Fortified Town of the Hellenistic Period on Mount Gerizim"], *Qadmoniot* 19 (1986) 91-101; idem, הר גריזים–עיר מקדש ["Mount Gerizim—A Temple City"], *Qadmoniot* 23 (1990) 70-96.

Hellenistic, Hasmonaean, and Roman periods, dated coins with Palaeo-Hebrew legends and the occasional inscription from a tomb or from the Temple area bring us up to 70 CE. We have mentioned above the occasional appearance of Palaeo-Hebrew writing on manuscripts which are inscribed basically in the Jewish character. These permit us to date one script by the other; the best study on this script is that of Mark McLean.[21] The dates of the Qumrân Palaeo-Hebrew scripts fall within the limits of the manuscripts in the Jewish hands—as might be expected. The earliest form of this writing at Qumrân is probably found in a manuscript of Deuteronomy (4Qpaleo-Deut^s or 4Q46) from the second half of the third century; 4QpaleoJob^c (4Q101) is of about the same early date. The latest of these manuscripts is 11QpaleoLeviticus (11Q1) from ca. 1–50 CE (see Plate 13). The relatively well-preserved Exodus scroll, 4QpaleoExod^m (4Q22), may be dated to ca. 100–50 BCE.[22]

In 1991 and 1996, two groups of manuscripts, mostly from Qumrân, were tested by radiocarbon dating methods, one group (1991) by the Institut für Mittelenergiephysik, Zürich, and the second (1996) by the NSF[23] Accelerator Mass Spectrometry Facility at the University of Arizona in Tucson.[24] These tests included one Palaeo-Hebrew manuscript (4QpaleoExod^m), and scrolls in Jewish scripts from across the spectrum. The results were remarkably in agreement with dates arrived at earlier on palaeographic grounds. But while the radiocarbon method gives a fairly broad range of dates, palaeographical analysis is more precise, often narrowing the range of dates to a half-century.

---

[21] "The Development and Use of Palaeo-Hebrew in the Hellenistic and Roman Periods" (Unpubl. Ph.D. diss., Cambridge, MA: Harvard University, 1982).

[22] The Palaeo-Hebrew manuscripts from Cave 4 are now published: P. W. Skehan, E. Ulrich and J. E. Sanderson, *Qumran Cave 4.IV: Palaeo-Hebrew and Greek Biblical Manuscripts* (DJD 9; Oxford: Clarendon Press, 1992). The editors follow the palaeographical datings of McLean. This volume also contains (pp. 7-13) a discussion, by P. J. Parsons, of the palaeographical dates of the Greek manuscripts from Cave 4.

[23] I.e. the National Science Foundation.

[24] See the contribution by G. Doudna to this Fiftieth Anniversary collection: "Dating the Dead Sea Scrolls on the Basis of Radiocarbon Analysis." Also G. Bonani, I. Carmi, S. Ivy, J. Strugnell and W. Wölfli, "Radiocarbon Dating of the Dead Sea Scrolls," *Atiqot* 20 (1991) 27-32; and A. T. J. Jull, D. J. Donahue, M. Broshi and E. Tov, "Radiocarbon Dating of Scrolls and Linen Fragments from the Judean Desert," *Atiqot* 20 (1996) 1-7.

Certain general shifts mark the evolution of the formal Jewish hand. Before proceeding to more a detailed description of the development of individual letters, we may underline one or two general traits of each period. The Archaic book hand is marked by two characteristics surviving from the end of the Persian era: the widely differing sizes of the letters below and above the ceiling line, and the preservation of variety in the width of strokes ("shading" stemming from a flexible reed pen), according to fixed fashions.[25] The Hasmonaean hand preserves in part the tradition of large and small letters, with letters hung from the ceiling line (usually marked in dry point on the leather). There is no sense of a baseline; but the tendency to uniformity of size—begun in the Aramaic or Archaic cursives of the third century—has set in, "infecting" the formal character. Shading becomes idiosyncratic. The Herodian hand breaks sharply with the tradition of variety in size according to fixed canons, and tends to standardize the height and breadth. Letters continue to be hung from the ceiling line, but a feeling for a baseline asserts itself in the instance of most letters, and occasionally a base guide is marked in dry point. Shading—if any—becomes monotonous. "Tittles" or *keraiai*,[26] which are archaic survivals or idiosyncratic flourishes in Hasmonaean scripts, develop and multiply to become standard parts of letters. In elegant hands new techniques of shading are often used.

In the pages that follow we shall deal in turn with three topics: the origin of the Archaic Jewish hand; the development of the formal Jewish hands; and the evolution of scripts in cursive traditions.[27]

2. THE ORIGIN OF THE ARCHAIC JEWISH HAND

The starting-point for the study of Jewish palaeography is the Persian chancellery hand in use at the end of the Persian Empire. This official Aramaic hand finds its origin in an elegant cursive script which took form in the sixth century and evolved into its classical style in the fifth and fourth centuries BCE. This standard Aramaic character was in regular use throughout the Persian Empire, from Asia

---

[25] Actually, the varieties of shading are controlled by the fashions of cutting the pen point, which change over time.

[26] Not to be confused with Medieval *tāgîn*!

[27] For detailed description of cursive and semicursive features of the Jewish scripts, see F. M. Cross, "The Development of the Jewish Scripts," in G. E. Wright (ed.), *Bible and the Ancient Near East*, 181-88.

Minor to North Arabia and Upper Egypt, and from Palestine to the eastern reaches of Iran. While it evolved steadily in these centuries, it remained relatively undifferentiated by local peculiarities in the western reaches of the Empire until Persian rule was swept away by the forces of Alexander in 331 BCE. So powerful was its sway that formal and lapidary Aramaic styles became moribund, and the chancellery hand, while cursive in its origin, was used not only for commercial and diplomatic correspondence and contracts, but as a fully formal script on stone monuments.

The immediate ancestor of the earliest *formal* Qumrân scripts has proved to be this standard Aramaic *cursive*. The earliest of the formal scripts from Qumrân is the old Samuel manuscript, 4QSam^b, which dates to the mid-third century BCE (See Plate 9, line 4).[28] I have designated it as "Archaic Jewish formal"—although one may prefer to describe it as "Proto-Jewish." This script is little influenced by the vulgar Aramaic cursive which developed in the third century BCE in Palestine and Egypt, when Greek replaced Aramaic for official purposes. On the other hand, the earliest Qumrân exemplar of the cursive tradition, the archaic manuscript of Exodus and Leviticus (4QExod-Lev^f, Plate 9, line 3), makes it evident that a cursive stream flowed in parallel to the formal, stemming from the vulgar Aramaic cursives of the third century. In the formal character of the mid-third century, the extreme difference in the length of various letters below the ceiling line continues, preserving the long slender letters of the classical tradition; in the cursive, however, letter forms become squat and more regular in size.

One very important development which was destined to modify radically the size and form of letters characterizes the fourth- and especially the third-century scripts. This is the trend to create what may be called "semi-ligatures," a tendency of the scribe to bend the final stroke of a letter in the direction of writing, i.e. to the position of forming the next letter. Especially affected were the long downstrokes of letters such as *kap*, *nun*, *pe* and frequently *ṣade*. However, other letters were also affected by the tendency: notably *mem* whose left oblique is bent upward to the left; and *lamed*, whose broad sweep down to the right tends to narrow, and in the course of the third century straightens and begins the development of a tick downward. Naturally this tendency was felt most strongly in the case of letters in

---

[28] Plates 9-14 are found at the end of the volume.

non-final positions, so that we see here the commencement of the development of "medial" forms of the letters. So-called "final" letters, actually the older forms of the letters, were preserved where the tendency to create semi-ligatures was not so strong. By the third century, the distinction between final and medial letters was full-blown, although different script traditions froze different sets of medial and final forms. In the course of time, certain forms were lost (e.g. final *lamed*), and secondary distinctions between final and medial forms were developed and then lost (e.g. the artificial distinction between medial and final *he*, and between medial and final *ʾalep* in certain cursive scripts).

3. THE DEVELOPMENT OF THE FORMAL JEWISH SCRIPTS

In Plate 10 we illustrate the evolution of the formal character in the Hasmonaean and Herodian periods. Out of scores of exemplars of the formal hands of the Hasmonaean period, we have chosen three typical specimens, the first from the transitional period at the beginning of the Hasmonaean development (4QDeut[a] or 4Q28), the second from the middle of the Hasmonaean period (4QDeut[c] or 4Q30, contemporaneous with the Great Isaiah scroll 1QIsaiah[a]), and the third a late transitional hand from the end of the Hasmonaean or the beginning of the Herodian period (4QSam[a] or 4Q51). The absolute dates for this series can be fixed between ca. 175 BCE and ca. 30 BCE.

Out of the great riches of manuscripts from the Herodian Age, we have chosen seven typical formal scripts (Plate 10, lines 4–10). The first two are Early Herodian; one of these is a fully formal script, appearing in the War Scroll from Cave 1 at Qumrân (1QM), while the second a popular Round or Rustic semiformal (4QNum[b] or 4Q27). The script of the War Scroll is an excellent example of the delicate, usually minuscule, formal script that evolved directly from the transitional hands of the type of 4QSam[a] (Plate 10, line 3). Its lapidary equivalent is found in the Tomb Inscription of the Benê Ḥezîr from about the turn of the Common Era. An additional five scripts have been chosen to represent the complex evolution of the late Herodian hand. 4QDan[b] (4Q113) and 4QDeut[j] (4Q37), especially the latter, exhibit the characteristic thick lines and squat configuration of the late formal scripts of Qumrân. Perhaps the latest formal hand at Qumrân is to be found in 4QPs[b] (4Q84). Its script is very nearly as evolved as the hand of another Psalms manuscript from the Naḥal Ḥever (Plate 10, line 9) which dates to the end of the first century of the Common Era

(5/6Ḥev–Se4 Ps). The final script in the series is from a dated Hebrew contract that was inscribed in 133 CE (Mur 24).

Perhaps it will be useful to single out a few salient features in the evolution of each letter of the alphabet in the formal series. A more detailed and nuanced discussion can be found in my long article, "The Development of the Jewish Scripts."[29]

ʾ*Alep* in the Archaic period is small, often with a crescent-shaped left leg (Plate 9, line 4). In the Hasmonaean period, the letter begins to enlarge, assuming by the end of the period a "standard" letter-size. In the Herodian period the left arm, and especially the right leg, develop more and more distinctive *keraiai* ("tittles"), while in the Late Herodian period the oblique axis and the left leg are penned as an inverted "V." This letter also becomes increasingly heavy-lined and squat.

Bet in the late Archaic and early Hasmonaean times is narrow, with the down-stroke curving softly into a short base. In the semiformal and semicursive scripts the *bet* becomes broad and enlarged, a development which invades the formal character of Hasmonaean times. At the end of the Hasmonaean period, the down-stroke is drawn almost vertically, and bends in a right angle to the horizontal base. In the Herodian period, the base-line is no longer penned from right to left, but rather from left to right, often breaking through the right down-stroke.

The changes in *gimel* are subtle. In the Archaic period the left leg of the letters moves down the right leg from near the top to the increasingly curved, or doubly-curved, middle or lower part of the right leg. In the Herodian period, the top of the right leg develops a *keraia*.

Dalet is a very narrow letter in the Archaic period, begun with a tick, and drawn without lifting the pen. In the Hasmonaean period the letter broadens under the influence of the semiformal *dalet*. By the end of this period, it is penned in two strokes. The tick enlarges, and the horizontal part of the head completes the first stroke. The pen is then lifted and the right down-stroke is drawn separately; in the Herodian period, the horizontal often breaks through the right leg owing to the change in the manner of penning the letter.

The typological shifts of *he* are complex, which makes it very useful in dating. The right leg is drawn first, then a shaded left horizontal is penned, attached slightly below the top of the right leg and usually slanting slightly down. The left leg is drawn down from

---

[29] F. M. Cross, "Development of the Jewish Scripts," 133-202.

the horizontal. In the Hasmonaean period, the leg is drawn continuously following the horizontal stroke, often being looped back in a triangular motion. In the Herodian period the fashion of making *he* once again changes, with the right leg penned upward (*sic!*), moving in a triangular motion into the horizontal, and then in another triangular motion into the left down-stroke, leaving triangular blobs of ink at the two top corners.

The Archaic *waw* begins with a curl, later becoming a hook, and a straight vertical. *Yod* is made either with a three-movement set of strokes, down to the left, up and around and down again to the right; or—typologically later— it is made in a two-movement inverted "V." In Hasmonaean times, the tops of both *waw* and *yod* become an angular hook, often shaded, so that a triangular effect is produced. In late Hasmonaean times the right down-stroke of *yod* lengthens and straightens, and in the early Herodian period *waw* and *yod* become virtually, if not actually, indistinguishable. Finally, in the late Herodian period *waw* and *yod* again are increasingly distinguished, with *waw* becoming slightly longer and *yod* tending to shorten.

Earlier on, *zayin* is a uncomplicated single down-stroke. But then, in the mid-Hasmonaean period, this letter develops to the right at the top of the down-stroke a bend or bulge which becomes a triangular tick or *keraia* in the Herodian Age.

Ḥet in the Archaic period is made with a right up-stroke, a crossbar, and a left down-stroke. The top corners are simple, with no evidence of looping from one stroke into another. In the Hasmonaean period there begins some tendency to loop, particularly at the upper right corner. In the Herodian period this looping tends to create a triangular bulge.

In the third century *ṭet* is made with the left vertical beginning high above the ceiling line, and descending into a curved or even bluntly pointed base, then angling up in an oblique stroke before finally curling to meet the left vertical at the ceiling line. In Hasmonaean scripts, the base straightens out towards the horizontal, and the left down-stroke shortens. At the end of the Hasmonaean and the beginning of the Herodian age, a new style of penning the *ṭet* makes its appearance. After the horizontal base is drawn, the right, curled stroke is drawn downward, and often in the Herodian period breaks through the lower horizontal base.

In the old Samuel scroll, *kap* has a "figure-3" shape. The medial and final forms in this period are similarly hooked at the top, left, and the final form curves little if at all as it plunges below the (theoretical) base-line. In the Hasmonaean period the form broadens, and in the Early Herodian period a new final form is introduced in which the top bar is shaded and eventually loops into the down-stroke.

After the disappearance of final (non-hooked) *lamed* that was found in the earliest Archaic formals, the small, hooked medial form comes to dominate in all positions. In the later periods its evolution is slow. Scribes sometimes experiment in penning *lamed* in varying styles, but the main line of evolution is not side-tracked. Intermittently in the Hasmonaean period, a hook develops at the top of the letter. In the Herodian period the hook becomes a *keraia*.

Medial and (especially) final *mem* are large letters in the Archaic period, extending well below a theoretical base-line. The right side of the medial form is drawn in the same pattern as the *kap* is made, and then the left arm is added last. Final *mem*, like medial *mem*, is often open. In the course of the Hasmonaean age, medial *mem* increasingly loses it long, slender form, and by the end of this period is of standard letter-size. The final form develops similarly, although not as dramatically. The left down-stroke cuts through the head of the letter, and is drawn vertically downward, in the mid- and late Hasmonaean period, touching the base. This base of the letter meets the right down-stroke and, like *kap*, the lower right part becomes increasingly angular. At the end of the Hasmonaean period, the left down-stroke of final *mem* moves to the right at its top and finally disappears, giving the form a box-like shape in Herodian times. In late Herodian times, the fashion of making the medial *mem* changes. The left diagonal is now drawn upward, and the former tick beginning the letter is penned last, a short vertical stroke drawn down into the oblique, sometimes cutting it.

Nun in non-final positions steadily shortens in the Hasmonaean period, in line with the trend toward uniform letter-size. In the Herodian period a tick rightwards at the top of the stroke—in both medial and final *nun*—becomes a *keraia*.

In the third century, *samek* in semicursive scripts loses its complex doubly-hooked head. The letter is drawn beginning with an upstroke on the left, into a looped head. The right side is curved around, but remains open at the base until the close of Hasmonaean period. In the Herodian period, the form is totally closed, and takes on a somewhat triangular shape.

ʿ*Ayin* in the Archaic and early Hasmonaean periods is a small letter drawn just under the ceiling line. It increases in size toward the end of the Hasmonaean period, following the general trend toward uniformity in letter-size. The right leg turns obliquely leftward, breaks through the left leg, and lengthens. The tendency for the ʿayin to rotate clockwise becomes fully developed in the Herodian period.

Medial *pe* in the Hasmonaean script ceases to be made with a gentle curve into the base, but, following a general trend in the Hasmonaean period (*bet, kap, mem, ṣade*), the right down-stroke turns in a right angle into a fully horizontal base. In the Herodian period the heads of both medial and final *pe* become curled under.

Medial *ṣade* follows the Hasmonaean tendency to turn a straight or gently-curved base into an angular one. The vertical down-stroke of the final form lengthens—influenced by other final forms, notably *kap* and *nun*. In the Herodian scripts the right arm develops a *keraia* at the top, and sometimes both arms have *keraiai*.

Qop in scripts from the Archaic era is small (but enlarging in the semiformal). A short down-stroke tends to lengthen in the Hasmonaean scripts, while in Herodian scripts the long "tail" persists with little change.

The changes in the development of *reš* are subtle. The narrow Archaic *reš*, which is frequently confused with *waw*, broadens in Hasmonaean scripts, and the ticked or sharp right shoulder becomes increasingly rounded.

The evolution of *šin*[30] is very slow in the Archaic and Hasmonaean periods. At the end of the Hasmonaean period, and persisting through the Herodian, the extreme rightdown-stroke develops a tick, and eventually a *keraia*.

Taw in the Archaic period is a very large letter, extending well below the (theoretical) base-line. The left leg is long and doubly curved. By mid-Hasmonaean times, however, *taw* has shrunken, following the general trend towards uniformity of letter-size. The left leg no longer ends in a curved flourish, but in an angular base. By Herodian times, the right leg has lengthened to roughly the same length as the left one.

4. SCRIPTS IN SEMICURSIVE AND CURSIVE TRADITIONS

The Jewish cursive script in the Herodian and post-Herodian period is now well known, thanks to the rich dated corpus of commercial and legal documents, especially from Murabbaʿât, Ḥever and Ṣeiyâl, that

---

[30] Of course, *śin* and *šin* are not distinguished.

were alluded to above.[31] Three specimens of this script are presented in Plate 13. The first of these is Mur 18 (the "Nero Papyrus"),[32] dated in the second year of Nero (55/56 CE); the second, a true cursive, is Mur 20,[33] dated probably in the year 117 CE; and the third (Ḥev/Se 8a), from an Aramaic contract of sale from 134 CE, is related to the older semicursive tradition.[34] Compare also Papyrus Yadin 10 from the early second century CE (before 125), and Ada Yardeni's discussion and charts of its script.[35]

The Herodian cursive is now relatively well known from ossuaries, from Qumrân (in unpublished texts), from the Bethphage Lid of the late first century BCE,[36] from the ostraca of Masada (before 73 CE),[37] from the Nero Papyrus mentioned above, and from an important group of ostraca (first half of the first century CE) that were published by Ada Yardeni, with an exemplary discussion of their script.[38]

The semicursive script springs from the crossing of two traditions, the early formal character and the cursive scripts of the second century BCE. From this combination, toward the beginning of the Hasmonaean era, it gains its integrity as a script type. On the other hand, it is a script quite sensitive to the cursive development, and its evolution is never wholly independent of the cursive. For this reason, it exhibits a considerable variety even in scripts of the same date; one exemplar may stand very close to the cursive tradition, another quite close to the formal script.

The semicursive script at Qumrân is represented largely in documents of the Hasmonaean age. In the Herodian period, the semiformal scripts, especially the Vulgar semiformal ones, seem

---

[31] See section 1.

[32] This manuscript, also knownas the "Nero Papyrus," was published by J. T. Milik in *Les grottes de Murabbaʿât* (DJD 2), 100-104 + pl. XXIX.

[33] See Milik in *Les grottes de Murabbaʿât* (DJD 2) 109-44 + pls. XXX–XXXI.

[34] J. T. Milik, "Deux documents inédits du Désert de Juda," *Bib* 38 (1957) 264-68 + pl. IV.

[35] In Y. Yadin, J. C. Greenfield and Ada Yardeni, "Babatha's *Ketubba*," *IEJ* 44 (1994) 75-99 + Palaeographical Chart.

[36] See J. T. Milik, "Le couvercle de Bethphagé," in *Hommages à A. Dupont-Sommer* (Paris: Andrien-Maisonneuve, 1971) 75-94 + Fig. 1; and J. Naveh, "Nameless People," *IEJ* 40 (1990) 108-23 + Figs. 1–3.

[37] Yadin and Naveh, *Masada I*; 6-67 + pls. I–LX.

[38] "New Jewish Aramaic Ostraca," *IEJ* 40 (1990) 130-52.

largely to replace the semicursive script in literary documents. The reappearance of the semicursive at Murabbaʿât and elsewhere, however, guarantees its continued use for some purposes—at least in certain scribal circles. Its rarity in extant documents of the Herodian period is not especially surprising since it must have served chiefly as a "chancellery" hand, i.e. for non-literary documents; even in the Hasmonaean period at Qumrân, it is a rare hand, especially rare in carefully-prepared biblical manuscripts.

The semicursive scripts, since they mix cursive and formal typological elements, provide extra, if interwoven and complex, criteria for dating. Since the script has a certain integrity in its tradition, an inner typology can be constructed. This is no simple task, owing, as we have noted, to the variety within the tradition.

In Plate 11 we have given three specimen scripts of an early mixed type, combining, in unstable fashion, formal and cursive traits: a marriage contract from 176 BCE,[39] the Nash Papyrus (line 2),[40] and the Murabbaʿât Ostracon (line 3).[41] These examples form a group apart.

The script of the Nash Papyrus and the Murabbaʿât Ostracon will not be studied in detail here. The Nash Papyrus stands very close to the formal tradition and can be fitted without difficulty into the formal typology in the transition between the Archaic and Hasmonaean eras, toward 150 BCE.[42] Roughly contemporaneous with the (more formal) hand of 4QDeutᵃ (Plate 10, line 1), it mixes with its formal characters, cursive forms of ʾalep, he, lamed, ʿayin, ṣade and taw. The Murabbaʿât Ostracon uses cursive forms more extensively, but its remaining formal traits prohibit the lowering of its date below ca. 100 BCE.[43] The

---

[39] Published by Kloner and Eshel, "An Aramaic Ostracon," 1-22.

[40] Published first by S. A. Cook, in *Proceedings of the Society for Biblical Archaeology* 25 (1903) 34-56 + plate; for a discussion of the script, see Albright, "A Biblical Fragment from the Maccabaean Age," 145-76.

[41] Mur 72, published by J. T. Milik, *Les grottes de Murabbaʿât* (DJD 2) 172-74 + pl. LII.

[42] Elsewhere the present writer has discussed the date and character of the Nash Papyrus and referred to the relevant literature: F. M. Cross, "Oldest Manuscripts from Qumrân," 148, n.3.

[43] The dating of the Murabbaʿât Ostracon (Mur 17) by Starcky and Milik, in *Les grottes de Murabbaʿât* (DJD 2) 94-99 + pl. XXVIII, is too late since comparison has been made *directly* with first century BCE Palmyrene and Nabataean inscriptions, which is an inadmissible procedure. The traits observed in the sister scripts are elements which persisted after the separation of the national scripts, but

cursive features of these manuscripts will be taken up when appropriate in the discussion of the detailed characteristics of the Qumrân semiformal scripts.

In Plate 12 a type series of characteristic semicursive scripts is presented: an early Hasmonaean biblical hand (4QXII[a] or 4Q76) in line 1; two developed Hasmonaean hands, one biblical (4QDan[c] or 4Q114) in line 2, and one from an Aramaic work, the Book of the Giants ar[b] (4Q530) in line 3;[44] and three late Hasmonaean hands, the last two of which may be as late as the beginning of the Herodian period (lines 4–6).[45]

The ʾalep of the early Hasmonaean semicursive is normally little differentiated from the contemporary semiformal character. In 4QXII[a], for example, ʾalep has become large, unlike most specimens in 4QDeut[a]; yet its form, with the bowed leg, is that of the Archaic semiformal and early Hasmonaean scripts. The cursive looped ʾalep which appears in the Nash Papyrus and the Murabbaʿât Papyrus, rarely appears in the semicursive hands of the Hasmonaean era. Its influence is felt, however, in the curious form of 4QDan[c] (Plate 12, line 2), and later, it reappears in simplified form, for example, in 6Q8 (Plate 12, line 6). The final ʾalep is derived not from the looped form, but from a simplified formal ʾalep which lost its left leg.

Bet undergoes a major change at the beginning of the Hasmonaean period. Even in the earliest part of this period (4QXII[a], Plate 12, line 1), bet has begun to be made in two non-continuous strokes, with the base an independent, shaded stroke made from left to right. In the Herodian cursive, a new form appears; developed from the Hasmonaean semicursive, this is the "figure 2" bet, made in a continuous motion, but with the base drawn from left to right in semicursive style.

---

which died out early in the Jewish tradition.

[44] The latter is among the Cave 4 documents being edited by É. Puech, *Qumran Cave 4.XXII: Textes en Araméen* (DJD 31; Oxford: Clarendon Press [forthcoming]).

[45] The first (line 4) is the so-called "Halakhic Epistle" (4QpapMMT[e]) in E. Qimron and J. Strugnell, *Qumran Cave 4.V: Miqṣat Maʿaśe Ha-Torah* (DJD 10; Oxford: Clarendon Press, 1994). The second (line 5) is a manuscript from Cave 4 (4QEn[g] ar or 4Q212), published by J. T. Milik in collaboration with Matthew Black, *The Books of Enoch: Aramaic Fragments from Qumrân Cave 4* (Oxford: Clarendon Press, 1976) pls. XXI–XXIV. The third (line 6) is a papyrus from Cave 6 (6Q8), which was edited by M. Baillet in M. Baillet et al., *Les 'Petites Grottes' de Qumran: Exploration de la falaise Les grottes 2Q, 3Q, 5Q, 6Q, 7Q, à 10Q, Le rouleau de cuivre* (DJD 3; Oxford: Clarendon Press, 1962) pl. XXIV, 8.

Gimel in 4QXII^a is undifferentiated from that of the Archaic series. As early as 4QDan^c (Plate 12, line 2), the right down-stroke begins to bow in the fashion of Hasmonaean formal *gimel*s, and in the late first century BCE shifts to a form drawn in a continuous stroke (Bethphage Lid, 4QEn^g ar).

Dalet in the early and late Hasmonaean semicursives is little differentiated from the semiformal Archaic style. The cursive *dalet*, made either with a simple head (Nero Papyrus) or with a head similar to cursive *reš* (Mur 117), belongs to a quite distinct tradition.

He in the early Hasmonaean semicursive manuscripts (4QXII^a) is undifferentiated from the earliest Hasmonaean formal *he* (4QDeut^a). In the developed hands (4QDan^c) it tends to narrow, with the cross-bar usually slanting up to the left, contrary to the formal development. Normally the cross-bar is heavily shaded. In the late Hasmonaean and early Herodian period, two forms of *he* are used, one formal in origin, the other cursive. In 4QpapMMT^e (Plate 12, line 4), the cursive form, retaining a most archaic shape,[46] is used as medial *he*; the formal *he* is used in the final position. A similar distinction obtains in the 6Q8 Papyrus and often in late Hasmonaean semicursives.

Waw and *yod*,[47] in the Hasmonaean semicursive hands, follow the pattern of development of the formal scripts. The broad, inverted "v" *yod* does not appear, however, and in some hands (especially in cursive or late scripts) *waw* is simplified into a slightly curved, headless stroke.

Zayin, throughout the Hasmonaean semicursive scripts, was made with a straight, simple stroke.[48] At the end of this period, and in the developed Herodian scripts, *zayin* has a head (6Q8) or is bent to the right at the top (Nero Papyrus).

Ḥet in 4QXII^a is little differentiated from early Hasmonaean formal types. A cursive tendency appears strongly in 4QDan^c, with the cross-bar slanting up to the left. The latter form, however, is still distant from the "N"-form *ḥet* (Bethphage Lid, Nero Papyrus). The *ḥet* of 4QEn^g ar is quite primitive also, warning against too late a date for its script. On the other hand, it may be that the cursive tendency that

---

[46] Regularly, the cross-bar slopes down from right to left, and the peak of the right leg stands high above the cross-bar.

[47] Occasionally 4QXII^a preserves a three-stroke *yod* of the Archaic type.

[48] 4QDan^c exhibits the slightly curved *zayin* of the Hasmonaean formal hands (4QDeut^c).

produced the cursive "N"-shaped *ḥet* was reversed in the late Hasmonaean semicursive under the influence of the formal hand.

The *ṭet* in the earliest semicursive scripts combines early and novel features. The left arm is quite high; at the same time the base is flat (4QXII[a]), and the right side is made independently, downward, joining the base-line at the right lower corner. It will be recognized that the latter trait is introduced into the formal script at the end of the Hasmonaean period. In certain late semicursive scripts this type is preserved in an evolved form: the left arm shortens and the base broadens (4QEn[g] ar). However, other semicursives follow instead the cursive trend (4QpapMMT[e]). The base of *ṭet* becomes yet broader, and characteristically the right stroke begins flush with the base-line, curling upward and down below it on the right. In the true cursive scripts, by the beginning of the Herodian period, this form begins to be made with a continuous stroke, giving rise to a new "S"-curved *ṭet*, which is comparable to the cursive Nabataean *ṭet*. The most primitive examples are found in the Bethphage Lid,[49] while one damaged specimen appears in the Nero Papyrus.[50] The even more evolved "S"-curved *ṭet* is standard, of course, in the post-Herodian cursives of Murabbaʿât.

Medial *kap* in 4QXII[a] is early in type: its head is normally narrow and ticked, and a slight tendency to the figure-three shape persists. On the other hand, the base is often straight rather than curved, sometimes giving the impression that it is drawn from left to right in the fashion of semicursive *bet* and *pe* (4Q530). The final *kap* of 4QXII[a] maintains wholly the old formal tradition (cf. 4QDeut[a]). In 4QDan[c], both medial and final *kap* are drawn with a new technique: the "head" in a single shaded stroke, and the right leg separately, beginning above the left stroke of the head. The medial form is, apparently, a transitory Hasmonaean type. This final form becomes popular, however, continuing into the later scripts (4QpapMMT[e], 4QEn[g] ar, 6Q8), and in the early Herodian period replaces the proper formal final *kap* in the formal scripts (1QM). Medial *kap* in the later semicursives is unstable in

---

[49] Cf. P. B. Bagatti and J. T. Milik (eds.), *Gli scavi del "Dominus Flevit,"* parte I, 102 + Fig. 24, col. 1. In older facsimiles of the Bethphage script, the form has gone unrecognized.

[50] J. T. Milik in *Les grottes de Murabbaʿât* (DJD 2) 100-04 + pl. XXIX, no. 18, line 7. In this essay the form is not given in Plate 13, line 1, owing to its damaged condition.

type. In 4Q530, a cursive form is used, the base stroke shaded and drawn from left to right. This form appears sporadically in the semicursive scripts (6Q8), and is regular in the Herodian and post-Herodian pure cursives (Nero Papyrus, Mur 117).

Lamed, as usual, is without special interest to the typologist, and evolves very slowly. 4QXII[a] normally uses a form derived from the old protocursive (4QExod-Lev[f]), used also in Archaic and early Hasmonaean scripts. In late scripts, *lamed* is strongly influenced by formal styles (4Q530, 4QpapMMT[e], 6Q8).

The development of medial and final *mem* in the semicursive scripts is both important for typological dating and most interesting. A variety of forms, many conserving old traditions lost in the other scripts, persist in the Hasmonaean semicursive. 4QXII[a] preserves a medial form of *mem* which resembles superficially the final form. But both the medial and final forms actually derive from the third-century cursive types which survive elsewhere in neither the formal nor the cursive series. The medial form is usually open at the bottom left, and the left down-stroke always cuts sharply through the cross-bar.

The medial and final forms are normally distinguished clearly. Final *mem* is longer and thinner, like the formal final *mem* (cf. 4QDeut[a]); however, this form is also normally closed at the bottom left.[51] In 4QDan[c], the old cursive medial *mem* and the final *mem* have fallen together. In later scripts, under the influence of the formal hand, this older semicursive form appears only in final positions (4QpapMMT[e]). As early as 4Q530, the "ovoid," cursive *mem* intrudes itself into semicursive scripts. In the early scripts it is often a simple elongated circle, usually with only the slightest projection to the left. But the form no doubt arises in the Archaic protocursive *mem*s of the type of 4QExod-Lev[f] and is highly developed in the cursive script before its first appearance in our extant literary texts. The more typical form is probably that of 4QpapMMT[e], with a fairly developed projecting arm.[52]

---

[51] Once in the extant fragments of 4QXII[a], which are quite extensive, a novel triangular *mem* is used in the final position, evidently deriving from an obscure cursive tradition. It appears again, not infrequently, in ossuary inscriptions, especially those in cursive traditions. Possibly it derives from a cursive biform of the Archaic semiformal final *mem* whose shoulder is often narrowed to a point (cf. 4QDibHam[a]); alternatively, it may derive from the protocursive *mem*, from which the ovoid cursive *mem* develops (cf. 4QExod-Lev[f], 4Q530).

[52] Actually, the form is excessively rare in this manuscript, appearing only once with certainty.

In the earlier semicursives this *mem* is made beginning with the projection, the pen moving clockwise. In later cursives the ovoid *mem* begins to be ligatured to following letters, so that the projection left is made last, often causing the top to open (cf. the Nero Papyrus). In the late Hasmonaean and early Herodian semicursives, a medial semicursive version of the formal medial *mem* is often used (4QpapMMT^e, 6Q8), and is very like the round semiformal *mem* of the early Herodian period. In some forms (6Q8), the left oblique stroke appears to be made first, as is the case in certain Herodian semiformal and (later) formal scripts.

Nun in non-final positions follows, for the most part, the development of its Hasmonaean formal counterpart. In the earlier scripts it is long, but in the later script it *shortens*, except in ligature with final *nun*. The Archaic curved down-stroke and the Herodian bent or ticked *nun* do not appear. Final *nun* usually follows the cursive pattern: a straight or slightly curved line extending far below the (theoretical) base-line.

Samek in the Hasmonaean semicursives normally follows a special cursive development. The form of 4QXII^a is exceptional, following the pattern of the Archaic semiformal *samek* (from which the early Hasmonaean formal *samek* stems). The latter form is open, the left stroke drawn upward, looping into the cross-bar. The form in 4QXII^a is, however, exceptionally long and narrow in the Archaic formal pattern. The standard semicursive *samek* only superficially resembles the form of 4QXII^a and later formal *samek*s. Actually, it is drawn like the Archaic formal *samek*, the left stroke downward, but without the characteristic Archaic hook.[53] The right portion is drawn clockwise, often in a simple curve producing a "D"-shaped *samek* (4QDan^c, 4Q530 [open at the base]). In some forms, usually of a later date, the right shoulder becomes angular (4QpapMMT^e), and often in late Hasmonaean and Herodian semicursive and cursive scripts the left down-stroke breaks downward below the curving base-line (4QEn^g ar, Nero Papyrus). This latter tendency does not develop systematically, however, and is rare in post-Herodian scripts.

The ʿ*ayin* of 4QXII^a is small, made with curved strokes in the fashion of early Hasmonaean formal ʿ*ayin*s. In the later scripts two forms emerge, the older, small "y"-form (4QDan^c; 4Q530; 4Qpap

---

[53] One or two cursive *samek*s from Cave 4 at Qumrân, though relatively late in date, actually preserve the hook.

MMT^e) and a cursive "y"-form made in a continuous stroke. A development of this latter form, shifted clockwise, appears in the Nero Papyrus. The post-Herodian semicursive of the type of XḤev/Se 8a (dated 134 CE) develops still another version of the "y"-form.

The evolution of *pe* in the semicursive scripts offers little of special typological interest. We have already noted above the tendency in certain scripts to draw the base-line from left to right in the fashion of *bet* and *kap* (4Q530). The looped *pe* of 4QDan^c is worthy of note, the form being ephemeral.[54]

Ṣade early in Hasmonaean times develops its characteristic semicursive form, being drawn without lifting the pen. The form persists throughout the Hasmonaean semicursives with insignificant changes. A distinct final form of *ṣade* is rarely used in the semicursive scripts.

Qop in the early Hasmonaean semicursive hands develops from earlier protocursive and semiformal styles. The tail is long and often separated from the head (4QXII^a), in considerable contrast to the usual Hasmonaean formal *qop*. Sporadically, the head is simplified, with the heavy, shaded stroke failing to loop back (4Q530, 4QpapMMT^e). In very late forms, the tail is made continuously with the loop of the head (4QEn^g ar). This latter style ultimately gives rise to the open *qop*s of the Herodian and later cursives (Nero Papyrus, Mur 117, XḤev/Se 8a [134 CE]).

The *reš* of 4QXII^a is narrow, sharply ticked on the left, but "round-shouldered" in the style of the Archaic and early Hasmonaean semiformal scripts. Both traits persist and, indeed, are often exaggerated in later semicursive scripts (4QDan^c, 4QpapMMT^e). In the Herodian and post-Herodian cursives (but not in the late semicursive), this form further evolves into a narrow "S"-curved *reš* (Nero Papyrus; Mur 117).

The letter *šin*[55] in 4QXII^a, and sporadically in later semicursives (4QpapMMT^e), exhibits an excessively archaic form. The right arms are not curved, and sometimes the upper right arm is high in the fashion of the third-century cursives. As early as 4QDan^c, the cursive *šin* invades the semicursive script. In the early exemplars of this *šin* the form is made with a shaded, slightly curved left down-stroke. The right arms are made in one continuous stroke, the point of the angle

---

[54] This form is vaguely reminiscent of the cursive Nabataean *pe*. It is more than doubtful, however, that there is any connection between the two.

[55] The letters *śin* and *šin* are not distinguished.

joining at about the mid-point of the left down-stroke. The lower left arm, especially, is gently curved in shape. In the semicursive hands this form persists until the Herodian period.

The Hasmonaean semicursive scripts normally use the looped, cursive *taw* that is familiar from the Nash Papyrus, but shows little development in the Qumrân scripts. In Herodian and Post-Herodian cursives the loop is often simplified and the right leg sometimes lengthens. 4QDan^c mixes the cursive *taw* and a relatively Archaic formal *taw*. Typologically, the latter is closest to the formal *taw* of the earliest Hasmonaean period.

In the legend to Plate 12, tentative dates have been assigned to the semicursive scripts described above. In general the typological sequence of the earlier Hasmonaean hands is clear: 4QXII^a, 4QDan^c, then 4Q530; and the absolute dating in the century between 150 and 50 BCE can hardly be far wrong. The later semicursive hands are more difficult to date and to place in typological sequence: 4QpapMMT^e, 4QEn^g ar, and 6Q8. On the one hand, their letters—especially the cursive forms—preserve Archaic characteristics remote from the Herodian cursive; on the other hand, the letter forms with formal traits often anticipate the (later) formal evolution. Again, the scripts in question combine different sets of cursive and formal elements in letter forms, making precise typological comparison difficult. It is quite possible that the order of the last three scripts as given in Plate 12 is incorrect. But in any case, all three belong to the late Hasmonaean period or, at the latest, to the beginning of the early Herodian era. A gap of considerable length must be posited between the latest of the semicursives of Qumrân and the extant Herodian cursives and post-Herodian semicursives.

SELECT BIBLIOGRAPHY FOR STUDIES IN JEWISH PALAEOGRAPHY

Albright, W. F. "A Biblical Fragment from the Maccabaean Age: The Nash Papyrus," *JBL* 56 (1937) 145-57.

Avigad, N. "The Palaeography of the Dead Sea Scrolls and Related Documents," *Scripta Hierosolymitana* 4 (1957) 56-87.

—. "Aramaic Inscriptions in the Tomb of Jason," *IEJ* 17 (1967) 101-10.

Birnbaum, S. *The Qumrân (Dead Sea) Scrolls and Palaeography* (New Haven, CT: American Schools of Oriental Research, 1952).

—. *The Hebrew Scripts Part I: The Text* (Leiden: Brill, 1971); *Part II: The Plates* (London: Palaeographica, 1954-1957).

Bonani, G., I. Carmi, S. Ivy, J. Strugnell and W. Wölfli. "Radiocarbon Dating of the Dead Sea Scrolls," ʿAtiqot 20 (1991) 27-32.

Cross, F. M. *The Ancient Library of Qumran* (3rd ed., Sheffield: Sheffield Academic Press, 1995), esp. Figs. 13-19 between pp. 128 and 129.

—. "The Development of the Jewish Scripts," in G. E. Wright (ed.), *The Bible and the Ancient Near East: Essays in Honor of W. F. Albright* (Garden City, NY: DoubleDay, 1961) 133-202.

—. "The Oldest Manuscripts from Qumrân," *JBL* 74 (1955) 147-72.

—. "The Scripts of the Dâliyeh Papyri," in P. and N. Lapp (eds.), *Discoveries in the Wâdī ed-Dâliyeh* (AASOR 41; Cambridge, MA: American Schools of Oriental Research, 1974) 25-27 + Chart of Scripts, pl. LIX.

Cross, F. M. and E. Eshel. "Ostraca from Qumrân," *IEJ* 47 (1997) 17-28.

Ephʿal, I. and J. Naveh. *Aramaic Ostraca from the Fourth Century BC from Idumaea* (Jerusalem: Magnes Press–Hebrew University–Israel Exploration Society, 1997).

Eshel, E. and A. Kloner. "An Aramaic Ostracon of an Edomite Marriage Contract from Maresha, Dated 176 BCE," *IEJ* 46 (1996) 1-22.

Geraty, L. T. "The Khirbet el-Kom Bilingual Ostracon," *BASOR* 2120 (1975) 55-61.

Jull, A. J. T., D. J. Donahue, M. Broshi and E. Tov. "Radiocarbon Dating of Scrolls and Linen Fragments from the Judean Desert," ʿAtiqot 28 (1996) 1-7.

Lemaire, A. *Nouvelles inscriptions araméennes d'Idumée au Musée d'Israël* (Paris: Gabalda, 1996).

McLean, M. D. "The Development and Use of Palaeo-Hebrew in the Hellenistic and Roman Periods" (Unpublished Ph.D. diss., Cambridge, MA: Harvard University, 1982). [available through University Microfilms]

Naveh, J. *The Development of the Aramaic Script* (Jerusalem: Israel Academy of Sciences and Humanities, 1970).

—. על חרס וגומא [*On Stone and Mosaic: The Hebrew and Aramaic Inscriptions from Ancient Synogogues*] (Jerusalem: Magnes Press, 1989).

Yadin, Y., J. C. Greenfield and Ada Yardeni, "Babatha's *Ketubba*," *IEJ* 44 (1994) 75-99 + Palaeographical Chart.

Yardeni, J. "The Palaeography of the 4QJer[a] Scroll," *Textus* 15 (1990) 233-68.

—. "New Jewish Aramaic Ostraca," *IEJ* 40 (1990) 130-52.

—. "Script" in E. Qimron and J. Strugnell, *Qumran Cave 4.V: Miqṣat Maʿaśe Ha-Torah* (DJD 10; Oxford: Clarendon Press, 1994) 21-25, 29-34 + Chart.

SCRIBAL PRACTICES REFLECTED IN THE TEXTS FROM THE JUDAEAN DESERT

EMANUEL TOV

1. INTRODUCTION

The documents from the Judaean Desert constitute the largest corpus of texts in non-lapidary scripts providing information about scribal habits in early Israel relating to biblical and non-biblical texts. These practices should be compared with other contemporary and earlier material in Hebrew and Aramaic in non-lapidary texts: i.e. material from the period prior to the third century BCE, involving *inter alia*, the Elephantine papyri and other Aramaic documents from the fifth and fourth century BCE. While these two groups of texts are very significant as comparative material for the present analysis, they provide only limited relevant information in that they may reflect mostly local Egyptian traditions. At the same time, the texts from the Judaean Desert continue the tradition of the Aramaic documents from the fifth century BCE in several important details. The Egyptian Aramaic corpus is significant, as it is extensive and ancient. But the corpus of documents from the Judaean Desert is larger and thus constitutes the largest corpus for our knowledge of scribal habits for Hebrew and Aramaic texts from ancient Israel prior to the early Middle Ages, from which time the first documents from the Cairo Genizah derive. Comparison of these practices with scribal habits of earlier cultures in the ancient Middle East and with contemporary Greek practices is mandatory, but because these texts were written in different languages and often on different materials, such a comparison is only partially relevant.

When referring to "scribal practices," we refer to various aspects: the copyists and their background; writing materials; technical aspects of the writing of scrolls (such as ruling, length of scrolls, sheets, and columns); writing practices (such as divisions between words, small sense units, and sections); special layout of poetical units; scribal marks; correction procedures; the scripts; special scribal characteristics of certain types of texts; and scribal traditions.

This summary article can only touch on some of these areas,[1] and even in the areas covered there is barely sufficient room to mention adequate examples or to document statements with footnotes.

2. TECHNICAL ASPECTS OF THE WRITING

Some technical aspects of the writing of scrolls have been studied for many scrolls in monographs as well as in the introductory paragraphs of the DJD editions in vols. 8 and following, but most aspects still need to be studied in detail. A start has been made in several monographic studies[2] mentioned below, and further studies

---

[1] A more extensive analysis of the scribes of the texts from the Judaean Desert has been presented in my articles "The Scribes of the Texts Found in the Judean Desert," in C. A. Evans and S. Talmon (eds.), *The Quest for Context & Meaning. Studies in Intertextuality in Honor of James A. Sanders* (BIS 28; Leiden: Brill, 1997) 131-52, and on writing materials and other technical aspects of the writing of scrolls in "Scribal Practices and Physical Aspects of the Dead Sea Scrolls," in J. Sharpe (ed.), *The Bible as Book* (London: The British Library, [in press]). In what follows, the reader will find a summary of my research on other aspects, which comprises a summary of two chapters of a monograph, *Scribal Practices and Approaches Reflected in the Hebrew and Aramaic Texts from the Judean Desert*, which is currently in preparation.

[2] For an initial analysis of several valuable technical data, see H. Stegemann, "Methods for the Reconstruction of Scrolls from Scattered Fragments," in L. H. Schiffman (ed.), *Archaeology and History in the Dead Sea Scrolls—The New York University Conference in Memory of Yigael Yadin* (JSOT/ASOR Monograph Series 2; Sheffield: JSOT Press, 1990) 189-220. See further C. Kuhl, "Schreibereigentümlichkeiten—Bemerkungen zur Jesajarolle (DSIa)," *VT* 2 (1952) 307-33; M. Martin, *The Scribal Character of the Dead Sea Scrolls* I–II (Bibliothèque du Muséon 44-45; Louvain: Publications Universitaires, 1958. Although this study is extremely detailed and helpful, it is based only on the major texts from Cave 1); H. Stegemann, "ΚΥΡΙΟΣ Ο ΘΕΟΣ ΚΥΡΙΟΣ ΙΗΣΟΥΣ—Aufkommen und Ausbreitung des religiösen Gebrauchs von ΚΥΡΙΟΣ und seine Verwendung im Neuen Testament" (Habilitationsschrift; Bonn: Friedrich-Wilhelms-Universität, 1969); J. P. Siegel, "Final Mem in Medial Position and Medial Mem in Final Position in 11QPs^a—Some Observations," *RevQ* 7 (1969) 125-30; idem, "The Employment of Palaeo-Hebrew Characters for the Divine Names at Qumran in the Light of Tannaitic Sources," *HUCA* 42 (1971) 159-72; idem, *The Scribes of Qumran. Studies in the Early History of Jewish Scribal Customs, with Special Reference to the Qumran Biblical Scrolls and to the Tannaitic Traditions of Massekheth Soferim* (Unpublished diss., University Microfilms, 1972); J. M. Oesch, *Petucha und Setuma, Untersuchungen zu einer überlieferten Gliederung im hebräischen Text des Alten Testament* (OBO 27; Freiburg [Schweiz]: Universitätsverlag; Göttingen:

must be underaken in the future. For example, a complete tabulation of the distinctive practice of using "guide dots" in the Qumran scrolls will allow for temporary conclusions on the causes and background of this practice. Similar conclusions may be drawn also from a study of the extent of scrolls,[3] sheets,[4] and of writing blocks, columns and margins,[5] *et cetera*.

2.1 Ruling

Almost all Qumran texts written in the square script had ruled lines since ruling of lines was the normal practice for most literary texts written on parchment in Semitic languages and in Greek, just as it had been in earlier times on cuneiform tablets and in lapidary Semitic inscriptions. On the other hand, the Qumran texts written on papyrus were not ruled (e.g. 4QpapMMT^e, 4QpapJub^h, and the Greek texts 4Q120 and 4Q127).[6]

Most Qumran parchment texts written in the square script (*not* the *tefillin*) and in the Palaeo-Hebrew script were ruled horizontally (indicating lines) as well as vertically (indicating the beginnings and often also the ends of columns); this was also the case in most medieval copies of the Masoretic Text and the Samaritan Pentateuch.

The so-called "blind" or "dry-point" ruling was usually performed with a pointed instrument, most likely a bone, which made a sharp crease in the parchment so that the leather could easily be split in two and even broken off (e.g. 1QapGen cols. 21–22; 1QIsa^a cols. 38, 48; and 11QT^a cols. 18, 22). In most cases the horizontal ruling on the sheets was continuous, starting at the right end to the right of the vertical line which indicated the beginning of the first column of the sheet, and continuing as far as the left border of the sheet beyond the left vertical line of the last column (For good examples, see 11QT^a, col. 27; and 11QtgJob, cols. 17–18). By the same token, vertical

---

Vandenhoeck & Ruprecht, 1979); idem, "Textgliederung im Alten Testament und in den Qumranhandschriften," *Henoch* 5 (1983) 289-321. Other initial studies are included in my own articles that are mentioned in the following footnotes.

[3] See section 2.3 below.
[4] Section 2.4.
[5] Section 2.5.
[6] E. G. Turner (*Greek Manuscripts of the Ancient World* [2nd ed., revised and enlarged by P. J. Parsons; London: University of London, Institute of Classical Studies, 1987] 5-6) discusses the possibility that an instrument was used in the writing of papyri in which there are no clear indications of any dry-point ruling.

ruling was usually continuous as well, extending beyond the written text into the top and bottom margins as far as the edges of the parchment (e.g. 1QIsa^a, cols. 2–4; 1QIsa^b, col. 8).

Only a few Qumran documents were not ruled, and consequently in these documents the distance between the lines of writing is irregular and the writing is not straight (e.g. 4QJer^c, 4QCant^b, 4QFlor). In a few cases, a double vertical ruling was applied to columns, especially before the first columns of each sheet. These columns were indicated with two dry lines spaced a few millimeters apart, while the writing started after the second vertical line. Examples are found in 4QNum^b before cols. 1, 10 and 15 at the beginnings of sheets; and in 1QH^a.

The ruling may have been executed by the scribes themselves, but more likely it was applied—often with the aid of guide dots (see below)—by the manufacturers of the scroll. There are several indications that sheets were ruled before the manufacturer knew exactly how many columns would be inscribed with text, while some columns (the "handling sheets") were not inscribed at all. To be noted are the presence of ruled columns after the last inscribed column of several compositions and the uninscribed ruled handling sheets at the ends of compositions.[7]

In a small number of Qumran texts that are written in the square and palaeo-Hebrew scripts single *guide dots* ("points jalons") or—more rarely—strokes were inscribed with the purpose of guiding the drawing of dry lines. These dots or strokes appear in the space between the right edge of the sheet and the beginning of the first column (usually close to its right side), as well as in the space between the last column and the left edge of the sheet. In similar fashion, E. G. Turner mentions several instances of such dots which appear in different positions in Greek papyrus scrolls: at mid-line; vertically with the initial letter or with the line beginnings; and before every line or every given number of lines.[8]

Only a small number of the Qumran texts (none of them found in other places in the Judaean Desert) bear witness to these guide dots. Examples include: 4QGen-Exod^a (frg. 19 ii); 2QpaleoLev; 4Qpaleo-Exod^m (small diagonal strokes in the left-hand margin of col. 1 and the right-hand margin of col. 2); 4QLev-Num^a; and 4QNum^b (cols.

---

[7] See 2.7 below.

[8] Turner, *Greek Manuscripts of the Ancient World*, 4.

19 and 24). The occurrence of these guide dots indicates that the scrolls in which they appear were prepared in a special way, probably at a special manufacturing centre or by a special scribal school. It is therefore significant that the majority of the non-biblical texts among the documents which contain guide dots reflect the characteristics of the Qumran scribal school.

2.2 Opisthographs and Palimpsests

Most parchment and papyrus texts were written on one side only, while some twenty of the documents from the Judaean Desert (half of them papyri) were inscribed on both sides (ὀπισθόγραφα or "opisthographs").[9] In addition, the enigmatic palaeo-Hebrew text from Masada pap paleoMas1o (Mas1039–320) was inscribed on both sides, but in two different handwritings.

Writing on both sides sometimes implies that the texts on the recto and verso are somehow related. For example, 4QpapCryptA MSM (4Q249) and 4Q250 (an unknown work) are both written in the Cryptic A script. Likewise, both sides of 4Q417 contain sapiential works, and different segments of 4QapocrMoses C appear on the recto and verso of 4Q377. More often, however, the contents of the two sides are not related, with the verso being used simply because of the scarcity of writing material. Two opisthographs from Qumran and many from Egypt are of this type, with a literary text on the recto and a documentary text of some kind on the verso. Thus, for instance, 4QNarrative Work and Prayer (4Q460) has on its verso a Greek text named 4QAccount of Cereal gr (4Q350), while another fragment contains on the recto 4QMishmarot C^c (4Q324) and on the verso an account in Aramaic or Hebrew (4Q355). In similar vein, a large collection of different compositions and different copies of one composition is found on the two sides of a papyrus containing on the recto 4QpapPrFêtes^c (4Q509), 4QpapDibHam^b (4Q505) and—once again—4Qpap PrFêtes^c, and on the verso 4QpapM^f (4Q496) and 4QpapDibHam^c (4Q506).

In addition to these manuscripts, *tefillin* were usually inscribed on both sides. On contracts the signatures were written on the verso. Finally, the number of *palimpsests* among the texts from the Judaean Desert is relatively small.

---

[9] See a list of such texts from Qumran in M. O. Wise, *Thunder in Gemini, and Other Essays on the History, Language and Literature of Second Temple Palestine* (JSPSup 15; Sheffield: Sheffield Academic Press, 1994) 133.

2.3 Length of Scrolls

Almost all Qumran fragments constitute parts of scrolls made of of parchment or papyrus. Unfortunately, insufficient information is available on the length of these manuscripts, since only very few complete scrolls have been preserved.[10]

2.4 Sheets

Scrolls consisted of sheets that were obtained from one or more different scroll manufacturers, and which were not necessarily prepared in the same way. In addition, they could have been ruled by different persons and for different purposes; there were thus differences between the sheets in the number of ruled lines (e.g. 1QpHab and 11QT^a) and in the practice of the guide rules.[11] It was probably easier to inscribe sheets separately, and then to sew them together. However, 4QLevi^a ar was inscribed to the very edge of the leather, and in one case (frg. 1, line 7) even beyond the edge, which proves that some sheets were inscribed only after they had been joined. After being joined, sheets could have been written by different scribes.

The *length* of most sheets in leather scrolls is between 21 and 90 cm. The natural limitations of the sizes of animal hides determined the different lengths of these sheets within each scroll, which varied more in some than in others. In two instances (MurXII and 11QpaleoLev^a), all the sheets are more or less of the same length, although insufficient data are admittedly available for these scrolls for a thorough assessment to be made. The *number* of sheets per scroll depends on the scope of the composition and the length of the individual sheets. This information can be calculated only for the scrolls of which both the beginning and end have been preserved. Thus, for instance, 1QIsa^a consists of seventeen sheets (with ten measuring between 35 and 47.7 cm and five between 48.7 and 62.8 cm, while the other are only 25.2 and 26.9 cm, respectively). 11QT^a is composed of nineteen sheets (with seven measuring between 37 and 43 cm and ten between 47 and 61 cm, while the last sheet is much shorter at only 20 cm). It should be noted that these

---

[10] For an analysis of the scope of Qumran scrolls, see E. Tov, "The Dimensions of the Scrolls Found at Qumran: Implications for an Understanding of Their Contents," *DSD* 5 (1998) [in press].

[11] See 2.1 above.

calculations on length and number pertain only to leather manuscripts, since well-preserved papyrus scrolls have not been found in the Judaean Desert.

In accordance with their different scope, sheets contain different numbers of columns. These are typically three or four in number (e.g. 1QIsa^a and 11QT^a), while as many as seven columns (1QapGen and 1QpHab) and even a single column (the first sheet of 4QDeut^n, the last sheet of 1QS, the last sheet of 4QDeut^q, and the first and last columns of 4QD^a) are exceptions. There is no general uniformity in the number of columns.

According to rabbinic prescriptions, sheets of scrolls were joined by sinews of ritually clean cattle or wild animals (cf. the tractate *Soperim* 1.1). On the other hand, J. B. Poole and R. Reed[12] have claimed that the stitching material which they examined was of vegetable origin and most probably derived from flax. It is not known, however, which specific manuscripts were consulted for this purpose.

It is not impossible that a damaged inscribed sheet was on occasion replaced with a repair sheet. This assumption has not been proven, but has been suggested for 4QJub^a (4Q216) and 4QDeut^n.

2.5 *Writing Blocks, Columns, and Margins*

The great majority of the texts from the Judaean Desert have been arranged in writing blocks that cover the greater part of the surface of the leather or papyrus, leaving margins on all sides of the inscribed surface. In *tefillin* and *mezuzot*, however, maximal use is made of the leather, with room being left only occasionally for such margins.

The inscribed surface usually has the shape of a column—certainly in literary compositions—and in texts consisting of more than one column, these follow one another. Only one document is known in which tiny sheets of parchment (four lines together with top and bottom margins) were stitched together vertically: 4QIncantation (4Q444). In the case of 4QApocryphal Psalm and Prayer (4Q448), the different arrangement of the columns probably derived from the adhesion of a reinforcement tab which necessitated a large margin at

---

[12] J. B. Poole and R. Reed, "The Preparation of Leather and Parchment by the Dead Sea Scrolls Community," in M. Kranzberg and W. H. Davenport (eds.), *Technology and Culture: An Anthology* (New York: Schocken, 1972) 143-68, esp. 164.

the beginning of the scroll (col. A). The sizes of columns differ in accordance with the number per sheet, the measurements of the sheets, and the conventions developed by the scroll manufacturers. The different parameters of the columns pertain to their width and length as well as to the margins that surround them (i.e. top, bottom, and intercolumnar margins).[13]

In some Qumran scrolls the height and width of the columns were fairly consistently fixed, but in most cases these parameters probably varied from sheet to sheet, and also within the individual sheets, in accordance with their measurements. Thus, for instance, the width of certain individual columns in 1QM and 4QLam differs by as much as 50 percent from other columns in the same scrolls. Considerable differences between the sizes of the columns are visible in 11QT^a and 8HevXIIgr, while even larger ones are evident in 1QIsa^a (cf. cols. 49 [16.3 cm] and 52 [8.8 cm]), in 1QS (cf. cols. 1 [9.7 cm], 2 [11.5 cm], and other columns measuring 16, 18 and 19 cm), and in 4QLam^a (where col. 3 is almost twice as wide as cols. 1 and 2). At the same time, a certain regularity in column sizes is noticeable. In most cases the available space in a sheet was evenly divided between the columns, but the unusual sizes of the sheets did not always allow for such uniformity. Columns which are unusually wide or narrow are generally found in the beginning or end of sheets.

The average number of lines per column in Qumran scrolls is probably 20, with a height approximately 14–15 cm (including the top and bottom margins). Larger scrolls contained columns from 25 to as much as 60 lines. Scrolls of the least dimensions contained merely 4–13 lines and their size was similarly small. For example, 4QIncantation (4Q444) is exceptionally minute, with only four lines written on tiny sheets of parchment (which include a top and bottom margin).

Small manuscripts include the Five Scrolls (the only exception being 4QQoh^a with 20 lines of 37 letter-spaces) and a few excerpted

---

[13] Exact details about the measures of the sheets in well-preserved scrolls have been listed for 1QIsa^a by J. C. Trever in M. Burrows (ed.), *The Dead Sea Scrolls of St. Mark's Monastery* (New Haven, CT: ASOR, 1950-51) xvii–xviii; for 11QpaleoLev^a by D. N. Freedman and K. A. Matthews, *The Paleo-Hebrew Leviticus Scroll (11QpaleoLev)* (Winona Lake, IN: Eisenbrauns, 1985) 7; for 11QT^a by Y. Yadin, *The Temple Scroll*, vols. 1–3 [Hebrew] (Jerusalem: The Israel Exploration Society, 1977) 11-12; and in most of the texts published in the DJD series from volume 8 onwards.

biblical books of various types that were intended for liturgical purposes (4QDeut[n] probably containing selections of Deuteronomy, 4QDeut[q] comprising Deuteronomy 32, and 4QPs[g] containing only Psalm 119. 4QExod[c] probably belongs to the same category). Other small compositions (up to 10 lines of text) that are written on scrolls of small dimensions are: 4QprEsther[a, b, d] ar (4Q550); 4QDanSuz(?) ar (4Q551); 4QCal. Document B[a] (4Q321); 4QToh A (4Q274); 4QapocrLam B (4Q501); 4QApocrMos[a] (4Q375); 4QApocalypse ar (4Q246); 4QZodiology and Brontology ar (4Q318); 4QShir[a] (4Q510); and 4QApocryphal Psalm and Prayer (4Q448).

There is a positive correlation between the length and the width of columns: the higher the column, the wider the lines. While it is in order to measure the width of columns according to the number of letters or letter-spaces (i.e. a space occupied by either a letter or a blank space between words) for purposes of reconstruction, for an overall understanding of the scroll it is more useful to calculate according to the width of the columns. Since individual sheets contained columns of varying width (see above), one should always be careful when linking a certain column-width with a specific scroll. An example of a scroll of very wide columns is 4QJer[b], with 21–24 cm or 115–130 letter-spaces to the column. Examples of narrow columns include the calendrical documents, which often contain merely a single word per line (such as the first fragment of 4QMMT[a] [4Q394]); column B of 4QApocryphal Psalm and Prayer (4Q448) with nine lines of 1–3 words; and all the poetical compositions that present the text stichographically with hemistichs, such as 4QNon-Canonical Psalms A (4Q380).

Scrolls were usually written with the same number of lines per column throughout the different sheets, or at least in the same sheet, but in some slight variations are to be found; for instance, 4QApocryphal Psalm and Prayer (9, 10 lines or 9.5 cm); 4QLam (10, 11 lines or 11.8 cm); and 4QapocrLam A (4Q179) with 13, 15 lines or 8.2 cm. On the one hand we note a remarkable degree of consistency in the number of lines in some scrolls, e.g. 4Qpr Esther[a, b, d] ar (7, 8 lines); 4QD[a, e, f, g] (20–25 lines); and 4QDan[a, b, c] (16–22 lines). On the other hand, a lack of consistency is recognizable in many other compositions. Some smaller Psalms scrolls were of a limited scope, probably containing only Psalm 119 (4QPs[g], 4QPs[h], 5QPs), while the longer ones contained all or most of the biblical Psalms; two copies of Ezekiel (4QEzek[a] and MasEzek) contain 42 lines per column, as opposed to 11 lines in 4QEzek[b]; in the *Hodayot*, 4QH[c] contains 12 lines per column in contrast to 1QH[a] which contains 41–42 lines; 4QShirShabb[a] and MasShirShabb contain 21 and 26 lines as opposed to 4QShirShabb[d] with 50 lines; the longer copies of Genesis (4QGen[b, e]) respectively contain 40 and 50 lines, as opposed to the smaller ones (4QGen[d, g, f]) with 11, 14 and 17 lines, respectively.

As for parallel copies of the same composition written with the same layout, only scanty evidence is available: in the overlapping sections of 4QDan[a] and 4QDan[b] (Dan 8:1–4), four lines have an identical layout and two lines approximately the same layout.[14]

In the Qumran texts the upper margin of the columns is usually smaller than the bottom margin. A detailed study of the measurements of the margins on a single scroll has been conducted by Yigael Yadin;[15] according to his calculations, the dimensions usually agree with the prescriptions that appear in the Talmud.

2.6 *The Written Text vis-à-vis Horizontal and Vertical Ruling*

Most literary texts from the Judaean Desert were ruled.[16] In the great majority of these cases the letters were suspended from the horizontal lines in such a way that the text was written flush with these lines. This procedure was also followed in Samaritan and Greek manuscripts. In a few Qumran texts, however, the letters were sometimes consistently written slightly below those lines; for instance, in 11QT[a] (with a distance of 0.1 cm; cf. cols. 45–48) and in the 4QHodayot-like text (4Q440). In other texts scribes more or less disregarded the guidance of the ruled lines; examples include a 4QText with a citation from Jubilees (4Q228); and 4Q522 (most clearly in frg. 9 where the letters were written irregularly between the lines, on and below the lines, and also through them). In 1QMyst (1Q27) and 4QApocrMoses[a] (4Q375) the words are more frequently written on the lines than under them.

Most texts were also ruled with a vertical line which served to

---

[14] See E. Ulrich, "Orthography and Text in 4QDan[a] and 4QDan[b] and in the Received Masoretic Text," in H. W. Attridge et al. (eds.), *Of Scribes and Scrolls, Studies on the Hebrew Bible, Intertestamental Judaism, and Christian Origins Presented to John Strugnell* (CTSRR 5; Lanham, MD: University Press of America, 1990) 29-42, esp. 38.

[15] Yadin, *Temple Scroll*, 1.15-17.

[16] See 2.1 above.

guide the right border of the writing surface. In addition, some were ruled with a left vertical line which indicated the end of the column.[17] Because of these vertical lines, the right border of the writing surface is usually straight, although occasional exceptions are to be found. For example, the writing surface at the right margin of 4QTest is not straight, with lines extending beyond the vertical line by as much as the width of one or two letters. As a rule, the writing surface at the left is not straight, even if it is demarcated with a vertical line. 4QApocalypse ar (4Q246), for instance, contains a perfectly ruled writing surface with clearly visible vertical lines. However, in frg. 1 ii, line 6 a complete word was written beyond this border, and in lines 3 and 9 the greater part of the last words exceeds the vertical line—probably because the scribe wanted to get as many words as possible in this scroll of small dimensions.

In fact, since the scribes left more or less equal spaces between the words in texts written with square characters it was virtually impossible to adhere to a straight left border of the writing surface (unless one of the devices mentioned below was used). But in texts written in the palaeo-Hebrew script it was relatively easy to adhere to the left border, since in these texts words were broken at the end of a line (i.e. split between lines). For example, in 11QpaleoLev^a, col. 3 the following words are split at the ends of lines: יה/וה, יש/ראל, ב/נו, א/ל, and א/תו. As a result of this splitting of words, virtually straight left margins could be obtained in these texts: for instance, in 4QpaleoExod^m, cols. 1, 6, 9 and in all the columns of 11QpaleoLev^a. It is interesting to note that a similar system was used in the medieval manuscripts of the Samaritan Pentateuch.

In contrast, in all texts written in square characters several lines either fall short of, or exceed, the vertical line at the left edge of the column, which was either drawn or existed in the scribe's mind.[18] In any event, the prescription of *Soperim* 2.3 for the number of letters which one may write beyond the vertical margin is not adhered to in most texts that are written in square characters. Whereas M.

---

[17] See 2.1 above.

[18] The amount of marginal observance in the scrolls from Qumran cave 1 was described in detail by M. Martin, *Scribal Character*, 1.109-17, and additional texts were described by E. D. Herbert, *Reconstructing Biblical Dead Sea Scrolls. A New Method Applied to the Reconstruction of 4QSam^a* (STDJ 22; Leiden: Brill, 1997).

Martin[19] stressed the scribal disregard of the ruled margin, E. D. Herbert[20] found that scribes often adhered not only to the ruled margin, but also to a "notional" margin, i.e. a margin which they had in mind. This margin could be either to the left (1QIsaa, 1QS) or to the right (1QpHab) of the ruled margin: for instance, 3.75 mm (cols. 1–27) or 5.25 mm (cols. 28–54) to the left in 1QIsaa. Sometimes scribes slightly exceeded the margin in order to keep parts of a phrase together.

While such vertical marginal lines at the left helped the scribes to obtain a neatly written writing block, as a rule adherence to the left margin was not a major concern for scrolls that were inscribed with square characters. Nevertheless, certain practices were employed to obtain this objective:

> (1) A few scrolls left extra spaces between words towards the end of the line ("proportional spacing"), so that it would be finished flush with the vertical lines (e.g. 4QNumb, 4QGenc, 4QGenf, 4QpaleoExodm 1:3–5; 19:11; and 38). This system is also known from medieval manuscripts.[21]
>
> (2) Cramming of letters into the existing space at the ends of the lines or writing them in a smaller size; e.g. 4QpsMose (4Q390) frg. 2 i, line 10; and 4QCommGen A I:5.
>
> (3) Writing of parts of words at the end of the line, only to be repeated in full in the next line. Examples: 1QIsaa cols. 2:11-12 and 41:10–11; Mur 42:5 (which has not been erased, *pace* the transcription in DJD 2).[22]
>
> (4) Line fillers, especially in papyri from Naḥal Ḥever.
>
> (5) Splitting of words between lines in texts that are inscribed in palaeo-Hebrew characters (see above), so that their margin was straighter than that of texts written in square characters in which words were not split between lines.
>
> (6) Writing of single letters or words above or below the last word in the line. For examples of single letters, see 4QDa frg. 10 i, line 6 (והשופטי‍ם); 4QpsMose (4Q390) frg. 2 i, line 7 (במועל‍ם); 1QIsaa col.

---

[19] Martin, *Scribal Character*, 1.112-13.

[20] Herbert, *Reconstructing Biblical Dead Sea Scrolls*.

[21] See M. Beit-Arié, *Hebrew Codicology—Tentative Typology of Technical Practices Employed in Hebrew Dated Medieval Manuscripts* (Jerusalem: Israel Academy of Sciences and Humanities, 1981) 87-88.

[22] J. T. Milik et al., *Les Grottes de Murabbaʿât* (DJD 2; Oxford: Clarendon Press, 1961) 156.

3:19 (Isa 3:19, בבתיכם). These letters were written under the line even though there was room to write them in the margin after the left marginal line. This was also standard procedure in the *tefillin*, see 4QPhyl A, B, G-I, J-K, L-N, S.

2.7 Beginnings and Ends of Scrolls

When the content of a specific scroll is known, as in the case of biblical scrolls or scrolls known from parallel compositions, external information may be combined with data on the content in order to determine whether or not the beginning or end of a composition has been preserved.

The beginnings of only a minority of the Qumran texts have been preserved, especially when scrolls were rolled up with their beginnings as the innermost section (e.g. 4QGen[b, g, k], 4QLev[c], 4QDeut[h], 5QKings, 1QIsa[a], and 4QIsa[a, b, j]). The ends of several manuscripts have been preserved as well, for instance: 11Qpaleo Lev[a], 4QDeut[q], MasDeut, 4QJudg[b], 1QIsa[a, b], 4QIsa[b, c], and MasPs[b]. There are no consistent patterns in the preservation and decay of these scrolls.

Special arrangements were made at the beginning and the end of scrolls to avoid the *handling* by users of the inscribed areas of sacred and non-sacred texts. This was done in two different ways at the beginnings and ends of the scrolls. At the beginnings two systems were used: (1) The scribe left an uninscribed area, which was always larger than the 1–2 cm of intercolumnar space, and sometimes extended to the size of a column. These segments at the beginning of the scrolls were generally unruled (e.g. 4QXII[d] [measuring 5 cm]; 1QM [9.75 cm]; 4QAgesCreat B frg. 2; 4QD[a] [4 cm]; 4QGen[b] [at least 8.9 cm]; and 4QPrayer of Nabonidus [4Q242]). However, the space was ruled in two instances (3QpIsa and 6Q20). (2) A separate, uninscribed handling *sheet* was attached to the scroll at its beginning. Such a beginning sheet was previously known in the (ancient) Greek and Latin manuscript tradition as a πρωτόκολλον (*protocollon*). Examples include 1QS, 1QSa, 4QGen[g] and 4QGen[k] (for all these, note the stitches), as well as the uninscribed fragment that appears on PAM 41.656. The stitches before the first column of 1QIsa[a] indicate the existence of such a separate sheet, which was reportedly seen by Metropolitan Samuel while it was still connected to the scroll.

The final column of the text was usually ruled beyond the last inscribed line of the composition as far as the end of the column, for instance: 1QpHab, 1QIsa[a], 4QText with a citation from Jubilees (4Q228), 4QCal. Document B[a] (4Q321), 11QtgJob, and 11QPs[a]. Beyond the last inscribed column, the end of the scroll was indicated by one of the following two systems:

(1) The final column was frequently followed by an uninscribed surface, which either was unruled (e.g. MasPs[b], 4QD[a] [at 9 cm], 4QDibHam[a] [4Q504] frg. 2 verso [7.2 cm]) or, more frequently, was ruled. In the latter case, the scroll contained this additional column with horizontal and vertical rulings because the manufacturer had provided the scribe with a quantity of ruled sheets since the precise contents of the surface needed for writing could not be calculated (e.g. 1QpHab, 4QMMT[f], 4QHodayot-like text [4Q440], 4QShir[b] [Q511], and 4QpsDan[c] ar). (2) A separate ruled or unruled uninscribed handling sheet was preserved at the end of 11QT[a], 11QApPs[a] (cf. PAM 43.988), and MasDeut, and was probably also attached to 1QS and 11QpaleoLev[a] after the stitches in the final columns. To be noted is the high frequency of texts from cave 11 in this group. The existence of such end-sheets is mentioned in *m. Yadayim* 3.4.

2.8 Titles of Compositions

Since the beginnings of most scrolls have been lost, insufficient information is available on the existence of titles or name tags to denote the content of compositions. There is, however, some evidence for the use of two different systems which *may* have been used concurrently for the same scroll:

(1) In some non-biblical scrolls the title of the composition was written as the first item of the running text, without any special layout, as also occurs for some of the Psalms:

1QM למשכיל סרך] המלחמה

1QSa וזה הסרך לכול עדת ישראל

1QS ספר סר]ך היחד (towards the end of the first line)

4QpapS[a] ספר סרכ היחד (end of the first line)

4QS[d] מדרש למשכיל על אנשי התורה המתנדבים (= 4QS[b] frg. 5, line 1)

4QD[a] לפרוש המשפטים למשכיל לב[ני אור (cf. DJD 18, 32)[23]

4QCryptA Words of the Maskil (4Q298) דבר]י משכיל אשר דבר לכול בני שחר. The composition itself was written in the Cryptic script, but the

---

[23] J. Baumgarten, *Qumran Cave 4.XIII: The Damascus Document [4Q256–4Q273]* (DJD 18; Oxford: Clarendon Press, 1996).

title in the square script, as in the case of 4QpapCryptA MSM (4Q249).[24]

4QPrayer of Nabonidus (4Q242) מלי צלעתא די צלי נבני.

(2) The title of the composition was written opposite the beginning of the scroll. When the scroll was rolled up with its beginning on the outside, the title would be visible if it was written on the verso, which is also the case when the scroll was tied with a thong. But if the title was written on the recto, the scroll had to be slightly opened. The following such titles are known:

The handle sheet of 1QS (סר[ך היחד ומן])

4QGen[h-title] (4Q8c), now detached from the main manuscript

4QDibHam[a] (דברי המארות)

4QpapCryptA MSM מדרש ספר מושה.

2.9 Uneven surfaces, damage, repair stitching, and patching

Uneven surfaces. At the time of preparation, some scrolls were of good quality; however, the surface of others was sometimes uneven, often showing scar tissue, for example: 4QRP[e] (4Q367) frg. 3, lines 5–14; 1QM; 11QPs[a]; 4QDeut[n] cols. 3:9 and 4:1–4, 7–8.

Damage. It has frequently been suggested that damage was inflicted on certain scrolls in antiquity, mainly by the swords of soldiers, even though there is no solid evidence for this assumption either in the historical descriptions or in the Qumran scrolls. Examples include 4QRP[c] (the diagonal crease in frgs. 12b iii and 23); XHev–Se 7 (Deed of Sale); and 4QpaleoGen–Exod[a] (frg. 19 i). Likewise, according to H. Stegemann, "Yadin's Temple Scroll was in part already damaged by its former readers in antiquity, mainly at its beginning and end, but also in the bottom parts of some other columns. Repairs dating to the first half of the first century CE are clearly visible. The first and the last sheet of the scroll with about four columns each were cut off and replaced by new sheets."[25]

Repair stitching. When a scroll was torn, it was often stitched both before and after the writing. Stitching sewn prior to the writing in a scroll made it necessary for the scribe to leave open segments in the middle of the text, which were frequently as extensive as two complete lines. Stitching that was done after the writing necessarily

---

[24] For the title, see section (2) a few lines below.

[25] H. Stegemann, "The Literary Composition of the Temple Scroll and Its Status at Qumran," in G. J. Brooke (ed.), *Temple Scroll Studies* (JSPSup 7; Sheffield: Sheffield Academic Press, 1989) 123-48, esp. 124.

rendered some of the words illegible (e.g. 4QJer^c, col. 23). Accordingly, when the stitching was made in the middle of an inscribed area it can usually be determined whether this occurred before or after the writing. When the stitching was done in the uninscribed margins—as in most instances—it cannot be determined when the scroll was actually stitched. Several tears in 1QIsa^a were stitched before the writing took place (e.g. col. 17, line 4 from the bottom) or after the parchment was inscribed (e.g. cols. 16 and 12, the latter with stitches in the full height of the column). In like fashion, tears in 4QJer^c were stitched both before the writing (e.g. cols. 4, 21 and 23) and after it (e.g. col. 23).

Patching. There is evidence of wear and tear in scrolls in antiquity in both uninscribed and inscribed areas. At times, a segment of a scroll was replaced with a patch that was stitched onto it. Most such patches were not inscribed (e.g. the back of cols. 23–24 and the front of col. 27 in 11QT^a),[26] but there is some evidence for inscribed patches. The only known inscribed patch from Qumran is in 4Qpaleo Exod^m, col. 8. In this case the results of the carbon-14 tests confirm a slightly later date for the patch than for the scroll itself.

Re-inking. It is not clear how many words in the texts from the Judaean Desert were re-inked in antiquity when the ink had become faint. Some examples are listed by M. Martin,[27] but it is difficult to evaluate the validity of his examples. In any event, the final column of 1QIsa^a was probably damaged in antiquity because of extensive usage of the scroll; as a result, the ends of lines 1–4, 6, 7, 9, 10 became so faint that they had to be re-inked.

3. WRITING PRACTICES

The writing practices reflected in the various texts found in the Judaean Desert differ internally in many respects. They often show a common idiosyncratic heritage, while other practices sometimes coincide with writing conventions that are known from other cultures. Some scribal conventions were developed uniquely for the purpose of writing documents in the palaeo-Hebrew or square script. Even the Copper Scroll imitated some of these traditions (notably in spacing systems, handling areas at the beginning of the scrolls, and in the arrangement of the text in sheets with columns). The analysis

---

[26] See Y. Yadin, *Temple Scroll*, plate 12*.
[27] M. Martin, *Scribal Character*, 2.424.

below implies writing practices that are reflected in the various texts found in the Judaean Desert to be identical, except where specifically remarked upon. Thus both sacred and nonsacred texts were written in the same scripts and orthographical systems, with the employment of the same systems of sense division, scribal marks, correction, etc.

3.1 Divisions between Words, Verses, Sections, Psalms, and Books

a. Divisions between Words

The overwhelming majority of the texts from the Judaean Desert use one of two systems for separating between words: either word-dividers of some kind (mainly dots) in texts written in the palaeo-Hebrew script, or spacing in texts written in the square script. Continuous writing (*scriptio continua*) is attested only in some texts or groups of texts. Probably all of the following texts were written continuously to effect economy of space, since they include final letters: all the *tefillin* and *mezuzot* from the different sites; the Copper Scroll (3Q15); Mur 1 (Genesis, Exodus, and Numbers), which was written almost continuously, with minute spaces between the words; and Mur 3 (Isaiah).

In the texts that were written in the palaeo-Hebrew script, most words were separated by dots, although similar graphic dividers were sometimes used. These dots were written on the line from which the letters were suspended (cf. 4QpaleoExod[m] and 11QpaleoLev[a]), so that they were positioned at the same level as the tops of the letters themselves. The word-dividers in 2QpaleoLev and 6QpaleoGen are shaped like small diagonal strokes, while in the enigmatic palaeo-Hebrew text pap paleoMas1o (Mas1039–320) the word-dividers resemble small triangles. At the ends of lines they were usually omitted (cf. 4QpaleoExod[l,m], 4QpaleoDeut[s], and 11QpaleoLev[a]), but they were written in 2QpaleoLev (possibly because at the end of the sheet they would have coincided with the guide dots). On the other hand, the scribe of 2QpaleoLev placed both the dots serving as word-dividers and short diagonal lines guiding the drawing of the horizontal lines at the end of the lines. The only known text written in the palaeo-Hebrew script in which words were not separated by any signs, but instead by spacing, is 4QpaleoDeut[r].

Words were separated by single spaces in most texts written in the square script, although in some cases this practice was not carried out consistently. Thus, for example, 4QTob[a] ar left only minimal spaces between words, even at the beginning of what constitutes a new chapter in the later division (4QTob^a ar frg. 2, line 9 = chapter 2:1). Finally, in some texts exceptions were made for small words that were joined to the next word, especially in the case of את and אל; examples include: 4QGen^c 1 ii 15 (אתכל), 4QGen^g (אתהשמים and אתהארץ, Gen 1:1); 1QIsa^a cols. 37:8 (אלתירא, Isa 41:2) and 34:13 (אלתשמ, Isa 41:10). A more detailed study of this practice needs to be conducted.

b. Divisions between Verses (Small Sense Units) in Biblical MSS

In the great majority of the texts from the Judaean Desert the sections (paragraphs) that are indicated by a system of spacing (i.e. open and closed sections[28]) were *not* subdivided into the smaller units which were later named "verses" in the transmission history of the Bible. While each section consists of a number of smaller units that were not separated in the known Hebrew manuscripts from the Judaean Desert, in Rabbinic tradition these were indicated with the term *pasuq*—a unit after which one "interrupts" (פסק) the oral reading and makes a pause. As a rule, such a unit equals the verse as known from the MT (i.e. a unit ending with a *silluq* accent). In actuality, however, what appears now to be a subdivision of sections into verses is no real subdivision at all, since the two systems were of a different origin. In the non-biblical texts no such subdivision of the sections developed in the later manuscript tradition.

Limited evidence for a division into verses may be behind the presence of extra spaces found in 4QDan^{a, d} and possibly also in 1QLev.[29] According to E. Ulrich, some spaces in 4QIsa^d coincide with the ends of verses;[30] however, the evidence is inconclusive, and there are more verses in this Qumran text which do not end with such a space. Some scholars[31] have offered similar evidence in the case of 1QIsa^a, where it should also be noted that the small space before col. 21:4 coincides with the beginning of Isa 26:21. But even though column 21 seems to provide a sizable number of instances in

---

[28] See section c below.

[29] In the latter case, there is insufficient information for a firm conclusion to be reached.

[30] E. Ulrich et al. (eds.), *Qumran Cave 4.X: The Prophets* (DJD 15; Oxford: Clarendon Press, 1997) 77.

[31] For example, A. D. Crown, "Studies in Samaritan Scribal Practices and Manuscript History: III. Columnar Writing and the Samaritan Massorah," *BJRL* 67 (1984) 349-81, esp. 376 (mentioning Isa 43:23ff.; 45:17).

which beginnings of verses were indicated by spacing, most beginnings of verses in the Great Isaiah scroll are not indicated in this manner. In short, evidence of this type is far from convincing—especially since the small spaces probably represent closed sections, which were for some reason smaller than the others.

At the same time, however, unequivocal evidence for an ancient division into verses is known for witnesses of the Aramaic and Greek Bible translations that have been discovered in the Judaean Desert and elsewhere. For instance, 4QtgLev (4Q156)[32] systematically denotes the ends of verses and half-verses by colons (Lev 16:12, 14a, 14b, 18a, 18b, 20, 21a); and 4QpapLXXLev^a [33] indicates a division at frg. 1, line 21 (after Lev 26:13). Outside of Qumran, P. Oxy 3522 does so for Job 42:11–12 (after 42:11, 12a); P. Fouad inv. 266[34] for Genesis and Deuteronomy; P. Rylands Greek 458[35] for Deuteronomy; and 8ḤevXIIgr[36] for the Minor Prophets. Several further examples can be provided.

c. Divisions between Sections

The writing block was subdivided into meaningful units (open and closed paragraphs) which were separated from each other by means of spacing.[37] This occurs in earlier Aramaic texts from the fifth and fourth centuries BCE, in the great majority of the biblical and non-biblical texts found in the Judaean Desert, and in most Greek texts from the Hellenistic period. However, such divisions are not found in documentary texts from both the Judaean Desert and the Hellenistic Greek corpus.[38]

---

[32] Ascribed by J. T. Milik to the second or first century BCE (R. de Vaux and J. T. Milik [eds.], *Qumrân Grotte 4.II: 2.Tefillin, Mezuzot et Targums* [DJD 6; Oxford: Clarendon Press, 1977] 86-89).

[33] Dating from the late second or early first century BCE.

[34] First or second century BCE.

[35] Dating from the second century BCE.

[36] End of the first century BCE.

[37] For a detailed description of the practices of the Qumran manuscripts, see E. Tov, "Sense Divisions in the Qumran Texts, the Masoretic Text, and the Ancient Translations of the Bible," in, *Interpretation of the Bible. Proceedings of the Ljubliana Meeting 1996* [in press].

[38] See J. T. Milik et al., *Les Grottes de Murabbaʿât* (DJD 2); A. Cotton and A. Yardeni, *Aramaic, Hebrew, and Greek Texts from Naḥal Ḥever and Other Sites* (DJD 27; Oxford: Clarendon Press, 1997); N. Lewis, *The Documents from the Bar*

d. Divisions between Psalms in the Book of Psalms

In the analysis of the types of spacing between units of different sizes, the Psalms comprise a special entity in that they are smaller than books and larger than verses. In a sense, each Psalm forms a distinct section in its own right. The indication of Psalms should be analyzed separately, since the beginnings and ends of these units are clearly denoted, while the indication of sections is always subjective. This assessment pertains mainly to the biblical Psalms, but also to other psalms from Qumran, such as 4QNon-Canonical Psalms A and B, 1-4QHodayot, and 4QBarkhi Nafshi. In the analysis of the layout of the biblical Psalms from Qumran, four different types of marking of the ends and beginnings of the biblical Psalms may be recognized, although these have been classified as five systems by G. H. Wilson.[39] The method of indicating of the psalms basically corresponds with the systems of open and closed paragraphs that was described above.[40]

e. Divisions between Books in Biblical Manuscripts

In scrolls containing more than one biblical book, spaces were left between successive books. Three blank lines were left in the middle of the column between what appears to be the last line of Genesis and the beginning of Exodus in 4QpaleoGen-Exod[l], preceded by at least one sheet of written text. This may also pertain to Exodus in 4QGen-Exod[a]—which begins more than halfway down the column—and to 4QExod[b], where Exodus starts in the middle of a column. But this rule is not adhered to in 4QLev[c], which commences at the top of a column; nor in 11QpaleoLev[a], which ends in the middle of a column but is not followed by Numbers. If the latter two scrolls in fact originally contained a single biblical book only, the aforementioned prescription does not pertain to them.

In MurXII, the equivalent of three lines was left between various books of the Minor Prophets, namely between Jonah and Micah, Micah and Nahum, and Zephaniah and Haggai.

Kochba Period in the Cave of Letters—Greek Papyri (Jerusalem: Israel Exploration Society-Hebrew University-Shrine of the Book, 1989).

[39] G. H. Wilson, *The Editing of the Hebrew Psalter* (SBLDS 76; Chico, CA: Scholars Press, 1985) 93-138.

[40] See section c.

3.2 Special Layout of the Text and Superscriptions of Poetical Units

While many of the poetic texts in the Bible are presented as running texts in the medieval representatives of the MT, a tradition developed in the Middle Ages of presenting the אמ"ת books (Job, Proverbs, and Psalms) and some of the songs of the Torah, the song of Deborah, and the acrostic in Lamentations as poetry. These traditions, as well as additional systems of layout in the poetical books and in the poems included in the prose books, were reflected already in the Qumran texts at an earlier stage of the transmission of the text. Some of the Qumran texts present a poetical layout, while others do not. Scrolls which do not present a special layout of the poetical sections disregard the poetic structure; instead they write the text as one continuous unit, separating the words of a stich into two lines when necessary.[41]

3.3 Scribal Marks and Procedures

The texts from the Judaean Desert, especially those from Qumran, contain various scribal markings, some of which recur in several specific texts. A few of these marks may have been simply scribbles —for example, in the bottom margin of 1QIsa[a] col. 32. However, most signs were written intentionally, even if their meaning is often unclear to us. Since there are hardly any differences between the scribal practices displayed in biblical and non-biblical documents, scribal signs occur in both types of text. Scribal markings have been identified—in varying degrees of frequency—in several texts, but more so in non-biblical than in biblical manuscripts. They may be subdivided into the following eight categories:

(1) signs pertaining to the division of the text into different paragraphs
(2) marks pertaining to scribal intervention, mainly for the correction of errors
(3) letters in the Cryptic A script denoting matters of special interest
(4) single palaeo-Hebrew letters denoting matters of special interest
(5) marks drawing attention to certain matters in the text
(6) marks written at the ends of lines as line-fillers

---

[41] For a detailed description of these systems, see E. Tov, "Special Layout of Poetical Units in the Texts from the Judean Desert," in J. Dyk (ed.), *Give Ear to My Words—Psalms and Other Poetry in and around the Hebrew Bible, Essays in Honour of Professor N.A. van Uchelen* (Amsterdam: Societas Hebraica Amstelodamensis, 1996) 115-28.

(7) separation dots between words

(8) marks numbering content units and sheets[42]

3.4 Correction Procedures and the Degree of Scribal Intervention

When copying from an existing text, most ancient scribes incorporated their thoughts on that text into the new version which they produced. Thus they added, omitted, and altered elements; all of these changes became part of the newly created text, in which the new features were not easily recognizable since they were not marked in a special way. In this section we are not referring to the new elements of this type, but rather to other cases of scribal intervention, namely the reactions of scribes or readers to the text that was already written. In the newly-created text scribes and readers inserted sundry changes, which are recognizable because the limitations of the ancient materials and the rigid form of the manuscript did not allow them to hide the intervention. These limitations were valid until the invention of printing and—even more so—of the computer. With such new techniques, scribal or editorial interventions are generally no longer recognizable. We have analyzed these aspects of the scribal activity elsewhere in greater detail.[43]

3.5 Notation of Variant Readings

It has been suggested by some scholars that some of the marginal notations in the Qumran scrolls reflect variant readings to the text of the present scroll that were copied from parallel scrolls containing

---

[42] For a detailed analysis, see E. Tov, "Scribal Markings in the Texts from the Judean Desert," in D. W. Parry and S. D. Ricks (eds.), *Current Research and Technological Developments on the Dead Sea Scrolls—Conference on the Texts from the Judean Desert, Jerusalem, 30 April 1995* (STDJ 20; Leiden: Brill, 1996) 41-77. A special study devoted to the cancellation dots, and other systems of correction is idem, "Correction Procedures in the Texts from the Judean Desert," in D. W. Parry and E. Ulrich (eds.), *Proceedings of the 1996 International Dead Sea Scrolls Conference, 15-17 July, 1996, Provo, Utah* (STDJ 30; Leiden: Brill [forthcoming]). For an analysis of the relevance of these practices for the study of the paratextual phenomena in the MT, see idem, "Paratextual elements in the Masoretic manuscripts of the Bible Compared with the Qumran Evidence," *Festschrift H. Stegemann*, in press.

[43] E. Tov, "The Textual Base of the Corrections in the Biblical Texts Found in Qumran," in D. Dimant and U. Rappaport (eds.), *The Dead Sea Scrolls—Forty Years of Research* (STDJ 10; Leiden: Brill, 1992) 299-314.

the same composition. Other scholars have posited that these marginal notations functioned as glosses. With one exception, however, the words written between the lines or in the margins should be viewed as corrections—probably on the basis of the scribe's *Vorlage*. There seems to be only one instance in 1QIsa^a of a gloss explaining a word in the text (at Isa 7:25), and a possible grammatical interpolation in the same scroll at Isa 44:3.

3.6 Palaeo-Hebrew Writing in Qumran texts and Its Background

The Qumran finds include several forms of writing in palaeo-Hebrew characters. Commencing with the texts which use the smallest number of these letters, the following three types of use of palaeo-Hebrew may be distinguished:

  (1) Individual palaeo-Hebrew letters used as scribal markings in the margins of texts written in square characters.
  (2) Divine names written in palaeo-Hebrew characters in texts written in square characters.
  (3) Texts written completely in palaeo-Hebrew characters.[44]

4. SPECIAL SCRIBAL TRADITIONS

In this final section several groups of texts are examined with the express purpose of determining whether they reflect special scribal characteristics.

4.1 Scribal Features of Sacred Texts?

Very little distinction, if any, was made between the writing of biblical and non-biblical texts. For example, the scribe who wrote 1QS, 1QSa and 1QSb, as well as the biblical 4QSam^c and some of the corrections in 1QIsa^a (e.g. at col. 33:7), employed the same system and notations throughout all five texts (including the use of four dots for the tetragrammaton). In addition, 1QS and 1QIsa^a also share three unusual marginal signs, which were probably inserted by the same scribe.[45] In a few cases, however, a distinction was made

---

[44] For an analysis of the background of the different uses of the palaeo-Hebrew characters in the Qumran texts, see E. Tov, "The Socio-Religious Background of the Paleo-Hebrew Biblical Texts Found at Qumran," in H. Cancik et al. (eds.), *Geschichte–Tradition–Reflexion, Festschrift für Martin Hengel zum 70.Geburtstag* (Tübingen: Mohr-Siebeck, 1996) 353-74.

[45] Note (1) the palaeo-Hebrew *waw* in 1QS col. 5:1 and 1QIsa^a col. 6:22; (2)

between biblical and non-biblical texts by certain scribes, although the evidence is not altogether clear-cut. The following three features may be listed:

(1) Biblical texts were inscribed on only one side of the parchment, as opposed to some non-biblical texts.

(2) Biblical texts found in the Judaean Desert were almost exclusively written on parchment (thus also *m. Megillah* 2:2; *y. Megillah* 1.71d). The relatively small number of papyrus fragments of biblical texts[46] probably derived from a special source, and may have served as personal copies. On the other hand, papyrus was frequently used for non-biblical texts.

(3) A special arrangement for the writing of the poetical sections was devised only for the biblical books (including Ben Sira!)—not for any of the non-biblical compositions, such as 4Q381 (Non-Canonical Psalms B), 1QH[a, b], 4QShirShabb and 4QBarkhi Nafshi. However, the stichographical arrangement of 4QNon-Canonical Psalms A (4Q380) is an exception.

4.2 Scribal Features of the Texts written in the Palaeo-Hebrew Script

Texts that were written in the square and palaeo-Hebrew scripts share many scribal features since both types of texts are exemplars of the same Hebrew writing tradition. An analysis of the differences between the two traditions has been presented elsewhere.[47]

4.3 Scribal Features of Tefillin

Most of the *tefillin* that were found in the Judaean Desert derive from Cave 4, with a few additional copies from Caves 1 and 8 and from Wadi Murabbaʿât and Naḥal Ṣeʾelim. Their scribal features include the following:

(1) Most of the known *tefillin* were inscribed on parchment of inferior quality with a rough surface and ragged borders. In other words, they were written on scraps of leather which were left over from hides during the preparation of larger scrolls. Such irregular material did not allow for the writing of even lines, let alone the

---

the sign in 1QS col. 7 (bottom margin) and 1QIsa[a], col. 22:10; and (3) the composite sign in 1QS col. 9:3, resembling a combination of the signs in 1QIsa[a] cols. 20:10 and 48:29 (figures 7 and 9 in Trever).

[46] 4QpapIsa[p], 6Q3 (Deuteronomy?), 6Q4 (Kings), 6Q5 (Psalms?), 6Q7 (Daniel).

[47] E. Tov, "Scribal Practices Reflected in the Paleo-Hebrew Texts from the Judean Desert," *Scripta Classica Israelica* 15 (1996) 268-73.

writing in columns (*pace* the instructions in *b. Menaḥot* 31b). The rectangular shapes of XQPhyl 1 and 2, however, are an exception.

(2) *Tefillin* were not ruled (thus also *b. Menaḥot* 32b; *b. Megillah* 18b). Nevertheless, the writing on these was usually very straight.

(3) For reasons of economy, the text was usually inscribed on both sides of the parchment, in contrast to biblical scrolls.

(4) No spaces were left between words, even though the scribes made used the final forms of letters. The *tefillin* thus employ the same system for separating letters as for separating words.

(5) Words were split between lines, as in inscriptions written in the "early" Hebrew and "square" (Assyrian) script and in Hebrew biblical scrolls written in the palaeo-Hebrew script, apparently due to considerations of space.

(6) Interlinear additions are found in most of the *tefillin* written in the "Qumran practice"[48] (their absence in some texts may be ascribed to the fragmentary state of preservation). On the other hand, such additions do not occur in the *tefillin* that are written with the spelling of the MT.[49] The second group thus reflects the prescription of *y. Megillah* 1:71c: "One may hang (the letter above the line) in scrolls, but one may not hang (the letter above the line) in *tefillin* or *mezuzot*."

4.4 Special Features of the Texts Written on Papyrus

Since the papyrus exemplars of literary works found in the Judaean Desert are generally considered to be private copies, an examination of the textual character of the papyrus fragments is in order. While several of these are too small for their character to be determined, the larger fragments of 1-2 Kings—and possibly those of Daniel—may be characterized as non-Masoretic. More specifically, they may be classed as independent, which could mean that these texts did not derive from Pharisaic circles. Most of the sectarian works are also evidenced in one or two papyrus copies.

Beyond the natural limitations of the material (for example: papyrus sheets were glued together, not stitched), the basic scribal tradition of writing on papyrus did not differ from writing on parchment. Finally, it should be noted that papyrus texts were not ruled.

---

[48] I.e. using a special system of orthography and morphology.

[49] I.e. with more sparing orthography.

SELECT BIBLIOGRAPHY

Herbert, E. D. *Reconstructing Biblical Dead Sea Scrolls. A New Method Applied to the Reconstruction of 4QSam^a* (STDJ 22; Leiden: Brill, 1997).

Kuhl, C. "Schreibereigentümlichkeiten—Bemerkungen zur Jesajarolle (DSIa)," *VT* 2 (1952) 307–333.

Martin, M. *The Scribal Character of the Dead Sea Scrolls I–II* (Bibliothèque du Muséon 44,45; Louvain: Publications Universitaires, 1958).

Oesch, J. M. *Petucha und Setuma, Untersuchungen zu einer überlieferten Gliederung im hebräischen Text des Alten Testament* (OBO 27; Freiburg [Schweiz]: Universitätsverlag; Göttingen: Vandenhoeck & Ruprecht, 1979).

—. "Textgliederung im Alten Testament und in den Qumranhandschriften," *Henoch* 5 (1983) 289–321.

Siegel, J. P. "The Scribes of Qumran. Studies in the Early History of Jewish Scribal Customs, with Special Reference to the Qumran Biblical Scrolls and to the Tannaitic Traditions of Massekheth Soferim" (Unpubl. diss., Waltham, MA: Brandeis University, 1972). [obtainable from University Microfilms]

Stegemann, H. "The Literary Composition of the Temple Scroll and Its Status at Qumran," in G. J. Brooke (ed.), *Temple Scroll Studies* (JSPSup 7; Sheffield: Sheffield Academic Press, 1989) 123-48.

—. "Methods for the Reconstruction of Scrolls from Scattered Fragments," in L. H. Schiffman (ed.), *Archaeology and History in the Dead Sea Scrolls—The New York University Conference in Memory of Yigael Yadin* (JSPSup 8; JSOT/ASOR Monograph Series 2; Sheffield: JSOT Press, 1990) 189–220.

Tov, E. "The Textual Base of the Corrections in the Biblical Texts Found in Qumran," in D. Dimant and U. Rappaport (eds.), *The Dead Sea Scrolls—Forty Years of Research* (STDJ 10; Leiden: Brill, 1992) 299-314.

—. "Special Layout of Poetical Units in the Texts from the Judean Desert," in J. Dyk (ed.), *Give Ear to My Words—Psalms and Other Poetry in and around the Hebrew Bible, Essays in Honour of Professor N. A. van Uchelen* (Amsterdam: Societas Hebraica Amstelodamensis, 1996) 115-28.

—. "Scribal Markings in the Texts from the Judean Desert," in D. W. Parry and S. D. Ricks (eds.), *Current Research and Technological Developments on the Dead Sea Scrolls—Conference on the Texts from the Judean Desert, Jerusalem, 30 April 1995* (STDJ 20; Leiden: Brill, 1996) 41-77.

—. "The Socio-Religious Background of the Paleo-Hebrew Biblical Texts Found at Qumran," in H. Cancik et al. (eds.), *Geschichte–Tradition–Reflexion, Festschrift für Martin Hengel zum 70.Geburtstag* (Tübingen: Mohr-Siebeck, 1996) 353-74.

—. "Scribal Practices Reflected in the Paleo-Hebrew Texts from the Judean Desert," *Scripta Classica Israelica* 15 (1996) 268-73.

—. "The Scribes of the Texts Found in the Judean Desert," in C. A. Evans and S. Talmon (eds.), *The Quest for Context & Meaning. Studies in Biblical Intertexuality in Honor of James A. Sanders* (BIS 28; Leiden: Brill, 1997) 131-52.

Turner, E. G. *Greek Manuscripts of the Ancient World* (2nd ed., revised and enlarged by P. J. Parsons; London: University of London, Institute of Classical Studies, 1987).

Ulrich, E. "Orthography and Text in 4QDan^a and 4QDan^b and in the Received Masoretic Text," in H. W. Attridge et al. (eds.), *Of Scribes and Scrolls, Studies on the Hebrew Bible, Intertestamental Judaism, and Christian Origins Presented to John Strugnell* (CTSRR 5; Lanham, MD: University Press of America, 1990) 29-42.

Wilson, G. H. *The Editing of the Hebrew Psalter* (SBLDS 76; Chico, CA: Scholars Press, 1985) 93-138.

DATING THE SCROLLS ON THE BASIS OF RADIOCARBON ANALYSIS[*]

GREG DOUDNA

In 1994 a battery of radiocarbon measurements on Judaean desert items, including eleven new Qumran texts, was conducted at the NSF[1] Accelerator Mass Spectrometry ("AMS") Facility at the University of Arizona in Tucson, as part of a collaboration that was implemented by Emanuel Tov.[2] These measurements have added important information to the data provided by earlier AMS radiocarbon datings (1991) that had been carried out in Zurich on eight Qumran texts and two Masada texts.[3]

The present study provides updated calibrations of both the Zurich and Tucson AMS radiocarbon results, undertakes analysis and interpretation of these data, and proposes a new framework for dating the Qumran scrolls.

---

[*] Support for this study is gratefully acknowledged from the Institute for Biblical Exegesis, University of Copenhagen. I thank Paula Reimer (University of Washington Quaternary Isotope Laboratory) for help with the computer program CALIB; Timothy Jull at the AMS Facility at the University of Arizona for prompt answers to many questions; Douglas Donahue of the same AMS Facility for discussion of an earlier draft of this paper; Bernard Weninger for insights concerning calibration and probability; Thomas Hougaard and Lisbeth Strange for consultation on questions of chemistry; Kaare Lund Rasmussen of the Radiocarbon Laboratory at the National Museum, Denmark, for consultation on technical questions; and Thomas Thompson, Niels Peter Lemche, Tilde Binger Frederick Cryer and John Strange for discussions of analysis in this paper. Any errors in fact or in argument are my own.

[1] I.e. the National Science Foundation.

[2] A. Jull, D. Donahue, M. Broshi and E. Tov, "Radiocarbon Dating of Scrolls and Linen Fragments from the Judean Desert," *Radiocarbon* 37 (1995) 11-19; A. Jull, D. Donahue, M. Broshi and E. Tov, "Radiocarbon Dating of Scrolls and Linen Fragments from the Judean Desert," ʿ*Atiqot* 28 (1996) 85-91.

[3] G. Bonani, M. Broshi, I. Carmi, S. Ivy, J. Strugnell and W. Wölfli, "Radiocarbon Dating of Fourteen Dead Sea Scrolls," ʿ*Atiqot* 20 (1991) 27-32; G. Bonani, S. Ivy, W. Wölfli, M. Broshi, I. Carmi and J. Strugnell, "Radiocarbon Dating of Fourteen Dead Sea Scrolls," *Radiocarbon* 34 (1992) 843-49.

1. WHAT IS AMS RADIOCARBON DATING?

AMS or Accelerator Mass Spectrometry is a method of conducting radiocarbon dating, which is itself the primary method used for dating organic materials and some inorganic materials. The radioactive carbon isotope ^{14}C ("carbon-14") is continually produced in the upper atmosphere in a reaction from the bombardment of nitrogen atoms by cosmic radiation. This new ^{14}C is quickly oxidized to become a component of $^{14}CO_2$ (carbon dioxide),[4] which circulates nearly uniformly throughout the world's atmosphere in each hemisphere over a span of several years.

Plants continuously absorb new ^{14}C by photosynthesis, and animals in turn absorb the ^{14}C by eating the plants. The ^{14}C is found in association with two stable isotopes, ^{12}C and ^{13}C (carbon-12 and carbon-13). When an organism dies, it ceases to be in equilibrium with its surroundings, and no longer takes in new carbon. The ^{14}C in the organism at the time of death decays at a constant rate (a half-life of about 5,730 years), but the atoms of the two stable isotopes do not. This is the key to the AMS method, which measures the ratio of ^{14}C to ^{13}C. Thereafter, by means of a second measurement of the $^{13}C/^{12}C$ ratio, the $^{14}C/^{12}C$ ratio can be determined. By this method the amount of ^{14}C decay that has occurred from the time of an ancient organism's death can be calculated.

But the amount of ^{14}C in the atmosphere varies through time, going up in certain years and down in others,[5] so a means of calibration is needed to translate today's measurements into calendar years. Radiocarbon measurements on tree rings of known dates provide such a calibration curve, going back some 11,000 years. For Dead Sea texts that are written on animal skin, a radiocarbon measurement yields an approximate date of the death of the animal that provided the skin. For papyrus, the radiocarbon date measures the date when the plant was cut.

The radiocarbon-dating method was invented and first applied in 1949 by Willard F. Libby, then at the University of Chicago. Among the items in Libby's early tests was a sample of linen from Qumran

---

[4] While most carbon dioxide found in earth's atmoshphere is either $^{12}CO_2$ or $^{13}CO_2$, a tiny fraction occurs with the less stable carbon-14 isotope as $^{14}CO_2$.

[5] Variability of ^{14}C production in the upper atmosphere correlates with changes in sun magnetic activity and in the earth's magnetic field (S. Bowman, *Radiocarbon Dating* [London: British Museum Press, 1990] 19).

Cave 1 which had been used to wrap a scroll. Libby conducted a single measurement on this linen in the fall of 1950 and reported the radiocarbon age of the linen as 1,917 years, plus or minus 200, prior to the year 1950.[6] Subsequently, this year (1950) became the standard used by radiocarbon laboratories around the world. By convention, all radiocarbon measurements today are reported as a number BP ("Before Present"), denoting the "radiocarbon age before 1950." Thus Libby's dating of the Qumran Cave 1 linen was BP 1917 +/- 200.[7] This measurement, however, was made before the necessity for calibration was known. (Libby's margin of error arose entirely from the counting of the radioactivity.) By modern calibration, Libby's measurement gives us 68% confidence that the date of the Cave 1 linen was somewhere between 160 BCE and 390 CE.[8] Although the margin of error was admittedly large in those early days, in the view of most scholars Libby's date weighed strongly against theories of a medieval dating for the scrolls which were then being argued.

In 1960 F. E. Zeuner reported two further radiocarbon measurements that were done in 1956 on a piece of charred roof-beam made of palm wood from Locus 86 at Qumran. The age measurements were the same in each case: a ^{14}C age of BP 1940 +/- 80. If the wood had been used immediately after cutting, this measurement would reflect a date of building activity at Qumran (some time before the date of the fire which had charred the wood). After allowing a factor

---

[6] W. F. Libby, "Radiocarbon Dates, II," *Science* 114 (1951) 291-96; O. R. Sellers, "Date of Cloth from the ʿAyn Feshka Cave," *BA* 14 (1951) 29.

[7] See item 37 in Table A at the end of this article.

[8] Calibrations in this article were done using a modified version of CALIB 3.0.3c (the University of Washington's Quaternary Isotope Laboratory Radiocarbon Calibration Program). The modification was done in Copenhagen and consisted of installation of a new decadal dataset that was constructed on the basis of corrections to the decadal curve presented in the final session of the 16th International Radiocarbon Conference held in Groningen in June, 1997 (cf. M. Stuiver, "Improving Radiocarbon Age Calibration," forthcoming in *Radiocarbon*). Details of the Seattle and Belfast datasets that were used in the construction of the decadal calibration curve are found in the notes to Table A. Computer programs for calibrating radiocarbon dates according to the 1997 system are also forthcoming (consult the journal *Radiocarbon* for information). The most current data at the time of writing of this article were used, but further corrections to the calibration system are expected.

for the age of the tree, calibratiοn of these measurements gives us 68% confidence that the cutting of the wood used to make that roof-beam occurred somewhere between 40 BCE and 110 CE.[9]

Until the late 1970's radiocarbon dating of parchment or papyrus texts was not practical because of the amount of sample material that would have to be destroyed by the conventional method (2-5 grams of the sample to obtain 1 gram of carbon). This problem was alleviated, however, with the development of AMS methods in which only 20-40 milligrams of parchment (or even less) are necessary.

2. CALIBRATION OF RADIOCARBON MEASUREMENTS ON THE SCROLLS

Radiocarbon measurements are converted to calendar dates on the basis of calibration data sets which are used by radiocarbon facilities throughout the world. In 1986 calibration data sets (or "curves") were published on the basis of extensive measurements—conducted at Seattle and Belfast—of tree rings in twenty- and ten-year intervals.[10] These sets were adopted as a single standard by the world's radiocarbon facilities at the Twelfth International Radiocarbon Conference at Trondheim (Norway) in 1985. In June 1997, at the Sixteenth International Radiocarbon Conference in Groningen (the Netherlands), the same laboratories announced updated calibration curves in light of a number of studies in the intervening years and also a correction in the Seattle data for a radon contamination factor that had offset previous dates by about 10 years.[11]

While AMS radiocarbon dates on Dead Sea items from both the Zurich and Tucson facilities were published on the basis of then-standard 1986 calibrations, the 1997 calibration data are more current and should be more accurate. All analysis and discussion of radiocarbon information in the field of Qumran studies should of course be carried out with recourse to the most accurate calibration information available. The calibrations of Dead Sea texts and linen

---

[9] F. E. Zeuner, "Notes on Qumrân," *PEQ* 92 (1960) 27-28. The calibration was done on the 1997 decadal system (see note 8), smoothed to 50 years with +/- 35 variance added to the averaged result of both radiocarbon measurements before calibration. This was based on Zeuner's estimate of 15-85 years for the age of the date palm.

[10] M. Stuiver and R. Kra (eds.), "1986 Calibration Issue," *Radiocarbon* 28 (1986).

[11] See note 8 above.

items in Table A at the end of this article have accordingly been made on the basis of the 1997 system.

The effect of the updated calibrations may be summarized in general terms as a slight, but noticeable, shift to younger calendar date ranges from previously reported dates for all Qumran texts on the order of less than a decade in most cases. But for certain texts the effect is greater and the date ranges become younger by several decades. It should be emphasized that these updated calibrations represent no change or correction in the actual radiocarbon measurements that were carried out by the laboratories. Calibrations done on the basis of the 1997 system represent simply a more accurate translation of the same laboratory measurements into calendar dates.

3. TEN- AND TWENTY-YEAR CALIBRATION CURVES

For the time-period of the scrolls there are two kinds of calibration curves in use within the radiocarbon profession: a 20-year ("bidecadal") curve based on average measurements of ^{14}C levels of tree rings in 20-year sequence intervals; and a 10-year ("decadal") curve based on average measurements of tree rings in 10-year intervals. The recommendation from within the radiocarbon profession is that the calibration curve should be used with intervals which most closely correspond to the time-span of formation of the sample material.[12] Since the Dead Sea materials tested at Zurich and Tucson—animal skin, papyrus, and linen—represent close to single-year determinations, the 10-year curve is more appropriate than the 20-year curve.[13]

The 20-year curve yields results that are easier to read because of greater "smoothing" of the wiggles in the calibration curve. Both Zurich and Tucson used the 20-year curve from 1986 in reporting calibrated dates for Dead Sea Scrolls. Calibrations from the 10-year curve are more "choppy" and difficult to read, since single radiocarbon measurements more frequently produce multiple calendar date ranges. These multiple ranges can be very confusing to those

---

[12] Bowman, *Radiocarbon Dating*, 48; M. Aitken, *Science-Based Dating in Archaeology* (London and New York: Longman, 1990) 114.

[13] The skin of the animals used to make scrolls will reflect levels of ^{14}C in years immediately prior to death (from eating plants which reflect current levels of atmospheric ^{14}C). An example of a 20-year period of formation of sample material is carbon that is derived from a piece of wood containing twenty growth rings.

who are inexperienced in reading statistics and laboratory data, thus rendering discussion more complex.

But there is a slight gain in accuracy for Dead Sea text-dating purposes when the 10-year curve is used. This somewhat greater accuracy has to do with the vicissitudes of ^{14}C production in the atmosphere. If the death of an animal, or the cutting of a plant used to make papyrus, happens to be in years of higher or lower ^{14}C in the atmosphere than was the average for the years prior or after, an accurate radiocarbon measurement will produce a calibrated calendar date range that is slightly offset from the true date. The only way to completely eliminate this variability factor is to use a 3- or 1-year curve that would be more appropriate for calibrations of the Scrolls, but which unfortunately does not exist for the time-period of these ancient documents.[14] A study for comparative purposes of the period 1510-1954 CE, for which single-year data do exist, has revealed about five years' average amount of under-reporting of error margins on single-year samples when these are calibrated according to a decadal calibration curve.[15] Accordingly, an additional uncertainty-factor—using this figure of five years—has been incorporated into all the calibrations of dates for Scrolls and linen in Table A and elsewhere in this article.

Radiocarbon measurements are not capable of producing precise dates to the year; instead, they give an average value with a standard allowance for error, i.e. +/- one sigma (1σ). The assumption is that this value for the radiocarbon date, like many other physical measurements, is normally distributed in a "bell-curve" (Gaussian) manner. The interval of +/- *one sigma* (1σ) means the laboratory

---

[14] "Whenever possible a single-year curve should be used, then a decadal one in preference to bi-decadal [for samples with a single season's growth]" (Bowman, *Radiocarbon Dating*, 48). "The calibration of [single-year samples] (against a decadal or bidecadal curve) will, in most instances, lead to underestimated cal-age uncertainty" (M. Stuiver, "A Note on Single-Year Calibration of the Radiocarbon Time Scale, AD 1510-1954," *Radiocarbon* 35 [1993] 68).

[15] About five years average additional difference between actual measurements for single years and the range of difference predicted on the basis of the decadal curve in the years 1510-1954 CE, is reported in Stuiver, "Improving Radiocarbon Age Calibration." Due to the nature of the mathematical formula used in adding further small uncertainties ("adding in quadrature"), the effect of this slight increase in margin of error on scrolls dates is very slight—in most cases not more than a calendar year or two after calibration.

reports with 68% confidence that the true date is somewhere within the reported date interval. An interval of +/- *two sigma* (2σ) is wider, and expresses 95% confidence that the true date is within that range. (A still wider three-sigma interval, though rarely used, would represent 99.7% confidence.)

While the Zurich facility reported its Dead Sea calibrated results only in one-sigma intervals or date ranges, Tucson reported both one- and two-sigma date ranges for its calibrated results. The relatively more narrow one-sigma ranges (at 68% confidence) seem more informative for dating Qumran texts—but at the cost of a one-third chance that the true date of what is being measured, in any individual case, is going to be outside these date ranges. Furthermore, the true date is also going to be outside even the two-sigma date ranges (at 95% confidence) in one out of twenty radiocarbon measurements. However, if a tested sample is free from unusual problems, any "misses" should be near to either end of the reported date ranges, as opposed to being far removed from one end or the other. (Throughout this article one-sigma ranges are quoted, unless otherwise indicated.)

4. CALIBRATION CURVE ANOMALIES

Figure 1 shows a segment of the 1997 decadal calibration curve which has been used in the calibrations in this article and which merits a brief examination. As an illustration of the anomalies in the calibration curve, note that the interval at 165-145 BCE is at about the same level as the flat stretch at 105-55 BCE. Dead Sea texts from within either of these two periods will be practically impossible to distinguish chronologically from one another by radiocarbon methods, since texts from within either of these time periods will yield the same measurements and generate the other possible date range each time in calibration. On the other hand, a drop in the curve between about 55 BCE and 5 CE means that radiocarbon dating should be capable of distinguishing texts older than 55 BCE from texts that are younger than 5 CE. A precipitous drop at 125-135 CE means AMS measurements should be able to distinguish texts older than this decade from texts that are younger. (However, it should be noted that five Dead Sea texts bearing internal dates measured in the Zurich and Tucson AMS batteries were from years *within* this 125-135 CE decade in which this sharp drop in the curve occurred.)

DATING AND RADIOCARBON ANALYSIS

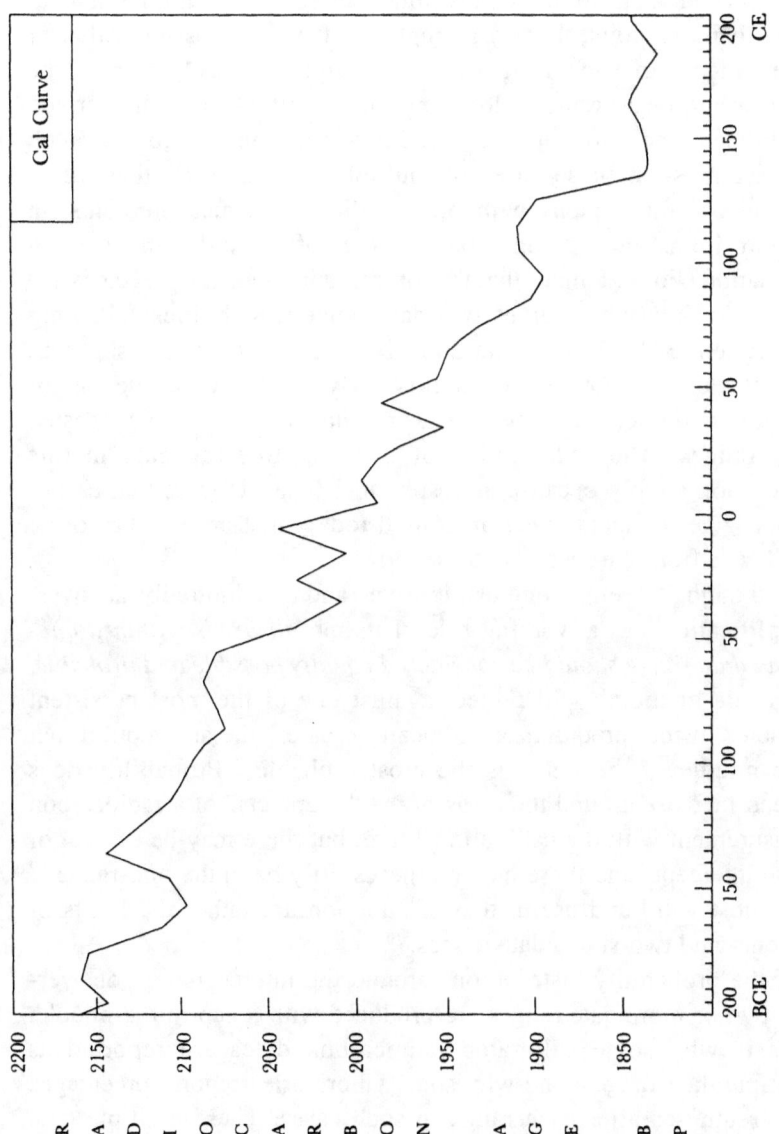

Figure 1. Section of the 1997 Decadal Calibration curve

Because of the variations in the calibration curve, a single radiocarbon measurement may intersect the calibration curve at more than one point, thereby giving more than one possible calendar date ranges. In such instances each range is possible; from the radiocarbon measurement alone one cannot tell which is the correct, or indeed the more probable, date range produced by such intersections. In these cases of multiple alternatives, other information or comparisons with other radiocarbon measurements on similar items in the same battery can often assist in such an evaluation. For example, the Tucson measurement for 1QIsa^a is BP 2141 +/- 32,[16] which gives two date range possibilities following calibration: 341-325 BCE and 202-114 BCE. From comparison with the dates of other Qumran texts, it is fairly clear that the true date of this text is reflected in the second, or younger, of the two suggested date ranges. The older range of 341-325 BCE appears in this calibration simply because atmospheric ^{14}C levels from that earlier period give numbers, when measured today, that are similar to the ^{14}C levels from the second date-period.

Although it seems counter-intuitive (and is admittedly an oversimplification), as a working rule of thumb *all areas within a one-sigma date range should be considered equally possible and probable.* This rule of thumb will protect against one of the most persistent fallacies in interpretation of radiocarbon dates: the assumption that "the middle of the range is the most probable." Probability does indeed increase around the areas of the "intercepts" of a radiocarbon measurement with the calibration curve, but there may be several of these intercepts and these may not necessarily be in the mid-range.[17] The most valid and useful foci of attention are rather the limits of the one- and two-sigma date ranges.

If the probability-distributions around the intercepts do not overlap, two or more date ranges are produced with a gap in the middle. This is why some calibrated radiocarbon dates are reported as multiple date ranges, and why some laboratories report percentages in parentheses after each range in such cases. These multiple date ranges do not represent the distinct results of separate tests. Nor do the percentages represent probabilities out of 100% for the true date

---

[16] See item 32 in Table A.

[17] The intercepts for each radiocarbon date are given in column VII of Table A at the end of this article.

(such that the true date can be known to be within one of the ranges). Instead, the multiple figures represent noncontinuous calibrated ranges from a single measurement, instead of a continuous range.

To render the data less confusing, in this article and in the table of Scrolls dates at the conclusion (Table A) date ranges that are separated by no more than 25 calendar years have had the gap removed, so that the two ranges have simply become a single longer one.[18]

5. ACCURACY AND PRECISION

A single measurement (or "run") at the best AMS facilities today cannot usually yield a reported margin of error of much less than +/- 60 radiocarbon years before calibration. Increased precision (i.e. reduction of margins of error) is accomplished by conducting several measurements and averaging them.[19] This is what both the Zurich and Tucson facilities did with the Dead Sea texts. All measurements on these documents represent combined results of multiple runs for each text, which involved separately-measured subsamples divided from the original samples. The number of runs for each text ranged from two to nine. By this means the margins of error before calibration were brought down to a low point of +/- 20 (4QEnastr^a, Tucson) and a high of +/- 68 (1QS, Tucson), with margins of error for all other items ranging between these two figures.

In reading a radiocarbon date, how reliable are the published margins of error? Results of large-scale laboratory intercomparison studies in the 1980's led to conclusions that "the 1σ expression typically underrepresents actual experimental variations."[20] In response to these studies many laboratories within the profession (amongst

---

[18] The outer ends, however, remain the same.

[19] "The measurements performed in a radiocarbon age determination are essentially those of experimental physics... [E]xperimental or observational errors arise from different causes and follow no simple laws. We find, quite generally in physics and other 'exact' sciences, that repeated measurements by the same scientist using the same equipment on a given specimen do not always produce the same result. ...much time and effort is spent in attempting to discover and eliminate the causes... Repetition of the measurements will, in general, tend to produce a statistical spread of results around the 'most probable' age..." (R. Switsur, "A Consideration of Some Basic Ideas for Quality Assurance in Radiocarbon Dating," *Radiocarbon* 32 [1990] 341-46, esp. 342-43).

[20] R. E. Taylor et al., *Radiocarbon Dating: An Archaeological Perspective* (Orlando, FL: Academic Press, 1987) 104.

them the Zurich and Tucson facilities) now include in their margins of error a factor for laboratory reproducibility, in addition to simple uncertainty in counting. This is designed to remove a major cause of systematic underreporting of margin of error in the past:

> It is important that users of radiocarbon results be aware of the limitations and possible pitfalls of quoted error terms. But many laboratories are scrupulously careful in their attempts to evaluate all sources of random error and to avoid systematic errors by continual self-checks and participation in intercomparison studies.[21]

Nevertheless, there are three additional factors which are not reflected in previously-published calibrations of AMS Scrolls dates or in the calibrations in the present article. Each of these factors represents potential additional uncertainties.

5.1 Possible Regional Geographic Variance

This factor, which may relate also to altitude and coastal/inland setting, is a subject of continuing investigation; the potential variance in the northern hemisphere is estimated to be no greater than 10-25 radiocarbon years.[22] Measurements on scrolls found near the Dead Sea are calibrated according to measurements on dated tree-rings from North American bristlecone pine and Irish oak-tree sequences which reflect atmospheric ^{14}C levels in North America and Europe. No study of regional variance yet exists for the Mediterranean or the Middle East, but in 1997 a team in Israel reported the beginnings of

---

[21] Bowman, *Radiocarbon Dating*, 41.

[22] "Although relatively fast transport in the troposphere causes atmospheric $^{14}CO_2$ to be fairly uniformly mixed near the earth's surface, small regional differences remain. General circulation and carbon reservoir model calculations predict regional 'age' differences of maximally 20 ^{14}C years within the northern hemisphere. Such inhomogeneity in atmospheric $^{14}CO_2$ alone can induce ^{14}C age offsets on the order of a decade between individual northern hemisphere dendrochronologies" (M. Stuiver and G. W. Pearson, "High-Precision Bidecadal Calibration of the Radiocarbon Time Scale, AD 1950-500 BC and 2500-6000 BC," *Radiocarbon* 35 [1993] 1-24, esp. 1-2). "^{14}C age differences of about 10 ^{14}C yr appear to be an upper limit for regional offsets in decadal or bidecadal calibration curves" (M. Stuiver, "A Note on Single-Year Calibration," 68). Measurements in North America suggest some regional variances exceed this 10-year estimate (P. Damon, "Note Concerning 'Intercomparison of High-Precision ^{14}C Measurements at the University of Arizona and the Queen's University of Belfast Radiocarbon Laboratories' by Kalin et al. (1995) and the Regional Effect," *Radiocarbon* 37 [1995] 955-59, esp. 957).

such a project: measurements on tree-rings from Cyprus as a first step toward producing a regional calibration curve for the Levant.[23] If a laboratory's results seem slightly offset from "true dates" after calibration, and the amount involved is small, it may well be that the calibration curve, not the laboratory, is actually offset. The laboratory could in fact be accurately measuring what was really there in the Middle East.

5.2 Systematic Offsets between Laboratories

The following representative statement from within the profession may be noted: "It is especially difficult to achieve precise intercalibration among laboratories and systematic differences of 20-30 yr are probably not unusual between laboratories".[24] International laboratory intercomparison studies within the profession work hard to identify and reduce or eliminate this phenomenon, and laboratories undertake continual checks on their own to detect and correct such offsets. It is often not known why these slight offsets occur (with the highly sensitive equipment in a modern high-precision laboratory this is not too surprising). An offset of a laboratory at the time of one set of measurements does not necessarily mean the laboratory will have the same offset on a later occasion, since its cause may have been corrected in the interim.

5.3 Contamination of Samples

Of particular concern for dating Dead Sea Scrolls is the possibility of contamination of individual samples with either modern or ancient carbon, which would obviously yield misleading dates. Prior to measurement of samples, radiocarbon laboratories follow procedures for cleaning that are designed to remove common types of contaminants (e.g. soil, dust, cigarette particulates); however, more specific treatments are also necessary to deal with unusual contaminants. This may prove difficult for a laboratory, particularly in dating objects that have been submitted from museums, if the history of usage of preservatives or chemicals is not known or if the laboratory is not alerted to look for specific kinds of contamination. If, for example,

---

[23] I. Carmi, N. Liphschitz, D. Segal, Y. Szabo and E. Mintz, "Is a Calibration Curve for the Levant Necessary?," presented at the 16th International Radiocarbon Conference, Groningen, 1997.

[24] J. C. Vogel, A. Fuls, E. Visser and B. Becker, "Pretoria Calibration Curve for Short-Lived Samples, 1930-3350 BC," *Radiocarbon* 35 (1993) 73-85, esp. 74.

some modern contaminant on a sample is not removed during the cleaning process, the measurement of the sample will give an erroneously young radiocarbon date. The problem here is not in the precision or accuracy of the AMS measurements, but concerns instead the possibility of unwanted items being measured.

In addition to uncertain documentation of the usage of chemicals on Dead Sea manuscripts during the past forty to fifty years in which they have been in the hands of human conservators, as well as unknown ancient variables, both the Zurich and Tucson laboratories reported difficulties in carrying out even routine cleaning procedures on Dead Sea text samples. The problem is that the cleaning involves immersion of the samples in acid and base solutions. But the Dead Sea manuscripts are so fragile that the samples simply dissolve or decompose rapidly in such solutions. Both laboratories reported that the strength of the acid and base solutions—as well as the the duration of time in which samples were immersed in them—had to be reduced (sometimes dramatically) from the intended procedures in order to have any sample material left for measurement.[25] Further discussion of sample contamination, and the extent to which the dates of scrolls may have been affected, will be undertaken later in this article.

5.4 Accurate Identification of Materials

Finally, the sample submitted to the laboratory must be accurately identified, and the linkage of the item being measured with the event one wishes to date must be secure. Radiocarbon laboratories are sometimes charged with producing erroneous dates that are almost

---

[25] The Zurich laboratory reported first testing tiny amounts of scrolls sample material in its regular "strong" solution strengths of hydrochloric acid, sodium hydroxide, and hydrochloric acid. When that dissolved the sample, one-half strength solution was tried with the same result, then one-fifth strength, and finally one-tenth strength. Only at one-tenth strength did the parchment material survive. One-tenth strength was then used at Zurich for all parchment sample pretreatment (Bonani et al., "Fourteen Dead Sea Scrolls" [1992], 846). The Tucson laboratory, applying the same acid-base-acid pretreatment, also diluted the strengths of solutions but, according to their report, not to the same extent of dilution as Zurich. Tucson reported: "We found that some partially gelatinized samples were very easily dissolved by NaOH [sodium hydroxide] solutions...and all samples were monitored during this process. Samples that started to dissolve in NaOH were removed from the solution as quickly as possible" (Jull et al., "Radiocarbon Dating of Scrolls" [1995], 12).

certainly cases of sample misidentification or misassociation. As is well known, many Qumran texts consist of smaller or larger numbers of fragments that have been joined and pieced together. These joins and fragment placements are not infallible, and mistakes are continually being discovered and corrected by subsequent editors. An example of such misidentification has already occurred so as to affect a radiocarbon date that was assigned to a Qumran text. One of the items measured in the Zurich AMS battery was reported as "4Q365 Pentateuchal Paraphrase." Subsequently, however, Emanuel Tov has argued that the piece measured at Zurich and identified as belonging to 4Q365 is in fact part of a different text altogether (perhaps a copy of the Temple Scroll).[26] If the two texts were copied by the same scribe, the radiocarbon date on the one may date the other as well. But the point is illustrated by this example.

6. INTERPRETATION OF RADIOCARBON DATA

An important principle in interpreting radiocarbon data is that single dates are not probative, but clusters of dates are. As a general rule, if a radiocarbon date is in line with a cluster of other dates of materials from the same context, this can become a powerful basis for confidence in the radiocarbon dating. But if an individual date differs from other dates or stands alone, it carries a weaker basis for confidence (regardless of published margins of error for that particular date).[27] This is why conducting radiocarbon measurements in batteries rather than single measurements is most important:

> Attention should be focused on the general *pattern* of ^{14}C values rather than on any individual ^{14}C age estimate. Only with a *suite* of ^{14}C values can problematic results be critically identified.[28]

---

[26] Cf. the comment of S. White, "4Q364 and 365: A Preliminary Report," in J. T. Barrera and L. V. Montanger (eds.), *The Madrid Qumran Congress* (STDJ 11.1; Leiden: Brill, 1992) 217-28, esp. 217 n.2, as well as Tov's own article in the same volume.

[27] "Little reliance should be placed on an individual ^{14}C 'date' to provide an estimate of age for a given object, structure, feature, or stratigraphic unit. A critical judgment of the ability of ^{14}C data to infer actual age can best be made with a suite of determinations... Concordance of values on different sample types or fractions of the same sample from well-defined stratigraphic contexts provides one of the strongest arguments for the accuracy of age assessments based on ^{14}C values" (Taylor, *Radiocarbon Dating*, 105).

[28] Taylor, *Radiocarbon Dating*, 142.

The Qumran texts are associated with each other in an archaeological context and in specific scribal and literary contexts as well. Individual radiocarbon data-points on Qumran texts must be evaluated not only in isolation (i.e. the numbers reported by the laboratory for that text), but also by how these results relate and cohere with radiocarbon data on other texts with which they are in association.

7. ZURICH'S MEASUREMENTS

After the development of the AMS method, there was a delay of an entire decade before serious interest developed and was acted upon within Qumran studies for utilizing this new procedure for dating Dead Sea texts. In 1990 the first battery of AMS measurments was carried out on Scrolls texts at the Institut für Mittelenergiephysik in Zurich at the initiative of Amir Drori, director of the Israel Antiquities Authority; this was in response to a request to him from Robert Eisenman and Philip Davies, that such testing be undertaken.[29]

Among the fourteen items tested at Zurich were samples from four texts bearing internal dates. These included a 4th century BCE deed of sale from Samaria, two deeds bearing dates from the early 2nd century CE, and an 8th century CE letter in Arabic. According to the scientific report, the Zurich laboratory was not told the true dates of these texts until after the AMS measurements had been completed.[30] In terms of 1997 calibration, the AMS-measured radiocarbon dates on these four items are in excellent agreement with the true dates of the texts. The true date of one text is within the reported one-sigma range of the AMS measurement, and the true dates of the other three are only 1, 2, and 5 calendar years, respectively, outside the one-sigma ranges (see Table A for details).

An unusual measurement from Zurich was the result obtained for 4QTQahat at a radiocarbon age of BP 2240 +/- 39,[31] which in terms of 1997 calibration is 385-349 BCE or 317-208 BCE at the one-sigma range[32] (The two-sigma range: 395-181 BCE). This result was

---

[29] Z. Kapera, "AMS Carbon-14 Dating of the Scrolls," *The Qumran Chronicle* 2 (1992) 39-43.

[30] Bonani et al., "Fourteen Dead Sea Scrolls," 29.

[31] See item 2 in Table A.

[32] With respect to the two date ranges: because of the irregular nature of the calibration curve, more than one such ranges are sometimes produced. Other

significantly earlier than the expected date, which led scroll scholars M. Broshi and J. Strugnell to report:

> The difference [for the Testament of Qahat] between the palaeographic and the radiocarbon dates is considerable. There is no doubt with regard to the palaeographic date (Late Hasmonean).[33]

In view of the absence before these AMS measurements of any independently-dated text in the script ("Hasmonean semiformal") in which 4QTQahat is written as a basis for chronological comparison or control, this statement from the Scrolls scholars' contingent of the radiocarbon report might be considered prematurely dogmatic.

The Zurich laboratory dated separate samples from 4QTQahat on two separate occasions and produced similar results each time[34] (but see below). Some members of the radiocarbon profession are not so quick as Qumran scholars to assume that the Zurich measurement on this text was erroneous. Nevertheless, the result has the appearance of an "outlier" (i.e. a measurement that differs from that of other similar items without known cause). Another Qumran text of the same genre and language (Aramaic), and identified as written in a similar type of scribal hand, is 4QLevi^a ar,[35] which was also dated at Zurich. The similarities between the two texts give grounds for thinking that 4QTQahat and 4QLevi^a ar should be contemporary. Zurich's date for 4QLevi^a ar was BP 2125 +/- 24, which calibrates to 197-105 BCE at the one-sigma range (two-sigma: 344-324 BCE or 203-53 BCE).[36]

Unexpected results are of interest because they may reflect information which was not previously known. But outliers are more

---

information (principally other radiocarbon dates on similar items) can serve to indicate which of the possible date ranges is most likely to refect the "true date" (see section 4 above, "Calibration Curve Anomalies").

[33] Bonani et al., "Fourteen Dead Sea Scrolls," 30.

[34] The Zurich measurements at each stage of testing of 4QTQahat are reported in Bonani et al., "Fourteen Dead Sea Scrolls," 847-48.

[35] Item 5 in Table A.

[36] On the palaeographic similarities of 4QTQahat and 4QLevi^a (formerly known as 4QTLevi^a), see É. Puech ("Le Testament de Qahat en araméen de la grotte 4 [4QTQah," *RevQ* 15 [1991] 23-54, esp. 27). All of the six texts of Aramaic Levi from Cave 4 are characterized as written in similar types of handwriting by M. Stone and J. Greenfield "213.-214b. 4QLevi^{a-f} ar" in G. Brooke et al. (eds.), *Qumran Cave 4.XVII: Parabiblical Texts, Part 3* (DJD 22; Oxford: Clarendon Press, 1996) 1-72.

frequently the result of errors. An unexplained outlier merits further study in an attempt to understand, if possible, why it has occurred, and whether it is a mistake or provides important new information. The Zurich laboratory reported:

> We cannot rule out possible contamination in this specific case [4QTQahat]. Two samples, collected at different times, were used for the ^{14}C dating of the Qahat manuscript. In both cases, subsamples subjected to ultrasonic cleaning alone yielded dates significantly older (c. 350 years) than those cleaned both ultrasonically and chemically. This indicates severe contamination which the chemical cleaning, constrained by the extreme solubility of the subsamples, may not have removed... It should be emphasized that no similar age discrepancy was found between the solely ultrasonic and ultrasonic and chemically cleaned subsamples of the other 13 scrolls that were dated.[37]

4QTQahat is a suspected outlier not simply because its radiocarbon age is older than that of 4QLevi^a ar whose scribal copy we would expect to be contemporary, but also because the radiocarbon age of 4QTQahat is markedly older than the radiocarbon dates of all other Qumran texts which have been dated. Furthermore, there is a ready mechanism which may account for the anomaly. That there was contamination from an older source on both samples from 4QTQahat before cleaning is a fact. If this contamination was successfully removed by the chemical pretreatment procedure, the radiocarbon date reported by Zurich may be an accurate date. But if some of this contamination was not removed despite the pretreatment procedures of the Zurich laboratory, then the radiocarbon date reported for 4QTQahat is older than the true date of this text. Present data suggests that this latter option is in fact the case.

8. 4Q258 COMMUNITY RULE (4QS^d)

A second example of apparent contamination affecting a Qumran text's radiocarbon date appears to have occurred in the battery of AMS measurements of scrolls done at Tucson. In 1994-95 the Tucson laboratory measured some twelve texts from Qumran (among other items), eleven of which had not previously received AMS measurements. In this battery the laboratory reported an age-measurement for a sample from 4QS^d (4Q258, an exemplar of the Community Rule) of BP 1823 +/- 24.[38] By 1997 calibration, this

---

[37] Bonani et al., "Fourteen Dead Sea Scrolls," 31.

[38] Item 18 in Table A.

measurement gives a calibrated date of 133-237 CE at one sigma (two sigma: 129-318 CE). This result was unexpected, since it is considerably later than believed possible for a Qumran text.[39] Yet this radiocarbon date was produced from five separate measurements on this particular sample in the Tucson accelerator which agreed with one another. However surprising, this *was* the date the Tucson laboratory was measuring for this sample. Because of the unexpected and puzzling date, a second sample from 4QS^d was cut from a different area of the text and sent to Tucson for dating.[40] The laboratory subjected this sample to extensive additional cleaning in acetone in an effort to knock out any possible contamination, and this time measured a radiocarbon age of BP 1964 +/- 45, which after calibration is 36 BCE-81 CE at the one-sigma range (two-sigma: 50 BCE-130 CE).

A common way in which laboratories test for the presence of sample contamination is by comparing dates on multiple samples of the same item that have been taken from different locations for inconsistent results. A simple test for inconsistency that is used within the radiocarbon profession is a "chi-square test," a mathematical procedure used to distinguish radiocarbon dates which have a greater degree of separation in their measurements than can be expected to have been produced by items of identical true ages (at a confidence level in this conclusion of 95%). According to this test, the radiocarbon measurements for the two samples of 4QS^d are inconsistent beyond acceptable margins of error. The practically certain explanation for the two results on 4QS^d is that some modern contamination was present that was not completely removed in the pretreatment on the first sample; and that this contamination or more of it was removed in the second attempt, or else it was not present to begin with in the second sample.

It should be noted that 4QS^d was redated because of an extraneous reason: the date produced by AMS was believed to be wrong on other grounds. As it turns out, the skepticism concerning the accuracy of the second-century CE radiocarbon date of the first

---

[39] 4QS^d is identified in a list of texts for which pieces were found by excavators in Qumran Cave 4 (see S. Pfann, "Sites in the Judean Desert Where Texts have been found," in E. Tov with S. Pfann [eds.], *The Dead Sea Scrolls on Microfiche. A Comprehensive Facsimile Edition of the Texts from the Judean Desert. Companion Volume* [Leiden: IDC and Brill, 1993] 109-19, esp. 112).

[40] Item 19 in Table A.

sample of 4QS^d was justified on radiocarbon grounds by the lack of repeatability in the second sample tested. But there is an important question raised by this procedure that demands consideration. Can it be known with certainty that the radiocarbon dates of no *other* scrolls might not be subject to *similarly illusory* late datings? But if, after calibration, such similarly inaccurate radiocarbon datings did not exceed 70 CE, it would not alert anyone to demand a redating (since it is commonly assumed that the scrolls were finally abandoned in the caves near Qumran in the second half of the first century CE). Were any other Qumran text radiocarbon results also erroneously late, but—owing to the accident of their radiocarbon dates not exceeding 70 CE—not redated?

9. YOUNG SCHOLARS PORING OVER TEXTS

The concern over contamination affecting radiocarbon measurements of Qumran texts is heightened by the knowledge of the identified and extensive use of at least one modern contaminant that was applied directly to the scrolls. Original members of the editing team organized by R. De Vaux, the excavator of Qumran, who worked in the 1950's on the texts housed in the Rockefeller Museum have reported that oil (such as castor oil) was brushed routinely onto manuscripts in order to improve the visibility of the letters.

> During the past season, the...excavated lot [of Cave 4 manuscripts] was... prepared and examined by the writer... In the worst cases, a non-acid oil must be used to reveal the script on the deteriorated surface of the leather (Cross, 1954).[41]
>
> We find that a very light brushing with a camel hair brush touched with a non-acid oil, like castor oil, will make the marl translucent and bring up the writing very clearly (Allegro, 1956).[42]
>
> Cleaning of the darker patches with oil, to bring out the writing—something chemically harmless, I am told, but some of us used it too generously in the early days; infrared film could probably have given us the same results without permanently darkening the surface (Strugnell, 1993).[43]

---

[41] F. M. Cross, "The Manuscripts of the Dead Sea Caves," *BA* 17 (1954) 2-21, esp. 14-15.

[42] J. M. Allegro et al., *The Dead Sea Scrolls* (Harmondsworth, Middlesex: Pelican, 1956) 44.

[43] J. Strugnell, "On the History of the Photography of the Discoveries in the Judean Desert for the International Group of Editors," in Tov with Pfann (eds.), *Companion Volume*, 122-34, esp. 125.

Here we get a picture of young scholars routinely applying castor oil to texts, oblivious to the havoc this process might be creating for future radiocarbon dates. (Yet how would they have known?) Castor oil comes from the seeds of the plant *ricinus communis*, and unfortunately contains modern carbon. If a Scrolls sample was contaminated with castor oil or some equivalent at the time of measurement, it would give an erroneously young radiocarbon date. The cleaning procedures reported by both laboratories as applied to the Qumran text samples—with the exception of four Qumran texts in the Tucson battery—would very unlikely have removed castor oil had any been present.[44]

On the texts it measured the Zurich laboratory followed a procedure which is often able to alert a laboratory to the presence of sample contamination. This consisted of dividing the original samples into subsamples, subjecting these subsamples to different levels of cleaning treatments, and comparing the results obtained.[45] If there is a discrepancy between the two subsamples' dates beyond expected margins of error, the laboratory is alerted to the presence of contamination. It was this method which revealed the existence of severe contamination affecting both of the samples from 4QTQahat. But in the seven other Qumran texts that were measured in the Zurich battery, the Zurich laboratory reported finding no significant disagreements in age-measurements among the subsamples from each text, given the different cleaning preparations. This information provides some basis for believing that most if not all of the remaining Qumran text AMS measurements in the Zurich battery were not affected by contamination.

This procedure of comparing measurements on subsamples that have undergone different levels of treatment was not done at Tucson.

---

[44] Both the Zurich and Tucson laboratories cleaned all samples with a standard "acid-base-acid" procedure (HCl, NaOH, HCl), as reported in Bonani et al., "Fourteen Dead Sea Scrolls" (1992), 846-49; and Jull et al., "Radiocarbon Dating of Scrolls" (1995), 11-13. This procedure is effective in removing most contaminants but would have had little effect (according to chemists) on castor oil embedded in parchment or papyrus material, had any been present. (A solvent such as acetone would be needed to remove castor oil.) All the Zurich samples received battering in ultrasound (in water), but none of these items received acetone cleaning. Samples from four Qumran texts in Tucson's battery—1QS, 4Q266, 4Q317, and 4Q258—received cleaning in acetone to remove visible glue.

[45] Bonani et al., "Fourteen Dead Sea Scrolls" (1992), 846-49.

Since the laboratory there was constrained in certain cases by very limited amounts of sample material it received, it used all of this scarce material for the purpose of "real" measurements. While aware of these circumstances, one nevertheless wishes that some check comparable to what was done at Zurich had been provided at Tucson. Since this kind of information does not exist for the Tucson data, we are blind on this particular point.

However, other information that was obtained in the Tucson battery is useful as a check on the incidence of sample contamination. For example, Tucson dated a sample from 4QpaleoExodus^m (4Q22) as having a ^{14}C age of BP 2044 +/- 65,[46] which after calibration is 164-144 BCE or 116 BCE-48 CE.[47] A repair patch which had been applied to this same text some time after its writing was also dated. The age of the patch was measured at BP 2024 +/- 39,[48] which after calibration gives 51 BCE-47 CE. The radiocarbon ages of the manuscript and patch are thus similar. Though not an infallible indicator, the agreement in these radiocarbon dates increases the confidence level that neither was significantly affected by contamination.

Another text is the Great Isaiah Scroll (1QIsa^a),[49] which was dated in both batteries. Zurich's date for 1QIsa^a was BP 2128 +/- 38,[50] which after calibration is 201-93 BCE. Tucson's date for 1QIsa^a was almost identical to that measured at Zurich,[51] at BP 2141 +/- 32 (341-325 BCE or 202-114 BCE after calibration).[52]

4QSam^c, which was dated at Zurich, and 1QS, dated at Tucson, are generally acknowledged to have been written by the same scribe.[53] If this is the case, both texts should produce similar radiocarbon dates,

---

[46] Item 26 in Table A.

[47] For the two date ranges, see note 32 above.

[48] Item 27 in Table A.

[49] I.e. the famous Isaiah scroll that was discovered among the first Dead Sea finds in 1947.

[50] Item 4 in Table A.

[51] Item 32 in Table A.

[52] According to the report in ʿAtiqot, the Tucson facility was not informed about the identity of this text or its age details until the measurements had been completed.

[53] F. M. Cross, "The Development of the Jewish Scripts," in G. E. Wright (ed.), *Essays in Honor of William F. Albright* (Garden City, NY: Doubleday, 1961) 133-202, esp. 198 n.116; E. Ulrich, "4QSam^c: A Fragmentary Manuscript of 2 Samuel 14-15 from the Scribe of *Serek Hay-yahad* (1QS)," *BASOR* 233 (1979) 1-4.

which is the case. Zurich's date for 4QSam^c was BP 2095 +/- 49,[54] which is 196-47 BCE after calibration, while Tucson's date for 1QS was BP 2041 +/- 68 (after calibration, 164-144 BCE or 116 BCE-50 CE).[55] The fact that these radiocarbon dates are in agreement with each other, within acceptable margins of error, increases confidence that neither was contaminated.

Between the two laboratories, seven texts bearing internal dates were measured: four at Zurich and three at Tucson.[56] After calibration six of these radiocarbon dates correspond well with the true dates of these texts. (In the seventh case, the Kefar Bebayou text measured at Tucson, the internal date falls at one edge of the two-sigma radiocarbon date range). Contamination did not significantly affect the radiocarbon dates of at least six, and perhaps all seven, of these manuscripts. All seven of these internally-dated texts were written on papyrus. Another of the Qumran texts on papyrus that was dated in Tucson's battery is 4QMidrash Sepher Moshe (4Q249),[57] for which Tucson measured a radiocarbon date of BP 2097 +/- 50 (196-47 BCE after calibration). This date is in agreement with most of the Tucson laboratory's radiocarbon dates for Qumran texts that are made of parchment (animal skin). Indirect means such as these strengthens confidence that most of Tucson's AMS parchment datings were not affected by contamination.

With respect to castor oil contamination, the samples from one of the texts named above (1QS) and from three other Qumran texts in the Tucson battery (4QD^a [4Q266], 4QPhases of the Moon [4Q317], and 4QS^d [4Q258]) received cleaning in acetone and ultrasound in order to remove visible glue. It can be assumed that this treatment would also have removed castor oil from these samples had any been present. 1QpHab can also be exempted as a likely castor oil candidate for two reasons. First, 1QpHab was never in the Rockefeller Museum in the 1950's where certain scholars are known to have been using the castor oil.[58] Second, the sample for 1QpHab was cut from the bottom edge of a large amount of blank space below the last lines

---

[54] Item 6 in Table A.

[55] Item 17 in Table A.

[56] See Table A for specific data.

[57] Item 23 in Table A.

[58] After a brief period in North America following its discovery, 1QpHab was housed at the Shrine of the Book in Jerusalem.

of the final column (13), which has no difficult letter readings and thus would not have required castor oil.

If it can be assumed that radiocarbon dates of the texts in the few paragraphs above were not contaminated, the uncertainty concerning contamination becomes reduced to four remaining Qumran texts in the Tucson battery for which the same kind of comparative information does not exist. These four texts are 4QpPs^a (4Q171), 4QMessianic Apocalypse (4Q521), 4QD^b (4Q267), and 4QEnastr^a (4Q208). The radiocarbon dates for these texts may well be accurate. However, the only basis for confidence from the information currently at our disposal that these dates were not contaminated with castor oil comes down to an assumption that the particular samples cut from these texts were not contaminated to begin with. This is likely to be a reasonable assumption in most cases.[59] But further individual cases of dates affected by contamination cannot *a priori* be excluded; caution should thus be exercised in relying upon individual dates from among this final group of four texts as a primary basis for argument.

10. 4Q171 COMMENTARY ON PSALMS (4QpPs^a)

The AMS measurement on the pesher 4QpPs^a, with its internal portrayal of a contemporary Teacher of Righteousness,[60] is of particular interest. The Tucson facility reported a measurement for this text of BP 1944 +/- 23 which gives a calibrated date of 29-81 CE at one sigma (two sigma: 3-126 CE).[61] The age of 4QpPs^a as represented in this radiocarbon measurement is younger than the age measured at Tucson for another of the biblical pesharim, the Commentary on Habakkuk (1QpHab). The Tucson date for 1QpHab was BP 2054 +/- 22, which after calibration is 88-2 BCE.[62] At the two-sigma level there are two calibrated date range possibilities for the date of 1QpHab: 160-148 BCE and 111 BCE-2 CE. Over a dozen exemplars of this type of commentary, known as the "continuous pesharim," were found at Qumran, only in single copies and being

---

[59] It is intrinsically unlikely that castor oil, applied to readings of difficult letters on some texts, would affect more than a fraction of samples that were cut from the margins of manuscripts chosen at random.

[60] 4QpPs^a frgs. 1–10 ii lines 18-20; iii 15-17; iv 8-10; and iv 26-27.

[61] Item 20 in Table A.

[62] Item 16 in Table A.

practically identical in formal and scribal characteristics, language, and motifs. There is thus good reason to expect that 4QpPs^a and 1QpHab should be contemporaneous both in composition and in their single scribal copies. If this analysis is correct, the apparent difference in radiocarbon dates for 1QpHab and 4QpPs^a may represent not a real difference in dates, but rather an anomaly in the radiocarbon measurements.

When viewed in isolation, it is difficult to judge whether the AMS date for 4QpPs^a or for 1QpHab is the stronger claimant for the hypothesized, approximately identical true date for both of these texts. Preference for the former (4QpPs^a) would offer significant vindication for Robert Eisenman, who since 1983 has argued for mid-first century CE themes and dates of composition in the pesharim, and who played a role in bringing about the start of AMS dating of the Scrolls.[63] However, with recourse to the interpretive framework that will be proposed at the end of this article,[64] the difference in dates between the two pesharim texts is accounted for on different grounds, with preference given to the AMS result on 1QpHab. Specifically, the proposal will be made that the true date for 4QpPs^a is better reflected by the radiocarbon date for its contemporary, 1QpHab, than by the radiocarbon date on itself.

11. MEASUREMENTS ON TEXTS WITH INTERNAL DATES

Three texts with internal dates from the years 128, 130 and 134-35 CE were measured in the battery at Tucson. Two of the internally-dated texts in the Zurich battery were also from this same period, bearing dates identified as 130-31 and 134-35 CE, respectively. The radiocarbon dates of these five contemporary Dead Sea texts are presented in Figure 2 (on the next page). The first two measurements are from Zurich (the papyrus deeds XḤev/Se 11 and Murabbaʿât 30),[65] and the bottom three from Tucson (the papyrus contracts Naḥal Ḥever 21 and the "Kefar Bebayou" text; and the papyrus deed Naḥal Ḥever 19).[66]

---

[63] R. Eisenman, *The Dead Sea Scrolls and the First Christians* (Shaftesbury, Dorset: Element, 1996).

[64] See sections 13 ("A Question of Evidence") and 14 ("The Single-Generation Hypothesis").

[65] See Table A, items 12 and 13, respectively.

[66] See also items 31, 33 and 34, respectively, in Table A.

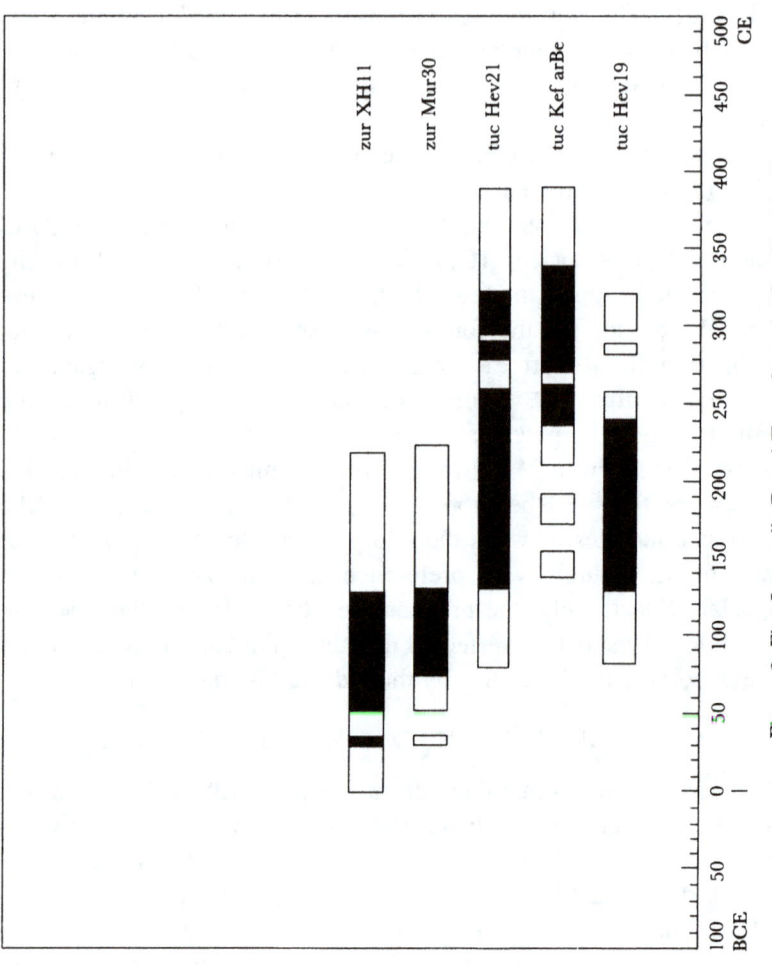

Figure 2. Five Internally-Dated Texts from the Bar-Kochba Era

These data show that Zurich's measurements are a little older than those of Tucson, and that one of the texts measured at Tucson (the "Kefar Bebayou" text)[67] seems to be more offset than the others. Interpreting the radiocarbon date for the Kefar Bebayou text is not clearcut. Its internal date is "the third year of the freedom of Israel," i.e. the third year of the Bar Kochba revolt; thus the document must have been written in either 134 or 135 CE. At Tucson the ^{14}C age of the Kefar Bebayou text was measured at BP 1758 +/- 36,[68] which after calibration gives a one-sigma date range of 237-340 and a two-sigma date range of 140-390 CE.

As it stands, the true date of the Kefar Bebayou text is just outside the calibrated two-sigma range for the radiocarbon date. The extent of this offset may, however, be misleading, since the calibrations of all five of these Bar-Kochba-era texts depend upon the position of a single data-point in the calibration curve, at 135 CE. As can be seen in Figure 1, the calibration curve reflects a sudden, steep drop between 125 and 135 CE. Two possibilities are that the Tucson laboratory may have been accurately measuring lower levels of ^{14}C in the atmosphere of Judaea in certain years than are reflected on the calibration curve,[69] or that Tucson's measurements may be indicating a lower data-point in the curve at 135 CE itself.[70] If so, this would weaken the visual impression that the Tucson laboratory is reporting—in this single point in the data at which there is an objective basis for checking—"later" than true dates. On the other hand, Zurich's two dates could be used to argue in precisely the opposite direction. It thus appears that the two laboratories are measuring on opposite sides of the calibration curve at this point.

Yet it is by no means certain that the two laboratories are measuring differently. If we suppose that the two Zurich texts were written on papyrus which had been manufactured several years before its use for writing, that papyrus, when it was living, would be

---

[67] This term comes from an early reading of a place-name in the text, although the reading is actually "Kefar Baru." See J. T. Milik, "Un Contrat Juif de l'an 134 après J.-C.," *RB* 61 (1954) 182-90; M. Broshi and E. Qimron, "A House Sale Deed from Kefar Baro from the Time of Bar Kokhba," *IEJ* 36 (1986) 201-14.

[68] Item 33 in Table A.

[69] In which a line was simply drawn between the measured points at 125 and 135 CE.

[70] Noted in Jull et al., "Radiocarbon Dating of Scrolls" (1995), 15-16.

placed in one of the earlier years likely to register significantly higher ^{14}C, as is reflected in the 125 CE data-point (with a ^{14}C level of BP 1898 +/- 11). Now let us suppose that the papyrus-sheets of the three texts dated by Tucson were freshly prepared at the time of their use for writing, and came from papyrus plants that had been cut in years after the sharp drop in ^{14}C levels which are reflected in the 135 CE point on the calibration curve in Figure 1 (i.e. at BP 1839 +/- 13). If this were the case, both laboratories would then have measured each of their texts accurately, with no actual difference between the two sets of results—despite the visual impression that a real difference exists. The anomaly arises because of the sharp drop at this particular point in the calibration curve, giving rise to differences that were greater than usual in this decade.

If, on the other hand, these five texts dated by the two laboratories were all written on papyrus from plants that were cut in the years of the dates written on them, the five radiocarbon dates could be reflecting a systematic offset between the two facilities. If such an offset existed, its correction would have the effect of either making the calibrated date ranges for the Zurich texts younger, or the calibrated date ranges for the Tucson texts older, or some combination of both. There is, however, insufficient information for us to know to which laboratory this offset would best be attributed or to quantify it, or—most importantly—to know that such an offset really existed at all.

12. LINEN: SCROLL WRAPPINGS

Two linen items were also dated in the Tucson AMS battery. One sample came from linen with an embroidered silk border that had been purchased from an antiquities dealer, and is recorded as from "Qumran Cave 2."[71] The AMS measurements gave a medieval date for this linen (BP 664 +/- 36, or 1279-1397 CE when calibrated at the two-sigma date range).[72] Since this linen is described as similar to medieval textiles that have been found by excavators at Wadi Murabbaʿât Cave 2, this has been suggested as the likely true site where the linen was discovered.[73] The AMS measurement supports the conclusion that the provenance of this item was misidentified; this

---

[71] The linen may well have been found at Murbbaʿât.

[72] Item 36 in Table A.

[73] See the comments of E. Tov and M. Broshi in Jull et al., "Radiocarbon Dating of Scrolls" (1996), 90.

linen had no material association with scrolls, and for purposes of dating Qumran texts is of no further relevance.[74]

But the other linen item which was measured at Tucson—identified as from "Qumran Cave 4"—does appear to be associated with the Qumran scrolls. Attached to this particular sample was a piece of leather thong, of the type that was used to hold scrolls. In the same box were further pieces of the thong, including a piece with slits; it is reportedly similar to other leather thongs that have been found with Qumran manuscripts.[75] The linen was reported to be similar in appearance to linen wrapping from Cave 1 in association with scrolls found there.[76] Therefore, in addition to the claim that this linen came from the cave, there seems good reason to link this linen item to the Qumran Cave 4 deposits of texts. This was the first time since 1950 that a linen wrapper which was used in association with the scrolls had been carbon-dated.

There are two grounds for special interest in this AMS measurement of a linen item from Cave 4. First, because of the difference in function and material of this item, the radiocarbon date on the Cave 4 linen may be exempt from the types of contamination that are of concern with respect to dating scrolls. Unlike the solubility problem that was reported by the laboratories during the cleaning of parchment and papyrus samples, there is no indication of a solubility problem in the cleaning of the linen.[77] In addition, scholars in the 1950's would not have used oils such as castor oil on linen in order to improve letter readings.

A second reason for interest is what the radiocarbon date for this linen may actually be measuring. The true date of the Cave 4 linen

---

[74] The linen pieces from Murabbaʿât Cave 2 to which this item is similar are estimated on art-historical grounds to date to the 12th-13th century CE (G. M. Crowfoot and E. Crowfoot, "The Textiles and Basketry," in P. Benoit, J. T. Milik and R. De Vaux [eds.], *Les Grottes de Murabbaʿât* (DJD 2; Oxford: Clarendon Press, 1961] 51-63, esp. 61). The art-historical estimate agrees well with the date for this item that was obtained by AMS measurement.

[75] Jull et al., "Radiocarbon Dating of Scrolls" (1995), 19 (citing an Israel Museum exhibit of comparative materials).

[76] A. Baginski, cited in Jull et al., "Radiocarbon Dating of Scrolls" (1995), 19.

[77] In the Zurich laboratory's description of cleaning of linen thread attached to 4QLevi^a ar, the use of full-strength acid and base solutions was reported, in contrast to a reduction to $1/10$ strength solutions in the cleaning of parchment samples (Bonani et al., "Fourteen Dead Sea Scrolls" [1992], 846).

item is presumably close to the date when the scroll it was wrapped around was deposited in the cave. If all of the large quantity of scrolls went into Cave 4 at about the same time, then the date of any linen wrapping on any of these manuscripts may reflect an approximate date of deposit for all of the scrolls from this cave. The AMS measurement on this linen may then be measuring something close to a date for the deposit of the scrolls in the caves. The Tucson laboratory's date on the Cave 4 linen was BP 2069 +/- 40,[78] which after calibration is 165-144 or 117-2 BCE.

13. A QUESTION OF EVIDENCE

Sometimes the most important questions are the unexpected ones. If the true date of the Cave 4 linen wrapping reflects a date of deposit for the scrolls in this cave, the question arises whether there is evidence for the existence of texts at Qumran later than the date that is reflected in the AMS measurement for the Cave 4 linen.

No reference or allusion to an historical figure, name, or event later than the mid-1st century BCE has been securely identified in any of the over 800 texts which are of uncontested Qumran provenance. On the basis of the 1994 Humbert and Chambon publication of R. de Vaux's Qumran excavation notes,[79] the wide-mouthed "scroll jars" that were found in association with the scrolls and also buried in the floors of certain rooms at Qumran can hardly be shown to have been buried there in De Vaux's Period II.[80] Other items that were found in some scroll-bearing caves and non-scroll-bearing caves—such as lamps and domestic pottery—attest to the presence of people camping in caves at some point in the mid-first century CE.[81] These items, however, are not securely associated with the scrolls.

Nor do present radiocarbon data provide secure grounds for confirming the existence of any textual activity at Qumran in the first-century CE. In an archaeological destruction layer, the greatest number of ceramics, coins and other artifacts are usually dated chronologically at the late end, just before the date of the destruction, with a "tail" of earlier dated items going back in time. This well-

---

[78] Item 35 in Table A.

[79] J-B. Humbert and A. Chambon, *Fouilles de Khirbet Qumrân et de Aïn Feshka* (NTOA Arch 1; Fribourg: Éditions Universitaires, 1994).

[80] I.e. 1st cent. CE, as distinguished from de Vaux's Period Ib (1st cent. BCE).

[81] On the basis of lamp datings.

known pattern of distribution which describes many archaeological finds[82] might be considered a useful hypothesis that is of relevance to the distribution of the dates of production of the Qumran texts. Let us suppose there to have been a flourishing text-production process during the period prior to the latest date when texts were deposited in the caves at Qumran (whenever that was). If so, texts from this last period of text production—when they have been dated by radiocarbon methods—would then show a spread of dates. The greatest number of radiocarbon dates in a distribution of this kind would be dispersed around the approximate generation of the date when the texts were deposited. But as in a bell-curve distribution, some of the radiocarbon dates of the texts would be a little older, and some a little younger, than the true date of deposit.

Paradoxically, the more radiocarbon datings that are done of items in the last decades of such a distribution, the greater the accumulation of dates which will appear slightly later than the true latest date of any of the texts involved. This could give the illusion of accumulating probability for a true later date for at least one of those texts —when in fact nothing is happening beyond a bell-curve phenomenon. Determining on the basis of radiocarbon data a terminus date for an archaeological destruction layer, or in this case, the latest date of deposit for a large number of texts, thus becomes a complex problem. In principle, this question should be amenable to statistical analysis using computer programs; however, such analysis assumes input of uncontaminated dates, or else a data base that is sufficiently large for the effects of a few contaminated dates to be absorbed and minimized.[83]

We are thus faced with a dilemma in interpretation. There are at least two apparent instances where contamination has affected results in the two batteries of Qumran text-datings; thus certainty cannot be assumed—at least in those cases where comparative measurements of differently-treated subsamples were not done—that one or two key radiocarbon dates at the critical late end of the spectrum are not contaminated. Out of twenty-one total items measured between the

---

[82] As well as distributions of copyright dates in modern libraries!

[83] For the complexities involved in statistical analysis of radiocarbon dates, note the discussion in S. Manning, *The Absolute Chronology of the Aegean Early Bronze Age: Archaeology, Radiocarbon, and History* (Sheffield: Sheffield Academic Press, 1995) 125-42.

two laboratories that are relevant to Qumran text datings,[84] there are five radiocarbon dates of Qumran items in which the bulk of the date possibilities after calibration lie in the first century CE. One of these (1QH[a]) is in the Zurich battery, and the other four are in the Tucson battery: 4QD[a] (4Q266), 4QMessianic Apocalypse (4Q521), 4QpPs[a] (4Q171), and 4QS[d] (4Q258).[85]

The published palaeographic dating estimates locate two of these texts, 4QD[a] (4Q266) and 4QMessianic Apocalypse (4Q521), in the first part of the first century BCE. With respect to the first text, Professor F. M. Cross wrote: "[4Q266] can be no later than the first half of the first century BC...before the Roman conquest of 63 BC... by palaeographical evidence,"[86] while Ada Yardeni characterized its script as "a semi-cursive hand [which]...should be dated to the first half or to the middle of the first century BCE."[87] The writing of 4Q521, meanwhile, has been characterized by É. Puech as "a type of formal Hasmonean script...in the first quarter of the first century, between 100 and 80 [BCE]."[88]

But the radiocarbon age reported by Tucson for 4Q266 was BP 1954 +/- 38,[89] which after calibration is 4-82 CE at one sigma (44 BCE-129 CE at two sigma). For 4Q521 Tucson measured an age of BP 1984 +/- 33,[90] which is 39 BCE-66 CE after calibration (at two sigma: 49 BCE-116 CE).

In light of the lack of a single internally-dated Hebrew or Aramaic manuscript in Palestine in the two century-period 150 BCE-50 CE for comparison, it might be suggested that the high-precision palaeographic estimates that have been given to these two texts are somewhat premature. Nevertheless, it would also be premature to declare that palaeographic estimates in the first part of the first century BCE that have been proposed for 4Q266 and 4Q521 must be

---

[84] I.e. nineteen texts, one repair patch, and one linen wrapping.

[85] The second sample.

[86] F. M. Cross, *The Ancient Library of Qumran* (3rd ed., Minneapolis: Fortress, 1995) 96.

[87] A. Yardeni in J. Baumgarten (ed.), *Qumran Cave 4. XIII: The Damascus Document* (DJD 18; Oxford: Clarendon Press, 1996) 26-30, esp. 26, 30.

[88] My translation from the French of É. Puech, "Une apocalypse messianique (4Q 521)," *RevQ* 60 (1992) 475-519, esp. 477, 480.

[89] Item 15 in Table A.

[90] Item 21 in Table A.

false on the basis of existing radiocarbon evidence. This assessment rests on the good agreement of the palaeographic estimates for these texts (early first century BCE) with strong patterns of other radiocarbon dates pointing to this same period for many Qumran texts, as well as the expectation that a small number of radiocarbon dates will not overlap with true dates even at the two-sigma uncertainty levels.

Since 4QpPs[a] has the youngest radiocarbon date for Qumran texts in either battery, its results are *a priori* of less secure confidence than the dates for the others. In addition to this general observation there is a specific reason for questioning the radiocarbon date of 4QpPs[a], i.e. the older radiocarbon date for 1QpHab, with which the scribal copy 4QpPs[a] ought to be contemporaneous.[91] If 4QpPs[a] is an outlier, the remaining dates in both batteries become in principle explicable as "measurement scatter"[92] of a larger pool of radiocarbon dates that converge in the first century BCE, and which are contemporaneous with the date of the Cave 4 linen.

It is, of course, possible that there are *other* grounds that are capable of documenting a 1st-century CE date for some Qumran texts. But such reasons for certainty do not include internal references within the texts, the dates of materials that were found in archaeological association, and existing radiocarbon data. The issue involved is one of evidence. If the three grounds just cited do not provide the needed certainty, how secure are other grounds which may be given for alleging the existence of scribal activity on any Qumran text that is datable to the first century CE?

Figure 3 (on the following page) lists calibrated radiocarbon dates for all Qumran texts and items associated with these texts that have received AMS measurements at Zurich and Tucson. It is these measurements on twenty-one distinct items which constitute our present database of radiocarbon information for dating Qumran texts. The following features should be noted: (a) For 4QS[d], the AMS measurement of the second sample (rather than the first) is regarded as the true radiocarbon date. (b) The single radiocarbon date for 1QIsa[a] is derived from a weighted average of the separate Zurich and Tucson dates (BP 2135 +/- 29). (c) AMS measurements

---

[91] See above, section 10: "4Q171 Commentary on Psalms (4QpPs[a])."

[92] "Measurement scatter" denotes a statistical spread around a "true date." A useful analogy is the blast from a shotgun at a target and the spread of the individual shotgun pellets.

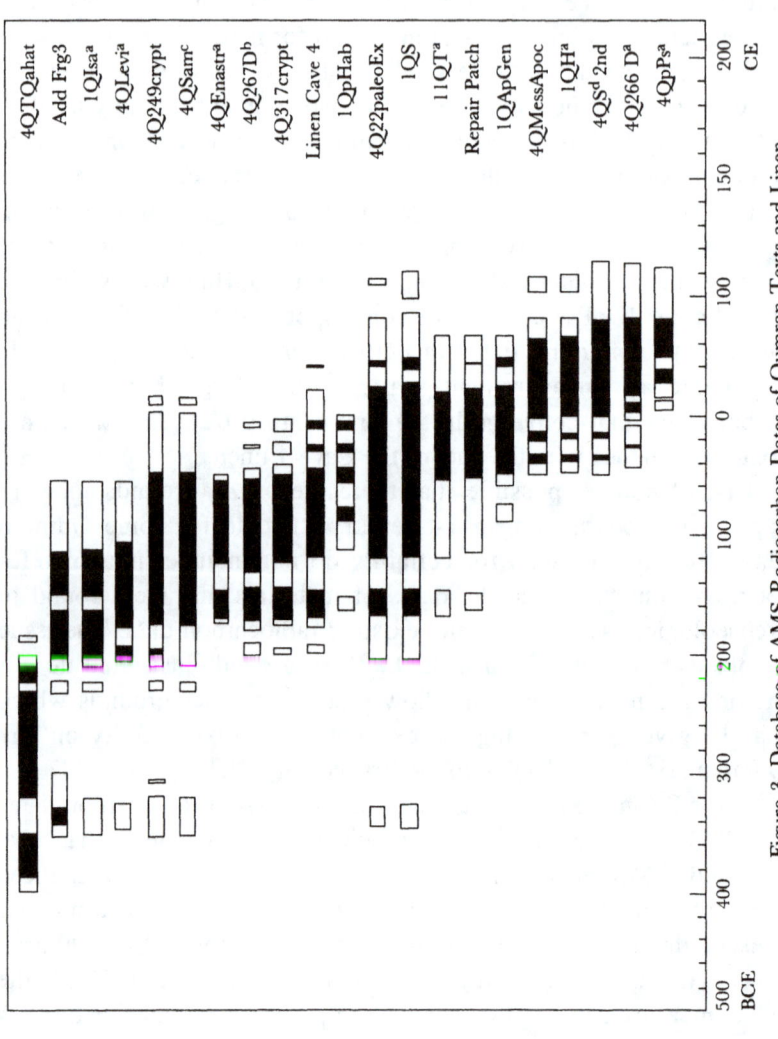

Figure 3. Database of AMS Radiocarbon Dates of Qumran Texts and Linen

for three economic texts with 4Q numbers that were dated in the Tucson battery (4Q342, 4Q344 and 4Q345) are not included because, according to their editors, these had nothing to do with Qumran.[93]

The striking thing about these data is the small difference between how this pattern of distribution would look were the texts all from a *floruit* of the same generation or two, instead of from various points within the presumed 200- or 300-year span of continuous scribal activity that is commonly believed to be represented in the Qumran texts.[94]

14. THE SINGLE-GENERATION HYPOTHESIS

Against this background, and in this collection that commemorates the Fiftieth Anniversary of the discovery of the Dead Sea Scrolls, I would like to propose a redating of the Qumran manuscripts on the basis of a new understanding of present radiocarbon information. In this new interpretation—which I term the "single-generation hypothesis"—most if not all of the radiocarbon dates reflect "measurement scatter" around a more narrow spread of true dates, and with a far greater number of contemporary texts, than has previously been considered.

According to this hypothesis, almost all scribal copies of Qumran texts come from a single generation. While the term "single generation" is to some extent arbitrary, it is convenient for expressing the notion that these documents represent contemporaneous scribal contexts to a far greater degree than has formerly been appreciated. The possibility is open that earlier texts also exist, including in principle a few from even a century or more earlier. But there will be no texts later than the date of the single generation. According to this hypothesis, most if not all AMS measurements on Qumran texts have measured not different true dates but instead virtually the same date—that of the single generation. The common view is that the Qumran texts reflect a lengthy duration of scribal processes that

---

[93] H. M. Cotton and A. Yardeni, *Aramaic, Hebrew, and Greek Documentary Texts from Naḥal Ḥever and Other Sites, with an Appendix Containing Alleged Qumran Texts* (The Seiyal Collection II) (DJD 17; Oxford: Clarendon Press, 1997) 283-84.

[94] Compare the discussion and illustrations in Aitken (*Science-Based Dating*, 96-98), and Taylor (*Radiocarbon Dating*) 139-42, concerning the distribution patterns of radiocarbon measurements around single events.

culminated in the second half of the first century CE. But in the single-generation hypothesis, the first century CE disappears from Qumran's textual horizon. These radiocarbon dates become an echo of a generation of widespread, diverse, and contemporaneous scribal activity whose date of *floruit*, as well as the text deposits in the caves near Qumran, were situated in the first century BCE.

If the single-generation hypothesis is correct, then the formal and semiformal Qumran scripts that have been called "Herodian" are actually older than the dates suggested for them by Professor Cross ("Development of the Jewish Scripts," and *Ancient Library of Qumran*, Figs. 17 and 18). In principle, no other class of palaeographic dating estimates on Qumran texts is challenged by the single generation hypothesis. The assumption that Qumran manuscripts written in "Herodian" scripts must indicate that scribes were writing as late as this period (ca. 30 BCE-70 CE), is regarded by the present writer as an uncorroborated scholarly construction.

SELECT BIBLIOGRAPHY

Aitken, M. J. *Science-Based Dating in Archaeology* (London and New York: Longman, 1990).

Bonani, G., M. Broshi, I. Carmi, S. Ivy, J. Strugnell, and W. Wölfli. "Radiocarbon Dating of the Dead Sea Scrolls," ʿ*Atiqot* 20 (1991) 27-32.

—. S. Ivy, W. Wölfli, M. Broshi, I. Carmi and J. Strugnell. "Radiocarbon Dating of Fourteen Dead Sea Scrolls," *Radiocarbon* 34 (1992) 843-49.

Bowman, S. *Radiocarbon Dating* (London: British Museum Press, 1990).

Caldarero, N. "Storage Conditions and Physical Treatments Relating to the Dating of the Dead Sea Scrolls," *Radiocarbon* 37 (1995) 21-32.

Goranson, S. "Radiocarbon Dating the Dead Sea Scrolls," *BA* 54 (1991) 172.

Humbert, J-B. and A. Chambon. *Fouilles de Khirbet Qumrân et de Aïn Feshka* (NTOA Arch 1; Fribourg: Éditions Universitaires, 1994).

Jull, A. J. T., D. J. Donahue, M. Broshi and E. Tov. "Radiocarbon Dating of Scrolls and Linen Fragments from the Judean Desert," *Radiocarbon* 37 (1995) 11-19.

—. "Radiocarbon Dating of Scrolls and Linen Fragments from the Judean Desert," ʿ*Atiqot* 28 (1996) 85-91.

Kapera, Z. J. "AMS Carbon-14 Dating of the Scrolls," *The Qumran Chronicle* 2 (1992) 39-43.

Laperrousaz, E.–M. "La datation d'objets provenant de Qumrân, en particulier par la méthode utilisant les propriétés du Carbone 14," in M. Delcor (ed.), *Qumrân: Sa piété, sa théologie et son milieu* (Paris-Gembloux: Duculot, 1978) 55-60.

Manning, S. W. "Section 2. Introduction," in *The Absolute Chronology of the Aegean Early Bronze Age. Archaeology, Radiocarbon, and History* (Sheffield: Sheffield Academic Press, 1995) 125-42.

Pardee, D. G. (chair of session). "Report and Discussion Concerning Radiocarbon Dating of Fourteen Dead Sea Scrolls," (Paper of G. Bonani et al., with discussion of Qumran scholars afterward), in M. O. Wise, N. Golb, J. J. Collins and D. G. Pardee (eds.), *Methods of Investigation of the Dead Sea Scrolls and the Khirbet Qumran Site. Present Realities and Future Prospects* (ANYAS 722; New York: The New York Academy of Sciences, 1994) 441-53.

Sellers, O. R. "Date of Cloth from the ʿAin Feshka Cave," *BA* 14 (1951) 29.

Shanks, H. "Carbon-14 Tests Substantiate Scrolls Dates," *BAR* 17/6 (1991), 72.

—. "New Carbon-14 Results Leave Room for Debate," *BAR* 21/4 (1995), 61.

Taylor, R. E. et al. *Radiocarbon Dating. An Archaeological Perspective.* (Orlando, FL: Academic Press, 1987).

Zeuner, F. E. "Notes on Qumrân," *PEQ* 92 (1960) 27-36.

TABLE A

CALIBRATED RADIOCARBON DATES ON
DEAD SEA TEXTS AND LINEN ITEMS

The table contains a great deal of helpful and complex information, but should be consulted in conjunction with the following notes.

General Comment:

The abbbreviation CE ("Common Era") is equivalent to AD, and BCE ("Before Common Era") to BC. Bibliography is in G. Bonani et al., "Radiocarbon Dating of Fourteen Dead Sea Scrolls" (1991 and 1992), and A. J. T. Jull et al., "Radiocarbon Dating of Scrolls" (1995 and 1996). Dates for the Bar-Kochba era may differ by a year from the identifications of earlier editors due to uncertainties in the dating of this period. The Libby measurement (item 37) is from W. F. Libby, "Radiocarbon Dates, II" (1951).

Column 2: Laboratory Number and Lab

In this column the name of the laboratory where each test was done is given in italics. Samples with ETH laboratory numbers were measured at the Institut für Mittelenergiephysik in Zurich, as reported in Bonani et al. Samples with AA laboratory numbers were measured at the NSF Arizona Accelerator Mass Spectrometry (AMS) Facility at the University of Arizona in Tucson, as reported in Jull et al.

Column 3: Sample Description

Sigla for items in sample descriptions follow the notation listed in E. Tov with S. Pfann in the *Microfiche Companion Volume*, except where these have been updated in the official DJD editions: e.g. 4QLevi[a] ar in DJD 22 (previously 4QTLevi[a], cf. item 5 in the Table). The listed items consist of parchment (animal skin), unless identified in the sample description as "pap" (papyrus) or as linen (e.g. items 1, 5 and 35). The language of the listed texts is Hebrew unless identified otherwise, notably as Aramaic (e.g. item 1) or Greek (e.g. item 31). The items Seiyal Collection 4Q342, 4Q344, and 4Q345 in the Tucson battery (28-30 in the Table) are not of Qumran provenance according to the editors,[95] and the association of "Additional Frg. 3" with 4Q365 is disputed.[96] In this column seven entries appear in bold face (items 1, 12, 13, 14, 31, 33, 34) for the purpose of representing the internal dates on seven texts; the calendar dates are as reported by the editors of these texts.

---

[95] H. Cotton and A. Yardeni, *Aramaic, Hebrew, and Greek Texts from Naḥal Ḥever and Other Sites* (DJD 27; Oxford: Clarendon Press, 1997) 283-84.

[96] S. White, "4Q364 and 365," 217 n.2 (see item 3 in the Table).

Column 4: Runs

This term denotes the number of separate measurements of subsamples.

Column 5: ^{14}C age (Year BP)

"BP" ("Before Present") in the ^{14}C age column is a convention among radiocarbon laboratories by which measured ^{14}C ages are reported by a single standard (which is defined as the number of radiocarbon years before 1950).

Column 6: One-sigma 1986 bidecadal calibration, published

The 1986 bidecadal calibration column contains calendar dates as reported by the laboratories in the original publications. These were based on a calibration system that was published in 1986.

Column 7: One-sigma (68% confidence) 1997 decadal calibration
Column 8: Two-sigma (95% confidence) 1997 decadal calibration

Calendar dates in the two 1997 decadal calibration columns are based upon an updated calibration that was announced by M. Stuiver[97] at the 16th International Radiocarbon Conference at Groningen in June, 1997. Calibrations were done with a privately-modified version of the computer program CALIB 3.0.3c from the University of Washington Quaternary Isotope Laboratory in Seattle. Modification consisted of installing a new decadal dataset that was constructed on the basis of the system described in Stuiver's paper as follows:

> Two Seattle datasets were averaged with a 1.3 error multiplier,[98] and these data were then averaged with the Belfast data with a 1.3 error multiplier.[99] Calibrations follow the intercept method of calculation. For convenience in reading these calibration data, date ranges have been combined in both 1997 columns in which intervals between ranges are separated by 25 or less calendar years. The outer ends of the outer calendar-year ranges remain the same.

As an estimate of the average amount of underreporting of margins of error when calibrations of parchment, papyrus and ^{14}C dates are carried out according to a decadal calibration curve,[100] an additional uncertainty of five years has been added in quadrature to the reported laboratory margins of error.

[Table A begins on the next page.]

---

[97] M. Stuiver, "Improving Radiocarbon Age Calibration."

[98] See M. Stuiver and B. Becker, *Radiocarbon* 35 (1993) 35-65; and M. Stuiver and B. Becker, *Radiocarbon* 28 (1986) 863-910.

[99] Cf. G. W. Pearson and F. Qua, *Radiocarbon* 35 (1993) 105-123.

[100] As reported for a study in a different time period in Stuiver, "Improving Radiocarbon Age Calibration."

TABLE A
CALIBRATED RADIOCARBON DATES ON DEAD SEA TEXTS AND LINEN ITEMS

READ THESE DATES →

No.	Laboratory Number and Lab	Sample Description	Runs	14C age (year BP)	One-sigma 1986 bi-decadal calibration, published	One-sigma (68% confidence) 1997 decadal calibration	Two-sigma (95% confidence) 1997 decadal calibration, intercepts in brackets
1	ETH-6637 Zurich	Wadi Dalyeh WDSP, pap Deed of slave sale ar (intrnl date: **352/51 BCE**)	3	2289 +/- 55	405-354 (55%) or 306-238 BCE (45%)	399-357 BCE or 287-234 BCE	408-[387]-203 BCE
2	ETH-6640, 7082 Zurich	4Q542 Testament of Qahat ar (4QTQahat)	4	2240 +/- 39	388-353 (34%) or 309-234 BCE (66%)	385-349 BCE or 317-208 BCE	395-[359, 272, 260]-181 BCE
3	ETH 6639 Zurich	Additional Frg. 3, assigned to 4Q365 (?)	3	2139 +/- 32	339-324 (12%) or 203-117 BCE (88%)	339-327 BCE or 202-112 BCE	351-296 or 230-[171, 137, 132]-53 BCE
4	ETH- 6651, 6813 Zurich	1Q Isaiah[a] (1Q Isa[a])	4	2128 +/- 38	335-327 (5%) or 202-107 BCE (95%)	201-93 BCE	351-296 BCE or 230-[169, 140, 127]-48 BCE
5	ETH-6641, 6642 Zurich	4Q213 Levi[a] ar, with linen thread	5	2125 +/- 24	191-155 (59%) or 146-120 BCE (41%)	197-105 BCE	344-324 BCE or 203-[168, 140, 125]-53 BCE
6	ETH-6643 Zurich	4Q53 Samuel[c] (4QSam[c])	2	2095 +/- 49	192-63 BCE	196-47 BCE	349-318 BCE or 228 BCE-[100 BCE]-18 CE
7	ETH-6652 Zurich	Mas11 paraJoshua, 1039-111	4	2086 +/- 28	169-93 BCE	166-49 BCE	196-[92, 68, 62]-2 BCE

DATING AND RADIOCARBON ANALYSIS

8	ETH-6812 Zurich	Mas1n, Sectarian frg., 1063-1747	2	1971 +/- 46	33 BCE-74 CE	38 BCE-78 CE	52 BCE-[28, 40, 50]-129 CE
9	ETH-6650, 6811 Zurich	11Q19 Temple Scroll (11QT[a])	5	2030 +/- 40	97 BCE-1 CE	53 BCE-21 CE	166 BCE-[43, 27, 23, 9, 3 BCE]-67 CE
10	ETH-6646, 6647 Zurich	1Q Genesis Apocryphon ar (1QApGen)	4	2013 +/- 32	73 BCE-14 CE	47 BCE-48 CE	89 BCE-[36, 33, 17, 13 BCE, 1 CE]-69 CE
11	ETH-6648, 6649 Zurich	1Q Thanksgiving Scroll (1QH[a])	5	1979 +/- 32	21 BCE-61 CE	37 BCE-68 CE	47 BCE-[26, 43, 48 CE]-118 CE
12	ETH-6644 Zurich	XHev/Se 11 pap Deed (intrnl date: **130/31 CE**)	3	1917 +/- 42	28-122 CE	32-129 CE	2-[80]-220 CE
13	ETH-6645 Zurich	Mur 30 pap Deed of sale (intrnl date: **134/35 CE**)	3	1892 +/- 32	69-136 CE	77-132 CE	32-[126]-224 CE
14	ETH-6638 Zurich	Khirbet Mird pap Private Letter Arabic (internal date: **744 CE**)	2	1289 +/- 36	675-765 CE	676-775 CE	660-[691, 703, 708, 751, 761]-803 CE
15	AA-13415 Tucson	4Q266 Damascus Document[a] (4QD[a])	5	1954 +/- 38	5-80 CE	4-82 CE	44 BCE-[34, 36, 58 CE]-129 CE
16	AA-13417 Tucson	1Q Habakkuk Commentary (1QpHab)	8	2054 +/- 22	104-43 BCE	88-2 BCE	160-148 or 111 BCE -[49 BCE]-2 CE
17	AA-13418 Tucson	1Q Community Rule (1QS)	3	2041 +/- 68	159 BCE-20 CE	164-144 BCE or 116 BCE-50 CE	344-323 BCE or 203 BCE-[46, 6, 4 BCE]-122 CE
18	AA-13419 Tucson	4Q258 Comm. Rule[d] (4QS[d]), first sample	5	1823 +/- 24	134-230 CE	133-237 CE	129-[221]-255 CE or 303-318 CE

TABLE A (continued) READ THESE DATES →

No.	Laboratory Number and Lab	Sample Description	Runs	^{14}C age (year BP)	One-sigma 1986 bi-decadal calibration, published	One-sigma (68% confidence) 1997 decadal calibration	Two-sigma (95% confidence) 1997 decadal calibration, intercepts in brackets
19	AA-16060 *Tucson*	4Q258 Comm. Rule[d] (4QS[d]), second sample	4	1964 +/- 45	11 BCE-78 CE	36 BCE-81 CE	50 BCE-[31, 39, 52 CE]-130 CE
20	AA-13420 *Tucson*	4Q171 Psalms Commentary[a] (4QpPs[a])	7	1944 +/- 23	22-78 CE	29-81 CE	3-[68]-126 CE
21	AA-13421 *Tucson*	4Q521 Messianic Apocalypse	4	1984 +/- 33	35 BCE-59 CE	39 BCE-66 CE	49 BCE-[24, 44, 46 CE]-116 CE
22	AA-13422 *Tucson*	4Q267 Damascus Document[b] (4QD[b])	5	2094 +/- 29	172-98 BCE	168-51 BCE	198-[98]-3 BCE
23	AA-13423 *Tucson*	4Q249 pap cryptA Midrash Sepher Moshe	6	2097 +/- 50	191-90 BCE	196-47 BCE	349-304 or 228 BCE-[103 BCE]-18 CE
24	AA-13424 *Tucson*	4Q317 cryptA Phases of the Moon	4	2084 +/- 30	164-93 BCE	166-48 BCE	196-[90, 70, 60]-1 BCE
25	AA-13425 *Tucson*	4Q208 Astronomical Enoch[a] (4QEnastr[a])	9	2095 +/- 20	166-102 BCE	167-53 BCE	172-[100]-48 BCE
26	AA-13426 *Tucson*	4Q22 paleoExodus[m] (4Q22)	2	2044 +/- 65	159 BCE-16 CE	164-144 BCE or 116 BCE-48 CE	342-324 BCE or 203-[47 BCE]-83 CE or 105-115 CE
27	AA-13426P *Tucson*	4Q22 paleoExodus[m], repair patch	4	2024 +/- 39	98 BCE-13 CE	51 BCE-47 CE	161-146 or 113 BCE-[40, 29, 21, 10, 1 BCE]-70 CE

DATING AND RADIOCARBON ANALYSIS

28	AA-13430 Tucson	Seiyal II/4Q342 Letter in Judeo-Aramaic	4	1934 +/- 47	14-115 CE	25-127 CE	43 BCE-[74 CE]-214 CE
29	AA-13431 Tucson	Seiyal II/4Q344 Debt Acknowledgement	3	1902 +/- 39	72-127 CE	68-131 CE	24-[87, 101, 122]-226 CE
30	AA-13432 Tucson	Seiyal II/4Q345 Sale of Land ar	5	2185 +/- 60	373-171 CE	361-168 BCE or 141-125 BCE	392-[346, 322, 226, 224, 205]-51 BCE
31	AA-13433 Tucson	5/6Hev 21 pap Purchase of a Date Crop gr (internal date **130 CE**)	3	1799 +/- 57	130-321 CE	132-324 CE	80-[236]-389 CE
32	AA-14984 Tucson	1Q Isaiah[a] (1QIsa[a])	3	2141 +/- 32	335-122 BCE	341-325 BCE or 202-114 BCE	351-295 or 230-[172, 136, 133]-53 BCE
33	AA-14986 Tucson	XHev/Se 8a pap Contract ar ("Kefar Bebayou") (intrnl date **134/35 CE**)	4	1758 +/- 36	231-332 CE	237-340 CE	140-[257, 302, 319]-390 CE
34	AA-14987 Tucson	5/6Hev 19 pap Deed of Gift gr (intnl d. **128 CE**)	4	1827 +/- 36	126-234 CE	131-240 CE	84-[218]-322 CE
35	AA-13434 Tucson	Qumran Cave 4 Linen with leather thong	2	2069 +/- 40	160-41 BCE	165-144 BCE or 117-2 BCE	197 BCE-[52 BCE]-46 CE
36	AA-13435 Tucson	"Cave 2" Linen (from Murabbaʿât?)	2	664 +/- 36	1279-1376 CE	1285-1310 CE or 1355-1386 CE	1279-[1299]-1397 CE
37	Libby (1950)	Qumran Cave 1 Linen	1	1917 +/- 200		160 BCE-390 CE	390 BCE-[126 CE]-600 CE

IMAGING THE SCROLLS: PHOTOGRAPHIC AND DIRECT DIGITAL ACQUISITION

GREGORY BEARMAN, STEPHEN J. PFANN,
AND SHEILA I. SPIRO

This topic has been divided into two sections. First, Stephen Pfann will discuss the history of photography of the Dead Sea Scrolls and the assorted image-collections that have arisen from that enterprise.[1] Second, Gregory Bearman and Sheila Spiro will cover newer digital imaging techniques and some technical photographic details.[2]

1. THE PHOTOGRAPHIC PROCESS

During the past half century, photographers have worked alongside editors to determine which available materials and photographic methods should be utilized to best represent each manuscript in order to aid in its decipherment. This collaboration between scholar and photographer, drawing upon their combined ingenuity and technical expertise, greatly increased the potential of the final product. Together they have succeeded not only in producing beautiful images of these rare manuscripts based upon what the naked eye can see, but more importantly, upon what the eye cannot see. In this respect, the importance and value of the resulting photographic images rival—or indeed even surpass—that of the scrolls themselves. The materials which the scholar and photographer work with have their limitations, must be carefully described, and include the following:

(a) The Dead Sea Scrolls. Since these manuscripts have inevitably continued to deteriorate in varying degrees since their discovery, gradual though that deterioration may be, the earliest negatives provide the best record of each manuscript in its optimal state of preservation. (b) The Negatives. Since these negatives have also deteriorated during the course of time (some substantially so), reproductions of the photographic archives have helped to preserve them

---

[1] See sections 1–5.
[2] Sections 6–9.

for posterity. (c) New Images and Editions. Several technological advancements have been made over the past decades which can help to draw better images from both the early negatives and from the scrolls themselves, even in their current state of preservation.

For these reasons, an overview of the history of photography, its participants, and the collections of negatives and their published editions, may be of help to the scholar and the interested layperson.

1.1 The Photography

Photography of the scrolls began with the first manuscripts to appear from Qumran Cave 1. The larger documents presented fewer problems for the photographers than the multitude of minute fragments which were scattered across the floors of virtually every cave in which manuscripts were found. Being in a better state of preservation, the larger, more complete scrolls were not subjected to the weathering, darkening, shrinking, and cracking that is typical of the less complete ones. Often the larger scrolls could be photographed with standard color or black-and-white film, with special consideration given only to lighting. But the others, which comprise more than ninety-eight percent of the manuscripts, required the attention of skilled and innovative photographers. It was soon discovered that darkened parchment fragments could be lightened, and carbon ink darkened, with the use of infrared film. Variations in darkness on a single assortment of fragments could thus be regularized by shading certain parts of the photographed area. In this way, certain manuscripts which were otherwise illegible were suddenly very readable on a photograph. The use of the infrared process was refined up through the photography of the scrolls from Cave 11 at Qumran during the late 1950's and early 1960's. Backlighting, however, was not used until rather recently. The older negatives were made of glass, but the greater portion of the negatives were of celluloid-based film.

1.2 The Photographers

Throughout the period since the first scrolls were retrieved from the Judean Wilderness many individuals have photographed portions of these priceless manuscripts. However, only a few professional photographers have been invited to photograph the scrolls—with the aid of their expertise systematically—in an effort to record them for all time. The first was John Trever, who was fortunate enough to be photographing plants at the time that the three best preserved scrolls arrived at the American School of Oriental Research (presently the W. F. Albright Institute) in Jerusalem. Trever photographed the scrolls using standard black-and-white film and later did the same in color.[3]

The scrolls which arrived on the other side of the border at the Hebrew University were more deteriorated, darker and difficult to read. During tests conducted at the laboratories of the Morgan Library in New York, it was discovered that they were best photographed on infrared film. Subsequently, the team of James and Helena Bieberkraut opened, cleaned and photographed all the manuscripts (with the exception of the Temple Scroll) that had been obtained by the Israelis,[4] generally on large format (13 x 18 cm) film.[5] Their photography included not only the scrolls from Qumran, but also those that had been excavated at Masada and during Yadin's Judean Desert Survey at Naḥal Ḥever.

The scrolls from most of the caves of Qumran, Wadi Murabbaʿât, Khirbet Mird, Wadi ed-Daliyeh and other minor sites in the Judean Wilderness of pre-1967 Jordan were photographed on 13 x 18 cm format film by Najib Albina of the Palestine Archaeological Museum. In general, he used broad-band infrared photography for all manuscripts on skin; this allowed the scholar both to distinguish between the carbon-black ink and the darkened skin tones of the background and to see the texture of the skin (which is useful information for reconstructing these fragmentary manuscripts).

The situation was particularly challenging with respect to the thousands of fragments recovered from the floors of Caves 4a and 4b[6] at

---

[3] J. C. Trever, *The Dead Sea Scrolls: A Personal Account* (Grand Rapids, MI: Eerdmans, 1977); idem, *The Untold Story of Qumran* (Westwood, NJ: Revell, 1965); see also F. M. Cross, D. N. Freedman and J. A. Sanders (eds.), *Scrolls from Qumrân Cave I: The Great Isaiah Scroll, The Order of the Community, The Pesher to Habakkuk from Photographs by John C. Trever* (Jerusalem: ASOR-Albright Institute of Archaeological Research-Shrine of the Book, 1972).

[4] Mainly by Eliezer Sukenik and his son Yigael Yadin.

[5] E. L. Sukenik, *The Dead Sea Scrolls of the Hebrew University* (Jerusalem: Magnes, 1955); Magen Broshi, "The Negatives Archive of the Shrine of the Book," in E. Tov, with S. J. Pfann (eds.), *Companion Volume to the Dead Sea Scrolls on Microfiche* (2nd ed., Leiden: Brill and IDC, 1995) 135-36.

[6] Cave 4 comprises two separate but adjacent caves which R. de Vaux decided to call together "Cave 4," since the Bedouin had not kept separate the manuscript

Qumran by Bedouin and the archaeologists. As the fragments were purchased, carefully cleaned, flattened, photographed and sorted, the individual manuscripts would "grow" as new fragments were added and gaps filled in. After the various scrolls were assigned to individual editors, improvements were made in the fragment configurations for each manuscript. These stages in the compilation of the fragments were photographed at regular intervals. Between three and five negatives were produced for each of nearly 600 manuscripts over the seven-year period of May 1953 to June 1960. This resulted in about five series of photographs in the PAM (Palestine Archaeological Museum) collection devoted to Cave 4 manuscripts.[7]

(a) May 1953 to June 1954 (PAM 40.575 to 41.139): the original plates of unsorted scroll fragments.
(b) June 1954 to July 1955 (PAM 41.140 to 41.762): the plates after general sorting.
(c) July 1955 to March 1956 (PAM 41.763 to 41.995): plates composed by the assigned editors, generally in a horizontal format.
(d) April 1956 to April 1959 (PAM 41.996 to 42.941): plates composed by editors, in a horizontal format.
(e) May 1959 to June 1960 (PAM 42.966 to 43.701): the final composition, in a vertical format.

In the case of Cave 11 (which had been discovered by Bedouin in 1956), each of the more complete scrolls found there was assigned to a new scholar connected with an agency which had contributed funds for the purchase of the manuscript. Albina produced one full set of

---

fragments which derived from each (cf. R. de Vaux and J. T. Milik, *Qumrân Grotte 4.II* (DJD 6; Oxford: Clarendon Press, 1977) 9-13.

[7] This involves especially those manuscripts which were assigned to F. M. Cross and Patrick Skehan (4Q1-127), J. T. Milik (4Q128-157 and 4Q196-363), J. Strugnell (4Q365-481), and J. Starcky (4Q521-575). The same is true, but to a lesser degree, for J. Allegro's "lot" (4Q158-186). M. Baillet joined the Cave 4 team only in 1958 after finishing his work on the Minor Caves (2Q-3Q, 6Q-10Q). The lateness of his assignment to the Cave 4 material and the difficult task of sorting and assembling the many plates of papyrus fragments meant that the final arrangement of his manuscripts was not completed until well into the 1970's—far beyond John D. Rockefeller's generous funding for the photography. Baillet's scrolls (4Q482-520) were thus not photographed in their final arrangements. For the most part, the plates for his volume (DJD 7) were composed of fragments that were pasted up from pieces clipped out of photographs representing the early stages of his work. With respect to the photographic process itself, see the accounts of F. M. Cross and J. Strugnell in the *Companion Volume*, 121-34.

initial photographs for each scroll: 11QpaleoLev[a] (PAM 42.171–175), 11QPs[a] (43.772–795), 11QtgJob (43.796–824), 11QApPs[a] (43.981–988), 11QShirShabb (43.989–992), and 11QNJ (43.994–44.002). The otherwise fragmentary manuscripts were left unsorted and were photographed on mixed plates (PAM 42.175–180; 43.794; 44.002–012; and 44.114–117).

The Temple Scroll (11QT[a]) was opened and photographed by David Shinhav and Ruth Yakutiel of the Israel Museum. This was one of the most challenging manuscripts to photograph: the ink was penned on the flesh side, instead of the usual hair side, which caused much of the lettering to be lifted from the surface and adhere to the back of the skin. Photographs of both the front and back sides of this scroll were taken in both standard black-and-white and infrared.[8]

After 1967, at the Israel Department of Antiquities (now the Israel Antiquities Authority), photographs of certain manuscripts which were housed at both the Shrine of the Book and the PAM were retaken on 35 mm format black-and-white film. Those of the Wadi ed-Daliyah manuscripts which were taken by Tsila Sagiv proved especially useful, since both front-lighting and back-lighting were used; the lines of the papyrus for both the verso and recto are thus visible simultaneously on each photograph.[9]

During the past decade Bruce and Kenneth Zuckerman of West Semitic Research photographed selected scrolls from the Shrine of the Book, the Rockefeller Museum and the Amman Archaeological Museum. The Zuckermans experimented successfully with various types of lighting (including backlighting) in order to produce improved images in color (i.e. color-balanced), infra-red and standard black-and-white formats. They also experimented with digital photography; besides investigating the potential value of the digitized images (and subsequent computer enhancement), they explored the possibility of utilizing it as an on-the-site guide for adjusting the settings for their film cameras. The negatives from their work are stored at West Semitic Research in Palos Verdes, California. For their work in digital imaging, see above.

---

[8] Y. Yadin, The Temple Scroll (3 vols., Jerusalem: Israel Exploration Society, 1983) esp. 1.5-8; idem, The Temple Scroll: The Hidden Law of the Dead Sea Sect (Jerusalem: Steimatzky, 1985) 46-54.

[9] This aids the scholar in matching the papyrus lines between disjointed fragments; cf. the Companion Volume, 129.

During the 1990's a new set of narrow-band infrared photographs of a large number of manuscripts from Caves 4 and 11 were taken by Tsila Sagiv. The advantage of these photographs over the earlier ones produced by Albina is that the skin tones are almost entirely muted, thus rendering the distinction between the carbon-black ink and the background much less ambiguous.

2. THE STATE OF THE ORIGINAL NEGATIVES

The original negatives that had been taken by John Trever of certain manuscripts from Cave 1 (1QIsa^a, 1QS, 1QpHab and a few fragmentary scrolls), are now stored at the Ancient Biblical Manuscript Center in Claremont, CA ("ABMC"). A second major collection of original negatives is housed at the Shrine of the Book. These represent a collection of early negatives that were produced from the scrolls housed at that facility. These negatives were made on the same types of film as those used by the PAM during the 1950's and early 1960's. But unlike the negatives which were produced at the PAM, all film stocks have remained stable throughout their existence.[10]

However, the vast majority of negatives (especially of fragments from Caves 2 to 10, and most from Cave 11) were produced at the Palestine Archaeological Museum (now called the Rockefeller Museum), and are presently housed at the Israel Antiquities Authority facilities at Har Ḥaṣovim in Jerusalem.

Many of the original negatives have suffered various forms of damage which compromise the excellence of the final product. In addition to the problems of broken, cracked or scratched glass-plate negatives (using Ilford and Kodak film), the main source of damaged negatives is the use of film produced by the Dupont Corporation.[11] In the PAM archives, negatives of this film type exhibit three forms of damage.

---

[10] Including those that were produced from Dupont film. The deterioration of similar Dupont negatives at the PAM seems due to the fact that they had not been thoroughly rinsed after processing (see below).

[11] Dupont Non-Color Sensitized "Cronar" Commercial-S Sheet Film (not infrared). "This is a non-color sensitized, medium-speed, fine grain film for general commercial photography" (Photo-Lab Index Lifetime Edition [New York: Morgan and Morgan, 1970] 8-03-1966). This type of deterioration concerns the PAM negatives collection only. Both the infrared and standard negatives at the Shrine of the Book, for example, remain in a relatively excellent state of preservation.

One, called "bluing," is due to the original development process. This blue tint, which affects some of the negatives, is due to procedural problems that arise during the development process. Negatives with this problem require that certain adjustments be made during the process of making reproductions because of the overall darkening of the negative.

Two more forms of damage are due to an on-going process of deterioration of the film which causes separation between the three components of the negative: the gelatin anti-hyaline surface, the celluloid base [or core], and the emulsion surface.[12] All of these forms of damage affect the celluloid base of the negative, only impacting the emulsion and gelatin surfaces indirectly. Separation between the celluloid base of the negative and the gelatin surface occurs due to two visible causes:

(a) *Reticulation,* or blistering due to shrinkage of the celluloid negative base. When this process occurs, the emulsion and gelatin surfaces separate to form regular raised, net-like patterns over both surfaces. At first these separations are limited to only a line or two extending across the surface of the negative. Gradually, however, more lines develop, forming increasingly denser net-patterns over the surface until total separation ultimately occurs and one or both surfaces separate totally from the negative body. This process affects first and foremost the gelatin surface, since the emulsion seems to exhibit more resilience to the shrinkage.

The separation and bowing (in lines) of the gelatin surface frequently causes refraction of light during the process of reproducing photographs. The result is a ghost-like web that extends throughout the image.

(b) *Separations due to crystallization.* This is the most damaging form of deterioration. Chemical substances that were once absorbed by the celluloid base of the negative are currently crystallizing. As the crystals grow, they create round separations between the negative base and the two surfaces (particularly the gelatin surface). At times the crystals penetrate the surfaces, creating holes; at other times the separation expands to join with other separations. Ultimately the body of the negative may crumble, leaving the two surfaces (emulsion and gelatin) hanging limp like two pieces of plastic wrapping. This phenomenon affects photographs made of objects and sites, and also non-infra-red photographs of manuscripts.[13]

---

[12] This phenomenon occurs mainly in pictures of papyrus documents, museum objects and at archaeological sites (such as Ein Feshka and Tell el-Farʿah [North]).

[13] In order to replace the missing or damaged negatives of the PAM collection, replacement negatives have recently been made directly from the "contacts" (i.e.

3. REPRODUCTIONS MADE FROM ORIGINAL NEGATIVES

Photographic reproductions are made from the original negatives in three forms: (1) as prints on photographic paper; (2) as diapositives (positive transparencies); and (3) as negative transparencies.[14]

A key factor in favor of the use of negative transparencies (against photographic paper) is that the emulsion surface of the film is relatively thick, and thus conveys a three-dimensional aspect to the layering of the photo-sensitive crystals. This allows darker areas in the image to be brightened by varying the light intensity through the layered emulsion. In the case of general viewing, this adjustment can be made on the light table or on the microfiche reader. If multiple exposures are made in the darkroom, then virtually every area on

---

one-to-one scale reproductions from negative transparencies printed on photographic paper. A complete set of these contacts was used by the museum to form a bound catalogue of the PAM and IAA photo collections; see section 4a). However, images produced on photographic paper have certain limitations: (a) There are far fewer steps on the gray-scale in a photograph than in an original negative, thus limiting the data received from the original. Images produced from the new negative become limited to the gray-scale levels preserved on the contact; (b) The brightness and contrast is limited to that which was set at the time when the photograph was made; and (c) The present replacement set has been made on 6 x 6 and 6 x 7 film size, which is less than 1/6 the size of the contact. Thus, any images that are made from these negatives suffer from reduction before an enlargement. For these, new replacements should be made from film which more closely approximates the size of the contact (and thus approximates the size of the original negative).

In a spirit of co-operation, the Ancient Biblical Manuscript Center at Claremont, CA, forwarded to the IAA replacement "diapositives" (for the term, see later in section 7) of many missing and damaged negatives—in the PAM and Shrine of the Book collections—that had been made from their set of R. Schlosser's diapositives. However, as is characteristic of diapositives, these replacements were generally high-contrast, thus lacking the refined gray-scale of the originals; cf. the examples of Schlosser's set of diapositives in E. Tov, with S. J. Pfann (eds.), *The Dead Sea Scrolls on Microfiche* (Leiden: Brill and IDC, 1993): PAM 40.063-65, 40.068, 40.070, 40.073-75, etc. The terms "high-contrast ... lacking the refined gray-scale" mean that traces of ink and faint lettering may be lost in the reproductions (as may be seen when a photocopying machine is used to reproduce pictures).

[14] Since a set of digital images has yet to be taken of the original negatives, much untapped information still resides in its optimal form in these negatives. Much of these data will best be obtained once recent advances in digital imaging are applied directly to the original negatives. (For the application of these advances to the scrolls, cf. the important work of G. Bearman and S. Spiro.) For an explanation of digital imaging of the scrolls, see section 9 below.

the image may be adjusted in order to achieve optimal clarity. If original negatives have been rephotographed on negative transparency film, the same information that is preserved in the three-dimensional emulsion of the original negative is passed on to the copies.

However, opaque prints made from negative transparencies on photographic paper have a rather two-dimensional layer of pigment. On the one hand, this medium does in fact preserve the image which has been dictated by settings made in the dark room at the time when the prints were made. On the other hand, on a print the darker areas have become "frozen" (i.e. locked into place) by those settings. Those areas cannot be brightened by intensifying the light on the printed surface. This holds true both for viewing the prints and for producing any successive generations of transparent negatives or prints from them.

Diapositives, since they are positive transparency films, produce a "like copy" of the original. In other words, a diapositive produces a negative transparency when it reproduces a negative transparency. Although a diapositive is by nature a true transparency film with a layered emulsion, it lacks the refined gray-scale of professional quality negatives. The resulting image often compares with that on high-contrast photographic paper. Because of this factor, its performance in the darkroom lacks the versatility of negative-transparency film.

4. SECOND GENERATION REPRODUCTIONS OF THE ORIGINAL COLLECTIONS

(a) *Prints*. As the original PAM negatives were produced, contact prints were made for each with the result that a complete set of contact prints was stored in an album at the Rockefeller Museum. These photographs are of fine quality and were made on good photographic paper. In other cases, reproductions from both the PAM and the Shrine of the Book negatives were limited to sets of full-sized prints that were produced for each editor for his or her work and for inclusion in the official publications.

(b) *Early Diapositives*. These were made from the original negatives of the PAM collection after 1967 on behalf of the late Prof. Y. Yadin. This incomplete collection is currently housed at the Shrine of the Book.

(c) *Later Diapositives*. High contrast diapositives were made from the original negatives (limited to the PAM collection) by R.

Schlosser on behalf of the Dead Sea Scrolls Preservation Council between 1984 and 1986. By this time, the original negatives were already showing signs of deterioration.[15] According to the IAA (Israel Antiquities Authority) staff photographer Tsila Sagiv, more than one copy of each negative was made at that time. The sets of photographs are stored in at least three locations: the Ancient Biblical Manuscript Center (Claremont, CA); the Huntington Library (San Marino, CA); and Duke University (Durham, North Carolina).

(d) *The Microfiche Edition Masters*. In 1993, under the joint editorship of E. Tov and S. Pfann, a set of microfiches was produced directly from the original negatives by P. Moerkerk, a photographer working for publishers E. J. Brill/IDC under the auspices of the IAA. These were made from the entire collection of original negatives that are stored at the IAA,[16] the Shrine of the Book, and the Hebrew University of Jerusalem. Multiple exposures (as many as five) of varying length were made of each negative. The photographer and Pfann viewed each of these test fiches in order to determine the correct settings for the final images to be included in the edition. In cases where the negative exhibited high variability in darkness, more than one image was included. Since the exposures were made directly from negative to negative on fine grain Fuji II High Resolution microfiche film, important information that is preserved only in the layered emulsion[17] has been preserved on each microfiche. The masterfiches are in the possession of the publishers in the Netherlands.[18]

5. FOURTH AND FIFTH GENERATION PUBLICATIONS

Images of the scrolls that appear in published volumes require at least two additional steps beyond the available source in the reproduction on the printed page or on microform transparencies.[19]

---

[15] For example, PAM 40.186 and 40.188-90.

[16] Both the PAM and IAA series.

[17] Which is typical of the transparent medium of negative film.

[18] For more details on the photography of this edition, see the *Companion Volume*, 6-16, which includes the account of the editors and of photographer P. Moerkerk.

[19] For example, the copies of the *Microfiche Edition* reproduced for general distribution are four generations or steps away from original negatives as follows: (1) the original negatives; (2) master fiches (positive transparencies, negatives pro-

5.1 Fourth-Generation Publications

(a) *Discoveries in the Judaean Desert.* The official *editio princeps* of scrolls includes PAM plates of the scrolls which came into possession of the Palestine Archaeological Museum. The plates for each volume are made from full-sized prints of the PAM negatives; since 1995 these prints have been digitized and "sharpened" by means of a photo-rendering program.[20]

(b) *The Dead Sea Scrolls on Microfiche.*[21] This comprehensive facsimile edition is the published version of the master fiches that were mentioned above.[22]

5.2 Fifth-Generation Publications

(a) *The Huntington Library Microfilm.* Based upon its own collection of Schlosser's second-generation negatives, the library's

---

duced from negatives); (3) negatives produced from the master fiches (from which the distribution copies were made); and (4) the published edition of the microfiches.

[20] This process increases the definition of the ink in the written text and of the edges of fragments. It must be borne in mind, however, that all digital images which have been rendered by a computer are based upon a certain degree of interpretive input from the computer programmer.

[21] See note 13 above.

[22] The reduction in resolution between the master fiches and the published copies was surprisingly minor. The fact that the successive generations were made (on a scale of one-to-one) on similar fine-grain film was helpful in achieving this, as was varying the exposure-time and the light-intensity through the layered emulsion. Such layering is a feature typical of negative transparencies, and can bring out virtually every line and trace of ink that was captured by the original negative. This is possible only in cases where, during each reproduction, the image is never on prints, but only on negative transparencies.

However, the size of the images in microform photography (whether microfiches or microfilm) creates at least two limitations. First, as they are viewed through microfiche/film readers, the images are reflected off two additional surfaces which diffuse light and decrease sharpness, even with the best readers. (The best images can be procured by viewing them on a light table through a 25x to 75x standing microscope.) Second, although the film used for each fiche is of fine grain, at a certain magnification the grains of film begin to appear. Thus when the film is magnified above 75x, the resolution begins to diminish. Digitized images that have been derived from a desk-top scanner are virtually unusable, but a slide or high-resolution transparency scanner achieves optimal results. As in the case of all microphotography, the potential for enlargement of the images for viewing is dictated by: (a) the fineness of the grain of the image itself; and (b) the quality of the equipment that is used for enlarging and viewing each image.

director W. Moffett gave permission for this set to be reproduced for the use of scholars. The resultant microfilms are of generally poor quality and are generally over-exposed.

(b) *The Facsimile Edition of the Dead Sea Scrolls (FEDSS)*. This was reproduced by the Biblical Archaeology Society from a set of small-format reproductions of the PAM series of negatives.[23] More than one print had been made from certain negatives in the series, in order to draw the best image from various parts of negatives that exhibited a high degree of variability in darkness.[24] An effort was made to limit the edition to unpublished manuscripts, and most of the prints in the collection that had been made from defective negatives were also eliminated. Thus not all PAM negatives were reproduced in these two volumes.

The fact that the images in the printed FEDSS volume actually represent fifth-generation reproductions weighs heavily upon the quality of the images. The text found on most of the fragments is generally readable. However, the edges of the fragments are often

---

[23] R. H. Eisenman and J. M. Robinson, *A Facsimile Edition of the Dead Sea Scrolls* (Washington, DC: Biblical Archaelogy Society, 1991). This set of reproductions came into the possession of R. Eisenman through the agency of a lawyer. The original source of the negatives has long been disputed; the rumor that they were willed to Eisenman by Najib Albina (who had moved to the United States after the Six Day War) must now be discounted. In December 1991, Stephen Pfann was assigned the task of determining the actual source of Eisenman's prints that were used for the FEDSS edition. The defective negatives were of special interest, especially those which had suffered gradual or recent damage. In the case of Plate 167 (PAM negative 41.159) no previous reproductions made from the original PAM negative had showed any damage. But when Schlosser photographed this glass negative (in 1984?), it was already broken and the two parts of the negative were imperfectly positioned by him. The resulting line in his diapositive was unique and is identical to the photograph that appears in the FEDSS volume. This precise mispositioning of the glass fragments, along with the light-setting and shadow, would be nearly impossible to reproduce a second time by another photographer. In view of this and cerain other indications, it is virtually certain that a set of Schlosser's negatives was the actual source used to produce Eisenman's prints.

[24] In such cases the best parts of each photograph were at times painstakingly cut out in order to create a composite of the negative. For the best examples, see Plates 49, 61, 64, 66, 80, 193, 215, 272, 273, 306, 339-341, 353, 409, 451, 457, 478, 538, 540, 547, 548, 564-566, 569, 572, 675, 677, 721, 756, 802, 893, 896, 906, 936, 1037, 1082, 1086, 1098, 1110, 1114, 1120, 1143, 1147, 1149, 1211, 1327, 1345, 1354, 1375, 1411, 1428, 1443, 1447, 1467, 1471, 1482, 1485, 1488, 1492, 1524, 1540, 1619, and 1683.

lost along with traces of ink, and the size of the images (often four plates to a page) at times makes the lettering too small to be clearly legible. However, until these volumes are superseded by the completion of the DJD series, this set will remain a handy reference tool for perusing most of the photographs in the PAM series.

6. EARLIER WORK AND FOCUS OF THIS ARTICLE

Our focus in this section will be recent imaging of the scrolls—which by definition includes both photographic and direct digital acquisition—and the newest techniques for both. As technologies have evolved, many museums and libraries are migrating their photographic collections to one or another of the available digital media. We will also discuss some issues that arise in this process.

In addition to our co-author's detailed examination on sections 5–9, consulting a number of sources will provide the reader with a more thorough and colorful narrative of the history of photography of the Dead Sea Scrolls. Most complete is the *Companion Volume* to the *Microfiche Edition* (recently updated),[25] which contains articles that provide details—both technical and anecdotal—about photography at the Rockefeller Museum into the mid-1980's. John Trever[26] has also written extensively of his experiences photographing the scrolls. The Dead Sea Scrolls Catalogue,[27] now being updated for posting on the Ancient Biblical Manuscript Center website, provides a comprehensive means of locating and cross-referencing the scrolls and briefly sketches the highlights of the story of the copies made by Robert Schlosser for safekeeping at the ABMC and the adventures that followed—not least of which was the release of a full set of the Schlosser photographs on microfiche by the Huntington Library in 1991, and two folio volumes of what are probably a set of Schlosser's photographs of unknown provenance.[28]

---

[25] E. Tov, with S. J. Pfann (eds.), *The Dead Sea Scrolls on Microfiche*; and the *Companion Volume*.

[26] J. C. Trever, *A Personal Account*; idem, *The Untold Story*. See also F. M. Cross, D. N. Freedman and J. A. Sanders (eds.), *Scrolls from Qumrân Cave I ... from Photographs by John C. Trever*.

[27] S. A. Reed, with M. J. Lundberg and M. J. Phelps, *The Dead Sea Scrolls Catalogue: Documents, Photographs and Museum Inventory Numbers* (SBLRBS 32; Atlanta: Scholars Press, 1994).

[28] See section 5.2 above.

(A carefully worded, contemporaneous account can be found in the *The Folio* 11:3 of 1991.)[29] Useful bibliographical information is available in the Oxford University Press/Brill[30] digital Dead Sea Scrolls library ("OUP/Brill collection"), and the FARMS Dead Sea Scroll database ("FARMS database")[31] the latter also providing a high-speed, unparalleled concordance and links between images and transcriptions. Most recently made available among a number of rumored or known private libraries of Dead Sea Scrolls negatives and photographs is the collection of John Allegro, now housed in the Manchester Museum;[32] in addition, some still have hope that Yigael Yadin's precious photographs are not lost forever. The interested reader is referred to the diverse works cited here for further details.

7. ULTRAVIOLET AND INFRARED PHOTOGRAPHY

The use of advanced techniques for acquiring new images directly from the scrolls is necessary only for a small subset of documents, usually small fragments. It is worth emphasizing at this point that the great majority of first generation Dead Sea Scrolls negatives at both the Rockefeller Museum and the Shrine of the Book remain in excellent condition and are suitably legible for most uses. Once they are digitized, information that is not visible to the unaided eye can often be recovered with simple image-processing. One problem frequently encountered in the early negatives is an imbalance of exposure in the presence of both light and dark fragments on a single plate. Najib Albina, photographer for the Palestine Archaeological Museum,[33] was aware of this and would use paddles outside the camera's field-of-view in order to block illumination of the lighter part.[34] The expense and logistical difficulties make re-imaging large numbers of fragments a less attractive option once the usefulness of

---

[29] This document is available on request from the ABMC.

[30] T. H. Lim (ed.), *The Dead Sea Scrolls Electronic Reference Library* (Oxford: Oxford University Press; Leiden: Brill, 1997).

[31] *The Dead Sea Scrolls on CD: The FARMS Electronic Database* (Provo, UT: Foundation for Ancient Research and Mormon Studies, 1997).

[32] G. J. Brooke (ed.), *The Allegro Qumran Collection on Microfiche* (Leiden: Brill, 1996).

[33] For further details on Albina's work, see section 1.2 ("The Photographers").

[34] *Applied Infrared Photography* (Publication M-28; Rochester, NY: Kodak, 1972).

the existing negatives and a half-century's deterioration of many fragments are considered.

Some basic data will assist most readers in the discussion that follows. Visible light is in the ~400-720 nm range,[35] with ultraviolet ("UV") below 400 nm and infrared ("IR") above 720 nm. The "blue" light referred to in this article is between 400 and 480 nm. The range of the team's cameras was in the "near IR," or up to 1,000 nm.

When the Dead Sea Scrolls were discovered, infrared photography was used from the outset. What suggested that IR would be appropriate or successful? By the 1950's both ultraviolet and IR illumination and photography already had a documented history in the examination of ancient documents. As early as 1910, UV was being used on palimpsests.[36] With the invention in the 1920's of a suitable UV source known as Wood's Lamp (which is still used by scientists around the world), UV reading of manuscripts became common. It has long been recognized that UV is particularly well-suited for iron-based inks, thus limiting the success of this approach to documents dated later than about the 3rd century CE.

It was to be another fifty years before the success of illumination in spectra above and below the visible one would be explained. Nevertheless, once the effectiveness of UV became apparent, it was only natural to try IR. The technology for UV imaging is easier and more readily apparent, which explains its routine use long before that of IR. Excitation occurs in the UV and the resulting fluorescence is in the visible part of the spectrum, thus facilitating both direct viewing and photography. Scholars would routinely examine fluorescing text under UV light and, if they desired, could take photographs with inexpensive black and white film. Since IR film was not developed until later, its use lagged behind that of UV. But by the 1930's IR was being used to improve readings of iron-based inks on burnt documents.[37] One of the manuscripts that was subjected to both UV and IR photography in the early use of this approach was *Beowulf*.[38]

---

[35] I.e. nanometers, by which wavelength is measured.

[36] Gustav Kogel, *Die Photographie historischer documente* (Leipzig: Harrassowitz, 1914).

[37] Lodewyk Benedikson, "Phototechnical Problems: Some Results Obtained at the Huntington Library," *Library Science* 57 (1932) 789-94; idem, "Charred Documents," *Library Science* 58 (1933) 243-44.

[38] A. H. Smith and F. Norman, "The Photography of Manuscripts," *London Mediaeval Studies* 1 (1937) 179.

Since infrared film is sensitive in both the red blue spectra, it is usually used with a blue filter. Although it is unclear precisely which filters Albina employed for the PAM photograph series, it was the use of filters by Bruce and Kenneth Zuckerman in the 1980's that renewed interest in applying IR photography to faded or darkened ancient manuscripts.[39]

In a series of photographic field trips to the Berlin Museum in 1991 and to Jerusalem in 1992, the Zuckermans observed that infrared photography yielded much better results when certain filters were used. Filters that yielded the best results were of the cut-on variety, i.e. filters which "cut on" (let in light) only at a specified fixed wavelength, and—in particular—those which blocked out the visible and blue part of the spectrum.[40] The specific filters they chose were Kodak 88A, 87 and 87C, which cut on at bandwiths of 740 nm, 750 nm and 810 nm, respectively. As IR film is sensitive only up to about 900 nm (and begins to decline before that), the result was photography over a bandwidth of ~90-160 nm. The explanation and, finally, the organized application of what began as a phenomenological result would have to wait a few years more until advances in electro-optic and detector technology would lead to the next step: electronic IR imaging.

8. IMAGING THE DEAD SEA SCROLLS

The authors became involved with imaging Dead Sea Scrolls in the summer of 1993 as a result of Gregory Bearman's work in electronic imaging and imaging spectroscopy. A physicist at the Jet Propulsion Laboratory (JPL), which is operated by the California Institute of Technology for the National Aeronautic and Space Administration (NASA), Bearman was involved with efforts to transfer NASA technology by determining commercial or academic applications of imaging and spectroscopy. Realising that the study of manuscripts might benefit from such technology, he approached the Ancient Biblical Manuscript Center in Claremont, CA; thus a collaboration was born between the ABMC, the JPL and the Zuckermans, with the purpose of exploring the application of these new technologies to the Dead Sea Scrolls.

---

[39] The Zuckermans would routinely photograph difficult documents with a variety of filters and in many exposures, in both UV and IR.

[40] I.e. the film recorded only reflected *infrared*.

Fortunately, a small fragment of the Genesis Apocryphon at that time resided in Los Angeles: The Getty Conservation Institute lent us a fragment from this scroll that had been provided by the Shrine of the Book for conservation studies. We used a new tunable filter that could be set to any wavelength in the IR with a very narrow bandpass,[41] and demonstrated that electronic imaging with a narrow bandpass filter provided excellent, real-time images. The major result of that work was presented at the 1993 Annual Meeting of the Society of Biblical Literature in Washington, DC.[42]

Media reports of that presentation prompted Magen Broshi, then Director of the Shrine of the Book in Jerusalem, to invite the ABMC to image the entire Genesis Apocryphon at the Shrine in the summer of 1994. (The visiting team also undertook a limited pilot program to demonstrate to the IAA the efficacy of their techniques.) The resultant images, which revealed a considerable amount of new text, were subsequently utilized by Matthew Morgenstern, Elisha Qimron and Daniel Sivan for their preliminary edition of the Genesis Apocryphon.[43]

A second ABMC-sponsored imaging field expedition took place in 1997, in collaboration with the Israel Antiquities Authority, the Israel Museum/Shrine of the Book and the editorial team, resulting in new electronic IR images of approximately 900 fragments that had been selected by editors of the scrolls and other scholars. In 1997 we borrowed a portable fiber-optic spectrometer for the purpose of taking reflectance spectra for ink and parchment. This effort explained not only why imaging in the infrared increases contrast between the ink and the parchment, even where no text is visible to the unaided eye, but also why narrow-band filters are effective on some fragments but not others. Simply stated, the contrast between the ink of the text and the parchment background determines legibility (Thus this paper is published in black ink on white paper!).

---

[41] 10 nm, which was much narrower than the ~90-160 nm of the Kodak filters which had been used previously.

[42] G. H. Bearman, Bruce Zuckerman, Kenneth Zuckerman, and J. Chiu, "Multi-spectral Imaging of Dead Sea Scrolls and Other Ancient Documents" (Paper presented at the Annual Meeting of the Society of Biblical Literature [Washington, DC], 20-23 November, 1993).

[43] M. Morgenstern et al., "The Hitherto Unpublished Columns of the Genesis Apocryphon," *Abr-Nahrain* 33 (1995) 30-52, esp. 30.

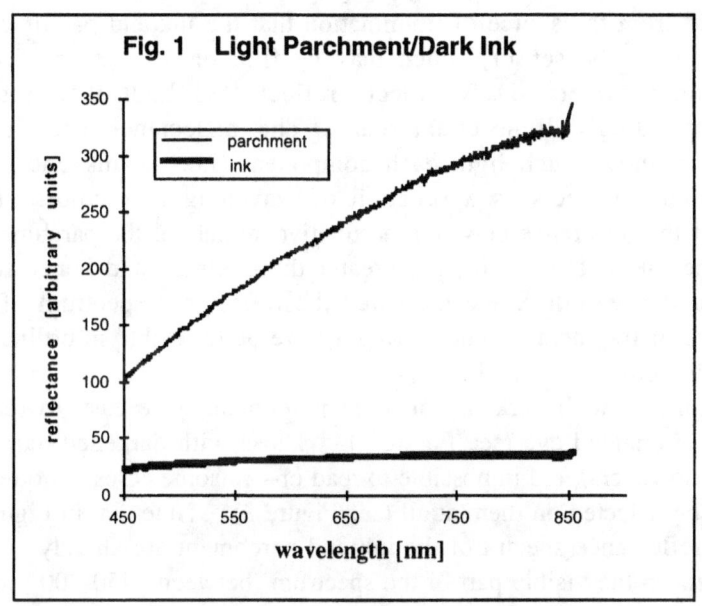

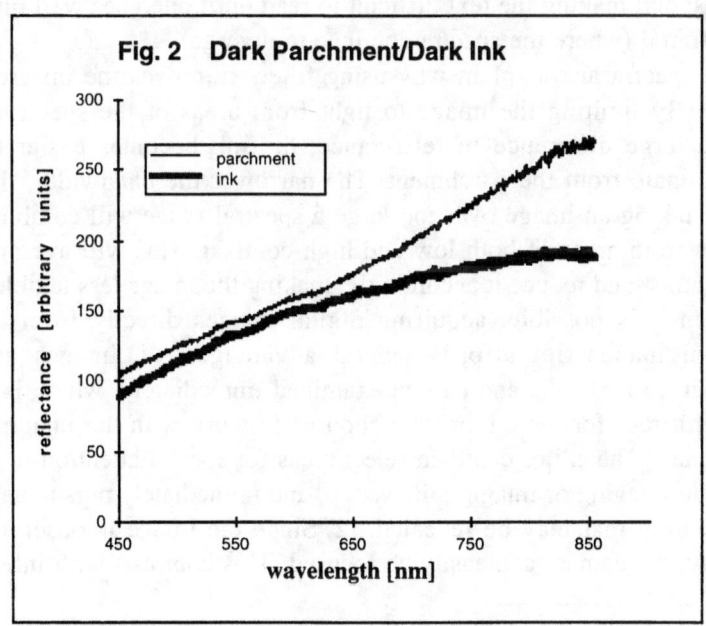

The contrast (quality) of any image is determined by the amount of light from the source of illumination that the ink and parchment reflect onto the sensor, which may be film or the sensor of an electronic camera. Dark objects reflect less light than their correspondingly light counterparts. The reflectance spectrum measures how much light each component (i.e. the ink and the parchment) reflects as a function of wavelength or color. The greater the difference between the relative signals of the parchment and the ink at the sensor, the greater the contrast, and hence the greater the legibility. We measured the reflectance spectrum of a number of fragments, some of which were quite legible in ordinary light, but others not at all.

Fragments with dark ink on light parchment were easy to read with the unaided eye (see Figure 1).[44] Those with darkened parchment, however, were impossible to read or—in some cases— no text could be detected on them at all (see Figure 2).[45] Note that in Figure 1 the reflectance spectra of the ink and parchment are already very different in the visible part of the spectrum (between ~450-700 nm). Compare Figure 2, where the ink and parchment have very nearly the same reflectance in the visible spectrum, thus providing little contrast and making the text difficult to read until one goes well into the infrared (where the spectra continue to diverge).

The spectra also explain why using filters improves the infrared image. By limiting the image to light from areas of the spectrum with a large difference in reflectance, the ink becomes easier to discriminate from the parchment. The narrower the bandwidth, the better; taking an image over too large a spectral range will combine signals from areas of both low and high contrast. This will average the contrast and reduce it accordingly, making the image less legible.

When it is possible, acquiring digital images directly from an original manuscript affords several advantages. (1) Images are obtained in real-time and can be examined immediately, which is a powerful tool for the editor who chooses to work with the imaging technician. The editor can then select areas for special attention (e.g. close-up imaging or imaging the verso), and immediately pursue new information that may be revealed. (2) Since the image is observed directly, the camera can easily be focused. This contrasts with infra-

---

[44] "Light Parchment/Dark Ink" on the previous page.

[45] "Dark Parchment/Dark Ink" on the previous page.

red photography, in which the photographer cannot see the images until they have been developed (usually later and off-site); focus obtained by a series of bracketing shots cannot guarantee success. (3) Since the images are acquired digitally, they are ready for digital image-processing techniques without the intermediate cost and delay of scanning. (4) Electronic imaging can work farther in the infrared spectrum than can film, thus obtaining images with better contrast.

Developing and maintaining a photographic, or image, archive has two main purposes—documenting and preserving the record of an invaluable discovery and making the best possible record available to future generations. Migrating the collection to one or more of the available digital media serves preservation of an image archive in a number of important ways, which are discussed in depth in a recent monograph by Michael Ester, who as director of the Getty Art History Information Program was responsible for setting program direction and policy and for managing its many projects in the US and Europe.[46] For the DSS collections the most important objective is to capture the contents of the photographs in a medium which: will not deteriorate physically or chemically over time; can be stored in multiple locations with complete image integrity; can be reproduced with identical quality from generation to generation, and can be organized and effectively searched in ways not possible with a photographic archive. Authorized projects have led to the creation of three important digital collections (each somewhat different) of images of early PAM and Shrine photographs of the Dead Sea Scrolls: at Oxford University Press (with pictures of 300 dpi[47]), the Foundation for Ancient Research and Mormon Studies (at 200 dpi), and the Ancient Biblical Manuscript Center (at 1,200 dpi, distributed not as a collection, but only on an image-by-image basis and strictly for scholarly use).

Future histories of Dead Sea Scrolls photography, or imaging,

---

[46] M. Ester, *Digital Image Collections: Issues and Practice* (Washington, DC: Commission on Preservation and Access, December 1996). Dr. Ester is a recognized expert in the field who has been generous with his guidance and counsel. The monograph is available from the Commission for US$15, and we highly recommend it as a thorough and thought-provoking treatment of the subject. It bears this disclaimer: "Reports issued by the Commission on Preservation and Access are intended to stimulate thought and discussion. They do not necessarily reflect the views of Commission members."

[47] I.e. dots per inch (see the discussion below).

must include the development of such digital libraries, which are an outgrowth of the same CCD[48] detector technology whose development has made infrared electronic imaging possible and even widely accessible. Digitizing (or scanning)[49] of major photographic collections and archives has become a mini-industry as, in the last decade, many humanities libraries have moved toward digitization of their textual and photographic collections into databases that can be interrogated by search engines. In the following section we will touch upon only the few aspects which seem of particular relevance to digital Dead Sea Scrolls libraries.

9. WHAT EXACTLY IS DIGITAL IMAGING?

To understand issues that are common both to acquiring direct electronic digital images of DSS and to digitizing existing image libraries, one must be aware of some basic principles. A digital image is composed of thousands of picture elements ("pixels"), much like a halftone newspaper photograph. The intensity or blackness of each pixel ("dynamic range" or "pixel depth") can range from zero (black) to a maximum value (white), as determined by the electronics of the camera acquiring the image. Although the human eye cannot discern much of the gray-scale, a computer can do so and pixel-depth information may prove vital. Most commercial cameras are 8 bits, providing a gray-scale of 255 or 2^8-1 (255 shades or intensities of gray); others range from 10 bits (2^{10}-1 = 1,023) to 16 bits (65,535).[50] Although far beyond what the human eye can appreciate, the computer has the information and greater pixel depth for providing better detail and dynamic range in both imaging and digitizing. Image-quality is to some extent a function of pixel-depth. The second common issue that directly affects text-legibility and image-quality is spatial resolution. Two questions must be asked: (1) How big is the detector (and thus the image field-of-view)?, and (2) What is the spatial resolution of the image (i.e. how much of the document's area does each pixel in the image represent—a micron, 100 microns, a millimeter)?

---

[48] I.e. a charge coupled device.

[49] The two terms will here be used interchangeably.

[50] The reader should be aware that electronic devices advertised as "36 bit-scanners" actually have 12 bits for each primary color channel—red, green and blue—for a *total* of 36 bits.

When an image is acquired digitally from the original manuscript, spatial resolution is set by the sensor size (1,024 x 1,024 pixels, etc.) and by the objective lens magnification. In 1993, we took most of our images with a half-column field-of-view, which resulted in a typical letter or character being 18 x 15 pixels, which was very legible. On loan from the Jet Propulsion Laboratory, the camera we used was of scientific grade and produced 16-bit images. For archival images these are ideal, since the dynamic range is huge, potentially storing up to 65,535 intensities of gray for later image-processing purposes. However, examination of the data showed that it spanned at most 12 bits; with proper adjustment of camera-noise, even 8 bits can provide excellent images at a far lower cost for equipment. In scanning, one has no power over the field of view, which was fixed when the photograph was made, and the "pixel" size is in a certain sense set by the size of the film grain.

The parameter over which some control is maintained is the sampling density, or dots per inch. A 600 dpi image means that each inch of the negative is sampled and digitized at 600 discrete spots along one dimension; in the final image, each dot corresponds to a pixel. A 600 dpi scan produces a file of reasonable size and is adequate for most purposes; increasing the sampling density also increases the file size. Although the increasing capacity of desktop computers makes it tempting to say "the more the merrier" and to employ scans of 3,000 dpi, for most of us to work in Adobe Photoshop with a 40-50 megabyte file is no easy task. The authors feel that the cost of the quality to be gained by increased sampling density becomes too dear somewhere between 1,200 and 2,000 dpi.

Scanning from a photographic negative is superior to doing so from a print, and scanning from the original is vastly preferable to scanning from second generation media:

> We have come to presume very little or no loss in converting film into digital form....[T]he significant quality degradation resulting from photographic duplication ... will, of course, be reflected in digital capture. Especially for long-term archival use, second generation film should be avoided whenever possible.[51]

The basis of the OUP/Brill collection consists primarily of prints from the collection housed in the Qumran Room of the Oxford

---

[51] Ester, *Digital Image Collections*, 10; see also the discussion by S. J. Pfann in sections 3-5 above.

Centre for Hebrew and Jewish Studies, supplemented by images from the *Microfiche Edition* and FARMS. The decision was made to scan these photographs at 300 dpi to balance image-quality that is acceptable for most purposes with manageability of file-size.[52] Images in the FARMS database were scanned from the ABMC's 5 x 7 transparencies at 200 dpi, as an illustrative enhancement to the project's main goal of providing a comprehensive database. The ABMC provides to scholars its high resolution images, those which have been acquired digitally during its Jerusalem expeditions, and those which have been scanned at 1200 dpi on CD-ROM from its 5 x 7 inch photographs. The images are provided at cost, and—by contract with OUP and the IAA—the scanned images are distributed only in single images or discrete sets, solely for academic use (and may be published only with the appropriate permission).

We will leave for the philosophers to discuss just what is an "archival" digital image.[53] The archaeologist, conservator and curator will likely provide answers that vastly differ from those offered by a textual scholar. Is it the one that most closely resembles the original? Should this original be as it was found, or as it is after some restoration? And exactly what is the "original"—the parchment itself as it was in the early 1950's? Or the scroll as it is now? Or is it the early photographs? Or should the archival image be the one that retains the most information? One can only be grateful that the Dead Sea Scrolls are of such great interest that we can have not only the debate, but also a sampling of types of images.

SELECT BIBLIOGRAPHY

Benedikson, L. "Phototechnical Problems: Some Results Obtained at the Huntington Library," *Library Science* 57 (1932) 789-94.

—. "Charred Documents," *Library Science* 58 (1933) 243-44.

Brooke, G. J., with the collaboration of Helen K. Bond. *The Allegro Qumran Collection on Microfiche* (Leiden: Brill, 1996).

Broshi, M. "The Negatives Archive of the Shrine of the Book," in Tov with Pfann (eds.), *Companion Volume*, 135-36.

Eisenman, R. H. and J. M. Robinson. *A Facsimile Edition of the Dead Sea Scrolls* (Washington, DC: Biblical Archaeology Society, 1991).

Lim, T. H. (ed.), with P. J. Alexander. *The Dead Sea Scrolls Electronic Reference Library* (Oxford: Oxford University Press; Leiden: Brill, 1997).

---

[52] T. H. Lim (ed.), *The Dead Sea Scrolls Electronic Reference Library*, vii–viii.

[53] Ester's monograph deals with these and many other issues in detail.

Reed, S. A. and M. J. Lundberg, with the collaboration of M. B. Phelps. *The Dead Sea Scrolls Catalogue* (SBLRBS 32, Atlanta: Scholars Press, 1994).

Smith, A. H. and F. Norman. "The Photography of Manuscripts," *London Mediaeval Studies* 1 (1937) 179.

Sukenik, E. L. *The Dead Sea Scrolls of the Hebrew University* (Jerusalem: Magnes Press, 1955).

Tov, E. (ed.), with the collaboration of S. J. Pfann. *The Dead Sea Scrolls on Microfiche* (Leiden: Brill and IDC, 1993).

—. *Companion Volume to the Dead Sea Scrolls on Microfiche* (2nd ed., Leiden: Brill and IDC, 1995).

Trever, J. C. *The Dead Sea Scrolls: A Personal Account* (Grand Rapids, MI: Eerdmans, 1977).

—. *The Untold Story of Qumran* (Westwood, NJ: Revell, 1965).

FARMS. *The Dead Sea Scrolls on CD: The FARMS Electronic Database* (Provo: Foundation for Ancient Research and Mormon Studies, 1997).

Yadin, Y. *The Temple Scroll.* (3 vols., Jerusalem: Israel Exploration Society, 1983).

—. *The Temple Scroll: The Hidden Law of the Dead Sea Sect* (Jerusalem: Steimatzky, 1985).

NEW TECHNOLOGICAL ADVANCES: DNA, ELECTRONIC DATABASES, IMAGING RADAR

DONALD W. PARRY, DAVID V. ARNOLD,
DAVID G. LONG, AND SCOTT R. WOODWARD

Three dissimilar technological innovations have been developed at Brigham Young University (BYU) and the Foundation for Ancient Research and Mormon Studies (FARMS).[1] Each of these was developed independently of the other and each contributes in its own unique way to Dead Sea Scrolls research.[2] Scott R. Woodward, from BYU's Department of Microbiology, has led a team of experts using DNA-techniques[3] to analyze several parchment fragments of the

---

[1] FARMS is a nonprofit educational foundation, independent of all other organizations. Its main reasearch interests include ancient history, language, literature, culture, geography, politics and law relevant to the scriptures.

[2] A number of recent technological advances, including radiocarbon dating, multi-spectral imaging, electronic digitization of texts, computer-assisted text reconstruction, and the creation and maintenance of internet Dead Sea Scroll sites have greatly benefited researchers; see, for example, G. Bonani et al., "Radiocarbon Dating of the Dead Sea Scrolls," ʿAtiqot 20 (1991) 27-32; G. A. Rodley, "An Assessment of the Radiocarbon Dating of the Dead Sea Scrolls," *Radiocarbon* 35 (993) 335-38; Gregory H. Bearman, Bruce Zuckerman, Kenneth Zuckerman and J. Chiu, "Multi-spectral Imaging of Dead Sea Scrolls and Other Ancient Documents" (Paper presented at the Annual Meeting of the Society of Biblical Literature [Washington, DC], 20-23 November, 1993); Gregory H. Bearman and Sheila I. Spiro, "Archaeological Applications of Advance Imaging Techniques," *BA* 59 (1996) 56-66; idem, "Imaging Clarified," in Donald W. Parry and Eugene C. Ulrich (eds.), *The Provo International Conference on the Dead Sea Scrolls: New Texts, Reformulated Issues, and Technological Innovations*, (STDJ 30; Leiden: Brill, 1998 [forthcoming]); Neil Silberman, "Digitizing the Ancient Near East," *Archaeology* 49/5 (1996) 86-88; Armin Lange, *Computer-Aided Text-Reconstruction and Transcription—CATT-Manual* (Tübingen: Mohr-Siebeck, 1993). In addition, the Orion Center for the Study of the Dead Sea Scrolls maintains a major Internet Site called "The Orion Home Page."

[3] The well-known abbreviation "DNA" denotes deoxyribonucleic acid.

Scrolls;[4] Donald W. Parry (Professor of Hebrew Language and Literature) has worked with a team from BYU and FARMS in the development of the Electronic Database of Dead Sea Scrolls materials;[5] and David V. Arnold and David G. Long (Department of Electrical and Computer Engineering) have developed a new and compact imaging-radar system that has archaeological applications for Qumran and its environs. This paper will set forth a brief description of each of these three innovations as they pertain to Dead Sea Scrolls research.

1. DNA AND THE DEAD SEA SCROLLS

A number of questions concerning the origin and production of the Dead Sea Scrolls may be addressed using DNA-analysis. Because these parchments were produced from animal skins, they may contain remnant DNA molecules. Within the last decade, new techniques in molecular biology have been developed that have made it possible to recover DNA from ancient sources. The molecular analysis of ancient DNA ("aDNA") from the Judaean Desert parchment fragments enables us to establish a genetic signature unique for each manuscript. The precision of this DNA-analysis will allow us to identify the species, population, and individual animal from which each parchment was produced.

1.1 Background

The ability to recover biomolecules, most importantly DNA, from ancient remains has opened new research that has many significant

---

[4] See Scott R. Woodward, Gila Kahila, Patricia Smith, Charles Greenblatt, Joe Zias and Magen Broshi, "Analysis of Parchment Fragments from the Judean Desert Using DNA Techniques," in Donald W. Parry and Stephen D. Ricks (eds.), *Current Research and Technological Developments on the Dead Sea Scrolls*, (STDJ 20; Leiden: Brill, 1996) 215-38.

[5] These include Noel B. Reynolds, professor of Political Science at BYU and president of FARMS; Steven W. Booras, electronic projects specialist at FARMS; and E. Jan Wilson, associate director of the FARMS Center for the Electronic Preservation of Ancient Religious Texts. In addition, a team of experts serve on the board of Advisors: Dr. Weston Fields, exective director of the Dead Sea Scrolls Foundation, and Professors Florentino García Martínez (Qumrân-Instituut), Dana Pike (BYU), Elisha Qimron (Ben Gurion University of the Negev), Lawrence H. Schiffman (New York University), David R. Seely (BYU), Shemaryahu Talmon (Hebrew University), Emanuel Tov (Hebrew University), and Eugene Ulrich (University of Notre Dame).

implications.[6] Access to aDNA provides the opportunity to study the genetic material of past organisms and to identify individual and population histories. Unfortunately, the DNA that has been recovered from archaeological specimens is of such a degraded nature that the usual techniques associated with DNA-fingerprinting cannot be used. However, the origin and identity of biological materials such as preserved skins or parchments may be detemined from modifications of the traditional procedures that involve the polymerase chain reaction ("PCR"), short segments of unique DNA from the mitochondria, and flanking short simple repeats from nuclear DNA.[7]

In 1984 the first reports on the retrieval of informative DNA-sequences from an extinct animal appeared,[8] followed by the cloning of DNA from the skin of an ancient Egyptian mummy[9] dated at 2,400 BP.[10] The rapid degradation of biomolecules begins immediately following death. Except in unusual circumstances, this process continues unabated until the molecules return to a native state. DNA, which occurs in large quantities in living tissue, degrades rapidly after death, and in most instances only small amounts of short DNA molecules can be recovered from dead tissue. This normally prevents recovery and analysis of DNA-sequences from ancient tissue.

However, the advent of PCR[11] in 1985 further opened the possibility of isolating DNA-sequences in extracts in which the majority of the molecules are damaged and degraded. Theoretically, a single intact copy of a target DNA-sequence, which needs only to be on the order of one hundred to two hundred base-pairs in length,

---

[6] Bernd Herrmann and Susanne Hummel, "Introduction," in B. Herrmann and S. Hummel (eds.), *Ancient DNA* (New York: Springer, 1994) 1-12.

[7] See Francis X. Villablanca, "Spatial and Temporal Aspects of Populations Revealed by Mitochondrial DNA," in Herrmann and Hummel (eds.), *Ancient DNA*, 31-58.

[8] See Russell Higuchi et al., "DNA Sequences from Quagga, an Extinct Member of the Horse Family," *Nature* 312 (1984) 282-84.

[9] See Svante Pääbo, "Molecular Cloning of Ancient Egyptian Mummy DNA," *Nature* 314 (1985) 644-45; Jörg T. Epplen, "Simple Repeat Loci as Tools for Genetic Identification," in Herrmann and Hummel (eds.), *Ancient DNA*, 13-30.

[10] BP ("before present") is equivalent in some scientific circles to BC or BCE.

[11] Randall K. Saiki et al., "Enzymatic Amplification of Beta-Globin Genomic Sequences and Restriction Site Analysis for Diagnosis of Sickle Cell Anemia," *Science* 230 (1985) 1350-54.

is sufficient for PCR, making it an ideal tool for aDNA studies. PCR products can be sequenced directly from a sample (which is preferable), or after cloning, making DNA-sequence comparisons an extremely useful tool for the study of kinship relationships between individuals and populations. The amplification of mitochondrial DNA ("mtDNA") from ancient bones and teeth dated from 750 to 5,450 years BP has been accomplished recently by a number of investigators.[12] In addition, aDNA has been used in the sex-identification of skeletal remains.[13] PCR has been successfully applied to the analysis of ancient mtDNA from a variety of soft tissue remains, including a 7,000-year old human brain,[14] an extinct marsupial wolf,[15] and—particularly relevant to this study—the

---

[12] Erika Hagelberg, B. Sykes and R. Hedges, "Ancient Bone DNA Amplified," *Nature* 342 (1989) 485; Erika Hagelberg et al., "Ancient Bone DNA: Techniques and Applications," in *Philosophical Transactions of the Royal Society of London B* 333 (1991) 339-407; Erika Hagelberg and J. B. Clegg, "Isolation and Characterization of DNA from Archaeological Bone," *Proceedings of the Royal Society of London B* 244 (1991) 45-50; S. Horai et al., "DNA Amplification from Ancient Human Skeletal Remains and Their Sequence Analysis," in *Proceedings of the Japanese Academy of Science* 65 (1989) 229-33; G. Hanni et al., "Amplification of Mitochondrial DNA Fragments from Ancient Human Teeth and Bone," *C. R. Academy of Science*, 3rd series, 310 (1990) 356-70; Susanne Hummel and Bernd Herrmann, "Y-Chromosome-Specific DNA Amplified in Ancient Human Bone," *Naturwissenschaften* 78 (1991) 266-67; D. A. Lawlor et al., "Ancient HLA Genes from 7500-year-old Archaeological Remains," *Nature* 349 (1991) 785-88; E. Beraud-Columb, J. M. Tiercy and G. Querat, "Human Beta-thalassemia Gene Detected in 7000-year-old Fossil Bones," in *Proceedings of the 3rd International Congress on Human Paleontology, Jerusalem, Israel, August 23-28, 1992* (1992) 146 (abstract); K. Thomas et al., "Spatial and Temporal Continuity of Kangaroo Rat Populations Shown by Sequencing," *Journal of Molecular Evolution* 31 (1990) 101-12; Scott R. Woodward et al., "Amplification of Nuclear DNA from Teeth and Soft Tissue," *PCR Methods and Applications* 3/4 (1994) 244-47; and Svante Pääbo, Russell G. Higuchi and Allan C. Wilson, "Ancient DNA and the Polymerase Chain Reaction," *Journal of Biological Chemistry* 264 (1989) 9709-12.

[13] Hummel and Herrmann, "Y-Chromosome-Specific DNA," 266-67; Svante Pääbo, "Ancient DNA: Extraction, Characterization, Molecular Cloning and Enzymatic Amplification," *Proceedings of the National Academy of Sciences* 83 (1989) 1939-43.

[14] See Lawlor et al., "Ancient HLA Genes," 785-88.

[15] R. H. Thomas et al., "DNA Phylogeny of the Extinct Marsupial Wolf," *Nature* 340 (1989) 465-67.

preserved museum skins of over thirty kangaroo rats.[16] Numerous reports document the successful extraction and amplification of aDNA from museum skins and field-collected specimens,[17] including both naturally-preserved (mummified) and actively-treated skins from a wide variety of organisms (especially birds and mammals).[18] Some of these skins have been subjected to the same conditions that we expect to exist in the scroll parchments, and the extraction procedures for such specimens are not substantially different from those we have used in previous studies of aDNA.

1.2 Methodology

Although there are many successful studies employing aDNA-analysis, numerous difficulties and methodological problems still arise. The PCR technology is extremely sensitive and can be easily affected by contamination from extraneous DNA material. The source of such contamination may be other personnel working in the field and laboratory or micro-organisms such as bacteria. Another problem is the presence of inhibitors of unknown origin in aDNA extracts that interfere with the PCR reaction.[19] In our laboratories, all work is routinely carried out using rooms, equipment, and reagents dedicated only to aDNA-analysis. All personnel wear masks and sterile gloves to minimize contamination, and extensive controls are routinely used in all stages of DNA-extraction and amplification. Specimens are thoroughly cleaned before sampling, and only sterile instruments that have been exposed to ultraviolet light to destroy DNA are used. Approaches have also been developed to overcome the inhibitor effect, either through dilution of the inhibitor prior to PCR[20] or via alternate purification techniques. Contamination by contemporary human DNA will not pose a serious problem to this study since it is easy to differentiate the contaminating human DNA from the animal DNA obtained from the parchments. The aDNA obtained from parchment fragments helps answer several questions:

---

[16] K. Thomas et al., "Spatial and Temporal Continuity," 101-12.

[17] R. H. Thomas et al., "DNA Phylogeny"; K. Thomas et al., "Spatial and Temporal Continuity"; M. Culver, personal communication.

[18] K. Thomas et al., "Spatial and Temporal Continuity."

[19] Hagelberg and Clegg, "Isolation and Characterization," 45-50; Pääbo, "Ancient DNA: Extraction."

[20] Hagelberg and Clegg, "Isolation and Characterization"; Pääbo, "Ancient DNA: Extraction."

What species of animals were used for parchment production?

It is currently thought that most of the scrolls were written on goat- or sheepskins, but variations in texture, color, thickness, follicle number, and distribution in the surviving parchments may indicate that other skins were also used. On the basis of microscopic examination of the distribution of hair-follicles that remain in the parchment fragments, W. Ryder[21] was able to determine four different groups that may have been the possible species of origin for twenty samples of parchment from the Dead Sea area. He determined that one sample group is derived from calf, one from a fine-wooled sheep, one from a medium-wooled sheep, and one from a hairy animal that could have been either a sheep or a goat. However, identification of the exact species is not possible on the basis of microscopic examination alone.

It is easy to suppose that scrolls destined to contain religious writings were produced from ritually clean animals. According to Maimonides, "A scroll of the Law or phylacteries written on skins not expressly tanned for those purposes, is unfit for use."[22] Evidence from biblical sources and from at least one of the Judaean desert manuscripts (the Temple Scroll) shows that very strict requirements were imposed on the purity of animal skins. In particular, the skins brought into the temple or the temple city had extra requirements placed on their origin and preparation. According to Y. Yadin, these skins had to be not only pure, but "entirely holy and pure."[23] In the Temple Scroll this requirement is stressed:

> Skin, even if it was made from the hide of a clean animal, unless the animal had been sacrificed in the Temple [should not be brought to the Temple city]. Such ordinary skins are, indeed, clean for the need of all labour in other cities, but "into the city of my temple they shall not bring [them]."[24]

Some of the parchments used at Qumran may have had less strict requirements for cleanliness and purity applied to them. It was therefore possible to use skins from species of animals that were clean, but not necessarily ritually pure or used for sacrifice in the

---

[21] W. Ryder, "Remains Derived from Skin," in *Microscopic Studies of Ancient Skins* (Oxford: Oxford University Press, 1965).

[22] Maimonides, as quoted by Yigael Yadin in *The Temple Scroll* (Jerusalem: Israel Exploration Society, 1983) 1.315.

[23] Yadin, *Temple Scroll*, 1.309.

[24] See the previous note.

temple. These clean, but not temple- or city-worthy, animals could have included a number of animal species such as gazelle, ibex, dishon or deer. By identifying the species of animal used for the production of a specific parchment, it may be possible to postulate a hierarchy of importance for the different manuscripts. Some would have been intended for use in the temple or synagogue and other important sites within the temple city or community, while others may have had lesser religious significance.

How many different manuscripts are represented in the collection of fragments at the Rockefeller and Israel Museums?

Unfortunately, most of the recovered parchment material is quite fragmented, making it difficult to establish physically contiguous pieces of manuscripts. It is estimated that the many thousands of fragments can be grouped into over eight hundred different scrolls, and it would be of tremendous value to determine exactly which fragments belong together. Obtaining DNA signatures unique to each manuscript will make it possible to sort out the physical relationships of scroll fragments. Such information should prove particularly useful in sorting out the huge number of small fragments that cannot be confidently grouped on the basis of fragment shape, style of handwriting, or text, and may well provide unique insights into the subsequent interpretation of the scrolls.

Which pieces can be grouped together as originating from the same scroll because they are from identical or related parchments?

Because individual animals can be identified by their unique genetic signature, it is theoretically possible to identify the unique origin of each of the parchment fragments based on their genetic information. Using the techniques of aDNA-analysis, pieces belonging to the same or closely-related skins can be grouped together. This should assist both in the reconstruction of manuscripts and in the verification of assemblies that were previously already made.

Did more than one scribe work on a single document, or did different scribes use parchment that originated from the same source for different manuscripts?

There are examples in which two or more scribes worked on the same manuscript, as was the case with the Temple Scroll, the Thanksgiving Scroll, and several other scrolls. If more than one scribe participated in the production of a single manuscript, which was then subsequently damaged and is today quite fragmented, the critical analysis based only on palaeography could falsely identify separate origins of what was a single text.

Because of their size, some manuscripts (i.e. the Great Isaiah Scroll, the Manual of Discipline and the Temple Scroll) are composed of parchments that were produced from a number of different animals. The Temple Scroll is written on nineteen separate sheets of parchment, each of which is thirty-seven to sixty-one centimeters in length.[25] It is probable that no more than two or four sheets were derived from the same animal. Analysis of fragments from each section of these scrolls will allow us to determine the degree of relatedness of the parchments in a single manuscript, and whether they are derived from identical or closely-related animals. This analysis can also be applied to repair patches, thus providing information about where a scroll was when it was patched.

Is the parchment for the patch from the same herd as the original manuscript? Does the patch represent a herd from a different region, reflecting mobility of either the original scroll or the herd?

Perhaps parchment was a trade item that was brought in from one or a number of different sources. The resulting data, revealing the level of relatedness of the parchment from a single scroll, will establish benchmarks that are valuable for the subsequent interpretation of the genetic data obtained by analysis of the aDNA from the fragments.

Does the collection represent a library from a single locality, or is it a collection representing contributions from a wide region?

Comparing DNA-fingerprints recovered from the parchments and those obtained from archaeological remains of animals found in ancient sites throughout Israel can determine the origins of individual parchments. In the ancient populations of domestic animals in Israel certain alleles[26] likely became fixed by inbreeding in local herds. This is especially true if a group such as that at Qumran was isolated and closed.[27] Biblical examples of the importance of sepa-

---

[25] *Temple Scroll*, 1.9-10.

[26] I.e. forms of a gene.

[27] James H. Charlesworth, *Jesus and the Dead Sea Scrolls* (New York: Doubleday, 1992), xxxiii; Emanuel Tov, "Textual Witnesses of the Bible," in idem, *Textual Criticism of the Hebrew Bible* (Minneapolis: Fortress, 1992) 102.

rating flocks and herds are reflected in Genesis 13:5–9, when Abram and Lot separate their herds to different locales, and again in 30:40, when Jacob separates his herds from those belonging to Laban.

It was apparently critical that animals for the production of skins for use in Jerusalem, the temple city, were derived from flocks and herds that were "known to their ancestors."[28] This suggests that flocks and herds were carefully observed and may have been guarded against "contaminating" crossbreeding. Such patterns of husbandry would effectively produce closed breeding-groups with predictable genetic consequences. Fixed allele patterns would establish specific markers in the population that could be used to identify and differentiate local herds. Analysis of aDNA that has been extracted from goat-bones excavated at Qumran and other archaeological sites within present-day Israel could reveal any fixed allele patterns and should be compared to the alleles found in the ancient parchments. Such an aDNA-analysis will determine if the sampled parchments were produced locally at Qumran or were collected from different locations. A test of the sensitivity of this procedure could be performed comparing genetic fingerprints from scrolls that were most likely composed at Qumran, such as the Rule of the Community (1QS), and others that were probably brought to Qumran other locations in Palestine, such as the Great Isaiah Scroll (1QIsa^a).[29] Another potential source of information about the origin of manuscripts is a comparison of DNA-sequence with "autograph" documents, several of which now appear to have been identified in the Qumran collections.[30] Since these autographs are considered to have been written by the people at Qumran, they can provide a genetic fingerprint of the parchment that was used by these individuals.

The molecular identification of parchment fragments involved a number of complex steps. We first demonstrated the ability to isolate and amplify aDNA from parchment on "modern parchment," animal skins that have been treated in a similar way to that which we believe

---

[28] Josephus, *Antiquities* (LCL 210; Cambridge, MA: Harvard University Press; London: Heinemann, 1966) 12 §146.

[29] Norman Golb, "The Problem of Origin and Identification of the Dead Sea Scrolls," *Proceedings of the American Philosophical Society* 124 (1980) 1-24; idem, "Who Hid the Dead Sea Scrolls?" *BA* 48 (1985) 68-82.

[30] See Golb, "The Problem of Origin," and idem, "Who Hid the Dead Sea Scrolls?"

was practiced in ancient times. To extract the DNA, the skin fragments were pulverized in liquid nitrogen, dissolved and lysed (i.e. disintegrated) in a highly chaotropic solution, and the DNA was recovered by collection on silica beads. We have extracted DNA from museum skins of rabbits and commercially-prepared deer- and sheepskins. These fragments were sequenced and shown to be specific for rabbit, deer, and sheep, respectively, and the procedures used were then repeated to obtain aDNA from the ancient parchment.

After we demonstrated that it was actually possible to obtain DNA from treated skins, the next step was to identify in modern goats—both domestic and wild—and other potential sources of parchment the appropriate DNA-sequence changes, or polymorphisms, that are capable of differentiating individuals, herds, or species. DNA was isolated from modern domestic goats, wild goats, sheep, ibex, and other animals that were possibly used for parchment-production and were then amplified using the polymerase chain reaction (PCR). From our preliminary results it is clear that unique DNA regions will be identified that will give good differentiation at both the species- and herd-levels.

1.3 The Results Obtained

We have begun to extract aDNA from small portions of parchment fragments of the Dead Sea Scrolls, to amplify biologically-active DNA using the polymerase chain reaction (PCR), to obtain DNA-sequences, and to identify unique genetic signatures of the fragments. This has shown that the process is feasible and can be used to re-establish the physical relationships of scroll fragments that may help clarify the translation and interpretation of the Scrolls.

We have extracted DNA from eleven small pieces (approximately 0.5 cm^2) of parchment from the area and time period corresponding to the Dead Sea Scroll parchments. DNA from these fragments has been successfully amplified and sequenced. The sequence of six of these fragments is most closely related to, but not identical with, that of both wild and domestic goats. It is significantly different from the human sequence, demonstrating that the parchment material was not contaminated by human DNA, neither in the handling of the parchment during collection nor during the laboratory manipulations. The number of differences between the aDNA and the contemporary goat-DNA is greater than was generally expected because of the accumulated normal evolutionary mutations over the intervening period of two thousand years. The aDNA is probably not from the same species as the contemporary goat samples. However, fewer differences occur between the ancient sample and the modern goat than between the ancient sample and either sheep or cow. This indicates a closer relationship to an animal such as a goat, rather than a cow or sheep. We then compared the first two of the eleven fragments with sequences that we have determined for the modern ibex and gazelle. These comparisons strongly suggest that these pieces were derived from a gazelle, ibex, or similar kind of animal.

We have also examined six fragments from five different sheets of the Temple Scroll, which have all proved to be derived from goats. For these pieces, no difference exists between ancient and modern goats at this gene locus. We are currently in the process of identifying individual DNA polymorphisms in those fragments to determine the degree of relatedness of the animals that were used to produce the parchment in the scroll.

We have also been able to isolate and amplify DNA from the archaeological bones of ibex and goats that were found at Masada. In most instances, horn-cores that have been identified by species are being used as the source of DNA. This demonstrates our ability to recover from ancient animal remains the necessary genetic information that will enable us to compare Dead Sea Scroll fragments with the animals from which they were derived. Such a comparison will allow geographical localization of the parchment sources.

In conclusion, we have demonstrated the ability to recover aDNA from the parchment on which the Dead Sea Scrolls were written. We have also shown that it is possible to recover authentic sequences from this material and to use it for making comparisons with other sequences. Our early results indicate that the skins from which the first two ancient fragments were derived are not domestic or wild goats, but are most likely a wild species of gazelle or ibex. We have also determined that seven other random scroll fragments are derived from goats, six of them from the Temple Scroll. These analyses differ from the earlier classifications that were made with recourse to microscopic analyses of similar parchment fragments from the same area by Ryder.[31] We have as yet not identified any parchment made from a species of sheep.

---

[31] W. Ryder, "Remains Derived from Skin."

This project is the beginning of a fruitful collaboration that will continue over the next few years. We hope that the analysis of DNA from parchment fragments will add a new level of critical analysis to Dead Sea Scrolls research.

2. THE DEAD SEA SCROLLS ON CD-ROM: THE FARMS ELECTRONIC DATABASE[32]

The FARMS Electronic Database has been produced in collaboration with the Ancient Biblical Manuscript Center (AMBC), Brigham Young University (BYU),[33] the Dead Sea Scrolls Foundation, E. J. Brill, the Israel Antiquities Authority (IAA), and Oxford University Press. It contains a fully-integrated and computerized collection of transcriptional texts and digitized images (or photographic images), as well as reference materials of importance for scholarly work on the Dead Sea Scrolls—the Hebrew Bible, an English translation of the Hebrew Bible, and the Septuagint. The texts include all the transcriptions that were published in the official DJD series through 1996, the preliminary versions of transcriptions to be published in 1997 or later, and many transcriptions that have been published in non-DJD venues (e.g. the Temple Scroll and the War Scroll). 800 digitized images, which were selected from the collection held at the Ancient Biblical Manuscript Center, correspond to these transcriptions.

New, more user-friendly features have been added to the Database since its preview presentation at the Provo International Conference on the Dead Sea Scrolls (15-17 July, 1996). The search-engine used is "WordCruncher," which has recently been considerably simplified at the front-end by BYU computer specialists via the addition of a second means of searching a word or phrase. In addition, the table of contents and interface have been modified so that the display is now similar to Windows 95. Access to the menus has also been facilitated, so that users can now be guided by either beginners' or advanced menus. A new coach system is in place, which—when activated at the "Help" menu—is designed to assist all users at every stage. If the

---

[32] For an early description of the Database, see Donald W. Parry and Steven W. Booras, "The Dead Sea Scrolls CD-ROM Database Project," in Parry and Ricks (eds.), *Current Research and Technological Developments*, 239-50.

[33] BYU developed the search engine "Wordcruncher" in the late 1980's so that researchers could access the Scriptures and other religious texts in English.

user desires help with a particular function, he or she can simply open the Help menu and receive a brief explanation. The Database also features an automatic lexicon or thesaurus; instead of the previous multi-step process for accessing the lexicon, users now simply press a single key. For this updated Database, WordCruncher has created a substring function for the Hebrew text, especially for searches, so that if a character exists in the middle of a triconsonantal root (for example), the search-engine can still conduct a root-search.

The Database has a number of functions that enable scholars and researchers to access the scrolls in ways that are not possible through other means. In addition to its function as an exhaustive concordance (even seeking and finding every question mark in a passage!), the Database offers complex, instantaneous and comprehensive searches of the transcriptional texts.[34] The search routine allows the user to design sophisticated searches of every occurrence of words, phrases or selected forms. It also permits searching a phrase, a single word, two words separated by other words, or a single letter, as one chooses. The user can even conduct a "wildcard search," entering two or three characters from the beginning, middle or end of a word—or on one, two or three lines of text—and the search-engine seeks all occurrences of the specified characters in the selected text.

The Database user may also access the transcriptional text by using the "WordWheel," which lists every word in the Database with the number of occurrences of specific words and the total count in a given text. The WordWheel presents the words in alphabetical order in the language of the text (Hebrew, English, Greek), and text-windows are created by clicking on a word with the mouse.

The Database also conducts sophisticated Hebrew verbal root-searches, regardless of affixal attachments (such as a prefix, suffix, or infix), including prepositions, the *waw* conjunction, and pronominal suffixes. For instance, one can search for a variety of constructions where one or more of the root-letters may be missing or arranged in a different order, such as III-*he* verbs, I-*nun* verbs, I-*yod* verbs, *hithpaʿel* verbs with sibilants that have undergone metathesis, and hollow verbs.

The results of the search (called "hits") are listed almost instantaneously and may be viewed in the Reference List display, or

---

[34] For a description and figures of the search routine, see Parry and Booras, "Dead Sea Scrolls CD-ROM Database Project," 244-47.

within a number of windows, with one reference per window. These windows may be adjusted (i.e. enlarged or reduced) to show one or several lines of text, the entire text, or may be scrolled down so the user can see all of the hits one after another. The user then prints the results of the search, or may store and retrieve them at a later date.

Two actual examples of the search routine are as follows: a simple word search reveals that the word בית occurs 2,109 times in the Bible and 194 times in the nonbiblical texts of the Qumran Caves; and the preposition על occurs 4,552 times in the Bible and 1,131 times in the nonbiblical Qumran texts. For these simple searches, the computer screen displays their number of occurrences, the name of the text source with references, and the context in which the searched words appear. After the required search words (בית and על) had been typed in, these searches each took less than one second each to complete.

A more Complex Search

The following letters were transcribed from a small fragment belonging to 4QSam[a]:

אׄ ו]
[ערב ו]נ
[ויה]

Although ערב is easy to locate in the Database by conducting a simple word-search, locating the reference in the books of Samuel is not as easy. After the characters ערב ו were entered "within 25 words" of ויה, the computer screen revealed a total of ten hits. But only one had all of the characters on the three lines of the small fragment, namely 1 Sam 14:24. Typing in the characters took a few seconds but WordCruncher's search-engine took less than one second to locate the ten hits. The fragment has accordingly been reconstructed as follows for the forthcoming edition in the DJD series:[35]

[	ההואׄ וׄ]יאל	24]	1
[	ה]ערב ונ]קמתי	]	2
[	[ויה]יׄ	25]	3

1 Sam 14:24-25

---

[35] F. M. Cross (with D. Parry), E. Ulrich, *Cave 4.XII: Samuel* (DJD 17; Oxford: Clarendon Press [forthcoming]).

The Database's approximately 900 images were scanned at 400 dpi on an Agfa Arcus II scanner. Each of these images is tagged to, and corresponds with, a particular transcriptional text. As the user reviews the transcriptions on the computer screen, he or she may click on an icon and view the corresponding digitized photographic images on the same screen. On occasion the user may also view alternate images (e.g. duplicate images taken under different conditions, with different methods and at different times). With the zooming capabilities[36] of the Database the user can examine high quality images at 500% of their actual size, often with little pixelization occurring. An example of a fragment from 4QSam^a (1 Sam 14:47-49) at 200% is presented on Plate 8.[37]

Beyond the advantages described in the previous paragraphs, the Database has other obvious benefits: convenience, protection of the originals, broad distribution, low cost, and the ability to manipulate the images. The Database is convenient and portable—one can carry the entire non-biblical Qumran library in the palm of one's hand and use it anywhere in the world where a computer and CD drive can be accessed. It also features high-quality digitized copies of the original scrolls and fragments, with no fear of mishandling these 2,000 year-old treasures. There is no limit to distribution of the Database (as permissions are granted), and so literally thousands of individuals may obtain a copy. Images and transcriptions may be distributed at relatively low cost to an individual or institution; and the images may be accessed through several types of commercial imaging-software (such as Adobe Photoshop). The user is thus able to cut and paste letters, words, or fragments, to enhance images via a number of techniques, to move fragments from one image to another (in the quest to identify the pieces), to flip, rotate, or manipulate images, and to carry out many other related tasks.

3. ARCHAEOLOGICAL APPLICATIONS OF IMAGING RADAR

During the past decade imaging radar has been applied to regions of potential archaeological interest.[38] For example, C. Elachi et al.[39]

---

[36] On the zooming capabilities and figures of the Database, cf. Parry and Booras, "Dead Sea Scrolls CD-ROM Database Project," 243-44.

[37] The Plates appear at the end of this volume.

[38] David V. Arnold and David G. Long are affiliated with the Microwave Earth Remote Sensing Laboratory, Electrical and Computer Engineering Department,

have shown that imaging radar can detect features buried under several meters of dry sand in the Sahara Desert, and D. Holcomb[40] describes how the subsurface capability of imaging radar can be used to provide a remote survey of the Taklamakan desert of northwestern China. D. Evans et al.[41] and F. El-Baz[42] have presented more recent radar images of the Taklamakan desert, revealing features such as waterways, ancient ruins and sections of the Great Wall of China. R. Blom et al.[43] have demonstrated that radar images can help in the detection of ancient roads.[44] In September 1994, a radar-image that was taken of Angkor in Cambodia from the Space-Shuttle by the Jet Propulsion Laboratory (in Pasadena)[45] showed how features covered by heavy vegetation may be discerned.[46] These studies and others show that imaging radar has the capability of detecting surface- and subsurface-features, as well as features obscured by heavy vegetation. This capability can be of significant assistance to the archaeological community, particularly if the technology can be made more widely available.

The imaging radar discussed above is officially termed "synthetic aperture radar" (SAR), a technology that has existed for more than thirty years. SARs are usually flown aboard large aircraft or

---

Brigham Young University in Provo, Utah. Many others have assisted Arnold and Long in the development of the imaging radar, including Douglas Thompson, Thomas Karlinsey, Perry Hardin, Elaine Alger, Gayle Miner and Adam Robertson.

[39] C. Elachi, L. E. Roth and G. G. Schaber, "Spaceborne Radar Subsurface Imaging in Hyperarid Regions," in *IEEE Transactions on Geoscience and Remote Sensing* 22/4 (1984) 383-87.

[40] D. W. Holcomb, "Shuttle Imaging Radar and Archaeological Survey in China's Taklamakan Desert," *JFA* 19 (1992) 129-38.

[41] D. L. Evans, E. R. Stofan, T. D. Jones and L. M. Godwin, "Earth from Sky," *Scientific American* 271/6 (1994) 70-75.

[42] See F. El-Baz, "Space Age Archaeology," *Scientific American* 277/2 (1997) 60-65.

[43] R. Blom, J. Zairins, N. Clapp and G. R. Hedges, "Space Technology and the Discovery of the Lost City of Ubar," in *Proceedings of the 1997 IEEE Aerospace Conference, 1-8 Feb. 1997, Aspen Colorado*, 19-28.

[44] These images are also found in the articles by Evans et al., "Earth from Sky," 70-75; and El-Baz, "Space Age Archaeology," 60-65.

[45] The JPL is is managed by the California Institute of Technology for NASA (the National Aeronautics and Space Administration).

[46] This image is available from the JPL website at http://www.jpl.nasa.gov.

spacecraft. Basically, SAR works by sending microwave energy-pulses towards the ground and processing the return echos, thus producing an image. Because of the complexity of SAR theory, a detailed discussion is not presented here; for further information the reader is referred to J. Curlander and R. McDonough,[47] S. Hovanessian,[48] W. Carrara et al.,[49] C. Jakowatz et al.,[50] or any of the many references contained in these works.

Even though the archaeological applications of SAR appear promising, the size, cost, and availability of SAR systems have limited their use by the archaeological community at large. In an attempt to make SAR technology more readily available and applicable to archaeology, we have developed a new compact SAR system. The Brigham Young University SAR ("YSAR") is small and inexpensive; even more important, it can be operated from a small four-to-six passenger aircraft, making the operating costs comparable to that required for optical surveys.

YSAR is flown at an altitude of 300 to 600 meters, producing images that are approximately 500 by 3,500 meters with a resolution of 1 meter. The system is operated at a microwave frequency of 2 GHz ("Gigahertz") which can allow some surface- and canopy-penetration. Many technical details related to YSAR can be provided, but for the sake of brevity we refer reders to detailed descriptions of YSAR to be found in D. Thompson et al.[51]

---

[47] J. C. Curlander and R. N. McDonough, *Synthetic Aperture Radar: Systems and Processing* (New York: Wiley, 1991).

[48] S. A. Hovanessian, *Introduction to Synthetic Array and Imaging Radars)* (Norwood, MA: Artech House, 1980).

[49] W. G. Carrara, R. S. Goodman and R. M. Majewski, *Spotlight Synthetic Aperture Radar: Signal Processing Algorithms* (Norwood, MA: Artech, 1995).

[50] C. V. Jakowatz, D. E. Wahl, P. H. Eichel, D. C. Ghiglia and P. A. Thompson, *Spotlight-Mode Synthetic Aperture Radar: A Signal Processing Approach* (Boston: Kluwer Academic Publishers, 1996).

[51] D. G. Thompson, D. V. Arnold, D. G. Long, G. F. Miner and T. W. Karlinsey, "YSAR: A Compact, Low-Cost Synthetic Aperture Radar," in *Proceedings of the 1996 International Geoscience and Remote Sensing Symposium, 27-31 May 1996, Lincoln Nebraska* (1996) 1892-94. Also see D. G. Thompson, D. V. Arnold, D. G. Long, G. F. Miner, T. W. Karlinsey and A. E. Robertson, "YSAR: A Compact, Low-Cost Synthetic Aperture Radar," in *Proceedings of the 1997 International Geoscience and Remote Sensing Symposium, 27 Jul.–1 Aug. 1997, Singapore* (1997) 386-88.

In September 1996, the YSAR system was taken to Israel to collect data over several archaeological sites, which was achieved during six flights at an altitude of 300 meters. We have processed some of these data and have created SAR images of the Zippori National Forest, Tel Safi and Qumran areas. Since this project is still in its early stages, we offer here only preliminary images of these sites. More analysis is needed to fully evaluate the archaeological information in these images, but so far the results have proved encouraging.

The Zippori site sits on a large hill and contains many partially-excavated ruins, some of which are largely covered with trees and brush. A sample SAR image of the area is shown in Figure 1.[52] Many rock fences, excavations, buildings, roads, and trees can be seen throughout the image. A set of 60 cm microwave corner-reflectors which were arranged in a cross and spaced 10 meters apart are indicated by the arrow. These corner-reflectors are used to help determine the performance of the SAR system.

Tel Safi is thought to be the ancient Philistine city of Gath. A SAR image of the site appears in Figure 2. The tel spans the middle portion of the image, and an arrow is again used to indicate the locations of the corner-reflectors. As was the case in the Zippori image, many surface features that reveal human activity are evident.

Qumran is situated on a shelf between a range of cliffs and the Dead Sea. Our main purpose was not to identify the locations of possible caves, but rather to observe past global traffic patterns and human disturbance. We hope such information may be helpful in developing a regional picture of ancient life in the area surrounding Qumran. SAR images that were taken near Qumran are shown in Figures 3 and 4. Both of these show the main road along the Dead Sea, and a large orchard is evident in Figure 3. Unfortunately, the region around Qumran was difficult to image due to random aircraft motion that was caused by excessive turbulence from thermal air-currents, which resulted in blurred images. A new SAR system which is currently being developed at Brigham Young University will solve this problem for future flights. However, even with the blurring effect, different features are evident in SAR imagery than are found in optical imagery. As we carefully compare the Qumran SAR imagery with corresponding optical imagery, we hope to find important differences between the two.

---

[52] Figures 1–4 appear on Plate 15 at the end of the volume.

As is evident from results obtained over the last decade, aerial SAR surveys have the potential of providing new information to the archaeology community; our efforts have made considerable progress toward making this technology more available. We have an ongoing program aimed at improving the overall performance and availability of SAR. In this connection, we recently received a grant from NASA to design and build an interferometric SAR, a system that will operate at 10 GHz and be capable of determining surface topography as well as producing radar images. The YSAR system which has been described in this paper is being rebuilt and integrated with the newer multiple frequency system, which will be well-suited for future aerial SAR surveys. Our team will also continue to analyze the information we have collected, to collect new data, and to assess the usefulness of SAR technology for the archaeological community.

SELECT BIBLIOGRAPHY

Bearman, G. H. and S. I. Spiro. "Imaging Clarified," in Parry and Ulrich (eds.), *The Provo International Conference on the Dead Sea Scrolls* [forthcoming].

Bearman, G. H., B. Zuckerman, K. Zuckerman and J. Chiu. "Multi-spectral Imaging of Dead Sea Scrolls and Other Ancient Documents" (Paper presented at the Annual Meeting of the Society of Biblical Literature [Washington, DC], 20-23 November, 1993).

Blom, R., J. Zairins, N. Clapp and G. R. Hedges. "Space Technology and the Discovery of the Lost City of Ubar," in *Proceedings of the 1997 IEEE Aerospace Conference, 1-8 Feb. 1997, Aspen Colorado*, 19-28.

Curlander, J. C. and R. N. McDonough. *Synthetic Aperture Radar: Systems and Processing* (New York: Wiley, 1991).

El-Baz, F. "Space Age Archaeology," *Scientific American* 277/2 (1997) 60-65.

Elachi, C., L. E. Roth and G. G. Schaber. "Spaceborne Radar Subsurface Imaging in Hyperarid Regions," in *IEEE Transactions on Geoscience and Remote Sensing* 22/4 (1984) 383-87.

Evans, D. L., E. R. Stofan, T. D. Jones and L. M. Godwin. "Earth from Sky," *Scientific American* 271/6 (1994) 70-75.

Holcomb D. W. "Shuttle Imaging Radar and Archaeological Survey in China's Taklamakan Desert," *JFA* 19 (1992) 129-38.

Hovanessian, S. A. *Introduction to Synthetic Array and Imaging Radars* (Norwood, MA: Artech House, 1980).

Lange, A. *Computer-Aided Text-Reconstruction and Transcription—CATT-Manual* (Tübingen: Mohr-Siebeck, 1993).

Parry, D. W. and S. D. Ricks (eds.). *Current Research and Technological Developments on the Dead Sea Scrolls* (STDJ 20; Leiden: Brill, 1996) 215-38.

Parry, D. W. and S. W. Booras. "The Dead Sea Scrolls CD-ROM Database Project," in Parry and Ricks (eds.), *Current Research and Technological Developments*, 239-50.

Parry, D. W. and E. Ulrich (eds.). *The Provo International Conference on the Dead Sea Scrolls: New Texts, Reformulated Issues, and Technological Innovations* (STDJ 30; Leiden: Brill, 1998 [forthcoming]).

Silberman, N. "Digitizing the Ancient Near East," *Archaeology* 49/5 (1996) 86-88.

Thompson, D. G., D. V. Arnold, D. G. Long, G. F. Miner and T. W. Karlinsey. "YSAR: A Compact, Low-Cost Synthetic Aperture Radar," in *Proceedings of the 1996 International Geoscience and Remote Sensing Symposium, 27-31 May 1996, Lincoln Nebraska* (1996) 1892-94.

Thompson, D. G., D. V. Arnold, D. G. Long, G. F. Miner, T. W. Karlinsey and A. E. Robertson. "YSAR: A Compact, Low-Cost Synthetic Aperture Radar," in *Proceedings of the 1997 International Geoscience and Remote Sensing Symposium, 27 Jul.–1 Aug. 1997, Singapore* (1997) 386-88.

Woodward, Scott R. et al. "Amplification of Nuclear DNA from Teeth and Soft Tissue," *PCR Methods and Applications* 3/4 (1994) 244-47.

Woodward, S. R., G. Kahila, P. Smith, C. Greenblatt, J. Zias and M. Broshi. "Analysis of Parchment Fragments from the Judean Desert Using DNA Techniques," in Parry and Ricks (eds.), *Current Research and Technological Developments*, 215-38.

ASSEMBLING AND RECONSTRUCTING MANUSCRIPTS

ANNETTE STEUDEL

In celebrating the fiftieth anniversary of the first Qumran finds, it is my distinct pleasure to present a special area of research on the Dead Sea Scrolls. While this area may not appear at first sight to be very sensational, it deals with what is fundamental to all Scrolls study—the establishment of the text. The roots of reconstructing manuscripts are found in the early years of Qumran investigation. Since the 1960's, however, its development as a method and its application are inseparably connected with the name of Hartmut Stegemann. In more recent times, the general awareness of the process of reconstructing Dead Sea Scrolls has emerged, which is reflected in several of the most recent editions in the DJD series.[1]

In discussion of the manuscripts that were discovered at Qumran, the term "Dead Sea Scrolls" is freqently used. While this is an appropriate designation, one should nevertheless be aware of an important fact. Among the more than 800 manuscripts found at Qumran there are only nine *scrolls* which are more or less well preserved: 1QIsa^a, 1QIsa^b, 1QGenAp, 1QS+Sa+Sb, 1QM, 1QH^a, 1QpHab, 11QPs^a, 11QT^a. Added to these are the completely preserved Copper Scroll (3Q15), the single sheet of leather containing 4QTest (4Q175),[2] and very probably the small square "card" containing 4QList of False Prophets ar (4Q339).[3] In reality,

---

[1] For example: J. Trebolle Barrera, "481a. 4QApocryphe d'Elisée," in G. J. Brooke et al. (eds.), *Qumran Cave 4.XVII: Parabiblical Texts, Part 3* (DJD 22; Oxford: Clarendon Press, 1996) 305–9, esp. 305; J. J. Collins and P. Flint, "244. 4Qpseudo-Daniel^b ar," in Brooke et al. (eds.), *Qumran Cave 4.XVII* (DJD 22) 123–31 + pls. VII-X, esp. 123; and G. J. Brooke, "252. 4QCommentary on Genesis A," in Brooke et al. (eds.), *Qumran Cave 4.XVII* (DJD 22) 185-207, esp. 186-87.

[2] See H. Stegemann, *Die Essener, Qumran, Johannes der Täufer und Jesus. Ein Sachbuch* (5th ed., Herder Spektrum 4128; Freiburg: Herder, 1996) 17.

[3] Although the right part of this unique document is unfortunately missing, the text is almost complete. According to its editors M. Broshi and A. Yardeni (in M. Broshi et al. [eds.], *Qumran Cave 4.XII: Parabiblical Texts, Part 1* [DJD 19;

all the other so-called "scrolls" exist only in a fragmentary form, very often in no more than tiny bits of pieces. So the Dead Sea Scrolls must still be regarded as a huge and incomplete jigsaw puzzle.

This article is in two parts, the first of which deals with the assembling of the many fragments from Qumran. The second part examines the feasibility and process of reconstructing scrolls out of these fragments, with particular emphasis on the necessity and purpose and of undertaking material reconstructions, the methods and techniques involved, the difficulties that arise, and some future prospects.

1. ASSEMBLING MANUSCRIPTS

Assembling Qumran manuscripts is a process that was basically completed in the thirteen years following the discovery of the first scrolls in 1947.[4] To a very large extent, this enterprise involves the material from Cave 4, where upwards of 15,000 fragments were found.[5] The laborious work of sorting all the single fragments and assembling these into different manuscripts was undertaken by the original team of editors in the 1950's and 1960's. This international and interconfessional team was constituted by Père R. de Vaux, who also served as Editor-in-Chief. The other members were J. T. Milik, J. Starky, D. Barthélemy, J. M. Allegro, J. Strugnell, F. M. Cross, P. W. Skehan and C. H. Hunzinger; the material from Cave 11 was later assigned to J. A. Sanders, J. van der Ploeg and A. S. van der Woude.[6] It is no exaggeration to say that the most significant single step in Dead Sea Scrolls research was made by these scholars. Besides grouping together the many fragments into discrete texts, they also prepared important editions[7] and the so-called "Card

---

Oxford: Clarendon Press, 1995] 77-79), its original size may have been 8.5 cm x 7 cm. The card was folded twice and was perhaps held together with a string passed through parallel holes at its left (and possibly also at its right).

[4] According to P. Benoit (in P. Benoit et al., *Les Grottes de Murabbaʿât* [DJD 2; Oxford: Clarendon Press, 1961] vi), the identification of the fragments was in principle concluded in 1960.

[5] P. Benoit, *Les Grottes de Murabbaʿât* (DJD 2), vi.

[6] A collection of unpublished photos from those early times of Qumran research is on exhibition by Alexander Schick in Westerland (Sylt), Germany.

Concordance," which is still extremely valuable and demonstrates the high quality of the early group's work.[8]

It is admirable—indeed, incredible—how this team managed to handle the enormous mass of fragments, since nearly everything was in disarray. As a rule it was only known from which cave, but not from which manuscript, individual pieces had come. Only on rare occasions were some fragments belonging to the same scroll found still adhering together.[9] It must be emphasized that this state of confusion had not been caused primarily by the Bedouin or archaeologists who excavated the caves or transported the fragments, but had already come about during the many centuries when the scrolls were lying in the caves. Most had not been deposited in jars, but had simply been stored in a virtually unprotected state. The chaotic state of the manuscripts is chiefly attributed to the wind

---

[7] For example, D. Barthélemy and J. T. Milik, *Qumran Cave I* (DJD 1; Oxford: Clarendon Press, 1955), and preliminary editions such as 11QMelch (11Q13) edited by A. S. van der Woude ("Melchisedek als himmlische Erlösergestalt in den neugefundenen eschatologischen Midraschim aus Qumran Höhle XI," *OTS* 14 [1965] 354–73 + pls. I–II). The only exception is J. M. Allegro's *Qumrân Cave 4.I* (4Q158–4Q186) (DJD 5; Oxford: Clarendon Press, 1968); on its inferior value see J. Strugnell, "Notes en marge du volume V des 'Discoveries in the Judaean Desert of Jordan'," *RevQ* 7 (1970) 163-276, esp. 163-67.

[8] The Card Concordance (ed. J. Strugnell), which was prepared by R. E. Brown, J. A. Fitzmyer, W. G. Oxtoby and J. Teixidor between 1952 and the early 1960's, includes the Hebrew and Aramaic non-biblical material from Caves 2 to 10 at Qumran, and serves a supplement to K.-G. Kuhn, *Konkordanz zu den Qumrantexten* (Göttingen: Vandenhoeck & Ruprecht, 1960). Although corrections are sometimes necessary (especially due to improved technology), in several cases the early readings of the Card Concordance are still better than those which have been presented subseqently by other scholars.

[9] Note, for example, 4QSongs of the Sage[b] (4Q511), frgs. 28 and 29 (in M. Baillet, *Qumrân Grotte 4.III [4Q482–4Q520]* [DJD 7; Oxford: Clarendon Press, 1982] 235); and—still sticking together—11QSongs of the Sabbath Sacrifice (11QShir Shabb[j]) frg(s). q (in C. Newsom, *Songs of the Sabbath Sacrifice: A Critical Edition* [HSS 27; Atlanta: Scholars Press, 1985] pl. XIX), which are unfortunately lost. It is a great pity that some information had obviously not been recorded during the process of separating layers of fragments or was lost later. Such notes would now be extremely helpful for the purposes of reconstructing manuscriptsm such as 11QNew Jerusalem (11Q18); cf. F. García Martínez "The Last Surviving Columns of 11QNJ," in F. G. Martínez et al. (eds.), *The Scriptures and the Scrolls. Studies in Honour of A. S. van der Woude on the occasion of his 65th birthday* (VTSup 49; Leiden: Brill, 1992) 178-92, esp. 180-83.

blowing through certain caves (notably 2 and 4), small animals such as rats,[10] and explorations of the caves by earlier looters or explorers[11].

But the following question now arises: How were these scholars, as they worked in the famous "scrollery" of the Palestine Archaeological Museum, able to determine exactly which fragments belonged to a certain manuscript and which were part of another? Various criteria for grouping fragments together were gradually established and refined by the team: the general appearance of the leather, its colour, the thickness and the preparation of the skin, the dimensions of the manuscript, the columns, the margins and the rulings, the ink, the trace of the pen, the hand (i.e. handwriting), the carefulness or carelessness of the scribe, the orthography, the language, the content and the genre.[12] Such a task is even more difficult than it seems to be—especially with respect to previously unknown compositions—because nearly all these features can vary within one and the same scroll. For example, from one sheet to another the skin may differ in thickness and colour, and the dimensions of the columns and the ruling may vary.[13] Moreover, two scribes may have produced a single manuscript,[14] a new pen may

---

[10] See the photograph of the rat nest containing fragments that was found at Murabba'ât (P. Benoit et al., *Les Grottes de Murabba'ât* [DJD 2], pl. II).

[11] Material reconstruction shows that in some instances larger fragments are missing where they would certainly be expected to be preserved—for example, 4QS^d (S. Metso, *The Textual Development of the Qumran Community Rule* [STDJ 21; Leiden: Brill, 1997]). Such fragments may well have been purchased by tourists during the early years of the Qumran finds.

[12] One rumour—certainly a humorous one!—is that the different *taste* of the fragments was also a criterion. The Qumran fragments surely taste rather similar, i.e. quite salty. According to laboratory tests, salt deposits were found on the glass plates between which the fragments used to be stored in the museum. See the information provided by curator L. Libman of the Rockefeller Museum, as reported by E. Hecht in *The Jerusalem Post Magazine*, March 1, 1996 ("Save our Scrolls," 17-18); as well as the article by E. Boyd-Alkalay and E. Libman elsewhere in this first volume of the Fiftieth Anniversary collection ("Preserving the Dead Sea Scrolls and Qumran Artifacts").

[13] The difference in leather, rulings and sizes of columns is illustrated by the first sheet (col. 8-9) and the second sheet (cols.10-12) of 4QMidrash on Eschatology^b (4Q177); cf. A. Steudel, *Der Midrasch zur Eschatologie aus der Qumrangemeinde (4QMidrEschat$^{a, b}$)* (STDJ 13: Leiden: Brill, 1994) 61-70.

[14] See, for example, 1QH^a and 4QD^a.

have been substituted at a certain point,[15] the orthography is often inconsistant,[16] and topics can easily change within the same text. It is thus amazing to what extent this first group of scholars' classification of the fragments still holds true today. Very rarely are fragments detected which do not in fact belong to the scroll to which they had been assigned all those years ago.[17]

In some cases, of course, it may prove impossible to decide with certainty whether a fragment belongs to a particular manuscript or not.[18] The process of reducing the number of unidentified pieces is still continuing, since a considerable number of such fragments still exists. Since significant finds or identifications might still be possible, it is worthwhile for scholars to study the photographic plates containing unidentified fragments in various DJD editions and in the Brill microfiche edition,[19] as well as the plates and remaining

---

[15] For example, in 4QD^a (4Q266): J. Baumgarten, *Qumran Cave 4. XIII: The Damascus Document [4Q266-273]* (DJD 18, Oxford: Clarendon Press, 1996) 26.

[16] For example, note—within the same fragment of 4QSapiential Work A (4Q418)—the spelling of כי\איכ (with and without *'alep*) in frg. 9, lines 11, 17; in frg. 55, lines 8, 11; and כול\וכל (plene and defective) in frg. 58, lines 2, 3.

[17] Many examples that exist involve the manuscripts from DJD 5; see the numerous corrections by J. Strugnell on 4Q183 ("Notes en marge du volume V"), and those of M. Horgan (*Pesharim: Qumran Interpretations of Biblical Books* [Washinghton: The Catholic Biblical Association of America, 1979]) on 4QpUnid. Yet to be fully solved is the problem with the fragments that were attributed by Allegro to 4QTanḥumim (4Q176); cf. Strugnell, "Notes en marge du volume V," 236; and M. Kister, "Newly-Identified Fragments of the Book of Jubilees: Jub 23: 21-23, 30-31," *RevQ* 12 (1987), 529-36. Recently É. Puech has noted that frg. 19 of the 4QMidrash on Eschatology^b (4Q177)—whose placement within the reconstruction was problematic and only tentatively adopted (A. Steudel, *Der Midrasch zur Eschatologie*, 112)—in fact belongs to 4Q525 (4QBeatitudes); see in É. Puech, *Textes Hébreux (4Q521–4Q528, 4Q576–4Q579)* (DJD 25; Oxford: Clarendon Press, [forthcoming]). The main reason for erroneous assignments of fragments is the widespread use of the formal tradition whose letters are more standardized—i.e. less characteristic; mistakes in assigning such fragments to a certain manuscript are thus more likely than in the case of those written in other scripts.

[18] This normally holds true for small fragments that preserve only a few letters, for example: frg. 17 of 4Q408 or 4QApocryphon of Moses^c? (*olim* 4QMorning and Evening Prayer).

[19] E. Tov (ed.) with S. J. Pfann (eds.), *The Dead Sea Scrolls on Microfiche. A Comprehensive Facsimile Edition of the Texts from the Judaean Desert, Companion Volume* (Leiden: Brill and IDC, 1993).

boxes of leather fragments and scraps housed in the Rockefeller Museum.[20]

A problem to have emerged only recently is extremely difficult to solve. It seems possible for the same scribe to have copied a work twice (or even more often?), which means that fragments that are counted as one manuscript in fact belong to two different scrolls. This may well be the case with 4Q418[21]; however, to this point we have no experience with other examples. If there is no actual textual overlap within a manuscript, such evidence will be discovered only by chance, mostly in the context of an attempted material reconstruction. Such material reconstructions may be helpful to sort out—via the identification of similar damage patterns—the fragments which belong to one or another scroll.[22]

Another question with respect assembling fragments which has not yet been properly dealt with concerns precisely the opposite phenomenon. Could manuscripts which are written by the same scribe, but which are now counted—especially because of their content—under separate numbers, in fact belong to one and the same scroll?[23] Possible examples of this kind are 4QpHos^b (4Q167) and

---

[20] Several encouraging examples have emerged. For example, among a group of unidentified fragments É. Puech found a number belonging to 1QH^a (É. Puech, *La croyance des Esséniens en la vie future: immortalité, resurrection, vie éternelle* [2 vols., Études bibliques, n.s. 21-22; Paris: Gabalda, 1993] 2.335-419). In addition,, H. Stegemann recently detected a yet unidentified piece of 4QD^d (4Q269).

[21] Cf. T. Elgvin, "Admonition Texts from Qumran Cave 4," in M. O. Wise et al. (eds.), *Methods of Investigation of the Dead Sea Scrolls and the Khirbet Qumran Site. Present Realities and Future Prospects* (ANYAS 722; New York: The New York Academy of Sciences, 1994) 179-96, esp. 180.

[22] A further hint for dividing a manuscript in two might be the existence of top margins of different size; on 4QSapiential Work A (4Q418) compare, for example, frgs. 128 (PAM 43.481) and 198 (PAM 43.474). While the size of bottom margins can vary from one sheet to another (rarely even within one sheet—cf. frg. 103 of 4Q418 on PAM 43.475), the top margins seem to be consistently of the same size within manuscripts among the Qumran finds (The only exception involving a slight difference is 1QpHab; note the difference of about half a centimeter between the first sheet [cols. 1–7] and the second [cols. 8–13]).

[23] Theoretically, even two scrolls with different hands might form a single manuscripts since there are a number of exemplars containing two different hands. Such cases, however, would be somewhat difficult to detect and to prove.

4QpMic (4Q168), which may come from a single pesher on the Minor Prophets.[24] Material reconstruction is a proper instrument whereby assumptions like this may be verified or falsified.

Last but not least, an important achievement of the first team of editors needs be mentioned: the identification of direct joins between tiny bits of fragments, whereby these pioneering scholars succeeded in combining hundreds of fragments. The care and precision in which they achieved this is demonstrated by the fact that in later times further material joins have been detected in relatively few cases—and only then by real experts.[25]

2. RECONSTRUCTING MANUSCRIPTS

2.1 Necessity, Aim and Advantage

As was mentioned above, virtually all Qumran manuscripts are preserved in a fragmentary state. In most cases the fragments of such scrolls—where there are no known parallel texts[26]—are presented in an edition only according to their size, starting with the largest fragment and ending with the smallest.[27] While this procedure is often inevitable and is certainly a cautious one, in many cases it is fruitful to go further—i.e. to attempt a material reconstruction of the scroll. Such material reconstructions may be accomplished with both leather and papyrus scrolls.[28]

---

[24] On this possibility, see J. Strugnell, "Notes en marge du volume V," 204.

[25] Scarcely has an old join ever had to be removed. One example is the misjoin of the right and the left parts of frg. 15 of 1QH^a in E. Sukenik's *Hodayot* edition, where both pieces come from different areas of the original scroll (cf. E. L. Sukenik [ed.], *The Dead Sea Scrolls of the Hebrew University* [Jerusalem: Magnes Press and the Hebrew University, 1955]). See H. Stegemann, "Methods for the Reconstruction of Scrolls from Scattered Fragments," in L. H. Schiffman (ed.), *Archaeology and History in the Dead Sea Scrolls. The New York University Conference in Memory of Yigael Yadin* (JSPSup 8; JSOT/ASOR Monographs 2; Sheffield: JSOT Press, 1990) 189-220, esp. 210 n.22.

[26] Of course, this statement does not include the biblical scrolls from Qumran.

[27] In some cases the logic of numbering and presenting fragments of a certain manuscript is no longer understandable, since it is neither guided by the size of the fragments nor seems to reflect purely material evidence; see, for example, 4QSongs of the Sage^b (4Q511).

[28] Reconstructing papyrus scrolls is much more difficult because of the fibres and our relative lack of experience with this material. The restoration of the only scroll made of neither skin nor papyrus, the Copper Scroll, was recently undertaken

The aim of a material reconstruction of scrolls is to acquire more information about a work which has been handed down in a fragmentary state, especially to gain more insight into its text, its structure, its content and its genre. Prior to their material reconstruction, some Qumran compositions had gone virtually unstudied by scholars, in that they were too fragmentary for any sense to be made of them.[29] However, following a thoroughgoing physical reconstruction both the appearance and the comprehension of several works has been advanced extensively.[30] The method involved is of particular importance in three respects:

(1) For those manuscripts which represent a formerly unknown work and which have no overlaping parallel text. Examples include the reconstruction of 11QMelchizedek (11Q13) by É. Puech,[31] and his proposed restoration of 4QMessianic Apocalypse (4Q521).[32]

(2) In cases where several copies of a work exist a material reconstruction is often worthwhile. We are now aware of a number of compositions that have undergone a complex process of redaction; two examples are the Rule of War (1QM, 4QM)[33] and—as was recently demonstrated in detail by S. Metso—the Community Rule (1QS, 4QS, 5QS).[34] Some scrolls in this

---

by experts at the Électricité de France (see their contribution in G. J. Brooke and P. R. Davies (eds.), *Copper Scroll Studies: Papers presented at the International Symposium on the Copper Scroll, Manchester, September 1996* (JSP Sup series; Sheffield: Sheffield Academic Press [in press]). É. Puech's re-reading of the Copper Scroll—based on this reconstruction—will appear in *NTOA* (Archaeological series) 2, edited by the University of Fribourg and Électricité de France.

[29] For instance, 4QMidrash on Eschatology^b (= 4QCatena A, 4Q177). Almost ignored for the same reason is 4QTanḥumim (4Q176), a work which is certainly Qumranic; no successful material reconstruction of 4Q176 has yet been achieved (on associated problems, cf. n.17 above).

[30] E.g. 4QMidrash on Eschatology^a (= 4QFlorilegium, 4Q174). The two-part structure of the composition (Introduction: interpretation of Deut 33 and 2Sam 7; Main Part: interpretation of selected psalms from the [Davidic] Psalter) became clear only after a material restoration. In addition, the fact that 4Q174 and 4Q177 are two copies of the same Qumran work—with 4Q174 representing the beginning, and 4Q177 the middle—became apparent only after a material reconstruction of both manuscripts (cf. Steudel, *Der Midrasch zur Eschatologie*, 126-28, 151).

[31] Puech, "Notes sur le manuscrit 11QMelkîsédeq," *RevQ* 12 (1987) 483-513.

[32] Puech, "Une apocalypse messianique (4Q521)," *RevQ* 15 (1992) 475-522.

[33] Unfortunately, no material reconstruction of the 4QM manuscripts has yet been attempted.

[34] S. Metso, *The Textual Development of the Qumran Community Rule* (STDJ 21; Leiden: Brill, 1997).

category may present only parts of a work or collection, while others present the whole.[35]

(3) Even for biblical manuscripts a material reconstruction can sometimes be profitable. One example is the restoration of 4QKings by J. Trebolle Barrera.[36] Some of the texts in this group may in fact turn out to be excerpted texts rather than "biblical" manuscripts (e.g. 4QDtn^n).

The immense advantage of a material reconstruction is that it is guided not by textual speculations but is instead oriented towards the physical evidence of the fragments. This procedure enables the scholar to ascertain the precise width of gaps between fragments as well as their order in the original scroll.

2.2 Method of Reconstructing Manuscripts

As far back as 1955, J. T. Milik undertook a material reconstruction of 1Q22 and of 1QSb in DJD 1.[37] But the actual method of material reconstruction of scrolls from scattered fragments—now also known as the "Stegemann-method"—was developed by H. Stegemann in his 1963 reconstruction of 1QH^a,[38] and further described in his famous English-language article of nearly three decades later.[39] This methodology has also been applied extensively

---

[35] For instance, the Rule of the Congregation (1QSa) and the Rule of the Blessings (1QSb) are represented only in one scroll, i.e. after 1QS; they are not included in any of the 4QS manuscripts. Another example may well be 4QMMT^b (4Q395), which according to E. Qimron and J. Strugnell (*Qumran Cave 4.V: Miqṣat Maʿaśe Ha-Torah* [DJD 10; Oxford: Clarendon Press, 1994] 14) probably had only the sections B and C of MMT, and is lacking the calendrical part A.

[36] J. Trebolle Barrera, "4QKings (4Q54)," in J. Trebolle Barrera and L. Vegas Montaner (eds.), *Proceedings of the International Congress on the Dead Sea Scrolls, Madrid, March 1991* (STDJ 11; Leiden: Brill, 1992) 229-46.

[37] J. T. Milik, *Qumran Cave I* (DJD 1) 91-97, 118.

[38] H. Stegemann, "Die Rekonstruktion der Hodajot" (unpublished diss., Heidelberg: University of Heidelberg, 1963). Independently, É. Puech also reconstructed 1QH^a and came to almost the same results as H. Stegemann; see É. Puech, "Quelques aspects de la restauration du Rouleau des Hymnes (1QH)," *JJS* 39 (1988), 38-55. These results have now been confirmed by the 4QH manuscripts. Unfortunately, no final publication exists of the reconstruction of 1QH^a, which results also in a new counting of columns and lines (it is often used beside or instead of the Sukenik system).

[39] This article, "Methods for the Reconstruction of Scrolls," constitutes a "handbook" for the reconstruction of manuscripts. It includes numerous illustrative examples, and for those who are interested in starting a material reconstruction working thoroughly through all the given instances is necessary (the time that it

by A. Steudel (1994);[40] and further ideas have been developed by D. Stoll (1996)[41] and S. Pfann.[42]

This method of reconstructing Dead Sea manuscripts from scattered fragments is based on the fact that they were originally "scrolls"—i.e. that they were rolled up when the natural process of decay started.[43] Its basic principle is to identify corresponding shapes of fragments and corresponding points of damage. Accordingly, those fragments or points of damage within a fragment which appear very similar to each other must come from successive layers of the original scroll. The distance between corresponding damage-patterns equals the circumference of the original scroll at the point from which they were originally situated; thus the smaller the distance between corresponding traces of damage, the closer to the end of the scroll we are.[44] Scrolls were usually stored rolled up in the correct direction, with the beginning of the text on the outside. In such cases distances decrease progressively from the beginning of the text (i.e. the right part of the scroll), towards the end (i.e. the left part).[45]

---

takes is in any case worthwhile!). Cf. also H. Stegemann, "How to Connect Dead Sea Scrolls Fragments," in H. Shanks (ed.), *Understanding the Dead Sea Scrolls. A Reader from the Biblical Archaeology Review* (New York: Random House, 1992) 245-55.

[40] A. Steudel, *Der Midrasch zur Eschatologie aus der Qumrangemeinde (4QMidrEschat$^{a, b}$)* (STDJ 13: Leiden: Brill, 1994).

[41] D. Stoll, "Die Schriftrollen vom Toten Meer—mathematisch oder Wie kann man einer Rekonstruktion Gestalt verleihen?," in H.-J. Fabry et al. (eds.), *Qumranstudien. Vorträge und Beiträge der Teilnehmer des Qumranseminars auf dem internationalen Treffen der Society of Biblical Literature, Münster, 25.-26. Juli 1993* (SIJD 4; Göttingen: Vandenhoeck & Ruprecht, 1996) 205-18.

[42] Pfann has observed horizontal breaks in the leather which were caused by the thongs used for tying rolled-up manuscripts; see S. Pfann, "4Q298. 4QcryptA: Words of the Maskil to All Sons of Dawn," in J. A. Fitzmyer et al. (eds.), *Qumran Cave 4.XV: Sapiential Texts, Part 1* (DJD 20; Oxford: Clarendon Press, 1997) 1-30 + pls. I–II, esp. 5-6.

[43] The only known exceptions—apart from the tefillin and mezuzot—are 4QTestimonia (4Q175) and 4QList of False Prophets (4Q339); cf. n. 3 above. Both manuscripts seem to have been single sheets of leather.

[44] In 11QPs^a, for example, note the progressive diminishment of distances between corresponding holes where the damage caused by a worm occurs between col. 14 and the end of the scroll.

[45] Note the imprints of the sewing seams in 11QT^a; cf. col. 25 with cols. 48 and 66.

In contrast, some scrolls were rolled up in the wrong direction, with the beginning of the text inside (i.e. these were obviously not been rolled back after usage). In such cases we find small distances between corresponding points of damage at the beginning of the scroll, which grow progressively larger the further one moves towards the end of the text.[46] The precise amount of increase/decrease from one layer to the next depends on the thickness of the leather and on how tightly a scroll was wrapped; normally this rate is approximately 0.1-0.3 cm.[47] In general, scrolls which were rolled in the wrong direction are usually more loosely wrapped than those which were rolled in the right direction.[48]

2.3 The Technical Process of Reconstruction

In reconstructing a manuscript the researcher must first ascertain whether direct joins between fragments exist. As a second step, one should look for definite connections of fragments that are provided by biblical quotations.[49] The third step is most important of all: in order to identify corresponding damage patterns it is necessary to compare all the pieces of a scroll with one another and also to check whether corresponding points of damage exist within a fragment.[50] For this purpose one has to prepare two sets of photocopies

---

[46] See, for example, 1Q22, 1QH, 1QM, 1QS/Sa/Sb, and 4Q174. Further examples are provided in H. Stegemann, *Die Essener*, 92.

[47] For papyrus scrolls the rate is higher, normally about 0.5 cm.

[48] Because of this feature, the decrease/increase may in some cases develop more irregularly than is the case for tightly rolled-up scrolls; see, for example, 1QS (which is referred to by T. Elgvin, "Admonition Texts from Qumran Cave 4," 566 n.17).

[49] One should avoid assuming at the outset the exact distance between fragments that share parts of the same biblical quotation, since it is often uncertain which text-tradition the quotation is following, or whether it is an abbreviated citation. Fragments whose relationhsip has been established or assumed by steps one and two must neccessarily be included in step three.

[50] This is the case when a fragment is larger than the circumference of the former scroll at that point. With regard to the placement of frgs. 9 and 10 of 4Qpap Apocryphon of Jeremiah B? (4Q384), M. Smith (in Broshi et al. [eds.], *Qumran Cave 4.XII* [DJD 19], 138) misunderstood H. Stegemann ("Methods for the Reconstruction of Scrolls," 194) by assuming that fragments with the same shape do not belong to the same column. This may well be the case when the circumference of the scroll is smaller than the width of the column; for example, see 1QS col. 3.

(xeroxes) of all the fragments of a manuscript,[51] to trace the shapes of the various fragments, and to mark features such as top and bottom margins, column dividers, sewing seams, intervals, etc.[52] In front of a strong light (whether artificial or sunlight) one of the photocopies is shifted around over the second until corresponding traces of decay are found. Furthermore, the distances between lines drawn with ink or a sharp instrument on different fragments must correspond with each other if the pieces are actually part of the same sheet. Alternatively, one set of photocopies and one set of transparencies may be used, in which case no additional extra light is necessary.[53] Fragments which correspond with each other must perforce be arranged on the same horizontal level. To ascertain whether a particular fragment has to be placed to the right or left of a corresponding one is often a matter of trial and error. Much patience is required, and only the reconstruction of the whole can ultimately prove whether a proposed arrangement is actually correct or not.[54]

In many cases it becomes possible to calculate the original length of a scroll that is now fragmentarily preserved.[55] A material recon-

---

[51] Care must be taken that both sets of copies are of exactly the same dimensions as the original, since photocopying machines sometimes slightly distort the image. Unfortunately, even the most recent DJD editions usually fail to indicate the scale of the printed plates, which has then to be verified with recourse to the original or the microfiche edition which in most cases present scales. Sometimes the scale of the photographs can vary in the same edition (e.g. 11QTemple Scroll^a).

[52] Although a rare occurrrence, it is helpful for purposes of reconstruction to identify any fragments that contain a "sheet number" (i.e. the letter used as numbering, usually placed in the right upper edge of a sheet). Two clear examples are 4QD^a (4Q266) and 4QS^b (4Q256) (J. T. Milik, "Numérotation des feuilles des rouleaux dans le scriptorium de Qumrân," *Semitica 27* [1977] 75-91). A sheet number is also probably found in 4QM^c (4Q493) (in M. Baillet et al. [eds.], *Qumrân Grotte 4.III* [DJD 7]), which may read *waw*—i.e. the fragment would come from the right edge of sheet number six. A further possible sheet number occurs in 4QExod^k (4Q21) (ed. J. Sanderson, in E. Ulrich and F. M. Cross [eds.], *Qumran Cave4.VII: Genesis to Numbers* [DJD 12; Oxford: Clarendon Press, 1994]).

[53] In the future computer technology will certainly help, but at present the enormous amount of data is still a problem; not only the shapes of fragments, but also cracks, imprints and folds, etc., in the skin have to be compared.

[54] When only a few fragments of a manuscript are preserved, this question must frequently be left open; cf. A. Steudel (ed.), "4Q425.4QSapiential-Didactic Work B" in Fitzmyer et al. (eds.), *Qumran Cave 4.XV* (DJD 20) 203-10 + pl. XVII.

[55] This is possible if the middle or the outer part of a scroll is preserved.

struction is often helpful to determine just how much of an original text has been preserved.[56]

Such reconstuctions, which have been made with recourse to photocopies, must inevitably be checked against the original manuscripts in the museum. Direct joins can be verified only via comparison with the original fragments, and many details that are of importance for the reconstruction process are often not mentioned in the editions and cannot be seen on the photographs—for example, the imprint of a fragment or of a sewing seam on the back of another fragment.[57] Similarities in the thickness and the colour of the leather may indicate that particular fragments belong to the same area of the original scroll; however, this is not necessarily the case, since thicknesses within a single sheet may vary and a fragment's colour—especially its darkening—is often dependent on its history after the scroll had fallen apart.[58] Yet another feature that can be investigated only with recourse to the original in the museum is the number of hairs per square centimeter of leather. Since this quantity varies in different parts of an animal's skin, fragments containing a similar number of hairs per square centimeter may come from the same area (and thus must be placed close to each other in the reconstruction).[59]

---

[56] For example, according to the material reconstruction of 4QSapiential Work A (4Q418), which Birgit Lucassen and I have been undertaking, less than half of the composition is preserved by this copy in fragmentary form.

[57] Material reconstruction of scrolls has become more difficult during the past few years, and measuring the thickness of the material has become almost impossible. One reason has been the adoption of a method in the museum whereby fragments are sewn between two layers of gauze so as to ensure better preservation, which usually prevents thorough investigation of a fragment's verso. Even more problematic is the method of gluing the fragments onto rice paper, which renders the verso totally inaccessible. Fortunately, however, curator L. Libman and her team at the Rockefeller Museum have proved most co-operative, by re-doing their painstaking work to facilitate examination of the necessary materials by the reconstructor.

[58] For instance, some fragments were used by rats to build their nests (cf. n.10 above). Moreover, some fragments changed colour after being treated with the oils and solvents that were used in the museum in order to preserve them (cf. frg. 1 of 4QMidrash on Eschatology[a] [4Q174]).

[59] This only holds true, of course, for fragments that belong to the same sheet. On a recently-developed technique that involves microscopic examination of the hair-follicle patterns on leather sheets, see S. Pfann, "4Q298," in Fitzmyer et al. (eds.), *Qumran Cave 4.XV* (DJD 20) 2-4.

Different possibilities exist for verifying or falsifying a material reconstruction. Important criteria are the width of the columns and the division of the sheets (i.e. the number of columns particular sheets contain), both of which are determined from, for instance, the material reconstruction.[60] Yet another criterion is both practical and aesthetic: once we have calculated the original length of a scroll, we can also calculate its original diameter. The results of a material reconstruction are called into question and must be thoroughly rethought if the diameter of the scroll turns out to be larger than the diameter of the opening of the scroll jars found at Qumran, or if its diameter is larger than its height.[61] In the final analysis, however, the most decisive evaluation of a material reconstruction is whether the text that results actually works.

2.4 Reconstrucing the Text

Unusual or conflicting textual evidence should, of course, give rise to a rethinking and often a redoing of the reconstruction. Yet the material reconstruction has to be taken seriously even when it leads to unexpected results. One example is the placement of frgs. 12 and 13 in the reconstruction of 4QMidrash on Eschatology[b] (4Q177).[62] The placement obviously disturbs the sequence of Psalms in this thematical midrash, which in general follows the biblical Psalter, by quoting verses of Psalm 6 (col. 11) *after* Psalm 17 (col. 10). While such textual evidence could militate against its suggested location, a

---

[60] The columns should be of reasonable width and generally about the same size within a scroll. However, these widths can vary significantly—even by some centimeters—before or after a sewing seam, and in the middle of a sheet. In reconstructing a scroll one has also to keep in mind the possibility of an inserted repair sheet, with (for example) only one column per sheet; but this is an exception.

[61] On this aspect, see D. Stoll, "Die Schriftrollen vom Toten Meer—mathematisch oder Wie kann man einer Rekonstruktion Gestalt verleihen?," in H.-J. Fabry et al. (eds.), *Qumranstudien. Vorträge und Beiträge der Teilnehmer des Qumranseminars auf dem internationalen Treffen der Society of Biblical Literature, Münster, 25.-26. Juli 1993* (SIJD 4; Göttingen: Vandenhoeck & Ruprecht, 1996) 205-18. A most promising project is that of Mireille Bélis (in cooperation with J.-B. Humbert) that deals with the numerous tissues in which scrolls were wrapped for protection, and which can frequently provide information on the dimensions of the manuscripts involved; see M. Bélis, "Des étoffes de lin pour protéger les manuscrits," in *Le Monde de la Bible* 107 (1997), 32.

[62] More details on this placement are found in Steudel, *Der Midrasch zur Eschatologie*, 142.

different placement in the original scroll is—from the material point of view—virtually excluded.⁶³ A closer examination of the text itself explains this evidence; while all the other quotations from the Psalter are cited in 4Q177 without a quotation formula, Psalm 6 is introduced by an אמר-formula, which serves to indicate the subordination of a quotation.⁶⁴ Thus Psalm 6 does not serve to guide the structure of 4Q177—which is a prominent function of the other Psalm quotations—but rather as an additional biblical quote that has been inserted for thematical reasons. This example illustrates how material reconstructions can force scholars to investigate a text more intensively.

But even more pivotal than a material reconstruction of a manuscript is a careful reading of the text itself. In order to provide a solid basis for the interpretation of a certain composition, all the remnants of letters have to be recognized, and should be *completely* indicated in the editions since they are sometimes of great importance for the restoration of text in the lacunae.⁶⁵ The traditional instruments for identifying and reading small traces of letters are magnifying glasses and microscopes, which help us to see more clearly the number of ink-strokes and the characteristic way in which these have been traced by the scribe. In more recent times, specialized software enables scholars to use the computer as a kind of photographic laboratory.⁶⁶ Computer technology, when used responsibly, has proved to be extremely helpful by (for example) obtaining sharper contrasts between the ink and leather; yet it cannot replace the eye and the judgement of a trained palaeographer.

Different schools of thought exist on how to accurately establish the precise amount of text that is to be restored in a lacuna. There

---

⁶³ A. Steudel, *Der Midrasch zur Eschatologie*, 67 n.1.

⁶⁴ This was already observed by G. J. Brooke, *Exegesis at Qumran. 4QFlorilegium in its Jewish Context* (JSOT Sup 29; Sheffield; JSOT Press, 1985) 136f., with regard to the quotation of 2 Sam 7:11b (col. 3:7).

⁶⁵ Taking into account the remains of all letters can also prevent superfluous scholarly discussions that are grounded on palaeographically impossible readings. One example is CD 11:21–12:1, which was for decades erroneously included in the Sabbath code of CD (cf. A. Steudel, "The House of Prostration CD 11:21–12:1 — Duplicates of the Temple," *RevQ* 16 [1993], 49-68).

⁶⁶ Note the handbook of A. Lange, *Computer Aided Text-Reconstruction and Transcription: CATT-Manual, with an Introduction by Hermann Lichtenberger and an Appendix by Timothy Doherty* (Tübingen: Mohr-Siebeck, 1993).

are two main methods for verifying whether an assumed restoration actually fits the required space: counting and drawing. The best way is to check a particular restoration is by using both methods; if these are carefully carried out, both should lead to the same result.[67]

2.5 Present Projects and Future Prospects

Material reconstructions of scrolls that are currently in progress include the 4QHodayot manuscripts,[68] which have already shown that "certain of the 4Q-manuscripts do not contain the large compilation of hymns found in 1QH^a, but smaller units of material."[69] H. Stegemann is working on several more reconstructions, including one of the 4QMMT material which will definitely differ from E. Qimron's[70] arrangement of 4QMMT C; and one of the 4QD manuscripts,[71] which will give rise to new views on the Damascus Document, indicate the original length of the composition and supply the reader with a composite text of the document. Further reconstructions in the making are those of 4QSongs of the Sage (4Q510-11)[72] and of the various scrolls of 4QSapiential Work A.[73] Countless other projects are waiting to be done. It would be worthwhile, for example, to restore 4QBeatitudes (in order to determine whether or not the Beatitudes come from the beginning of the composition, as occurs in Matthew), to proceed further with 4QMessianic Apocalypse (for the purpose of assessing the precise

---

[67] It makes no difference whether one counts "cleared letter spaces," by assigning different values to various letters (such as *he* and *waw*) and to spaces between words, or whether one takes into account "units of signs" on the basis that in the long run the varying sizes of letters equalize each other. The method developed by E. Herbert (*Reconstructing Biblical Dead Sea Scrolls. A New Method Applied to the Reconstruction of 4QSam^a* [STDJ 22; Leiden: Brill, 1997]) is a rather sophisticted one.

[68] This reconstruction is being conducted by E. Schuller with H. Stegemann.

[69] E. Schuller, "Prayer, Hymnic, and Liturgical texts from Qumran," in E. Ulrich and J. VanderKam (eds.), *The Community of the Renewed Covenant: The Notre Dame Symposium on the Dead Sea Scrolls* (CJA 10; Notre Dame: University of Notre Dame Press, 1994), 153-71, esp. 168.

[70] In Qimron and Strugnell, *Qumran Cave 4.V* (DJD 10).

[71] Hartmut Stegemann, in collaboration with A. Maurer and A. Steudel.

[72] By A. Maurer (Ph.D. dissertation, Göttingen: University of Göttingen).

[73] By Birgit Lucassen and A. Steudel. The results of this reconstruction will differ significantly from that of T. Elgvin, "The Reconstruction of Sapiential Work A," *RevQ* 16 (1995) 559-80.

character of this work), and (for the same reason) to restore 4QTanḥumim (4Q176).

2.6 Limits of the Material Reconstruction

It must be pointed out that not every scroll is reconstructable, even if there appears to be sufficient material for a successful restoration to take place.[74] Nature has its own rules, and every fragment has its own history after the scroll has fallen apart.[75] One cannot predict at the outset whether or not the reconstruction of a certain manuscript will ultimately be possible. It is possible that, even after intensive attempts to achieve a reconstruction, a larger fragment may still remain unplaced (i.e. with no space for it in the suggested sequence). In this case the entire reconstruction must be called into question, impelling the researcher not to suggest any order at all for the fragments, or—better still—to communicate that the attempt has failed.[76] Despite such caveats, in numerous cases attempting a material reconstruction is eminently worthwhile. But the method that has been described here should only be applied only with great care and responsibility.[77]

SELECT BIBLIOGRAPHY

Baumgarten, J. *Qumran Cave 4.XIII: The Damascus Document (4Q266-273)* (DJD 18, Oxford: Clarendon Press, 1996).

Bélis, M. "Des étoffes de lin pour protéger les manuscrits," in *Le Monde de la Bible* 107 (1997), 32.

---

[74] One such case may be the non-canonical Psalms manuscript 4Q381.

[75] A specific problem surrounding material reconstruction has arisen comparatively recently, notably with respect to the 4QS, 4QD and 4QH manuscripts which exist in several copies. A reconstruction may sometimes include large gaps where no actual fragment is preserved, with about half a meter of the original scroll represented by no leather at all. In such cases precise measurement obviously becomes very difficult, if not impossible.

[76] In particular, this concerns fragmentary manuscripts whose beginning and end is preserved.

[77] We cordially extend an invitaiton to scholars who are interested in learning or practising the method of material reconstruction to join Prof. H. Stegemann's group that works regularly in Göttingen or during the Summer in Jerusalem. This method is much easier learnt through practice than through pure theory or reading articles. By working together with trained colleagues and experts, many misunderstandings—frequently with serious consequences—can be avoided and expert advice for special cases is readily available.

Chazon, E. תעודה ליטורגית מקומראן והשלכותיה: דברי המאורות (Ph.D. diss., Jerusalem: Hebrew University, 1991). To be published as *The Words of the Luminaries: A Liturgical Document from Qumran and Its Implications (4QDibHam)* (STDJ series; Leiden: Brill [forthcoming]).

Cross, F. M. *The Ancient Library of Qumran* (1st ed., London: Epworth, 1958; 3rd ed., Minneapolis: Fortress, 1995).

Elgvin, T. "Admonition Texts from Qumran Cave 4," in M. O. Wise et al. (eds.), *Methods of Investigation of the Dead Sea Scrolls and the Khirbet Qumran Site. Present Realities and Future Prospects* (ANYAS 722; New York: The New York Academy of Sciences, 1994) 179-96.

—. "The reconstruction of Sapiential Work A," *RevQ* 16 (1995) 559-80.

García Martínez, F. "The Last Surviving Columns of 11QNJ," in F. García Martínez et al. (eds.), *The Scriptures and the Scrolls. Studies in Honour of A. S. van der Woude on the Occasion of His 65th Birthday* (VTSup 49; Leiden: Brill, 1992) 178-92 + pls. III–IX.

—. "De la découverte à la publication," *Le Monde de la Bible* 86 (1994) 6-8.

Herbert, E. D. *Reconstructing Biblical Dead Sea Scrolls. A New Method Applied to the Reconstruction of 4QSam^a* (STDJ 22; Leiden: Brill, 1997).

Horgan, M. P. *Pesharim: Qumran Interpretations of Biblical Books* (Washington, DC: The Catholic Biblical Association of America, 1979).

Kister, M. "Newly-Identified Fragments of the Book of Jubilees: Jub 23: 21-23, 30-31," *RevQ* 12 (1987) 529-36.

Lange, A. *Computer Aided Text-Reconstruction and Transcription: CATT-Manual, with an Introduction by Hermann Lichtenberger and an Appendix by Timothy Doherty* (Tübingen: Mohr-Siebeck, 1993).

Metso, S. *The Textual Development of the Qumran Community Rule* (STDJ 21; Leiden: Brill, 1997).

Milik, J. T. and D. Barthélemy. *Qumran Cave I* (DJD 1; Oxford: Clarendon Press, 1955) pls. XVIII–XIX (1Q22) and p. 119 + pls. XXV–XXIX (1QSb).

—. "Numérotation des feuilles des rouleaux dans le scriptorium de Qumrân," *Semitica* 27 (1977) 75-91.

Newsom, C. *Songs of the Sabbath Sacrifice: A Critical Edition* (HSS 27; Atlanta: Scholars Press, 1985).

Pfann, S. "4Q298. 4QcryptA: Words of the Maskil to All Sons of Dawn," in J. A. Fitzmyer et al. (eds.), *Qumran Cave 4.XV: Sapiential Texts, Part 1* (DJD 20; Oxford: Clarendon Press, 1997) 1-30 + pls. I–II.

Puech, É. "Notes sur le manuscrit 11QMelkîsédeq," *RevQ* 12 (1987) 483-513.

—. "Quelques aspects de la restauration du Rouleau des Hymnes (1QH)," *JJS* 39 (1988) 38-55.

—. "Fragments d'une Apocryphe de Lévi et le personnage eschatologique. 4QTestLévi^{c-d}(?) et 4QAJa," in Trebolle Barrera and Vegas Montaner (eds.), *International Congress on the Dead Sea Scrolls, Madrid*, 449-501.

—. "Une apocalypse messianique (4Q521)," *RevQ* 15 (1992) 475-522.

—. *La croyance des Esséniens en la vie future: immortalité, resurrection, vie éternelle* (2 vols., Études bibliques, n.s. 21-22; Paris: Gabalda, 1993) esp. 2.335-419 on 1QH.

—. "Déchiffreur de manuscrits," *Le Monde de la Bible* 86 (1994) 9-11.

Schuller, E. *Non-Canonical Psalms from Qumran. A Pseudepigraphic Collection* (HSS 28: Atlanta: Scholars Press, 1986 [A preliminary reconstruction is suggested here]).

Steck, O. H. "Zur Abfolge Maleachi—Jona in 4Q76 (4QXIIa)," *ZAW* 108 (1996) 249-53.

Stegemann, H. "Die Rekonstruktion der Hodajot" (unpublished diss., Heidelberg: University of Heidelberg, 1963).

—. "Methods for the Reconstruction of Scrolls from Scattered Fragments," in L. H. Schiffman (ed.), *Archaeology and History in the Dead Sea Scrolls—The New York University Conference in Memory of Yigael Yadin* (JSPSup 8; JSOT/ASOR Monograph Series 2; Sheffield: JSOT Press, 1990) 189-220.

—. "How to Connect Dead Sea Scrolls Fragments," in H. Shanks (ed.), *Understanding the Dead Sea Scrolls. A Reader from the Biblical Archaeology Review* (New York: Random House, 1992) 245-55.

—. *Die Essener, Qumran, Johannes der Täufer und Jesus. Ein Sachbuch* (5th ed., Herder Spektrum 4128; Freiburg: Herder, 1996). English version: *The Library of Qumran. On the Essenes, John the Baptist and Jesus* (Grand Rapids: Eerdmans, 1998).

Steudel, A. *Der Midrasch zur Eschatologie aus der Qumrangemeinde (4QMidr Eschat$^{a, b}$)* (STDJ 13: Leiden: Brill, 1994).

Stoll, D. "Die Schriftrollen vom Toten Meer—mathematisch oder Wie kann man einer Rekonstruktion Gestalt verleihen?," in H.-J. Fabry et al. (eds.), *Qumranstudien. Vorträge und Beiträge der Teilnehmer des Qumranseminars auf dem internationalen Treffen der Society of Biblical Literature, Münster, 25.-26. Juli 1993* (SIJD 4; Göttingen: Vandenhoeck & Ruprecht, 1996) 205-18.

Strugnell, J. "Notes en marge du volume V des 'Discoveries in the Judaean Desert of Jordan'," *RevQ* 7 (1970) 163-276.

Tov, E. (ed.), with the collaboration of S. J. Pfann. *The Dead Sea Scrolls on Microfiche. A Comprehensive Facsimile Edition of the Texts from the Judean Desert* (Leiden: Brill and IDC, 1993).

Trebolle Barrera, J. and L. Vegas Montaner (eds.), *Proceedings of the International Congress on the Dead Sea Scrolls, Madrid, March 1991* (2 vols., STDJ 11; Leiden: Brill, 1992) 229-46.

Trebolle Barrera, J. "4QKings (4Q54)," in Trebolle Barrera and Vegas Montaner (eds.), *International Congress on the Dead Sea Scrolls, Madrid*, 229-46.

PRESERVING THE DEAD SEA SCROLLS AND QUMRAN ARTIFACTS

ESTHER BOYD-ALKALAY AND ELENA LIBMAN

After the discovery of the first scrolls some 50 years ago, systematic archaeological searches were carried out in the Qumran area north of the Dead Sea. In the nine years that followed (Up to 1956), eleven caves were investigated in the area of Qumran.[1] The purpose of this contribution to *The Dead Sea Scrolls After Fifty Years* is to report the efforts that have been made at preserving the manuscripts and artifacts found in these caves, and to describe both the earlier and current procedures involved.

1. RESTORATION AT THE PALESTINE ARCHAEOLOGICAL MUSEUM

Most of the Dead Sea Scrolls were written on hides, while some were inscribed on papyrus. Over a period of some 300 years,[2] various ancient methods of treating hides, the many additives that were used,[3] and tanning with various vegetables in varying concentrations, yielded a variety of skins of different thicknesses and colours ranging from pale yellow to dark brown. Of course, the colour also depends on the nature of the skin and the kind of damage it has suffered over the years. Some of the scrolls were found wrapped in linen cloths in jars, while others were in niches in the walls of caves, or on the floor buried in dust and partially disintegrated due to the action of water, insects and moulds. When a standard price was offered for each fragment found, the Bedouin cut up into small pieces the manuscripts they found with a view to reaping greater profits.

After two thousand years in the caves, the scrolls passed into the hands of scholars in Jordanian Jerusalem who began processing them on the premises of the the Palestine Archaeological Museum (later to be renamed the Rockefeller Museum). In late 1952 or early 1953, an

---

[1] For a recent account, see J. VanderKam, *The Dead Sea Scrolls Today* (Grand Rapids: Eerdmans, 1994) 1-12, esp. 12.

[2] I.e. the 300 or so years from the date of the earliest Qumran manuscripts (ca. 250 BCE) to the date of the latest ones (68 CE).

[3] Such as oil, alums, and other minerals.

international team was formed with the task of preparing an edition of the Dead Sea Scrolls. These pioneers were faced with a daunting task: sorting and ordering a huge number of fragments in the "Scrollery," a large room containing some twenty trestle tables where pieces of manuscripts were placed between sheets of glass. The plates totalled more than 1,000 and contained many thousands of fragments. The initial task—taking infra-red photographs and sorting and deciphering individual fragments—was completed ca. 1960.

Photographs dating from the fifties seem to show a lack of present-day awareness of environmental control. After being systematically moistened and flattened between two sheets of glass, scrolls were sorted "according to the text." Unfortunately, in the course of sorting, adhesive tape was used as backing and connecting material. At that time cellulose tape ("Sellotape") was newly invented and came highly recommended by its manufacturers (the 3M Company). This tape was glued—sometimes in several layers—on the leather and even onto the text itself. In some cases fragments were "encapsulated" between two layers of adhesive tape. In many cases the adhesive has penetrated the parchment and has soaked through to the other side; as a result, several fragments appear black and greasy, or are completely transparent.

Most of the papyri and parchments were placed between sheets of ordinary window glass without framing. Fragments lay loose between these glass plates, and would sometimes slip out. Plates were frequently piled three or four high, which caused additional pressure on the fragments themselves—thus accelerating the process of penetration of the greasy sticky mass into the scrolls. Moreover, the glass tended to be dusty, dirty, and sometimes cracked.

It is interesting to note that the description provided here on the early condition of the Dead Sea Scrolls almost coincides with that offered by one of the first scholars of the scrolls, John Allegro, in his letter to the Editor of the *Observer* on 11 December, 1966:

> ... on a recent visit to the museum, I saw for myself just how perilous is the situation. Fragile fragments, which have been out of their desert habitat now for more than 14 years, are lying still between the glass plates where we left them many years ago, mostly unsecured, and in some cases, as I was horrified to see, subjected to intolerable pressure by the plates lying on top of one another in a large cabinet ...

In 1962 Sir Francis Frank of the British Museum wrote to Father Roland de Vaux: "The fragments must first be freed of the cellulose acetate tape which was used to hold them together."[4] Many specialists who viewed the scrolls in these early years stressed that the edges of some pieces bore a black sticky substance which seemed—in the view of H. Plenderleith, Keeper of the Research Laboratory at the British Museum—due to the long-time influence of water on leather.[5] To make matters worse, the fragments were stuck to the glass, which could not be lifted without damaging the manuscripts themselves.

In his report on the state of the scrolls in 1962, Plenderleith recommended carrying out several urgent measures: sterilization of the leather to eliminate fungi and bacteria, flattening the fragments, and moisturizing them with an evaporation of water mixed with glycerin (up to 90% RH [relative humidity]). His technical notes—which were written in 1955—describe how Plenderleith attempted to separate and analyze fragments contained in three boxes which had been sent to London:

> Exposure overnight at 75% relative humidity caused insufficient relaxation of the parchment. A further 6 hours at 80% relative humidity made the membrane limp and various strata could be separated by careful manipulation with an ivory paper knife. A complication presented itself in the form of black bituminous substances which permeated the tissue and prevented the membrane from being separated. This substance was the ultimate decomposition product of the animal membrane. It seems likely that this gelatinization and later congealation had been caused by the prolonged action of water. The method eventually adopted was to expose the scroll fragments at 100% relative humidity for a few minutes and then to transfer them to a refrigerator for a like period. The degree of freezing was sufficient to congeal the surfaces of the black material while leaving the membrane sufficiently limp.

Following his arrival in Jordanian Jerusalem in March 1962, Plenderleith attempted to unroll a rigid scroll. When the method just described failed, he carried out a dissection with the appropriate tools, using as support the thinnest white silk, spread thinly with polyvinyl acetate and brought into intimate contact with the cleaned flat surface of the scroll. Plenderleith recommended that the leather be sterilized in order to eliminate fungi and bacteria. We are not able to ascertain whether this procedure was in fact carried out.

---

[4] F. Frank, Unpublished letter to R. de Vaux (1962).

[5] H. Plenderleith, "Unpublished notes and reports" (1962). See also A. E. Werner, Unpublished report (1966). Werner was a British conservator who visited the Palestine Archaeological Museum in order to assess the condition of the Scrolls.

In her report of Oct.–Dec. 1963, Ms Valerie Foulkes of the British Museum described the procedure of the restoration of scrolls, which consisted of removing all sorts of patches from the fragments, moistening and flattening the leather, and then fastening them with thin strips of silk—using gum arabic—or with gold beater's skin, using PVA[6] glue. In addition, she employed a special dressing for softening leather ("British Leather Dressing") that had been developed at the British Museum. This dressing was used for softening the leather (from the reverse), consolidating the surface (from the obverse), and making the script more legible. Since the dressing produced a glittering film on the surface of the leather, Foulkes thinned it with benzene, because she considered it dangerous to remove the adhesive tape from the papyri and from very damaged parchment fragments.[7]

The adhesive tape was removed with a scalpel and—as was recommended by Plenderleith—with trichloroethylene. Gummed silk strips or gold beater's skin and PVA adhesive were then used to join the fragments. On the surface of the leather Foulkes found water-soluble crystals which, after analysis, were found to be salt crystals. She believed it necessary to remove these crystals using the same British Leather Dressing.

We regret to report that the present condition of the fragments is alarming. The leather, which has been treated with British Leather Dressing, is now badly darkened and appears greasy and glossy. In many cases the text is almost illegible against this dark background. It thus transpires that the temporary improvements carried out in the 1960's did not arrest or slow the deterioration of the scrolls.

In the 1970's and 1980's half of the parchments and some of the papyri were forwarded to the Israel Museum Laboratory for restoration. According to preserved notes and documentation, much of the adhesive tape was removed by scalpels and greasy spots of adhesive were eliminated using wads of cotton dampened with trichloroethylene. Many fragments were then backed with white lens-tissue paper (sometimes in several layers) with the help of perspex glue in a solution of acetone or toluene and polyvinyl acetate. Some of the glass plates were replaced by acid cardboard of the kind available in Israel at the time, and the fragments were treated with thymol.

---

[6] I.e. polyvinyl acetate.

[7] V. H. Foulkes, "Unpublished notes and reports" (1963).

We thus see that in earlier years the Dead Sea Scrolls passed through many hands in different venues, were exposed to drastic environmental changes, and were treated by various methods. Unsuitable treatments in the nineteen-fifties, -sixties and -seventies—which involved excessive humidity, leather dressings, PVA glue and perspex solution—accelerated the rapidly deteriorating condition of these ancient and precious manuscripts. The main obstacle that still confronted the conservators was the adhesive tape, which had to be removed without delay; however, this proved to be an inexorably lengthy process.

2. THE WORK OF THE ISRAEL ANTIQUITIES AUTHORITY

In 1991 a laboratory for the conservation of the scrolls was established by the Israel Antiquities Authority on the premises of the Rockefeller Museum. The conservators include Esther Boyd-Alkalay, Elena Libman, Tatyana Bitler, Tatyana Treiger and Asia Vexler; several are well-known to editors of the Scrolls as they visit the Museum to work on their respective editions.

It was soon realized that removal of the adhesive tape and stains would take many years, thus diverting our attention from other necessary tasks. We thus decided to launch a "first-aid programme" as an emergency measure, which entailed removing the fragments from the acid boards and glass plates and placing them between acid-free cardboard. This procedure was accomplished in two main phases. First, a work record was established, whereby the condition of the fragments was fully documented. This provided: (a) a scheme showing their position and where they had been secured with adhesive tape; (b) a description of the damage suffered by the skin and the text; and (c) a record of the kinds of intervention that had been introduced previously or had been carried out by ourselves. Second, the fragments were attached to lens tissue with hinges of Japanese paper in the order shown on the original photographs that had been taken by scholars in the 1950's. In cases where the adhesive tape covered the fragment completely, thus preventing the use of hinges, the fragment was placed in a pocket of Japanese paper and the pocket was then attached to the sheet of lens tissue. This sheet, in turn, was enclosed in acid-free boards in passe-partout form. The upper board carries the shelf number and a color code that indicates the condition of the fragments.

The purpose of this temporary measure was to dispense with the glass and acid board mounting, and this has now been completed. In tandem with this emergency first-aid treatment, a procedure was initiated with a view to removing the adhesive tape. After initial experiments using blank samples of parchment, we decided to exclude parchment glue and adhesives based on organic solvents due to the difficulty of reversing their effects and—in some cases—the creation of a rigid surface when they are used. Instead, we found that water-based adhesives such as methylcellulose (abbreviated "MC") were far safer and more suitable. This type of adhesive is placed on Japanese tissue in a thin layer, left to dry on a false plate to form a film, and is then applied in patterns cut from tissue with a little moisture. A light application of water-based adhesives relaxes the skin and activates the linking of the proteins in them; however, problems arise when gelatinized areas are involved. We therefore settled on using MC glue in its cold jelly condition, or Clucel G that has been dissolved in ethanol (5%).

In our quest for the best method of conservation we studied many papers on similar themes (notably reports by the British conservators who had worked on the scrolls in the 1960's). We also carried out a vast number of experiments (on uninscribed fragments!) using different adhesives (such as parchment glue) and backing materials (e.g. a thin layer of modern parchment). Modern parchment and gold beater's skin were excluded because of their different constitutions in comparison with ancient leather. We also tried to work on a suction disk; however, this method appears to be very time-consuming and demands the constant presence of a conservator. Moreover, it requires a large quantity of solvents to permeate individual fragments, which are already very dry and brittle. But eventually, in consultation with specialists in the field of restoration—notably members of the International Committee at the Getty Conservation Institute—we arrived at a method that is most appropriate for the conservation of the Dead Sea Scrolls.

3. THE RESTORATION METHOD OF THE MANUSCRIPTS PROPER

Before work on the leather commences, each fragment is checked under a microscope. Then delaminated areas of leather are reinforced by MC glue in its cold jelly state, with a tiny quantity of glue being carefully introduced into every peeling. After the glue has dried a little, the fragment is pressed under a small weight (comprising silicon release paper, filter paper, and a small sack of sand). Then the damaged areas are temporarily fastened from the recto with Japanese paper and MC glue which has been previously prepared on the glass. With the help of a heated surgical scalpel—or, alternatively, a scalpel and hot air gun (Leister Blower Unit)—the adhesive tape is removed piece by piece (about 1.5 cm^2 at a time).

Unforunately, in many cases the surface which was covered by the adhesive tape is still coated with a thick layer of greasy and sticky glue, which of course must be removed as soon as possible. This procedure is carried out under a protective hood in order to ensure the safety of the conservator. The fragment in question is placed on the Mylar film (i.e. a flexible and transparent sheet) with the coated side up. A strip of filter paper is then folded into a "harmonica" shape and dampened with a solvent (usually MEK[8] or acetone), and put into a small glass. After the glass has been placed upside down for one or two minutes on the spot containing the unwanted glue, the softened sticky mass is removed using a small eraser and tiny tweezers. The entire procedure is repeated until the surface of the fragment is no longer sticky.

At this stage we may begin removing the dark spots and extracting the greasy glue which have penetrated the parchment. First, a mineral powder (Fuller's Earth) is strewn on the dark spot, and one or two drops of solvent (MEK or acetone) are placed in the centre. The fragment is then covered by another film of Mylar and a heavy piece of glass. Only after the powder has completely dried can it be removed from the surface of the leather using a fine brush. Needless to say, the poulticing process is rather time-consuming, since the powder takes about three hours to dry. However, it is possible to work simultaneously on several fragments. The remaining powder is then removed, using a tiny eraser, under a microscope.

For reinforcing weak or torn areas, we use Japanese paper that has been prepared in advance on glass with MC glue dissolved in distilled water. It normally suffices to dab the deficient area several times with a slightly damp cotton wad over the layer of Japanese paper that has been placed on the fragment, and to dry it under pressure (using silicon release paper, filter paper and a small sack of sand). Such reinforcing treatments are extremely time-consuming and sometimes have to be repeated. The Japanese paper that has been temporarily

---

[8] I.e. Methy-ethyl Ketone

glued on the recto of the fragment may be easily removed from the parchment without causing any damage to the text.

Samples of damaged blank skins were analyzed in the laboratories of the Getty Conservation Institute before and after treatment. Since solvents not only remove the oils of the adhesive tape but may also dry the skins and extract their natural oils, we limit the treatment with solvents to reducing the dark and sticky residues which make the text illegible. We have achieved very good results in uncovering texts that had been completely obscured by stains, using an earth poultice together with solvents. We are pleased to report no loss of natural oils from the skins.

It must be noted that the removal of the adhesive tape cannot be standardized due to variations both in adherence of the tape and in the extent of oxidation of the oils that it contains. An additional problem is the other sorts of patches that were were also used to "reinforce" the scrolls. Following the reinforcement on the recto (described above), such old patches are removed with recourse to a different method. Lens tissue with perspex glue is eliminated with acetone (sometimes with methylene chloride) and replaced by Japanese paper using MC glue. In cases where patches have been affixed with PVA glue, the adhesive is softened with a tiny quantity of MC glue and is removed with a surgical scalpel. Several samples are very complicated, since they carry different types of patches on top of each other. The restored fragments are kept in acid-free passe-partout and are attached with hinges of Japanese paper.

Another method of mounting fragments is to place them between two pieces of stabil-tex that has been stretched on cardboard frames and sewn around with stabil-tex thread. A space of 2-3 mm is left between thread and fragment to let the latter "breathe." This procedure seems to be most appropriate for preserving and exhibiting the scrolls. Editors deciphering the texts often require a direct view of both sides of the fragments, which are now presented to the reader enclosed in a frame made of two clear perspex plates in such a way that the perspex does not come into contact with the actual manuscript. The frames can thus be turned over without damaging the fragments.

At first glance the state of preservation of papyrus manuscripts seems to be much better than the parchment scrolls. Since the sticky mass of adhesive tape has not penetrated the papyri and has remained on the surface, it may be less troublesome to remove this glue from the surface of the papyri than from parchment. However, removing the adhesive tape itself from such a fibrous material as papyrus without causing damage is problematic to say the least. Since a good amount of the papyri fragments bear text on both sides, adhesive tape has often been glued on the script—which highly complicates the process of removing tape. We attempted several methods, notably the use of chemical sustances and laser rays, but with mixed results. At the present time, the "hot air method" (using a heated surgical scalpel or a hot-air gun) seems to be the most effective. At the same time that the adhesive tape is removed, tiny strips of Japanese paper with MC glue are used to fix and unite the papyrus fragments in order to acieve a permanent reinforcement. Cotton wads dampened with a solvent (MEK or acetone) serve to remove any adhesive residues from the papyrus surface. The protruding papyrus fibres may be softened with a brush dampened in distilled water, and are then pressed down and dried under a press.

Unlike the parchment fragments, papyrus pieces cannot be mounted between a net. The older method of placing them between two sheets of glass is also unsatisfactory in our view, owing to the fragile composition of glass (to judge by the many examples of broken and cracked glass in the Scrollery). It was thus clear to us that a new method of mounting papyrus manuscripts had to be invented, which is described as follows. A laced pattern of Japanese paper is cut according to the shape of the papyrus fragment. This is carefully fixed in stages, using tiny hinges, onto both sides of the fragment, with care being taken to avoid the actual script. The edges of the cutout are then glued to the cardboard frame. Finally, the entire "sandwich" is placed between two sheets of polycarbonate. The tissue pattern thus serves both to reinforce and to stretch the papyrus.

4. INTERNATIONAL CO-OPERATION AND FUTURE PROSPECTS

The Dead Sea Scrolls constitute an almost virgin field for research, not least in the area of manuscript conservation. Beginning in 1992, a team of conservators and scientists from the Getty Conservation Institute has come to our assistance. In several important studies, these scholars have investigated the precise nature of damage to the scrolls, including physical changes which have occurred, the effect of the climate in the caves, the origin of the minerals found in the scrolls, and the actual causes of physical, chemical and biological deterioration. More recently, studies have been carried out inside the actual caves where the scrolls were found; these are to be published by the Getty Institute. (One example: an investigation of temperature and relative humidity conditions shows that RH levels fluctuate not only with changes in seasonal temperatures, but also with changes in day-time and night-time temperatures.)

Joint studies between the Israel Antiquites Authority and the Getty Institute include ongoing examination of samples of leather, ink, salt crystals, and mould fungi. Early results show the inks on the scrolls to be carbon-based, and that the mould fungi are (fortunately) in an inactive state. Furthermore, we now attribute the overall bad state of the leather to the great quantity of salt crystals that has been deposited on the scrolls. Delamination of the parchment surface seems due to a process whereby salt—depending on changes in humidity—first dissolves, then crystallizes, and tears the surface of the leather. These results, however, are preliminary and need to be more fully substantiated.

The storage room at the Rockefeller Museum is maintained at a constant temperature and under controlled humidity. One of our current foci is to provide more effective buffering materials by housing the acid-free boards that contain the fragments in acid-free boxes. A future priority will be to replace with suitable shelves the shallow drawers in which these boards are presently stored.

It is an unfortunate fact that aging and deterioration of the scrolls cannot be halted—but we will be most relieved if this process can at least be slowed. We are attempting to achieve this goal with as little intervention as possible, and by using methods that are reversible. We trust and hope that our work will contribute to the future preservation of these two-thousand year old treasures.

SELECT BIBLIOGRAPHY

Foulkes, V.H. Unpublished notes and reports (1963).

Ginell, W. S. *Report on the Dead Sea Scrolls* (Marina del Rey, CA: The Getty Conservation Institute, 1993).

Plenderleith, H. Unpublished notes and reports (1955, 1962).

Reed, E. *Ancient Skins, Parchments and Leather* (London and New York: Seminars Press, 1972).

Schilling, M. and W. S. Ginell. *The Effects of Relative Humidity Changes on Dead Sea Scrolls Parchment Samples* (Marina del Rey, CA: The Getty Conservation Institute, 1993).

Werner, A. E. Unpublished report (1966).

PLATES

PLATE 1: Khirbet Qumran: Plan of Site in Periods Ib and II
(from R. de Vaux, *Archaeology and the Dead Sea Scrolls*, Plate XXXIX)

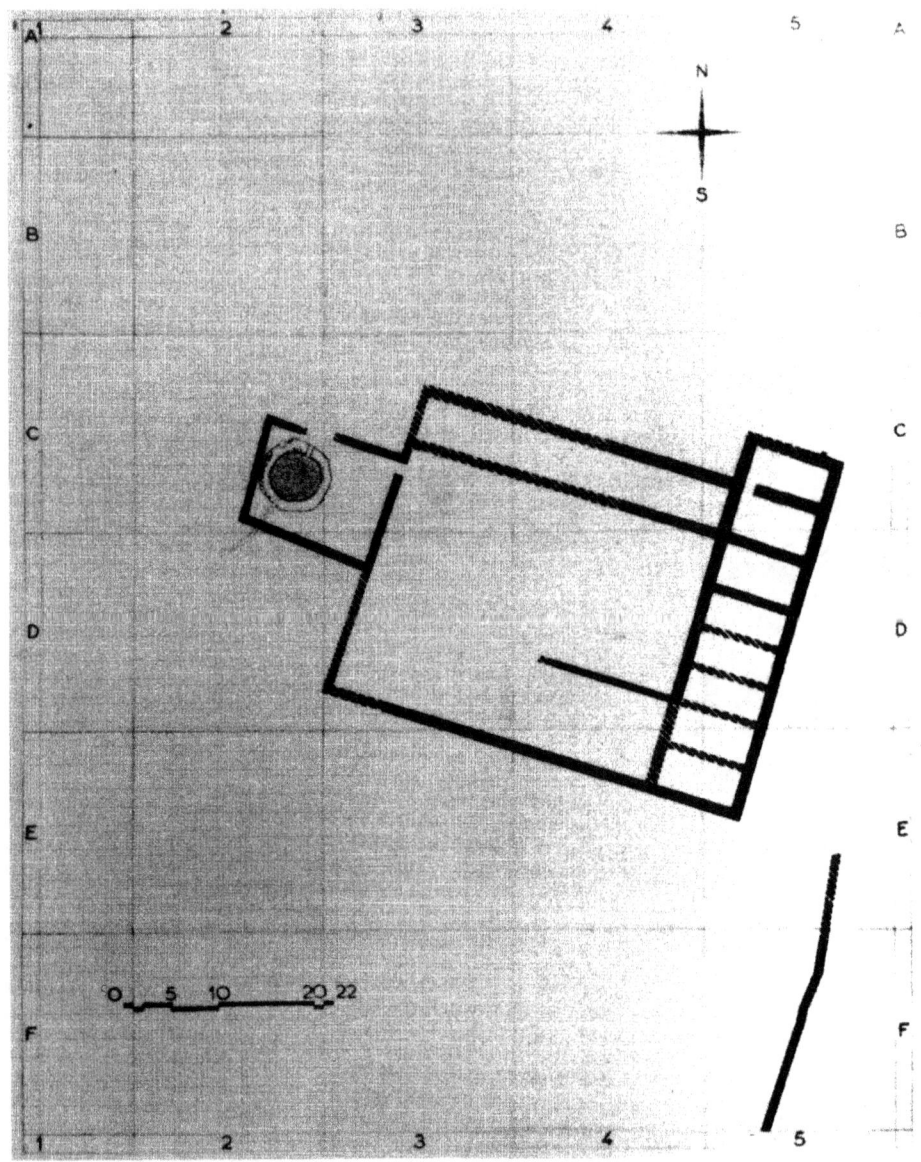

PLATE 2: Khirbet Qumran: Plan of the Iron Age Settlement
(from R. de Vaux, *Archaeology and the Dead Sea Scrolls*, Plate III)

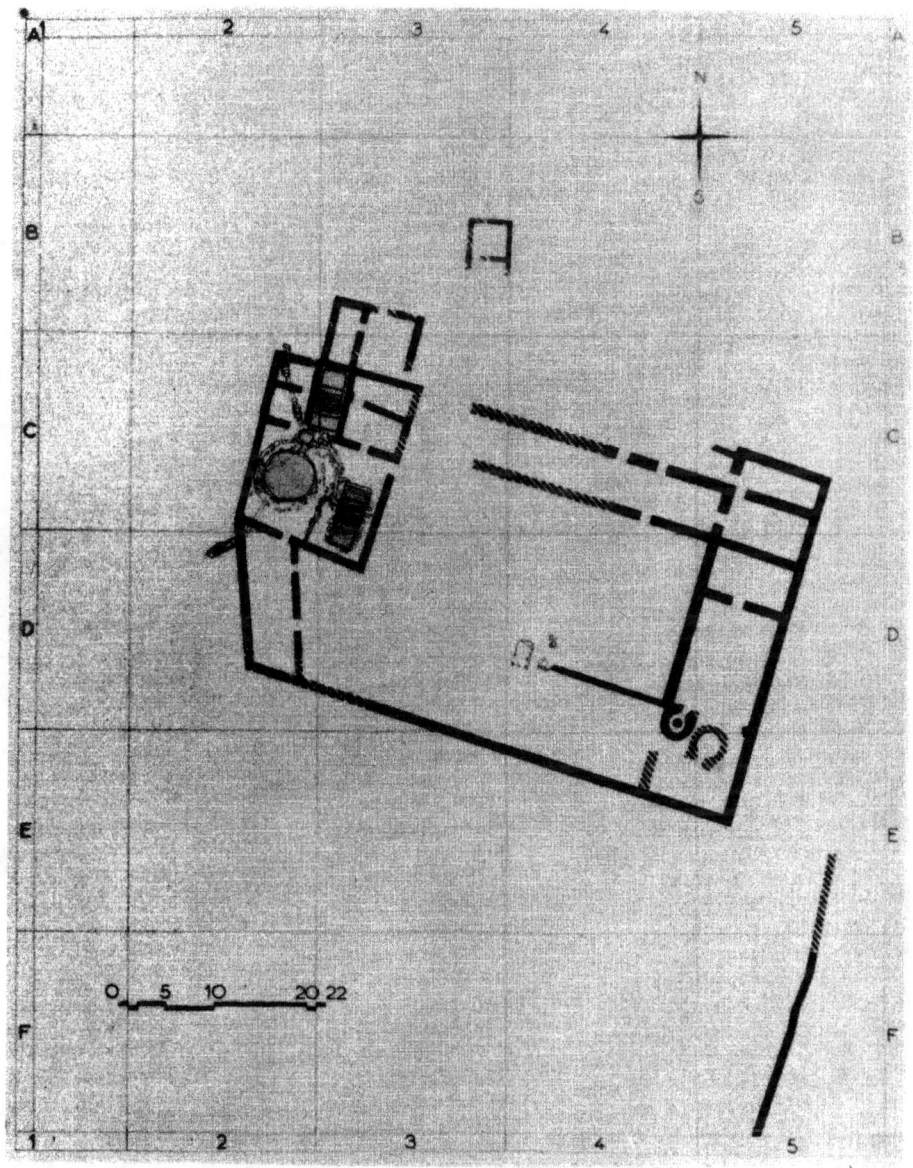

PLATE 3: Khirbet Qumran: Plan of Period Ia
(from R. de Vaux, *Archaeology and the Dead Sea Scrolls,* Plate IV)

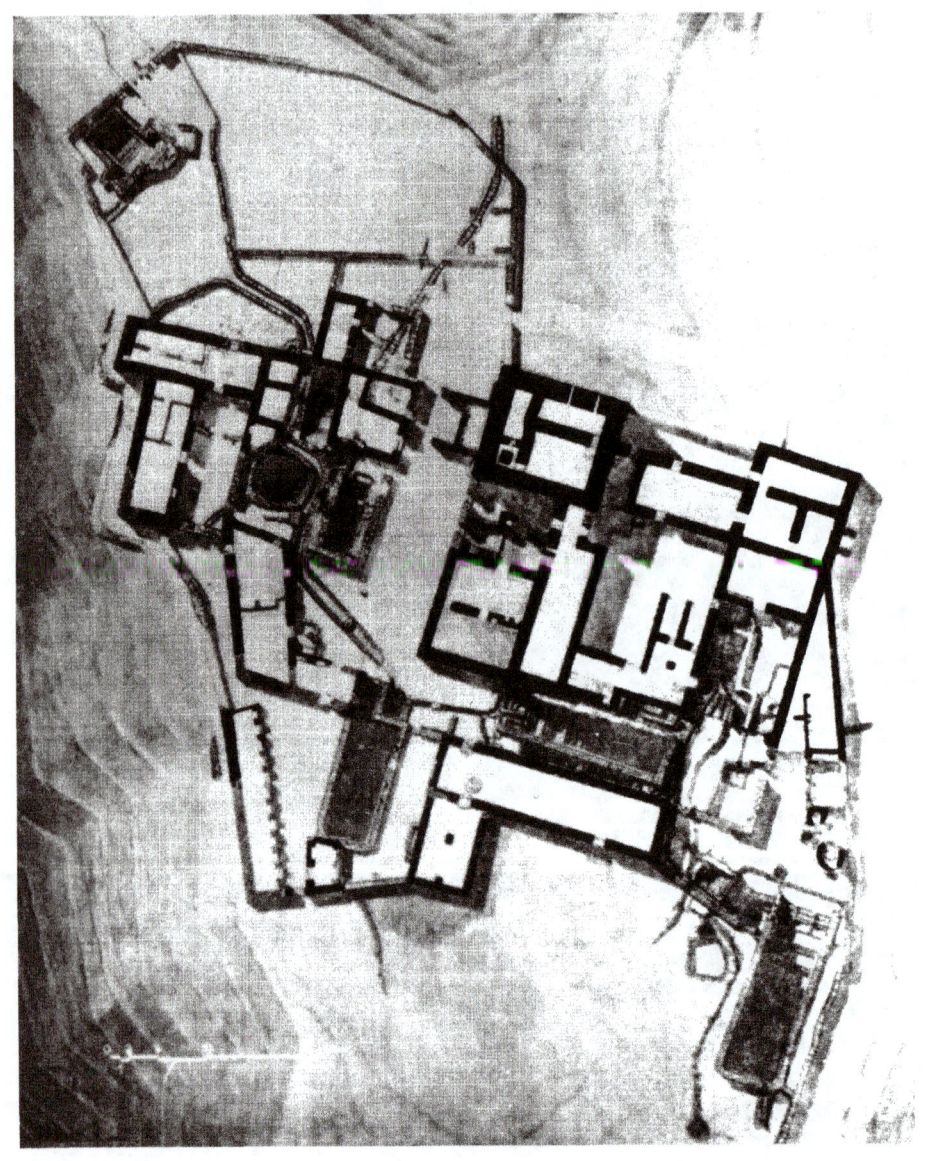

PLATE 4: Khirbet Qumran: Plan of Period Ib
(from R. de Vaux, *Archaeology and the Dead Sea Scrolls*, Plate VI)

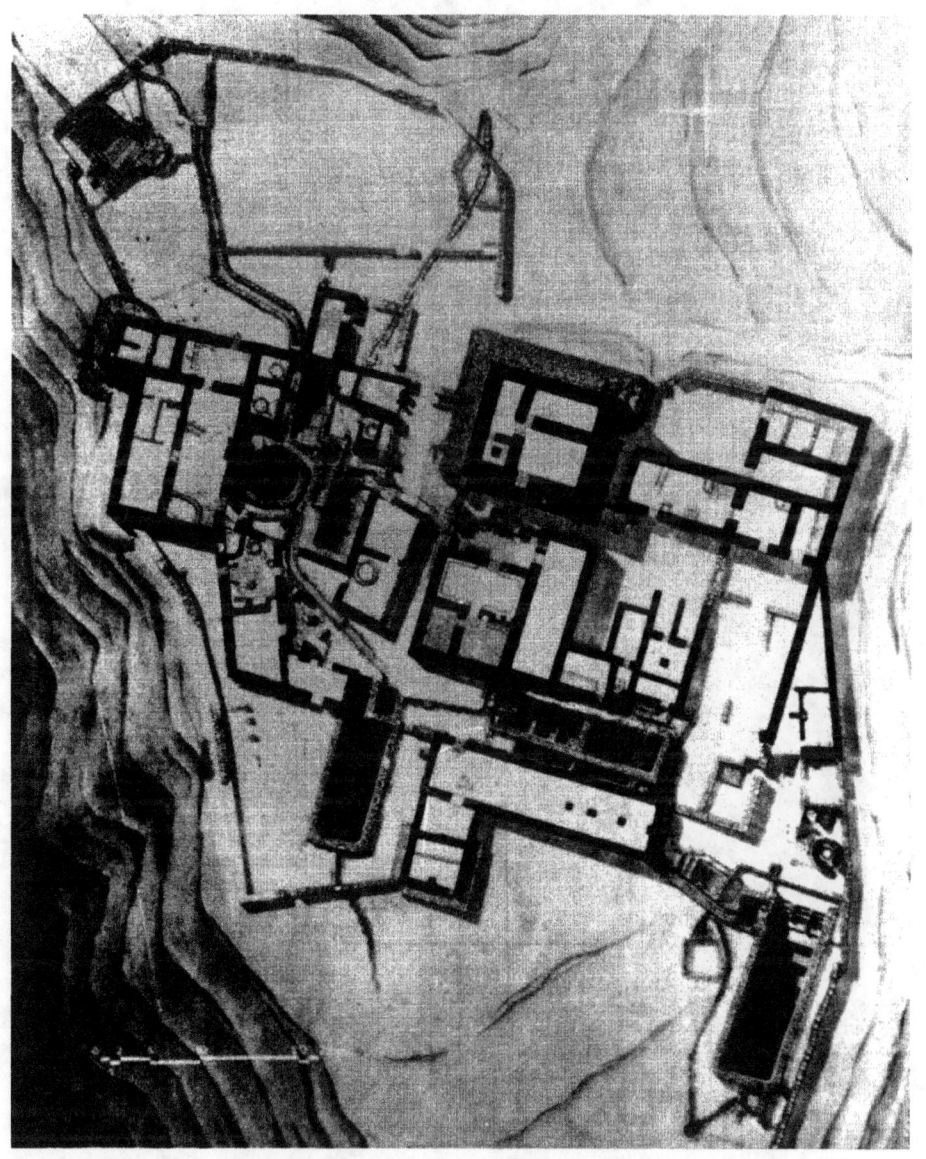

PLATE 5: Khirbet Qumran: Plan of Period II
(from R. de Vaux, *Archaeology and the Dead Sea Scrolls,* Plate XVII)

PLATE 6: Khirbet Qumran: The Pool in L48-49, split by the earthquake
(from R. de Vaux, *Archaeology and the Dead Sea Scrolls*, Plate XVI)

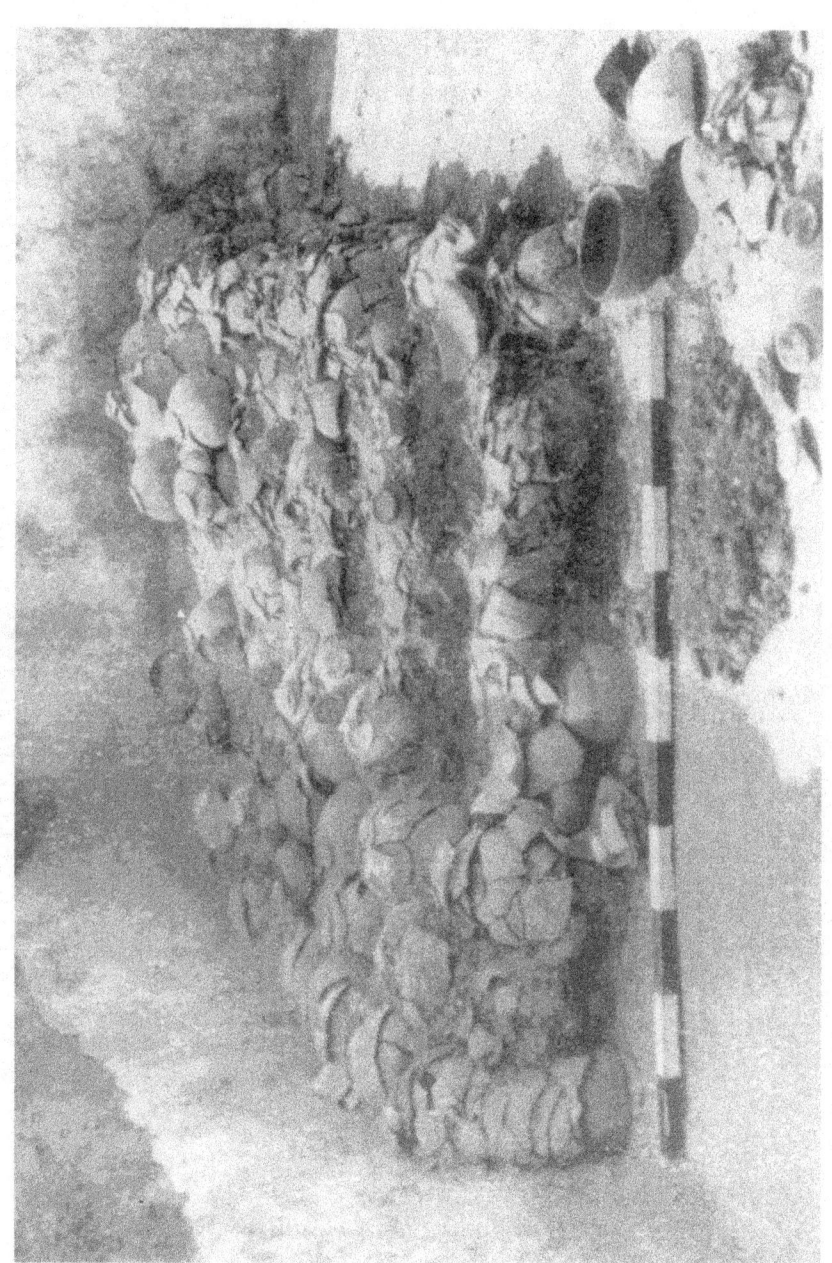

PLATE 7: Khirbet Qumran: Pottery in the Pantry (L.89)

PLATE 8: Fragment from 4QSamᵃ (1 Samuel 14:47-49) at 200%

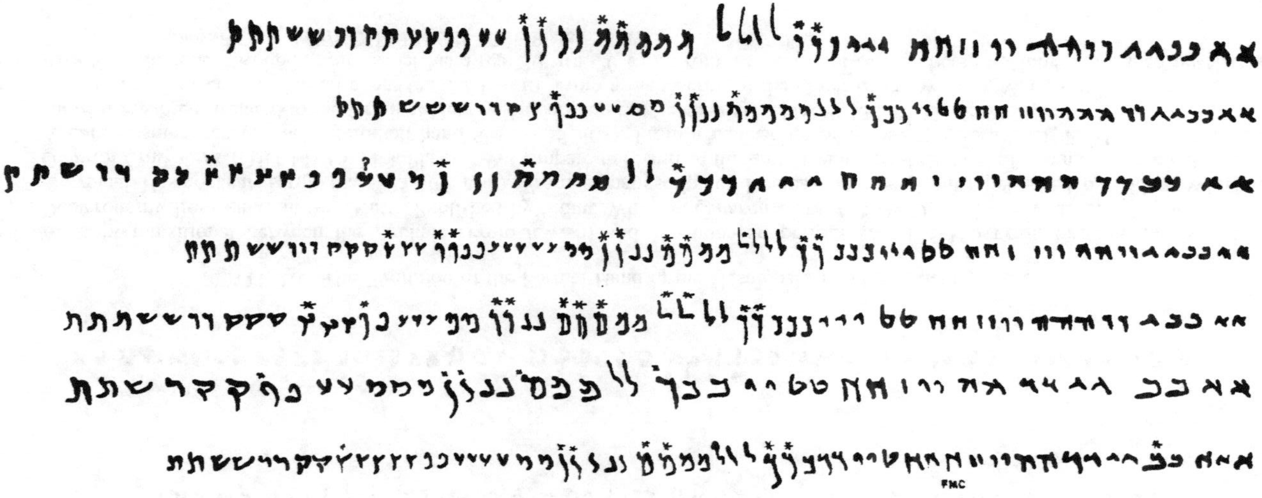

PLATE 9: Early Aramaic and Proto-Jewish Scripts

Line 1. The classical Aramaic cursive of the late Persian Empire, ca. 400 BCE. From Papyrus Luparensis, *CIS (pars secunda)* 1.1, 146 A, B, Table XVII.
Line 2. An Aramaic Vulgar cursive of the early third century BCE from Egypt. From the Edfû Papyri published by Sayce-Cowley, *PSBA* 29 (1907), Plates 1 + 2.
Line 3. An Archaic proto-Jewish hand of the mid-third century BCE. The script contains letter forms which eventually evolve into the early Jewish cursive character. This manuscript, 4QExod-Lev^f (4Q17) is now published in *Qumran Cave 4.II* (DJD 12) 133-44.
Line 4. An Archaic proto-Jewish formal hand of the mid-third century BCE. From a manuscript of 4QSam^b [4Q52] published in part in F. M. Cross, "The Oldest Manuscripts from Qumrân," *JBL* 74 (1955) 147-72, esp. Figs. 6 and 2, line 2.
Line 5. An Archaic proto-Jewish formal hand of ca. 200 BCE. From a manuscript of Jeremiah from Qumrân (4Q Jer^a). See E. Tov, "The Jeremiah Scrolls from Qumran," *RevQ* 14 (1989) 189-205, esp. Plate 3.
Line 6. An Archaic or Early Hasmonaean semiformal script of ca. 175-150 BCE. From a manuscript of Qohelet from Qumrân (4QQoh^a). Cf. J. Muilenburg, "A Qohelet Scroll from Qumran," *BASOR* 135 (1954) 20-28.
Line 7. An Archaic or Early Hasmonaean semiformal script of ca. 175-150 BCE. From a manuscript published by M. Baillet, *Qumrân Grotte 4.II* (DJD 7, 4Q504, 4QDibHam^a) 137-77 + Plates 49-53.

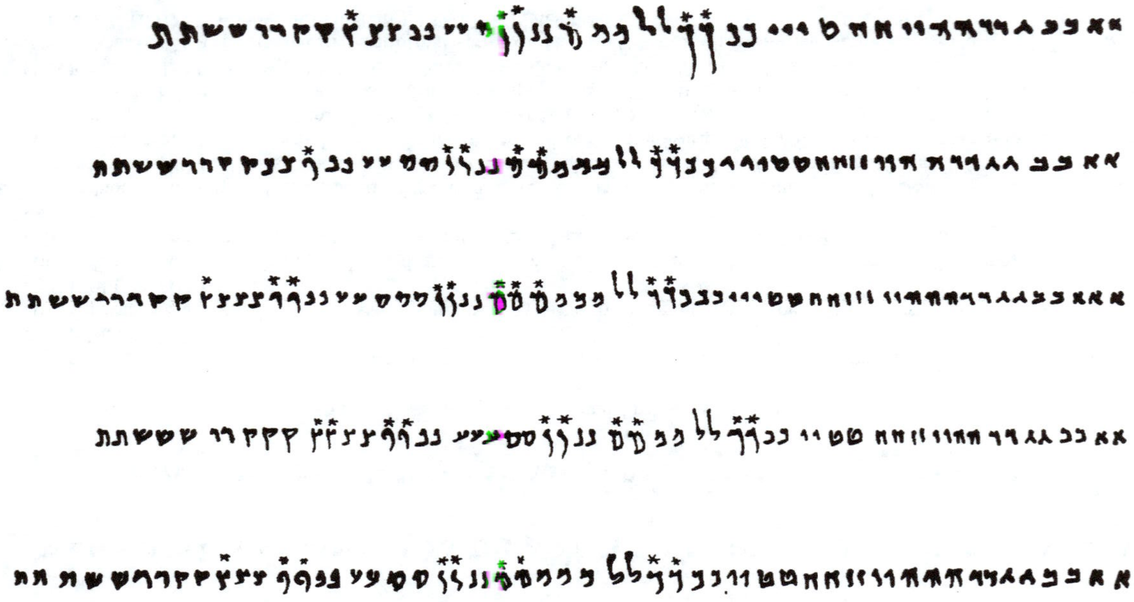

PLATE 10: The Evolution of the Formal Hand in the Hasmonaean and Herodian Periods

Line 1. A script transitional between the Archaic (Proto-Jewish) and Hasmonaean periods (ca. 175-150 BCE). From a manuscript of Deuteronomy from Qumrân (4QDeut^a). Published by Sidnie White in *Qumran Cave 4.IX* (DJD 14) 7-8 + Plate 1.
Line 2. A typical Hasmonaean script (ca. 125-100 BCE). From a manuscript of Deuteronomy (4QDeut^c) published by Sidnie White in *Qumran Cave 4. IX* (DJD 14) 15-34 + Plates 3-9. Compare the hand of the great Isaiah scroll (1QIsa^a) of about the same date.
Line 3. A Late Hasmonaean or Early Herodian hand (ca. 50-25 BCE). From a manuscript of Samuel (4QSam^a). Cf. F. M. Cross, "A New Biblical Fragment Related to the Original Hebrew Underlying the Septuagint," *BASOR* 132 (1953) 15-26.
Line 4. A typical Early Herodian formal script (ca. 30-1 BCE). From a manuscript of the Order of the War (1QM[1Q33]).
Line 5. An Early Herodian "Round" semiformal hand (ca. 30 BCE-20 CE). From a manuscript of Numbers (4QNum^b) published by Nathan Jastram, in *Qumran Cave 4.VII* (DJD 12) 205-67 + Plates 38-49.

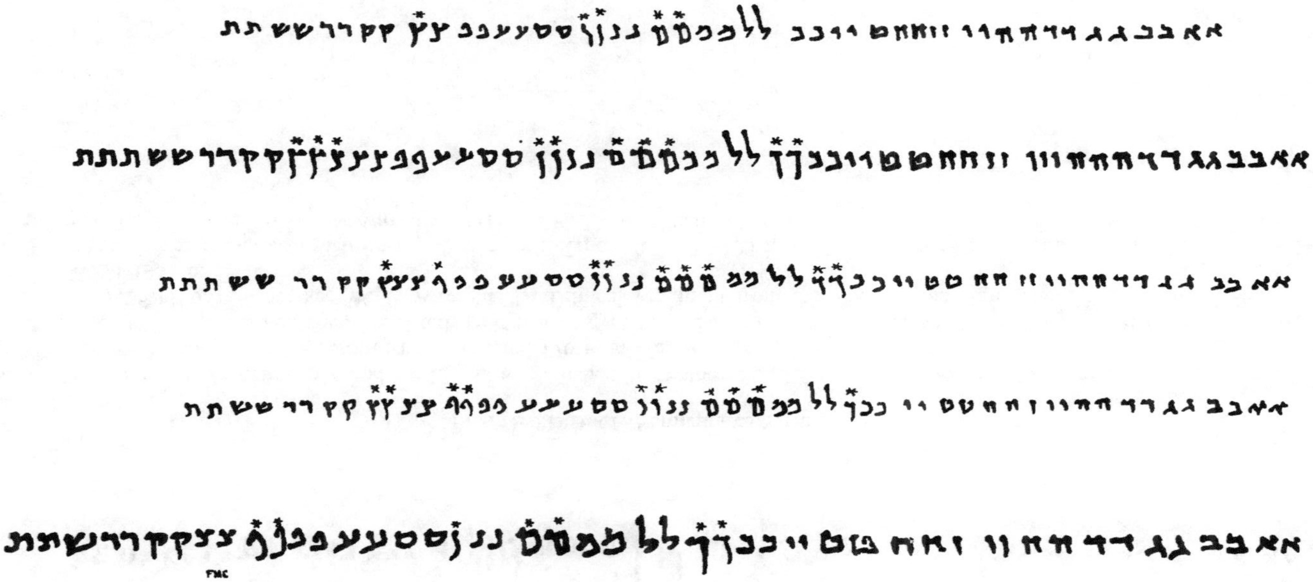

PLATE 10: *Continued*

Line 6. A developed Herodian formal script (ca. 20-50 CE) from a manuscript of Daniel (4QDan^b). Cf. E. Ulrich, "Daniel Manuscripts from Qumran, Part 2: Preliminary Editions of 4QDan^b and 4QDan^c," *BASOR* 274 (1989) 3-26.

Line 7. A Late Herodian formal script (ca. 50 CE) from a manuscript of Deuteronomy (4QDeut^j). Published by J. A. Duncan in *Qumrân Cave 4.XI* (DJD 14) 75-91 + Plates 20-23.

Line 8. A Late Herodian formal script (ca. 50 CE-68 CE). From a manuscript of Psalms from Qumrân (4QPs^b), published by P. W. Skehan, *CBQ* 26 (1964) 313-22. This script represents the classic book hand of the First Jewish Revolt, the prototype of the post-Herodian biblical hand.

Line 9. A post-Herodian biblical hand (ca. 75-100 CE). From a manuscript of Psalms from the Naḥal Ḥever (5/6Ḥev-Se4 Ps).

Line 10. A formal Jewish script from a Hebrew contract (Mur 24) dated in 133 CE, published by J. T. Milik, *Les grottes de Murabbaʿât* (DJD 2) 122-34 + Plates 35-37.

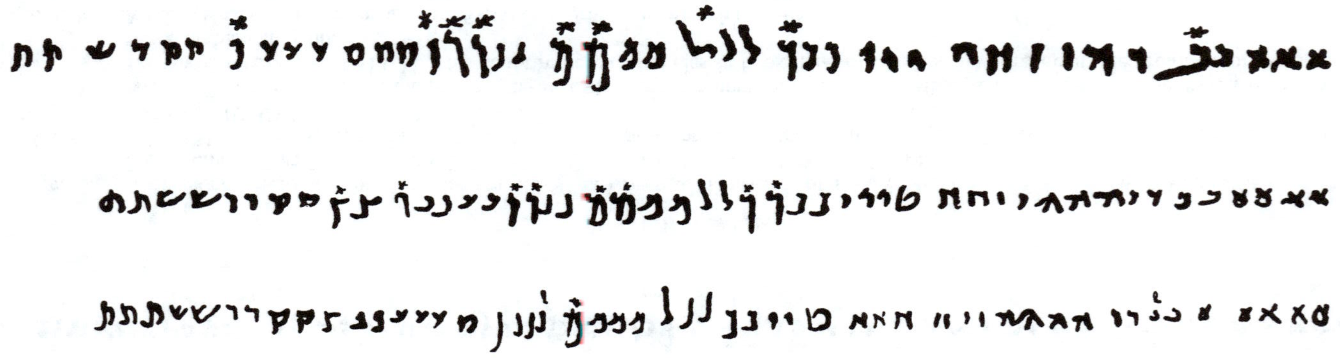

PLATE 11: Early Semicursive Scripts

Line 1. The script of an ostracon dated to 176 BCE published by Esther Eshel and Amos Kloner, "An Aramaic Ostracon of an Edomite Marriage Contract from Maresha, dated 176 BCE," *IEJ* 46 (1996) 1-22.

Line 2. An early Jewish semicursive, or mixed hand from Egypt (ca. 150 BCE). From the Nash Papyrus, published by S. A. Cook, *PSBA* 25 (1903) 34-56; see W. F. Albright, "A Biblical Fragment from the Maccabaean Age: The Nash Papyrus," *JBL* 56 (1937) 145-76.

Line 3. A Jewish semicursive script from the Judaean Wilderness (ca. 125-100 BCE). From a Murabbaʿât ostracon (Mur 72) published by J. T. Milik, *Les grottes de Murabbaʿât* (DJD 2) 172-74 + Plate 52.

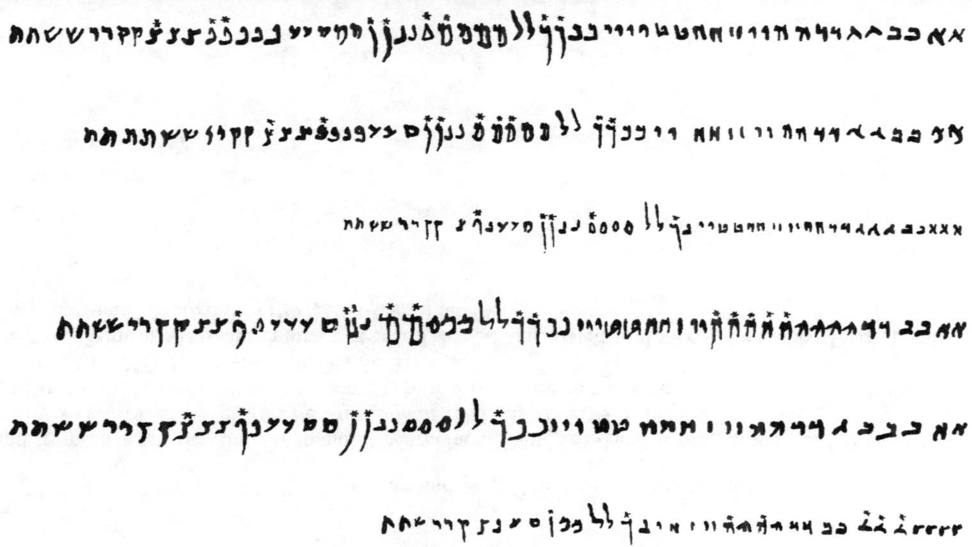

PLATE 12: Semicursive Scripts from Qumran

Line 1. A semicursive hand from a manuscript of the Twelve Minor Prophets (4QXII^a [4Q76]), dating to ca. 150-100 BCE. See provisionally, R. E. Fuller, "Text Critical Problems in Malachi 2:10-16," *JBL* 110 (1991) 47-57 + Plate.
Line 2. A semicursive script from a manuscript of 4QDaniel^c (4Q114], dating to ca. 100-50 BCE. Cf. E. Ulrich, "Daniel Manuscripts from Qumran, Part 2: Preliminary Editions of 4QDan^b and 4QDan^c," *BASOR* 274 (1989) 3-26.
Line 3. An unusual semicursive from a non-biblical Aramaic work (Book of Giants ar^b [4Q530]), 100-50 BCE. To be published by E. Puech.
Line 4. A late Hasmonaean semicursive script from a papyrus document (4QpapMMT^e [4Q398]), dating to ca. 50-25 BCE. Published by E. Qimron and J. Strugnell in *Qumrân Cave 4.V* (DJD 10) Plates 7, 11-13 + 8, 14-17. A palaeographical discussion of the text is given by A. Yardeni, pp. 29-34.
Line 5. A hand from a manuscript containing part of the Enoch literature (4QEn^g ar [4Q 212]), dating to ca. 50-1 BCE. Published by J. T. Milik, with the collaboration of Matthew Black, *The Books of Enoch: Aramaic Fragments from Qumrân Cave 4* (Oxford: Clarendon Press, 1976), Plates 21-24.
Line 6. A script used in an Aramaic papyrus from Cave VI (6Q8), edited by M. Baillet in *Les 'petites grottes' de Qumrân* (DJD 3) 116-18 + Plate 24.

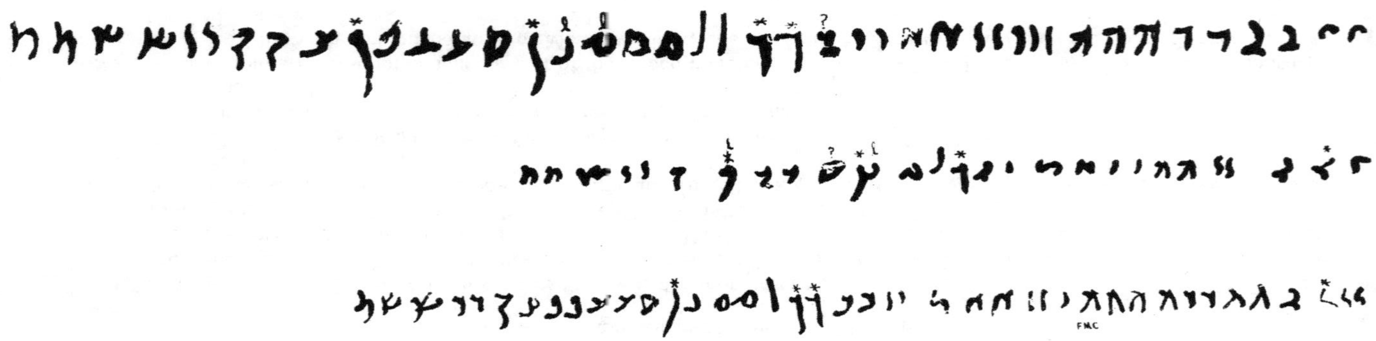

PLATE 13: Herodian and Post-Herodian Cursive Scripts

Line 1. A cursive hand from an Aramaic contract found at Murabbaʿât (Mur 18) dated it the second year of Nero (55/56 CE). The papyrus was published by J. T. Milik, *Les grottes de Murabbaʿât* (DJD 2) 100-104 + Plate 29.
Line 2. A cursive hand from an Aramaic marriage contract, probably dating to the year 117 CE (Mur 20). Published by J. T. Milik, *Les grottes de Murabbaʿât* (DJD 2) 109-14 + Plates 30-31.
Line 3. A semicursive hand from an Aramaic contract of sale (Hev/Se 8a), dated in 134 CE. Published by J. T. Milik, "Deux documents inédits du Désert de Juda," *Biblica* 38 (1957) 264-68 + Plate 4.

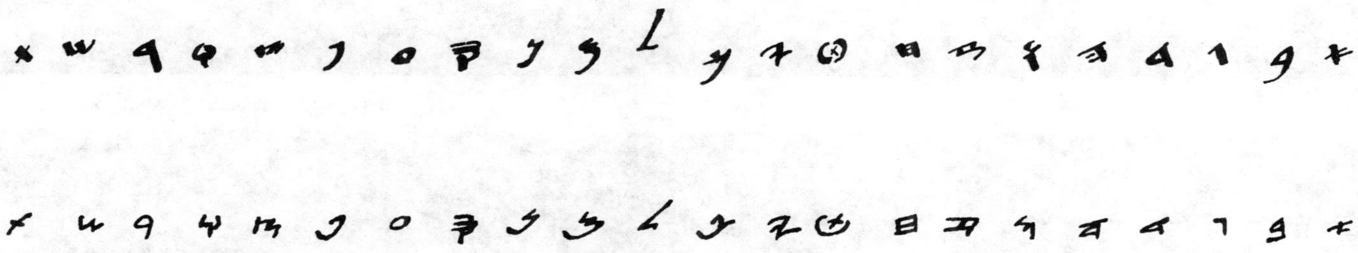

PLATE 14: An Old Hebrew Script and a Palaeo-Hebrew Script from Qumran

Line 1. The Hebrew script of the Lachish Letters from ca. 600 BCE.
Line 2. The script of the Leviticus Scroll from Cave 11 (11QpaleoLev[a] [11Q1]), dating to the first century BCE. Published by David N. Freedman and K. A. Mathews, with contributions by R. S. Hanson, *The Paleo-Hebrew Leviticus Scroll: 11QpaleoLev* (Winona Lake, IN: Eisenbrauns, for the American Schools of Oriental Research, 1985).

Figure 1: SAR image of ruins in the Zippori National Forest, Israel

Figure 2: SAR image of ruins at Tel Safi, Israel

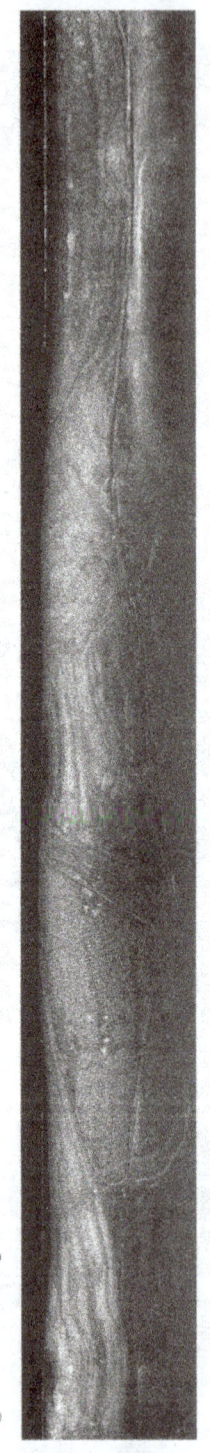

Figure 3: SAR image of the region near Qumran, Israel

Figure 4: Another SAR image of the region near Qumran, Israel

www.ingramcontent.com/pod-product-compliance
Lightning Source LLC
Chambersburg PA
CBHW052043290426
44111CB00011B/1596